POINT BLANK

SOCIAL INSTITUTIONS AND SOCIAL CHANGE

An Aldine de Gruyter Series of Texts and Monographs

Edited By
Michael Useem • James D. Wright

Mary Ellen Colten and Susan Gore (eds.), **Adolescent Stress: Causes and Consequences**

G. William Domhoff, **The Power Elite and the State: How Policy is Made in America**

Glen H. Elder, Jr. and Rand D. Conger, **Families in a Changing Society: Hard Times in Rural America**

Paula S. England, **Comparable Worth**

Paula S. England and George Farkas, **Households, Employment, and Gender: A Social, Economic, and Demographic View**

Richard F. Hamilton and James D. Wright, **The State of the Masses**

Gary Kleck, **Point Blank: Guns and Violence in America**

James R. Kluegel and Eliot R. Smith, **Beliefs About Inequality: Americans' Views of What Is and What Ought to Be**

David Knoke, **Organizing for Collective Action: The Political Economies of Associations**

Dean Knudsen and JoAnn L. Miller (eds.), **Abused and Battered: Social and Legal Responses to Family Violence**

Robert C. Liebman and Robert Wuthnow (eds.), **The New Christian Right: Mobilization and Legitimation**

Theodore R. Marmor, **The Politics of Medicare** (*Second Edition*)

Clark McPhail, **The Myth of the Madding Crowd**

Clark McPhail, **Acting Together: The Organization of Crowds**

John Mirowsky and Catherine E. Ross, **Social Causes of Psychological Distress**

Carolyn C. and Robert Perrucci, Dena B. and Harry R. Targ, **Plant Closings: International Context and Social Costs**

Robert Perrucci and Harry R. Potter (eds.), **Networks of Power: Organizational Actors at the National, Corporate, and Community Levels**

David Popenoe, **Disturbing the Nest: Family Change and Decline in Modern Societies**

James T. Richardson, Joel Best, and David G. Bromley (eds.), **The Satanism Scare**

Alice S. Rossi and Peter H. Rossi, **Of Human Bonding: Parent-Child Relations Across the Life Course**

Roberta G. Simmons and Dale A. Blyth, **Moving into Adolescence: The Impact of Pubertal Change and School Context**

David G. Smith, **Paying for Medicare: The Politics of Reform**

Walter L. Wallace, **Principles of Scientific Sociology**

Martin King Whyte, **Dating, Mating, and Marriage**

James D. Wright, **Address Unknown: The Homeless in America**

James D. Wright and Peter H. Rossi, **Armed and Considered Dangerous: A Survey of Felons and Their Firearms**

James D. Wright, Peter H. Rossi, and Kathleen Daly, **Under the Gun: Weapons, Crime, and Violence in America**

POINT BLANK

Guns and Violence in America

Gary Kleck

ALDINE DE GRUYTER
New York

About the Author

Gary Kleck is Professor, School of Criminology and Criminal Justice, Florida State University. His research centers on violence and crime control with special focus on capital punishment, crime deterrence, gun ownership, gun control, and the impact of economic conditions on violent behavior. Results of his research have appeared in major sociology journals. Dr. Kleck received his Ph.D. in Sociology from the University of Illinois, Urbana-Champaign.

ALDINE DE GRUYTER
A division of Walter de Gruyter, Inc.
200 Saw Mill River Road
Hawthorne, New York 10532

The paper used in this publication meets the minimum requirements of American National Standard for Information Sciences—Permanence of Paper for Printed Library Materials, ANSI Z39.48-1984. ♾

Library of Congress Cataloging-in-Publication Data

Kleck, Gary, 1951–
Point blank : guns and violence in America / Gary Kleck.
p. cm. — (Social institutions and social change)
Includes bibliographical references and index.
ISBN 0-202-30419-1 (cloth)
1. Violence—United States 2. Firearms—Social aspects—United States.
3. Gun control—United States I. Title. II. Series.
HN90.V5K56 1991
303.6′0973—dc20 91-16780
CIP

Manufactured in the United States of America

10 9 8 7 6 5 4 3 2 1

To my wife Diane and my children Matthew and Tessa
To my parents, William and Joyce Kleck
and to my mentor, David Bordua

AUTHOR'S VOLUNTARY DISCLOSURE NOTICE

The author is a member of the American Civil Liberties Union, Amnesty International USA, and Common Cause, among other politically liberal organizations. He is a lifelong registered Democrat, as well as a contributor to liberal Democratic political candidates. He is not now, nor has he ever been, a member of, or contributor to, the National Rifle Association, Handgun Control Inc., or any other advocacy group on either side of the gun control issue, nor has he received funding for research from any such organization.

Contents

PART II. EFFECTS OF GUNS ON VIOLENCE

Acknowledgments

Many people have helped me with the work in producing *Point Blank*, a massive task that would have taken even longer without their generous help. I am happy to have the chance to properly thank them for their contributions. My colleague Professor Britt Patterson collaborated with me on the analyses of the city-level data, reported in Chapters 5 and 10, and my former student, Professor Karen McElrath collaborated on the analysis of the individual-level assault data, reported in Chapter 5. Over the years, my many graduate assistants have helped gather mounds of data. These include Byron Johnson, Tracy Griffith, Susan Sayles, Wes Johnson, and Miriam DeLone. It was always a pleasure to work with all of them.

I am grateful for the extremely close readings and searching critiques of previous drafts of the book provided by Don Kates and my colleague Professor Leroy Gould. Also, thanks to James Wright not only for reading the manuscript but also for suggesting the book's title. Dr. Paul Blackman of the National Rifle Association also read the manuscript and shared his encyclopedic knowledge of the gun control field with me. Although I could not always make changes in accordance with his many strong criticisms, the book is nevertheless stronger for his comments. Others who were given an opportunity to read and comment on the manuscript included Barbara Lautmann, of the Center to Prevent Handgun Violence, and Professors Philip Cook and Colin Loftin.

Many of the datasets analyzed for this project were supplied by the Inter-University Consortium for Political and Social Research. They are listed in the References. Neither the collectors of the data nor the Consortium bear any responsibility for the analyses or interpretations presented here. The Federal Bureau of Investigation provided unpublished city arrest data for 1979–1981 which were used in the city-level analyses, and the National Technical Information Service supplied the 1979–1981 Mortality Detail Files datasets. The National Rifle Association provided counts of NRA membership in each of the 170 largest U.S. cities. Thanks are due in particular to that organization's Mary Rose, for painstakingly compiling the figures. Finally, William Kleck, of the Audit Bureau of Circulation, supplied unpublished county-level gun magazine subscription figures (Thanks, Dad!).

I am grateful to various sources for giving permission for me to use previously published material. The University of California Press has given permission to use copyrighted material in Chapter 4 that was adapted from *Social Problems,* Vol. 35, No. 1, February, 1988, pp. 1–19. The University of North Carolina Press has given permission to use copyrighted material in Chapter 5 that was adapted from *Social Forces,* Vol. 69, No. 3, March, 1991, pp. 1–21.

The Florida State University Foundation provided travel funds so that some of the findings of this research could be presented at the annual meetings of the American Society of Criminology and the American Sociological Association. The Bureau of Justice Statistics and the American Statistical Association sponsored the First and Second National Workshops on the National Crime Surveys and thereby underwrote much of my education on the NCS. Thanks to Colin Loftin and the rest of the Workshop staff, as well as the rest of the participants, for a tremendously enriching experience.

The staff of the FSU Computing Center provided computing advice and data entry services, while Paul Hanna of the College of Social Sciences helped in acquiring many computer datasets. The staff of Strozier Library, and especially Ann Foche and the rest of the Documents Department staff, were an invaluable asset.

Finally, I wish to thank my mentor, Professor David Bordua, for inspiring me to undertake the project, and my wife Diane, for inspiring me to complete it.

Preface

By 1990 there were probably more than 200 million guns in private hands in the United States, and around half of American households contained a gun. Over 30,000 people a year are killed with guns in suicides, homicides, and accidents (Chapter 2), and Americans use guns for defensive purposes as many as a million times a year (Chapter 4). There is little doubt that gun violence and gun control are issues of vital national importance and worth debating. There is considerable reason to doubt, however, whether most gun debates are worth listening to.

The main issues and arguments in the debate over controlling firearms in the United States have not changed substantially from those summarized in 1926 in a debate outline titled "Outlawing the Pistol" (Berman 1926). What is remarkable is that so few of the component issues of the debate have been resolved in the intervening decades. The quality of the disputation has generally been abysmal. As one critic noted, "Any careful observer of the battle must be distressed at the ignorance, ill-will, and dishonesty apparent on both sides" (Caras 1970, p. 122). Others have described the level of argumentation as "debased," and asserted that "the gun control debate has been conducted at a level of propaganda more appropriate to social warfare than to democratic discourse" (Bruce-Briggs 1976, pp. 37–8). The discussion can fairly be described as a dialogue of the deaf (Kennett and Anderson 1975, p. 232). In a proper debate, each side understands, responds to, and tries to undercut the assertions of the other side; in the Great American Gun War each side simplifies, caricatures, and sometimes willfully distorts the arguments of the other, setting up and knocking down their respective straw men with ease. Partisans then wonder how their opponents could possibly hold to such obviously absurd views. Rather than directly engaging the best arguments actually made by the adherents of the opposing position, the debaters argue past one another. Thus, it is not surprising that the debates generally leave everyone exactly where they began, with their biases intact.

Perhaps the greatest obstacle to acquiring an understanding of the facts surrounding the gun control debate is the firm conviction of many on both sides that most of the critical facts are self-evident. Is it not obvious that widespread private gun ownership deters crime? Alternatively, it is not indisputable that the availability of guns increases the homicide rate and plays a large role in America's high violence rates? How could the possession and use of deadly weapons *not* raise the murder rate? The debaters begin with premises that are so thoroughly taken-for-granted that they never consider evaluating them. Self-examination is redundant and doubt is out of the question.

The scholar's faith is that knowledge matters, and that there exists an open-minded audience ready to consider seriously the full range of pertinent ideas and evidence bearing on an issue. It is to this audience that this book is directed. The time when it was necessary to arouse public concern about guns and violence is long past. Quite the contrary—constructive discussion possibly leading to reasonable public policies has become nearly impossible in this context of fever-pitch emotionalism. This book is written deliberately to work against this atmosphere of hysteria and extremism. There will be no dramatic and heart-rending accounts either of people killed by attackers armed with guns or of people killed because they did *not* have a gun for self-defense. In short, there will be no attempts to manipulate readers by stimulating their viscera and bypassing their minds. Readers who seek that sort of material need only turn on their television or open a newspaper or magazine for an ample supply.

While the gun control debate will not be advanced with emotional appeals, neither can it be settled by logical argumentation without factual material. Both sides in the debate use arguments that are *both* emotionally powerful and logically valid to buttress their positions and to undercut the claims of their adversaries. As with most complex and heavily disputed topics, people of intelligence and good will have reasonable differences about guns and gun control, which will not be resolved through logical argumentation alone. If one's goal is to seek the types and levels of gun regulation that will produce the greatest good for the greatest number, then one prerequisite is more and better empirical information.

The gun debate has been unusually statistically oriented, perhaps because intelligent adherents on both sides recognize that most of the key questions are not a matter of *whether* certain costs and benefits are produced by gun control or gun ownership, but rather a matter of *how much* cost or benefit there is, and for how many people. How many lives are lost from criminal use, or saved by defensive use, of guns; how many robberies or assaults are facilitated by criminal possession of guns or deterred by victim possession; how much reduction in crime is produced by gun controls, at what cost in law enforcement dollars and loss of civil liberties and privacy? This book is devoted to providing information about these questions, and thus to make public, democratic debate on the issue of gun control a productive exercise rather than a hollow political ritual.

Organization of the Book. The book covers a broad span of issues bearing on the impact of guns on violence and how best to regulate (or not regulate) firearms in order to reduce violence and crime. In Part I, Chapter 1 considers the political and ideological obstacles to understanding the problem of gun violence and doing something about it, and identifies common flaws in the arguments to which readers are likely to have been exposed. Chapter 2 assesses the extent and nature of gun ownership and use, for legitimate and illegitimate purposes, examining who owns guns and how and why they acquire, own, and use them. Part II covers the effects of gun ownership and use on all major forms of violence and crime linked with firearms. Chapter 3 examines the involvement of specific subtypes of guns and ammunition in violent crime. Chapter 4 explores the effects on violence of guns in the hands of victims and prospective victims. Chapter 5 addresses the effect of gun availability and use on assaultive crime, rape, and robbery. Chapter 6 assesses the relevance of weaponry and gun control to suicide. Chapter 7 gives extended attention to the often neglected topic of gun accidents. Part III examines attempts to regulate guns, what controls have been tried and how well enforced gun laws are (Chapter 8), how much public support there is for various forms of gun control (Chapter 9), the effects of the major existing forms of control on crime and violence, and various untried policy options (Chapter 10). Finally, Part IV outlines what lessons for making public policy may be drawn from the evidence (Chapter 11).

The book reports both original research and assessments of existing evidence drawn from a wide variety of academic disciplines, from criminology and sociology to law and medicine. It is addressed primarily to a general scholarly audience of criminologists, but much of it has been written so it will be understandable to a general nonscholar audience. The discussion is sufficiently nontechnical for nonspecialist scholars to understand most of the material, but some technical material cannot be covered briefly and in a way that is understandable to the general reader.

PART I

ISSUES OF GUN CONTROL AND GUN OWNERSHIP

CHAPTER

1

Ideology, Politics, and Propaganda

Ideological Ironies and Crosscurrents

One of the ironies of the gun control struggle is how traditional political positions often become reversed when the issue is guns. Although twentieth-century liberals have usually supported expanding the state's power to regulate business, they have generally opposed expanding its authority to regulate the behavior of individuals. They have commonly opposed restrictions on free speech, public demonstrations, political associations, sexual behavior, abortion, drug use, and pornography. More specific to criminal justice matters, they have usually opposed the expansion of the power and authority of police and prosecutors to search homes, interrogate suspects, gain confessions, and seize contraband. And although conservatives have opposed expanding the state's power to regulate business, they generally have supported expanding the state's authority and power to regulate private behavior of which they disapprove, and to enforce laws that concern behaviors mainly engaged in by lower class persons, including so-called "street crime." Liberals usually give a broad reading to the Bill of Rights regarding individuals rights of criminal suspects, privacy, and limits on governmental power in general, whereas conservatives give it a narrow one, especially regarding the rights of criminal suspects and dissenters. Liberals generally oppose increasing the scope and severity of penalties for typically lower-class forms of criminal behavior, whereas law-and-order conservatives support the death penalty, mandatory sentencing, and more severe punishment of crime. More generally, liberals oppose expanding the scope of the criminal law to include more "victimless crimes," i.e., prohibited categories of behavior that involve no unwilling victim, such as illegal drug use or gambling (Stinchcombe et al. 1980).

When the issue is gun control, liberals and conservatives switch places. Many liberals support gun laws that confer broad power on government to regulate individual behavior, especially in private places, whereas conservatives oppose them. Some liberals dismiss the Second Amendment to the Constitution as an outmoded historical curiosity that never really guaranteed an individual right to keep and bear arms, whereas conservatives defend a view of this amendment that is every bit as broad as the American Civil Liberties Union's (ACLU) view of the First Amendment regarding free speech or the Fourth, Fifth,and Sixth Amendments as they pertain to suspects' rights.

Some liberals seek to pass gun control laws that create and expand a category of victimless crime (gun possession), whereas some conservatives oppose the effort, citing all the arguments liberals use to oppose laws restricting drug use, gambling, pornography, and sexual conduct: the laws create black markets, criminalize and stigmatize otherwise noncriminal people, encourage discriminatory law enforcement, are impossible to effectively enforce, invite police corruption and abuse of authority, and divert law enforcement resources from areas in which they are more effectively deployed (Kessler 1980). Although murder and robbery with a gun are not victimless crimes, laws banning the mere possession, acquisition, sale, or carrying of firearms clearly encompass "victimless" behaviors. An especially noteworthy example of this particular reversal can be found in the work of Edwin Schur, the principal popularizer of the "victimless crime" concept (Schur 1965). Schur is also a strong supporter of gun control, who shows no apparent awareness of any possible contradiction—"Effective general gun control . . . is one of the few public policy measures directly aimed at controlling crime that could really have a beneficial impact" (Schur 1974, p. 237). Other proponents of the victimless crime perspective have been more intellectually consistent in applying it to gun law violations as well as to the behaviors traditionally discussed under that heading, drugs, gambling, prostitution, and so on (Kaplan 1979; Kessler 1980; Kates 1984a).

It is a mildly amusing pastime to read virulently anticontrol propaganda written by obviously ultraconservative authors, who rail against improper warrantless searches of gun owners' homes and gun dealers' business premises, sounding for all the world like spokesmen for the ACLU (e.g., the March/April and September/October 1987 issues of *The Gun Owners,* newsletter of Gun Owners of America). On the other hand, the writings of otherwise liberal proponents of gun control are frequently most remarkable for what they leave out—any discussion of the search-and-seizure issues that make effective enforcement of many gun laws so problematic or of evidence of discriminatory enforcement (Kates 1986). Even when these concerns are confronted, however superficially, they are commonly dismissed as minor (e.g., Drinan 1976). At one point the city attorney of Berkeley, California, which had what was arguably the most liberal city government in the United States, was even researching the legality of establishing the nation's first neighborhood "weapons checkpoints," allowing random police searches of cars for weapons (Levine 1987).

The current ideological lineup on gun control has shallow historical roots. Before 1963, gun control was not a salient issue for most Americans. Only two Gallup polls from the 1930s up to 1959 asked even a single question on the issue (Crocker 1982). Support for gun control was not a major tenet of liberalism before that time. Indeed, in the nineteenth and early twentieth century, gun control laws were most often targeted at blacks in the South and the foreign-born in the North, and were supported by persons who would clearly not be recognized today as liberals. The stated motives behind support were often overtly racist and xenophobic, revolving around a desire to control "dangerous populations," including not only racial and ethnic minorities, but also radicals, anarchists, union organizers, and other "troublemakers." Southern gun laws during the antebellum and immediate postwar years were explicitly limited to blacks. And although those during and after Reconstruction were written in race-neutral language, they too were aimed at, and largely enforced against, blacks (Kennett and Anderson 1975, pp. 50–1, 81, 153–5, 167; Kates 1979a, pp. 12–22; Kessler 1984, pp. 476–8). In the North, legislative activity on guns were most intense during the period of rapid immigration from about 1890 to World War I, and proponents often justified their proposals with references to the dangers of violent foreigners, anarchists, and other radicals, rather than just the "criminal classes" (Kennett and Anderson 1975, pp. 163, 167, 174, 177–8, 183, 213; Kates 1979a, pp. 15–22).

Between World War I and the assassination of President John Kennedy in 1963, there was still little clear conservative–liberal lineup on gun control, and limited legislative activity (Kennett and Anderson 1975, pp. 187–215). John Kennedy was himself a gun owner and life member of the National Rifle Association. Ownership and even carrying of firearms were common among prominent liberals of earlier eras, such as Theodore Roosevelt, Eleanor Roosevelt, and columnist Drew Pearson (Kennett and Anderson 1975, p. 235; Kates 1986). However, since 1963, liberalism and support for gun control have become closely linked in the public mind. Surveys have documented a rough association between gun control support and a wide variety of other opinions conventionally associated with liberalism. Interestingly, it turns out that this link is solely due to higher gun ownership among conservatives—gun-owning liberals are no more likely to support gun control than gun-owning conservatives (Chapter 9).

Further, not all liberals take a procontrol stance. A book published in 1979 was titled *Restricting Handguns: The Liberal Skeptics Speak Out* (Kates 1979a). Its editor was a former law clerk to radical lawyer William Kunstler and had helped draft civil rights legislation for the U.S. House of Representatives. Its preface was written by U.S. Senator and leading Vietnam War opponent Frank Church, and its contributors included the cofounder of American Amnesty International, the Vice President of the Southern California ACLU, various civil rights activists, and a former legal aid lawyer who worked for Cezar Chavez' United Farm Workers and who took part in the earliest Freedom Rides of the civil rights movement. All expressed concerns, rooted in liberal principles, about the wisdom of gun control in its more restrictive forms. The book's chapters documented the antiblack and anti-immigrant origins of many gun control laws, reinstated the Second Amendment as an important part of the Bill of Rights, and argued the importance of gun ownership for deterring government oppression. The contributors asserted that guns provided the only effective means of defense for minorities and dissidents deprived of legal protection by hostile authorities, and argued from a feminist position that guns are vital "equalizers" for women with a need to protect themselves from violent, physically stronger men.

It is interesting in this connection that support for gun control is often one of the few "liberal" positions taken by otherwise dyed-in-the wool conservatives, including William F. Buckley, Jr., who once flirted with a procontrol position, former Du Pont executive and self-described conservative Pete Shields, chairman of Handgun Control, Inc., and dozens of law-and-order big city police chiefs (Shields 1981; Alviani and Drake 1975, p. 52). Taking a procontrol stand allows such individuals to thereby display their open-mindedness and ability to rise above rigid ideological categories, by endorsing a position that has a liberal reputation, but is not really all that alien to the rest of their generally conservative beliefs.

Radical scholars such as Raymond Kessler (1984) have asserted that gun laws are fundamentally conservative or even reactionary, having in times and places served a variety of conservative political functions beyond simple crime control, including (1) increasing citizen dependence on the state for protection, (2) facilitating repressive action by governments, (3) reducing popular pressures for more fundamental reforms that might reduce crime, and (4) enabling selective enforcement against dissident political groups and racial and ethnic minorities. In sum, it is by no means clear that the intellectually natural position for liberals is support for restrictive gun controls or that the natural position of conservatives is opposition.

The Appearance of Reason—Fallacies in Gun Control Reasoning

By disposing of some of the more specious arguments for and against gun control, the air can be cleared so as to focus with fewer distractions on the more valid arguments. Therefore, some of the more common fallacies are discussed immediately. Of course, throughout the book, many dubious claims made by adherents of both sides will be compared with the evidence. Right now it suffices to cover only some of the more general and widely disseminated fallacies.

Fallacies in Anticontrol Argumentation

The Overmotivated Criminal

Gun control opponents argue that criminals cannot be disarmed or prevented from committing crimes through gun control because they will always be willing and able to either get a gun or to commit the crime without a gun. There is certainly some merit to this argument, as even proponents will concede. It is, however, an exaggeration, one that is based on a conception of criminal motivation that sees every criminal as powerfully motivated and driven to commit crime regardless of the obstacles. Like noncriminals, however, criminals do many things that are casually or only weakly motivated. Indeed, much crime is impulsive or opportunistic, with criminals committing some crimes only if it requires little effort and entails little risk (Feeney 1986). Certainly, gun control is unlikely to have much effect on crime committed by criminals with the strongest and most persistent motivation to commit crimes, such as drug dealers, emotionally disturbed mass murderers, professional hit men, terrorists, or political assassins. However, it is not at all impossible for crime preventive effects to be achieved among the more weakly or temporarily motivated criminals who may make up the majority of the active offender population. Note also that if conservative opponents of gun control really believed this argument, they would not support proposals to prevent crime through deterrence produced by more severe penalties. Offenders as strongly motivated as they allege most criminals to be would not be deterred by any penalty, no matter how severe.

Anything Short of Total Success is Utter Failure

Opponents of gun laws, like opponents of any law, like to point to the failures of the laws—how many crimes are committed even in places with strict gun laws, how many criminals have guns despite the laws, and so on. This argument, however, is a non sequitur; it does not follow that gun laws are ineffective. All laws are violated and thus less than completely effective, and most important criminal laws are violated frequently, as a glance at criminal statistics indicates. Even some laws widely supported by the population have been violated by a majority of the population, as self-report surveys of the population have long shown (e.g., Wallerstein and Wyle 1947). Yet no one concludes that the thousands of homicides committed each year mean that laws prohibiting murder are ineffective and should be repealed. It is unreasonable to oppose a law merely because some people will violate it.

A more sensible standard to apply is to ask whether the benefits of the law exceed its costs, i.e., whether the world will, on balance, be a better place after the law is in effect. It is impossible to directly count the number of successes, i.e., the number of crimes deterred or otherwise prevented by the existence of laws prohibiting the acts, since one can never count the number of events that do not occur. And no matter how many failures there are, it is always possible that there are still more successes. The only way one can assess the relative balance of successes and failures is to compare jurisdictions having a law with those lacking the law, or to compare jurisdictions before and after they adopt a law, to see if there is, on balance, less crime with the law than without it. Just counting failures settles nothing.

Criminals Will Ignore the Law

A corollary to the previous fallacy is the assertion that many criminals will ignore gun laws and get guns anyway. This is indisputably true, but not especially decisive regarding the desirability of gun control, since it does not address the number of successes of gun control. There is no clearly established minimum level of compliance that must be achieved before a law is to be judged a success. And if there were such a standard, it certainly could not reasonably be 100%, and would not necessarily be even 50% or any other similarly high level. It is even conceivable that if just 1 or 2% of potentially violent persons could be denied a gun, the resulting benefits might exceed the costs of whatever measure produced this modest level of compliance.

As it happens, there appears to be some compliance with gun laws even among the "hard-core" felons incarcerated in the nation's prisons. A survey of over 1800 felons in 11 state prisons found that 25% of felon gun owners reported having registered a firearm and 15% reported having applied for a permit to purchase or carry a gun, percentages that would have been higher had felons in states without such legal requirements been excluded from the computations (Wright and Rossi 1986, p. 84). Although the self-reported compliance levels were low, as one would expect in a sample of felons, they were also not zero. Among potentially violent persons not in prison, who are probably less persistently and seriously involved in law-breaking, compliance levels would presumably be even higher.

One Thing Leads to Another

Gun control supporters often wonder how the National Rifle Association (NRA) and other gun owner organizations can possibly oppose some of the more modest and apparently inoffensive regulations. Opponents reply that today's controls, no matter how limited and sensible, will just make it that much easier to take the next, more drastic step tomorrow, and then the next step, and the next, until finally total prohibition of private possession of firearms is achieved. They argue that gun control is a "slippery slope" on which it is hard to stop halfway, and that many proponents do not want to stop with just the more limited restrictions.

This fear is not completely unreasonable, as bills calling for a national ban on private possession of handguns have been introduced in Congress (Alviani and Drake 1975, pp. 55, 57) and much of the general public does favor prohibitions. In national opinion polls, about 40% of Americans say they support bans on the private possession of handguns, and one in six even support a ban on possession of *any* guns. Since about 75% of all Americans favor registering gun purchases and about 70% favor requiring police permits to buy a gun (Chapter 9), this means that *most* supporters of these moderate controls also favor a total ban on private handgun possession. If this is so among ordinary nonactivist supporters of gun control, it almost certainly is true of activists and leaders of gun control advocacy groups.

There have always been enough prominent prohibitionists willing to air their views in a highly visible way to lend credence to fears about a movement toward total prohibition. For example, criminologist Marvin Wolfgang, in a letter to the editor of *Time* magazine, advocated a total national ban on possession of all firearms (July 5, 1968, p. 6), a sentiment echoed by noted sociologist Morris Janowitz (*Time*, 6-21-68).

Most leaders of gun control advocacy groups eventually became cautious about publicly describing their prohibitionist intentions, but earlier in the debate some were quite open about them. In 1969, one of the leading gun control advocacy groups was the National Council for a Responsible Firearms Policy (NCRFP). Its Secretary, and a member of its Board of Directors, was J. Elliott Corbett. Responding to a letter writer who evidently had complained that the NCRFP's support for a moderate handgun control bill did not go far enough, Corbett wrote: "I personally believe handguns should be outlawed . . . Our organization will probably officially take this stand in time but we are not anxious to rouse the opposition before we get the other legislation passed. It would be difficult to outlaw all rifles and shotguns because of the hunting sport. But there should be stiff regulations. . . . We thought the handgun bill was a step in the right direction. But, as you can see, our movement will be towards increasingly stiff controls" (reproduced in the *Congressional Record*, 3-4-69). Other advocates have expressed similar support for a one-step-at-a-time or incrementalist strategy. In a 1990 television documentary, a reporter asked the mayor of Stockton, California why she supported restrictions on so-called "assault rifles" while leaving much more powerful hunting rifles unregulated. She replied "I think you have to do it one step at a time . . . banning semi-assault [sic] military weapons . . . is the first step" (ABC-TV documentary, "Guns," broadcast 1-24-90).

Leaders of procontrol advocacy groups such as Handgun Control and the Coalition to Stop Gun Violence (previously the National Coalition to Ban Handguns) used to assure audiences that they were interested only in regulating handguns, so hunters and sport shooters who used rifles and shotguns had nothing to fear from them (e.g., Fields 1979; Shields 1981, p. 124). Yet, once "assault rifles" became a highly publicized issue, leaders of these groups immediately pushed for strict controls on semiautomatic rifles (Chapter 3). This kind of policy shift undercuts their credibility regarding their ultimate intentions, and feeds the worst paranoia of anticontrol extremists. In Don Kates' words, this sort of "extremism poisons the well," making it all the harder to get people to seriously consider more reasonable alternatives (1984b, p. 533).

It would be unfair to generalize from such cases to all supporters of moderate controls. Undoubtedly, many of those who insist they are not interested in further controls are sincere. Unfortunately, it is impossible for gun owners to know for sure which gun control supporters are sincere, how numerous they are, whether they will continue in the future to adhere to their commitment to limited controls, and whether they will dominate the gun control movement in the future. There are uncomfortable historical parallels between the gun control movement and the Temperance movement. The latter movement was originally directed toward regulating alcohol and encouraging, as its name suggested, moderation in drinking and a reduction in alcoholism. Yet it eventually evolved into the national Prohibition movement, which completely banned the production and sale of alcohol, and thereby criminalized millions of Americans (Gusfield 1963, esp. pp. 74, 96–110).

The political advantages of an incrementalist strategy are obvious. If one imagines a hypothetical scale of gun control restrictiveness going from, say, one (least restrictive) to ten, it is easier to move incrementally from level one to level two, then from two to three, and so on, up to level ten, than it is to jump straight from level one to level ten. Each single step looks less radical than a leap of several steps.

However, this is true about all solutions to any social problem. The fact that such escalation *could* happen says nothing about whether it *will* happen. The belief that "one thing inevitably leads to another" would preclude action of almost any kind, since a minor dose of any given solution to any problem could always lead to an overdose. It might be argued that use of the death penalty for murder or long mandatory prison sentences for serious violent crimes might lead to applying them to petty theft, then to minor traffic violations, and eventually to spitting on the sidewalk or speaking an unkind word to one's neighbor. Yet one never hears conservative gun control opponents applying this line of reasoning to their preferred solutions to crime. If such thinking is unreasonable in those examples, it is equally unreasonable to apply it to gun control, in the absence of any evidence showing the gun issue to be significantly different in this respect.

The fact remains that although most Americans support moderate gun controls such as requiring a permit to buy a gun, decades of lawmaking and propaganda have not persuaded a majority of them to support a general ban even on private possession of handguns, never mind all guns. The efforts of gun prohibitionists notwithstanding, the historical record does not support the view that public support for gun control has increased inexorably over the years; indeed it has remained fairly stable regarding most moderate controls, and even declined slightly with regard to handgun bans (Chapter 9). Nor does the record support the view that gun law has inevitably gotten more restrictive. Indeed, the gun lobby's victories in passing state preemption laws (Chapter 8), the 1986 amendments weakening the federal 1968 Gun Control Act, and recent liberalization of state gun carrying laws (Blackman 1985, p. 13

suggest an opposite trend in restrictiveness. A few minor procontrol victories notwithstanding (Chapter 3), so far, at least, one thing has not lead to another. Regardless of their prohibitionist intentions, the more extreme gun control advocates have not, with few exceptions, been successful in moving very far toward banning guns. Opponents frequently cite New York City as an example of a place where originally moderate laws evolved, through gradual amendment and exploitation of administrative discretion, into virtual prohibition. As will be discussed in Chapter 8, there is merit to this claim as it pertains to New York City, but opponents can cite very few other examples, leading to the conclusion that such an evolution has been the exception rather than the rule with gun controls.

To Reduce Crime, We Should Get Tough with Criminals, Not Gun Owners

It may surprise some readers to learn that gun owner groups do support some kinds of gun control—severe, mandatory penalties for persons who commit crimes with firearms. However, this sort of "get tough with criminals" approach is usually regarded as an alternative to the measures most people have in mind when the term "gun control" is used, rather than being gun control itself. That is, opponents recommend "criminal control" as an alternative to gun control. However, proponents point out that to regard these as forced-choice alternatives is an error, since there is nothing to prevent governments from doing both (Shields 1981, pp. 123–4). Indeed, this is precisely what most governments do. The same legislators who support gun control proposals are often quick to point out also how "tough on criminals" they are, and the same is even true of some leaders of procontrol groups (e.g., Shields 1981, p. 156).

Nevertheless, both proponents and opponents who consider this an effective approach to crime reduction, as distinguished from a cynical but effective propaganda strategy, are on empirically weak ground. A long series of "get tough" strategies have been tried, carefully evaluated, and found to be either ineffective in producing significant crime reductions or hopelessly expensive. These failed strategies include longer prison terms mandatory prison terms, use of capital punishment, "selective incapacitation" of career criminals, increasing police manpower, and reducing procedural restraints on police and prosecutors (see Chapter 8, and the excellent book-length assessment by Walker 1989). While there are many promising alternatives to gun control for reducing violence, the "get-tough" approach is not one of them.

Fallacies in Procontrol Argumentation

The Undermotivated Offender

Just as opponents of gun control envision the typical criminal to be so strongly motivated that no gun law could possibly restrain him, proponents envision the opposite: weakly motivated offenders who could be prevented from committing crimes merely by placing procedural obstacles or delays in their way, making the acquisition of a gun marginally more expensive or difficult. The truth, of course, lies somewhere between these extremes. At least a few murderers are weakly or only temporarily motivated to kill their victims, and some are ambivalent or unclear in their intentions. Proponents exaggerate this image, however, by suggesting that killers rarely intend to kill, that the fatal outcome of their assaults was largely the product of weapon availability and chance. They argue that this implies that some criminals can be prevented from getting guns, and that many killers will *not* do whatever it takes to kill and will not kill using other means if they are denied guns (e.g., Zimring 1968). As will be discussed in Chapter 5, there is little direct empirical support for this idea and the evidence presented to support it usually has little clear bearing on the issue. Most homicides are unpremeditated, most develop out of arguments, and many involve combatants who knew one another, but none of these facts imply anything about how strongly killers wanted to kill or how angry they were at the time of the attack. Consequently, they imply nothing about whether most assaulters still would have killed had they not had a gun, or about whether they could have been prevented from getting a gun by gun control laws (see Chapter 5; Wright et al. 1983, pp. 189–206).

It is necessary, however, for this imagery to be maintained if proponents are to argue that gun control can reduce crime. They must believe in the existence of a substantial number of persons who are willing and able to break serious laws such as those prohibiting murder, assault, and robbery, yet who are not willing or able to break gun control laws. If someone lacks the first attribute, preventing them from getting guns would be pointless for crime control; if they lacked the second, it would be impossible.

Guns That Are Good for Just One Thing—Murder (Targeting the "Bad" Types of Guns)

In the face of a U.S. civilian stock of over 200 million guns (half of U.S. households have at least one firearm—Chapter 2), many gun law proponents have narrowed their political efforts, targeting specific types of guns, which they argue are "good for only one thing—to kill" (Shields 1981, pp. 38, 46). These proponents in effect differentiate "good" (or at least not-so-bad) types of guns, like the old family deer rifle, from "bad" types of guns. At various times, the especially dangerous, "bad" subcategory has been (1) handguns, (2) the cheap, small handguns known as "Saturday Night Specials," (3) so-called "assault rifles," (4) machine guns, and (5) plastic guns. Proponents argue that these weapons are only useful for committing crimes, and sometimes even imply that they are never used for any other purposes (Fields 1979; Shields 1981). Because the guns have no legitimate purposes, it is argued, there can be no valid objection to outlawing them.

The logical problem with this position is that whatever technical attributes guns have that make them suitable for committing crimes necessarily also make them useful for a variety of lawful applications. This issue is discussed at length in Chapter 3.

Gun Control Is Worthwhile Even if Just One Life Can Be Saved

This argument is convenient for gun control proponents since it relieves them of the need to establish just why they consider a gun-linked problem to be serious or to demonstrate that their proposals will save a large number of lives. Advocates will at times cite data documenting the large number of lives supposedly lost due to guns, yet at other times (usually after doubt has been cast on their figures) hint that the number of lives lost due to guns is not really an important matter because every human life is infinitely valuable. Almost any plausible gun control measure is bound to save at least one life, somewhere, sometime in the future. Therefore, it is implied, only a cold-hearted monster could deny the wisdom of a policy that could save that life.

There are two problems with this argument. First, it ignores the costs of gun control, in particular the possibility that gun control could cost lives by denying effective defensive weaponry to at least a few people who need and could successfully use guns in self-defense—almost any control that saved lives could also cost at least one life (Chapter 4). Second, most major social problems have multiple possible solutions, each costing something, and each having some potential for reducing the problem. However, since resources are limited, choices inevitably must be made as to which strategies the resources should be invested in. More resources devoted to some strategies means less available for others. Consequently, the adherents of one particular strategy are obliged to at least roughly assess the potential benefits that strategy would produce rather than merely arguing that it does not matter whether a proposed policy would save one life or a 1000 lives. It is unlikely that many people would seriously argue that a problem resulting in 1000 deaths is no more important than one resulting in one death, so numbers do matter. In any case, it is doubtful if advocates really believe to the contrary—most invoke the "one life" argument only when one of their numerical claims regarding the harms of guns is challenged as being inflated.

Procontrol propagandists sometimes avoid making meaningful assessment of the seriousness of a particular gun-related problem if the effort would not yield a supportive result. They frequently note that more than three fifths of homicides are committed with guns, but when targeting assault rifles or machine guns are silent on how many crimes are committed with these weapons, and do not cite any meaningful standard by which one could judge criminal use of these guns to constitute a serious problem. Proponents do note that gun suicides outnumber suicides by any other means, a meaningful comparison, but do not indicate what standard should be used to judge gun accidents to be an important source of mortality among children (e.g., Schetky 1985). Or sometimes they use a standard of comparison that is uninformative or misleading, as when proponents state that fatal gun accidents are the fourth leading cause of *accidental* death among children aged 14 and under (Center to Prevent Handgun Violence 1989). Although approximately accurate (they are the fifth leading cause rather than the fourth), the ranking is not very enlightening, since it conceals the fact that only the first of the leading accidental causes, motor vehicle accidents, is responsible for a large number of child deaths. Out of more than 20,000 deaths, from all causes, of children age 1 to 14 in 1987, over 4000 were due to motor vehicle accidents, compared to about 250 due to gun accidents (National Safety Council 1989). If gun accidents are responsible for only 1% of child deaths, then the only standard by which this can be regarded as a major source of child mortality is the one which states that every human life is infinitely valuable and that all causes of death therefore are "major." But by this standard, comparisons among causes of death are pointless.

Common Problems of Persuasion

Members of advocacy groups on both sides of the great American gun debate share some rhetorical difficulties in common. Each side is committed to overstating the problem it addresses. For the procontrol forces, that problem is the contribution of guns to violence and crime, while for the anticontrol forces that problem is the procontrol forces. Each side faces a delicate dilemma in their propaganda efforts, one familiar to fund raisers everywhere—they must convey the enormity of the problem, yet also instill confidence in their own effectiveness by pointing to their victories and the progress they have achieved. Thus the NRA must simultaneously convince its current and potential members and contributors that it is facing a powerful gun control movement that is a serious threat to gun owners' rights if not checked, but also convince them that the NRA has beaten the enemy in the past and can do so again in the future, if they are just given the support they need. Likewise Handgun Control, Incorporated (HCI) and the Coalition to Stop Gun Violence (CSGV) overstate the connection between guns and violence, and speak darkly of the NRA's vast political power, seemingly unlimited funds (largely derived, it is inaccurately hinted, from economically self-interested gun manufacturers), and their victories over majority public opinion, while also boasting of their own organization's growing membership and recent legislative victories (e.g. Handgun Control Incorporated 1989; National Coalition to Ban Handguns 1988). To believe both sides, one would have to believe that both parties to the conflict are simultaneously weak and strong, triumphantly victorious and headed toward ignominious defeat. Each set of advocacy groups serves as the demon with which the other side can rally the troops, raising morale and money. The public is not enlightened by this war of words because neither set of advocates has any stake in merely presenting the plain unvarnished truth, even to the extent that flawed and biased human minds can understand it. Quite the contrary—to tell the truth and nothing but the truth would place one side at a distinct disadvantage if the other side did not also lay down their propaganda weapons. As a consequence, the intended audience for these propaganda efforts is inundated with an avalanche of misinformation, half-truths, irrelevancies, trivialities, and outright falsehoods. And this bad information drives out the good, either displacing it because there is only so much attention that can be paid to any given issue, or rendering accurate information useless because it cannot be recognized as such, being so thoroughly intermixed with the disinformation that only the most diligent and unusually well informed readers and viewers can and will separate the two.

CHAPTER

2

Ownership and Uses of Guns

The heart of this book is concerned with the relationships among guns, violence, and gun control. However, to understand these issues it is necessary to first appreciate how common gun ownership is, who owns guns, why they own them, how they get them, and what they use them for. How easily and cheaply guns can be regulated depends to a great extent on how numerous they are. How easily people can be dissuaded from getting, having, keeping, carrying, or using guns depends heavily on why they own them. And how one interprets the relationships between gun availability and crime will depend on how well one understands the impact of crime on gun ownership, in addition to the impact of guns on crime.

Size of the Civilian Gun Stock

Although a few nations may have shares of their households with guns rivaling those of the United States, this country almost certainly has more firearms in civilian hands than any other nation in the world.[1] Exactly how many guns there are, however, will never be known with certainty.

There are two major ways to measure the size of the civilian gun stock, i.e., the number of guns in the possession of private persons, other than the on-duty arms of the police or military. First, one can cumulate the number of guns manufactured for the civilian market in the past, subtract guns exported out of the country, and add guns imported into the country. Second, one can survey a representative sample of the population and ask whether they own guns, and how many they own. Table 2.1 shows the figures resulting from the first procedure. The data indicate that this cumulated total (hereafter the "production-based estimate" for short), for all gun types, probably passed the 200 million mark sometime around 1988. The handgun total is over 65 million. If one makes the simple assumption that uncounted additions to the gun stock have equalled uncounted losses, the figures imply that for every 100 Americans there are more than 80 guns of all types, including 27 handguns. There are, however, numerous flaws in these data, discussed at length in Appendix 1.

Several major points can be noted about the figures in Table 2.1. First, the existing private stock of guns in the United States is enormous. Even if it was conservatively (and unrealistically) assumed that no gun survived past its fortieth birthday, all older guns being lost, confiscated, worn out, or corroded, and it was assumed that there were *no* uncounted additions to the stock, there were still nearly 150 million guns, over 50 million of them handguns, in the civilian stock as of 1990. Second, most of the gun stock has been produced since the mid-1960s, and thus most guns are still relatively new and not likely to wear out or corrode soon. This is especially true of handguns, but is also true of all gun types. Third, of the nearly 200 million guns in the cumulated stock as of 1990, about one-third were handguns; the rest were long guns. Long guns are clearly much more common than handguns. Fourth, among recent additions to the firearms stock, handguns have claimed an increasingly large share. As recently as 1962 only 29% of annual additions were handguns, compared to 45% in 1987. During the 1960s and 1970s the demand for handguns increased faster than the demand for long guns. Fifth, the increasing annual additions of guns was not solely due to population increases, since the per capita rates in the last two columns also show large increases. The rates of increase in per capita ownership turned sharply upward right around 1963, also a watershed year for crime rate increases. From 1963 to 1987, the rate for handguns increased by 145%, and the rate for all guns increased by 83%. Thus the biggest increases occurred among the type of guns most frequently owned and used for self-defense and for committing crimes.

The other major way of measuring the size of the gun stock, as well as the prevalence of gun ownership in the population, is through surveys of representative samples of the nation's population. Table 2.2 displays the results of 45 national surveys conducted between 1959 and 1990. (There were no national surveys asking a gun ownership question before 1959). All of the surveys asked whether there was a gun of some kind in the respondent's (R) household, and most asked more specifically whether there was a handgun in the household. With one exception, only since 1980 have any national surveys asked whether the R owned any of the household guns. The surveys indicate that since at least 1959 about one out of two U.S. households have owned a gun.

The survey-based estimates have all the widely discussed deficiencies of survey data [e.g. see Deming (1944) 1978 for a classic enumeration]. Rs can forget, not be aware of, or lie about guns in their households. They can even misunderstand what the question means, failing to understand that air guns should not be reported, or that guns kept in a vehicle, garage, or barn, or at a business should be reported along with those in their house or apartment. Some Rs may not know about the gun ownership of other household members, some Rs may forget about guns long gathering dust in an attic or basement, and some may no longer think of an antique family heirloom as a firearm. Perhaps the most important problem with the survey data is the possibility that some Rs intentionally conceal their gun ownership. These problems with the survey estimates, and others, are discussed in detail in Appendix 2.

There is a major gap between most estimates of the gun stock based on surveys and those based on production and import/export figures. The most conspicuous seeming discrepancy is that survey results indicate no trend in general gun ownership prevalence, while the production-import estimates indicate enormous growth in the size of the total gun stock from about 1965 to 1990. Even the handgun prevalence figures from the surveys indicate no significant change from 1978 to 1990. Appendix 2 covers some of the possible reasons, stressing flaws in the survey data and especially respondent reporting failure. There is, however, another possible explanation for the gap. It is possible that survey respondents have been generally accurate in their reports of gun ownership, but that gun ownership has increased greatly among segments of the population largely excluded from survey samples, including transients, young minority males, illegal immigrants, and criminals. It may be these groups, which, though a relatively small share of the entire population, absorbed a disproportionate share of the guns, especially handguns, produced in the 1960s and 1970s. Evidence concerning gun possession trends in some of these groups will be presented later in the chapter.

By international standards the fraction of U.S. households with guns in extremely high. The nearest known competitor is Switzerland, where about a third of households have guns, mainly due to military service requirements (Killias 1990). Nevertheless, household prevalence in the United States is probably actually *lower* today than it was in earlier periods, when the country was predominantly rural. There are indirect indicators of gun ownership available for much longer periods of time than production or survey data. Table 6.5 in Chapter 6 shows the percentages of suicides and homicides committed with guns, and compares these with the production-based gun ownership estimates. These indicators are necessarily "noisy," reflecting both gun availability and inclinations of violent people to choose guns for their aggressive or suicidal purposes. Although the two measures often show similar trends, they also moved in opposite directions during 1945–1951, 1976–1983, and, to a lesser degree, 1958–1963. If the gun share of homicides were used as an indicator of long-term trends in a general gun ownership, it would indicate that gun ownership had declined since the 1920s. In 1920–1926, 71% of U.S. homicides were committed with guns (Brearley 1932, p. 68). Since at that time six states in the South and West, where a high share of homicides were committed with guns, were not yet a part of the national vital statistics system, the figure almost certainly would have been higher had those states been included. By 1989, the national figure was down to 62% (U.S. FBI 1990).

Table 2.3 provides estimates of the size of the U.S. gun stock, based on national surveys that asked Rs how many guns they owned. They all support the view that there was a huge number of guns in private hands. All but one of the estimates, however, are substantially lower than production-based estimates for the same years (Table 2.1). Flaws in these estimates and reasons for the discrepancy are discussed in Appendix 2.

Table 2.4 displays information on the combinations and numbers of guns owned by gun-owning households and individuals. Part A shows that most households with guns have long guns (85%), and that most (56%) own *only* longguns, whereas only one-seventh of owning households have only handguns. However, it will be this handgun-only type of household that will be of special interest later because it may be the type most likely to have guns for crime-related reasons (Bordua et al. 1979). Conversely, two-thirds of households with handguns also have long guns. This fact is significant because it suggests that when handguns are used in crimes or for defense (at least when in the home), the use was often the result of a choice between different types of guns, rather than the fact that only handguns were available. This would support the view that there is something about handguns that gun users regard as especially suitable for defensive and criminal purposes. An even more important implication is that if handguns were restricted, most current handgun owners would not even have to acquire new guns in order to have substitute firearms to use. The implications of this substitution possibility will be discussed in detail in Chapter 3.

Part B of Table 2.4 attempts to provide more realistic estimates of the number of guns owned per owner than were reported in Table 2.3. It has been assumed that the true fraction of households and individuals owning guns is 10% higher than survey figures indicate, to adjust for the underreporting previously discussed (see Appendix 2 for a justification). These survey figures were combined with the production cumulation figures in Table 2.1 to roughly estimate the numbers of guns owned per owner. Based on this procedure, among households owning guns, an average of over four guns are owned, considerably higher than most survey data suggest. The distribution, however, is undoubtedly skewed to the right, with a few households owning very large numbers of guns, and most households owning a few, based on the Table 2.3 survey results. Among households with a handgun, the average number of handguns owned is about 2.8. Among individuals age 18 or over who own guns, the average number owned is about 3.4, and among individuals with handguns, the average is about 2.0. Both these data and survey data support the conclusion that although gun ownership is widespread in the United States, a large share of the guns may also be in relatively few hands (see also Cook 1983, pp. 78–9).

Regardless of the major source on which one relies, it is clear that the number of guns currently in private hands in the United States is very large, whether the number is 100 or 200 million. One straightforward policy implication is that policies that seek to reduce gun violence by reducing the overall supply of guns, as distinct from reducing the number possessed by high-risk subsets of the population, face an enormous obstacle in this huge existing stock. Even if further additions to the stock could somehow be totally and immediately stopped, the size of the stock and durability of guns imply that, in the absence of mass confiscations or unlikely voluntary surrenders of guns, it might be decades before any perceptible impact became apparent.

Who Owns Guns?

In a nation where at least half of the households have a gun, it would be difficult to regard gun ownership as an unusual or deviant status. Nevertheless, gun owners do differ from nonowners in some respects, as the figures in Table 2.5 demonstrate. These figures were computed from the combined 1980, 1982, and 1984 General Social Surveys conducted by the National Opinion Research Center (for details of the surveys, see Davis 1984). These surveys were superior to previous national surveys in that they asked whether each *respondent* (R) owned a gun, rather than asking only whether someone in the household did. This made it possible to relate attributes of the R to whether the R owned guns, a procedure whose value was first demonstrated by Bordua and his associates in the late 1970s (Bordua et al. 1979).

For descriptive purposes, the following material discusses bivariate relationships between gun ownership and other variables. The reader is strongly cautioned against drawing causal inferences before the results of multivariate analyses are discussed later. Males are far more likely to personally own guns than females, although many women live in households with guns that belong to a male in the household. Whites are much more likely to own guns or handguns than blacks, although the difference is much smaller for handguns. Most of this racial difference is due to the facts that most blacks live in big cities and that gun ownership is low in big cities. Black households in rural areas are just as likely to have a gun as white households in those areas, and racial differences in other kinds of places are small (Stinchcombe et al. 1980, p. 107). Guns are more common among whites in those ethnic groups that immigrated earlier to the United States than in more recently arrived white ethnic groups. Gun ownership is higher among middle-aged people than in other age groups, presumably reflecting higher income levels and the sheer accumulation of property over time. Married people are significantly more likely to own guns than unmarried persons. Protestants are more likely than others to have guns, and Jews are far less likely to have guns. Middle and upper income people are significantly more likely to own than lower income people, but consistent with the stereotype of gun ownership as a working class attribute, persons with manual jobs are more likely to own guns (contrast with Wright and Marston 1975). There is little association between gun ownership and education.

Along with the gender difference, perhaps the strongest differences in gun ownership are by size of place—rural people are far more likely than urban residents to own guns, including handguns. By region, gun ownership is highest in the Rocky Mountain states (not the South, as some might believe), followed by the Southern states, the Midwest, then the Pacific states. Finally, it is the Middle Atlantic states, and, even more so, New England, which stand out as the oddities, showing far lower levels of gun ownership than the rest of the nation.

Political conservatives are more likely to own guns than liberals. Not surprisingly, hunters are far more likely to own guns than nonhunters. About 40% of persons admitting to a nontraffic arrest record report personally owning a gun, and 21% reported a handgun, compared to only 28 and 15%, respectively, among persons not reporting an arrest record. However, differences are slight in terms of household ownership. There is no significant relationship between respondent gun ownership and approval of violence (as measured by the sum of approving responses to five approve–disapprove items describing hypothetical acts of violence), although there is a statistically significant relationship between respondent handgun ownership and approval of violence. Finally, contrary to what might be common expectation, persons afraid to walk in their neighborhoods or afraid in their homes at night are significantly *less* likely to own guns or handguns, and those burglarized or robbed in the year prior to the interview were slightly less likely to own guns.

Perhaps what is most striking about this entire set of relationships is the absence of consistent indications of a link between gun ownership and criminal or violent behavior by owners. Whereas self-reported arrestees were somewhat more likely to report gun ownership, the difference was a rather modest one for R ownership of handguns, the type of gun most frequently involved in violence, and the difference in household ownership of a handgun was nonsignificant. There was a relationship between handgun ownership and approval of violence, but gun ownership was not consistently higher in segments of the population in which rates of actual violent behavior are higher. It is true that both gun ownership and violence are more frequent among males and Southerners. On the other hand, gun ownership is also higher among whites than among blacks, higher among middle-aged people than among young people, higher among married than unmarried people, higher among richer people than poor, and higher in rural areas and small towns than urban areas, patterns that are all the reverse of the way in which violent criminal behavior is distributed. In short, gun ownership is not consistently higher in places and groups where violence is higher. This should serve as the first broad hint that the relationship between guns and violence is not so close, simple, or consistent as might be thought.

For the most part, there has been very little change in recent decades in the patterns of gun ownership, or changes in who owns guns. The major patterns of gun ownership in the early 1980s (Table 2.5) were also evident in survey data from 1959 (Wright et al. 1983, pp. 87, 89) and throughout the period from 1973 through 1987 (U.S. Bureau of Justice Statistics 1988, pp. 167, 169). Further, when Wright and his associates combined data from a 1959 survey and a 1976 survey, they found that the predictors of gun ownership did not interact with the year of the survey, indicating that the effects of the variables had not changed over time (1983, p. 92). The press gave considerable attention to claims that gun ownership increased sharply among women in the 1980s, but beyond a survey sponsored by a gun manufacturer, there is little credible evidence for the assertion. The percentage of women reporting they personally owned a gun in the General Social Surveys (GSS), was 11 in 1980, 14 in 1982, 11 in 1984, 12 in 1985, and 14 in 1987 (U.S. Bureau of Justice Statistics 1988, p. 169). Given that these estimates all had a margin of error due to random sampling error of about two percentage points, they do not support a claim of increasing gun ownership among U.S. women from 1980 to 1987.

There was, however, one important shift in the social distribution of gun ownership in recent decades. During the period of the nation's fastest increases in violent crime rates, from 1964 to 1974, gun ownership apparently increased more among criminals than it did among noncriminals. There are several scattered pieces of evidence supporting this claim. The most direct evidence of such a trend would be survey data comparing persons with and without a criminal arrest or conviction. Although the GSS asked both gun ownership and arrest questions, these surveys began only in 1973, too late to indicate trends over the entire period of interest. Earlier gun ownership surveys did not ask any criminal record questions.

The next most direct evidence would be survey information on other groups with high rates of violence. Black homicide victimization rates are many times higher than white rates, and one pair of surveys indicated that household handgun ownership increased from 1972 to 1978 much more for blacks than for whites (Kleck 1984a, p. 129). However, another pair of surveys showed less of an increase for nonwhites than for whites from 1959 to 1976 (Wright et al. 1983, p. 89). Neither comparison quite pertains to the time period of interest. Further, the contradictory results may be at least partly due to the small numbers of black households in the surveys (typically only about 150), which leads to very unstable estimates. Other evidence is less direct, though more reliable. The proportion of homicides, aggravated assaults, and robberies involving guns increased rapidly from 1964 to 1974, suggesting increasing gun availability among persons who commit violent crimes. Further, the fraction of homicides involving guns increased much faster among blacks than among whites over this period, again suggesting that gun availability may have been increasing faster among blacks than among whites. On the other hand, it is possible that what changed over this period was criminals' *preferences* in weapons to use in assaults, rather than relative gun levels among blacks and whites.

Although the GSS data do not concern the period of interest, they do point to a possible continuation of this trend into the 1973–1984 period. Gun and handgun ownership among persons without arrest records remained fairly stable over this period, whereas ownership fluctuated erratically among self-admitted arrestees over this span (Table 2.6). Since the number of arrestees included in each survey was about as small as the number of blacks, these estimates are subject to the same instability as annual estimates by race. Therefore, the percentages for the four surveys from the 1970s have been averaged together and compared with the averages for the three surveys from the 1980s. The resulting figures indicate that the trends hypothesized for the 1964–1974 period may have continued through the 1980s—household ownership of guns in general, but especially of handguns, increased more for arrestees than for nonarrestees, from the 1970s to the 1980s.

Why People Own Guns

Stated Reasons

There are two ways one can answer the question "Why do people own guns?" The simplest way is to report the reasons people give when they are asked the question. These reasons tend to be utilitarian, reflecting the uses to which gun owners put, or anticipate putting, their guns. When the questions refer to all guns, without differentiating them by type, the most frequently given *main* reasons for owning guns are, in descending order: hunting, self-protection, sport or target practice, and gun collecting. In a 1978 national survey, 74% of all gun owners reported that hunting was *one* of the reasons they owned guns, 65% mentioned protection, 40% sport or target shooting, and 21% gun collecting (DMI 1979, p. 71). Very similar results had been obtained in a 1975 Harris poll (Crocker 1982, p. 256). Some people also can state honestly that they have no particular reason for owning a gun since they may have inherited one or received it as a gift.

When the question pertains just to handguns, the leading reason for ownership is protection. About half of handgun owners report that defense or protection is their main reason for having a handgun, leaving half who own them for other, mainly recreational, reasons. However, among persons in a 1977 Illinois survey who owned *only* handguns, 67% reported that protection was their primary reason for owning the guns, with 73% citing protection as a primary or secondary reason (Kleck 1984a, p. 105). No other single reason for owning handguns rivals protection. In a 1978 national survey, 45% of handgun owners stated that protection at home or work was their most important reason for owning, with another 8% owning for a law enforcement or security job, arguably also defensive reasons for owning. The next most common reasons were target shooting, cited by 17%; gun collecting, cited by 14%; and hunting, cited by 9% (DMI 1979, p. 40).

Owners of long guns are most likely to own them primarily for hunting or target shooting, although in the 1977 Illinois survey, even among persons in households with only long guns, 11.4% owned them at least partly for protection (Bordua et al. 1979, p. 231). It should be stressed, however, that in all these surveys "protection" could have been understood by Rs to refer to protection from dangerous animals as well as defense against humans. The most important conclusion to be derived from these data is that most owners of guns in general, and long guns in particular, own them primarily for reasons unrelated to crime; rather, they own them for a variety of recreational reasons, especially hunting. On the other hand, about half of handgun owners, and some long gun owners as well, own guns mainly for protection, and it may be this subset of owners that is most relevant to understanding the relationship between levels of gun ownership and violence. The share of all gun owners having guns for protection may also be increasing. In a 1986 national survey, 30% of all households keep a gun at home "for security reasons" (DIALOG 1990). Since 42% of households reported a gun in 1986 (Table 2.2), this means that about 71% (30/42 = 0.71) of gun-owning households kept a gun at least partly for protection in 1986, compared to 65% in 1978 (DMI 1979).

Modeling Gun Ownership

Another way to explain why people own guns is to develop and test a statistical model predicting gun ownership. Prior research of this type will be reviewed. Interest will first focus on the possible effects of criminal victimization and fear of crime on gun ownership, since these links will be important later in interpreting aggregate-level relationships between gun ownership levels and rates of crime and violence. These can be regarded as situational determinants of gun ownership, because it is assumed that when crime levels change or people relocate into areas with a different crime level, the motivation to get a gun for defensive reasons changes as the situation changes. Situational determinants can be contrasted with cultural determinants, which are likely to be more lasting mental attributes that people retain over time and carry with them as they move from place to place, to some degree independent of situation. Thus, persons raised to believe in rural values or a Southern regional culture conducive to gun ownership are likely to retain these cultural attributes for a time, even after they leave the social settings when they were socialized and where these cultures flourish, carrying their culture with them even when they move into social situations less conducive to keeping firearms.

Fear, Victimization, and Gun Ownership

Some scholars have expressed doubt that fear of crime and prior criminal victimizations motivate gun ownership (Wright et al. 1983). Nevertheless, it is argued here that the weight of the best available evidence is at least weakly supportive of the idea that crime affects handgun ownership, although interpretation of the evidence is clouded by the fact that it may simultaneously reflect both the effects of fear or victimization on gun owning and the effects of gun ownership on fear and victimization.

Evidence on these issues has been very mixed. Williams and McGrath (1976), Lizotte and Bordua (1980; Lizotte et al. 1981), McClain (1983), Hill et al. (1985), Young (1986), and Smith and Uchida (1988) all found support for the idea that fear, prior victimization, or perception of high or increasing crime rates motivates gun acquisition, at least for some people, while Wright and Marston (1975), DeFronzo (1979), Stinchcombe et al. (1980), and Young (1985) generally failed to detect significant positive associations. Generally the supportive studies were methodologically more satisfactory, but all were seriously flawed. Most used datasets not originally designed to study gun ownership, such as the General Social surveys (GSS), which did not ask questions about many important possible determinants of gun ownership. Some of the surveys asked only about household gun ownership, making it difficult to relate respondent (R) attributes such as fear of crime to the R's own gun ownership. The earlier studies used simple cross-tabular analytic methods with few simultaneous controls for possibly confounding variables (Wright and Marston 1975; Williams and McGrath 1976; Stinchcombe et al. 1980).

Some examined ownership of guns in general rather than just handguns, even though it was mainly handgun ownership that was assumed to be motivated by concerns about crime. The significance of the problem was first demonstrated by Williams and McGrath (1976), who found that pistol ownership was positively and significantly related to both fear of crime and prior victimization, whereas general gun ownership was related to neither.

Some researchers attempted to isolate "protection" owners in GSS datasets by defining them as nonhunting gun owners who lived in a household with a handgun (Hill et al. 1985) or as people who personally owned guns (of any kind) but did not hunt (Young 1986). Although the former is somewhat better than the latter, both result in frequent classification error. For more than a quarter of gun owners, and half of handgun owners, the primary reason they own guns is *neither* protection nor hunting; these nonhunting owners would be misclassified as protection owners by Hill et al. and Young. Further, many hunters also consider protection to be one reason they own guns; these protection owners would be misclassified as not protection owners (DMI 1979, pp. 71, 118).

These studies also relied on crude measurement of fear of crime, usually using the GSS question asking whether the R was afraid to walk near his or her home at night. Since most guns owned for defensive reasons are kept in the home, one might expect gun acquisition to be more closely related to fear in the home. The 1982 GSS included a question about fear at home; Young (1986) found it to be significantly and positively related to gun ownership for non-Southerners, though not for Southerners.

Clearly the best studies of gun ownership done to date are those of Lizotte and Bordua (1980; Lizotte et al. 1981).[2] Though the studies covered only Illinois, the researchers avoided all of the problems mentioned thus far. They used data generated by surveys designed specifically to research gun ownership, measured respondent as well as household gun ownership, could directly identify Rs who owned guns for protection, specified multivariate models of gun ownership, estimated their models with logistic regression methods, and used a three-item measure of fear of crime and a five-item measure of prior victimization. In addition, they explored the possible causal paths through which actual crime levels, perceived crime levels, prior victimization, and fear of crime might affect gun ownership. They found that county crime rates positively affected Rs' perceived level of crime, which in turn positively and significantly affected fear of crime. Both fear and prior victimization were significantly and positively associated with gun ownership for protection.

Some ancillary findings from the Illinois surveys are important to note. Bordua and his associates asked respondents why they owned guns and thus could distinguish those who owned only for protective reasons, mainly for protection, secondarily, or not at all for protection. They found that though women were far less likely to own guns than men, they were more likely to own solely for protection. Likewise, though blacks were generally less likely than whites to own guns, they were more likely than whites to own solely for protection. In particular, 9.8% of all Illinois black female respondents owned a gun solely for protection, compared to only 2.4% for the white males, who otherwise were most likely to own guns. These findings are significant in light of the symbolic imagery used by gun control advocates to justify disarming defensive gun owners. Bordua has noted that these advocates paint a picture that stresses the "obstructionist refusal of 'rednecks' to join the twentieth century" but downplays "disarming frightened black women whose frontier is now." He further suggested that "The common stereotype held among gun control proponents of a Daniel Boone lingering on from yesterday should perhaps give way to that of a black nurse hoping to make it to tomorrow" (Bordua 1988, pp. 37, 42).

Although the Lizotte–Bordua studies are the most authoritative to date, both they and their predecessors share important flaws. First, there is the knotty problem of causal order. Whereas fear of crime and criminal victimization might affect gun ownership, gun ownership could also influence the level of fear and the likelihood of victimization. If people buy guns to provide themselves with some security against crime, then one would expect that gun ownership could reduce fear of crime (DeFronzo 1979; Hill et al. 1985). Clearly this is what gun owners believe they experience. As will be discussed in Chapter 4, results from a number of national surveys have all indicated that most protection gun owners feel safer because they have a gun in their home, whereas almost none feel less safe. If these self-assessments are accurate, the net effect of home gun possession on gun owners is to reduce fear of crime. In surveys done at a single point in time, it is impossible to disentangle the possible negative "reassuring" effects of gun ownership on fear, and deterrent effects on victimization, from the positive "motivating" effects of fear and victimization on gun ownership. The results of prior survey studies may reflect an undifferentiated combination of both effects. Since the effects are of opposite sign, almost any observed association is compatible with the hypothesis that fear and victimization motivate defensive gun acquisition. For example, even a net negative association could be interpreted as indicating a strong fear-reducing effect of gun ownership, in combination with a weaker positive motivating effect of fear on gun acquisition. Likewise, the absence of any relationship significantly different from zero could simply be interpreted as an indication of the two opposite-sign effects canceling each other out, the "reassuring" effects of gun ownership being roughly equal in size to the motivating effects of fear on gun acquisition (a point noted by Wright et al. 1983, p. 129).

Indeed, if one had to interpret existing survey results as bearing on one causal link or the other, one would have to say that the surveys bear more on the effects of gun ownership on victimization and fear of crime than the effect of victimization and fear on gun ownership. The R's fear has always been measured as of the time of the survey, and victimization measured for the period (usually a year) just prior to the interview. In contrast, gun ownership is a continuing status resulting from a gun acquisition that occurred at some time in the past, usually the rather remote past—in one national survey the median span of gun ownership was 23 years (Quinley 1990). Thus gun acquisition is usually temporally prior to victimization and fear of crime as measured in these surveys. A present-time emotion cannot cause a behavior in the past. Further, current fear is unlikely to be a good proxy for fear prior to gun acquisition in the past, especially 23 years in the past. Perhaps the best way to interpret the results of the best survey studies is to conclude that the net relationship between fear and gun ownership is positive, suggesting that the positive motivating effect of victimization and fear on gun ownership may be greater, on average, than the fear-reducing effects of gun ownership. Whether there is actually any effect of fear on gun acquisition cannot be definitively established until research focuses on recent gun buyers and/or uses a panel design to assess this temporal/causal sequence.

Although the authors of at least two studies have raised these causal order issues (DeFronzo 1979; Hill et al. 1985), only DeFronzo attempted to deal with them, and he was unable to satisfactorily do so for technical reasons. He specified a nonrecursive model in which fear was allowed to affect household handgun ownership, but handgun ownership was also allowed to affect fear, estimating the model with two-stage least-squares methods on GSS data (males only). For estimates to be consistent and unbiased, this sort of model must be properly identified (see Johnston 1972 for a discussion of the identification issue). In this application, this meant that DeFronzo had to specify at least one variable that had a direct causal effect on fear, but not on handgun ownership, and at least one variable that had a direct causal effect on handgun ownership, but not on fear. Such variables are called "instruments" and the plausibility of results derived from estimation of nonrecursive models depends largely on the credibility of assumptions about the instruments. DeFronzo's key assumption was that the R's age would affect fear, but not handgun ownership (p. 356). This is not a plausible assumption, in light of the significant bivariate relationship between age and gun ownership observed in Table 2.5 and in light of the commonsensical expectation that the probability of owning most consumer durables is likely to increase with age, as people accumulate possessions over time. Indeed, other researchers have routinely specified age as a determinant of handgun or protective gun ownership (e.g., Hill et al. 1985; Lizotte et al. 1981). Consequently, this model was probably underidentified and its estimates biased and inconsistent. In fairness, there is little DeFronzo could have done, since the GSS just do not provide any strong instruments for estimating this reciprocal relationship. For what it is worth, DeFronzo concluded that handgun ownership appears to reduce fear, whereas fear has no apparent effect on handgun ownership.

The second major problem characterizing most of these studies is a conceptual one. It is a mistake to think that the only way gun ownership can be a response to crime is through the emotional experience of fear. Instead, gun acquisition, even for protective reasons, may be a fairly unemotional act of prudence and planning for the future. Persons acquiring guns may get them not because they are afraid but simply because they recognize the possibility of becoming a crime victim in the future and wish to give themselves another option for dealing with such a situation should it arise. Under this rational decision-making model, some people in effect make rough predictions of the likelihood of their future victimization and the probability that it will occur in circumstances where their possession of a gun might help. If this model is correct, gun ownership is indeed a response to crime, but the effect does not have to be mediated by either fear of crime or even experience with criminal victimization. Prior victimization would be but one of many possible predictors of future victimization. (Indeed, some people may even fall prey to the irrational gambler's fallacy that once they have been victimized, they have "had their one" and thus have less need to prepare for another victimization.)

Two prior studies related gun ownership to actual (as distinct from perceived) crime rates in surrounding areas. Lizotte et al. (1981, p. 501) found a weak indirect connection between reported crime rates in the R's county of residence and owning a gun for protection—crime rates affected perception of county crime rates compared to other counties, which in turn affected fear of crime, which influenced the likelihood of protective gun ownership. Smith and Uchida (1988, pp. 100–1) found that reported crime rates indirectly affected the likelihood of buying a weapon for protection by increasing the perception of a rising crime rate and of the perceived likelihood of burglary or robbery victimization in the future.

The rational decision-making explanation ties together all of the existing survey research results just reviewed, the fact that large numbers of gun owners, especially handgun owners, say they own guns for protection, and also the results of aggregate studies that indicate that increases in crime rates can drive up gun ownership rates (discussed in a later section). However, it should be stressed that this perspective does not preclude the possibility of some individuals acquiring guns in response to fear. There can be multiple paths to protective gun ownership.

Confidence in the Criminal Justice System

There is another way in which protective gun ownership may be a response to crime. People may acquire guns not merely because they perceive high or rising crime risks, but also because they believe the police and the rest of the criminal justice system cannot adequately protect them from these risks, leading them to the conclusion that they must rely at least partly on their own resources, including gun ownership, for security. In a 1970 national survey, Rs were asked "Do you think that people like yourself have to be prepared to defend their homes against crime and violence, or can the police take care of that?" (Feagin 1970, p. 805). Among Rs who believed they had to defend their homes and could not leave it to the police, 60% of whites and 33% of blacks reported a gun in their household, whereas among those who felt they could rely on the police, only 35% of whites and 27% of blacks reported a gun.

Lizotte and his colleagues (1981) constructed a two-item index of confidence in the police, consisting of the item used in the Feagin study and another one in which Rs rated how important they thought police patrols would be in reducing crime. They found that a perception of the police as ineffective indirectly affected ownership of a gun for protection by increasing fear of crime, which in turn increased the likelihood of protective gun ownership (p. 501). Later research by Young (1985), using more limited data from the Detroit area, also indicated that gun ownership was higher among persons with less confidence in the ability of the police to provide adequate protection. Smith and Uchida (1988) found that defensive weapon ownership was higher among persons less satisfied with the "quality of police services in their neighborhood" (p. 97). Unfortunately, this latter measure reflected all aspects of police activity, not just the crime control activity that occupies only a minority of police time (Reiss 1971). Nevertheless, using a wide variety of measures of both confidence in the police *and of gun or weapon ownership,* these researchers all found that protective gun/weapon ownership was positively associated with a perception that the police were not sufficiently effective or could not adequately protect the citizenry (see also McDowall and Loftin 1983 for an extended discussion). On the other hand, Whitehead and Langworthy's (1989, p. 274) analysis of a 1982 national survey indicated no net effect of confidence in the police on household gun ownership. This anomalous finding may be due to the failures to measure the R's personal gun ownership or to distinguish defensive or handgun ownership from less crime-related types of gun ownership.

Aggregate-Level Studies of the Effect of Crime Rates on Gun Ownership Rates

Another way to assess the effects of crime on gun ownership is to use information on aggregates such as states or cities to measure the association between levels of gun ownership and levels of crime, civil disorder, and other sources of insecurity. In two national time series studies, Kleck (1979, 1984a) found that rates of total gun ownership, handgun ownership and even long gun ownership were positively and significantly affected by homicide rates. Because of the high correlation between homicide and robbery rates, the effects of these two crime rates on gun ownership could not be separated, but either variable included in the handgun equation by itself showed a positive and significant effect. These studies are superior to others because they utilized models that allowed for reciprocal causation between gun ownership and crime rates, i.e., crime rates could affect gun ownership levels, and gun ownership rates could affect crime rates. Further, production-based data were used to measure gun ownership levels, thereby counting both legal and illegal gun ownership. Using Kleck's data and a somewhat different estimation technique, Magaddino and Medoff (1984) also concluded that the homicide rate positively affected handgun ownership levels.

Bordua and Lizotte (1979) examined the relationship between rates of licensed gun ownership and crime rates in Illinois counties. They concluded that crime rates had no effect on rates of legal ownership among men but did have significant positive effects on women's ownership. However, the authors acknowledged that they could not separate ownership of handguns from long guns, noting the latter are far more common than the former. It may be for these reasons, and because much protective gun ownership is illegal, that the authors found no effect of crime rates on legal ownership among men. Further, they did not model the reciprocal relationship between gun ownership and crime rates.

Clotfelter (1981) studied six states, relating crime rates and the frequency of riots during various periods during the 1960s and 1970s to various measures of legal handgun acquisition. The latter apparently measured applications to purchase handguns or perhaps the number of permits granted; it is unclear which was measured, or whether the same thing was measured in all of the states. In these six states, there was no significant relationship between the murder rate or the rate of other violent crimes and the rate of legal handgun acquisitions when a time trend variable was included in his regression equations, but acquisitions were positively and significantly related to nonmurder violent crime rates when the trend variable was omitted. Handgun acquisitions were also related to frequency of riots in the United States as a whole, though not to riot frequency within the states. Clotfelter did not model the possible reciprocal relationship between gun ownership and crime rates, in effect assuming that the former had no effect on the latter. Further, his results pertained only to legal acquisitions; their generalizability to handgun acquisition in general is unclear. Because the need for defensive guns is greatest in groups and areas in which law-breaking is highest, it would not be surprising if a large fraction of defensive gun acquisitions were unlawful and therefore not measured by gun purchase permits and the like.

Finally, in a sophisticated time-series analysis of the issuance of permits to purchase handguns in Detroit, McDowall and Loftin (1983) modeled the reciprocal relationship between gun ownership and crime. They found that the violent crime rate had a significant positive effect on handgun permits issued, and also that permit issuance was higher when police strength was low. As with the previous two studies, the generalizability of these findings to unlawful gun acquisitions is unknown.

If findings of the more sophisticated studies are weighted more heavily, the entire set of results from aggregate-level studies indicates that crime rates positively affect gun ownership rates. This conclusion thus accords with the admittedly ambiguous findings of the best individual-level survey studies, supporting the claim that gun ownership, especially handgun ownership, is often, though not exclusively, a response to the threat of a crime.

Additional support for this thesis comes from an examination of the trends in handgun sales during the 1960s and 1970s (Table 2.1). This was a period of both sharply increasing production and importation of handguns and rapid crime rate increases and civil disorders.

Gun Ownership as Pathology

Some researchers have proposed models of gun ownership, especially protective ownership, that stress pathological or abnormal causes. They have proposed that gun ownership is a result of racial prejudice, or punitiveness or aggressiveness toward criminals (Young 1985). Others have suggested that gun ownership may be the result of psychological abnormalities such as paranoia, violence-proneness, inability to control aggressive impulses, an unusual need for power, or felt sexual inadequacies (e.g., Bakal 1966; Sherrill 1973; Diener and Kerber 1979).

Stinchcombe and his associates argued that gun ownership is caused by "punitiveness" toward criminals (as well as gun ownership increasing punitiveness) (1980, p. 105). Using GSS data on household gun ownership, they found that persons favoring capital punishment and harsher criminal courts were more likely to own guns. However, this was true only for whites, and the differences in household gun ownership between those favoring and those opposing these views were typically only about five or six percentage points. Because they controlled only for race and sex, it would seem that this small association could be spurious, attributable to rural residency, age, and other variables that are positively associated with both gun ownership and "punitiveness" toward criminals, or to education, being Jewish, and other variables that are negatively associated with both gun ownership and punitiveness. Further, it is possible that the items used to measure punitiveness were instead merely indicators of a general political conservatism.

Young (1985) asserted that among white males in Detroit interviewed in 1979, racial prejudice toward blacks caused "aggressive attitudes towards criminals," which in turn caused nonhunting household gun ownership. He found no direct effect of racial prejudice on gun ownership. However, he did find that (1) racial prejudice was significantly related to favoring capital punishment and getting tough on crime, and (2) favoring capital punishment and getting tough on crime (believing stricter law enforcement will reduce crime, and that courts are too lenient) were marginally related to gun ownership (two-tailed significance levels of .10 and .06, respectively).

There were many problems with this analysis. First, the equations predicting "tough on crime" and "capital punishment" appeared to be substantially misspecified, with the former containing six predictors, only one of them significant at even the .10 level, and the second containing six predictors, only three of them significant. Second, treating racial attitudes as causally antecedent to crime control attitudes is questionable. Third, it is possible that the items in Young's "prejudice" index and the crime control opinion items were all just measures of different aspects of a general conservatism, rather than causes of one another. Young conceded that a scale of conservatism was indeed positively and significantly correlated with the crime control attitude measures, but claimed that, in an analysis not reported in the paper, "the relationships among the variables presented here were unaffected by the presence of conservatism" (p. 478). This begged the question, since the problem was not just that conservatism should have been controlled as a separate variable, but rather that both prejudice and the crime control attitudes were aspects of a single underlying "conservatism" variable, a suspicion that his findings supported rather than refuted. In any case, even taking the results at face value, if the effect of prejudice is purely an indirect one through crime control attitudes, and these attitudes in turn were only marginally significant predictors of gun ownership, it would seem that support for the racial prejudice hypothesis in this study was weak.

Although Young was aware of the research and cited it in other connections, he omitted any mention of the null findings of Lizotte and his colleagues regarding the effect of racial prejudice. Using a much larger statewide sample, the latter researchers found that "racist attitudes did not predict owning a gun for protection" (Lizotte et al. 1981, p. 503). They did find that perception of blacks in the R's neighborhood increased the probability of crime victimization and increased the perception of an above-average crime rate in the R's county, and that these in turn increased fear of crime, which in turn increased the likelihood of owning a gun for protection. In short, the perceived presence of blacks in the neighborhood may have served as an indicator of high crime levels, elevating the perception of crime risk and thereby indirectly increasing protective gun ownership. This interpretation is supported by the findings of Smith and Uchida (1988, pp. 100–1), which indicated that the size of the nonwhite share of an R's neighborhood population had a positive effect on the purchase of protective weapons, but that all of this effect was mediated by household victimization experiences and the R's perceived risk of future victimization.

Lizotte and his colleagues did not report testing for the specific indirect links that Young proposed. In other work using these data, Bordua and associates (1979) reported that people who owned guns solely for defensive reasons were very likely to own only handguns and were disproportionately black and female. This could help explain why, at least among studies of samples including both blacks and whites, little racial prejudice was found among defensive or handgun owners.

Although scholars have occasionally argued that gun owners are more racist or punitive than average, it has mostly been nonscholars who have asserted or implied that gun owners are somehow psychologically abnormal (e.g., Bakal 1966; Sherrill 1973). Barry Bruce-Briggs (1976, p. 59) commented on one variant of this theme:

> A common assertion in the dispute in that gun owners are somehow mentally disturbed. The weapon is said to be a phallic symbol substituting for real masculinity, for "machismo." The historian Arthur Schlesinger, Jr. has written of the "psychotic suspicion that men doubtful of their own virility cling to the gun as a symbolic phallus and unconsciously fear gun control as the equivalent of castration." When queried about the source of this suspicion, he responded that he thought it was a "cliche." Such statements never cite sources because there are no sources. Every mention of the phallic-narcissist theory assumes it is well known, but there is no study or even credible psychoanalytic theory making the point.

Although there may be no scientific basis for this notion of gun ownership as compensation for felt sexual or penile inadequacies, there has been scholarly discussion of the related idea that a gun can bestow "feelings of power and virility" on its owner (Diener and Kerber 1979, p. 227). That a gun, or any other tool, does in fact bestow power seems incontrovertible; whether people acquire guns as compensation for an unusual lack, or perceived lack, of other sources of power is another matter. There is only one scholarly study of any value on personality attributes of gun owners, and it was a very small scale study comparing 37 male gun owners recruited with a newspaper ad with 23 nonowners living on the same blocks (Diener and Kerber 1979). Subjects were given three paper-and-pencil personality tests, including the California Psychological Inventory (CPI), and filled out a questionnaire. The authors concluded that "there was no evidence in the present study that the *average* gun-owner exhibits atypical personality characteristics. The gun owners did not differ appreciably from a normative sample of college students on the CPI subscales, nor did the gun-owners show an unusual profile compared with the nonowner matched sample" (p. 236). However, they also noted findings indicating that "gun-owners tended to be more open-minded and tended to have a higher need for power" and were less affiliative and sociable than nonowners (p. 234), though their scores on the pertinent scales were not significantly different from national norms. Because the authors stated that "no evidence emerged that gun owners were more personally insecure than nonowners" (p. 237), it is unclear what the "need for power" might denote. The authors cautioned that it may simply reflect a greater desire of gun owners to control their environments, and that "this motivation for gun ownership should thus be viewed skeptically" (p. 236). At this point, there is no research-based foundation for attributing gun ownership to psychological abnormalities.

Cultural Determinants of Gun Ownership

As the term will be used here, culture refers to mental attributes such as norms and values that are shared by the members of social groups, and that are learned in interaction with other members. They may also be transmitted from one generation to the next. Cultural attributes are possible causes of gun ownership. In contrast to situational determinants of gun ownership, such as residence in a high crime area or the perception of a high risk of personal victimization, cultural determinants would tend to be more persistent and probably also more difficult to change. Consequently, to the degree that gun ownership is due to cultural causes, it might be more difficult to deliberately reduce through gun control laws.

Many authors have suggested that gun ownership results from membership in subcultural groupings and the acceptance of subcultural norms and values. Bruce-Briggs (1976, p. 61) contrasted "two alternative views of what America is and ought to be," views that sociologists would identify as elements of two distinct subcultures: "On the one side are those who take bourgeois Europe as a model of a civilized society: a society just, equitable, and democratic; but well ordered, with the lines of responsibility and authority clearly drawn, and with decisions made rationally and correctly by intelligent men for the entire nation." On the other side are persons whose "model is that of the independent frontiersman who takes care of himself and his family with no interference from the state. They are 'conservative' in the sense that they cling to America's unique pre-modern tradition—a non-feudal society with a sort of medieval liberty writ large for everyman." In the gun-hunting subculture of rural and small town America, a boy's introduction to guns and hunting is an important rite of passage—Bruce-Briggs called the first gun at puberty the "bar mitzvah of the rural WASP" (p. 41).

Stinchcombe and his associates (1980) portrayed much gun ownership as resulting from membership in a rural hunting culture originating in the early settlement of the American frontier. They argued that the culture is found today primarily in rural areas and small towns and among ethnic and religious groups whose ancestors came to the United

States early in its pre-industrial history. Persons with a family tradition of hunting, and an exposure, especially in the South and West, to regional values and norms encouraging hunting are more likely to own guns. The authors showed that contemporary gun ownership was in fact higher in these social locations. However, they did not convincingly distinguish situational determinants of gun ownership from cultural ones, failing to establish whether gun owning resulted from association with like-minded others or whether it was linked with a family tradition of gun ownership or hunting or with socialization in the South.

Lizotte and his colleagues (1981), in contrast, developed evidence directly supporting a subcultural explanation of ownership of guns for sporting purposes. Independent of the fact that gun owners were themselves more likely to hunt, they were also more likely to have friends who hunt, and were more likely to reside in counties in which there were many other hunters, and in which many residents subscribed to magazines devoted to hunting and other outdoor sports, indicating ample opportunities for association with like-minded persons. Sport owners were also more likely to have parents who owned guns, to have obtained their first gun at an early age, and to have been trained in gun use, suggesting socialization into a sporting gun culture. Concerning a possible protective gun subculture, the authors found that although persons who owned guns for protection were more likely to have friends who also owned for the same reason, there was no evidence of socialization into a gun-owning subculture. Protective gun owners commonly obtained their first guns as adults, without training in gun use, and without any family background in gun ownership. Finally, the authors found no evidence that gun-ownership was part of a subculture of violence. Neither proviolent attitudes nor racially prejudiced views predicted either sport or protection gun ownership.

Other authors have focused on region-based subcultures of gun ownership, stressing especially the higher rates of gun ownership in the South. Note, however, that gun ownership is even higher in the Rocky Mountain states, and nearly as high in parts of the Midwest (Table 2.5). Consequently, the exclusive regional focus on the South may be unduly narrow. Many studies of national survey data have found that Southerners are more likely than average to own guns, yet most could not separate cultural from situational effects because they did not distinguish where people were raised from where they currently resided (e.g., Newton and Zimring 1969; Wright and Marston 1975; Williams and McGrath 1976; Stinchcombe et al. 1980; Hill et al. 1985). For example, it is possible that people in the South are more likely to own guns because more of the region's population was reared in rural areas where hunting was common, rather than because they were socialized into a regional subculture. O'Connor and Lizotte (1978) used national GSS data in an attempt to separate the effects of socialization in the South (measured by residence in the South at age 16) from the presumably more situational effects of residing in the South at the time of the interviews. The authors concluded that although gun ownership was affected by current residence in the South, it was not affected by residence at age 16; this undercuts the regional subcultural explanation. However, since 88% of those raised in the South were also living there at the time of the interviews (computed from p. 424), it was hard for them to separate the effects of the two region measures. Either measure predicted gun ownership when included as a predictor by itself, but multicollinearity prevented both measures from being significant predictors when included simultaneously. The authors preferred a model including only current residence in the South, mainly on the rather technical grounds that it had fewer parameters to estimate (p. 427).

Using the 1982 GSS and similar sets of variables, Young (1986) found that, among women, nonhunting respondent gun ownership was positively and significantly related to being in the South at age 16, but not to current residence; the opposite was found for men. Thus, at least for this problematic measure of gun ownership, the subcultural model was supported over the situational model for women, whereas the opposite was true for men. Also using GSS data on males only, but with more refined regional measures that sidestepped the multicollinearity problem, Dixon and Lizotte (1987) found that household gun ownership was higher among males both raised and currently residing in the South than among those either reared outside the South or currently residing outside the South. The results were thus consistent with the existence of a Southern subculture of gun ownership. The authors also concluded that this regional effect on gun ownership was not mediated by a regional subculture of violence, finding no links between region and violent attitudes or between violent attitudes and gun ownership. They did, however, report evidence that those both raised and currently residing in the South are more likely to have "defensive" attitudes, and that such attitudes in turn positively predict household gun ownership.

Finally, the present author's own analysis of the GSS data can be briefly summarized (Kleck 1990). It was a multivariate probit analysis based on a sample combining the 1980, 1982, and 1984 GSS surveys. The strongest and most consistent predictors of gun ownership were hunting, being male, being older, higher income, residence in rural areas or small towns, having been reared in such small places, having been reared in the South, and being Protestant. The social origins of Rs consistently predicted having firearms, suggesting that early socialization into gun owning subcultures is important in explaining gun ownership. However, traits such as racial prejudice and punitiveness toward criminals were not important. Most gun ownership in the general public is related to outdoor recreation such as hunting and its correlates, rather than crime. However, ownership of handguns may well be linked with fear of crime and prior burglary victimization, though findings are necessarily ambiguous due to questions of causal order.

The pattern of results as a whole was fully compatible with the thesis that gun ownership is a product of socialization into a rural hunting culture. The findings support a simple explanation of the high level of gun ownership in the United States. Unlike European nations with a feudal past, the United States has had both widespread ownership of farmland and millions of acres of public lands available for hunting. Rather than hunting being limited to a small land-owning aristocracy, it has been accessible to the majority of ordinary Americans. Having the income and leisure to take advantage of these resources, millions of Americans have hunted for recreation, long after it was no longer essential to survival for any but an impoverished few. Rather than high gun ownership being the result of a lack of strict gun control laws, it is more likely that high gun ownership discouraged the enactment of restrictive gun laws, and that the prevalence of guns was mostly a product of the prevalence of recreational hunting.

One final category of causes of gun ownership would be gun control laws themselves. Gun laws could either discourage gun ownership, as many of them are intended to do, or in some cases could actually encourage gun acquisition. Some laws, although probably having little long-term impact on gun ownership, may encourage people, during the period the laws are being considered, to buy guns in a soon-to-be-prohibited category, e.g., when sales of "assault weapons" increased in 1989 as relevant laws were being debated. The impact of gun laws on gun ownership levels will be addressed in Chapter 10.

Uses of Guns

The uses to which people put guns are to some extent implied by owners' stated reasons for having guns. People use guns primarily for outdoor recreational activities such as hunting and target and sport shooting, for protection against threats both human and animal, and in connection with a variety of miscellaneous pursuits such as gun collecting [see Olmstead (1988) for an account of gun collecting as "morally controversial leisure"].

Just as the most common reasons for owning guns are recreational, so the most common uses of guns are recreational. According to data from the 1980 National Survey of Fishing, Hunting, and Wildlife-Associate Recreation (U.S. Fish and Wildlife Service 1982a), in 1980, among U.S. residents age 16 or older, 17.4 million persons hunted, each for an average of 19 days per year, five hours per hunting day, for a total of 330 million hunting days. Some idea of the value placed by hunters on these activities can be derived from the fact that hunters spent over $8.5 billion that year on hunting (pp. 45, 67, 82). These survey results are supported by hunting license data, which indicate there were 16 million hunting license holders in the United States in 1985 (U.S. Bureau of the Census 1987, p. 221). Contrary to claims that handguns are useless for hunting or that there is no legitimate sporting use for handguns (e.g., Stinchcombe et al. 1980, p. 115), 1.3 million people (about 7% of hunters) hunted with handguns in 1980, mostly during special handgun hunting seasons, for a total of over 10.7 million days of participation (U.S. Fish and Wildlife Service 1982a, p. 82; Wright et al. 1983, pp. 58–9).

The other major category of recreational use of guns is sport shooting, which can cover more formal target shooting such as trap or skeet shooting and the shooting of paper targets, or less formal "plinking"—shooting of tin cans, natural inanimate targets found in the woods, and so forth. Target shooting accounted for 149 million days of participation, by 10.4 million participants age 16 or over in 1975; plinking accounted for 84 million days of participation by 5.7 million participants (U.S. Fish and Wildlife Service 1977, pp. 54, 55, 64, 85). By comparison, in Chapter 4 it is estimated that guns are used for defensive purposes about a million times a year, with about 600,000 of the uses involving handguns. Thus, although far more serious, defensive uses are rare in comparison with recreational uses.

However, the main reason guns are a major source of public concern is their use in acts of violence. Like defensive uses, these too are very rare in absolute terms, but altogether too frequent in terms of their human cost. Tables 2.7 to 2.9 cover all the major quantifiable forms of gun violence, including deaths, nonfatal injuries, and nonfatal violent crimes. Table 2.7 covers all forms of death involving guns. In 1985, about 31,600 persons were killed with guns. The majority of these, 55%, were suicides, not criminal homicides. Only 37% were homicides, 5% were fatal gun accidents, and 1.5% each were due to legal intervention (police officers killing suspects in the line of duty) and to death where it was undetermined whether injury was intentionally or accidentally inflicted. Among all deaths due to "external cause," i.e., accident, suicide, or homicide, guns were involved in 22% of them, and handguns in about 13% of them. The majority of all gun deaths involve handguns, mainly because 79% of the gun homicide deaths involved handguns. Guns were involved in 1.5% of all deaths, from all causes, in 1985. However, they were involved in 59% of suicides, 60% of homicides, and 1.8% of accidental deaths in 1985. Each of these will be discussed in detail in Chapters 5–7.

To put the 31,600 gun deaths in perspective, it may help to provide a point of comparison. As with gun deaths, it can be argued that deaths due to medical incompetence are avoidable, premature deaths, that might be prevented through legal actions. The Harvard Medical Practice Study estimated that 6895 short-term nonpsychiatric hospital patients died in 1984 due to negligent medical practice in New York State (1990, p. 6–21). In that year there were 37.9 million hospital admissions in the United States, compared to 2.8 million in New York State (U.S. Bureau of the Census 1986, p. 95). If the rate of negligence was as high in the rest of the nation, the New York figures extrapolate to about 93,329 people killed by negligent medical care in the United States in 1984, triple the gun total.

Whereas the death data are generally quite reliable, the figures concerning nonfatal gunshot woundings in Table 2.8 are more questionable because there is no national system for gathering comprehensive nonfatal injury data. Surveys such as the National Health Survey (U.S. National Center for Health Statistics 1976a) cover samples that are large, but not large enough to get precise estimates of rare events such as gun injuries. Further the survey does not distinguish self-inflicted and other-inflicted injuries, or accidental versus intentional injuries. Its estimate of 170,000 plus or minus 75,000 "gun injuries" in 1975 also apparently included injuries that did not actually involve any gunshot wounding, such as those due to people dropping a gun and breaking a toe, or temporarily losing their hearing for a day or two as a result of shooting without hearing protection.

The present estimates are instead extrapolations based on the fairly reliable death counts, multiplied by estimates of the ratio of nonfatal gunshot wounds to fatal wounds. The estimates of the ratios are based on local studies of fairly small numbers of cases, but they seem reasonable. One would expect the nonfatal-to-fatal ratio to be highest for accidents, since the shooters were not trying to hurt anyone, and to be lowest for suicide attempts, since these commonly involve the shooters placing a gun against or close to their heads (Chapter 6). Consistent with these expectations, the ratios used here are 14.5 for accidents, 5.25 for intentional, other-inflicted assaults, and 0.181 for suicide attempts. The total estimated number of nonfatal gunshot wounds for 1985 was about 130,000, but this estimate should be taken with a large grain of salt. Note, however, that it is well within the 95% confidence interval estimate from the National Health Survey.

Finally, Table 2.9 provides the most complete available estimate of crime incidents involving guns. Based on the National Crime Surveys (NCS), which interview representative samples of the U.S. population age 12 or over, the figures cover both incidents reported to the police and those not reported, and both major and minor crimes. It should be stressed that few of these incidents involve crime victims being shot. Homicides were already covered in Table 2.7, and few of the nonfatal crimes covered in Table 2.9 involved gunshot wounds, though there is some overlap with the events counted in Table 2.8. Most of the incidents involved a threat by a person armed with a gun, i.e., an assault but not an injury. Only about 2.4% of handgun crimes in the NCS involve a victim being shot (U.S. Bureau of Justice Statistics 1990a, p. 5). In 1985, guns were involved in about 6% of the rapes, 17% of personal robberies, 52% of commercial robberies, and 9% of assaults (attacks or threats without any elements of theft or rape). There were over 650,000 violent crimes involving guns in some way, over 540,000 of them, or 82% of the gun crimes, involving handguns. Guns were involved in about 12% of all violent crimes, and handguns in about 10%. The majority of the gun crimes were assaults, with no element of theft or rape.

Relative to the total number of guns, the number of gun crimes is small. Even if each gun used to further a crime was used only once, thereby spreading crime involvement around to the maximum number of guns, the fraction of guns involved in crime in any one year would be 0.3% for all guns, 0.9% for handguns and 0.09% for long guns (using the 1985 gun figures from Table 2.1). Over a gun's lifetime, however, the fraction of guns involved in crime would necessarily be higher. Cook (1981b) developed a simple formula to estimate this fraction and Kleck (1986b) applied it to data concerning the cheap, small handguns known as "Saturday Night Specials." Since evidence reviewed there indicated that these weapons were no more likely than other handguns to be involved in crime, the resulting estimates should be applicable to handguns in general. Taking account of the fact that the same gun can be used in many crimes, it was estimated that even under a very generous set of assumptions, at most 6.7% of handguns sold in a given year would ever be involved in even one crime. Under more plausible sets of assumptions, the fraction was under 2%. As long guns are twice as numerous as handguns, yet account for only about a sixth of gun crime (Table 2.9), the fraction would be well under 0.5% for rifles and shotguns, and under 1% for all guns.

The main significance of these figures is that they imply that if gun restrictions were indiscriminantly aimed at reducing gun availability in the general population rather than just some high-risk subsets, for every one gun seized (or kept out of civilian hands) that would eventually be involved in crime, perhaps about 100 "noncriminal" guns would have to seized, with the ratio probably in excess of 50 even for handguns (see also Wright et al. 1983, p. 320). In estimating this same fraction, Cook (1981b) used somewhat unrealistic assumptions about how widely gun crime would be spread among crime-involved handguns, but still arrived at estimates that support the same qualitative conclusion: even among the more crime-involved type of gun, handguns, the number of guns that would never be involved in crime exceeds the number that would eventually be criminally used by a ratio of at least ten-to-one. Thus control measures aimed at the general public face a significant "needle-in-the-haystack" obstacle to disarming the violence-prone minority of gun owners.

How Are Guns Acquired?

The ways in which people obtain guns are of obvious relevance to their regulation. Much gun law is concerned largely with regulating the sale and purchase of guns (the two are legally distinct in that different parties to the transaction are regulated) and these regulations mostly cover transactions involving licensed gun dealers, in particular those operating retail businesses (U.S. Bureau of Alcohol, Tobacco and Firearms 1980; Blose and Cook 1980). Every person in the United States in the regular business of selling guns is required to have a federal firearms dealer's license, and many must have a state license as well. The problem with this focus is that many guns are acquired through other, largely unregulated, channels. Even among members of the general, largely noncriminal, population, about 36% of guns were acquired by their present owners from private parties, most commonly as a gift (DMI 1979, p. 71).[3] Although nominally regulated in some jurisdictions, these transactions are largely invisible to legal authorities under existing law, and they are, as will be seen, even more common routes to gun possession among criminals. The data in Table 2.1 imply that there were about 4.3 million new guns sold at retail in 1987. Since there is about one used gun acquired for each new gun (Newton and Zimring 1969, pp. 13–14), this implies over 8.6 million total gun acquisitions each year, about 3.1 million (0.36 × 8.6 million) of them involving nonretail sources, and 5.5 million involving guns, both new and used, acquired from licensed retail sources.

The best work on criminal acquisition of guns was done by Wright and Rossi (1986), who surveyed over 1800 imprisoned felons in 10 states about their guns. Among 943 felon handgun owners, by far the most common means of obtaining the most recently acquired gun were "from a friend" (36%) and "off the street" (15%), with another 4.5% getting a gun from a family member. Only about 16% had obtained their most recent handgun by a purchase from a retail dealer, while only 2.9% mentioned a "black market source" and only 4.7% got the gun from a fence. Consequently, the focus of some scholars (e.g., Moore 1981) on black market enterprises as sources of criminal guns appears to be misdirected. Criminals do get their guns from unlicensed sources, but rarely from black market dealers. Thus most of these felons' guns were obtained outside of licensed, easily regulated channels, yet not from persons in the business of illegal gun selling.

It is important to stress the chief limitation of the Wright–Rossi prison survey, which the authors acknowledge. The felons filling out the questionnaires must be regarded as an especially serious, criminally active, and strongly motivated set of criminals. First-time criminals, and infrequent or petty offenders do not often get sent to prison. Yet much of the rationale for gun control is based on the belief that relatively weakly motivated, infrequent offenders can be disarmed or prevented from acquiring guns through firearms regulations. Consequently, the subset of the criminal population that is arguably most relevant to gun control was necessarily heavily underrepresented in this and other prison surveys. Among less "hard-core" criminals, gun transactions probably resemble those in the general public more than those typical among the inmates, with more purchases through licensed channels and fewer thefts and illegal purchases.

The Wright–Rossi survey also confirmed an important fact first noted by Burr (1977)—the main reason criminals acquire handguns is not to commit crimes, but rather for self-protection. When the felon gun owners were asked the reasons why their most recent guns were obtained 58% cited protection as a "very important" reason for getting their most recent handguns, with another 26% citing protection as "somewhat important." This was far and away the most frequently cited reason, with only 28% citing "to use in crimes" as "very important" and 20% citing this reason as "somewhat important" (Wright and Rossi 1986, p. 137). Criminals live among, and routinely associate with, other criminals, much more so than do members of the general public, and they are crime victims as well as victimizers. Consequently, their motivation to acquire guns for self-protection may be even stronger than it is among noncriminals.

Conclusions

There were probably over 200 million guns in private hands in the United States by 1990, about a third of them handguns. Gun ownership increased from the 1960s through the 1980s, especially handgun ownership. Some of the increase was due to the formation of new households and to income increases enabling gun owners to acquire still more guns; however, a substantial share of the increase was also a response to rising crime rates among people who previously did not own guns. Most handguns are owned for defensive reasons. Therefore, part of the positive association sometimes observed between gun ownership levels and crime rates is due to the effect of the latter on the former, rather than the reverse. Nevertheless, most guns, especially long guns, are owned primarily for recreational reasons unconnected with crime.

Gun owners are not, as a group, psychologically abnormal, nor are they more racist, sexist, or violence-prone than nonowners. Most gun ownership is culturally patterned, linked with a rural hunting subculture. The culture is transmitted across generations, with gun owners being socialized by their parents into gun ownership and use from childhood. Defensive handgun owners, on the other hand, are more likely to be disconnected from any gun subcultural roots, and their gun ownership is usually not accompanied by association with other gun owners or by training in the safe handling of guns. Defensive ownership is more likely to be an individualistic response to life circumstances perceived as dangerous. This response to dangers, however, is not necessarily mediated by the emotion of fear, but rather may be part of a less emotional preparation for the possibility of future victimization.

Probably fewer than 2% of handguns and well under 1% of all guns will ever be involved in even a single violent crime. Thus, the problem of criminal gun violence is concentrated within a very small subset of gun owners. These criminal gun users most commonly get their guns by buying them from friends and other nonretail sources, or by theft. Therefore, gun regulation would be more likely to succeed in controlling gun violence if it could effectively restrict nonretail acquisitions and possession of guns by a small high-risk subset of gun owners.

Table 2.1. Size of the U.S. Civilian Gun Stock, 1945–1987[a]

	Additions to Stock			*Cumulated Stock*[b]		*Guns/1000 population*[c]	
Year	*Handguns*	*Longguns*	*Total*	*Handguns*	*Total*	*Handguns*	*Total*
1899–1945	12657618	34251565	46909183	12657618	46909183	94.9	351.6
1946	176745	1356620	1533365	12834363	48442548	91.2	344.3
1947	264256	1836669	2100925	13098619	50543473	91.3	350.8
1948	444034	2215524	2659558	13542653	53203031	92.7	362.6
1949	262504	1940925	2203429	13805157	55406460	92.9	371.1
1950	278038	2217583	2495621	14083195	57902081	93.5	381.3
1951	348373	1738210	2086583	14431568	59988664	94.1	389.6
1952	454229	1503422	1957651	14885797	61946315	95.6	396.1
1953	415857	1583063	1998920	15301654	63945235	96.7	402.3
1954	376455	1236362	1612817	15678109	65558052	97.3	405.0
1955	429237	1399846	1829083	16107346	67387135	98.0	408.2
1956	534964	1513834	2048798	16642310	69435933	99.5	413.1
1957	538032	1442544	1980576	17180342	71416509	100.8	417.2
1958	519362	1227579	1746941	17699704	73163450	102.1	420.1
1959	648672	1526066	2174738	18348376	75338188	103.9	425.3
1960	602843	1560034	2162877	18951219	77501065	105.4	430.6
1961	561742	1473809	2035551	19512961	69536616	106.6	434.6
1962	598649	1467719	2066368	20111619	81602984	108.3	439.3
1963	676062	1555762	2231824	20787672	83834808	110.3	444.8
1964	744273	1778620	2522893	21531945	86357701	112.6	451.8
1965	1013300	2107921	3121221	22545245	89478922	116.5	462.4
1966	1212817	2309250	3522067	23758062	93000989	121.5	475.5
1967	1673417	2413345	4086762	25431479	97087751	128.8	491.7
1968	1725383	2799776	5214500	27846203	102302251	139.7	513.1

(continued)

Table 2.1. (*Continued*)

Year	*Additions to Stock*			*Cumulated Stock*[b]		*Guns/1000 population*[c]	
	Handguns	*Longguns*	*Total*	*Handguns*	*Total*	*Handguns*	*Total*
1969	2414724	3084186	4809569	29571586	107111820	146.8	532.0
1970	1673227	3132686	4805913	31244813	111917733	153.3	439.4
1971	1777862	3233186	5011048	33022675	116928781	160.1	567.3
1972	2106883	3269316	5376199	35129558	122304980	168.7	587.7
1973	1781261	3930432	5711693	36910819	128016673	175.9	610.3
1974	2175818	4394790	6570608	39086637	134587281	184.9	627.0
1975	1995077	3332767	5327844	41081714	139915125	192.8	657.1
1976	2026689	3708975	5735664	43108403	145650789	200.8	678.5
1977	1914050	3183161	5097211	45022453	150748000	208.1	696.7
1978	1972498	3444020	5416518	46994951	156164518	215.3	715.6
1979	2231088	3493255	5724343	49226039	161888861	219.2	720.9
1980	2481230	3311496	5792726	51707269	167681587	227.5	737.9
1981	2612200	2868968	5481168	54319469	173162755	236.5	753.9
1982	2469671	2486464	4956135	56789140	178118890	244.8	767.8
1983	1943069	2111304	4054373	58732209	182173263	250.7	777.6
1984	1904029	2382563	4286592	60636238	186459855	256.4	788.5
1985	1684754	2357532	4042286	62320992	190502141	261.0	797.9
1986	1538080	1985856	3523936	63859072	194026077	264.9	804.8
1987	1957901	2386535	4344436	65816973	198370513	270.6	815.5

[a] All figures are domestic production, minus exports, plus imports, for each year within each gun type category. Shipments to the military are excluded. 1982–1987 import figures for the federal fiscal year were used for corresponding calendar years (e.g., federal fiscal year 1985 is 10-1-84 to 9-30-85 and was used for calendar year 1985). See Appendix 1 for further details and limitations of the data.

[b] As of end of calendar year.

[c] Based on resident population as of July 1.

Sources: Number of guns: 1945–1968—Newton and Zimring (1969, p. 174); 1969–1972—Zimring (1975, pp. 168–69—Table 4, ATF column; Table 5); U.S. Bureau of the Census (1976, p. 156); U.S. Bureau of Alcohol, Tobacco and Firearms (BATF) (1975); 1973–1981—U.S. BATF (1974, 1984); 1982–1983—Howe (1987); 1984–1987 (and 1982–1983 import figures)—U.S. BATF (1989a). Population estimates, all years—U.S. Bureau of the Census (1987, p. 7).

Table 2.2. National Survey Estimates of Gun Ownership, 1959–1990[a]

Survey Dates	% Households Owning		% Respondents	Survey Organization
	Any Gun	Handgun	Owning Any Gun	
7/23–28/59	49	16	—	Gallup
1/7–12/65	48	16	—	Gallup
1966	48	—	—	Gallup[b]
4/?/68	51	—	—	Harris
5/22–6/16/68	44	—	33	CBS News[c]
1968	50	17	—	Gallup[d]
10/?/68	49	20	—	Harris[e]
1/?/71	51	—	—	Harris
5/26–29/72	43	16	—	Gallup
3–4/?/73	47	20	—	NORC
3–4/?/74	46	20	—	NORC
3/7–10,28–31/75	44	18	—	Gallup
10/3–6/75	47	19	—	Gallup
10/?/75	47	—	—	Harris
9/29–10/8/75	41	21	—	DMI[f]
3–4/?/76	47	21	—	NORC
3–4/?/77	50	21	—	NORC
1/?/78	51	—	—	CBS News
4/20–5/15/78	44	24	—	Cambridge[g]
5/19–6/9/78	47	24	—	DMI[h]
12/9–12/78	48	20	—	DMI[h]
2/?/80	45	—	—	Gallup
3–4/?/80	48	23	29	NORC[i]
1/18–22/81	43	23	—	L.A. Times
4/12–16/81	44	21	—	L.A. Times
4/?/81	44	23	—	NBC News
1981	47	27	—	ABC News[i]
3–4/?/82	45	21	29	NORC[i]
1982	47	26	—	ABC News[i]
5/20–23/83	40	18	—	Gallup[j]
3–4/?/84	45	22	26	NORC[i]
1/11–16/85	42	24	—	ABC News[i]
3–4/?/85	44	23	29	NORC[i]
6/?/85	44	22	—	Gallup[i]
4/11–14/86	42	20	—	Gallup[k]
3–4/?/87	46	25	28	NORC[l]
2–4/?/88	41	23	26	NORC[k]
"Early 1989"	49	29	—	?[m]
2/?/89	49	—	—	YCS[n]
2/?/89	—	24	—	Decima[k]

(continued)

Table 2.2. (*Continued*)

Survey Dates	% Households Owning		% Respondents	Survey Organization
	Any Gun	Handgun	Owning Any Gun	
2/28–3/2/89	47	25	—	Gallup[o]
2–4/?/89	46	25	31	NORC[k]
3/15/89	52	—	—	CBS/NYT[k]
3/23–29/89	45	27	—	Harris[k]
3/20–4/10/90	46	27	—	CSUR[p]

[a] All surveys without a superscript on the survey organization's name are from Crocker (1982, p. 255). All surveys cover the noninstitutionalized resident population, age 18 or over, of the lower 48 states, except the DMI surveys, which were based on registered voters.

[b] Computed from Stinchcombe et al. (1980, p. 111, Table 34).

[c] Computed from separate black–white percentages in Erskine (1972, p. 459), assuming 90% of sample was white and 10% was black.

[d] Gallup (1984, p. 119).

[e] Newton and Zimring (1969, p. 10).

[f] U.S. Congress (1975a).

[g] Cambridge Reports, Inc. (1978).

[h] Decision/Making/Information (DMI) (1979).

[i] U.S. Bureau of Justice Statistics (1987b, pp. 169–70).

[j] Gallup (1984, p. 118).

[k] Computer search of DIALOG databank's POLL file.

[l] U.S. Bureau of Justice Statistics (1988, pp. 167–9).

[m] Killias (1990).

[n] Yankelovich Clancy Shulman (Quinley 1990, p. 17).

[o] Gallup (1990, pp. 88–9).

[p] Center for Social and Urban Research, University of Pittsburgh (Mauser and Margolis 1990, p. 17).

Table 2.3. Number of Guns, Based on Household Survey Data

	Surveys: Handguns								
	Harris Oct. 1968			*DMI May/June 1978*			*Gallup May 1983*		
	No.	*%*[a]	*Group Mean*	*No.*	*%*	*Group Mean*	*No.*	*%*	*Group Mean*
	1	83	1	1	68	1	1	56.25	1
	2	11	2	2	18	2	2	25.00	2
	3	4	3	3–4	9	3.5	3	12.50	3
	4	1	4	5–9	2	7.0	4+	6.25	7
	5+	1	9	10+	2	15.0			
Mean[b]		1.300			1.725			1.875	
% households with guns		20			22.7[c]			18	
Gun-owning households		12.2 million			17.3 million			15.1 million	
Estimated guns		15.8 million			29.8 million			28.3 million	

(*continued*)

Table 2.3. (Continued)

	Surveys: All guns											
	Harris Oct. 1968			*Gallup Oct. 1975*			*Gallup March 1989*			*Time/CNN Dec. 1989*		
	No.	*%*	*Group Mean*	*No.*	*%*	*Group Mean*	*No.*	*%*	*Group Mean*	*No.*	*%*	*Group Mean*
	1	41	1	1	42.5	1	1	31.8	1	1	22.9	1
	2	26	2	2	25.0	2	2	22.7	2	2	17.7	2
	3	12	3	3	20.0	3	3	11.4	3	3	18.8	3
	4+	20	7	4	7.5	4	4+	34.1	7	4–5	16.7	4.5
				5+	5.0	9				6–8	13.6	7
										9+	10.3	15
Mean	2.735			2.275			3.501			4.410		
% households with guns	49			47			47			48[d]		
Gun-owning households	29.8 million			33.4 million			42.7 million			44.6 million		
Estimated guns	81.5 million			76.0 million			149.4 million			196.5 million		

[a] % figures refer to the percent of gun-owning households that own the indicated number of guns.
[b] Mean number of guns (handguns) per gun (handgun)-owning household. See Appendix 2 for method of computation and justification for category means in the upper (e.g., 4+, 5+) categories.
[c] Average of figures from three surveys in 1978 (Table 2.2).
[d] Average of figures from six surveys in 1989 (Table 2.2).
Sources: Harris, 1968: Newton and Zimring (1969, pp. 9, 175–6); Gallup, 1975: Gallup (1976, p. 586); DMI, 1978; DMI (1979, p. 70); Gallup, 1983, 1989: Gallup (1984, p. 119; 1990, p. 89); Time/CNN: Quinley (1990, p. 2).

Table 2.4. Household Gun Ownership Patterns

	A. Household Gun Combinations, as of 1973–1977	
	% of all households	*% of gun-owning households*
Any gun(s)	48.1	100.0
Any handgun(s)	21.2	44.0
Any longgun(s)	41.1	85.4
Both handgun(s) and longgun(s)	14.2	29.5
Only handgun(s)	7.0	14.6
Only longgun(s)	26.9	56.0

	B. Guns per Owner, c. 1982	
	All Guns	*Handguns*
Adjusted % households owning	51.3	24.4
Estimated number households owning	42,815,940	20,397,293
Adjusted % persons age 18+ owning	30.9	16.7
Estimated persons age 18+ owning	52,328,157	28,305,622
Gun stock as of end of 1982	178,118,890	56,789,140
Guns per gun-owning household	4.160	2.784
Guns per gun-owning individual age 18+	3.404	2.006

Sources: A: Published marginals in codebooks for 1973, 1974, 1976, and 1977 General Social Surveys (Davis 1984 and previous years). B: Adjusted percentages owning guns are from combined 1980, 1982, and 1984 General Social Surveys, with each proportion shifted up 10% to adjust for underreporting of gun ownership. Gun stock figures are for 1982, from Table 2.1. The estimated number of U.S. households in 1982 was 83,527,000 and the number of persons age 18 or over was 169,292,000 (U.S. Bureau of the Census, *Statistical Abstract of the United States 1988*).

Table 2.5. Who Owns Guns?[a]

Respondent/Household Characteristic	% Respondents Owning		% Households Owning	
	Gun	Handgun	Gun	Handgun
Total population	28.1	15.2	46.6	22.2
Sex				
Male	49.0	25.5	54.4	28.0
Female	12.8	7.7	40.2	17.9
Race				
White	29.3	15.7	48.4	22.9
Black	19.3	12.5	30.5	18.5
Other	22.9	7.1	34.9	9.2
Ethnic group[b]				
Black	19.3	12.5	30.5	18.5
New stock white	21.4	10.5	36.0	15.5
Transition stock white	32.2	18.1	53.8	26.4
Unclassified and others, white	32.5	16.5	51.4	23.4
Old stock white	30.6	16.5	50.4	24.5
Age				
18–24	17.6	7.2	41.4	15.9
25–39	26.7	14.5	45.4	21.9
40–64	33.6	19.6	53.9	27.1
65 and over	28.8	14.2	39.6	18.5
Marital status				
Never married	19.2	10.1	34.3	16.6
Divorced	25.2	16.7	34.5	19.2
Separated	17.7	9.9	26.0	12.1
Widowed	24.3	12.3	30.5	14.4
Married	32.7	17.3	56.1	26.5
Religion				
Protestant	32.6	17.9	53.0	25.9
Catholic	20.3	10.0	35.5	15.4
Jewish	5.3	3.3	12.3	7.7
None	24.0	13.4	37.7	19.4
Family income				
Under $10,000	21.5	10.4	32.6	13.8
$10,000–19,999	28.8	15.3	47.5	21.4
$20,000–24,999	33.6	18.0	55.7	27.7
$25,000 or more	33.2	19.9	55.4	30.1
Occupation				
Professional, technical	20.9	13.1	36.8	21.1
Manager, administrator, sales workers	33.8	20.8	49.4	26.5
Clerical	15.4	9.4	41.8	20.1

(continued)

Table 2.5. (Continued)

Respondent/Household Characteristic	% Respondents Owning		% Households Owning	
	Gun	Handgun	Gun	Handgun
Craftsmen, Operatives	42.8	21.1	54.4	25.2
Farmers, farm laborers	73.4	19.2	79.7	20.1
Service Workers	16.8	10.5	37.5	19.0
Education				
(last grade completed)				
0–7	29.9	14.6	42.6	18.2
8–11	29.4	13.7	46.3	19.3
12	29.7	15.9	52.7	24.8
1–3 years of college	27.5	16.8	45.3	24.3
4 years of college	21.5	13.4	35.8	20.0
Over 4 years college	24.7	15.6	37.4	22.5
Size of place of residence				
Under 5,000 population	42.8	18.7	67.9	26.5
5,000–49,999	26.9	15.9	45.9	23.5
50,000–249,999	22.9	13.1	37.3	17.9
250,000–999,999	19.3	13.4	32.4	20.2
1,000,000 or more	10.5	6.9	18.6	11.7
Region				
New England	13.0	4.5	24.2	8.7
Middle Atlantic	19.7	8.4	33.0	12.3
East North Central	26.5	13.5	44.2	19.7
West North Central	30.8	11.8	55.4	17.3
South Atlantic	32.3	17.7	52.5	26.6
East South Central	37.4	23.3	59.4	32.3
West South Central	34.8	24.6	55.5	35.2
Mountain	39.8	21.6	60.8	31.2
Pacific	25.6	16.0	40.8	22.7
Political views				
Liberal	23.6	12.6	39.4	18.9
Moderate	26.7	13.2	47.5	21.5
Conservative	34.3	20.1	52.4	27.5
Hunter				
Yes	72.4	37.3	84.6	42.1
No	19.0	10.6	38.7	18.0
Arrest record				
(nontraffic)				
Yes	36.6	20.4	49.2	25.6
No	27.1	14.5	46.0	21.8

(continued)

Table 2.5. (Continued)

	% Respondents Owning		% Households Owning	
Respondent/Household Characteristic	*Gun*	*Handgun*	*Gun*	*Handgun*
Approval of violence (0–5 scale)				
0	19.1	6.2	32.5	9.8
1	24.9	13.2	43.0	18.3
2	24.7	14.0	44.9	22.7
3	30.7	17.9	51.0	25.5
4–5	35.3	19.9	48.4	24.4
Afraid to Walk in own area				
Yes	18.0	11.7	38.1	19.8
No	36.3	18.2	52.9	24.3
Afraid at home at night				
Yes	25.3	15.7	40.9	20.8
No	30.2	15.4	47.0	22.2
Burglarized in past year				
Yes	26.5	17.3	39.6	23.2
No	28.3	15.0	46.8	22.1
Robbed in past year				
Yes	23.6	15.2	32.8	19.1
No	28.2	15.2	46.5	22.3

[a] No answer, do not know, and other missing responses have been excluded before calculating percentages.

[b] Classified as in Stinchcombe et al. (1980, p. 110), in the order in which group entered United States: 5, old stock whites—English, Scots, Canadian, Scandinavian; 4, unclassifiable, multiple countries, missing cases, whites; 3, transition stock whites—German, Irish, and French; 2, new stock whites—Eastern, Southern European, Hispanic, Oriental, and other whites; 1, blacks (listed last because they have only recently been integrated into the social structure in such a way as to encourage gun ownership).

Source: Analysis of 1980, 1982 and 1984 General Social Surveys, combined (Davis and Smith 1984).

Table 2.6. Trends in Gun Ownership by Arrest Record[a]

Year	% Households with				% Respondents with			
	Gun		Handgun		Gun		Handgun	
	Yes[b]	*No*[c]	*Yes*	*No*	*Yes*	*No*	*Yes*	*No*
1973	50.7	47.7	20.3	20.1	—	—	—	—
1974	43.9	46.9	22.3	19.7	—	—	—	—
1976	44.7	48.3	28.5	21.6	—	—	—	—
1977	46.8	51.1	19.2	20.9	—	—	—	—
1980	51.1	47.6	24.3	23.2	40.7	27.4	20.9	15.6
1982	52.4	45.6	26.8	21.3	39.4	28.0	21.3	14.5
1984	44.6	45.5	25.3	21.2	29.2	25.5	18.9	13.5
% change, from 1973–77 to 1980–84	+6.1	−4.7	+12.8	+6.4	—	—	—	—

[a] These surveys did not ask about personal respondent gun ownership before 1980. All missing data were excluded before computing percentages.

[b] Arrest record.

[c] No arrest record.

Source: Author's tabulations from Cumulated General Social Surveys, 1973–1984 (Davis and Smith 1984).

Table 2.7. Gunshot Deaths, U.S. 1985[a]

	Category of Death					
ICD[b]	*Accident* *E800–949*	*Suicide* *E950–959*	*Homicide*[c] *E960–969*	*Legal Inter.*[d] *E970–977*	*Undetermined*[e] *E980–989*	*Total*
Total deaths	93459	29453	19380	496	2826	145612
By Firearms	1649	17369	11621	486	481	31606
% of total, by firearms	1.8	59.0	60.0	98.0	17.0	21.7
% of gun deaths	5	55	37	1.5	1.5	22
Estimated deaths by gun type						
Handguns	604	8063	9189	461	237	18554
Shotguns	683	6223	986	15	149	8056
Hunting rifles	359	3078	1446	10	95	4988
Military firearms	3	5	0	0	0	8

[a] All firearms deaths exclude deaths due to explosives. Deaths due to "late effects" of injury have all been proportionally allocated across the subcategories (firearms, handguns, etc.). The row weapon labels are the ones used in the category names in the ICD. Apparently, "hunting rifles" is used to designate all rifles except those used by the military.

[b] ICD, International Classification of Diseases cause-of-death codes, 9th revision, 1975.

[c] Firearms homicides have been allocated across gun type categories in accordance with the distribution of firearms murders and nonnegligent manslaughters reported in the 1985 Uniform Crime Reports (U.S. FBI 1986, p. 10); most of the firearms homicides in the vital statistics database were not specified as to gun type. Although the same problem characterized suicides and gun accidents, there was no alternative national source to use for allocating unspecified gun type cases across gun type categories. Therefore, for suicides and gun accidents, such cases were allocated in accordance with the distribution of deaths in which gun type was specified.

[d] Legal intervention covers killings by police in the line of duty. Counts exclude executions, none of which involved guns. The published figures have been doubled to adjust for widespread failure by medical examiners to note police involvement in such killings, leading to misclassification of these deaths (actually ICD categories E970–977) as general homicides (E960–969). True counts of killings by police are at least double the vital statistics counts (Sherman and Langworthy 1979). This adjustment resulted in 243 additional legal intervention deaths and 243 fewer general homicide deaths. There are no breakdowns of these deaths by gun type; it was asumed that 95% of legal intervention gun homicides involved handguns, 3% shotguns, and 2% rifles.

[e] Injury undetermined whether accidentally or purposely inflicted.

Sources: U.S. NCHS (1988, pp. 212, 218, 220, 222, 224, 305); U.S. FBI 1986 (p. 10, used only for allocating gun homicides across gun type subcategories).

Table 2.8. Estimated Nonfatal Gunshot Woundings, U.S. 1985

Nonfatal Gunshot Woundings Connected with	*Number*
Accidental shooting[a]	23910
Suicide attempt[b]	3137
Criminal assault[c]	99645
Legal intervention assault[c]	2552
Undetermined[d]	1997
Total	131241

[a] Data in Waller and Whorton (1973, p. 353) indicate that there were 58 nonfatal gun accidents and 4 fatal ones in 1967 in Vermont, a state in which physicians were required by law to report all persons treated for gunshot wounds, no matter how minor. This implies a ratio of 14.5 nonfatal accidental gunshot wounds for every fatal one. Since there were 1649 fatal gun accidents in 1985 (Table 2.9), this indicates there were about 14.5 × 1649 nonfatal gun accident woundings.
[b] Studies reviewed in Chapter 6 indicate that 84.7% of gun suicide attempts are fatal, implying a ratio of nonfatal to fatal attempts of 15.3/84.7 = 0.181; 17,369 gun suicides times 0.181 = 3137 nonfatal gun suicide attempts.
[c] Studies reviewed in Cook (1985) indicate about 16% of criminal gunshot woundings known to the police are fatal, implying a nonfatal to fatal ratio of 84/16 = 5.25; 11,621 gun homicides (i.e., fatal criminal assaults) times 5.25 = 99,645 nonfatal criminal gunshot woundings. The same ratio was applied to legal intervention killings.
[d] Undetermined whether accidentally or purposely inflicted. The nonfatal–fatal ratio applied was computed by combining the totals for the rest of the categories, yielding a ratio of 4.152; 481 "undetermined" deaths times 4.152 = 1997.

Table 2.9. Violent Crime Incidents Involving Guns, U.S., 1985[a]

Crime Type	Total Incidents	With Weapon		With Gun		With Handgun		With Other Gun	
		%	Number	%	Number	%	Number	%	Number
Rape	132920	20.2	26850	6.1	8082	4.5	6041	1.5	2041
Personal robbery[b]	878810	51.1	449072	17.0	149541	16.2	142356	0.8	7185
Completed	577780	53.7	310268	20.1	116350	19.3	111386	0.9	4964
With injury	188180	47.6	89574	8.2	15496	7.9	14959	0.3	537
w/o injury	105460	56.6	59690	26.1	27517	25.0	26383	1.1	1134
Attempted	301030	46.1	138775	11.1	33445	10.3	30947	0.8	2498
With injury	73130	47.3	34590	7.9	5811	7.9	5811	0.0	0
w/o injury	227900	45.7	104150	12.2	27704	11.1	25204	1.1	2500
Assault	3969970	29.6	1174636	9.1	362962	6.7	267817	2.4	95145
Aggravated	1257640	93.4	1174636	28.9	362962	21.3	267817	7.6	95145
Simple	2712330	0.0	0	0.0	0	0.0	0	0.0	0
Commercial robbery[c]	260561	65.2	169886	52.4	136534	48.0	125057	4.4	11477
Total	5242261	34.7	1820444	12.5	657119	10.3	541271	2.2	115848

[a] Because the NCS defines any assault involving a weapon as an aggravated assault, simple assaults, by definition, never involve weapons of any kind.

[b] Includes incidents that started as burglaries but developed into robberies when there was a confrontation between victim and offender.

[c] The National Crime Surveys (NCS) ceased gathering data on commercial robberies in 1976, so data from that year were used to estimate the number of commercial robberies in 1985, by multiplying the ratio of commercial robberies in 1976 to the number of personal robberies in 1976, times the number of personal robberies in 1985. The percentages of commercial robberies that involved weapons, guns, etc. in 1976 were then applied to this 1985 estimate. Note that this table omits criminal homicides, which are covered in Table 2.7, but it includes some criminal assaults involving gunshot wounds, thus overlapping to a degree with Table 2.8.

Source: U.S. Bureau of Justice Statistics (1978, pp. 22, 51, 60; 1987b, pp. 45, 56).

CHAPTER

3

Searching for "Bad" Guns: The Focus on Special Gun Types

Introduction

Gun ownership is commonplace in the United States, with about half of households having at least one. Consequently, restrictions on the acquisition, possession, and use of guns impinge on the lives of millions of Americans, not just a small or peculiar subset of them. This is the essential political obstacle that faces advocates of stricter gun control—legislators who vote for strong gun laws must face the prospect of offending large numbers of gun-owning voters at the next election. Perhaps in response to this simple political fact, many advocates of more restrictive controls have directed their focus away from measures that regulate all types of guns and toward those that regulate special subtypes of firearms, i.e., types of guns owned by smaller numbers of voters that are consequently more vulnerable to regulation.

Procontrol groups have increasingly stressed the need to control various special weapon categories such as machine guns, "assault rifles," plastic guns, "Saturday Night Special" handguns, and "cop-killer" bullets. For each weapon or ammunition type, it is argued that the object is especially dangerous or particularly useful for criminal purposes, while having little or no counterbalancing utility for lawful purposes. A common slogan is "This type of gun is good for only one purpose—killing people." The specific weapon type so described shifts from one year to the next. Sometimes the weapon is itself a new technological development, sometimes it is merely a newly popular device that has been around for years, and sometimes the weapon and its involvement in crime are not new in any sense other than the degree of media attention given to them.

What remains a constant is the effort to identify and more strictly regulate guns (or ammunition) that are regarded as *especially* dangerous and criminally useful, i.e., to search for especially "bad" guns that are even more problematic than guns in general. Although this strategy solves the political problems associated with regulating the more popular gun types, it also entails difficulties regarding the effectiveness of the regulations. First, when the gun type to be regulated is rare in the noncriminal general public, it usually is also rare among criminals as well, and thus not widely used in crime. This limits the potential impact of the regulations. Second, the same technical characteristics of guns that make them useful for criminal purposes almost always also increase their utility for a variety of lawful purposes as well, such as self-defense. Third, and most seriously, successful restrictions on availability of some gun types would lead criminals to substitute other weapon types, and in some cases the most likely substitutes would be more dangerous than the weapons targeted for control.

Types of Guns

To understand what follows it is necessary to clarify some of the distinctions between major types of firearms. Therefore the principal categories of guns are defined below.

Firearm: A weapon capable of firing a projectile by producing a controlled explosion or rapid chemical reaction. As used in this book the term is restricted to hand-held small arms. BB guns and CO_2 pellet guns are not firearms.

Handgun: A small firearm with a short barrel (rarely more than eight inches) and no buttstock, designed to be fired with the hands only, not from the shoulder.

Revolver: A repeating handgun employing a revolving cylinder that moves cartridges (most commonly five to nine) into alignment with the barrel.

Semiautomatic Pistol: A repeating handgun with a spring-loaded magazine that pushes cartridges into the chamber. It fires only one shot per trigger pull, but each shot causes successive rounds to be chambered (i.e., it is autoloading), ready to be fired. The rate of fire is somewhat higher than that of the revolver. Magazines commonly hold 5–17 cartridges.

Long Gun (or shoulder weapon): A larger firearm with a long barrel and a buttstock, designed to be fired with the buttstock held against the shoulder. It includes rifles and shotguns.

Rifle: A long gun with a rifled barrel (spiraling grooves on the inside of the barrel); most rifles fire a single bullet with each trigger pull. Cartridges can be fed into firing position by movement of a hand-operated bolt, lever, or pump after each shot, or fed by a semiautomatic mechanism similar to that described above for pistols.

Shotgun: A long gun with one or two barrels, each of which is smooth on the inside and fires a shotshell, discharging a large number of round pellets (usually from 15 to over 400), or sometimes a single large rifled slug. Ammunition can be chambered by operating a pump action for each round, by a semiautomatic mechanism, or the gun may have one or two barrels each of which holds one shotshell. Most hunting shotguns hold 2–5 rounds, most "military and police" shotguns hold 5–9 rounds, and some exotic varieties can hold 20 or more (Warner 1988).

Machine Gun: Unlike the weapons described above, this gun can fire in fully automatic mode, i.e., it can fire multiple shots per trigger pull, firing as long as the trigger is held down and ammunition remains. The term usually denotes a fully automatic weapon firing rifle caliber ammunition.

Submachine Gun: A fully automatic weapon that fires handgun ammunition and can be operated by a single person.

Assault Rifle: In its original meaning this term denoted a "selective fire" military rifle capable of either fully automatic, 3–5 round burst, or semiautomatic fire, firing ammunition of intermediate power. Recent journalistic usage has altered the term to refer to rifles capable only of semiautomatic fire, but which are military in appearance or lineage (i.e., adapted from military guns).

Machine Guns

It has been unlawful since 1934 for Americans to possess fully automatic firing weapons without special permission from the U.S. Department of Treasury; registering a machine gun involves being fingerprinted, undergoing a background check, and paying $200 for a tax stamp (Kennett and Anderson 1975, pp. 206–11). Even this exception was curtailed in 1986 with the passage of the Firearms Owners' Protection Act, which "froze" the number of machine guns legally possessed by private individuals at the 1986 level (Hogan 1986). As of April 19, 1989, there were 193,084 machine guns legally registered in the United States, with about 103,000 of these owned by private individuals. The rest belonged to police departments and other governmental agencies (U.S. Bureau of Alcohol, Tobacco and Firearms 1989a). The number of illegally owned machine guns is unknown.

Edward D. Conroy, head of the Miami office of the Bureau of Alcohol, Tobacco and Firearms (later BATF Deputy Director in charge of enforcement), was quoted in 1985 as asserting that "machine gun hits are almost commonplace" in Miami, and that "there are even brazen attacks at stoplights, with grandma and the kiddies getting greased along with the target" (*Newsweek* 10-14-85, p. 48). Are machine gun killings "almost commonplace," either in Miami or the nation as a whole? Certainly if such events were common anywhere in the United States, they should have been common in the "machine gun Mecca" of Miami, since drug dealers were reputedly the type of criminal most likely to use machine guns, and alleged drug killings made up an unusually large share of killings in that city (Wilbanks 1984). Further, according to BATF officials, the Miami area was the nation's leading locale for illicit machine gun sales (*Tallahassee Democrat* 1-14-90, p. 10D). In 1980, Miami's homicide rate hit its all-time high (Wilbanks 1984). According to Dr. Joseph Davis, medical examiner of Dade County, of 569 total homicides, five or six involved machine guns (one homicide involved multiple gun types). This was less than 1% of all homicides (*Miami Herald* 8-23-84, p. 19A). Although there are no comparable national figures, almost certainly the figure was still lower for the United States.

Presumably this handful of machine gun homicides involved illegally owned machine guns. Concerning machine guns legally registered with the Treasury Department, the Director of BATF testified before Congress that he knew of fewer than 10 crimes of any kind committed with a legally possessed machine gun (no time period specified) (Higgins 1986). Even this small total could have included violations of gun regulations, such as moving a registered weapon across state lines without notifying BATF.

Some rough idea of the sorts of guns commonly carried and used by criminals can be obtained from records of firearms confiscated by police. Machine guns are apparently so rare in these samples that they are not even mentioned in tabulations by gun type (e.g., Los Angeles Police Department 1989). Even among guns seized from drug dealers, machine guns are extremely rare. A total of 420 weapons, including 375 guns, were seized during drug warrant executions and arrests by the Metropolitan Area Narcotics Squad (Will and Grundy counties in the Chicago metropolitan area) from 1980 to 1989. None of the guns was a machine gun. Three were Uzis and three were MAC 11s, guns that are normally semiautomatic, but can be converted to fully automatic fire. Drug dealers apparently rarely use machine guns, preferring medium-bore handguns and shotguns (Mericle 1989).

Machine guns fire bullets at extremely high rates, normally 400–1000 rounds per minute, or about 7–17 rounds per second. As a result, they are difficult to aim accurately with controlled fire. Except at the closest ranges, it is almost impossible for a shooter to make more than the first round hit a human-sized target. Thus a shooter with a machine gun fires more rounds in a given span of time, but with less chance of any one round hitting what was aimed at. These two facts work in opposite directions regarding the dangerousness of the weapon, and it is unclear whether the net effect of using fully automatic fire is to increase or decrease the chances of an intended victim being wounded. Soldiers using assault rifles are commonly trained to fire single shots when they need accurate fire in combat. Very high rates of fire are even criticized by military firearms experts as tending to waste ammunition and to produce few hits, due to excessive dispersion (e.g., Ezell 1983, p. 67).

Although it is not clear that fully automatic fire makes a gun more dangerous to an intended target, machine guns increase the likelihood that innocent bystanders will be accidentally shot in those rare incidents in which a shooter fires into a crowd. Whereas the likelihood of hitting one specific intended victim is not increased by the use of automatic fire, the chances of hitting *someone* in the crowd would be increased.

As Mr. Conroy's remark suggests, some law enforcement personnel believe that incidents of "grandma and the kiddies" or other innocent bystanders being killed by automatic fire are commonplace, especially in shootings related to drug trafficking. This is untrue. Killings of innocent bystanders, under any circumstances, constitute less than 1% of homicides, even in big cities and even in the 1980s, when their frequency increased (Sherman et al. 1989). A large share of them, though not necessarily a majority, may well be related to drug trafficking (p. 312), but there is no evidence that any significant share involves fully automatic guns. Even in the peak homicide year of 1980, in Dade (Miami) County, Florida, probably the drug trafficking capital of the United States at the time, there was only one case of an innocent bystander being accidentally killed in a drug-related shooting (of 569 homicides, about 112 of them allegedly drug-related), and that case did not involve a machine gun (based on my examination of homicide summaries in Wilbanks 1984). Ordinarily the people killed in drug-related incidents are involved in drug trafficking themselves, are killed intentionally, and thus are neither "innocent" nor bystanders. Innocent bystanders are rarely killed in such incidents, by automatic fire or otherwise, because the typical drug killing occurs in an isolated or private location rather than a crowded city street and shots are thus unlikely to hit anyone other than the intended target.

It should be stressed, however, that even though machine gun killings of innocent bystanders are currently almost nonexistent, this does not mean that they could not become common in the future if restrictions on machine guns were eased. Although, oddly enough, gun control advocates rarely mention it, the *de facto* federal machine gun ban in place since 1934 may well be an example of a successful gun control effort. Although the large size and greater cost of machine guns and the difficulty in aiming them accurately probably would have discouraged extensive criminal use anyway, the fact remains that machine guns were banned and subsequently have rarely been used in crime.

Assault Rifles and Assault Weapons

According to official Department of Defense definitions, as well as usage in standard firearms reference works, an assault rifle (AR) is a "selective fire" military rifle, i.e., one capable of firing both fully automatically and semiautomatically (and sometimes in short bursts of 3–5 rounds) (U.S. Department of Defense 1980, p. 105; Ezell 1983, p. 515). However, the term "assault rifle" took on a very different meaning in common journalistic usage in the late 1980s, usually referring to weapons capable of firing only in a semiautomatic mode, and having a "military" appearance. There is no official definition of the term in its journalistic usage, and this usage is clearly inconsistent with official military definitions. The term "assault rifle" in quotes will be used to refer to the journalistically defined weapon type and the term without quotes to refer to true assault rifles.

An even vaguer term "assault weapons" (AW), also began to appear in the news media in the late 1980s. The term seemed to encompass semiautomatic pistols and a few shotguns as well as "assault rifles," although it too appears to be restricted to weapons conceptualized as "military-style" guns. Most firearms, no matter what their current uses, derive directly or indirectly from firearms originally designed for the military; "military-style" appears to signify a modern or contemporary military appearance. For example, plastic stocks are supposedly more "military" in appearance than wood stocks, a loop for a lanyard is military-style, having a nonreflective surface is more military than a shiny one, and so on. Mechanically, there are no significant differences between the semiautomatic rifles labeled "assault rifles" and other semiautomatic centerfire rifles sold to the civilian market for hunting and target shooting, such as the Ruger Mini-14/5R Ranch Rifle and the Valmet Hunter (Warner 1988, pp. 298, 302).

Legislators and other policy makers have also had difficulties defining "assault weapons." They have had to tackle the difficult task of developing a definition that simultaneously satisfied two conflicting requirements: (1) it identified the attributes that supposedly make AWs more dangerous than other guns, and (2) was sufficiently limited so as to not restrict gun models popular among large numbers of voters. The chief attributes that are supposed to make AWs more dangerous than other guns are their semiautomatic capability, which provides a higher rate of fire than other guns (and allegedly make it easy to convert the guns to a fully automatic capability), and their ability to accept large-capacity magazines. However, if a law restricted all guns with such attributes, millions of voters would be affected. About 300,000–400,000 semiautomatic centerfire rifles and about 400,000–800,000 semiautomatic pistols are sold each year in the United States (U.S. Bureau of the Census 1989; Howe 1987), and a December 1989 national survey indicated that 27% of U.S. gun owners reported ownership of at least one semiautomatic gun (Quinley 1990, p. 3), which would imply that about 13% of all U.S. households own such guns. Most of these semiautomatic firearms can accept large magazines.

As a way out of this conflict, many policymakers have thrown up their hands and declined to identify the dangerous attributes of AWs. Instead, the proposed bills include long lists of specific makes and models of guns that have little in common beyond (almost always) a semiautomatic loading mechanism and (usually) an arguably "military" appearance. Typical of such efforts is that of the Florida Commission on Assault Weapons (Florida 1990), which listed no less than 66 different guns in a survey designed to gather data on AWs from police agencies. The list lumped together handguns, rifles, and shotguns, both those usually sold with large magazines and those sold with small ones, large caliber and small caliber, foreign-made and domestic. Although the guns on the list were almost all semiautomatic, so were a large number of guns left off the list, such as the very popular Colt Model 1911A1 .45-caliber pistol and the Beretta Model 92 9-mm pistol. Legislation passed in California and New Jersey, as well as a federal ban on importation, defined the restricted weapon category using similarly heterogeneous lists of specific gun models (Cox Newspapers 1989).

The difficulties with this political compromise are obvious. If semiautomatic fire and the ability to accept large magazines are not important in crime, there is little reason to regulate AWs. On the other hand, if these *are* important crime-aggravating attributes, then it makes little crime control sense (though ample political sense) to systematically exclude from restriction the most widely owned models that have these attributes, since this severely limits the impact of regulation.

There is nothing new about either semiautomatic firearms in general or "assault rifles" in particular. Semiautomatic firearms were produced in large numbers beginning in the late nineteenth century, and true assault rifles were introduced into military use during World War II, (Ezell 1983, pp. 17, 514–5). Semiautomatic "assault rifles" did become more popular among civilians during the 1980s—gun catalogs indicate a substantial increase in the number of models of "paramilitary" rifles shown between 1973 and 1988 (compare Koumjian 1973 with Warner 1988). However, this is less significant than it appears, because it reflects little more than a demand for guns with military-style cosmetic details, rather than a criminologically significant shift in mechanically different gun types. Mechanically, "assault rifles" are semiautomatic centerfire rifles. Trends in sales of semiautomatic centerfire rifles were basically flat in the period from 1982 to 1987, and were substantially lower in the 1980s than in the 1970s (see Table 3.1). The major trend in recent years has not been a shift to mechanically different types of rifles, but rather a shift in consumer preferences regarding guns' appearance, and a substantial shift away from domestic sources to foreign sources of semiautomatic rifles. In light of this latter trend, President George Bush's move in 1989 to ban imports of foreign "assault rifles" makes more sense as trade protectionism than as gun control. Similarly, proposed state controls were heavily aimed at foreign-origin AWs (e.g., Florida 1990).

Among handguns, there was a trend towards semi-automatic pistols and away from revolvers in the 1970s and 1980s. In 1973, 28% of handguns produced by U.S. manufacturers were semiautomatic pistols, compared to 58% in 1987 (Howe 1987; U.S. Bureau of Alcohol, Tobacco and Firearms 1989b). This trend was characteristic of the general flow of guns into the general population's stock of guns, implying increases in the average magazine capacity and rate of fire of U.S. handguns. It seems likely that a similar trend occurred among criminals, though it is unknown whether the trend was any stronger among criminals. It also is unclear whether such a trend would have caused any increases in violent crime or influenced the outcomes of many criminal assaults.

Although there was no upward trend in sales of semiautomatic centerfire rifles in the general public from the early 1970s to the late 1980s, it might be argued that the prevalence of ownership and use of these and other weapons in the broad AW category increased among criminals during this period. There are no reliable quantitative trend data for this period, partly because the matter did not become an issue until late in the period. The best available information appears to be that pertaining to trends in Dade County (Miami), Florida. An informal 1990 survey of all seven firearms examiners in that county yielded the unanimous opinion that AW use in shootings had been slowly and steadily declining since 1981 (Florida 1990, pp. 156–7).

It was commonplace for news sources in the late 1980s to refer to "assault rifles" as the "favored" weapon of criminals, or, more specifically, of drug dealers and youth gangs (e.g., *New York Times* 2-21-89; *Newsweek* 10-14-85, p. 48). There is no hard evidence to support such a claim, either for criminals in general or for these specific types of criminals. Analyses of samples of guns seized by police from criminals indicate that only a small fraction can be described as "assault weapons." This fraction was less than 3% ("assault rifles" only) in Los Angeles in 1988 (Trahin 1989), 0.5% ("assault-type long guns") in New York City in 1988 [*White Plains Reporter Dispatch* 3-27-89, pp. A8, A9 (Associated Press wire service story)], 8% ("assault weapons") in Oakland, California, less than 3% (semiautomatic rifles, including sporting ones) in Chicago, and 0% ("assault weapons" covered under the 1989 federal import ban) in Washington, D.C. (*New York Times* 4-3-89, p. A14). Of 217 homicides committed in 1989 in Dade County (Miami) Florida, 3 or 1.4% involved an "assault weapon" (Florida 1990, pp. 140–3). In Massachusetts (excluding Boston) during 1984–1988, there were 559 criminal homicides, about 295 of them involving guns (U.S. FBI 1985–1989). Of these, 5 involved "assault rifles" (*Boston Globe* 3-16-89, p. 12), i.e., 0.9% of the homicides and about 1.7% of the gun homicides. With the exception of the Oakland data, available evidence indicates that AWs constituted no more than 3% of crime guns in the nation's big cities. In the face of such evidence, even a spokesman for Handgun Control, Inc., which advocated tighter restrictions on AWs, conceded that assault weapons "play a small role in overall violent crime" (emphasizing, however, that they could become a problem in the future) (*New York Times* 4-7-89, p. A15).

This spokesman's use of the term "overall violent crime" may have been intended to hint that "ARs" or AWs might be commonly used by special criminal subgroups such as drug dealers and youth gang members. For example, a spokesman for the U.S. Drug Enforcement Administration asserted that "you can count on coming across them on every single narcotics raid" (*Los Angeles Herald Examiner* 1-23-89, p. A-1). The limited available hard evidence contradicts the claim that "assault weapons" are favored by these groups. Records of the previously mentioned Chicago-area narcotics unit indicated that only 6 of 375 guns seized in drug raids, or 1.6% could be described as AWs (Mericle 1989).

In Los Angeles, beginning in 1983, police and newspapers reported an epidemic of so-called "drive-by" shootings allegedly involving gang members using "assault weapons" to fight over control of drug trafficking. However, when queried about the guns seized from gang members, the head of the city's largest police gang detail admitted that (as of 1985) the unit had not confiscated any AWs: "We've seized only shotguns and handguns, but I have *heard about* the purchase of Uzis and military assault rifles" (*Crime Control Digest* 5-13-85, p. 2; emphasis added). Presumably "AR" use was even less common among gang members in cities lacking the vocal concern over gang use of "ARs" that characterized Los Angeles.

Probably the most extensive data on the involvement of AWs in crime were gathered by the Florida Assault Weapons Commission (1990), which distributed a survey on the topic to virtually every police agency in the state. The Commission defined AWs very broadly, providing agencies with a list of 66 models of handguns, rifles, and shotguns. The survey covered the period 1986–1989 and inquired about guns involved in crimes as well as all guns confiscated or recovered after being abandoned. Of 136 agencies eventually returning the survey, 18 were "unable to provide information" and another three provided unusable data. Of the remaining 115 agencies, 86 reported "no experience with assault weapons" or "no assault weapons listed." Of the 29 agencies with some experience with AWs, only two reported experience with more than two such guns. Of 2522 guns "seized or abandoned" and recovered by the police, only 90 (3.6%) were AWs under the broad definition used. If nonreporting agencies were predominantly those without any contact with AWs, the true figures for AW involvement in crime would all be lower. In sum, in Florida, a state in which drug-linked AW use was purportedly very common, most police agencies, even over a 4-year period, had apparently never come across even a single AW.

Lest it be thought that such negative evidence dissuaded those who believed that "assault weapons" were popular crime weapons, consider a widely published newspaper series produced by the Cox newspaper chain. Rather than study general samples of guns seized by police from criminals committing gun crimes, the reporters studied a more eccentric subset of seized guns—those for which a "trace request" had been processed by BATF.

A trace request is submitted when police have seized a gun and decide they want to track down its previous history, from manufacture or importation to wholesale purchase to first retail purchase. About 35,100 trace requests were sent to BATF in 1987 (Cox Newspapers 1989, p. 3). Cox claimed that about 1 in 10 "gun crimes" results in a trace request. In fact, only about 1 of 6 of these trace requests involved a gun used to further a violent crime such as homicide, assault, or robbery. The rest were linked only with technical gun violations (illegal possession, sales, etc.), "narcotics" violations, or other "miscellaneous" offenses (BATF 1990). Thus, there are only about 5600 traces per year of guns used to further violent crimes. Compared to about 360,000 such crimes known to the police in 1987 (U.S. FBI 1988), this means that fewer than 2% of violent gun crimes result in a trace. Thus, requesting a trace is strictly optional and clearly not very common.

It also is apparently not random. For example, there seems to be a disproportionate tendency to request a trace when a gun is linked with drug trafficking or other "organized" crime (Cox Newspapers 1989, p. 4). For whatever reason, "assault weapons" are substantially overrepresented among guns traced, relative to their share of all guns used in violent crimes. Cox claimed that 10% of U.S. "crime guns" (i.e., among those few that were traced) were "assault weapons." However, they also provided a "city-by-city" breakdown that allows comparisons with the previously cited police data taken from the entire stock of guns seized from criminals. The latter data indicated that 3% of seized guns in Chicago were semi-automatic rifles, whereas Cox found that 10% of traces concerned "assault weapons." The corresponding figures were 3% ("assault rifles") of all confiscated gun vs. 19% for Los Angeles trace requests, under 1% ("assault rifles") of all guns vs. 11% of New York City's trace requests, and 0% ("assault weapons" covered under federal import ban) vs. 13% of trace requests from Washington, D.C. Part of these huge discrepancies is due to the fact that the Cox reporters defined "assault weapons" more broadly than did police departments in these cities—the Cox definition encompassed 64 different weapons (p. 1). However, Cox reported that 90% of the traced "assault weapons" were of just 10 different models, 6 of which were "assault rifles" clearly counted in the police estimates based on confiscation stocks. Most of the difference, therefore, was probably due to the simple fact that guns on which trace requests are filed are not representative, by gun type, of the firearms used in crime. Consequently, the Cox trace request data could not provide a reliable basis for judging the share of crime guns that are "assault weapons." It is worth noting that the Cox Chain began publishing their "assault weapons" series on May 21, 1989, over a month and a half after publication of the *New York Times* and Associated Press articles in which the more representative police confiscation figures were reported.

About the time that news stories started to report on how rarely "assault rifles" were used in crime (ca. April 1989), the Cox chain and other newspapers shifted their emphasis to the broader, more vaguely defined category dubbed "assault weapons" (AWs), an amorphous category that included many semiautomatic pistols and a few shotgun models, apparently with military-style cosmetic details, as well as "assault rifles." Thus, the emphasis was shifted to semiautomatic handguns. The Cox chain claimed that criminals "preferred" AWs in some sense, documenting their claim by showing that the fraction of traced guns that were AWs exceeded a rough guess from BATF on the fraction of all U.S. guns that were AWs (Cox 1989, p. 4).

Could it be that criminals "prefer" semiautomatic pistols in this same sense? Trace requests are misleading for judging the types of guns generally used by criminals, but no other national source covers all guns seized by police or a representative sample of seized guns. However, one can examine a local police sample of seized guns and compare it with guns recently added to the general U.S. gun stock. Zimring (1976) showed that the majority of guns used by criminals are relatively recently manufactured guns, so these would be the appropriate set of guns to use in the comparison. In a sample of guns seized in the first 3 months of 1989 by the Los Angeles Police Department, 49.8% of the handguns were semiautomatic pistols (Los Angeles Police Department 1989). Among the 7.08 million handguns added to the U.S. stock (the number domestically manufactured, plus imports, minus exports) from 1984 to 1987 (1988 data were not yet available), about 3.89 million were semiautomatic pistols.[1] Thus, about 55% of the handguns bought by the general, largely noncriminal public were semiautomatic pistols, while only about 50% of those seized from criminals fell into this category. Los Angeles criminals in 1989 did not "prefer" semiautomatic weapons in the sense of going out of their way to obtain them in numbers disproportionate to their share of the recently sold handgun stock. Rather, criminals were just using the same kinds of handguns as recent noncriminal gun buyers were obtaining. If the higher rate of fire and larger magazines of these weapons were important to criminals, they were no more important to them than to noncriminal gun buyers.

"Assault rifles" are clearly much larger than the handguns criminals really do favor, and even "assault weapon" handguns such as Uzis are generally larger than other handguns. Since criminals say they favor more concealable handguns, this may largely explain why so few criminals use assault weapons.

AW pistols are no more lethal than either non-AW semiautomatic pistols (since they differ only cosmetically) or revolvers. Moreover, "ARs" are less lethal than ordinary civilian hunting rifles and the standard military rifles of the World War II era. Based on scattered experience in treating wounds purportedly inflicted with "assault rifles," some emergency room physicians have asserted that these guns create especially devastating and lethal wounds that are unusually hard to treat (*New York Times* 2-21-89). However, specialists in the wounding effects of military rifle ammunition, experienced in treating battlefield wounds, contradict this claim (Fackler 1989; Mohler 1989). Dr. Martin L. Fackler (1989), Director of the Wound Ballistics Laboratory at the Letterman Army Institute of Research, has noted that typical "assault rifles" fire smaller-than-average ammunition, and has shown through ballistics experiments that this ammunition has milder wounding effects than civilian hunting ammunition or regular infantry rifle cartridges. This is partly because the military cartridges commonly used in "assault rifles" have smaller, pointed bullets, which tend to produce smaller wounds, which are correspondingly less lethal. The more lethal hollow point or "dum-dum" bullet often used in hunting ammunition was forbidden for military use by the 1899 Hague Peace Conference. In addition to serving life-saving humanitarian purposes, the smaller, pointed full-metal-jacketed bullet has military advantages. By wounding rather than killing enemy soldiers, it not only removes the soldier from combat, but also requires the enemy to devote resources to evacuating and treating him. Further, the light weight of the bullets allows soldiers to carry more rounds. In short, rather than being designed to kill human beings, the military ammunition commonly used in assault rifles was designed in such a way as to reduce the likelihood it would kill.

Nevertheless, compared to the ammunition used in the middle-caliber handguns that criminals commonly use, "AR" ammunition is indeed more lethal, as is rifle ammunition in general. Fackler described the "AR" ammunition as being intermediate in power between handgun ammunition and regular infantry rifle cartridges (and, by implication, civilian hunting ammunition). Thus, if many criminals in the future did start using "ARs" in place of handguns it would result in higher fatality rates in assaults and other crimes. Because of the limited concealability of "ARs," it is unlikely that criminals would adopt them. But even if at least some types of criminals did seek out rifles as an alternative to handguns, they would have an ample supply of more lethal substitute rifles available to them even in the absence of "ARs."

While "ARs" are not unusually lethal relative to other rifles, they do have other technical attributes potentially relevant to criminal violence: (1) they are capable of firing single shots as fast as the shooter can pull the trigger, and (2) they can accept magazines that hold a large number of cartridges. It is unclear whether either of these attributes is of substantial criminological significance. "ARs" are capable of firing at a rate somewhat faster than other gun types, but it is unknown how often violent incidents occur in which this higher rate of fire would have any impact on the outcome of the incident. For example, even in a rare mass shooting such as the 1989 Stockton schoolyard killing of five children, the killer fired 110 rounds in 3 to 4 (or more) minutes, or about 28–37 rounds per minute (*Los Angeles Times* 1-18-89, p. 3; 1-19-89, p. 9). The same rate of fire can be achieved with an ordinary double-action revolver using speed-loaders to reload. Further, there was nothing to stop Purdy from continuing his attack for another 3 or 4 minutes. The higher rate of fire was unnecessary for Purdy to carry out his murderous intentions—he did all the shooting he wanted to do in 4 minutes and then killed himself.

The effective rate of fire of any gun is limited by its recoil. When a shot is fired, the force of the bullet leaving the barrel causes the gun to move back toward the shooter and off of its original aiming alignment. It cannot be fired at the same target again until the shooter puts it back in line with the target. Thus the somewhat higher rate of fire of semiautomatic weapons cannot be fully exploited, reducing the effective difference between these weapons and revolvers.

Ordinary revolvers can easily fire six rounds in 3 seconds without any special skill on the part of the shooter or modification to the weapon. Even assuming a semiautomatic gun could fire at twice this rate, it would only mean that a shooter could fire six rounds in 1.5 instead of 3 seconds. The issue comes down to this: How many violent incidents occur each year in which a shooter has 1.5 seconds to shoot the victim(s), but not 3 seconds? Such incidents are probably fairly rare, although there are no hard data on the matter.

Critics of "ARs" have also pointed to the high total *volume* of fire of which the weapons are capable, due to their large magazines. It should be noted that magazines for these weapons are almost always detachable, and the weapons are usually capable of accepting many different common magazine sizes, whether one containing only 3 rounds, or one containing 30 or more (Warner 1989). Thus, the high volume of rounds is not, strictly speaking, an attribute of the gun itself, but rather of the magazine. Likewise, most of the millions of ordinary semiautomatic pistols sold in the United States for decades are also capable of accepting box-type magazines that can have very large capacities. Consequently, one legal difficulty in distinguishing "ARs" from other semiautomatic rifles, or AWs from other semiautomatic handguns, is that most varieties of all of these weapon categories accept box-type magazines. Since such magazines can be either big or small, it means that the unrestricted civilian-style guns are just as capable of using a large-capacity magazine as are the restricted modern military-style AWs. Consequently, rational controls based on concern over large ammunition capacity would have to either ban large magazines or ban all guns capable of receiving types of magazines that sometimes have large capacities. The former alternative would be very difficult to enforce, whereas the latter alternative would mean banning large numbers of hunting rifles and most semiautomatic pistols, and thus would negate the chief political benefit of restricting only rare weapons.

It is doubtful whether a high volume magazine is currently relevant to the outcome of a large number of violent incidents. The rare mass killing notwithstanding, gun assaults usually involve only a few shots being fired. Even in a sample of gun attacks on armed police officers, where the incidents are more likely to be mutual combat gunfights with many shots fired, the suspects fired an average of only 2.55 times (New York City Police Department 1989, p. 6). On the other hand, if high-volume guns did become popular among criminals in the future, this could change for the worse. Further, although "ARs" are not unique in any one of their attributes, they are unusual, although not unique, in combining the lethality of rifles, a potentially large ammunition capacity, *and* a high rate of fire. It is possible that the combination of all three attributes could have a crime-enhancing effect greater than that generated by any one of the attributes.

Whereas semiautomatic firearms offer a rate of fire only somewhat higher than other common gun types, fully automatic weapons have much higher rates of fire. "ARs" sold on the civilian market are not capable of fully automatic fire, but it has been argued that this distinction is a minor one because "ARs" are so easily converted to fully automatic fire (*Newsweek* 10-14-85, pp. 48–9). The *New York Times,* in an editorial, even told its readers that "many semiautomatics can be made fully automatic with a screwdriver, even a paperclip" (8-2-88). Eight months later, a *New York Times* feature article about a federal ban on importation of "ARs" gave its readers a rather different view of the "issue of whether or not such guns are easy to convert from semiautomatics to illegal fully automatics":

> The staff of technical experts at the [Bureau of Alcohol Tobacco and Firearms] disassemble, test and examine samples of all semiautomatic weapons marketed in the United States to make formal determinations on this question. Any model found to be readily convertible to automatic fire would be declared illegal. None of the five types included in the import ban had been declared readily convertible, *nor have any domestic semiautomatics now on sale.* (4-3-89; emphasis added)

Thus, none of the semiautomatic guns available for sale in the U.S., whether "ARs" or not, was readily convertible to fully automatic fire as of 1989. Two semiautomatics, the MAC-10 and MAC-11, were sold in the United States, but in 1982 were declared by the BATF to be "readily convertible" to automatic fire and their further sale was banned (Hancock 1985). Of course, it is trivially true that almost any gun can be converted to fully automatic fire, given sufficient expertise, time, tools, and added parts. Given unlimited resources, one could also fabricate an entire machine gun from scratch. However, data on weapons seized by police indicate that criminals almost never have both the resources and the inclination to perform a conversion. Of over 4000 guns confiscated by the Los Angeles Police Department in a 1-year period, only about a half dozen (1/6 of 1%) were formerly semiautomatic guns successfully converted to fully automatic fire; only about a dozen showed evidence of even an attempt to perform a conversion (Trahin 1989).

All rifles fire bullets at high velocity, which increases the likelihood they can penetrate body armor of the sort police officers wear. This has given rise to concern about "ARs" by some police. One big city police official was quoted in the *Los Angeles Times* (5-25-90) as saying "We're tired of passing out flags to the widows of officers killed by drug dealers with Uzis." Are large numbers of police officers killed by drug dealers using Uzis? It is easy enough to test this narrow claim about Uzis. According to the Chief of the FBI's Uniform Crime Reporting Program, from 1980 when the Uzi was first imported into the U.S., through 1989, not one police officer in the U.S. was killed by a drug dealer with an Uzi. Only one case in their files involved an officer killed with an Uzi under any circumstances, but this was in Puerto Rico and did not involve a drug dealer (Wilson 1990a).

The police official's claim might generously be interpreted to broadly refer to all AWs rather than just Uzis, and all criminals, not just drug dealers. For the 10-year period 1980–1989, of 810 officers feloniously killed in the United States and its territories, 33 (4%) were killed by "assault weapon" models covered by federal restrictions either passed or pending as of January, 1991. For 1986–1989, of 284 killings, 14 involved rifles and three involved handguns covered under such restrictions (U.S. Congressional Research Service 1991, p. 6). Thus, 4% involved "ARs" and 5% involved AWs, averaging about four AW killings of police officers in the United States per year.

For the entire nation in 1988, there were 78 police officer killings, of which 5–8 involved AWs (U.S. Congressional Research Service 1991, p. 6). Based on case descriptions published by the FBI, there were at most four, and possibly *no* police officers, killed by drug dealers using any kind of "assault weapon" anywhere in the U.S. in 1988 (U.S. FBI 1989, pp. 31, 33, 37).

"Assault rifles" are of particular concern to police because some of these weapons, like civilian hunting rifles, are capable of penetrating police body armor. ("Assault weapon" handguns are no more capable of penetrating body armor than ordinary revolvers.) In the United States in 1988, five officers wearing body armor were killed by gunshot wounds inflicted anywhere other than in the head, regardless of the gun type used (U.S. FBI 1989, p. 13). At least four of these, however, involved bullets that passed between body armor panels or in lower torso areas below the area covered by protective vests (U.S. FBI 1989, pp. 28, 31, 35–6, 38). In sum, killings of police officers with bullets penetrating body armor, fired from AWs or any other kinds of guns, were almost nonexistent.

Have the very rare killings of police officers by assailants using "assault rifles" increased in recent years? Table 3.2 presents relevant data covering 1970–1989. The figures indicate that killings of police officers generally declined over this period, the number and fraction involving guns declined slightly, and the number and fraction involving rifles declined slightly. The maximum number that could have involved "ARs" (i.e., involved rifles with calibers common among "ARs") has always been very small (nine or fewer in any single year) and has shown no consistent trend over this period.

To summarize, "assault rifles" and "assault weapons" are rarely used by criminals in general or by drug dealers or juvenile gang members in particular, are almost never used to kill police officers, are generally less lethal than ordinary hunting rifles, and are not easily converted to fully automatic fire. They offer a rate of fire somewhat higher than other gun types and can be used with magazines holding large numbers of cartridges, but there is at present little reason to believe either attribute is relevant to the outcome of any significant number of gun crimes.

Plastic Guns

An even rarer weapon type has been the focus of regulatory efforts. A federal law passed in 1988 required that all guns contain a certain minimum amount of metal, thereby banning guns made entirely of nonmetallic materials such as plastic. These weapons were of concern to legislators because they would not be detectable by metal detectors such as those used at airports, outside courtrooms, and in prisons and other secure facilities. They would thus be ideal, for example, for use by persons intent on hijacking airplanes. Such weapons *are* detectable by the X-ray machines used to examine luggage–even a plastic squirt gun is perfectly visible if the machinery is working properly (Astrophysics Research Corporation 1986).

What was unusual about this law was that it banned a nonexistent weapon type. At the time it was proposed, no all-plastic gun had yet been manufactured. A few weapons such as the Glock 17 pistol were made partly of plastic, but had enough metal to set off properly functioning metal detectors (*New York Times* 5-5-86, p. A15). Consequently, it is safe to say that no crime had ever been committed with an all-plastic gun. Since production of such a gun may have been technically feasible, sponsors promoted the law as a preventive measure, rather than as a cure of an existing problem.

"Cop-Killer" Bullets

Some gun control efforts focus on ammunition rather than guns. An example is a 1986 federal law that banned the manufacture, importation, or sale of armor-piercing bullets made with any of seven hard metals such as bronze. Ordinary bullets are made of lead, a soft metal. Bullets made of hard metals can more easily penetrate the soft body armor worn by police officers, so advocates of such legislation referred to the bullets as "cop-killer bullets." This was something of a misnomer since, at the time the law was voted on, there were no documented cases of a policeman being killed by such a bullet. Congressional committees could find only 18 cases, over an 18-year period, in which criminals were even found in possession of armor-piercing ammunition (*Los Angeles Times* 12-18-85, p. 16). [None of this prevented the *New York Times* from asserting that hard-alloy ammunition was "favored by narcotics traffickers and other criminals" (7-20-85, p. 22).]

The softness of ordinary lead bullets causes them to expand on hitting a target, increasing the bullet's cross-sectional area and thereby widening the wound cavity created by the bullet. Thus, although a bullet made of hard materials will tend to penetrate into a body further, thereby lengthening the wound cavity, it will also tend to create a narrower wound cavity than an ordinary lead bullet. Consequently, for civilians and police officers without body armor, the physical attributes that make bullets capable of penetrating body armor do not necessarily increase the average size of wound cavities and thereby make the bullets more lethal. Armor-piercing bullets may thus be significant in influencing the outcome of a gun attack only with shots fired at body armor, by increasing the probability of the round reaching the wearer's body.

In this connection, bullets capable of penetrating body armor continue to be legally available. The federal law provided an exemption for "bullets primarily intended to be used for sporting purposes" (*Los Angeles Times* 12-18-89, p. 16), and much ordinary hunting rifle ammunition still on the market is capable of piercing body armor. This law might, in the future, be responsible for preventing killings of armor-wearing police officers who otherwise would have been killed had this ammunition been more widely available, but there is no evidence from past experience to support this speculation, since criminals have not used hard-alloy ammunition. However, as with plastic gun legislation, one can always speculate that this ban discouraged development of a possible future problem.

"Saturday Night Specials"—Small, Cheap Handguns

All of the aforementioned attempts to regulate special types of guns and ammunition were relatively unimportant simply because the targeted objects are so rarely used by criminals. However, this is not true of controls over so-called "Saturday Night Specials" (SNS), small, cheap handguns. Although the desirability of focusing regulatory efforts on this type of gun is questionable for many reasons, this is not because criminals rarely use them.

Small, cheap handguns have been commonplace in America since the nineteenth century, and there have been attempts to legally restrict more concealable handguns at the federal level since as early as 1915 (Kennett and Anderson 1975, pp. 98–9, 156, 197–8). The vast majority of the guns used in violent crimes are handguns (Table 2.8), and, correspondingly, a great deal of gun control legislation is directed specifically at handguns. Some legislation is more specifically aimed just at SNSs. Supporters of such measures argue that SNSs are especially suited for criminal uses and have little or no legitimate use (Cook 1981a; Shields 1981). In their most extreme form, arguments for control of SNSs state or imply that all or most of them are used for crime (Iveson 1981, p. 791) or, conversely, that most crime handguns are SNSs (Burr 1977). In either case it is asserted that SNSs are more likely to be involved in crime than other types of handguns. None of these claims is supported by the best evidence.

Handgun Control Inc. (HCI) is the nation's leading gun control advocacy group. The principal legislation it has pushed for is the Kennedy–Rodino Handgun Crime Control Act, which would, among other things, ban the manufacture and sale of SNSs (Shields 1981, p. 147). Pete Shields, the Chairman of HCI at the time the bill was proposed, asserted in 1981 that "Saturday Night Specials . . . are the preferred weapon of the criminal" (p. 157), and that "Although expensive handguns are sometimes used in crime, the real enemy in the American Handgun War remains the small, cheap, easily concealable handgun" (p. 46). This was a curious claim in light of the conclusions of a report sponsored by the Police Foundation and published 4 years earlier. This generally pro-control report's most widely cited conclusion was also the one most prominently summarized by the Foundation's President, Patrick Murphy, in the report's preface: "This evidence clearly indicates that the belief that so-called Saturday Night Specials (inexpensive handguns) are used to commit the great majority of these felonies is misleading and counterproductive" (Brill 1977, p. v). Shields and/or the HCI staff had clearly read this report, since widely separated parts of it were cited at least twice in Shields' book (pp. 44, 113). Since no subsequent information undercut the Police Foundation conclusion, it is especially difficult to understand the basis for Shields' claims.

Part of the explanation may lie in the way the SNS was defined. It is possible to either exaggerate or minimize the prevalence of SNSs among crime guns simply by manipulating definitions to suit one's purposes. Some supporters of SNS controls have created an impression of high prevalence by implicitly defining a SNS as any small handgun. Shields, however, defined SNSs as handguns that were both cheap *and* small

(1981, p. 46), and claimed that 68% of handguns used by criminals in one study were SNSs (p. 148). However, examination of the source on which the claim was based revealed that the figure merely referred to the fraction of handguns that had a barrel length of 3 inches or less (see Burr 1977, Appendix 4–7), i.e., the fraction that met the small size requirement, but not necessarily the low price requirement.

In this book, SNSs are defined as small, cheap handguns. This general description was operationalized by a definition used in at least two reports by BATF. This was the closest thing to an "official" definition in existence and it effectively captures both the ideas of small size, indexed by short barrel length and small caliber, and of low retail price. BATF (1976b, 1977) defined an SNS as a handgun that had all three of the following traits: (1) a retail price (ca. 1976) of less than $50, (2) caliber of .32 or smaller, and (3) a barrel length of 3 inches or less. This definition will be used in this book as well, modifying the price limit to account for inflation where necessary.

The best available information (summarized in Kleck 1986b) indicates the following about SNSs. Only about 10–27% of crime handguns (in the 1970s) fit the BATF definition of SNSs. Thus, most crime handguns are not SNSs, nor do they claim a share even approaching a majority. Because only about 10% of violent crimes involve a handgun, SNSs are involved in only about 2–7% of all violent crimes. Further, the SNS share of crime guns appears to be no larger than the SNS share of the general civilian handgun stock—at least 20% of all handguns introduced into the civilian stock were SNSs. Thus, there is no strong reason to believe that criminals are any more likely to use SNSs than noncriminal members of the general public are. More specifically, criminals are no more likely to use cheap or small caliber handguns than noncriminal gun owners. Therefore, there is no meaningful sense in which criminals can be said to "prefer" SNSs. On the other hand, there is some mixed support for the idea that criminals prefer short-barreled handguns over longer-barreled ones, though the weapons tend to be middle or large caliber and of good quality. At most, perhaps 7%, and more realistically 1–2%, of SNSs will ever be involved in even one violent crime. In sum, most handgun criminals do not use SNSs, and most SNSs are not owned or used for criminal purposes. Instead, most are probably owned by poor people for protection.

One policy implication of the last conclusion is that gun control efforts directed specifically at SNSs, such as the Kennedy–Rodino bill (Shields 1981, pp. 146–8), would have their greatest impact in reducing the availability of defensive handguns to low income people. The identical observation was made by liberal critics about the ban on importation of SNSs contained in the Gun Control Act (GCA) of 1968 (Sherrill 1973). Effective SNS-specific measures would disproportionately affect the law-abiding poor, since it is they who are most likely to own SNSs and obey the laws, and who are least likely to have the money to buy better quality, and therefore higher-priced, weapons.

A law that banned gun ownership by all persons with an annual gross family income under a given dollar amount would obviously be unfair and probably unconstitutional. Banning low-priced variants of a given product is functionally equivalent to such a law, as it has the same consequences. Drafters of existing SNS legislation did not define the SNS by retail price but rather by various criteria closely related to price. In some state laws the prohibited guns are defined by the temperature at which they melt, cheap guns being made of metal that melts at a relatively low temperature. In the federal GCA the guns banned from importation were defined as those "not suitable for sporting use" (a definition that takes no account of the fact that the predominant reason for ownership of handguns is defense and not sport—Chapter 2). The definition was administratively applied through the use of a list of "factoring criteria" that gave points for each gun feature that supposedly made the gun more suitable for "sporting uses"—a longer barrel, adjustable sights, or better quality metal (U.S. Internal Revenue Service 1969b). However, almost all of the features that earned points toward the minimum "qualifying score" were features that would also raise the price of the gun. Regardless of what definition of SNS is used, the handguns that fall within its purview are mostly the low-priced guns that poor people are most able to afford.

Supporters of SNS restrictions commonly adhere to two claims: (1) SNSs are dangerous in the hands of criminals, capable of killing or grievously wounding, and (2) SNSs are useless for self-defense. Supporters assert that despite their low power, difficulty in aiming, and relative unreliability, SNSs can be lethal weapons when used by criminals, and at the same time imply that somehow this confers no defensive utility when the weapon is in the hands of a crime victim defending against a criminal. Certainly, good quality handguns are better for defensive purposes than poor quality handguns, but the same is true with respect to criminal purposes. Regardless of how good or bad the SNS is at hurting or intimidating human beings, it is the same technological device in the hands of a criminal or of a victim. Therefore, to whatever degree its technical characteristics limit its utility for defensive purposes, they must also limit its utility for offensive purposes. If a crime victim cannot hit his or her victimizer with an SNS or do any serious damage to his body, then a robber, or assailant should also find it hard to hit and seriously harm his victim using the exact same type of weapon. And if criminals can seriously harm their victims with SNSs, then obviously victims can credibly threaten (and sometime inflict) similar grievous bodily harm to their victimizers. Philip Cook put the matter succinctly: "it seems doubtful that there are any guns that are 'useless' to legitimate owners, yet useful to criminals. Any gun that can be used in self-defense has a legitimate purpose, and therefore is not 'useless.' Similarly, any gun that can be used in crime can also be used in self-defense" (1981a, p. 1737).

What would be the most likely consequences of policies that effectively reduced or eliminated the manufacture or sale of SNSs? Among that small segment of the criminal population that uses SNSs to further crimes, most would presumably continue to use the SNSs they already had, while newcomers who sought such a gun could obtain them through theft and unregulated purchases, trades, and other transactions with friends, relatives, and occasionally black market dealers. Among those who somehow were denied access to an SNS, the easiest adaptation would be to purchase a marginally more expensive handgun. When Wright and Rossi asked the felons in their sample what they would do if they could not get an SNS, 68% of those classified as handgun predators (persons who frequently used handguns in crime) said they would get bigger, more expensive handguns; another 18% said they would saw off a shoulder weapon, i.e., a rifle or a shotgun (1986, p. 216). Police officials have reported that this substitution of better quality handguns has in fact occurred (*Washington Post* 12-27-89, p. A6).

Whereas it might not be easy for the law-abiding poor to buy a more expensive gun, few career criminals willing to assault and rob would lack the additional $50–100 it would take to purchase a gun not falling into the SNS category. As with policies intended to raise the price of illegal drugs by inducing scarcity, the greater cost of handguns could be passed on to crime victims in the form of additional crimes yielding the cash needed to buy more expensive handguns.

Some efforts to restrict SNSs do not force anyone to pay even slightly higher prices for handguns, and thus may not even slightly reduce handgun acquisitions. Maryland's 1988 law banning the sale of SNSs established a Handgun Roster Board to decide which models of handguns were banned. The board approved over 700 handgun models for sale, and disapproved only eight (another 100 or so models, some no longer in production, became banned by default because they were not submitted for approval) (*Washington Post* 12-5-89, p. D1). Although the handful of banned models were generally cheap, many equally cheap models were approved. Consequently, handgun buyers were not obliged to spend even one more dime to purchase a gun. Similarly, laws that define SNSs solely by melting point necessarily leave some guns legal that have low prices despite good-quality metal. This can be achieved through cost savings in other areas—smaller size, poorer workmanship, fewer safety features, and so on.

Considering the obvious flaws of a policy focusing solely on SNSs, why would anyone advocate it? One answer is that SNSs may not be the real target of the policies, but rather that all handguns are. Given the somewhat obscure and technical definitions that are actually used in legislation and administrative regulations, it would be easy to manipulate such a definition in a politically low-profile way such that *most* handguns fell within the SNS category. For example, bills introduced in Congress since 1968 used "factoring criteria" based on "size, quality of construction, caliber, safety features, and miscellaneous equipment" to define what handguns could be legally manufactured and sold in the United States. One major bill would have banned from domestic manufacture all handguns that failed to meet these factoring criteria. According to a BATF estimate, *54%* of the handguns manufactured in the United States would have failed this test (U.S. Congress 1975b, p. 124). Bruce-Briggs has gone so far as to claim that both sides in the gun control debate view SNS regulation as little more than the first step toward more wide-ranging controls: "Actually, neither side cares much about the 'Saturday night special' one way or another. The interdictionists advocate its regulation as a stepping stone toward tight licensing of handguns or the licensing of all guns, while the organized gun owners fear it as a camel's nose in the tent" (1974, p. 50). Confirming this, advocates of controls over special weapons often openly describe their efforts as a "first step" or a "step in the right direction" (see Chapter 1).

Another plausible explanation of support for SNS-specific gun regulation is suggested by some remarks of Philip Cook, who discussed the merits of defining SNSs according to metal quality as a way of avoiding "overt economic discrimination," candidly noting that such "subtle approaches may be more acceptable politically" (1981a, p. 1740). Prohibiting those types of firearms that poor people can best afford is the next best thing to an overtly discriminatory policy of banning gun ownership by poor people. The latter alternative would be unlikely to survive a constitutional challenge, but the former has survived so far. No one especially likes shoddy goods of any kind, so it is easier to build coalitions to support restrictions on poor quality guns than to support similar restrictions on those better quality guns that are actually more dangerous and more widely used by criminals.

The main advantage of SNS-only legislation appears to be the political one of being aimed largely at politically weak, predominantly nonvoting segments of the population, i.e., at those unable or unlikely to retaliate at election time against the sponsors of such measures. SNS-specific control policies combine the politically attractive features of restricting production and sale of shoddy goods and of disarming only the politically weak "dangerous classes." It is worth noting in this connection that from their origins in the Reconstruction-era South, SNS laws were commonly directed specifically at disarming blacks (Kates 1979a, pp. 12–15, 19). That the burden of SNS restrictions would fall disproportionately on black gun owners may not have escaped the notice of critics. According to Bruce-Briggs, the label for this gun type was derived from the racist phrase "nigger-town Saturday night" (1976, p. 50). Similarly, liberal journalist Robert Sherrill (1973) described the SNS provisions of the 1968 GCA as "ghetto control" rather than gun control.

Presumably, supporters of SNS restrictions are not driven by a concern that criminals armed with SNSs are not getting good value for their gun dollar, nor are they worried about the fact that cheap guns sometimes fail to fire when the trigger is pulled, or are not very accurate. These technical flaws associated with low price and poor quality are virtues where the reduction of gun violence is concerned. Instead, supporters believe that SNS restrictions could disarm a significant share of the violent criminal population. This belief may derive from an implicit assumption that marginal increases in the costs of guns, achieved by eliminating the low-price segment of the market, would produce marginal reductions in gun ownership among predominantly poor violent criminals. This assumption in turn relies on the idea that at least some criminal gun ownership is so weakly motivated that gun cost increases of, say, $50–100 would deter some gun acquisition. Unfortunately, among both criminals engaged occupationally in robbery, and impulsive "in-the-heat of passion" killers, gun ownership seems to be motivated primarily by fear of victimization, a fairly strong motivator (Burr 1977; Wright and Rossi 1985).

Some supporters justify SNS restrictions by arguing that they are aimed at reducing the availability of concealable guns, rather than simply making it harder for poor people to get guns, asserting that it is the size of the guns rather than their cheapness that is their key attribute.

The value of SNS restrictions may thus lie in their potential for reducing gun carrying by reducing the concealability of handguns. When SNSs are defined by barrel length, the cut-off length is commonly 3 inches. For example, the Kennedy–Rodino bill mentioned earlier used BATF "Factoring Criteria" to define the handguns whose manufacture and sale it would ban, and these criteria require that an acceptable revolver have "a barrel length of at least 3 inches" (U.S. Internal Revenue Service 1969b). Since the most common barrel length for revolvers is probably 4 inches (Warner 1988), one could not place the cutoff much higher than 3 inches without making the control measure look less like an SNS measure and more like one aimed at most handguns. However, even the shortest snub-nosed revolvers on the market already have barrels at least 1 inch long (Warner 1988). Under a ban on SNS production, it is a safe assumption that manufacturers of revolvers with barrels under 3 inches would find their most economically sensible adaptation to be to lengthen their barrels to just over 3 inches. Therefore, a requirement for 3 inch minimum would increase gun length by, at most, 2 inches. Assuming the intent of SNS control is to make handguns less concealable, they would reduce handgun carrying only to the extent that criminals find an additional inch or two in barrel length renders a gun insufficiently concealable for their purposes. It seems scarcely credible that any significant number of handgun criminals fall into such a category. This is not to say that some have not argued to the contrary. For example, Philip Cook (1981c) advocated a sales ban on short-barreled handguns, describing it as a measure that could somehow prevent "a few hundred homicides each year and a few thousand robberies and rapes."

An SNS-specific control policy could be worse than merely ineffectual. If it actually did deprive any criminals of SNSs, some would adapt by substituting larger and/or marginally more expensive guns, which would imply the substitution of larger caliber, longer barreled handguns. Wounds inflicted with larger caliber handguns are more like to result in a death; longer barreled guns fire bullets with greater accuracy and a higher muzzle velocity, thereby presumably increasing their deadliness (Zimring 1972). Consequently, among those persons who previously would have used SNSs but who, as a result of the control policy, substituted larger handguns, the attack fatality rate would almost certainly increase. The next section makes a similar argument concerning substitution of long guns for handguns.

In view of these considerations, it is inadvisable to establish restrictions on smaller caliber and/or shorter barreled handguns in the absence of restrictions at least equally strong applying to more lethal handguns. Restrictions applying exclusively to SNSs run a strong risk of increasing the fraction of gun assaults resulting in death, by inadvertently encouraging substitution of more lethal weaponry.

Handguns

Regulations aimed solely or largely at handguns are not just common—they are the *predominant* form of gun control in the United States (Chapter 8). This focus is understandable, since it is clear that handguns are the preferred weapon of criminals who use guns. Certainly any restrictions applied to handguns are directed at the heart of the gun violence problem. Unlike restrictions on machine guns, "ARs", plastic guns, and "cop-killer" bullets, policies aimed solely at restricting handguns cannot be criticized for dealing with a weapon type rarely used for criminal purposes.

However, the fact that handguns are the dominant crime weapon does not logically lead to the conclusion that it is advisable to apply restrictions *exclusively* to handguns. The substitution problem noted in connection with restrictions on SNSs applies with even greater force to restrictions imposed on handguns in general. Prospective violent offenders unable to easily obtain handguns would presumably seek substitutes, and for many of them the most satisfactory substitute would be a long gun. This would be socially undesirable because long guns are generally more lethal than handguns. That is, a given wound inflicted by a long gun is more likely to kill the victim than an otherwise similar handgun wound. Thus, any restrictions that induced violent persons to acquire long guns as substitutes for handguns could increase the death rate of gun attacks (Kates and Beneson 1979).

Whether this increase would in fact occur, and whether the total number of homicide deaths would be thereby increased, would depend on three parameters: (1) the "substitution fraction" (S), defined here as the fraction of persons using long guns in attacks, among those persons who would have used handguns in the absence of handgun-only restrictions, (2) the ratio of the fatality rate of long gun attacks over the fatality rate of handgun attacks, assuming all else, including intensity of attacker motivation, was equal, (D_2), and (3) the ratio of the fatality rate of handgun attacks over the rate for attacks with less lethal weapons such as knives, assuming all else, including intensity of attacker motivation, was equal (D_3). The higher these parameters are, the more likely it is that handgun restrictions would produce a net increase in homicide deaths. If few violent people substituted long guns, it would not matter much if long guns were much more lethal than handguns. Likewise, if long guns were only slightly more lethal than handguns, it would not matter how much long gun substitution occurred. Thus the critical question is: How high can these parameters get before one could anticipate undesirable effects of handgun-only restrictions?

In Appendix 3, a formula is derived that shows how these parameters are related, and how low they must be to avoid a handgun-only control policy from resulting in a net increase in homicide deaths. The results are shown in Table 3.3. They indicate that under even the most optimistic combination of assumed deadliness ratios, S must remain under 0.62 if a handgun-only policy is to avoid producing a net increase in homicide deaths. And under all but the most favorable conditions (i.e., very low D_3 and D_2), S must stay under 0.44 for the policy to succeed. Evidence reviewed in Kleck (1984b) indicated that 54–80% of homicides occur in circumstances in which long guns could be substituted for handguns, that most surveyed felons say they would carry a sawed-off long gun if they could not get a handgun, and that the deadliness of the substituted long guns would almost certainly be at least 1.5–3 times greater than that of handguns.

For a handgun-only policy to reduce the number of homicides, an extremely optimistic set of circumstances would have to apply. For example, even if one assumed knives were only one-fifth as deadly when used in attacks as handguns, and long guns were only 1.5 times as deadly as the handguns for which they were substituted, the policy still could succeed only if fewer than 62% of attackers substituted long guns (first row of Table 3.3). As noted in Appendix 3, even this substitution level might not be achieved. And it is important to remember that if the substitution level could somehow be kept this low, the policy would only avoid making things worse; it would save lives only to the extent that the substitution level dropped *below* this point. Even if the substitution fraction were as low as 0.5, savings in lives would be slight.

Once one assumes, probably more realistically, that substituted long guns would be at least twice as deadly as handguns ($D_2 \geq 2$), a handgun-only policy that successfully eliminated handguns could not avoid increasing the number of homicides unless the substitution fraction were kept below 44% (second row of Table 3.3), a level that seems improbable. Consequently, although it is not impossible for restrictions that apply only to handguns to reduce the number of homicides, it does seem highly unlikely.

Even specialists in gun issues have misunderstood the issues involved in the substitution problem. Consider, for example, a bizarre criticism of an earlier version (Kleck 1984b) of this policy simulation. Zimring and Hawkins (1987, p. 73) argued that the methods used to estimate deadliness ratios in that study lead to the absurd conclusion that some guns could kill three people for every one person shot! A careful reader would not be able to find anything in the study that actually implied such a thing, but it is worth examining this claim for what it reveals about how Zimring and Hawkins thought about weapon lethality. They drew an impossible conclusion from the simulation because they confused weapon lethality (one *input* into the attack process) with assault fatality rates (an *output* measure of the results of the attack process). The simulation assumed that some weapons could be 3, 5, or even 10 times as lethal as other weapons; there is no reason to doubt the plausibility of these assumptions. However, this does *not* imply, as Zimring and Hawkins apparently thought, that observed assault fatality rates would necessarily be 3, 5, or 10 times higher. Fatality rates have a logical upper limit of 100%—there cannot be more deaths than persons attacked. In contrast, the intrinsic deadliness of weapons has no logical upper limit. The degree to which one weapon is more deadly than another is limited only by the ingenuity of humans in devising tools of destruction. For example, suppose a very powerful type of shotgun killed victims in 60% of attacks. Would the fact that fatality rates cannot go over 100% imply that no weapon could be twice as deadly, purely on the basis of its technical attributes, as this shotgun? Clearly not, since this "reasoning" would imply the truly absurd conclusion that even a hydrogen bomb is not in any sense even twice as deadly as the shotgun. It was Zimring and Hawkins' inability to maintain the distinction between inherent weapon lethality and the observed assault fatality rates associated with weapons that led them to their absurd conclusions. Further, since the true fatality rate of handgun woundings, if all nonfatal woundings were counted, is probably under 10% (Chapter 5), this means that it would be mathematically possible (though unlikely) for even observed long gun wound fatality rates to be as much as 10 times higher than observed handgun wound fatality rates.

The present analysis was based on the beginning assumption that the policy would be completely effective in taking handguns away from violent people. Given the implications of Table 3.3, under most sets of assumptions, it would be just as well if the handgun-only policy failed to achieve its proximate goal of reducing handgun availability. The more successful it were at reducing handgun availability, the larger the scale of the counterproductive effects resulting from long gun substitution.

Fortunately, existing handgun-only policies probably are not very effective, and thus have not reduced handgun availability enough to stimulate much long gun substitution among violence-prone people (see Chapter 10).

One of the political temptations of handgun-only control is that it appears to be a satisfactory compromise between doing nothing about gun violence, which would alienate procontrol voters, and restricting all gun types, which would alienate many long gun owners. It is tempting to assume that the *results* of this apparent compromise policy would correspondingly lie somewhere between the results of a policy of doing nothing and the results of one restricting all guns. This assumption is false—the "middle" course of restricting only handguns is worse than either of the other two alternatives. It may be unrealistic to expect legislators to resist the political temptations of handgun-only controls, but they should know that there can be serious costs to lawmaking based solely on political convenience.

Conclusions

A clear policy recommendation follows from what should be the first principle of weapons regulations: Never place restrictions on a subcategory of weapons without also placing restrictions at least as stringent on more deadly, easily substituted alternative weapons.

Focusing on specialized weapon categories will be an unproductive, but unfortunately increasingly popular gun control strategy in the forseeable future. The very features that make the piecemeal approach ineffective also make it politically attractive. Thus, policies focusing on machine guns, "assault rifles," plastic guns, and armor-piercing bullets are inoffensive to most voters and have little cost, but they also address weapons that are only very rarely used by criminals.

So far, this is merely a special case of a political universal applying to any policy area—weak approaches carry less risk to policymakers, while also having less impact on the target problem. However, many special-weapon gun control measures are worse than this, since they have serious potential for making the violence problem worse. Policies targeting only less lethal weaponry, such as handguns generally or "Saturday Night Specials" specifically, can increase the gun death total by encouraging the substitution of more lethal types of guns.

Table 3.1. Trends in Production and Importation of Semiautomatic Centerfire Rifles, 1972–1987

Year	*Domestic Production Semiautomatic Centerfire Rifles*	*Rifles Imported*[a]	*Estimated Total Sales, Semiautomatic Centerfire Rifles*[b]
1972	360,000	194,713	457,356
1977	186,000	169,669	270,357
1982	284,000	175,145	371,572
1987	149,000	413,780	355,890

[a] Includes all imported rifles, not just semiautomatic centerfire. Available data do not provide separate counts for imported rifle subtypes.
[b] Assumes half of imported rifles were semiautomatic centerfire.
Source: U.S. Bureau of the Census (1989).

Table 3.2. Police Officers Feloniously Killed, by Weapon Type, U.S., 1970–1989

		Number					% of Total Killed with				
Year	Total Deaths	Guns	Handgun	Shotgun	Rifle	Possible Assault Rifle[a]	Guns	Handgun	Shotgun	Rifle	AR
1970	100	93	73	12	8	—	93	73	12	8	—
1971	129	124	97	11	16	—	96	75	9	12	—
1972	116	111	77	18	16	—	96	66	16	14	—
1973	134	127	93	13	21	—	95	69	10	16	—
1974	132	128	95	21	12	—	97	72	16	9	—
1975	129	127	93	13	21	—	98	72	10	16	—
1976	111	95	66	16	12	—	86	59	14	11	—
1977	93	83	59	11	13	5	89	63	12	14	5
1978	93	91	66	11	14	9	98	71	12	15	10
1979	106	100	76	6	18	5	94	72	6	17	5
1980	104	95	69	13	13	8	91	66	12	12	8
1981	91	86	69	5	12	4	95	76	5	13	4
1982	92	82	60	17	8	5	89	65	5	18	9
1983	80	74	54	8	12	8	92	68	10	15	10
1984	72	66	46	11	9	3	92	64	15	12	4
1985	78	70	58	9	3	3	90	74	12	4	4
1986	66	62	51	3	8	4	94	77	5	12	6
1987	73	66	48	9	9	8	90	66	12	12	11
1988	78	76	62	2	12	7	97	79	3	15	9
1989	67	57					85				

[a] A gun was considered to be a possible "assault rifle" if it was a rifle (or submachine gun, in a few cases) of any of the following calibers: .22, .223, 7.62 mm (.308 Win), 9 mm, .45, or "caliber not reported." The true number of deaths actually involving "assault rifles" is almost certainly smaller than these figures; they should be regarded as upper limit estimates.
Source: U.S. FBI (1971–1989).; U.S. Congressional Research Service (1991, p. 6).

Table 3.3. Substitution of Long-guns for Handguns[a]

D_3	D_2	S
1/5	1.5	.62
	2	.44
	3	.29
	4	.21
	5	.17
1/4	1.5	.60
	2	.43
	3	.27
	4	.20
	5	.16
1/3	1.5	.57
	2	.43
	3	.25
	4	.18
	5	.14
1/2	1.5	.50
	2	.33
	3	.20
	4	.14
	5	.11

[a] S = substitution fraction at the point where handgun-only policy has no net effect on number of homicides; D_3 = ratio of deadliness of knives over deadliness of handguns; D_2 = ratio of deadliness of long guns over deadliness of handguns.

PART II

EFFECTS OF GUNS ON VIOLENCE

CHAPTER

4

Guns and Self-Defense

Chapter 5 will address the effects of aggressors' possession of guns on their violent behavior. However, first this chapter addresses the effects of guns in the hands of potential victims of crime. Chapter 2 showed that millions of Americans own guns for defensive reasons. Now it is time to consider what the effects of that mass phenomenon might be. This chapter addresses the use of armed private violence for protection and the control of predatory criminal behavior, particularly violent crime and residential burglary. Extended attention will be given to the defensive utility of guns and whether predatory crime is deterred by armed self-help.

The ownership and use of guns for defensive purposes should have been of considerable interest to scholars in many areas, but has largely been ignored. For example, the prevalence of guns in America holds great significance for the "routine activities" approach to crime, which conceptualizes criminal incidents as the convergence in time and space of "likely offenders and suitable targets in the absence of capable guardians" (Cohen and Felson, 1979, p. 590). This approach has been important in expanding the interests of criminologists beyond their traditional emphasis on the supply of "likely offenders." The aspect of the routine activities perspective of interest here is what makes a guardian capable of preventing violations. The primary, ultimate source of "capability" is the appearance of being able and willing to use force, or to mobilize the forceful capabilities of others. At some times, crimes can be deterred or disrupted merely by the presence (or apparent possibility of presence) of an individual who is awake and able to telephone the police to dispatch officers armed and ready to use force. When the police are too remote or otherwise not able to respond quickly enough, the ability, real or apparent, of a prospective guardian to use force can be a critical contributor to how "capable" the guardian is. Whether a person is armed with a deadly weapon is therefore an important element of capable guardianship. Further, given the fact that at least half of all U.S. households and a quarter of retail businesses keep firearms (Crocker 1982; U.S. Small Business Administration 1969), gun ownership must surely be considered a very routine aspect of American life and one of obvious relevance to the activities of criminals.

The paucity of scholarly attention to civilian use of guns for defense may be partially due to the very limited visibility of such acts. Criminology texts do not report estimates of the frequency of defensive uses of guns. Published police-based crime statistics such as those found in the Uniform Crime Reports do not cover the subject and such incidents are rarely reported in the national news media. It is also possible that scholars feel shooting or threatening to shoot another person, even in self-defense, is so morally repugnant and utterly barbaric that it is preferable not to address the subject at all (Goode 1972; see also Tonso 1984 re. scholars' attitudes toward firearms). It could even be argued that to study the matter seriously might imply some endorsement and encourage the indiscriminant spread of the behavior.

Ignoring this issue might have serious costs. For example, a rational assessment of the impact of the more restrictive types of gun control laws requires an understanding of the consequences of disarming large segments of the civilian population. If civilian gun possession deters crime, reductions in general civilian gun ownership would amount to a reduction in a source of crime control as well as reduction of a possible cause of crime. Very different sorts of gun control would be called for under these circumstances than would be the case if one could assume that gun ownership has no desirable impact on crime rates.

These may have been ignored up until recently because students of violence thought they already knew everything they needed to know about whether guns can be effectively used by victims for self-defense. As far back as 1932, one noted homicide scholar stated that "the possession of firearms gives a false sense of security and encourages recklessness and arrogance. Those most experienced in such matters generally agree that it is almost suicidal for the average householder to attempt to use a firearm against a professional burglar or robber" (Brearley 1932, p. 76). These views have been echoed almost without modification in subsequent decades by scholars and gun control advocates (Shields 1981, pp. 48–53, 125; Newton and Zimring 1969, pp. 66–8; Yeager et al. 1976).

The Nature of Defensive Gun Use

Gun ownership for self-protection, and defensive gun use, must be distinguished from other forms of forceful activity directed at criminals, such as vigilantism, or activities of the criminal justice system (CJS) such as police making arrests. All of these can be coercive and all may be done by armed persons. However, vigilantism and CJS activity share a purpose that self-defensive actions do not—retribution. Whereas the CJS and the vigilante both seek to punish wrong-doers, the first lawfully, the second unlawfully, the defensive gun user seeks to protect the bodily safety and property of himself and others. Elements of vengeance may be mixed with the concern for self-preservation, but retribution is not an essential or even necessarily a common part of self-defense. Both the defensive gun user and the vigilante act independently of crime control professionals, but whereas the vigilante's actions are unlawful, a given self-defensive action may or may not be lawful—this is not one of its defining attributes. Both the vigilante and the defensive gun user act partly in response to a perceived lack of effectiveness of the CJS in preventing crime, but the former acts collectively, in concert with like-minded individuals, whereas the latter ordinarily acts alone (Brown 1969). It therefore is an oxymoron to refer to a defensive gun user as a "lone vigilante." Both the goals and actions of defensive gun users are more individualistic and less social than those of vigilantes.

Similarly, gun ownership for protection can be contrasted with other forms of private self-protection. Gun ownership, like defensive gun use, is individualistic and requires little preexisting social organization, unlike either vigilantism or legal collective activities such as neighborhood watch or patrol activities. This means that gun ownership can flourish in socially disorganized areas in which collective crime control strategies would flounder. Further, gun ownership is largely passive self-protection—once a gun is acquired, the owner rarely does anything with it. Only a minority of defensive owners actually use their guns for self-protection; the rest just keep the gun in a bureau drawer or similar location, where it is available for use should the need arise. This contrasts sharply with neighborhood crime control strategies, which may require considerable investment of time and effort from each participant.

Gun ownership is low-visibility protection. Unlike the activities of either police officers in marked patrol cars or of neighborhood patrol members, gun ownership of any one prospective crime victim is generally invisible to criminals. Although the occasional home or business might bear a sign saying "These premises protected by Smith and Wesson," with the image of a gun displayed, most armed premises would be externally indistinguishable from unarmed premises. This has two important implications. First, gun owners ordinarily should not enjoy any more benefit from whatever deterrent effects mass gun ownership may exert than nonowners. Whereas owners bear the costs of gun ownership, their unarmed neighbors share in any deterrent benefits. On the other hand, only gun owners will be able to actually use a gun to disrupt a criminal attempt made against them. Second, criminals usually cannot avoid the risk of running into an armed occupant merely by carefully choosing which home or store to victimize. They are forced to treat this risk as a real possibility for *any* occupied premises. This sets defensive gun ownership apart from other, more visible, self-protective measures because it makes displacement of criminals from armed to unarmed targets less likely. Criminals can shift from heavily patrolled neighborhoods to less heavily patrolled ones, but they cannot so easily shift to occupied homes or stores which they can be confident contain no armed occupants.

Gun ownership costs more money than simple measures such as locking doors, having neighbors watch one's house, or avoidance behaviors such as not going out at night, but it costs less than buying and maintaining a dog, paying a security guard, or buying a burglar alarm system. Consequently, it is a self-protection measure available to many low-income people who cannot afford more expensive alternatives. Gun ownership is not a replacement or substitute for these other measures, but rather is more accurately thought of as complement to them—an additional measure that might prove useful, for at least some crime victims, some of the time.

The Frequency of Defensive Gun Use: Survey Data

In any one year the fraction of the population that is the victim of serious violent crime or burglary is fortunately rather low, despite public fears about the ubiquity of crime. For example, even if minor violent crimes, such as assaults without injuries, are considered together with serious ones, only an estimated 3% of the U.S. population was the victim of a violent crime in 1982 (U.S. Bureau of Justice Statistics 1985b, p. 3). Consequently the fraction of the population that has any reason to use a gun against a criminal in any one year is correspondingly low. Further, most crimes occur away from the victim's home or place of employment and thus in places in which even gun-owning victims are not likely to have access to their weapons.

At least eight national or state-wide surveys have asked probability samples of the general adult population about defensive gun use. The results and other noteworthy features of these surveys are summarized in Table 4.1. The surveys differ in many important respects. Some asked about uses of all types of guns, whereas others were confined to handguns. Some covered a specific time period, asking if the respondent (R) used a gun in, e.g., the past 5 years, whereas others asked whether the R had ever used a gun defensively at any time in the past. Given the widely varying ages of Rs and differing spans of time guns were owned, the former method of asking the question is clearly more informative. Some of the survey questions asked about "self-defense," a term that may narrowly suggest defense of one's own bodily safety to some Rs, whereas others asked more broadly about "protection," which could include protection of other people and of property. Some questions asked only about the R's personal experiences, whereas others asked about defensive uses by anyone in the R's household. Most surveys asked the defensive uses questions of all Rs, but three of these "pre-screened" Rs through question funnelling, asking the question only of those who reported currently having a handgun or gun in the household. Most surveys specifically excluded guns used while in the military or as part of police duties, but some did not. Perhaps most important of all, only some of the surveys distinguished defensive uses against animals from uses against human threats. The 1978 DMIa survey indicated that 44% of the Rs who reported a gun use for protection had used guns only against animals (DMI 1979, p. 48).

The most informative of the surveys were the 1981 Hart poll and the 1990 Mauser survey. These were the only surveys to cover a national population, ask about defensive uses during a specific limited time period, ask the question of all respondents, distinguish civilian use from other uses, and distinguish uses against humans from uses against animals. The results of the Hart survey as reported here were first published in Kleck (1988); they were obtained privately from Hart Research Associates, Inc. (Garin 1986). In this survey, 6% of the adults interviewed replied "yes" to the question: "Within the past five years, have you yourself or another member of your household used a handgun, even if it was not fired, for self-protection or for the protection of property at home, work, or elsewhere, excluding military service or police work?" Those who replied "yes" were then asked "Was this to protect against an animal or a person?" Of the total sample, 2% replied "animal," 3% "person," and 1% "both." Therefore, 4% of the sample reported gun use against a person by someone in their household. The Mauser survey was basically the same as the Hart survey except that it asked about defensive use of all guns, not just handguns. Its results indicated that 3.8% of U.S. households had used a gun for protection in the previous 5 years.

These and most of the rest of the percentages reported in Table 4.1 are percentages who reported defensive use, out of the entire sample. If the figures are calculated as a percentage of gun owners, they are much higher. For example, in the Cambridge Reports survey, 17% of the total sample reported personally owning a handgun for protection or self-defense. Only these persons were asked about defensive use of handguns. The original source indicates that 3% of the total sample reported personally using a handgun for defensive purposes at some time in the past. Thus, about 18% (3/17) of protective handgun owners had actually used their guns at least once for defensive purposes. Among all handgun owners, irrespective of reasons for ownership, the fraction is somewhat smaller. In the Hart survey, among Rs reporting an operable handgun in their household, 10% reported a household member using a handgun defensively against a person in the previous 5 years.

Like crime victimization prevalence figures, the defensive gun use percentages are small. However, when translated into absolute numbers, as crime figures are commonly reported, the percentages imply large numbers of defensive uses. In 1980 there were 80,622,000 U.S. households (U.S. Bureau of the Census 1982). Applying the 4% figure from the Hart survey yields in an estimate of 3,224,880 households with at least one person who used a handgun defensively at least once during the period 1976–1981. Conservatively assuming only one use per household over the entire period, there were about 644,976 defensive uses of handguns against persons per year, excluding police or military uses. There is considerable room for sampling error associated with the point estimates. The 95% confidence interval estimate of the proportion of household handguns used defensively against person over the past 5-year period is .029–.051, implying from 468,000 to 822,000 uses per year.

The Hart survey asked only about handgun use, ignoring defensive uses of the far more numerous long guns (rifles and shotguns). And the DMI surveys, which did ask about all gun types, did not ask about a specific limited time period. An all-guns estimate can be based on an extrapolation of the Hart survey handgun results. In 1985 the ratio of all gun crimes over handgun crimes was 1.214 (Table 2.11). If it is assumed that crime victims' gun choices resemble those of criminals, this ratio can be applied to the 645,000 defensive handgun uses to get a rough estimate of about 783,000 defensive uses of guns of all types. Applying the same ratio to the 4% handgun prevalence figure yields an estimate of 4.856% for all guns, with a 95% confidence interval estimate of 3.756–5.956%, implying 606,000–960,000 defensive uses of all guns.

The Hart-based estimates were confirmed by the more recent Mauser (1990) national survey. Mauser found that 3.79% reported a defensive use of a gun of any kind, a figure within the all-guns 95% interval estimate derived from the Hart survey conducted 9 years earlier. The difference between the 3.79% Mauser result and the Hart-based 4.856% therefore could be due to random sampling error, but it could also reflect genuinely declining defensive uses guns from 1976–1981 to 1985–1990, paralleling the decline in criminal uses of guns. The Mauser estimates imply an average of 691,000 defensive gun uses per year over 1985–1990.

The magnitude of these figures can be judged by comparison with an estimate of the total number of crimes in which guns were used, based on the Uniform Crime Reports (UCR) count of homicides and National Crime Survey (NCS) victimization survey estimates of assaults, robberies, and rapes. Including minor assaults in which the gun was not fired, and including both crimes reported to the police and unreported crimes, the total for handguns in 1980 was about 580,000; the corresponding figure for all gun types was about 740,000. For 1985, there were about 540,000 handgun crimes and 660,000 gun crimes (Chapter 2). Thus the best available evidence indicates that guns are used about as often for defensive purposes as for criminal purposes.

Confidence in the estimates derived from the Hart survey is increased by the consistency of these results with those of the other surveys summarized in Table 4.1.[1] Appendix 4 develops alternative estimates of the number of defensive uses, based on three other surveys (two national and one state) not as satisfactory as the Hart and Mauser polls. All three of these surveys yield estimates of defensive gun uses even larger than the estimates based on the Hart and Mauser surveys. Therefore one cannot attribute the large estimates of defensive gun uses to technical peculiarities of the Hart and Mauser surveys, and it would be wrong to claim that they depend on just one or two surveys.

Another way of comparing the frequency of offensive uses of handguns with defensive uses is to compare direct survey estimates of the prevalence of household experience for each type of event. The Hart survey indicated that 4% of all households had used a handgun defensively at least once in the 5-year period preceding the survey. Assuming the uses were evenly distributed throughout the period, at least 0.8% of households used a handgun defensively in any one year, 1976–1981. The NCS survey for 1980 indicated that about 5.5% of U.S. households had experienced a violent crime in 1980 (from figure 6, U.S. Bureau of Justice Statistics 1981, p. 3) and that about 10.3% of violent crimes involved guns (U.S. Bureau of Justice Statistics 1982a, pp. 57–9). Generously assuming that 90% of these gun crimes involved handguns, about 0.5% (0.055 × 0.103 × 0.90 × 100%) of U.S. households in 1980 experienced a handgun crime. The 90% confidence interval estimate for household handgun victimization is 0.44–0.56% (computed from procedures in U.S. Bureau of Justice Statistics 1982a, p. 95), whereas the interval estimate for defensive handgun use was 3.2–4.8% over the 5-year period, or 0.64–0.96% over a 1-year period. Based on household prevalence figures, then, civilian experience with defensive use of handguns appears to be more common than experience of handgun victimization.[2]

Problems with the Surveys

It should be emphasized that these surveys do not permit an assessment of the legal or moral character of the defensive gun uses reported, and one necessarily relies on the honesty of Rs as to the defensive character of the acts referred to. This is important because of the character of much violence. Many homicides and assaults are episodes of mutual combat involving two people fighting back and forth rather than one clear aggressor who is morally at fault and one totally guiltless victim (Luckenbill 1977). Wright and Rossi (1985, pp. 27, 29) have also pointed out that predatory criminals frequently victimize other criminals much like themselves. In any given incident, who one concludes was doing the "defending" may depend on which party one asks. Thus the gun use surveys may count some incidents as defensive gun uses that in legal terms were criminal assaults by the R; still others may have been acts of criminal vengeance.

The opposite problem applies to the victim surveys used to estimate the total number of crimes committed with guns. Strictly speaking, victim surveys do not even attempt to determine who is the victim and who the aggressor in an assault. The relevant survey questions simply ask whether the R was "knifed, shot at, or attacked" in the previous 6 months (Gove et al. 1985, p. 458; U.S. Bureau of Justice Statistics 1982a, p. 82). The R is labeled a "victim" partly by virtue of being the party to the assault who was selected to be interviewed. This creates some problems. For example, if an R had criminally attacked or tried to rob (without a gun) someone who defended himself with a gun, the R could honestly report that he had been shot at or threatened with a gun. He would therefore be counted as a victim of a gun assault, even though neither he nor his attacker was the victim of any gun crime.

In short, the incidents described as defensive uses in gun user surveys and as gun crimes in victim surveys overlap. Even if just one party uses a gun, the same incident may be describable as either a gun assault or a defensive use of a gun, depending on which party to the event happens to be questioned. Many instances of mutual combat could accurately be regarded as involving both aggressive and defensive uses of guns. Incidents can be misreported in either direction in both kinds of surveys. It therefore is not clear how, or even whether, these problems affect comparisons between the number of gun crimes and the number of defensive gun uses.

There is a problem, however, affecting all surveys that could consistently contribute to a net undercount of both defensive and criminal gun uses. It has often been recognized that criminals will be among the persons least likely to be interviewed in general population surveys, because of their low income, high mobility, time spent incarcerated, and possible reluctance to be interviewed even if successfully contacted (e.g., Cook 1985). Since it is criminals who are in most frequent contact with other criminals, it is they who are both most likely to be victimized and most likely to have reason to use guns defensively. Relative to their share of the population, criminals should claim a disproportionate share of both defensive gun uses and gun crime victimizations. Therefore, victimization and gun use surveys share a sampling bias that contributes to underestimating both criminal and defensive gun uses.

As to the comparison between numbers of defensive gun uses and criminal gun uses, it is possible there are biases that lead to more undercounting of defensive uses than criminal uses. The results of both victimization and gun use surveys, like all survey results, can be affected by recall failure and telescoping. Despite the highly dramatic nature of crime incidents, victims nevertheless frequently fail to recall them in survey interviews, even when questioned as little as 6 months after the events (U.S. LEAA 1972). The main difference between the two survey types is that the recall period is only 6 months for the national victim surveys, whereas it was 5 years in the Hart and Mauser gun use surveys, and was the R's lifetime in most of the rest of the surveys.

This suggests there is more recall failure in the gun use surveys. Consistent with this idea, the Field survey found that 1.4% of Rs recalled a defensive handgun use just in the past year, yet only 8.6% recalled such a use over the span of their entire lives. A December 1989 national survey found that gun owners had personally owned guns for a mean of 23.4 years. Assuming the "past year" experience of the Field sample was representative of earlier years of handgun ownership, and assuming little repeat usage of guns for defense, the lifetime prevalence of handgun defensive use could have been as high as 23.4 times as high as the 1.4% past year prevalence, or about 33%, instead of the 8.6% lifetime figure reported. Given the large number of owners with extremely long histories of handgun ownership, and thus the skewed distribution of ownership spans, one might expect the cumulative percentages of owners experiencing defensive uses to be even higher than this. In any case, there seems to be considerable recall failure in the gun use surveys, which would contribute to underestimation of defensive gun uses. Unless telescoping is also far greater for the Hart and Mauser gun use surveys than for the victim surveys, to at least the same degree as recall error, this implies that the estimate of defensive gun uses is less complete than the estimate of gun crimes based on victim surveys.

One survey that almost certainly is not adequate for estimating the total number of defensive gun uses is the National Crime Survey. Respondents in that survey are not asked about defensive actions unless they first give an affirmative answer to screener questions asking about victimization experiences in general. If respondents underreport the kinds of incidents in which guns are most commonly used defensively, then defensive gun uses will also be underestimated. As will be seen later (Table 4.5), about 40% of defensive gun uses are connected with assaults in the home, most of these presumably being instances of family violence. Perhaps another 10% or so are linked with commercial robberies. The latter type of incident is not covered at all in the NCS, and the former is severely undercounted. The true count of spouse assaults may be 12 times higher than the NCS estimate, and the true count of rapes may be 33 times as high as the NCS estimate (Loftin and MacKenzie 1990, pp. 22–3).

Police, security guards, armed forces personnel, and, to a lesser extent, correctional officers are especially likely to use weapons for defensive purposes, due to the violence-related nature of their occupations and the fact that they are commonly armed with a gun during the work hours. Since such people are eligible for inclusion in the victim and gun use surveys, one would expect them to account for a disproportionate share of the defensive gun uses. Recall that the Hart and Mauser surveys excluded police and military uses of guns (but not, however, off-duty uses of guns by police officers and military personnel). The size of the share of defensive uses attributable to these sorts of users is relevant to assessing NCS information used later to evaluate the effectiveness of defensive gun uses, since that information is derived from questions that did not exclude any uses by persons with these violence-related occupations. Although the gun use surveys did not obtain sufficiently detailed occupational detail to assess this, the NCS did. In the 1979–1985 sample, members of these occupations accounted for 15.4% of self-protection gun uses. They do therefore account for a disproportionate share of the NCS-counted gun uses, but still a relatively small fraction. And again it should be stressed that on-duty uses by such persons were explicitly excluded from the surveys used to estimate the number of defensive gun uses.

Shooting in Self-Defense

Most uses of guns for either criminal or defensive purposes are probably much less dramatic or consequential than one might think. Only a tiny fraction of criminal gun assaults involves anyone actually being wounded, even nonfatally, and one would expect the same to be true of defensive gun uses. More commonly, guns are merely pointed at another person, or perhaps only referred to ("I've got a gun") or displayed, and this is sufficient to accomplish the ends of the user, whether criminal or noncriminal. Nevertheless, most gun owners questioned in surveys assert that they would be willing to shoot criminals under the right circumstances. The 1989 Time/CNN survey found that 80% of gun owners thought they would get their guns if they thought someone was breaking into their home, and 78% said they would shoot a burglar if they felt threatened by that person (Quinley 1990, p. 9).

Despite this stated willingness of gun owners to shoot under certain circumstances, most defensive uses of guns do not in fact involve shooting anyone. Although the surveys listed in Table 4.1 did not delve into much detail about the circumstances in which guns were used defensively, or the manner in which they were used, most did ask whether the gun was fired. Results generally indicate the gun was fired in less than half of the defensive uses; the rest of the times the gun was merely displayed or referred to, in order to threaten or frighten away a criminal.

Self-Defense Killings

The rarest, but most serious form of self-defense with a gun is a defensive killing. Although shootings of criminals represent a small fraction of defensive uses of guns, Americans nevertheless shoot criminals with a frequency that must be regarded as remarkable by any standard. Although the FBI does not publish statistics on self-defense killings, it does compile unpublished counts of civilian justifiable homicides (CJH) gathered through their Supplementary Homicides Reports (SHR) program. For a variety of reasons the FBI SHR totals for CJHs represent only a minority of all civilian legal defensive homicides (CLDHs). First, some cases that even local police label as CJHs are not reported as such to the FBI. Wilbanks (1984, p. 3) reports that police in Dade County were unwilling to spend much time properly recording homicides where prosecution of the killer was not to be pursued. Second, many homicides ultimately ruled noncriminal by prosecutors or judges are reported to the FBI as criminal homicides because that is how the initial police investigation treated them. Homicides are classified, for FBI Uniform Crime Reporting purposes, solely on the basis of the initial police investigation.

Third, and most significantly, in jurisdictions that follow legal distinctions between justifiable and excusable homicides fairly closely, most CLDHs will be recorded as excusable rather than justifiable, and thus are not eligible to be counted by the FBI. The magnitude of this last problem is suggested by findings concerning Detroit homicides. Over the period from 1969 to 1980, while 344 cases of civilian homicides were labeled justifiable, another 741 were labeled excusable (Dietz 1983, p. 203). Excusable homicides can include some accidental deaths, but accidental vehicular homicides were excluded from these excusable totals and it is known that there were only 123 accidental deaths from guns in Detroit over this period.[3] About half of fatal gun accidents are self-inflicted (Chapter 7), so only about 62 of the accidental gun deaths were accidental homicides (i.e., one person killing another), and many of these would be labeled negligent manslaughters rather than excusable homicides. Thus, few of the 741 excusable homicides were accidental deaths. Likewise, homicides by police officers are almost invariably labeled justifiable (Wolfgang 1958; Wilbanks 1984), so they are unlikely to claim any significant share of the excusable homicides. Instead, most of these excusable homicides appear to be CLDHs, and thus are not counted by the FBI as CJHs. (See Appendix 5 for explanation of the various categories of noncriminal homicides and the FBI classification scheme.)

Because no national data exist distinguishing between the different types of CLDHs, data from single legal jurisdictions like cities and counties must be relied on to judge the relative frequency of each homicide type. Table 4.2 summarizes information from six unusually detailed local homicide studies. Although the character of homicide may differ somewhat from city to city, the results nevertheless suggest that there are sharp differences from place to place in the way authorities classify homicides as noncriminal. Row 12 of the table indicates that the fraction of intentional civilian homicides labeled as CLDHs varied from 1.6 to 19.5% over the six jurisdictions.

The Detroit and Dade County results yielded middle-range values on this fraction, came from two regionally distinct parts of the country, and are also the most recent. Thus they seem to be most likely to be representative of the contemporary United States as a whole. Therefore these results will be used, in combination with the national SHR counts of civilian justifiable homicides, to roughly estimate national totals for CLDHs. One way to do this (Estimation Method I) is to assume that self-defense homicides grow out of criminal threats to life, as indexed by murders and nonnegligent manslaughters reported to the FBI, and that the ratio of the former to the latter will be roughly the same for the United States as a whole as it is for Detroit and Dade County. The combined totals for these two local areas were 1062 killings counted by the FBI as murders and nonnegligent manslaughters (U.S. FBI 1981, pp. 74, 107) and 145 killings known to be CLDHs (Table 4.2), giving a ratio of the latter to the former of 0.1365. Multiplying this number by the national total of 23,044 murders and nonnegligent manslaughters (which includes some misclassified CLDHs) (U.S. FBI 1981, p. 41) yields an estimate of 3146 CLDHs for the United States in 1980.

Alternatively, the national counts of civilian justifiable homicide reported to the FBI could be used as a starting point, with an adjustment for its incomplete coverage of CLDHs (Estimation Method II). In 1980 there were 145 CLDHs in the two sample jurisdictions, of which only 36 were reported to the FBI as CJHs (tabulations from 1980 SHR dataset, ICPSR 1984), yielding a ratio 4.167 CLDHs to every CJH counted in the SHR program. Multiplying this times the 1980 national SHR total of 423 CJHs yields an estimate of 1704 CLDHs. Of the 423 CJHs, 379, or 89.6% involved guns, so it is estimated that about 1527 (.896 × 1704) CLDHs involved guns, based on the lower estimate, or 2819 (.896 × 3146) based on the higher estimate. In sum, about 1500–2800 felons were killed by gun-wielding civilians in self-defense or some other legally justified cause in 1980.

The degree to which these estimates are meaningful for the nation as a whole is heavily dependent on the representativeness of the two local jurisdictions chosen as regards the critical ratios used in the estimates. However, the evidence indicates that the relative prevalence of CLDHs among homicides is not unusually high in these two areas. Row 14 of Table 4.2 indicates that the ratio of CLDHs to murders and nonnegligent manslaughters was 0.242 in the Bensing and Schroeder study of the Cleveland area, much higher than in Detroit and Dade County. Likewise, Kellermann and Reay (1986) found that in King County (Seattle) Washington during 1978–1983 there were 9 legal self-protection homicides and 41 criminal homicides with a gun kept in the home. Because vehicular and other accidental homicides were excluded from the criminal homicide total, it does not include negligent or involuntary manslaughters and thus is roughly equivalent to a count of murders and nonnegligent manslaughters. Therefore, the ratio of CLDHs to murders and nonnegligent manslaughters was 0.220, far higher than the one used to estimate national CLDH totals in the present study. Since the ratio was lower in the Wolfgang and Rushforth et al. studies and somewhat indeterminate in the Lundsgaarde study, it seems justifiable to regard the ratio based on Detroit and Dade County as a middle-range value. In any case, it is not claimed that the resulting numbers are anything more than rough estimates intended to support the very general claim that civilians use guns to legally kill a large number of felons each year.

The various estimates are summarized in Table 4.3. The police homicide estimates are simple totals for deaths by legal intervention as compiled by the vital statistics system (Estimation Method I) (U.S. NCHS 1983, pp. 35–6), which were then doubled (Estimation Method II) to adjust for the fact that only about half of police killings get reported as such to the national vital statistics system (Sherman and Langworthy 1979, p. 552). FBI/SHR counts of police justifiable homicides are also reported here. Regardless of which counts of homicides by police are used, the results indicate that civilians legally kill far more felons than police officers do. The figures imply that, of 23,967 civilian (not by police) homicide deaths in the United States in 1980 (U.S. NCHS 1985b), about 1700–3100, or 7.1–12.9% were legal civilian defensive homicides.

Even if one had complete national counts of all homicides eventually declared lawful by the legal system, they would very likely understate certain categories of defensive homicide. Gillespie (1989, pp. xii–xiii) reviewed five local studies of homicides in which women killed their husbands or men with whom they lived intimately and concluded that the majority were self-defense killings. She estimated that there were as many as 500 such killings each year, but then described case after case of women killing (usually with a gun) abusive husbands or boyfriends that resulted in the women being convicted for criminal homicide, even in incidents in which the circumstances seemed to clearly justify such a claim.

The following examples, adapted from brief case narratives in Wilbanks (1984, pp. 193–374), help give the flavor of typical defensive gun killings (V = victim, i.e., the aggressor who was shot, O = "offender" who used gun defensively to kill aggressor).

Case 566

V (Latin male) and O were both roomers in a "fleabag" hotel. O was a black male and did not speak or understand Spanish. V provoked O, pulled a knife on him and backed him into a corner (other Latins present tried to calm the V to no avail). O (a soft-spoken and quiet man) pulled out a gun and fired a warning shot. When the V kept coming the O fired again and killed the V (p. 373).

Case 228

Black male V entered black female O's bedroom and told O not to be afraid as he just wanted to have sex. O got out her shotgun (by her bed) and advised V to leave. When V put his right leg on the bed, he was shot by the O. O keeps a loaded shotgun by her bed as she has been burglarized several times. V had a knife in his possession when he advanced on the O. O stated that she had never seen the V before (p. 270).

Case 288

Two victims entered a pawn shop and attempted to pawn a bad stereo that the store employee refused to accept. One V then jumped over the counter, armed with a revolver, and both victims were shot by the co-owner of the store (p. 278).

Case 566 is a clear case of excusable homicide, involving simple self-defense against an attacker, whereas cases 228 and 288 would probably be classified under FBI guidelines as justifiable homicides, involving defense against rape and robbery, respectively. A few homicides, though treated by authorities as noncriminal, are of a more dubious moral and legal character than these examples. The following incident is illustrative.

Case 159

V and another person were burglarizing a residence when they were surprised by the owner of the house. Both V and accomplice ran from the house as owner fired shots and struck the V (p. 159). Although the victim was clearly committing a felony against the shooter, the latter was apparently no longer in danger when he fired his gun at the fleeing burglars. Only four or five of the 72 civilian justifiable homicides in this dataset were similarly questionable, but Case 159 does illustrate that homicides can be legally classified as noncriminal even though they seem to be criminal (or might be under some legal doctrines). Likewise, cases that appear to be legitimate cases of self-defense can be wrongly classified as criminal homicides. It is not known what the relative balance of these two types of errors are in general samples of homicides, so one cannot be sure whether they contribute to an overcount or an undercount of CLDHs, though the Gillespie book strongly suggests that there is a net undercount of defensive killings among female-against-male homicides.

Defensive Woundings

Nonfatal gun woundings are far more frequent than fatal shootings. Cook (1985) reviewed data that indicate that only about 15% of gunshot wounds known to the police are fatal, implying a ratio of about 5.67 (85/15) nonfatal gun woundings to each fatal one. Assuming the same applies to legal civilian defensive shootings, there were between 8700 and 16,600 nonfatal, legally permissible woundings of criminals by gun-armed civilians in 1980. Combining the defensive killings and nonfatal woundings, there are about 10,000–20,000 legal shootings of criminals a year, which would be less than 2% of all defensive gun uses. The rest of defensive gun uses, then, involve neither killings nor woundings but rather misses, warning shots fired, or guns pointed or referred to.

That defensive gun uses, with or without a wounding, are so common is not surprising in view of how many Americans own guns for defensive reasons and keep them ready for defensive use. A 1989 national survey found that 27% of gun owners have a gun *mainly* for protection, and 62% said that protection from crime was at least *one* of the reasons they owned guns (Quinley 1990). This translates into about 14 million people who had guns mainly for protection, and about 32 million who had them at least partly for protection (using data on number of individual gun owners from Table 2.4). Thus, even a million defensive gun uses of some kind per year would involve only about 3% of defensive gun users, hardly an implausibly high fraction.

Further, many gun owners, and almost certainly a majority of those who own guns primarily for protection, keep a household gun loaded.

The 1989 survey found that 24% of gun owners always keep a gun loaded, and another 7% had a gun loaded at the time of the interview although they did not do so all the time, for a total of 31%. Guns were most commonly kept in the bedroom, where they would be ready for nighttime use (Quinley 1990, pp. 4–6, 9).

Apparently nearly all of the guns kept loaded are handguns. Although the national survey did not address this issue, a 1977 telephone survey of Illinois adults found that 35.4% of households that owned only handguns, and 31.9% of households that owned both handguns and long guns, kept a gun loaded, compared to only 1.6% of households that owned only long guns. Black gun owners were four times as likely as white owners to keep a gun loaded, Chicago residents were twice as likely to do so as other Illinois residents, and households with no adult male were twice as likely as other households to have a loaded gun (Bordua 1982). In short, keeping a gun loaded was most common in households in which vulnerability to victimization was highest.

Carrying Guns for Protection

Carrying firearms for protection is one of the most active forms of gun use for both defensive and criminal purposes. Persons who wish to have guns available for defensive purposes in public spaces must necessarily carry guns, legally or illegally, to do so. Unlawful carrying of guns probably accounts for the majority of arrests for weapons violations (Bordua et al. 1985), and virtually all gun crime committed in public places necessarily involves carrying of firearms. Millions of Americans carry guns every year. A February 1985 national Roper survey indicated that 17% of U.S. adults regularly carried with them some device for self-defense, and 30% of these, or 5% of all U.S. adults, regularly carried guns (DIALOG 1990). This would have been about 9 million people. At most, 1.5 million gun carriers could be police, security guards, and the like (U.S. Bureau of the Census 1988, p. 389), leaving at least 7.5 million regular civilian defensive gun carriers. Given that handguns are involved in about 600,000 crimes, with only some of these involving carrying, one implication of these numbers is that over 90% of gun carriers carry without any intention of committing a crime. Note that some of the carrying involved keeping a gun in the owner's car or truck, rather than carrying on the person. Also, some of the guns may be carried in rural areas for protection against animals rather than criminals.

Carrying guns implies carrying deadly weapons in public spaces.

What makes spaces public is that almost anyone may freely move through them without invitation. Unlike home spaces, they are places where unplanned encounters between strangers routinely occur. Such encounters are inherently more dangerous than encounters between family members, friends, and others who interact in private spaces, because the actors share no previously established understandings, commitments, emotional bonds, or sets of obligations to restrain the open expression of hostility. Most people recognize this special character of public contacts with strangers, and exercise caution accordingly. Gun carrying could have a number of effects in this setting. Carrying a gun might make people foolhardy, encouraging them to take unnecessary risks, and perhaps even seek out risks. Or, by giving its possessor the quiet confidence of knowing he has a power advantage, a gun might prevent a potentially conflictual situation from progressing to the point where hostility was openly expressed, thereby making the resort to weapons unnecessary. Alternatively, display of the weapon could deter the unarmed party from further escalation of hostilities. On the other hand, once the situation did escalate to open hostilities, use of the gun might make it more likely conflict could lead to a death.

Although gun laws regulating the carrying of firearms have been studied, especially the Massachusetts Bartley–Fox law (Pierce and Bowers 1981), and carrying by felons has recently been examined (Wright and Rossi 1986), research on carrying by the general public is virtually nonexistent (Blackman 1985). A major review of research on guns and violence did not review a single study on the subject (Wright et al. 1983). And the handful of relevant studies are flawed and of limited generalizability. A 1962 study was descriptive in nature and limited to urban black arrestees, finding that 70% of 50 St. Louis blacks convicted of carrying concealed weapons did so because they anticipated attack (Schultz 1962). The findings also suggested that, among lower class blacks, the people who carry guns for self-protection and the people who use them in violence are to a great extent the same people, i.e., the two groups heavily overlap. Thus carrying can be a prelude to both legitimate defensive uses of guns by noncriminals and to criminal assaults by the carriers.

Hassinger (1985) conducted a mail survey of Jefferson County (Birmingham) Alabama residents who had a legal permit to carry firearms. In this county, 10% of the adult population was licensed to carry a handgun. The most frequently endorsed reason for carrying a pistol was the belief that "the police cannot be everywhere; the pistol is a prudent precaution" and the second most common reason was worry about being a victim of crime (p. 115). The main sources of information that lead to these concerns about crime were "actual prior incidents," "news reports about crime," and "common knowledge (word of mouth) about crime" (p. 117). Unfortunately this survey had a return rate of only 21%, raising questions about generalizability.

Bankston et al. (1986) conducted a mail survey of Louisiana driver's license holders, which included an item that read: "Please indicate how often you do the following to protect yourself and your property . . . Carry a firearm when you leave home." The possible responses were never, occasionally, frequently, and always (p. 7). The authors' regression analysis indicated that gun carrying was more likely, other things being equal, among persons with a crime victimization experience, people fearful of crime, younger people, males, and residents of Northern Louisiana, the area with the more traditionally Southern, non-Cajun, culture. Unfortunately there is strong indication that the sample surveyed was seriously biased. This survey indicated that 56.5% of white Louisiana households owned handguns, although only 37% of white households in the West South Central region (Louisiana, Texas, Oklahoma, and Arkansas) in the 1984 General Social Surveys reported a handgun (analysis of ICPSR 1985). Handgun owners appear to have been substantially more likely to return questionnaires. A return rate of less than 50% and the lack of follow-up mailings presumably contributed to this problem.

Psychological Effects of Keeping Guns for Protection

Before addressing the objective outcomes of actual defensive uses of guns, a more subjective issue should be addressed. If some people get guns in response to crime or the prospect of being victimized in the future, as indicated in Chapter 2, does gun ownership have any reassuring effects? Once a gun is acquired, does it make its owner feel safer? Reducing fear would be an intangible benefit distinct from any objective utility a gun might have when it is actually used for defensive purposes.

A December, 1989 national survey of 605 U.S. gun owners asked the following question: "Does having a gun in your house make you feel more safe from crime, less safe, or doesn't it make any difference?" Of the gun owners 42% felt more safe, only 2% felt less safe, and the rest said it made no difference (Quinley 1990). Since only 27% of the owners had a gun mainly for protection from crime, and only 62% had a gun even partially for protection from crime, it is not surprising that some owners felt having a gun made no difference in their feelings of safety—it presumably was not supposed to make any difference, since their guns were owned for recreational reasons. Assuming that those who felt safer fell largely among those 62% (or 27%) of owners who had guns for protection, one can infer that a majority of defensive gun owners do feel safer from crime, or at least claim to feel that way. When asked "Overall, do you feel comfortable with a gun in your house or are you sometimes afraid of it?," 92% of gun owners said they were comfortable, 6% were sometimes afraid, and 2% were not sure (p. 10).

A 1990 national survey indicated that nearly all defensive gun owners feel safer because they have a gun. Among persons whose primary reason for owning a gun was self-defense, 89% replied "yes" to the question: "Do you feel safer because you have a gun at home?" Among gun owners who did not feel safer, 96% were persons whose primary reason for owning was something other than defense (Mauser 1990).

These surveys confirmed what previous surveys had indicated. For example, in a national survey conducted in January 1981, Rs were asked: "How do you feel about having a gun in your house? Do you think it makes things safer or do you think it makes things more dangerous?" This question wording differed from that of the CNN/Time poll in that it focused on perception of actual dangers, a matter that is partly objective and partly subjective, rather than how the gun made Rs feel. Among Rs in gun owning households giving nonmissing responses, 58% felt having a gun in their house "makes things safer," 30% felt things were about the same, and 11% felt it made things more dangerous (tabulation of data in Los Angeles Times 1981). In sum, most gun owners, including many who do not even have a gun for defensive reasons, feel comfortable with guns, feel safer from crime because of them, and believe their guns actually do make them safer from crime.

Effectiveness and Risks of Armed Resistance to Criminals

Of course, gun owners may be deceiving themselves. Their feelings of greater security, however real in emotional terms, may lack a factual foundation. Regardless, the belief that guns provide effective self-protection for at least some people some of the time is nearly universal. Even proponents of stringent gun control who assert the guns are not effective defensive devices for civilians nearly always make exceptions for police officers and the like. The rationale for police having guns is based at least partly on the idea that police need and can effectively use guns for defending themselves and others. Doubts about the defensive utility of guns, then, appear to rest on any of three beliefs: (1) civilians do not need any self-protective devices, because they will never confront criminals, or at least will never do so while they have access to a gun, or (2) they can rely on the police for protection, or (3) they are not able to use guns effectively, regardless of need.

There is certainly some merit to the first belief. Most Americans rarely face a threat of serious physical assault, and some will never do so. Nevertheless, National Crime Survey (NCS) estimates indicate that 83% of Americans will, sometime over the span of their lives, be a victim of a violent crime, all of which by definition involve direct confrontation with a criminal (U.S. Bureau of Justice Statistics 1987c, p. 3). Further, the most common location for such a confrontation is in or near the victim's home, i.e., the place where victims would be most likely to have access to a gun if they owned one (Curtis 1974, p. 176). Although it cannot be stated what share of these incidents will transpire in a way that would allow the victim to actually use a gun, it is clear that a large share of the population will experience such an incident.

The second idea, that citizens can depend on police for effective protection, is simply untrue. It implies that police can serve the same function as a gun in disrupting a crime in progress, before the victim is hurt or loses property. Police cannot do this, and indeed do not themselves even claim to be able to do so. Instead, police primarily respond reactively to crimes *after* they have occurred, questioning the victim and other witnesses in the hope that they can apprehend the criminals, make them available for prosecution and punishment, and thereby deter other criminals from attempting crimes. Police officers rarely disrupt violent crimes or burglaries in progress; even the most professional and efficient urban police forces rarely can reach the scene of a crime soon enough to catch the criminal "in the act" (Walker 1989, pp. 134–5). More generally, the idea that modern police are so effective in controlling crime that they have rendered citizen self-protection obsolete is widely at variance with a large body of evidence that police activities have, at best, only very modest effects on crime (Walker 1989, Chapter 7).

The third idea, that civilians are not generally able to use guns effectively, requires more extended consideration. Gun control proponents sometimes argue that only police have the special training, skills, and emotional control needed to wield guns effectively in self-defense. They hint that would-be gun users are ineffectual, panic-prone hysterics, as likely to accidentally shoot a family member as a burglar (e.g., Alviani and Drake 1975, pp. 6–8; Yeager et al. 1976, pp. 3–7). Incidents in which householders shoot family members mistaken for burglars and other criminals do indeed occur, but they are extremely rare. Studies reviewed in Chapter 7 indicate that fewer than 2% of fatal gun accidents (FGAs) involve a person accidentally shooting someone mistaken for an intruder. With about 1400 FGAs in 1987, this implies that there are fewer than 28 incidents of this sort annually. Compared with about three quarters of a million defensive uses of guns, this translates into about a 1-in-26,000 chance of a defensive gun use resulting in this kind of accident.

It has been claimed that many people who attempt to use guns for self-protection have the gun taken from them by the criminal and used against them (e.g., Shields 1981, pp. 49, 53; McNamara 1986, p. 989). Although this type of incident is not totally unknown, it is extremely rare. In the 1979–1985 NCS sample, it was possible to identify crime incidents in which the victim used a gun for self-protection and lost a gun to the offender(s). At most, 1% of defensive gun uses resulted in the offender taking a gun away from the victim (author's analysis of NCS data). Even these few cases did not necessarily involve the offender snatching a gun out of the victim's hands. Instead a burglar might, for example, have been leaving a home with one of the household's guns when a resident attempted to stop him, using another household gun. Thus, the 1% figure represents an upper limit estimate of the relative frequency of these events.

It is important to distinguish at this point two discrete issues: (1) the effectiveness of individual instances of civilian gun use against criminals in preventing injury and the completion of the crimes involved, and (2) whether such actions deter criminal attempts from being made in the first place. Actual defensive use of guns by victims in specific criminal attempts could *disrupt* the attempt, preventing the criminal from injuring the victim or obtaining property. On the other hand, the general fact of widespread civilian gun ownership, or ownership by specific individuals or identifiable groups, could *deter* some criminals from making the criminal attempts in the first place. It is even hypothetically possible that defensive actions could often be effective in preventing completion of crimes, yet fail to exert any general deterrent effect on the criminal population; the opposite could also be true. Nevertheless, one would expect, a priori, that gun ownership would be more likely to deter if defensive gun uses were effective in disrupting those individual crimes in which victims used guns.

Preventing Completion of the Crime

It has been argued that resistance by crime victims, especially forceful resistance, is generally useless and even dangerous to the victim (Block

1977; Yeager et al. 1976). Although evidence supports this position as it applies to some forms of resistance, it does not support the claim as it applies to resistance with a gun. Yeager and his colleagues (1976) examined data from victim surveys in eight large U.S. cities, which included information on the fraction of robberies and assaults that was completed against the victim and on victim use of self-protection measures. They did not report results separately for victims resisting with a gun but analyzed a category including victims using any weapon to resist. For robbery, the completion rate was 37% in crimes where the victim resisted with a weapon, a rate lower than that of any other form of self-protection and far lower than among those who did not resist in any way (p. 13). Because guns are regarded as more intimidating and deadly weapons than knives and other lesser weapons, one would expect gun-armed resisters to experience lower completion rates than victims resisting with other weapons. Therefore, had gun resisters been separately analyzed by Yeager et al., the results should have indicated even greater effectiveness of gun resistance relative to other forms of self-protection.

This is confirmed by the national data reported in Table 4.4, which break out gun-armed resistance from other armed resistance. The figures are derived from analysis of the 1979–1985 incident-level files of the NCS public use computer tapes (ICPSR 1987). This dataset contains information on over 180,000 sample crime incidents reported by nationally representative samples of noninstitutionalized persons aged 12 and over. Respondents were asked if they had been a victim of crime in the previous 6 months, if they used any form of self-protection, if they were attacked, if they suffered injury, and if the crimes were completed. For assaults, "completion" means injury was inflicted; thus completion and injury rates are the same for assaults. For robbery, "completion" means the robber took property from the victim. The figures in Table 4.4 indicate that robbery victims who resisted with a gun or with a weapon other than a gun or knife were less likely to lose their property than victims using any other form of self-protection or who did not resist at all.

The remarkably successful outcomes of defensive gun uses might seem surprising if one imagines the incidents to involve shootouts between criminal and victim. This, however, does not describe most gun uses. Among the 1979–1985 violent incidents reported in the NCS, 70.4% of defensive gun uses were against offenders who did not even have a gun (or at least none visible to the victim). Even in the remaining cases it is unlikely that many involved the victim and offender shooting at one another, since less than a quarter of gun assaults involve a gun actually being fired (U.S. Bureau of Justice Statistics 1986b) and under

40% of defensive gun uses involve the defender shooting. More commonly, gun-armed defenders face a criminal without a gun, thus have a strong power advantage, and successfully prevent the completion of the crime without shooting.

Avoiding Injury

Data on attack and injury rates in robberies and assaults, by victim protection method, for the entire nation are also shown in Table 4.4. Robbery and assault victims who used a gun to resist were less likely to be attacked or to suffer an injury than those who used any other methods of self-protection or those who did not resist at all. Only 17.4% of gun resisters in robberies, and 12.1% in assaults, were injured. The misleading consequences of lumping gun resistance in with other forms of forceful resistance (ala Yeager et al. 1976; Cook 1986) are made clear by these data, since other forms of forceful self-protection are far more risky than resisting with a gun. After gun resistance, the victim course of action least likely to be associated with injury is doing nothing at all, i.e., not resisting. However, this strategy is also the worst at preventing completion of the crime. Further, passivity is not a completely safe course either, since a quarter of victims who did not resist were injured anyway. This may be because some robbers use violence preemptively, as a way of deterring or heading off victim resistance before it occurs. Thus they may use violence instrumentally to ensure victim compliance, against those victims for whom this seems to be a safe course of action (Conklin 1972, Chapter 6). Other robbers may simply enjoy assaulting victims for its own sake, using violence expressively (Cook and Nagin 1979, pp. 36–7).

Some analysts of robbery data have uncritically assumed that where crimes involve victims who resisted and were also injured, resistance must somehow have led to the injury (e.g., Yeager et al. 1976). Although it is tempting to assume that resistance to a robber provokes attack, the reverse may also be true. That is, victims otherwise reluctant to resist may do so out of desperation or anger after being attacked by the robber—injury may provoke victim resistance. The regular NCS surveys before 1986 did not establish the sequence of offender attack and victim self-protection actions. Consequently it is not certain if any of the 17.4% of robberies with an injured, gun resisting victim involved an attack provoked by the victim's resistance. Nevertheless, even after acknowledging that their police record data did not allow them to confidently establish the sequence of events, Zimring and Zuehl (1986, p. 19) asserted that active victim resistance escalates victim risk of death and recommended that victims refrain from resisting.

Based on work of a former Zimring collaborator, it is evident that such a conclusion is questionable. In a study of robberies reported to the Chicago police in 1975, Block (1977) examined offense reports to determine which came first, victim resistance or robber use of force. In robberies in which the victim resisted with force (including the use of weapons), victim resistance came *after* the offender's initial use of force in 68% of the cases (1977, pp. 81–2). Presumably 32% involved resistance first, then offender use of force. If this applied nationally to the 17.4% of robbery gun resisters who were injured, it would mean that only about 6% (.32 × .174 = .058) were injured after they used their guns to resist. And since some of these injuries surely would have occurred even without resistance, it means that fewer than 6% of these victims provoked the injury by their use of a gun. In any case, even if all gun resister injuries had been directly caused by the resistance, a dubious assumption, it is still clear that a robbery victim's resistance with a gun rarely provokes a robber into injuring him. Based on the present findings and those of Block, the chances of this happening are probably less than 1 in 20.

In contrast, Block noted that among victims who resisted nonforcefully, by fleeing or yelling for help, it was resistance that came first in 70% of the cases. The evidence is thus compatible with the hypothesis that active physical resistance without a gun often provokes offender attack, whereas resistance with a gun deters attack.

These conclusions are supported by special NCS data. Questions about the sequence of resistance and injury were asked in a limited one-month-only Victim Risk Supplement (VRS) administered to 14,258 households as part of the NCS in February 1984. In assaults that involved both *forceful* self-protection actions and attack on the victim, the victim actions preceded attack in only 9.8% of the incidents. For assaults involving *nonforceful* resistance, only 5.7% of victim actions preceded attack. For robbery incidents with both attack on the victim and self-protection actions, *forceful* self-protective actions never preceded attack, whereas in only 22% of similar incidents involving *nonforceful* victim actions did the victim actions precede the attack (author's analysis of VRS data). Thus, even in those few incidents in which forceful resistance was accompanied by attacks on the victim, the sequencing was rarely compatible with the contention that the victim's resistance provoked the attack. The national NCS data, then, even more strongly indicate that forceful victim resistance rarely provokes attack. The best available evidence indicates that gun-armed victim resistance to robbery or assault almost never provokes the offender to injure the victim.

Rape and Resistance

The previous discussion addressed gun resistance only in robberies and assaults. Rape, the third major violent crime covered in NCS data, had to be excluded because there are so few relevant sample cases to analyze. Less than 1% of NCS rape victims report resistance with a gun (e.g., U.S. Bureau of Justice Statistics 1985c). However, one may gain some strong hints about the results of gun resistance by examining all instances of armed resistance by rape victims. Grouping together instances of resistance with guns, knives, or other weapons, Kleck and Sayles (1990) found, in a multivariate probit analysis of national victim survey data, that rape victims using armed resistance were less likely to have the rape attempt completed against them than victims using any other mode of resistance. These results confirmed those of Lizotte (1986) using city victim surveys. Further, there was no significant effect of armed resistance on the rapist inflicting additional injury beyond the rape itself. In view of the robbery and assault findings indicating that gun resistance is generally more effective than armed resistance using other weapons, it would seem to be a reasonable inference that the same would be true for rape. Indeed, this would seem especially likely with rapes, given that rape victims are nearly all women, and guns are the weapon type whose effectiveness is least dependent on the physical strength of its user.

The Police Chief's Fallacy

Some police officers advise people to refrain from armed resistance should they be confronted by a criminal. For example, Joseph McNamara, Chief of the San Jose Police Department, testified before a Congressional committee considering gun legislation: "We urge citizens not to resist armed robbery, but in these sad cases I described, the victims ended up dead because they produced their own handguns and escalated the violence. Very rarely have I seen cases in which the handgun was used to ward off a criminal" (McNamara 1986, p. 989). Why do some police give such advice? While some, like Chief McNamara, a strong gun control advocate, may be motivated by political considerations, it is doubtful if this is true for most officers. Instead, police advice may well logically follow from the resistance experiences of victims with whom officers have had contact. The problem with relying on this sample of resistance cases is that it is substantially unrepresentative of the experiences of crime victims in general—the cases McNamara and other police officers have seen are not like those they have not seen, and the latter outnumber the former by a wide margin.

Most crimes are not reported to the police, and the crimes most likely to go unreported are the ones that involve neither injury nor property loss, i.e., those that had successful outcomes from the victim's viewpoint. For example, among robberies reported to the NCS, only 24% of those with no injury or property loss were reported to police, whereas 72% of those with both were reported. Likewise, assaults without injury are less likely to be reported than those with injury (U.S. Bureau of Justice Statistics 1985d, p. 3). By definition, all successful defensive gun uses fall within the no-injury, no-property-loss category, and thus are largely invisible to the police. Consequently, police never hear about the bulk of successful defensive gun uses, instead hearing mostly about an unrepresentative minority of them dominated by failures. To conclude that armed resistance is ineffective or dangerous, based on the experiences of this sort of unrepresentative sample of victims, can be called, in honor of Chief McNamara, "the police chief's fallacy." At present, advising victims to not use guns to resist criminal attempts seems imprudent at best, dangerous at worst. As Ziegenhagen and Brosnan (1985, p. 693) have commented: "victims can and do play an active part in the control of crime outcomes regardless of well-intentioned but ill-conceived efforts to encourage victims to limit the range of responses open to them. Victims can, and do, exercise a range of optional responses to robbery far beyond those conceived of by criminal justice professionals."

An Exercise in Ingenious Speciousness

When gun control advocates and public health scholars consider whether keeping a gun for defensive purposes is sensible, they frequently bring up one of the oddest statistics in the gun control debate. In 1975 four physicians published an article based on data derived from medical examiner files in Cuyahoga (Cleveland) County, Ohio. They noted that during the period 1958–1973, there were 148 fatal gun accidents (77% of them in the home) and 23 "burglars, robbers or intruders who were not relatives or acquaintances" killed by people using guns to defend their homes. They stated that there were six times as many home fatal gun accidents as burglars killed. (This appears to have been a miscomputation—the authors counted all 148 accidental deaths in the numerator, instead of just the 115 occurring in the home. Although the value of the number does not matter much, the correct ratio was five rather than six.) On the basis of these facts, the authors concluded that "guns in the home are more dangerous than useful to the homeowner and his family who keep them to protect their persons and property" and that "the possession of firearms by civilians appears to be a dangerous and ineffective means of self-protection" (Rushforth et al. 1975, pp. 504–5).

These conclusions were a breath-taking non sequitur. The first thing to note about whether guns are "ineffective" means of self-protection is that the authors presented no evidence of any kind having any bearing on the issue—no counts of defensive uses, no estimates of the fraction of defensive uses that prevented completion of crimes or resulted in injury—nothing. As to how dangerous keeping a gun for protection is, the authors could only cite accidental gun deaths. Yet they did not establish that any of the accidents occurred in connection with defensive uses or even that the guns involved were owned for defensive reasons. The connection between the accidents and defensive gun ownership was simply assumed, rather than demonstrated.

The main flaw, however, in the authors' reasoning was in treating the 6–1 ratio as if it were somehow a cost–benefit ratio, a comparison that could say something about the relative benefits and risks of defensive gun ownership. The ratio cannot serve such a purpose. The numerator is not a meaningful measure of risk for the average gun-owning household, and the denominator has no bearing at all on the defensive benefits of keeping a gun. As will be shown in Chapter 7, gun accidents are largely concentrated in a very small, high-risk subset of the population—for everyone else, the risks of a fatal gun accident are negligible. Therefore the population-wide accident rate is an exaggeration of the risk born by the typical defensive gun-owning household. And the number of burglars killed does not in any way serve as a measure of the defensive benefit of keeping a gun. As Barry Bruce-Briggs, commenting on this article, wryly noted, "The measure of the effectiveness of self-defense is not in the number of bodies piled up on doorsteps, but in the property that is protected" (1976, p. 39). To assess defensive benefits might entail estimating the number of burglars captured, frightened off, deterred from attempting burglaries, or displaced to unoccupied premises where they could not injure any victims. The authors measured none of these things. As previously noted, well under 1% of defensive gun uses involve a criminal being killed. And the one protection-related item the authors did count is not even itself a benefit. Defensive gun owners do not have guns for the purpose of getting a chance to "bag a burglar." Being forced to kill another human being, burglar or not, is a nightmare to be suffered through for years.

Even this number was artificially reduced by excluding killings of intruders who were relatives or acquaintances; the authors apparently felt that killings by, e.g., a wife defending herself against a homicidally abusive husband, or a woman defending herself against an estranged husband or ex-boyfriend trying to kill or rape her, were not legitimate defensive homicides suitable to be counted along with shootings of burglars (see Kates 1990, pp. 24–32 for an extended discussion of this exclusion).

The benefit of defensive gun ownership that would be parallel to innocent lives *lost* to guns would be innocent lives *saved* by guns. However, it is impossible to count the latter, so it will never be possible to form a meaningful ratio of genuinely comparable quantities.

Bruce-Briggs described this sort of study as "ingeniously specious" (1976, p. 39) and briefly dismissed it. Most serious gun scholars ignore this particular study (e.g., the massive review by Wright et al. does not mention it at all), but it is a favorite of procontrol propagandists (e.g., Yeager et al. 1976, p. 4; Alviani and Drake 1975, p. 8). It was even unwittingly replicated 11 years later by two other physicians (Kellermann and Reay 1986) who apparently were unaware of the Rushforth et al. study (or at least did not cite it) or of the harsh criticism to which it had been subjected. This later analysis had all the same problems as its predecessor, used the same specious reasoning, and, inevitably, arrived at essentially the same non sequitur conclusion: "The advisability of keeping firearms in the home for protection must be questioned."

Crimes Involving Defensive Gun Use

What crimes are defensive gun users defending against? Evidence from NCS surveys is unreliable on this point. In addition to the reasons previously discussed, the doubts victims may have about the legality of their gun uses may further contribute to an underreporting of defensive uses. Also, since crimes involving victim gun use usually involve neither property loss nor victim injury, victims are especially likely to forget or otherwise fail to report them to interviewers, just as they fail to report them to police.

Two very different sources of information suggest that assaults at home are the most common crimes involving victim gun use, followed by burglaries and retail store robberies. Table 4.5 displays the results of the 1976 Field poll of California (Field Institute 1976) and data from medical examiner records concerning civilian justifiable homicides committed in Dade County in 1980 (compiled from Wilbanks 1984, pp. 190–374). The Field poll addressed only handgun use and indicated locations of gun uses, while the medical data covered all gun types but did not usually indicate the location of homicides. Nevertheless, the results are compatible concerning the crimes with which defensive gun uses are associated.

The California survey data indicate that 62% of uses are connected to assault or rape. The medical examiner data indicate a figure of 65% for these offenses, while also showing that nearly all of these uses are connected to assault other than rape. "Theft at home" in the California survey apparently included burglary, and the justifiable homicide data suggest that burglary accounts for most of the cases in this category. "Theft elsewhere" in the California survey would include retail store robberies, and the robbery category among justifiable homicides may consist largely of uses linked to such crimes. This interpretation is supported by information on the locations of civilian justifiable homicides in California in 1982, 86% of which involved guns. Police records showed that 32% occurred in the killer's residence, 23% in a business location (especially in robbery-prone businesses such as liquor stores and bars), 14% on the street or sidewalk, and 30% elsewhere (California 1983, p. 67). This set of California homicides excluded pure self-defense homicides (i.e., killings not involving any other felonies besides an assault on the defender) and thus is not strictly comparable with the Dade County defensive homicides, most of which were pure self-defense killings. This at least partially accounts for the smaller share of California homicides occurring in the home, since it means that cases such as those involving women defending themselves against abusive husbands or boyfriends would ordinarily be excluded. Therefore the California data do not undercut the conclusion that most defensive gun uses occur in the home and involve defense against assaults. Home defenses against burglars and retail store defenses against robbers each accounts for substantial minorities of the uses.

Deterrence

Gun Deterrable Crimes

To deter a crime means to cause a criminal to refrain from even attempting the crime, due to fear of some negative consequence. If there is a deterrent effect of defensive gun ownership and use, it should be facilitated by a criminal being able to realistically anticipate a potential victim using a gun to disrupt the crime. The types of crimes most likely to be influenced by this possibility are crimes occurring in homes—where victims are most likely to have access to a gun—and in the kinds of business establishments where proprietors keep guns. In line with the preceding information about where defensive uses commonly occur, crimes such as assault in the home, residential burglary, and retail store robbery would seem to be the most likely candidates to be deterred. About one in eight residential burglaries occurs while a household member is present (U.S. Bureau of Justice Statistics 1985a, p. 4), and, by definition, all robberies, rapes, assaults, and homicides involve direct contact between a victim and an offender. To be sure, in many of these incidents the offender has the initiative, often taking the victim by surprise, and the situations often develop too quickly for victims to get to their guns. On the other hand, the most common single location for violent crimes, especially homicides and assaults between intimates, is in or near the home of the victim or the home of both victim and offender, where access to a gun would be easier (U.S. Bureau of Justice Statistics 1980, p. 22; Curtis 1974, p. 176).

Strategic attributes of some crime types make them better-than-average candidates for disruption by armed victims. For example, violent acts between intimates are typically part of a persistent, ongoing pattern of violence (Wilt et al. 1977). Prospective victims of such violence may not ordinarily be able to predict the exact time of the next violent episode, but they often are able to recognize the usual precursors of repetitive violence. Wives and girlfriends of violent men, for example, may understand well the significance of their husband or boyfriend getting drunk and verbally abusive (Gillespie 1989). This implies a distinct tactical difference between violence among intimates and other crimes. Victims of intimate violence can take advantage of behavioral cues that serve as advance warning signs and can ready themselves accordingly. In the most threatening situations, advance preparations could include securing a weapon.

Plausibility of Deterrent Effects

Demonstrating deterrent effects of criminal justice system punishment has proven difficult (e.g., Blumstein et al. 1978) and the same must certainly be true for the private use of force, which is even less well measured than the risk-generating activities of the criminal justice system. Therefore, the following evidence should be regarded only as suggestive.

Results from deterrence research have been highly mixed and often negative. Why should one expect deterrence from the armed citizenry when the legal system appears to have so little impact? The deterrence doctrine states that punishment deters more as its certainty, severity, and celerity (promptness) increase (Gibbs 1975). One obvious difference between the risk for the criminal from criminal justice activity and that from civilian gun use is that the maximum potential severity of citizen self help is far greater than legal system responses to crime. The maximum legal penalty a burglar, robber, or even a murderer is likely to face is a few years in prison: only 20 persons were legally executed, all for murders, between mid-1967 and mid-1984 (U.S. Bureau of Justice Statistics 1984b). In contrast, thousands of criminals are killed by gun-wielding private citizens every year.

The frequency of defensive gun uses roughly equals the total number of U.S. arrests for violent crime and burglary, which numbered about 988,000 in 1980 (U.S. FBI 1981, p. 190). Being threatened or shot at by a gun-wielding victim is about as probable as arrest and substantially more probable than conviction or incarceration. This is not surprising since there are only about 600,000 police officers in the United States, fewer than a quarter of whom are on duty at any one time (U.S. Bureau of the Census 1982, p. 184). There are, on the other hand, tens of millions of civilians who have immediate access to firearms and are well motivated to disrupt crimes directed at themselves, their families, or their property.

Finally, victims who use guns defensively almost always do so within minutes of the attempted crime. In contrast, when an arrest occurs, it can follow the crime by days or even weeks. At the very soonest, it comes after the several minutes it takes a patrol car to respond to a citizen's call. In any case, the average swiftness of even arrest is much lower than for victim gun use, whereas the celerity of conviction and punishment is lower still. If the possibility of deterrence due to CJS activities is taken seriously, then so should the possibility of deterrence due to private gun ownership and defensive use.

Evidence from Surveys of Criminals

There is direct, albeit not conclusive, evidence on the deterrent effects of victim gun use from surveys of imprisoned criminals. Wright and Rossi (1986) interviewed 1874 felons in prisons in 10 states and asked about their encounters with armed victims and their attitudes toward the risks of such encounters. Among felons who reported ever committing a violent crime or a burglary, 42% said they had run into a victim who was armed with a gun, 38% reported they had been scared off, shot at, wounded, or captured by an armed victim (these were combined in the original survey question), and 43% said they had at some time in their lives decided not to commit a crime because they knew or believed the victim was carrying a gun (my tabulations from ICPSR 1986).

Concerning the felons' attitudes toward armed victims, 56% agreed with the statement that "most criminals are more worried about meeting an armed victim than they are about running into the police, 58% agreed that "a store owner who is known to keep a gun on the premises is not going to get robbed very often," and 52% agreed that "a criminal is not going to mess around with a victim he knows is armed with a gun." Only 27% agreed that committing a crime against an armed victim is an exciting challenge" (my tabulations from ICPSR 1986). Further, 45% of those who had encountered an armed victim reported that they thought regularly or often about the possibility of getting shot by their victims. Even among those without such an encounter the figure was 28% (Wright and Rossi 1986, p. 149). These results agree with earlier findings from less sophisticated surveys of prisoners (Firman 1975; Link 1982).

Many objections to prison survey research on deterrence concern flaws whose correction would tend to strengthen conclusions that there are deterrent effects. For example, Zimring and Hawkins (1973, pp. 31–32) discussed the "Warden's Survey fallacy" whereby prison wardens concluded that the death penalty could not deter murder since all the killers on death row to whom they spoke said the penalty had not deterred them. Clearly, prisoners are biased samples of criminals and prospective criminals, since their presence in prison itself indicates that deterrence was not completely effective with them. In view of this bias, prison survey results supporting a deterrence hypothesis are all the more impressive. Such doubts about the validity of prisoners' responses to surveys are discussed throughout the Wright and Rossi book (1986, but especially pp. 32–38). Being "scared off by a victim" is not the sort of thing a violent criminal is likely to want to admit, especially in prison, where maintaining a fearless image can be essential to survival. Therefore, incidents of this nature may well have been underreported. Even more significantly, the most deterrable prospective criminals and those deterred from crime altogether will not be included in prison samples. These results, therefore, may reflect a minimal baseline picture of the deterrent potential of victim gun use.

Quasiexperimental Evidence

Increases in actual gun ownership are ordinarily fairly gradual, making interrupted time series analyses of such increases inappropriate. However, highly publicized programs to train citizens in gun use amount to "gun awareness" programs that could conceivably produce sharp changes in prospective criminals' awareness of gun ownership among potential victims. The impact of these programs can be assessed because they have specific times of onset and specific spans of operation that make it easier to say when they might be most likely to affect crime.

From October 1966 to March 1967 the Orlando Police Department trained more than 2500 women to use guns (Krug 1968). Organized in response to demands from citizens worried about a sharp increase in rape, this was an unusually large and highly publicized program. It received several front page stories in the local daily newspaper, the *Orlando Sentinel,* a co-sponsor of the program. An interrupted time series analysis of Orlando crime trends showed that the rape rate decreased by 88% in 1967, compared to 1966, a decrease far larger than in any previous 1-year period. The rape rate remained constant in the rest of Florida and in the United States. Interestingly, the only other crime to show a substantial drop was burglary. Thus, the crime targeted decreased, and the offense most likely to occur where victims have access to guns, burglary, also decreased (Kleck and Bordua 1983, pp. 282–8).

Green (1987, p. 75) interpreted the results of the Orlando study as indicating a partial "spillover" or displacement of rape from the city to nearby areas, i.e., a mixture of absolute deterrence of some rapes and a shift in location of others. Unfortunately, the possibility of displacement can never be eliminated when considering any location-specific crime control effort, be it a local job training program, an increase in police manpower or patrol frequency, or a gun training program.

Green also suggested that the apparent rape decrease might have been due to allegedly irregular crime recording practices of the Orlando city police department, without, however, presenting any evidence of police reporting changes over this period, beyond the sharp changes in the rape rates themselves.

A much smaller training program was conducted with only 138 people from September through November 1967 by the Kansas City (Missouri) police, in response to retail businessmen's concerns about store robberies (U.S. Small Business Administration 1969, pp. 253–6). The city had a population of 507,000 (U.S. Bureau of the Census 1982, p. 23), so the participation rate was less than 1/90 of that achieved in Orlando. Nevertheless, results from the Kansas City program are consistent with the hypothesis that the program caused crime levels to be lower than they otherwise would have been. Table 4.6 displays crime trends in Kansas City and its metropolitan area, as well as robbery trends in the rest of Missouri, the region of which Kansas City is a part, and in the United States. Whereas the frequency of robbery increased sharply from 1967 to 1968 by 35% in the rest of Missouri, 20% in the region, and 30% in the United States, it essentially levelled off in Kansas City and declined by 13% in surrounding areas, even though robberies had been increasing in the 5 years prior to the training program and continued to increase again in 1968. Thus, the upward trend showed a distinct interruption in the year immediately following the program. This cannot be attributed to some general improvement in conditions generating robbery rates elsewhere in the nation, since robbery rates were increasing elsewhere. Nor can it be attributed to improvements in conditions producing violent crime in general in Kansas City, since robbery was the only violent crime to level off—a pattern not generally evident elsewhere. Something occurred in the Kansas City area in the 1967–1968 period that caused an upward trend in robberies to level off, something that was not occurring in other places and that was specifically related to robbery. Interestingly, Kansas City also experienced a leveling off in its sharply upward trend in burglary, suggesting a possible "by-product" deterrent effect such as that suggested by the Orlando data.

These two gun training episodes are not unique. They resemble instances of crime drops following gun training programs elsewhere, including decreases in grocery robberies in Detroit after a grocer's organization began gun clinics, and decreases in retail store robberies in Highland Park, Michigan, attributed to "gun-toting merchants" (Krug 1968, p. H571).

Awareness of the risks of confronting an armed victim may also be increased by highly publicized instances of defensive gun use. After Bernhard Goetz used a handgun to wound four robbers on a New York City subway train on December 22, 1984, subway robberies decreased by 43% in the next week, compared to the 2 weeks prior to the incident and decreased in the following 2 months by 19% compared to the same period in the previous year, even though nonrobbery subway crime increased and subway robberies had been increasing prior to the shootings (*Tallahassee Democrat* 1985; *New York Times* 1985a,b). However, because New York City transit police also increased manpower on the subway trains immediately after the shootings, any impact uniquely attributable to the Goetz gun use was confounded with potential effects of the manpower increase.

Finally, the hypothesis of deterrent effects of civilian gun ownership is supported by the experience of Kennesaw, Georgia, a suburb of Atlanta with a 1980 population of 5095 (U.S. Bureau of the Census 1983c, p. 832). As a way of demonstrating their disapproval of a ban on handgun ownership passed in Morton Grove, Illinois, the Kennesaw city council passed a city ordinance requiring heads of household to keep at least one firearm in their homes. Only a token fine of $50 was provided as a penalty, citizens could exempt themselves simply by stating that they conscientiously objected to gun possession, and there was no active attempt to enforce the law by inspecting homes. It is doubtful that the law substantially increased household gun ownership; the mayor of Kennesaw guessed that "about 85% of Kennesaw households already possessed firearms before the ordinance was passed" (Schneidman 1982). Nevertheless, in the 7 months immediately following passage of the ordinance (March 15, 1982 to October 31, 1982), there were only five residential burglaries reported to police, compared to 45 in the same period in the previous year, an 89% decrease (Benenson 1982). This drop was far in excess of the modest 10.4% decrease in the burglary rate experienced by Georgia as a whole from 1981 to 1982, the 6.8% decrease for South Atlantic states, the 9.6% decrease for the nation, and the 7.1% decrease for cities under 10,000 population (U.S. FBI 1983, pp. 45–7, 143).

This decrease, however, is not conclusive evidence of a deterrent effect, since small towns have small numbers of crimes and trends can be very erratic. It is not clear that any deterrent effect, no matter how large, would be detectable in an area with monthly crime trends as erratic as those found in small towns. For example, an ARIMA analysis of monthly burglary data found no evidence of a statistically significant drop in burglary in Kennesaw (McDowall et al. 1989). This study, however, was both flawed and largely irrelevant to the deterrence hypothesis. The Kennesaw ordinance pertained solely to household gun ownership, and thus its deterrent effects, if any, would be evident with *residential* burglaries. This study blurred any such effects by using a data source that lumped all burglaries together (see their footnote 1). The difference between the two numbers apparently can be very large—the authors report 32 total burglaries for 1985, whereas a *New York Times* article, which the authors cited, reported only 11 "house burglaries" for that year (Schmidt 1987). The authors also used raw numbers of burglaries rather than rates. Kennesaw experienced a 70% increase in population from 1980 to 1987. Burglary increases due to sheer city growth would obscure any crime-reducing effects of the ordinance. The effects of these two errors can be very large, as indicated below:

Raw Number or Rate?	Total Burglaries or Just Residential	% Change 1981–82	% Change 1981–86
Raw	Total	−35	−41
Rate[a]	Total	−40	−56
Raw	Residential[b]	−53	−80
Rate[a]	Residential[b]	−57	−85

[a] Based on linear interpolation of 1980 and 1987 population figures reported in Schmidt (1987).
[b] Based on counts of "house burglaries" reported in Schmidt (1987).

Thus the authors' methods apparently obscured much of the decrease in the residential burglary rate. Also, their use of total burglary data ignores the implications of an extended discussion in Kleck (1988, pp. 15–16, immediately following the Kennesaw discussion cited by the authors), in which it was argued that a major effect of residential gun ownership may be to displace burglars from occupied homes to less dangerous targets (see also next section). As nonresidential targets (especially stores and other businesses left unoccupied at night) would fit into the latter category, one would expect a displacement from residential burglaries to nonresidential burglaries, as well as a shift from occupied residences to unoccupied ones. Thus, the hypothesized deterrent effect on occupied residential burglary could easily occur with no impact at all on total burglaries. Consequently, the exercise by McDowall and his colleagues has no clear relevance to the hypothesis stated in Kleck (1988).

Even as a test of the impact on total burglary, this study was affected by two other related flaws. The authors specified an intervention model that assumed an abrupt and *permanent* change in crime. However, a deterrence model stresses the critical importance of increases in offenders' perceptions of risk. Any such subjective shift is almost certainly temporary, fading along with memories of the passage of the ordinance. A temporary-change model would be theoretically preferable, regardless of issues of fit to the data. The authors report that a model assuming a temporary effect did not fit the data as well as the one they preferred, but that may be due to a related problem. Although the intervention occurred in March of 1982, the authors extended their times series all the way to the end of 1986. Although more time points are desirable from a narrow statistical viewpoint, a longer postintervention period will also tend to obscure any effects that were temporary and followed by rising crime rates. This suspicion is supported by the authors' footnote 3 and Figure 1, which indicate that, beginning about 3 years after the intervention, total burglaries increased substantially (probably at least partly due to the large population increases and related changes). When the authors excluded 1986 time points, the parameter measuring impact of the intervention reversed sign, going from small positive to small negative. This raises the possibility that if the time series had been limited just to time points closer to the intervention (say, within 3 years), this alteration alone might have made the impact parameter negative and significant, supporting the deterrence thesis.

It needs to be stressed that the results of the natural quasiexperiments are not cited for the narrow purpose of demonstrating the short-term deterrent effects of gun training programs or victim gun use. There is no reason to believe that citizens used the training in any significant number of real-life defensive situations, nor any solid evidence that gun ownership increased in the affected areas. Rather, the results are cited to support the argument that routine gun ownership and defensive use by civilians may have a pervasive, *ongoing* impact on crime, with or without such programs or incidents. This impact is intensified and made more salient at times when criminals' awareness of potential victims' gun possession is dramatically increased, thereby offering an opportunity to detect an effect that is ordinarily invisible. A few diverse examples of how this awareness might come to be increased have been described. Other examples would be general stories in the news media about gun ownership, increases in gun sales, and so on.

Guns and the Displacement of Burglars from Occupied Homes

Residential burglars devote considerable thought, time, and effort to locating homes that are unoccupied. In interviews with burglars in a Pennsylvania prison, Rengert and Wasilchick (1985) found that nearly all the 2 hours spent on the average suburban burglary was devoted to locating an appropriate target, casing the house, and making sure no one was home. There are at least two reasons why burglars make this considerable investment of time and effort: to avoid arrest and to avoid getting shot. Several burglars in this study reported that they avoided late night burglaries because it was too difficult to tell if anyone was home, explaining "That's the way to get shot" (Rengert and Wasilchick 1985, p. 30). Burglars also stated that they avoided neighborhoods occupied largely by persons of a different race because "You'll get shot if you're caught there" (p. 62). Giving weight to these opinions, one of the 31 burglars admitted to having been shot on the job (p. 98). In the Wright-Rossi survey, 73% of felons who had committed a burglary or violent crime agreed that "one reason burglars avoid houses when people are at home is that they fear being shot" (unpublished tabulations from ICPSR 1986).

The nonconfrontational nature of most burglaries is a major reason why associated deaths and injuries are so rare—an absent victim cannot be injured. Don Kates (1983a, p. 269) argued that victim gun ownership is a major reason for the nonconfrontational nature of burglary and is therefore to be credited with reducing deaths and injuries by its deterrent effects. This possible benefit is enjoyed by all potential burglary victims, not just those who own guns, because burglars seeking to avoid confrontations usually cannot know exactly which homes have guns, and therefore must attempt to avoid all occupied premises.

Under hypothetical no-guns circumstances, the worst a burglar would ordinarily have to fear would be breaking off a burglary attempt if faced with an occupant who called the police. A typical strong, young burglar would have little reason to fear attack or apprehension by unarmed victims, especially if the victim confronted was a woman or an elderly person. Further, there would be positive advantages to burglary of occupied premises since this would give the burglar a much better chance to get the cash in victims' purses or wallets.

To be sure, even under no-guns conditions, many burglars would continue to avoid occupied residences simply because contact with a victim would increase their chances of apprehension by the police. Others may have chosen to do burglaries rather than robberies because they were emotionally unable or unwilling to confront their victims and thus would avoid occupied premises for this reason. However, this does not seem to be true of most incarcerated burglars. Prison surveys indicate that few criminals specialize in one crime type, and most imprisoned burglars report having also committed robberies. In the Wright and Rossi survey, of those who reported ever committing a burglary, 62% also reported committing robberies (my secondary analysis of ICPSR 1986). Thus, most of these burglars were temperamentally capable of confronting victims, even though they presumably preferred to avoid them when committing a burglary.

Results from victim surveys in three foreign nations indicate that in countries with lower rates of gun ownership than the United States, residential burglars are much more likely to enter occupied homes. A 1977 survey in the Netherlands found an occupancy rate of 48% for all burglaries, compared to 9% in the United States the previous year (Block 1984, p. 26). In the 1982 British Crime Survey, 59% of attempted burglaries and 26% of completed burglaries were committed with someone at home (Mayhew 1987). And Waller and Okihiro (1978, p. 31) reported that 44% of burglarized Toronto residences were occupied during the burglaries, with 21% of the burglaries resulting in confrontations between victim and offender. The differences between the United States and Great Britain and Canada cannot be explained by more serious legal threats in this country, since the probability of arrest and imprisonment and the severity of sentences served for common crimes are at least as high in the latter nations as in the United States (Wilson 1976, pp. 18–19; U.S. Bureau of Justice Statistics 1987b).

If widespread civilian gun ownership helps deter burglars from entering occupied premises, what might this imply regarding the level of burglary-linked violence? NCS data indicate that when a residential burglary is committed with a household member present, it results in a threat or attack on the victim 30.2% of the time (U.S. Bureau of Justice Statistics 1985a, p. 4). Although only 12.7% of U.S. residential burglaries are against occupied homes, the occupancy rate in three low gun-ownership nations averaged about 45%. What would happen if U.S. burglars were equally likely to enter occupied premises? In 1985 the NCS counted 5,594,420 household burglaries, with about 214,568 resulting in assaults on a victim (5,594,420 × .127 × .302). Now assume a 45% occupancy rate and assume that 30.2% of the occupied premise burglaries resulted in assaults on a victim, the same as now. This would imply about 760,282 assaults on burglary victims, 545,713 more than now. This change alone would have represented a 9.4% increase in all NCS-counted violent crime in 1985. If high home gun ownership rates in the United States really do account for the difference in burglary occupancy rates between the United States and other nations, these figures indicate that burglary displacement effects of widespread gun ownership could have a significant impact on violence rates.

To briefly summarize, gun use by private citizens against violent criminals and burglars is common and about as frequent as legal actions like arrests, is a more prompt negative consequence of crime than legal punishment, and is more severe, at its most serious, than legal system punishments. On the other hand, only a small percentage of criminal victimizations transpire in a way that results in defensive gun use; guns certainly are not usable in all crime situations. Victim gun use is associated with lower rates of assault or robbery victim injury and lower rates of robbery completion than any other defensive action or doing nothing to resist. Serious predatory criminals perceive a risk from victim gun use that is roughly comparable to that of criminal justice system actions, and this perception may influence their criminal behavior in socially desirable ways. Nevertheless, a deterrent effect of widespread gun ownership and defensive use has not been conclusively established, any more than it has been for activities of the legal system. Given the nature of deterrent effects, it may never be convincingly established.

The most parsimonious way of linking these previously unconnected and unknown or obscure facts is to tentatively conclude that civilian ownership and defensive use of guns deters violent crime and reduces burglar-linked injuries. Although one cannot precisely calculate the social control impact of gun use and ownership any more than one can for the operations of the legal system, the available evidence is compatible with the hypothesis that gun ownership may exert as much effect on violent crime and burglary as do CJS activities.

It should be stressed that even if the deterrent effects of civilian gun ownership and use are comparable to those due to the operations of the CJS, they are not necessarily huge. The impact of the legal system on crime rates does not appear to be very large (Walker 1989). Therefore, although there are clearly benefits to an armed citizenry, the possibility that its crime-reducing effects are as large as those of the CJS is not in itself necessarily very impressive.

Conclusions

Does the widespread use of guns for defensive purposes constitute vigilantism? Certainly there are some parallels. Vigilantism, in the true sense of collective private force used for social control purposes, flourished where legal controls were weakest, such as frontier areas. And research on today's world indicates that private citizen crime prevention activities in general are more common where police are less numerous (Krahn and Kennedy 1985). It is commonplace to draw an analogy between conditions in the Western U.S. of the nineteenth century and high crime neighborhoods in today's cities. The analogy is especially close regarding the limited effectiveness of urban law enforcement agencies in controlling crime. However, it is also true that contemporary private efforts to collectively control crime, such as neighborhood crime watch organizations, are least effective and enduring in precisely those areas that most need them—disorganized high crime areas occupied largely by transient populations of socially isolated strangers (Greenberg et al. 1984). The social disorganization and lack of cultural consensus that encourage criminal behavior also hinder any kind of effective collective action to control crime. Under the anomic conditions characterizing large U.S. cities, it is no more possible to form lynch mobs than it is for ghetto residents to maintain stable neighborhood watch or patrol organizations or for the police to control crime. Instead, more individualistic efforts, whether violent or not, prevail. The late twentieth century substitute for vigilantism is individualistic resistance to criminals by those directly victimized.

It is a tragic fact of life that economic injustice, a history of racism, and other factors have created dangerous conditions in many places in America. Police cannot realistically be expected to provide personal protection for every American, and indeed are not even legally obliged to do so (Kates 1990). Although gun ownership is no more an all-situations, magical source of protection than the police, it can be a useful source of safety in addition to police protection, burglary alarms, guard dogs, and all the other resources people exploit to improve their security. These sources are not substitutes for one another. Rather, they are complements, each useful in different situations. Possession of a gun gives its owner an additional option for dealing with danger. If other sources of security are adequate, the gun does not have to be used; but where other sources fail, it can preserve bodily safety and property in at least some situations.

One can dream of a day when governments can eliminate violence and provide total protection to all citizens. In reality, the American legal system has never even approximated this state of affairs, and is unlikely to do so in the foreseeable future. The "fiscal crisis of the state" limits the resources available for public services such as criminal justice (O'Connor 1973) and democratic values continue to slow the advance of totalitarian state alternatives to private social control. If predatory crime can be reduced, hopefully without sacrificing democratic values, the private resort to violence for social control should decline. In the meanwhile, the widespread legal use of guns against criminals will persist as long as Americans believe crime is a serious threat and that they cannot rely completely on the police as effective guardians. Until then, scholars interested in gun control, crime deterrence, victimology, the routine activities approach to crime, and in social control in general need to consider more carefully the significance of millions of potential crime victims armed with deadly weapons.

Implications for Crime Control Policy

Much of social order in America may depend on the fact that millions of people are armed and dangerous to each other. The availability of deadly weapons to the violence-prone may well contribute to violence by increasing the probability of a fatal outcome of combat (but see Chapter 5 and Wright et al. 1983, pp. 189–212). However, it may also be that this very fact raises the stakes in disputes to the point where only the most incensed or intoxicated disputants resort to physical conflict, with the risks of armed retaliation deterring attack and coercing minimal courtesy among otherwise hostile parties. Likewise, rates of commercial robbery, residential burglary injury, and rape might be still higher than their already high levels were it not for the dangerousness of the prospective victim population. Gun ownership among prospective victims may well have as large a crime-*inhibiting* effect as the crime-*generating* effects of gun possession among prospective criminals. This could account for the failure of researchers to find a significant net relationship between rates of crime such as homicide and robbery, and measures of gun ownership that do not distinguish between gun availability among criminals and availability in the largely noncriminal general public (e.g., Cook 1979; Kleck 1984a)—the two effects may roughly cancel each other out (see also Bordua 1986).

Guns are potentially lethal weapons whether wielded by criminals or victims. They are frightening and intimidating to those they are pointed at, whether these be predators or the preyed upon. Guns thereby empower both those who would use them to victimize and those who would use them to prevent their victimization. Consequently, they are a source of both social order and disorder, depending on who uses them, just as is true of the use of force in general. The failure to fully acknowledge this reality can lead to grave errors in devising public policy to minimize violence through gun control.

Some gun laws are intended to reduce gun possession only among relatively limited "high-risk" groups such as convicted felons, through such measures as laws licensing gun owners or requiring permits to purchase guns. However, other laws are aimed at reducing gun possession in all segments of the civilian population, both criminal and noncriminal. Examples would be the aforementioned Morton Grove handgun possession ban, near approximations of such bans (as in New York City), prohibitions of handgun sales (such as that in Chicago), and restrictive variants of laws regulating the carrying of concealed weapons. By definition, laws are most likely to be obeyed by the law-abiding, and gun laws are no different. Therefore, measures applying equally to criminals and noncriminals are almost certain to reduce gun possession more among the latter than the former. Because very little serious violent crime is committed by persons without previous records of serious violence (Chapter 5), there are at best only modest direct crime control benefits to be gained by reductions in gun possession among noncriminals, although even marginal reductions in gun possession among criminals might have crime-inhibiting effects. Consequently, one has to take seriously the possibility that "across-the-board" gun control measures could decrease the crime-control effects of noncriminal gun ownership more than they would decrease the crime-causing effects of criminal gun ownership. For this reason, more narrowly targeted gun control measures such as gun owner licensing and permit-to-purchase systems seem preferable.

People skeptical about the value of gun control sometimes argue that although a world in which there were no guns would be desirable, it is also unachievable. The evidence presented in this chapter raises a more radical possibility—that a world in which no one had guns would actually be *less* safe than one in which nonaggressors had guns and aggressors somehow did not. As a practical matter, the latter world is no more achievable than the former, but the point is worth raising as a way of clarifying what the goals of rational gun control policy should be. If gun possession among prospective victims tends to reduce violence, then reducing such gun possession is not, in and of itself, a social good. Instead, the best policy goal to pursue may be to shift the distribution of gun possession as far as practical in the direction of likely aggressors being disarmed and likely nonaggressors being armed. To disarm noncriminals in the hope this might indirectly help reduce access to guns among criminals is not a cost-free policy.

These categories are, of course, simplifications—some people are both serious aggressors and victims of serious aggression, and most people are at least occasionally aggressors in some very minor way. However, although it is clear these two groups overlap to some extent, it is equally clear that they can and are routinely distinguished in law, e.g., in statutes that forbid gun possession among persons with a criminal conviction and allow it among others. Further, although a great deal of violence is committed by persons without criminal convictions, it is also true that convicted felons are far more likely to be violent aggressors in the future than nonfelons. The idea that a significant share of serious violence is accounted for by previously nonviolent "average Joes," as in the "crime-of-passion" domestic homicide, is largely a myth (Kleck and Bordua 1983).

Consequently, a rational goal of gun control policy could be to tip the balance of power further in prospective victims' favor, by reducing aggressor gun possession while doing little or nothing to reduce nonaggressor gun possession. This would contrast sharply with across-the-board restrictions that apply uniformly to aggressors and nonaggressors alike. In view of this chapter's evidence, this sort of "blunderbuss" policy would facilitate victimization because legal restrictions would almost certainly be evaded more by aggressors than nonaggressors, causing a shift in gun distribution that favored the former over the latter. The general public already seems to be aware of these issues. In an April 1989 CBS News/*New York Times* national survey, 67% of U.S. adults answered "Yes" to the question "Do you think prohibiting the public from having guns would give criminals an added advantage?" (DIALOG 1990).

The following remarks, although over two centuries old, are still pertinent to consideration of across-the-board gun controls. They were written by Cesare Beccaria:

> False is the idea of utility that sacrifices a thousand real advantages for one imaginary or trifling inconvenience; that would take fire from men because it burns, and water because one may drown in it; that has no remedy for evils, except destruction. The laws that forbid the carrying of arms are of such a nature. They disarm those only who are neither inclined nor determined to commit crimes. . . . Such laws make things worse for the assaulted and better for the assailants; they serve rather to encourage than to prevent homicides, for an unarmed man may be attacked with greater confidence than an armed man. (1963 [1764], pp. 87–8)

Table 4.1. Percent of the Adult Population That Has Used Guns for Protection

Survey:	*Field*	*Cambridge Reports*	*DMIa*	*DMIb*	*Hart*	*Ohio*	*Time/ CNN*	*Mauser*
Area	California	U.S.	U.S.	U.S.	U.S.	Ohio	U.S.	U.S.
Year of interviews	1976	1978	1978	1978	1981	1982	1989	1990
Population covered	Noninstitutionalized adults	Noninstitutionalized adults	Registered voters	Registered voters	Registered voters	"Residents"	"Firearm owners"	Residents
Gun type covered	Handguns	Handguns	All guns	All guns	Handguns	Handguns	All guns	All guns
Time span of use	Ever/1,2 years	Ever	Ever	Ever	5 years	Ever	Ever	5 years
Distinguished uses against persons?	No	No	No	Yes	Yes	No	No	Yes
Excluded military, police uses?	Yes	No	Yes	Yes	Yes	No	Yes	Yes
"Self-defense" or "protection"?	Protection	Protection or self-defense	Protection	Protection	Protection	Self-defense	Self-protection	Protection
Defensive question asked of:	All Rs	Protection handgun owners	All Rs	All Rs	All Rs	Handgun owners	Gun owners	All Rs
Defensive question referred to:	Respondent	Respondent	Household	Household	Household	Respondent	Respondent	Household
Used gun (%)	8.6[a]	3	15	12/7[b]	4[c]	6.5	n.a.	3.8
Fired gun (%)	2.9	2	6	n.a.	n.a.	2.6	9–16[d]	n.a.

[a] 8.6% ever, 3% in past 2 years, 1.4% in past year.
[b] Defensive uses against persons or animals, 12%. Use against persons only, 7%.
[c] Refers to respondent or any member of household.
[d] 9% used for self-protection, 7% used "to scare someone." Some of the latter could be nonoverlapping defensive uses.
Sources: Field Institute (1976), Cambridge Reports (1978), DMI (1979), Garin (1986), Ohio (1982), Quinley (1990), and Mauser (1990).

Table 4.2. Civilian Legal Defensive Homicides in Six Local Studies[a]

	Row	*Bensing and Schroeder (1960) Cuyahoga County (Cleveland) 1947–1953*	*Wolfgang (1958) Philadelphia 1948–1952*	*Rushforth, et al. (1977) Cuyahoga County (Cleveland) 1958–1974*	*Lundsgaarde (1977) Houston 1969*	*Dietz (1983) Detroit 1980*	*Wilbanks (1984) Dade County (Miami) 1980*
Total sample homicides	(1)	662	625	3371	~312	583	569
Criminal homicides	(2)	505	588	?	282	493	478
Murders, nonnegligent manslaughters	(3)	505	Est. 502[b]	?	281	487	478
Estimated unintentional excusable homicides	(4)	?	23	?	Up to 12	~4	5
Involuntary/negligent manslaughters	(5)	?	Est. 86[b]	?	1	6	0
Justifiable police homicides	(6)	35	14	~110	10	13	14
Estimated intentional civilian homicides	(7)	627	502	~3261	~289	560	550
Justifiable civilian homicides (CJH)	(8)	122	8	~329	19	16	72
CJH reported on SHRs	(9)	n.a.	n.a.	n.a.	n.a.	12	24
Other civilian legal defensive homicides	(10)	0	n.a.	?	At least 1	57	0
Total civilian legal defensive homicides (CLDH)	(11)	122	8	~329	At least 20	73	72
Ratio, (11)/(7)	(12)	.195	.016	.101	At least .069	.130	.131
Ratio, (11)/(1)	(13)	.184	.013	.098	At least .064	.125	.127
Ratio, (11)/(3)	(14)	.242	.024	?	At least .071	.150	.151

[a] (7) = (1) − (4) − (5) − (6) and (11) = (8) + (10). Homicides were classified according to their final legal classifications as reported in the study, whether police, coroner, or court-determined. See Appendix 5 for explanation of different types of homicides.

[b] 14.7% of criminal homicide offenders prosecuted were charged with involuntary manslaughter. .147 × 588 = 86. 588 − 86 = 502.

Sources: Bensing and Schroeder (1960, pp. 5, 59, 80), Wolfgang (1958, pp. 24, 228, 301, 303), Rushforth et al. (1977, pp. 531–533), Lundsgaarde (1977, pp. 68–69, 162, 219, 236, 237), Dietz (1983, pp. 203), and Wilbanks (1984, pp. 29–30, 57, 70–72, 154).

Table 4.3. Estimated U.S. Totals, Police and Civilian Legal Defensive Homicides (LDHs), 1980[a]

Homicide Type	Justifiable Homicides Reported to FBI/SHR	Estimated Total LDHs	
		Estimation Method I	*Estimation Method II*
Police, gun	368	303	606
Police, nongun	14	8	16
Police, total	382	311	622
Civilian, gun	379	2819	1527
Civilian, nongun	44	327	177
Civilian, total	423	3146	1704

[a] SHR, Supplementary Homicide Reports. Estimation methods—see text.

Sources: Analysis of 1980 U.S. Supplementary Homicide Reports computer tape; U.S. NCHS (1983, pp. 35–6).

Table 4.4. Attack, Injury, and Crime Completion Rates in Robbery and Assault Incidents, by Self-Protection Method, U.S., 1979–1985[a]

	Robbery				*Assault*		
Method of Self-Protection	*(1) Percent Completed*	*(2) Percent Attacked*	*(3) Percent Injured*	*(4)[b] Number Times Used*	*(5) Percent Attacked*	*(6) Percent Injured*	*(7)[b] Estimated Number Times Used*
Used gun	30.9	25.2	17.4	89,009	23.2	12.1	386,083
Used knife	35.2	55.6	40.3	59,813	46.4	29.5	123,062
Used other weapon	28.9	41.5	22.0	104,700	41.4	25.1	454,570
Used physical force	50.1	75.6	50.8	1,653,880	82.8	52.1	6,638,823
Tried to get help or frighten offender	63.9	73.5	48.9	1,516,141	55.2	40.1	4,383,117
Threatened or reasoned with offender	53.7	48.1	30.7	955,398	40.0	24.7	5,743,008
Nonviolent resistance, including evasion	50.8	54.7	34.9	1,539,895	40.0	25.5	8,935,738
Other measures	48.5	47.3	26.5	284,423	36.1	20.7	1,451,103
Any self-protection	52.1	60.8	38.2	4,603,671	49.5	30.7	21,801,957
No self-protection	88.5	41.5	24.7	2,686,960	39.9	27.3	6,154,763
Total	65.4	53.7	33.2	7,290,631	47.3	29.9	27,956,719

[a] See U.S. Bureau of Justice Statistics (1982) for exact question wordings, definitions, and other details of the surveys.

[b] Separate frequencies in columns (4) and (7) do not add to totals in "Any self-protection" row since a single crime incident can involve more than one self-protection method.

Source: Analysis of incident files of 1979–1985 National Crime Survey public use computer tapes (ICPSR, 1987). Series incidents and those occurring outside the U.S. were excluded.

Table 4.5. Crimes Associated with Defensive Uses of Guns

1976 Survey of Californians (Handgun Uses Only)			*1980 Dade County (Miami) Civilian Justifiable Homicides*		
Crime	*Frequency*	*%*	*Crime*	*Frequency*	*%*
Assault or rape at home	40	41	Assault	46	64
Assault elsewhere	20	21	Rape	1	1
Theft at home	19	20	Burglary	6	8
Theft elsewhere	11	11	Robbery	19	26
All other reasons for use	7	7			
Total	97	100	Total	72	100

Sources: California survey—Field Institute (1976); Dade County justifiable homicides—compiled from short narrative descriptions in Wilbanks (1984, pp. 190–374).

Table 4.6. Crime Trends in Kansas City and Comparison Areas, 1961–1974

	Kansas City, Missouri						*K.C. SMSA, excluding K.C.*							*Robbery*	
Year	*Robbery*	*MNNM*	*Agg. Asslt.*	*Rape*	*Burg.*	*Auto Theft*	*Robbery*	*MNNM*	*Assault*	*Rape*	*Burg.*	*Auto Theft*	*Missouri, excl. K.C. SMSA*	*West North Central*	*U.S.*
1961	1169	49	1194	222	6020	1995	202	14	135	42	2430	622	2266	5702	106670
1962	1069	49	946	147	5337	2336	239	21	184	38	2680	840	2166	5597	110860
1963	1164	60	935	197	5600	2911	347	20	234	47	2937	958	2277	6241	116470
1964	1180	48	1126	205	6484	2701	270	26	745	83	3416	1109	2505	6594	130390
1965	1212	71	1180	209	7219	3054	261	25	770	100	4234	1148	2722	6938	138690
1966	1574	59	1315	205	7495	3689	432	27	674	124	4917	1414	2763	8022	157990
1967	2120	62	1711	231	9455	4835	644	41	760	93	6612	1925	3241	10624	202910
1968	2171	92	1995	307	10020	4929	563	33	874	170	6219	2319	4374	12724	262840
1969	2679	105	1921	375	12269	6926	559	33	879	174	6733	2810	5245	14272	298850
1970	2982	120	1805	401	11265	5570	712	38	1102	183	7554	2815	5699	16279	349860
1971	2473	103	1961	371	11550	5408	641	48	1389	173	8104	2666	5419	14582	387700
1972	2092	71	1960	344	9472	3921	742	35	1295	200	8391	2607	5513	14928	376290
1973	2333	81	2433	302	10394	3884	715	64	1288	185	10073	2554	6153	16571	384220
1974	3002	109	2575	363	13406	3719	1087	57	1856	201	12585	2761	6264	19894	442400
% change, 1967–68	2	48	25	33	6	2	−13	−20	15	83	−6	20	35	20	30

Notes: Figures before 1961 for Kansas City are not comparable with later years (U.S. FBI, 1962:131). The Kansas City Metropolitan Police Department firearms training program sessions were held in September through November, 1967. MNNM = murders and nonnegligent manslaughters, SMSA = standard metropolitan statistical area.

Sources: Annual issues, Uniform Crime Reports (U.S. FBI, 1962–1975).

CHAPTER

5

Guns and Violent Crime

Several facts about violent crime in America are indisputable. The United States has a high level of violence, it has a large number of guns, and a very high share of its homicides are committed with guns. Further, relative to other industrialized nations, the United States has more violence, more guns per capita, and a higher fraction of its violent acts committed with guns. From these simple facts, some draw a simple conclusion: America's higher level of gun ownership causes its higher rate of violence (for an example of this reasoning, see Sloan et al. 1990). This conclusion is a non sequitur. Even if 100% of violent acts were committed with guns, it would be a logical possibility that every single gun death and crime would have occurred by other means even if there were no guns, and that high gun ownership levels had no impact on violence rates. Further, it is possible that there is a causal connection between the two, but that it is high violence rates that cause high gun ownership levels, rather than the reverse.

Whether guns in some sense cause violence cannot be inferred from these facts; this inference requires more complicated analysis of a considerably larger set of facts. Two approaches to the question are used here, one at the level of individual incidents of violence and the other at the level of city rates of violent crime. Two questions are addressed. First, are incidents of violence in which the aggressor possesses a gun more likely than otherwise similar incidents to result in an attack on the victim, injury to the victim, or the victim's death? Second, do areas with higher rates of gun ownership have, as a result, higher rates of violence? It should be emphasized that this chapter addresses the effects of the *aggressor's* possession and use of weapons on the outcomes of violent incidents and on rates of violence; the effects of the victim's possession or use were addressed in the last chapter.

Guns and Power

Individual power has primarily been conceptualized by social scientists as deriving from lasting attributes of persons and from their position in the social structure, e.g., from social class position, gender, age, and race (e.g., Wrong 1988, Chapters 6–8). For example, in the family violence literature (e.g., Strauss et al. 1980), power is typically viewed as deriving from family role and gender. All of these sources of power, however, ultimately derive to some extent from a capacity to use physical force and violence, either exercised by the actor or by agents the actor can call upon. And capacity to use force in turn often relies partly on a rather transitory attribute of the person, the possession of weaponry.

Indeed, the single most important factor that sets human violence apart from aggression among lower animals is arguably man's greater technological capacity to inflict harm. The tools of death available to humans are vastly more lethal than even the most deadly natural equipment of animals. Whereas interpersonal conflict of some sort is inevitable and universal, it may be factors such as use of weaponry that determine whether verbal conflict escalates to violence, whether physical attacks are completed by reaching their target, and whether they inflict serious injury or death when they do.

The power that weaponry confers has been conventionally treated as exclusively violence-enhancing—it was commonly assumed that weapon possession and use act only to increase the likelihood of the victim's injury and death (e.g., Newton and Zimring 1969). This is an unduly restrictive conceptualization of the significance of weaponry. A broader perspective starts with a recognition of weapons as sources of power, used instrumentally to achieve goals by inducing compliance with the user's demands. The ultimate goal behind an act of violence is not necessarily the victim's death or injury, but rather may be money, sexual gratification, respect, attention, or the humiliation and domination of the victim. Power can be, and usually is, wielded so as to obtain these things without inflicting injury. Threats, implied or overt, usually suffice and are often preferred to physical attack. The inflicting of injury may even be an indication that the preferred mode of exercising power failed.

Weapons are an important source of power, especially so in a nation such as the United States, where half of the households possess a gun. As such, they are frequently wielded to achieve some emotional or material goal—to obtain sexual gratification in a rape or money in a robbery, or, more frequently, to frighten and dominate victims in some other assault. All of these things can be gained without an attack, and indeed the possession of a gun can serve as a substitute for attack, rather than its vehicle.

Issues of Assault Outcomes

Violent crimes occur within hostile or threatening situations, which can be categorized into the "hierarchy of violence" illustrated in Figure 5.1. A "threatening situation" is an encounter in which one person (the "victim") is either physically attacked or perceives that another person

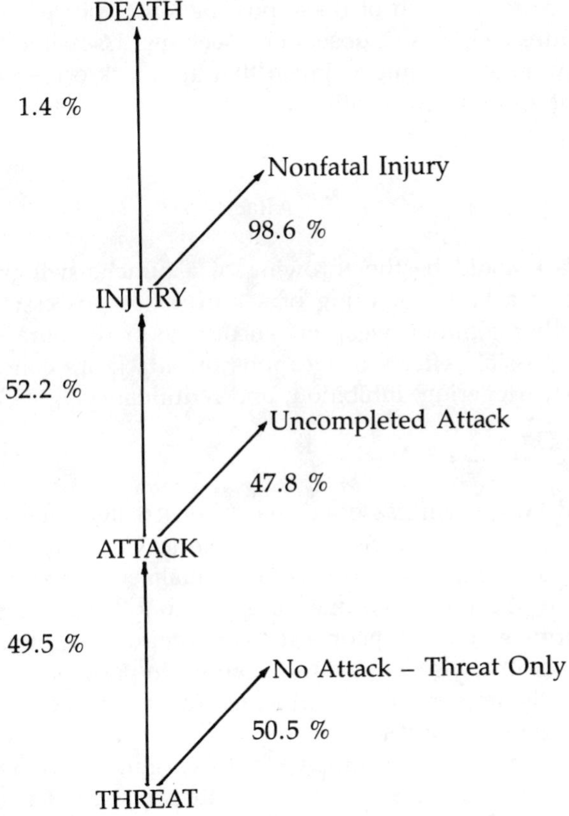

Figure 5.1. The hierarchy of violence. Percentages are weighted. Those below INJURY are from the 1979–1985 NCS stranger violent incident sample. Those above INJURY are from the merged 1982 NCS and SHR dataset.

(the "aggressor") is threatening them with physical harm in some way, including verbal threats, menacing gestures, or other actions. Most threatening situations never proceed beyond mere threat. Aggressors obtain what they want from a threatening speech or gesture, or limit their aggression to words out of fear of the consequences of doing more. (In the common law, to threaten to hurt another person is assault, regardless of whether any actual attempt to physically injure is made.)

In the 1979–1985 National Crime Surveys (NCS), half of assaults were mere threats, without any attack. And of those assaults involving an attack, only about half were completed, i.e., resulted in an injury. Finally, based on combined NCS and FBI Supplementary Homicide Reports (SHR) data for 1983, only about 1% of those attacks that caused injury resulted in death. Each of these possible outcomes of threats is separately addressed, with subsequent sections assessing the impact of weaponry on attack, injury, given that an attack occurred, and death, given that an injury was inflicted.

Attack

An attack could be the throwing of a punch, swinging of a club, thrusting of a knife, or firing of a gun. Does possession of guns or various other common weapons encourage or discourage attack? The principal possible effects of weapons on attack are conceptualized as facilitation, triggering, inhibition, and redundancy.

Facilitation

An Old West saying asserted that "God created men—Colonel Colt made them equal," or alternatively, "Colonel Colt made all men six feet tall." Just as a gun can serve as an "equalizer" for victims of attacks (Chapter 4), it can do the same for aggressors. It has long been argued that firearms give some people the courage to attempt aggressive acts they would otherwise be afraid to attempt. In particular, a weapon may be especially important in facilitating the aggression of weaker aggressors against stronger victims.

There is some empirical support for this argument. For example, Cook (1982, p. 257) used police data from 50 cities to show that guns are more commonly used in homicides in which the attacker was older and presumably weaker, and the victim younger and presumably stronger. Likewise, wives or girlfriends killing their husbands or boyfriends were more likely to use guns. Table 5.1 furthers this analysis by using national data and examining three different measures of attacker–victim power differentials. The data indicate that gun use in homicides is more common when (1) the victim is male rather than female, (2) the victim is male and the attacker is female, compared to the reverse situation, (3) the attacker is outside the "physical prime" ages of 16–39, compared to other ages, (4) the attacker is outside the "prime" age span and the victim is in that age span, compared to the reverse situation, (5) there is a single attacker, compared to a group of attackers, and (6) there is a single attacker and multiple victims, compared to the reverse situation. In each of these comparisons, gun use was more likely when the attacker(s), if not armed with a gun, would usually be less powerful than the victim, due to gender, age, or numbers. These findings do not conclusively prove that guns facilitate attacks that would not otherwise have occurred. It is possible that the minority of attackers who choose guns are so strongly motivated that, although they would prefer to use a gun, they would still attack without a gun, even with the odds against them. Nevertheless, the results are quite consistent with the equalizer hypothesis.

Unlike other common personal weapons, guns permit effective attack from a great distance. As one gun control advocate put it, "a gun may not be necessary to kill another, but at fifty yards it's certainly a help." Guns therefore can facilitate long-range attacks. However, few assaults occur at ranges longer than the length of the average barroom or kitchen. Studies of general samples of gun attacks do not report ranges, but inferences can be made from attack locations. In a 17-city study of crimes known to police, 61% of criminal homicides and 49% of aggravated assaults (with or without guns) occurred in indoor locations (Curtis 1974, p. 176). Given the dimensions of most rooms, virtually all of these must have involved ranges no greater than 20–30 feet.

Information on attack ranges is available for a near-complete national sample of one special type of gun attack. FBI data on the gunshot killings of 960 police officers killed in 1970–1987 indicated that 72% of the attacks involved a range of 10 feet or less, and 87% a range of 20 feet or less (U.S. FBI 1971–1988; e.g., the 1984 issue, p. 14). Generally speaking, then, gun attacks usually occur at ranges short enough that other weapons could have been used had the attacker been willing to close the distance and make physical contact with the victim.

However, for some attackers, maintaining a distance of just a few feet or even inches from their victim may be essential to carrying out an attack. It has been hypothesized that guns may facilitate attack by persons too squeamish to come into physical contact with their victims or to use messier methods to injure them (Wolfgang 1958, p. 79). Some prospective attackers may be psychologically incapable of doing something as distasteful and ugly as plunging a knife into another human being's chest cavity or bashing in their skull with a blunt instrument, yet are perfectly capable of shooting their victim. Guns provide a more impersonal, emotionally remote, and even antiseptic way of attacking others, and could allow some attackers to bypass their inhibitions against close contact with their victims. There is some experimental evidence that people are less willing to inflict pain on others if it requires physical contact with the victim (Bandura 1973, p. 177). However, these acts of laboratory aggression were done on the orders of experimenters and directed at "victims" against whom the subjects had no serious grievances. Whether the phenomenon can be generalized to serious real-world violence, and how many attackers need a gun for this psychological facilitation, are both unknown.

Triggering

Experimental psychologists Berkowitz and LePage (1967) proposed the "weapons effect" hypothesis, which stated that the sight of a weapon could elicit aggression from angered persons, due to the learned association between weapons and aggressive behavior. Thus, they believed that weapons can trigger attacks by angry persons. The "weapons effect" studies all used experimental designs and most were conducted in laboratories. In a typical study, subjects (Ss) were led to believe they were participating in some sort of learning experiment in which they supposedly administered painful electric shocks to another S each time this person failed to respond properly. Some Ss were exposed to weapons, others were not. Experimenters tested to see if Ss exposed to weapons aggressed more than the controls.

There were many variations on this basic pattern. Some researchers conducted experiments in natural settings. In one especially imaginative study conducted by Turner and his associates (1975), a confederate of the experimenters intentionally stopped a pickup truck at an intersection and refused to move when the light turned green, even though it was clear he was capable of doing so. The Ss were the drivers stuck behind the truck and their aggression was measured by whether they honked their horns. The experimental stimulus was whether or not the truck had a rifle in a gun rack visible to Ss.

Table 5.2 summarizes the results of 21 studies of the "weapons effect" hypothesis, emphasizing the way in which findings relate to how realistic the conditions of the experiments were. Overall, the findings are extremely mixed—studies have been almost evenly divided between those that were supportive and those that were unsupportive. The degree of realism of the experiments, and their relevance to real-world conditions of weapons-linked violence in the United States, varied widely, and this appears to have influenced the results. For example, whereas some studies exposed Ss to real weapons, others exposed them only to toy weapons or pictures or films of weapons. In some studies Ss believed they were inflicting physical pain in the form of electric shocks to another person, whereas in others they engaged in play "aggression," honked car horns, or were merely asked how much aggression they would *like* to inflict on the target. Some studies used adults and adolescents as Ss, i.e., persons in age groups likely to commit serious acts of violence and to be exposed to guns in an aggressive context. Others used children. Some studies were conducted in the United States, where both gun ownership and gun violence are common, whereas others were conducted in foreign nations where both are rare. The general pattern of findings, summarized in Part B of Table 5.2, is that the more closely the experiments simulated real-world situations of weapons-linked aggression in the United States, the less likely they were to support the weapons hypothesis. Supportive findings seem to be heavily dependent on various artificial experimental conditions prevailing.

Nevertheless, there were a few moderately realistic studies that yielded some support for the "weapons effect" hypothesis, and several substantive findings from this literature are worth noting. First, some studies indicated that weapons elicited aggression only if Ss assigned an aggressive meaning to them. For example, in the pick-up truck experiment, the gun was sometimes paired with a bumper sticker that read "vengeance," and at other times with one that read "friend." The sight of the gun elicited more horn-honking only when paired with the violent meaning (Turner et al. 1975). Other scholars interpreted a failure to discover a weapons effects to the rural setting of their study—where hunting was common, more positive meanings were attributed to guns, reducing their aggressive cue value (Halderman and Jackson 1979).

Second, some studies found that guns could inhibit aggression among some subjects, as well as elicit it. Fisher et al. (1969) found inhibiting effects for women. Turner et al. (1975) found inhibiting effects for both men and women under a variety of conditions. Fraczek and Macaulay (1971) found inhibiting effects for highly emotional Ss, speculating that such persons had learned to be especially fearful of the consequences of their aggression.

One study found the "weapons effect" occurred only among people who had no prior experience with guns (Buss et al. 1972). This is especially important for a number of reasons. First, the Ss in most of these studies were college students, commonly in psychology classes. College students and college-educated persons are less likely to own guns, and therefore less likely to have real-world contact with them (see Table 2.5). Thus, the unrepresentative nature of the student subject pool may have artificially increased support for the hypothesis.

This finding also helps explain another pattern evident in Table 5.2—studies with foreign Ss were much more likely to support the hypothesis than those with U.S. Ss. There is little tradition of recreational ownership and use of guns among the mass of Europeans, and far less gun ownership of any kind than in the United States.

The findings can be tied together to provide a straightforward explanation for these patterns. The "weapons effect" has been detected only among people with no prior experience with guns. Persons with direct experience have gained it largely in nonaggressive, recreational contexts. Persons without such experience know guns only through the aggression-laden contexts of military service or gunplay in television and films. Members of the inexperienced group, which would include most children, college psychology students, and Europeans, are therefore more likely to attribute an aggressive meaning to guns, which apparently is essential for the "weapons effect" to occur.

The relevance of this body of research to real-life gun violence is further cast in doubt by the fact that the weapons to which Ss were exposed were either associated with the victims of the aggression, or with no one at all; they were almost never associated with the S whose aggression was being assessed. In the only study that actually associated a weapon with Ss, no weapons effect was observed [Buss et al. (1972) had some Ss fire a BB gun before being assessed for aggression]. Consequently, none of the studies provided any evidence directly supporting the idea that possessing a gun encourages physical aggression, or that the "trigger pulls the finger."

At best, some of the studies inadvertently concerned the effect of gun possession by *victims* of aggression on the behavior of aggressors. The analysis of victim survey data in Chapter 4 indicated that aggressor attack was *less* likely when the victim used a gun in self-defense. How can the conflict between real-world experience and the findings of half of the experimental studies be reconciled? One way would be to hypothesize that the sight of a gun in the possession of a prospective target of aggression increases the aggressor's aggressive *arousal*, i.e., it stimulates anger, but that it inhibits actual physical attack because the would-be aggressor fears a dangerous counterattack by the victim. Since no such counterattack was likely in the experiments, aggressors were free to act on their aggressive impulses in a way that would be unlikely in real life.

Inhibition

In an early study of victim survey data from eight cities, Hindelang (1976, p. 263) concluded that "when a gun is involved in a victimization, both the victim and the offender appear to be more restrained and interested in avoiding an attack with the weapon." Thus, not only does victim defensive use of a gun inhibit aggressor attacks (Chapter 4), but even the aggressor's possession of a gun can inhibit his own aggression, as well as that of his victim. In many assaults the aggressor not only lacks an intent to kill, but specifically wants to *avoid* killing his victim. Instead, he may want only to frighten or to hurt without killing. Possession of a lethal weapon gives such an assaulter more killing power than he needs or wants, and to attack would risk inflicting more harm than the assaulter wanted. The possession of deadly weapons raises the stakes into what may seem to be an all-or-nothing situation—kill or do not attack at all. Assuming the intentions of assaulters as a group cluster predominantly at the less deadly end of the continuum, one effect of aggressor possession of guns and other deadly weapons could therefore be inhibition of attack behavior. As previously noted, a number of "weapons effect" experiments indicated that the sight of weapons could inhibit aggression under some conditions.

Redundancy

A deadly weapon empowers its possessor to terrify, coerce compliance with demands, deter another's aggression, nonfatally injure, or kill. Power increases the likelihood its user will get what he wants, whatever that may be. If most assaulters do not want to kill, then a lethal weapon enables its user to achieve other goals. In robberies, the robber's use of a gun ensures compliance with his demands for money and deters the victim from resisting, convincing the victim that the robber has the capacity to inflict death or serious injury (Luckenbill 1982). Without a gun it would often be impossible for the robber to achieve this without actually attacking. Threat with a gun can thereby serve as a substitute for actual attack, rather than its vehicle. In short, possession of a gun can make a physical attack *unnecessary.* Supporting this idea, at least nine prior studies found that robbers armed with guns are less likely to injure their victims than robbers without guns (Normandeau

1968; Conklin 1972; Feeney and Weir 1973; MacDonald 1975, p. 138; Hindelang 1976, p. 213; Block 1977; Cook and Nagin 1979, p. 35; Luckenbill 1981; U.S. Bureau of Justice Statistics 1986b).

This pattern need not be limited to acquisitive crime such as robbery. Aggressors in ordinary anger-instigated assaults have their own peculiar goals whose attainment can, if they have a weapon, be achieved without attacking. Those who want to frighten, humiliate, or dominate their victims can do so by merely pointing a gun, without firing it. On the other hand, without a gun, nothing short of attack may suffice. The same qualities of weapons that make them dangerous if used to attack can preclude the necessity of actually doing so. Simple percentage analysis of early National Crime Survey (NCS) victimization survey data indicated that the fraction of assaults resulting in attack and the fraction resulting in injury were both lower in those involving gun-armed offenders than for those with either offenders armed with other weapons or unarmed offenders (Hindelang 1976; U.S. Bureau of Justice Statistics 1986b, p. 4). Likewise, King (1987), using analysis of variance on later NCS data, also found lower rates of injury for gun-armed offenders in assault as well as robbery.

A combatant may also regain a favorable situational identity through the use of a weapon to control others and to compel their unwilling obedience. He can demonstrate to his victim, to himself, and to any bystanders that he cannot be pushed around, and that he must be granted respect, or at least fear. The weapon can be used to place its possessor into a superordinate position in situations in which this might otherwise be impossible to achieve without an actual attack.

One combatant's use of a lethal weapon may also give his opponent a socially acceptable excuse for not retaliating for an insult or other challenge to his self-image: "only a fool attacks someone with a gun." The failure to retaliate, which might otherwise be regarded by witnesses as evidence of cowardice, is instead viewed as mere prudence in the face of greatly unequal power. The extreme imbalance of power can thus prevent an escalation to physical violence by exacting from the weaker opponent some gesture of deference or an exit from the scene.

Injury

If an attack does occur, it may or may not be completed, i.e., result in injury by a bullet reaching its target, a knife penetrating skin, or a fist or club bruising flesh or smashing bone. The attributes of weapons that can facilitate attack may also reduce the attack completion rate by encouraging attacks at a longer range, against more formidable opponents or under more difficult conditions. It is possible to shoot a victim from a great distance, but the rate at which this is achieved is likely to be far lower than the rate at which thrown punches land. Concerning the more common close range gun attacks, those unfamiliar with firearms marksmanship might assume that shooters are virtually certain to hit their target. This assumption is not born out by the real-life experiences of persons shooting under conditions of emotional stress. NCS data covering the United States from 1979 to 1987 indicate that only 19% of incidents where an attacker shot at a victim resulted in the victim being hit, i.e., suffering a gunshot wound (U.S. Bureau of Justice Statistics 1990a, p. 5). In contrast, corresponding data on NCS-reported knife attacks indicated that about 55% resulted in a knife wound [U.S. Bureau of Justice Statistics 1986b, p. 4; 9.8% of knife attacks involved a knife wound, while another 7.9% involved an attempted knife attack without injury—9.8/(9.8 + 7.9) = 0.55].

Even individuals trained and presumably mentally prepared to shoot under stressful conditions, such as police officers, commonly have difficulty hitting their targets. A study of shots fired by New York City police officers, who unambiguously intended to shoot their adversaries (warning shots were excluded), found that of 2303 shots fired "in defense of life" or to "prevent or terminate crime," only 39% wounded the opponent (computed from Fyfe 1979, pp. 318, 320). One would expect this rate to be even lower among the mass of civilians lacking the training and relative emotional preparedness of police officers, and the NCS data supported this expectation. Thus, there is reason to expect that the net effect of gun use would be to decrease the fraction of attacks resulting in injury.

Death

Only about one in seven gunshot woundings known to the police results in death (Cook 1985, p. 96). Because many minor nonfatal gunshot woundings never come to the attention of authorities, the true death rate is almost certainly lower than this. Most gunshot wound victims probably do not seek medical treatment. Even among those willing to report such incidents to the NCS, only half reported receiving any kind of medical treatment (U.S. Bureau of Justice Statistics 1986b, p. 5). Since unreported crime incidents tend to be either less serious or regarded by victims as private or embarrassing matters, the fraction of unreported gunshot woundings that resulted in medical treatment is probably even lower than half. Consequently, large numbers (probably a majority) of nonfatal gunshot wounds never result in medical treatment and consequently never come to the attention of either doctors or the police. This results in overstated fatality rates in gunshot woundings. Cook's review of the evidence suggested that about 15% of gunshot woundings known to police result in death. If it is assumed that only half of nonfatal woundings (and all fatal woundings) are reported or known to police, the true fatality rate would be about 8% (based on a doubling of nonfatal woundings counted).

Nevertheless, gunshot wounds are more likely to result in death than those inflicted by a knife, the weapon generally assumed to be the next most lethal, among those that could be used in the same circumstances as guns. Although widely cited data from a single city indicated the gun attack death rate to be five times that of knife attacks (Zimring 1968, p. 728), other police-based and medical studies limited to woundings indicate a ratio of gun and knife wounding death rates of about 3–1 or 4–1 (Wilson and Sherman 1961, pp. 640–2; Ryzoff et al. 1966, p. 652; Block 1977). Further, figures in Table 5.3, based on national homicide data and NCS-based estimates of nonfatal woundings, also support a 4–1 ratio.

In Chapter 3, it was fairly simple conceptually to compare long guns with handguns, especially rifles with handguns. Both categories of weapons produce injury in very similar ways—by propelling small objects at high velocity. Likewise, Zimring's (1972) comparisons of smaller caliber guns with higher caliber guns, despite some empirical problems, was understandable at a conceptual level. On the other hand, knives (or clubs, hands, feet, etc.) produce injury in ways very different from guns. It is harder to get a handle on what people mean when they say guns are more lethal than knives, since this is very much an "apples and oranges" comparison. Cook (1982, p. 249) describes the "objective dangerousness pattern" to define what he means by gun–knife lethality differences, stating that "Gun attacks have a higher probability of killing the victim than knife attacks in otherwise similar circumstances." However, this defines lethality or "objective dangerousness" in a somewhat circular way—we want to know how weapon lethality affects assault outcomes, yet Cook uses assault outcome to define weapon lethality. The definition also does not explain *why* guns should more often produce lethal outcomes. It is not self-evident, from the point of view of either physics or medicine, that very small fast-moving objects such as bullets should produce more serious injury than much larger but slower-moving objects such as knives. Finally, it is not in fact known that gun attacks have a higher probability of killing the victim *in otherwise similar circumstances,* since the available evidence indicates that gun and knife attacks rarely occur in genuinely "similar circumstances," thus affording few opportunities for making the necessary comparisons in any direct or simple way.

Zimring (1968) compared a set of handgun attacks with a heterogeneous sample of attacks involving a miscellany of stabbing and cutting instruments, finding that the fatality rate was five times higher in the latter sample than in the former. However, as Kates (1979b, p. 18) and Wright and his colleagues (1983, p. 199) have pointed out, Zimring was lumping presumably serious attacks using heavy, long-bladed knives in with fairly trivial cases of people scratched with pen knives and possibly even forks and beer can openers! It would be far-fetched to suppose that people who attack with a fork are, on average, comparable in motives, intentions, or strength of aggressive drive with people who shoot others with a handgun.

Wright et al. (1983) argued that a more informative comparison would have been between handgun attacks and just those "knife" attacks committed with long-bladed cutting instruments. As it happened, such research had already been done, long before Zimring's work. At least one medical study compared very similar sets of wounds (all were "penetrating wounds of the abdomen"), and found that the mortality rate in pistol wounds was 16.8%, while the rate was 14.3% for ice pick wounds and 13.3% for butcher knife wounds (Wilson and Sherman 1961, p. 643). This is far from Zimring's 5–1 ratio, yet is based on a study that met Cook's "similar circumstances" condition far better than the work by Zimring on which Cook relied.

Clearly, only some of the difference in death rates of attacks with different weapons, however large or small that may be, is attributable to the technical properties of the weapons themselves. Part of the difference is due to the greater "lethality" of the users of the more deadly weapons. Those with more lethal intentions, a greater willingness to hurt others, or a stronger instigation to aggress choose more serious weaponry, regardless of how vague their intentions are, or how impulsively and even unconsciously these might be arrived at. Thus, weapon lethality and attacker lethality should be closely associated (Cook 1982, pp. 247–8), and thus can easily be confused with one another.

A gun does not get used in an assault simply because it "happened to be there." Although it is rare that an aggressor obtains a gun to commit a specific act of violence, more seriously violent people are more likely to have acquired guns in the past (usually for "defensive" purposes) and are more likely to keep them available for use, e.g., by carrying them on their person (Wright and Rossi 1986). Further, when the gun is actually used in an attack, it is almost always the result of a choice, however hastily made, among weapon alternatives. It surely is a rare gun homicide that occurs where a knife or blunt instrument is not also available. And certainly every gun killer also has hands and feet with which to attack the victim. For a variety of reasons, then, guns are *chosen* by aggressors.

Furthermore, this choice is not made randomly. The people who choose to use guns are different from those who choose other modes of attack. Reanalysis of data from a prison survey by Wright and Rossi (1986) indicates that as aggressor "seriousness" increases, weapon seriousness increases—killers and other assaulters with more extensive records of prior violence were more likely to have been armed in their attacks, more likely to have used guns, and even somewhat more likely to have used long guns (Table 5.4). This suggests that on average, a criminal gun user's willingness to do violence and inflict serious injury is greater than that of criminals who do not use guns. In addition, those who, at the time of the attack, intend to inflict serious, possibly lethal harm on their victim would presumably be more likely to select a weapon perceived to be more lethal.

If the wounding fatality rate of guns is four times higher than that of knives when the attackers are not matched regarding their lethality, then this ratio would necessarily be less than 4–1, though probably higher than 1–1, if attacker lethality were somehow controlled. Perhaps a reasonable, tentative "guesstimate" of the true guns-vs.-knives lethality ratio might be the average of these two ratios, or about 2.5–1.

Attackers who choose guns over other weapons, then, are more violent people, apart from the weapons they use. Consequently, unless one can somehow control for "attacker seriousness" in assaults, it is logically impossible to use data on the frequency of fatal outcomes in assaults to separate the effects of a weapon's technical properties from the closely associated effects of the attacker's willingness to seriously hurt the victim. Prior research has not measured or controlled for attacker seriousness, so it is impossible to tell from prior studies of assault fatality rates (e.g., Zimring 1968, 1972; Block 1977) whether fewer people would die if nongun weapons such as knives were substituted for guns by the same highly motivated attackers who currently use guns. Since attackers who use guns and those who use knives are likely to be quite different at the time of the attacks, the fact that gun attacks are more likely to result in death by itself says nothing about whether it was the weapon that was responsible for the more frequent fatal outcomes of gun attacks. Consequently, it is impossible to tell from such data whether fewer assault victims would die if attackers were somehow induced to substitute knives for guns.

It is impossible to directly measure strength of an aggressor's motivation at the time of a real-life assault or to do experiments with serious, armed violence. It would also be pointless to ask attackers about their intentions after the fact, even if they were capable of recalling them. For an aggressor to admit that he intended to kill his victim would constitute a giant step toward a death sentence, or at least a very long prison term. Likewise, one cannot measure or control for attacker motivation by noting the location of wounds inflicted (e.g., Zimring 1972), especially for gun attacks. Given the difficulty of aiming guns accurately, the exact location of gunshot wounds is to a great extent a product of chance rather than aggressor intent (Cook and Nagin 1979, p. 7).

Therefore, to isolate the effects of weaponry itself on assault outcomes one cannot directly control for offender motivation, but only for presumed correlates of motivation. In the analysis of individual violent incidents reported later, the efforts of previous researchers are improved on in this respect only to the extent that the controls introduced are indeed correlated with an attacker's aggressive drive or the lethality of his intentions.

Another issue must be distinguished from that of the relative motivation strengths of gun and knife attackers. To what degree is the motivation of gun attackers strong and unambiguous? If every gun killer had, even for just a few minutes, a very strong aggressive drive and a single-minded intent to kill regardless of the risks and effort needed, then it would do no good to deprive them of guns—they would do whatever was necessary to kill their victims by other means in those few minutes. Arguing against this contention in a 1968 article, Zimring concluded (p. 736) that "a *substantial proportion* of all homicides can be thought to be ambiguously motivated" (emphasis added). By 1972, he had upgraded the weak "substantial proportion" to a majority. Summarizing the 1968 article, he asserted that "*most* homicide is not the result of a single-minded intention to kill at any cost" (emphasis added) (p. 97). Either in its weak or strong forms, the claim was not supported by the evidence Zimring presented; all of it was either irrelevant to the ambiguity claim, unclear as to whether it was supportive, or contrary to the claim.

Before assessing Zimring's evidence, it is worth noting that the killer's cognitive ambiguity may not be all that pertinent to an assessment of whether gun control could prevent homicide. It is possible that most gun killers are ambiguously motivated in the sense that they do not, at the moment of attack, have a clear mental image of their victim dead. On the other hand, they may have a very strong aggressive drive and a willingness to seriously hurt their victim, without regard for exactly how serious an injury they inflict. Under such circumstances, killers deprived of guns could still be sufficiently angry, for a long enough time, to inflict lethal injuries at just as high a rate as they would have with guns. The key concept is the emotional one of strength and persistence of aggressive drive, rather than the cognitive concept of ambiguity of motives. If gun killers typically have a very strong drive to hurt their victims, then they might well not be satisfied until they had inflicted very serious injury, even if it took greater energy and a few more seconds of time to do so with a knife or club.

Zimring (1968) presented four kinds of evidence intended to support his "ambiguous motives" thesis: (1) killers and victims usually know each other before the killing, (2) most killings result from altercations, (3) most gun homicide victims are killed with a single wound, and (4) in most homicides, the killer or victim had been drinking. (It should be noted that most of Zimring's evidence pertained to all homicides, not just gun killings, even though it is only the traits of gun killers that are relevant to the issue of whether gun scarcity would reduce homicides.) Taking Zimring's points in order:

1. There is no evidence that fights between people who know each are less likely to involve a strong, persistent or unambiguous intent to kill than conflicts between strangers. Indeed, a prior relationship could provide the basis for the development of intense hatred and an accumulation of long-standing grievances. As Wright (1990) has noted, prior relationships tell us nothing about how ambiguous aggressors' motives are.

2. Altercations are unpremeditated and therefore allow less time for an aggressor to rethink his intentions, or to consider the long-term costs of an act of violence. This might well *reduce* aggressor ambivalence. Further, in conflicts in which time passes before the prospective aggressor decides to attack, the strength of the aggressive drive should dissipate. Consequently, the frequency of altercation homicides could easily be seen as *supportive* of the view of killers as unambiguously motivated, rather than the reverse.

3. Similarly, alcohol consumption could reduce ambivalence and inhibit the operation of an aggressor's conscience, strengthening rather than weakening his "single-mindedness."

4. Finally, the fact that a single shot was fired in most homicides may reflect little more than the fact that a single shot sometimes suffices to kill, and that even lethally minded killers stop shooting once the victim is dead. Consequently, there is no reason, on the basis of Zimring's evidence, for believing that all, most, or even a large minority of gun killings are ambiguously or weakly motivated. (For good critiques of the ambiguity thesis, see Hardy and Stompoly 1974, pp. 103–10; Wright et al. 1983, pp. 191–7).

For all one can tell at this point, the majority of gun killers are, at the time of the attack, strongly motivated enough to kill even if no guns were available. On the other hand, the opposite could also be true. Existing evidence does not permit any strong conclusions one way or the other. Nevertheless, it is not ordinarily assumed that the outcomes of intentional human actions are other than what the actors intended. It would seem a reasonable, though rebuttable, assumption that most aggressors who kill their victims intended to do so, and most aggressors who do not kill their victims did *not* intend to do so. If this assumption were generally correct, then it could well be the case that most gun killers have a fairly unambiguous intent to kill and therefore would be likely to kill their victims even if deprived of guns.

Closely related to the "ambiguous motives" thesis is another proposition with even less empirical support. This one can be called the "average Joe" thesis, which states that even though hardened felons cannot be denied guns through gun control, most killers are basically law-abiding citizens who lost their tempers and killed someone only because a gun was there. Such individuals could be effectively denied guns with the right gun laws; these laws could therefore have a significant impact on murder rates, even if they had little impact on rape, robbery, and other violent crimes supposedly committed by "hard-core" criminals. The evidence advanced by gun control advocates in support of this thesis overlaps the evidence Zimring used to support his "ambiguous motives" thesis: (1) killers and victims often knew each other before the killing, and (2) murders are commonly impulsive "acts of passion" (Shields 1981, p. 124; other examples cited in Kates 1990, p. 46). As with the ambiguity evidence, both of these factual claims are accurate, yet neither implies anything about whether most, or many, gun killers are basically "average Joes" who would obey gun laws—even hardened felons willing to violate gun laws often kill people they know, and frequently commit crimes impulsively.

More to the point, the average killer has a long history of criminal conduct in his or her past (see studies reviewed in Kleck and Bordua 1983, pp. 291–4). This is true not only for killings by professional robbers and Mafia hit men, but also for the perpetrators of domestic "crime-of-passion" homicides. To be sure, only a portion of this history is recorded in police files—most violence goes undetected by the police, and this is particularly true of domestic violence (Strauss et al. 1980). Nevertheless, even if one examines only information known to the police, it is clear that the typical domestic homicide is preceded by many previous acts of serious violence. For example, in 90% of domestic homicides in a Kansas City study, police had responded to a disturbance call at the same address during the previous 2 years, with a median of 5 previous calls (Wilt et al. 1977). This is not to say that everyone who kills with a gun has a prior record of serious criminal conduct. There is a first time for every criminal, and no doubt there have been a few individuals who committed a gun homicide as their first serious act of violence. However, this appears to be a rare exception to the general rule that most people who are seriously violent now, with or without guns, have been seriously violent in the past. On the other hand, this does not prove that there are no gun killers who could be prevented from getting a gun by the right gun laws. Even gun killers fall along a continuum of willingness and motivation to break laws, and a sizable number of them may fall far enough toward the low end of the scale that gun laws could work, by making acquisition or possession of a gun difficult or risky enough for them to refrain from doing so.

Guns in Robbery and Rape

Only about 20% of robberies and less than 10% of rapes involve offenders armed with guns, and in many of these cases guns were incidental to the crime—they happened to be there, but were not actually used to threaten or harm the victim (U.S. Bureau of Justice Statistics 1986b). Further, of the 31,606 gun-related deaths in 1985 (Chapter 2), less than 7% were homicides linked with robbery or "sex offenses" (computed from U.S. FBI 1986, pp. 12, 41). Nevertheless, guns do sometimes play a role in these crimes and this role is worth some discussion.

Robbery

The following generalizations are consistent with, though certainly not proven by, the best available evidence on guns and robbery.

1. Gun ownership levels have no effect on total robbery rates (Murray 1975; Brill 1977; Cook 1979; McDowall 1986). Note, however, that this does not necessarily mean that the immediate availability of guns for robbery, and the rate of gun carrying, does not have an impact on total robbery rates.
2. Gun ownership levels positively affect the rate of gun robberies, but negatively affect the rate of nongun robberies, thereby increasing the fraction of robberies involving guns (Cook 1979; 1987).
3. Injuries are more common in nongun robberies; therefore decreases in gun use among robbers would increase the fraction of robberies resulting in injury (Cook 1980).
4. Victims of gun robberies are less likely than victims of nongun robberies to resist the robber; resisting victims are in turn generally (excepting those who resist with guns—Chapter 4) more likely to be injured than nonresisting victims (Hindelang 1976; Cook and Nagin 1979, p. 37).

Analysts typically attribute the lower injury rate among gun robbery victims to their lower rates of resistance. Although this may be part of the explanation, it should also be noted that gun robbers are less likely to attack or injure their victims, compared to unarmed robbers or those using nongun weapons, even controlling for resistance (Cook and Nagin 1979, p. 37). Further, since resistance often follows injury (Chapter 4; Block 1977), it is not clear that the resistance-injury association indicates that resistance provokes robber attack. To the extent that injury precedes resistance, one cannot explain the lower injury rates of gun robberies by victim resistance patterns.

5. When injuries are inflicted on robbery victims, those inflicted by gun-armed robbers are no more likely to result in hospital treatment of some kind than those inflicted by other robbers. Injuries inflicted by gun-armed robbers are more likely to result in hospitalization *overnight* than those inflicted by unarmed robbers, but they are about the same in this respect as injuries in knife robberies and somewhat *less* likely to result in overnight hospitalization than those inflicted by robbers armed with weapons other than guns or knives (Table 5.6 concerning hospitalization in all violent crimes; Cook 1987, p. 361, concerning hospital treatment and hospitalization overnight among robbery victims). Thus,

if knives were substituted for guns, there is currently no empirical basis for believing that the fraction of injuries requiring hospital treatment or overnight hospitalization would decrease. On the other hand, for the 3% of robbery victims who received overnight hospitalization (Cook 1987, p. 361), the average length of stay is longer for robbery victims wounded by guns (Table 5.6).

6. Murder of the victim is more likely in gun robberies than nongun robberies (Cook 1987). However, it is unclear whether it is the lethality of guns or the greater lethality of robbers who use guns that is responsible for this pattern, for reasons previously discussed. Gun reductions may or may not produce any reduction in robbery murders, depending on the impact of gun scarcity on the number of robberies, how much of an increase in the number of injuries occurs, and how much the injury fatality rate declines, assuming it declines at all (Wright et al. 1983, pp. 209–12). Further, almost all of those robber murders were committed with handguns, and gun control efforts usually cover only handguns (Chapter 8). Most incarcerated felons say they would substitute the more lethal long guns if they could not carry handguns (Wright and Rossi 1986, p. 217), suggesting that laws inducing handgun scarcity would increase the fraction of robbery attacks resulting in death by inducing substitution of long guns (Chapter 3).

7. Guns enable robbers to tackle more lucrative and risky targets such as businesses rather than more vulnerable ones like women, children, the elderly, and so on (Hindelang 1976; Cook 1976). Reducing gun availability could cause robbers to switch from the former to the latter, shifting the burden of robbery to those most vulnerable to injury and least able to absorb the financial losses. Injuries to more vulnerable victims could well result in death more often.

8. Finally, the data in Table 5.5 indicate that robbers armed with guns are more likely to complete their crimes, i.e., get away with the victim's valuables. This is presumably at least partly due to the aforementioned fact that victims are less likely to resist gun-armed robbers; although the impact of victim resistance on injury is uncertain, resistance clearly reduces the likelihood of robbery completion. Thus, if fewer robbers were armed with guns, more victims would probably manage to retain their valuables.

In sum, gun control policies that managed to reduce gun possession among robbers would have the desirable effects of increasing the rate at which robbers failed to get their victims' property and *possibly* reducing the number of robbery victims killed. On the other hand, gun scarcity would also probably increase the number of robbery injuries and shift the burden of victimization to victims less able to bear the burden, without reducing the number of robberies. Therefore, it is difficult to say whether the overall set of social consequences of gun scarcity would make an effective gun control policy a success with regard to robbery.

Rape

In the typical male offender–female victim rape, the rapist has a substantial power advantage over the victim even without a weapon. Therefore, use of a weapon by most rapists is probably redundant. It is unknown how large a subset of the 10% of rapes committed by rapists armed with guns actually required a gun to attempt or complete the crime. However, the data in Table 5.5 do indicate that rapists with guns are more likely than unarmed rapists to complete the crime. The differences between rapes by rapists armed with guns and those armed with knives, the weapon most likely to be substituted in the absence of guns, is fairly small (6.8 percentage points). In a multivariate analysis, Kleck and Sayles (1990, p. 155–6) found that armed rapists were more likely to complete their rapes than unarmed rapists, but they could not establish that gun-armed rapists differed from those with knives or other weapons. On the other hand, they found no effect of rapist weapon possession on injury beyond the rape itself.

With this previous research in mind, the impact of guns on violence is now addressed in two ways. First, a nationally representative sample of individual violent incidents is analyzed to see how the aggressor's possession or use of weapons relates to attack, injury and death of victims. Then aggregate level data on cities are used to estimate the net impact of gun ownership levels on violence rates.

Individual-Level Analysis

Problems in Previous Research

Previous studies of weapon effects in violent incidents have all suffered from one or more of four problems. First, all studies using incidents known to the police or treated by physicians have analyzed samples that were biased regarding the dependent variable, i.e., some measure of assault outcome, including death. Police-based or hospital-based studies examined samples in which incidents of minor violence had been systematically selected out because they were not regarded as serious enough to bother reporting to the police or did not require medical treatment. Alternatively, other studies bias the sample by excluding the most serious cases, homicides. Second, the studies typically analyzed local samples, usually limited to a single city. Weaponry varies sharply across localities, not only in general availability (e.g., fewer guns in urban areas than rural areas, more in the South than elsewhere), but also in its distribution across weapon subcategories (a higher fraction of guns owned being handguns in urban areas, etc.) and in reasons for ownership (more crime-oriented ownership, either for criminal or defensive purposes, in urban areas) (Chapter 2). Consequently, there may be very limited generalizability of findings from urban-only or single-jurisdiction studies (e.g., Zimring 1968; Wilson and Sherman 1961; Felson and Steadman 1983). Third, analysis in these studies has commonly been unsophisticated, relying on simple percentage table methods, and often bivariate analysis at that. This is particularly a problem because there were no controls for any correlates of assaulter motivation or aggressive drive levels. Fourth, with few exceptions (e.g., Cook and Nagin 1979), prior research on real-life violence has ignored the distinction between weapons' effects on whether the aggressor attacks the victim (rather than merely threatening) and their effects on whether an attack is completed, i.e., produces an injury. Either only the attack outcome is studied, or the two are lumped together into a combined attack-and-injury variable, usually labeled "injury" (e.g., King 1987; Block 1977).

The present study (adapted from Kleck and McElrath 1991) goes beyond the work of others by using nationally representative samples of violent incidents covering the full range of seriousness from very minor threats to homicides, covering both incidents reported to the police and those not reported, using multivariate analytic techniques, distinguishing between attack, injury, and death as outcomes of violent situations, and controlling for a number of likely correlates of offender motivation strength. The present study is unique in combining nationally representative samples of both fatal and nonfatal violent incidents in a single analysis.

Before describing the multivariate analysis, it is worth noting the bivariate association between offender weapon possession and use and the outcomes of violent incidents. The figures in Table 5.6 are based on all violent crime victimizations lumped together, from the 1973–1982 National Crime Surveys. The main interest focusses on the comparison between guns and knives. The data indicate that offenders who possess guns are less likely to attack victims than offenders with knives, or any other weapons for that matter. Gun users are also less likely to injure their victims, and this is true both for all aggressors and just among those who attacked their victims. If one interprets receiving medical care as an indication the victim was seriously injured, victims of gun users are less likely to be seriously wounded than knife victims. Most of this is due to the low rate of attack and injury in gun incidents, but even just among incidents with injury, gun victims are slightly less likely to receive medical care than knife victims. If hospital care is indicative of an even more serious injury, then the preceding pattern is repeated, except that hospital care is slightly more likely among those injured by guns than among those injured by knives. Finally, among the small share of victims who received hospital care, victims of gun injuries had a median hospital stay about 2 days longer than those hospitalized for knife injuries. In sum, even at the bivariate level, there is little evidence in the NCS that gun possession and use make serious outcomes more likely in violent incidents.

Problems in Analyzing Violent Incidents

The National Crime Surveys (NCS) cover a representative sample of the noninstitutionalized U.S. population age 12 and over. Respondents (Rs) are asked whether they have been a victim of crime in the previous 6 months and are questioned about the details of the crime incidents they recall. At least three "reverse record checks" studies have found that Rs' ability or willingness to recall crimes is worse for assaults than for any other crime type—as few as 36% of assaults known to police were reported to NCS interviewers (Dodge 1981; Murphy and Dodge 1981; Turner 1981). These studies indicated that it was violent incidents among persons who knew one another that were most likely to go unreported. For example, only 22% of assaults involving relatives were reported, compared to 54% of those involving strangers (Turner 1981). This problem is addressed by limiting analysis to stranger cases, where there is less room for underreporting to bias results.

Other known patterns of bias concern R's race and education. Blacks appear to underreport violent incidents, especially less serious incidents, more than whites. And less educated persons consistently report fewer incidents, especially minor ones, than more educated persons (Skogan 1981). By recalling (or defining as assaults) a larger number of assaults without attack or injury, better educated Rs make it seem that their assaults are less likely to result in these outcomes, with an opposite, equally artificial pattern for blacks compared with whites. The result is that the measured fraction of assaults resulting in attack or injury may be artificially elevated for blacks and for less educated people. These effects were roughly controlled for by including education and race of victim in all initial versions of equations.

Some minor assaults may be recalled only because they were repeated, i.e., part of an ongoing pattern. Although serious assaults are generally recalled in any case, minor assaults, i.e., those without attack or injury, may be more likely to be recalled if they were repeated than if they were isolated. This could make it artificially appear that repeated incidents are less likely to involve an attack or injury. In NCS terminology, a "series" incident is an incident that was one of three or more incidents occurring in the 6-month recall period, which were so similar that the R could not separately describe them. Although not all repeated assaults are "series" incidents, all series incidents are repeated crimes. This effect is controlled by including a measure of whether an incident was a series case.

What is the relationship between these biases and weapon involvement in violence? Could the fraction of assaults involving attack or injury be distorted by response biases that vary across weapon categories? Certainly the NCS coverage of nonfatal assaults is incomplete for both assaults involving attack and/or injury and those involving neither. Although the NCS covers minor assaults better than police records, Cook (1985) has shown that the NCS covers the most serious assaults, such as gunshot woundings, *less* completely than do police records. That is, these gun cases, involving both injury and more serious weaponry, are frequently missed in the NCS. However, whether this is more true for serious-weapon assaults than for minor-weapon assaults is unknown, since minor-weapon assaults may be covered in the NCS at just as low a rate as the more serious ones. The undercoverage of the NCS may simply have been more easily detected with gun assaults because of unusually complete police knowledge of assaults requiring medical treatment—physicians are commonly required by law to report gunshot wounds to the police. Consequently, it is unclear whether the relative average seriousness levels of NCS assaults are distorted by these underreporting problems more in some weapons categories than in others.

Methods of the Present Analysis

Samples

Two datasets are analyzed. The first, used to analyze the attack and injury outcomes, is the set of all NCS violent incidents that occurred in the United States in 1979–1985 and that involved victims and offenders who were strangers to one another. The NCS covers only victims age 12 or over. The present sample is as inclusive as possible, to avoid introducing additional sample bias by needlessly excluding relevant cases. The only exception was the decision to exclude nonstranger cases, motivated by a judgment that the advantages of reducing the response bias associated with violence among intimates outweighed the sample-biasing effects of this exclusion. This NCS sample includes series incidents, as well as incidents with multiple victims or offenders. All cases involve at least a threat of violence, although they may also involve the elements of other crimes besides assault. Thus, the sample includes incidents classified as rape or robbery in the NCS Type-of-Crime classification. Dummy variables measure whether the elements of rape, robbery (theft plus force), or burglary (illegal entry) were also involved in an incident.

The second dataset, used to analyze the death outcome, is a merger of all NCS stranger violence incidents for 1982 and all Supplementary Homicide Reports (SHR) intentional stranger homicides of victims age 12 and over for 1982, including both civilian and police justifiable homicides. The year 1982 was used simply because it was in the middle of the time span covered in the first dataset. The SHR program, run by the Federal Bureau of Investigation and based on police offense reports, records information on the victim, offender (when known), and circumstances of about 90% of U.S. homicides. To maintain comparability between the NCS and SHR datasets, homicides of victims under age 12 were excluded, and negligent (unintentional) manslaughters were excluded because the NCS is intended to cover only intentional acts. NCS incidents occurring outside the United States were also excluded because the SHRs cover only homicides occurring within U.S. police jurisdictions. All other relevant cases were retained, including incidents involving multiple offenders or multiple victims, and civilian or police justifiable homicides. All variables that existed in some form in both sources were identified and given a common coding scheme. A weight was computed that equalled the NCS incident weight for NCS cases and a number slightly larger than one for SHR cases (see Appendix 6). The resulting merged dataset was a national sample of intentional stranger assault incidents, both fatal and nonfatal, weighted up to represent national totals.

Estimation Techniques

All three dependent variables were binary, so some form of probit was generally used to estimate equations. Ordinary least squares (OLS) regression was used for preliminary screening with the ATTACK and INJURY models before applying the more computationally expensive maximum likelihood estimation techniques. A very liberal significance level ($p < .30$) was used in the screening, to avoid prematurely excluding a relevant variable. Because of the extreme distribution of the DEATH variable, even preliminary screening had to be done with probit.

All final versions of the INJURY and DEATH equations were estimated with bivariate probit with a correction for nonrandom sample selection (Van de Ven and Van Praag 1981; Greene 1985). This correction was necessary because of the way the samples were subdivided into increasingly serious subsets. First, all assaults were examined to determine why some involved an attack and others did not. Then analysis was limited to cases with an attack, to analyze why only some attacks resulted in injury. Finally, cases with injury were analyzed to explore why only some injuries resulted in death.

To estimate INJURY equations on the full assault sample would muddle the distinction between attack and injury—estimated models of the INJURY variable would reflect processes affecting ATTACK, as well as those affecting INJURY, given attack. However, selecting only cases with an attack for estimation of the INJURY equation is a nonrandom selection that could bias the coefficient estimates (Berk 1983). To correct for this bias, a "selection" equation was estimated that modeled the inclusion of cases into the sample on which the "substantive" equation was estimated. The ATTACK equation predicts whether an incident will involve an attack. The INJURY equation was estimated only on cases that involved an attack, since those without an attack obviously could not result in injury. Therefore the ATTACK equation in effect predicts whether a case will be "selected" for inclusion in the sample on which the INJURY equation was estimated. A similar procedure was used to estimate the substantive DEATH equations, with an INJURY equation being used as the selection equation, since only cases involving injury were "eligible" to result in death. The sample selection correction procedure works by including a measure of the predicted probability of a case not being selected for the sample as a variable in the substantive equation (Heckman 1979; Van de Ven and Van Praag 1981).

Definitions of Key Variables

Table 5.7 lists the variables included in the individual-level analyses, with their means and standard deviations. Most of the variables are binary, representing the presence or absence of an attribute. Because some incidents involve more than one offender, the offender dummies indicate whether there was at least one offender with the indicated trait. Thus, when MALEOFF is 1, it means there was at least one male offender; there could also have been female offenders. To avoid near-perfect collinearity, at least one dummy variable representing a category of some larger variable was always excluded from each equation. For example, both MALEOFF and FEMOFF, dummies representing the two possible categories of offender sex, could not both be included in an equation, since if there was no male offender, it would always indicate the presence of a female offender, and vice versa.

The dependent variables, ATTACK, INJURY, AND DEATH, are necessarily generic—they reflect attack, injury, or death involving *any* weapon (or no weapon). Therefore, an incident with a gun present and involving an attack and/or injury did not necessarily involve a gunshot wound. Rather, a gun-armed assaulter may have fired the gun and missed, used it only to threaten, used it as a blunt instrument, or not used it all, instead attacking and/or injuring the victim with fists or feet or with some other nongun weapon. Table 5.7 lists three different versions of each gun variable. In the ATTACK analyses, the gun variables measure whether guns were present, i.e., whether the offender possessed them in a way evident to the victim. In the INJURY analyses, the gun variables measure whether a gun was actually used to *attack* the victim, i.e., whether the victim was shot or shot at. And in the DEATH analyses, the variables indicate whether the victim actually suffered a gunshot wound. In all cases, a victim could be confronted with an offender with more than one type of weapon, and be attacked or injured in more than one way. However, less than 0.1% of assaults involve more than one weapon type being used in an attack.

Equations were estimated not only for the full sample of stranger violent incidents, but also for each of three subsets. First, to see whether results were distorted by lumping robbery, rape, and confrontational burglary incidents in with "pure" assaults, estimates were obtained for the "nonfelony" subset of violent incidents that did not have the elements of theft, rape, or illegal entry. Second, it might be argued that victim recall is poor for series incidents since the information obtained refers to the average features of multiple incidents, rather than any one specific incident. Therefore, estimates were obtained for the "nonseries" subset excluding series incidents. Finally, one could argue that some assaults involve "victims" who were really aggressors and that variables referring to the "victim" were actually describing the offender, and vice versa (see Appendix 6). On the assumption that victims reporting incidents to the police were more likely to regard themselves as true victims, cases in which the victim or a member of the victim's household reported to the police were separately analyzed.

Most of the variables in each equation were included as likely correlates of offender "motivation," broadly conceived as how willing and able (apart from weaponry possession) aggressors were to attack, injure, or kill victims. Offender attributes (MALEOFF, AOLE11, AOGE30, BLACKOFF) were included because they reflect differing levels of willingness to aggress—males, persons age 12–29, and blacks commit serious violent acts more frequently than others. Victim attributes (MARRIED, GUNOCC) were included because they reflect differing levels of difficulty or risk to the aggressor in attacking and trying to injure the victim—married victims are more likely to have a spouse nearby, while victims employed as a security guard or police officer are more likely to possess a gun. (On the other hand, people in gun-carrying occupations are also more likely to encounter more seriously violent persons.) ROBBERY, RAPE, and BURGLARY were included on the assumption that robbers, burglars, and rapists have longer and more serious records of prior violence than simple assaulters and are therefore more willing to use violence in a sample incident. (On the other hand, these types of aggressors also have goals other than hurting the victim, which could reduce attacks and injuries.) The power differential variables (AGEDIF, SEXDIF, and NUMDIF) were included on the assumption that aggressors with a power advantage would be more willing to attack and injure because they were at less risk of effective counterattack from the victim. (On the other hand, they would also have less need to attack or injure to get what they wanted.) SUMMER was included on the assumption that people are more easily and strongly angered when the weather is hot. Finally, DARK and INSIDE were included because darkness and an inside location should make witness identification or interruption of the crime less likely and thus could reduce situational inhibitions against attack.

Findings

In Tables 5.8–5.10, the excluded weapon category was "no weapon present" (or "no weapon used"), so coefficients reflect the effect of each weapon category relative to weaponless assaults, i.e., those involving only hands, feet, etc. All equations were significant at a level less than .001.

Attack

The findings in Table 5.8 indicate that the net effect of the presence of deadly weaponry in threatening situations is to *reduce* the probability of attack by the possessors of the weapons. The negative association is significant for handguns, "other" guns (mostly rifles and shotguns), and knives. The apparent effect of the presence of less lethal "other" weapons (blunt objects, broken bottles, etc.) is to increase the probability of attack. Thus, as lethality of the weapons present increases, the probability of attack decreases. Equation 1 shows the ordinary least-squares estimates for the full sample of stranger violent incidents, while Eq. 2 presents the full sample probit estimates. The findings are substantively identical and hence not dependent on the estimation procedure used. The findings also hold regardless of whether felony-linked assaults are excluded (Eq. 3), series incidents are excluded (Eq. 4), or the analysis is restricted just to those cases reported to the police (Eq. 5). Since the "weapons effect" thesis is intended to apply only to angry persons, the present findings are relevant to the extent that it can be assumed that aggressors in the sample incidents were angry. If the "weapons effect" does exist, the findings indicate that the conditions necessary for it to produce a net assault-triggering effect are rarely met in real-life violent incidents, or if the effect does operate, its impact is outweighed by attack-reducing effects of deadly weaponry.

Notice that the education and series variables have the expected negative signs. Better educated respondents are more likely to report assaults in which an actual attack did not occur, and the reported series incidents were more likely to be threats without attack than nonseries incidents. Victim race, on the other hand, was unrelated to ATTACK.

Injury

The findings in Table 5.9 indicate that, given an attack, the use of guns has a statistically significant net negative association with victim injury. The use of knives and "other weapons" in an attack was positively associated with injury. The general pattern of findings is that the more lethal the weapon used in an attack is, the less likely it is that it will be used to actually inflict an injury. These findings hold regardless of the estimation procedure used (Eqs. 6–8). This is important because the correction for sample selection bias used in the bivariate probit estimates will improve estimates only if the sample selection equation models the selection process reasonably well, something of which one can not be certain. Since the procedure corrects for the probability of a case being included in the sample, if the selection process cannot be accurately modeled, it amounts to the same thing as either failing to include a relevant variable in the equation (sample selection bias as a specification error—Heckman 1979) or including a poor measure of that needed control variable.

Death

The findings in Table 5.10, based on analysis of the merged SHR/NCS assault and homicide dataset, indicate that, given a wounding, the wound is more likely to be fatal if it is a gunshot wound. The results suggest the existence of a clear hierarchy of weapon lethality, with gun woundings the most likely to result in death, then injuries produced by knives, then "other weapons," then blunt objects, and finally, hands and feet. These findings are largely independent of estimation procedure used (Eqs. 12–14) and data subsamples analyzed (Eq. 14 vs. Eqs. 15 and 16).

The only missing data indicator variable (see Appendix 6) with a coefficient significantly different from zero in any of the equations was UNDRACEO, indicating that missing data patterns were random with respect to DEATH, except that incidents where the offender's race was unknown were more likely to be fatal.

Discussion of the Individual-Level Findings

These findings support a more complex picture of the significance of firearms in American violence than has commonly been a part of the debate over gun control. The possession of guns appears to both inhibit attack and reduce the probability of injury, given attack, while also increasing the probability of death, given an injury. What would be the net effect on deaths of a reduction in aggressor possession of guns in threatening situations? To answer this question, a DEATH equation was estimated on the full sample of stranger violent incidents, not just those with injuries. The equation included all variables that were available in the combined SHR/NCS dataset and that appeared in any of the three equations for attack, injury, or death. It was estimated with OLS and probit. The results are shown in the last two columns of Table 5.11, which summarizes the sizes of the effects of the weapon variables on each of the assault outcomes.

Note that OLS coefficient estimates are unbiased when the dependant variable is binary, and their values can be interpreted as linear probability coefficients (Aldrich and Nelson 1984, pp. 13, 18). The linear probability interpretation is most meaningful when the predictors, as a group, take on average values, since this is where OLS slopes are essentially identical to slopes estimated with methods assuming nonlinear relationships, such as probit or logit.

The aggressor's possession of a handgun in a violent incident apparently exerts a very slight net positive effect on the likelihood of the victim's death. The linear probability interpretation of the OLS coefficient implies that the presence of a handgun increases the probability of the victim's death by 1.4%. Thus, the violence-increasing and violence-suppressing effects of gun possession and use almost exactly cancel each other out. This small an association is statistically significant, however, because of the very large (n = 14,922) sample size.

The effects of aggressor weaponry are quite substantial when taken stage by stage, i.e., when separately examining attack, injury, and death. This is why impressive-appearing results can be obtained when researchers examine, for example, only the last stage, looking solely at the impact of guns on the likelihood of the victim's death, among those wounded. Guns probably do substantially increase the probability that a wounding will result in death. The effects of guns, however, are very small when one assesses the overall net impact of all of their effects, both positive and negative, at all stages of violent incidents. The explanation for this apparent contradiction is simple: gun possession and use have opposite sign effects at the various stages, which largely cancel each other out.

Note also the effect of omitting any direct measure of aggressor motivation. More seriously violent people use more serious weaponry (Table 5.2), and it seems reasonable to assume that, on average, the intensity of the aggressor's desire to seriously hurt the victim, at the moment of attack, would also be positively correlated with the presence of "serious" weaponry. Since aggressor motivation is almost certainly positively associated with the probability of a victim being killed, this means that omitting direct measures of motivation tends to bias the gun coefficients in a positive direction, making it seem that gun use has more of a positive effect than it really does. Consequently, the slight apparent net positive effect of guns on the death outcome would be reduced, and could easily disappear altogether, if motivation could be properly measured and controlled.

Nevertheless, at this point it seems that there may be some slight net effect on the likelihood of the victim's death that could be attributed to guns. Taken at face value, the results suggest that aggressor possession of guns may increase the net probability of the victim dying in a violent incident by about 1%. This would lead to the expectation that laws that were effective in reducing gun possession among aggressors in violent incidents could slightly reduce the homicide rate. On the other hand, gun possession among potential victims may deter some aggressors from initiating violent incidents in the first place. Any laws that reduced gun possession among potential victims, including those who are also sometimes aggressors, could thereby encourage assaults. The net impact on the homicide rate of these opposite effects could be positive, negative, or zero, depending on their relative magnitudes. These conclusions help explain the findings of prior research, which indicated that trends in aggregate gun levels had no net effect on homicide rates (Kleck 1984a).

The findings also imply that if gun possession were reduced among aggressors in violent situations, total assault injuries would increase, the fraction of injuries resulting in death would decrease, and the total number of homicides would remain about the same. This appears to be precisely what happened in Boston after implementation of the Bartley–Fox law. After gun carrying, and thus the immediate availability of guns in some violent situations, was reduced, total assault injuries increased substantially, but with no significant change in homicides, implying a drop in the fraction of injuries resulting in death (see Chapter 10).

Three limitations of this analysis are important to note. First, it is unclear what response biases may be affecting NCS data. It is possible that a large fraction of gun assaults, even those not involving attack or injury, are remembered just because they involved guns, with many minor nongun assaults going unremembered or unreported. The result would be that an artificially higher fraction of nongun assaults would appear to have resulted in attack, injury, or death, relative to gun assaults, making the gun–nongun differences appear smaller than they really are. Second, the NCS and SHR provide data on only a few of the variables that may influence assault outcomes, having no direct measures of assaulters' motives or the strength of their aggressive drives. This increases the possibility of the models being misspecified due to the exclusion of variables associated with both weapon variables and assault outcomes. Finally, the findings are based on violent incidents between strangers. Whether weapons effects are different in violence among nonstrangers is unknown.

Although the individual-level analysis has the merit of getting closer to the phenomenon, it cannot show what the net overall effect of gun ownership levels is on total rates of violence. For example, even if the net effect of gun possession among aggressors in violent incidents is to increase the probability of the victim's death, there are still other gun effects related to gun possession among prospective victims. As indicated in Chapter 4, not only does the victim's possession of a gun often disrupt a criminal attempt and prevent injury, but the fact of mass gun ownership might deter some prospective aggressors from making criminal attempts in the first place. Therefore, the overall net impact of gun ownership levels on violence rates is assessed using data on cities.

Aggregate-Level Analysis of Gun Ownership and Violence Rates

Previous Research on Gun Ownership Levels and Crime Rates

What is the impact of widespread gun availability on crime rates? Do areas with more guns have, as a result, more crime? Do increases in gun ownership over time increase crime rates? At least 18 previous studies have addressed these questions and are summarized in Table 5.12. The table covers only studies in which there was an attempt to actually measure gun ownership levels, rather than merely assuming differences across cases.

The first thing that is apparent from this table is that there have been an enormous variety of ways of measuring aggregate gun levels—over a dozen of them—with few researchers using the same measures. The survey measures are the most direct ones and would seem to have the highest face validity; yet, as was noted in Chapter 2, there are reasons to question the validity even of survey responses. Whether these problems affect comparisons across aggregate cases, however, is unknown. Further, survey measures are available only for the nation as a whole or for broad regions of the nation.

Other measures are less direct, relying on the relative frequency with which guns are used to commit acts of violence, such as the percentage of homicides committed with guns. Studies using these measures all relied on just one or two indicators. Further, with the exception of Cook (1979), researchers using these measures failed to validate them in any way, such as establishing that they correlate well with more direct survey measures. The "% gun use" measures also raise the possibility of artifactual associations with crime rates. For example, the number of gun homicides is a component in the numerators of both the percentage of homicides committed with guns and either the gun homicide rate or the total (gun plus nongun) homicide rate. This would tend to create a positive association between the gun ownership measure and the crime rate, even if there were no causal relationship. Whereas a few like Cook (1979) took steps to avoid this problem, most other researchers did not.

Even more critically, these kinds of measures reflect not only the availability of guns but also the preference of the criminal population for using guns (Brill 1977, pp. xvi, 20). Whereas availability certainly affects how often criminals choose guns, it has also been seen that offender seriousness affects this choice as well. Consequently, these measures, if used by themselves, tend to confound gun availability with what might be called the "average lethality of the criminal population." In short, the same problem of separating gun effects from associated effects of criminals' lethality that afflicted individual-level research also plagues aggregate-level research.

Even some of the more sophisticated researchers in the field have failed to adequately appreciate this problem. For example, Cook (1987, pp. 372–3) found that city rates of robbery murder were more strongly associated with the gun robbery rate than with the nongun robbery rate, and concluded that this was "strong evidence that gun robberies are . . . intrinsically more dangerous than other robberies." In fact, such findings are not necessarily even weakly supportive of this conclusion, since one would expect precisely this pattern even if gun use had no causal impact on the likelihood of a robbery resulting in the victim's death. If gun use is a good indicator of robber willingness to kill, then the gun robbery rate would be a better indicator of average robber lethality than the nongun robbery rate; the rate of robberies by more "lethally minded" robbers should obviously relate more strongly to robbery murder rates than the rate of robberies by less "lethally minded" robbers. Whether this explanation completely accounts for Cook's findings is unknown. The point is, analyses using aggregate data cannot resolve the matter.

Miscellaneous other gun measures are unsatisfactory. As the empirical results reported later in the chapter will show, the fatal gun accident rate does not correlate significantly with survey gun ownership measures (see also Cook 1979), nor do rates of gun magazine subscriptions. The hunting license rate is marginally significantly correlated with the total gun ownership rate but its association with the handgun rate is not quite statistically significant. This suggests that it serves best as an indicator of long gun ownership, consistent with the fact that most hunting is done with rifles and shotguns. Gun owner license or registration rates are satisfactory as measures of legal gun ownership, but not of total ownership. Similarly, gun magazine subscription rates might serve, at best, as indirect measures of legal long gun ownership. Subscription rates are probably best regarded as indicators of the prevalence of a mostly noncriminal "gun sporting culture" (Bordua and Lizotte 1979) rather than a measure of gun ownership per se. It would be preferable to have separate measures of criminal and noncriminal ownership; however, if only one can be measured, then for purposes of assessing the impact of gun ownership on violence rates, it is criminal ownership that is more relevant. Counts of the number of gun purchase permits also tap only legally acquired guns, and measure only additions to the stock of guns, rather than the total stock.

For time series analyses, a measure that is both very direct and avoids the possibility of artifactual associations is available. Researchers can cumulate the total number of guns domestically manufactured, minus exports, plus imports, up to a given year, thereby measuring trends in the available stock of guns. However, as noted in Chapter 2, this measure fails to count some additions and deletions of guns from the stock and its use necessitates assuming that these errors are roughly equal and cancel each other out.

The findings of previous aggregate studies are summarized in Table 5.12. Their findings are almost exactly evenly split between 12 findings that support the idea that higher gun levels increase crime and 11 findings that do not. All but a handful of the studies are technically very weak. They rely on small samples, sometimes including as few as nine, or even four cases; only Bordua (1986) had more than 50 cases. In combination with the multicollinearity that typically characterizes aggregate data, this implies very unstable results. Eight of the studies did not control for any other factors that might be associated with gun ownership and could affect crime rates, making it impossible to check whether any observed associations between gun and violence levels were spurious; 11 studies controlled for no more than two other variables.

The most critical flaw is the failure to model the two-way relationship between crime rates and gun levels. As shown in Chapter 2, higher crime rates can cause more people to acquire guns for self-defense, whether or not this effect is mediated by the experience of fear. Consequently, any significant positive associations generated in studies failing to model the possible two-way relationship will at least partially reflect the effect of crime rates on gun rates. Whether there is also any effect of guns on violence is impossible to detect from these findings. Of 18 studies, the problem was statistically addressed in only four, and one of these almost certainly did not succeed in modeling the relationship. McDowall and Loftin (1988) used a simultaneous equation model of a Detroit homicide time series, a model that assumed that homicide rates could affect gun rates. However, their model was underidentified unless a single exclusion restriction was valid (see Johnston 1972 for an explanation of simultaneous equation techniques). They assumed that the Detroit riot of 1967 increased the gun ownership rate, but did *not* otherwise affect homicide rates. In view of Daniel Glaser's (1978, pp. 230–1) strong theoretical rationale for a major impact of ghetto riots on subsequent black violence, this critical assumption lacked a priori plausibility.

Of the three studies that may have adequately modeled the reciprocal causation, two found no impact of gun levels on total violence levels

(Kleck 1984a; McDowall 1986); the third (Kleck 1979) found an impact. However, the second Kleck study was a replication of the first, with a longer time series; the second study's findings therefore should be given greater weight. Note that the robbery findings in the second Kleck study were based on a model that did *not* test for reciprocal causation, so it shares the same flaw as other studies that found a supposed positive impact of gun levels on crime rates. McDowall (1986, pp. 141–3) interpreted his panel design results to indicate that the gun robbery rate positively affected gun ownership levels in the general public, but that the total robbery rate did not have such an effect. He did not provide any explanation for this combination of effects. He also did not report any results assessing Cook's (1979) claim that higher gun levels increase the robbery murder rate. In sum, the best one can say is that the literature fails to make a consistent or convincing case for an impact of guns on violence rates. Put more negatively, one could say that the literature has little of a persuasive nature to say on the matter, and that the few studies that adequately addressed the key technical problems have generally found no impact of gun levels on violence levels.

International Comparisons

One of the least productive lines of inquiry in the gun control debate has been to compare the United States with other nations. It is unproductive because the game has been played in such a way that either side can win regardless of whether there is any merit to their claims. Gun control supporters like to selectively contrast the high gun ownership/high violence United States with nations having both low gun ownership and low violence rates (homicide data are usually cited), such as Great Britain or Japan, concluding that low gun ownership must have contributed to the low violence rates. Opponents selectively cite high gun/low violence nations such as Switzerland or low gun/high violence nations such as Mexico, and conclude that gun ownership either has no impact on violence, or actually reduces it. Obviously, pairwise comparisons of two selected cases is useless for establishing causal connections, or the lack thereof [see Sloan et al. (1988) for a particularly egregious example]. Out of any large number of possible pairings, it is safe to say that at least a few pairs can be found to appear to support either side.

In some cases the comparisons of nations are patently ridiculous. To do no more than compare homicide rates in Japan and the United States and claim to know whether any of the huge difference in homicide rates is attributable to differences in gun ownership levels is far-fetched. The two nations differ enormously on almost all hypothesized determinants of homicide rates, including degree of social solidarity, cultural and ethnic homogeneity, history of racial conflict, hierarchical rigidity, obedience to authority, subjective sense of unjust deprivation, and so on. Further, most of these differences are not currently measured, making it impossible to empirically disentangle effects of these other variables from effects of gun ownership on homicide.

One way one might crudely and partially control for United States–Japan cultural differences is to compare homicide rates among Japanese-Americans, who live where guns are plentiful, with the homicide rates of their presumably culturally similar brethren in Japan, where private gun ownership is nearly nonexistent. Certainly this pair of populations is more comparable than the population of Japan compared with the entire U.S. population. Up through 1979, the FBI reported homicide arrests sorted by racial breakdowns which included "Japanese." For the period 1976–1978, 21 of 48,695 arrests for murder and nonnegligent manslaughter were of Japanese-Americans, or 0.04% (U.S. FBI 1977–1979). Applying this fraction to the total of 57,460 homicides yields an estimate of 24.78 killings by Japanese-Americans for 1976–1978, or about 8.26 per year. With 791,000 persons of Japanese ancestry in the United States in 1980 (U.S. Bureau of the Census 1984), this translates into an annual rate of 1.04 homicides per 100,000 population. For the same 1976–1978 period, the annual homicide rate in Japan averaged 2.45 (United Nations 1982, pp. 192, 718). Thus, crudely controlling for Japanese culture in this way indicates that in Japan, where civilian gun ownership is virtually nonexistent and gun control laws are extremely strict, the homicide rate is 2.3 times as high as it is among Japanese-Americans living where guns are easily available and gun laws are far less restrictive.

It is possible that the Japanese-American homicide rate was underestimated due to a failure of police officers to consistently note Japanese ancestry of homicide arrestees. However, even if the true Japanese-American share of U.S. homicide arrests were doubled to adjust for this hypothetical data flaw, the homicide rate in Japan would still be higher. A critic could object that there are still many uncontrolled differences between these two populations, and such a critic would be quite correct. These sorts of primitive cross-national comparisons tell us little about the guns–violence link. One would hope, however, that this criticism would be even-handedly applied to all such comparisons, whether used to spuriously buttress either progun or antigun arguments. The preceding exercise merely served to demonstrate that one simple "control" can make an entire cross-national violence rate difference disappear altogether, and even reverse its direction.

The reasoning used in cross-national comparisons is also very selective. Great Britain is often compared with the United States and it is noted that the former not only has a much lower total homicide rate, but also a lower *gun* homicide rate. This fact is supposed to nail down the claim that it is gun ownership that causes the homicide rate differences. However, the absurdity of the logic becomes evident once it is applied to nongun homicides. Britain's rates of knife homicide and of killings with hands and feet are also far lower than the corresponding rates in the United States, but no one is foolish enough to infer from these facts that the lower violence rates were caused by a lower rate of knife ownership in Britain, or to the British having fewer hands and feet than Americans (Greenwood, 1972, p. 37).

In earlier research, a major obstacle to judging whether gun ownership accounts for any of the homicide rate differences between nations was the absence of any actual data on gun ownership levels in the foreign nations compared to the United States. Some previous comparisons had to rely on very indirect indicators of gun levels, such as the gun homicide rate. Curtis (1974, pp. 110–1) compiled data on a miscellany of nations, foreign cities, tribes, and groups of cities, and found a high correlation between the *gun* homicide rate and the *total* homicide rate, similar to the intra-U.S. state-level analysis of Seitz (1972). Apparently both authors believed the association somehow bore on the issue of whether homicide rates were causally affected by gun ownership levels. As previously noted, this association is at least partly an artifact of the presence of gun homicides as a component in the numerator of both the gun homicide rate and the total homicide rate. Curtis did note that the size of the correlation fluctuated wildly, from +0.96 to −0.92, depending on which exact set of cases was included.

What Curtis did not report was another interesting correlation. If one uses his data to compute the correlation (across 25 cases) between the total homicide rate and the *percentage* of homicides committed with guns, it is 0.065, not significantly different from zero. One would think the percentage of homicides committed with guns would be at least a rough indicator of gun availability, at least among violence prone people; this is certainly how many researchers have previously used it (e.g., Brearly 1932; Fisher 1976; Brill 1977; Cook 1979). Thus, Curtis' data indicated that, cross-nationally, there was not even a bivariate association between the homicide rate and an indirect indicator of gun ownership.

Recently, international data based on a more direct measure of gun ownership have become available. Telephone surveys asking about gun ownership were conducted in early 1989 in 14 countries, including the United States. The percentage of households with guns in 11 of these countries was reported by Killias (1990, p. 171), along with their homicide rates. Killias did not statistically analyze his data beyond noting pairwise cross-national comparisons. Generally speaking, nations with higher gun ownership levels had higher total homicide rates—secondary analysis of the published figures yielded a correlation coefficient of 0.774 for the nine nations on which Killias had complete data. Further, the correlation between gun prevalence and the *gun* homicide rate was 0.74. Killias concluded that higher gun ownership levels cause higher homicide rates.

However, what Killias did not note was the fact that countries with higher gun ownership had higher *non*gun homicide rates as well—that correlation was 0.74, just as high as the correlation with gun homicides. This pattern of findings strongly suggests either of two interpretations. (1) Gun ownership levels are a *response* to high violence rates, rather than a cause (as found in Kleck 1984a). The data make more sense from this perspective than from Killias', since one would expect both gun and nongun homicides to increase fear and motivate the acquisition of guns for defense, but one would not expect gun ownership levels to increase nongun homicide rates. (2) Alternatively, gun ownership levels, along with the percentage of homicides committed with guns, may serve as indicators of the population's willingness to inflict lethal violence on others. This too would explain why both gun and nongun homicides should be equally correlated with gun ownership levels—both are influenced by the same "population lethality" variable. Either explanation accords more closely with the full set of associations than the assertion that higher gun ownership levels cause higher homicide rates.

At this point it is safe to say that cross-national comparisons do not provide a sound basis for assessing the impact of gun ownership levels on crime rates.

A City-Level Study of Gun Levels and Violent Crime Rates

The following analysis is a city-level cross-sectional study of the impact of gun ownership levels on violent crime rates (and is adapted from Kleck and Patterson 1991). Data were gathered on all 170 U.S. cities that had a population of 100,000 or larger in 1980. Cities are the smallest, most homogeneous unit or area for which crime data are nationally available. A majority of the reported violent crimes in the United States occurred in these 170 cities (U.S. FBI 1981, p. 173), so the following analysis covers the areas in which most of the violent crime problem is located. Cities smaller than 100,000 could not be included in the sample because person-level vital statistics mortality data, including homicide and suicide data, do not identify locations of deaths for cities with populations smaller than 100,000 (U.S. NCHS 1983, p. 8). These data were needed to obtain city counts of specific subcategories of deaths, such as gun homicides and gun suicides. These counts were essential as components in dependent variables and important as indirect indicators of gun ownership.

Table 5.13 lists the variables used in the city-level analysis of the impact of gun ownership levels. The dependent variables are the rates per 100,000 resident population of homicide, aggravated assault, robbery, rape, and burglary. For the first three of these categories, data were available that allowed separate analyses of rates of violence with guns, without guns, and gun and nongun crimes combined. The analysis covers all of the major categories of crime in which firearms are involved with any significant frequency.

Burglary is rarely committed with guns (Yeager et al. 1976, p. 7). Guns are seldom of much utility to burglars because they rarely confront victims. However, burglary was analyzed for two reasons. First, since residential burglaries occur in the location where a gun-owning householder usually keeps his gun, widespread gun ownership could have a deterrent effect on burglars. However, it has also been argued that the main effect of gun ownership may be to displace burglars from occupied homes to unoccupied homes (Chapter 4; Kleck 1988). Although this would be beneficial in reducing confrontations between burglars and victims, thus reducing burglary-linked injuries, it would not necessarily result in a net reduction in the total burglary rate. Second, analyzing burglary serves as a useful test in detecting spurious or coincidental associations between gun ownership levels and violence rates. For example, if it were found that gun ownership has more of an apparent positive effect on burglary than it does on crimes that frequently involve guns, it would suggest that rather than having a causal effect on violence rates, gun ownership may merely be associated with some other factor that affects crime rates but that was omitted from the models.

The violence rates were averaged over the 3 years, 1979 to 1981, thus bracketing the Census year of 1980 for which data on many of the control variables were available. Three years were covered rather than a single year to minimize the potential measurement error produced by misclassification. Some of the smaller cities had fewer than a half dozen homicides per year; thus misclassification of just one or two homicides as other kinds of deaths could substantially alter a single year's official count. This should reduce error variance. The dependent variables were expressed in natural logs. This transformation made the initially skewed distribution of the dependent variable (and therefore of the residuals) more nearly normal, and stabilized the variance of the residuals, reducing heteroscedasticity.

Models of violence rates were estimated using LISREL methods (Joreskog 1973; Joreskog and Sorbom 1981a,b), primarily because the gun ownership level was not directly measured and was treated as a latent construct. Also, LISREL was appropriate for estimating models in which a simultaneous reciprocal relationship was specified between violence rates and gun levels, based on the idea that higher violence rates could motivate gun acquisition, in addition to gun ownership increasing violence rates.

The structural models therefore each contain two endogenous variables: the crime rate and gun ownership. For purposes of estimation, crime rates were assumed to be perfectly measured, whereas gun ownership was treated as a latent construct with multiple indicators (i.e., four to five indicators or manifest variables—see Smith and Patterson 1985). For purposes of scaling the latent construct, in each measurement model one loading was constrained to the value of 1.00 (Stapleton 1977; Joreskog and Sorbom 1981a).

Exogenous variables presented in the models represent only a subset of variables that were initially hypothesized as affecting violence rates. Exogenous variables remaining represent those that showed a significant association with violence rates below the .10 level of significance using OLS. In the models these variables were treated as if they were perfectly measured.

Measuring aggregate levels of gun availability for cities is problematic. One fairly direct method would be to use survey data. Although many national surveys have asked gun ownership questions, the surveys do not provide sufficient cases for single-city estimates for most of the cities, even when many surveys are combined. Instead gun availability was measured using multiple indirect indicators. For cities, Cook (1979) used a simple index consisting of the average of two indicators: the percentage of suicides committed with guns and the percentage of nonfelony-related homicides committed with guns. He showed this measure to be highly correlated with survey measures of urban household gun prevalence aggregated over nine census regions, indicating validity for purposes of cross-sectional analyses. Earlier researchers had used similar indirect measures (Brearley 1932, p. 71; Seitz 1972; Curtis 1974, p. 110; Brill 1977, p. 20). These measures were improved by using a total of as many as five indicators of city gun ownership levels: (1) percentage of suicides committed with guns, 1979–1982, (2) percentage of homicides committed with guns, 1979–1982, (3) percentage of aggravated assaults known to the police committed with guns, 1979–1980, (4) percentage of robberies known to the police committed with guns, 1979–1980, and (5) percentage of the dollar value of all stolen property reported to the police that was due to firearms thefts, 1979–1981. Four other indicators were also evaluated: the fatal gun accident rate, the rate of subscriptions to gun/outdoor sport magazines, the rate of National Rifle Association members, and the rate of contributors to the Second Amendment Foundation, another gun owners group. However, in a factor analysis these did not load with the other indicators.

Validation of the Gun Ownership Measure

Following Cook (1979), the validity of the gun indicators was assessed by measuring their associations with survey-based measures of gun ownership. As previously noted, there are insufficient cases in national surveys for the gun prevalence of most cities to be measured. Instead, the results of three national surveys, the General Social Surveys for 1980, 1982, and 1984, were combined to compute reported gun ownership prevalence figures for the nine major U.S. census regions, among persons living in places of 100,000 or larger population. Comparable measures were computed for each of the gun indicator variables, weighting each city measure by the city's population and calculating a weighted big city regional measure for each of the nine regions.

All but one of the five indirect gun indicators were strongly correlated with the survey measures of gun availability in the nine regions, and the indicators were highly correlated among themselves. The only indicator about which there is some doubt is one of the two used by Cook (1979)—the percentage of homicides committed with guns. It was correlated only 0.38 with the survey-based percentage of households reporting a gun, over the nine regions, an association not significantly different from zero. The other indicators showed the following correlations with the percentage of households reporting a gun: 0.69 for percentage of aggravated assaults committed with a gun, 0.83 for percentage of robberies committed with a gun, 0.86 for percentage of suicides committed with guns, and 0.90 for percentage of the value of reported stolen property attributable to guns. The stolen guns measure, not previously used in gun research, was the best single indicator of gun ownership. These results were confirmed using survey-based measures of respondent (as opposed to household) gun ownership and both household and respondent ownership of handguns.

All of the indicators were more strongly associated with survey measures of handgun ownership than with gun ownership in general. Thus the measure may mainly tap handgun ownership. This is not surprising, since most of the indicators seem to be oriented to measuring gun availability among criminals, and handguns are the predominant gun type involved in crime. On the other hand, the indicators are also less strongly associated with gun ownership among self-reported arrestees than with gun ownership among nonarrestees. Thus, the indicators seem to most strongly reflect noncriminal handgun ownership. In any case, these distinctions are a bit tenuous, since survey-measured ownership among self-reported arrestees and among nonarrestees are highly correlated with each other, indicating that criminal and noncriminal ownership are highly correlated. This would mean that if they could be separately measured for cities, each could serve as a good surrogate for the other, but also that it would be hard to empirically distinguish their separate effects. Consequently, it would seem prudent to interpret the indicators as reflecting general gun ownership, i.e., ownership in the entire population, without distinguishing ownership among criminals from ownership among noncriminals (see Kleck and Patterson 1990 for further details of the validation.)

In each model, when the dependent variable could bear an artifactual association to one of the gun ownership indicators, that indicator was deleted. Thus, the percentage of homicides involving guns was omitted from the homicide model, the gun percentage of assaults was omitted from the aggravated assault model, and the gun percentage of robberies was omitted from the robbery model.

Most of the violence predictors besides the gun ownership indicators were simply measures of the relative sizes of population groups that have especially high or low violence rates, of the prevalence of statuses that frequently give rise to violence, such as divorce, alcoholism, and unemployment, or of social integration, isolation, or transience. They were chosen on the basis of a review of prior studies of violence and crime rates done at the city or metropolitan area level—those that had been consistently found to be significant predictors were specified in initial versions of the corresponding models.

A few of the predictors are sufficiently uncommon to require comment. College enrollment was specified as a predictor of violence rates as a way of controlling for prevalence of city residents with low current income but predominantly middle class origins, culture, and economic prospects, a group both low in violence and high in support for gun control (Wright et al. 1983). Mortality data were used to roughly control for the size of substance-abusing segments of city populations. Alcoholic liver disease deaths per capita served as an indicator of alcohol abuse, whereas per capita deaths due to nonmedical accidental poisoning by opiates served as an indicator of opiates abuse. Since it is questionable how consistently substance abuse-linked deaths are recorded as such on death certificates, estimates for these variables should be interpreted cautiously.

As with nearly all aggregate analyses of violence, the present study uses ratio variables, with city population being the denominator in many variables, both exogenous and endogenous. Many critics have argued that the presence of common components in ratio variables can lead to biased, tautological, or artifactual associations. Firebaugh and Gibbs (1985, p. 715) recommended that if one seeks unbiased coefficient estimates in a regression model containing both endogenous and exogenous variables with a common component (commonly population size) in the denominator, one should also include one divided by the common component as another predictor. Thus all models include one divided by resident population (in 100,000s) as a predictor of violence rates, in addition to those predictors that were computed by dividing some number by the population in 100,000s.

There is another problem related to use of population figures. Computing aggregate crime variables as per capita rates is conventionally done to control for the size of the population at risk of either committing crimes or being victimized in crime. Standard city resident population figures, however, are not completely adequate for this purpose because they do not count nonresident persons at risk, including daily commuters and visitors such as tourists and business travelers. The omission of commuters was controlled by including as a separate predictor the city population as a fraction of the surrounding metropolitan area, on the assumption that cities located in much larger metropolitan areas are likely to have more commuters, in which case resident population would be a more serious underestimate of the population at risk. The contribution of short-term visitors was controlled by including as a separate predictor a "visitors index": the per capita total receipts for hotels, motels, and other lodging places, for the metropolitan area in which a city is located, for 1977. This is an especially important control for cities with large numbers of tourists relative to resident population, such as Las Vegas, Orlando (Disney World), and Miami.

The relationships between gun ownership and crime levels were treated as reciprocal, based on the assumption that although gun levels may affect violence levels, crime and violence may also motivate gun acquisitions (Kleck 1984a). The rate of subscriptions to gun-related magazines and the state hunting license rate were used as indicators of recreational interest in firearms and the prevalence of a gun sporting subculture. They served as instruments that should have a direct effect on gun ownership but not on violence or crime rates, thereby permitting identification of the model.

Tables 5.14 and 5.15 present the main statistical results. In each model the value of PSI represents the unexplained variance in the endogenous variables, since these coefficients come from a standardized solution in which the variance of the latent variable, gun ownership, has been scaled to 1.0. Thus, for example, the proportion of the variance explained in total homicide rates is 1 − .256 = .744 (Joreskog and Sorbom 1981a). The tables also present the degrees of freedom, chi-square, and goodness of fit index for each of the models (see Wheaton 1988; Bollen and Liang 1988; Bollen 1989 for discussions of overall model fit).

Because the estimated models are quite large, estimates are reported in two tables, one covering estimated effects of control variables and the other covering estimated effects of gun laws and gun ownership. Table 5.14 reports standardized LISREL parameter estimates for the control variables used in each of the five models. These estimates indicate, for example, that city assault rates are significantly higher in cities in which poverty (RPOV), alcohol abuse (ALCHLSM), and divorce (CNTDIVRT) are high but significantly lower in areas with large college enrollment rates (COLLEGE) and areas in which the city population makes up a smaller percentage of the metropolitan area population (PCTSMSA). Because these effects are secondary to this book's concerns, the remainder of these findings are left to the interested reader.

Table 5.15 presents standardized LISREL solutions for estimated effects of gun ownership on the five total crime rates as well as the rates for gun and nongun violence rates for three of the types of violence (homicide, assault, and robbery). In addition, the estimated effects of violence rates on gun ownership are shown.

With two exceptions, levels of general gun ownership had little apparent effect on violence rates (see coefficients in Gun ownership row of each panel). One exception is the homicide model where gun ownership appeared to have a significant *negative* effect on the violence rate. The only result in Table 5.15 that supports the view that gun levels have a net positive effect on crime or violence as for burglary, a crime that rarely involves guns. Because it is implausible that gun ownership would increase the frequency of crimes that do *not* involve guns, and not increase crimes that *do* involve guns, the association is probably due either to a coincidental association of gun ownership with an omitted variable that affects burglary rates, or to a positive effect of burglary rates on gun ownership that has not been adequately modeled.

Based on the individual-level findings, a reasonable prediction about aggregate rates would be that gun availability would have a negative effect on rates of assaults resulting in attack and on rates of assaults with injury, whereas the overall net effect on the homicide rate should be essentially zero, or perhaps slightly positive. Unfortunately, FBI data count total aggravated assaults, which include both threats and actual attacks, and both attacks with injury and those without. The city-level data indicate that gun levels have no net impact on aggravated *assault* rates, i.e., on the total rate of both threats and attacks combined, but they cannot tell us the net impact of gun levels on rates of attack or of assault injury. The city data also indicate that gun levels have no net effect on the total homicide rate, as would be expected based on the results of the individual-level analysis.

Note that it is possible that having a gun emboldens some people to enter into situations, settings, and confrontations likely to result in violence. Once in such a situation, the net effect of an aggressor having a gun on the probability of inflicting a death may be zero, yet gun availability could still increase the total homicide rate by increasing the rate at which people enter into such "assault-prone" situations. This possibility cannot be directly assessed because there are no data on the frequency of such encounters.

As expected, homicide and rape rates appear to have a positive effect on gun ownership, confirming national time series findings (Kleck 1979; 1984a), and supporting those survey studies that found gun ownership to be related to crime rates in surrounding areas (Chapter 2). However, results did not support such an effect for assault, robbery, or burglary (Table 5.15).

Although the measurement of gun availability is probably superior to any previously used in aggregate-level research, it is not adequate for the purpose of distinguishing gun ownership among more violence-prone subsets of the population from ownership levels in the general public. Also, some of the indicators of gun ownership can each also be interpreted as indicators of the seriousness of violent motivations of a city's residents. If a large fraction of a city's aggressors selects serious weapons such as guns to carry out their intentions, this may indicate that a large fraction of them was seriously intent on producing a death. Note, however, that this problem would tend to positively bias the apparent effect of "gun ownership" on violence, i.e., make it seem there was more of an effect than their really was, since weapon effects would be confounded with the effects of aggressor "seriousness." Thus, correcting this flaw would tend only to strengthen the present conclusions that gun ownership levels have no net positive effect on violent crime rates.

Analysts always need to be skeptical about restrictions used to achieve identifiability in structural equation models. The key identification restrictions needed to model the assumed reciprocal relationship between gun ownership and violence rates were the exclusion of gun magazine subscription rates and hunting license rates from the crime equations. Interest in hunting and other gun-related sports was assumed to affect gun ownership rates but to not directly affect crime rates. Some have argued that such interests may reflect, or even generate, proviolent attitudes, but Krug (1968), Eskridge (1986), and Bordua (1986) have all found hunting license rates to have small-to-moderate *negative* associations with violence rates.

Why do gun ownership levels have no apparent net positive effect on violent crime rates, either in the present study or in many previous ones? For burglary and rape, guns are rarely involved (U.S. Bureau of Justice Statistics 1987a), and rarely necessary or helpful in committing those crimes. Thus there was no strong a priori reason to expect a positive effect of gun ownership on these crimes.

There was also no support for the idea that gun ownership deters burglars in a way that produces a net negative effect on the total burglary rate, since the apparent effect was positive. However, the deterrence hypothesis received only a partial test, since home gun ownership should mainly affect residential burglary, whereas the published FBI data cover nonresidential burglaries as well. Since another effect of victim gun ownership might be displacement of burglars from occupied homes to unoccupied homes and nonresidential targets (Chapter 4; Kleck 1988), it is not clear what the net effect would be on total burglary rates. A more relevant test will have to focus on residential burglaries separately, with an attempt to measure occupancy of burglary targets.

The lack of any apparent effect of gun levels on the crime rates could be due to counterbalancing effects of opposite sign, with criminal ownership increasing violence and noncriminal ownership decreasing it due to deterrent effects of ownership among prospective victims. If this were so, it might still be useful to reduce gun levels among criminals if measures used to accomplish this did not also reduce gun levels among noncriminals to an equal or greater degree.

As previously noted, robber gun possession can have a mixture of both positive and negative effects on robbery rates. Also, gun ownership by prospective victims, especially retail store owners, may deter some robbery attempts (Chapter 4; Wright and Rossi 1986, pp. 141–59; Kleck 1988). The present results confirm the findings of the two best previous studies of city gun ownership and robbery rates, which also found no evidence of a net impact of gun ownership levels on the total robbery rate (Cook 1979; McDowall 1986). They are consistent with an interpretation that effects of opposite sign cancel each other out so as to produce no net effect on the total robbery rate. The findings also indicate that gun ownership levels increase gun robbery and decrease nongun robbery, producing no net effect on total robbery rates (Table 5.15, third panel), just as Cook (1979) and McDowall (1986) found. Because gun robberies are less likely to involve injury, the results are consistent with the hypothesis that higher gun levels reduce robbery injury rates.

In assaultive crimes such as homicide and aggravated assault, gun availability also seems to have a mixture of positive and negative effects. The present aggregate level findings are consistent with a claim that the negative, violence-reducing effects of gun availability, noted in the individual-level analysis, may outweigh the violence-increasing lethality effect, since the findings indicate a net negative association of gun ownership with city homicide rates. It certainly is possible that gun ownership among prospective victims could deter some homicidal attacks. Nevertheless, this surprising result is not emphasized, partly because it contradicts the findings of time series research indicating no net effect, positive or negative, of gun ownership levels on the homicide rate (Kleck 1984a).

It might be argued that positive effects of gun ownership levels are not evident in a sample of U.S. cities because there is little meaningful variation in gun ownership, all U.S. cities supposedly being awash in guns. Empirical evidence indicates otherwise. There is great cross-city variation in all of the indirect indicators of gun ownership (Table 5.12). Surveys have likewise always indicated tremendous variation across U.S. regions. For example, only 24% of New England households reported a gun, compared to 61% in Rocky Mountain states (Table 2.5). Likewise, variation within states, across counties is very large, whether measured with surveys or gun license data (Bordua et al. 1979). Further, if one cumulates results from 11 national General Social Surveys (GSS) conducted between 1973 and 1989, direct survey measures of gun prevalence can be computed for very large cities, with reasonably large sample sizes. These data indicate enormous cross-city variation in gun ownership within the United States, from very high rates greater than any known to exist outside the United States, to very low rates below those common in the Western European nations often compared with the United States. For example, while the percentage of households reporting a gun was about 61% in Houston and 56% in Birmingham (and probably still higher in many smaller cities), it was only 6% in New York City and 7% in Boston (author's analysis of GSS data).

Nevertheless, one might argue that all of this variation is at a relatively high level, and that one could observe the lower crime rates that would result from lower gun ownership rates only if the latter got down to *very* low levels—levels that are not only lower than those commonly observed in the United States, but are also lower than the 9–33% household gun prevalence levels found in Western European nations (see Killias 1990). Therefore, data from another nation with indisputably low levels of gun ownership are now analyzed.

An English Test of the Link between Guns and Crime Rates

The leading study of English gun control was conducted by Colin Greenwood, who compiled tables of data on gun crimes and rates of legal gun owners in all 47 English police force areas, as of 1969 (1972, pp. 220–23). Greenwood performed no statistical analysis of these data, but informally concluded that "the rate of armed crime is in no way connected with the density of firearms in the community. Indeed, if anything, the reverse appears to be true. The legitimate use of firearms is largely a rural pursuit, and crime is largely a city pursuit" (p. 219).

It is worth analyzing Greenwood's data, both to more rigorously confirm his null finding, and to test his urban/rural explanation. His counts of crimes were translated into per capita crime rates and correlation coefficients between the rate of legal gun owners (firearms or shotgun certificate holders per 100 households) and the rates of "robberies involving firearms" and rates of "indictable offenses firearms" were computed. It was not possible to do more extensive multivariate analyses because Greenwood's police areas do not correspond to the areas for which other data are available.

Greenwood was correct: the legal gun owner rate correlated −.17 with both crime rates. However, although legal gun ownership rates are indeed higher in rural areas, this does not account for the absence of a positive association between gun ownership and crime. Greenwood classified each of the 47 areas of England into four urban–rural types: (1) Rural, (2) Rural/Urban, (3) Urban/Rural, and (4) City or Urban (these two have been combined together, as only one area was "Urban"). Correlations of the legal gun ownership rate even *within* these areas (i.e., controlling for urbanness) were all nonsignificant and were negative in two of the four area types (correlations with the indictable firearms offenses rate were −.12, −.47, .48, and .05 within the four types of areas, respectively). This corresponds with the results of similar county-level multivariate analyses performed on Illinois legal gun-owner data by David Bordua and his colleagues (Bordua 1986; Bordua and Lizotte 1979; Bordua et al. 1979). Legal gun ownership is generally either unrelated or negatively related to gun crime rates, even controlling for urbanness. Note that this is true of *gun* crime rates—if legal gun ownership levels are unrelated to gun crime rates, they are even less likely to be related to total crime rates (Table 5.15). Note also that there were no controls for the possible positive effect of crime rates on gun ownership; doing so would presumably reduce even further any impression of a positive effect of gun ownership on crime rates.

It should not be thought that gun ownership did not vary across English areas—the rate of certificate holders per 100 households varied from an extremely low 0.4 in Liverpool to a surprisingly high 16.7 in rural Suffolk. In the latter area, legal gun ownership was higher than all self-reported gun ownership, legal and illegal, is in some areas of the United States. Therefore, considerable variation in legal gun ownership rates at a generally very low level was unrelated to variation in crime rates, just as was true with considerable gun variation at higher levels in the United States. On the other hand, if criminal gun ownership could somehow have been separately measured, results might have been different.

Conclusions

When aggressors possess guns, this has many effects on the outcome of violent incidents, some tending to make harmful outcomes more likely, some making them less likely. Gun possession probably facilitates some attacks by less powerful aggressors against more powerful victims, and may elicit aggression in at least some circumstances, whereas gun ıse probably increases the probability of death if a wound is inflicted. On the other hand, possession of guns has the overall effect of reducing the likelihood of attack, probably because it often makes attack unnecessary, and of reducing the probability of an injury being inflicted, perhaps due to the difficulty of aiming guns accurately. The aggregate level analysis of violent crime rates indicated that the net impact of all the various individual effects of gun possession, among prospective victims and aggressors combined, was not significantly different from zero.

Consequently, the assumption that general gun availability positively affects the frequency or average seriousness of violent crimes is not supported. The policy implication is that there appears to be nothing to be gained from reducing the general gun ownership level. Nevertheless, one still cannot reject the possibility that gun ownership among high-risk subsets of the population may increase violence rates. Likewise, the immediate availability of guns produced by gun carrying might increase violence rates even if gun ownership levels do not. Further, gun controls might also be justified on the basis of their potential for reducing deaths from suicides and gun accidents. These last two topics are addressed in Chapters 6 and 7.

Table 5.1. Guns and the Facilitation of Homicide[a]

	% of Homicides Involving Guns (Base Frequencies in Parentheses)	
	Sex of Attacker	
	Male	Female
Sex of victim		
Male	68.4 (9096)	63.5 (1779)
Female	59.6 (2737)	39.2 (268)
	Age of Attacker	
	16–39	Other
Age of victim		
16–39	68.3 (7529)	72.5 (3758)
Other	49.5 (2919)	61.9 (3155)
	Number of Attackers	
	2 or more	One
Number of victims		
2 or more	70.3 (91)	69.4 (301)
One	60.7 (1492)	66.0 (12035)

[a] Cases are murders or nonnegligent manslaughters that ocurred in the United States in 1980 and were reported to the FBI's SHR program.

Source: 1980 Supplementary Homicide Reports (ICPSR 1984a).

Table 5.2. Summary of "Weapons Effect" Experimental Studies
A. Results of Individual Studies[a]

Studies	*Measure of Aggression*	*Real Weapon?*	*Subjects*	*Weapon Linked with Aggressor?*
Supportive				
Berkowitz and LePage (1967)	M	M	M	L
Boyanowsky and Griffiths (1982)	L	M	L	L
Caprara et al. (1984)	M	L	L	L
Frodi (1973)	L	M	L	L
Leyens and Parke (1975)	L	L	L	L
Mendoza (1972)	L	L	L	L
Page and O'Neal (1975)	M	L	M	L
Simons et al. (1975)	L	M	M	L
Simons and Turner (1975)	M	M	M	L
Turner and Goldsmith (1976)	L	L	L	L
Mixed Findings				
Fraczek and Macaulay (1971)	M	M	M	L
Turner et al. (1975)	L	M	M	L
Contrary				
Buss et al. (1972)	M	L	M	M
Cahoon and Edwards (1984)	L	M	M	L
Cahoon and Edwards (1985)	L	M	M	L
Ellis et al. (1971)	M	M	M	L
Fisher et al. (1969)	M	M	M	L
Halderman and Jackson (1979)	L	M	M	L
Page and Scheidt (1971)	M	M	M	L
Tannenbaum (1971)	M	L	M	M
Turner and Simons (1974)	M	M	M	L

[a] M, study was more relevant to real-world gun violence in United States; L, study was less relevant or realistic. In Panel B, the first study condition listed, of each pair, is considered to be the more relevant and realistic one.

(continued)

Table 5.2. (Continued)
B. Patterns of Findings in Studies

Characteristic	*Condition*	*Results*[a]
Type of aggression Ss believed they were inflicting	Painful electric shocks	4/1/6
	Play aggression, horn honking, hypothetical aggression, etc.	6/1/3
Weapon stimulus	Real weapons	5/2/7
	Toy weapons, pictures, etc.	5/0/2
Subjects	U.S. adults, adolescents	4/2/9
	Non-U.S. or children	6/0/0
Weapon associated with aggressor?	Yes	0/0/1
	No	10/2/8
Overall relevance to real violence in United States	High[b]	2/1/4
	Low	8/1/5
All studies		10/2/9

[a] Number of studies with findings generally (1) supportive of / (2) mixed / (3) contrary to "weapons effect" hypothesis.
[b] "High" overall relevance means Ss were U.S. adults or adolescents, believed they were inflicting physical pain on another person, and were exposed to real weapons; "Low" means all other studies. (There were no studies with all three of these attributes and the weapon was also associated with the aggressor.)

Table 5.3. Assault Wound Death Rates by Weapon Type, U.S. 1988

	Total	*Gunshot Wound*	*Knife Wound*	*Injury from Other Weapon*	*No Weapon*
Simple assaults	860000	0	0	0	860000
Aggravated assaults[a]	571000	22190	40062	325956	33118
Homicides[b]	18901	11869	3744	2069	1220
Assaults + homicides	1449901	34059	43806	328025	894338
Death rate[c]	0.0130	0.3485	0.0855	0.0063	0.0014

Ratio of gunshot death rate over knife death rate = 4.08

[a] Aggravated assaults completed with injury—gunshot and knife wound figures reflect the fact that only some injuries inflicted by attackers possessing guns or knives actually involved injuries inflicted by those weapons.
[b] Murders and nonnegligent manslaughters, excluding those linked with robbery or rape. Killings involving guns of unknown type were allocated across gun type categories according to the distribution among cases with known gun type. Killings where weapon type was among cases with known gun type. Killings where weapon type was not stated at all were similarly allocated.
[c] Homicides/(assaults + homicides). The absolute size of these death rates is far too high, due to a serious undercount of woundings in the NCS (Cook 1985). They are computed only for purposes of comparing the gun rate with the knife rate, on the assumption that gun and knife woundings are roughly equally undercounted.
Sources: Assaults: U.S. Bureau of Justice Statistics (1989a) for total number of assaults, U.S. BJS (1989b, p. 64) for assault distribution by weapon type. Homicides: U.S. FBI (1989, pp. 12–14, 47). Fraction of gun and knife assaults with injury that involved gunshot or knife wounds: U.S. BJS (1986b).

Table 5.4. Offender "Seriousness" and Weapon "Seriousness"[a]

	Self-Reported Lifetime Arrests			
Weapons Used[b]	*1*	*2–5*	*6 or More*	*Total*
No weapon	21	55	29	105
Nongun weapon	20	69	92	191
Handgun only	37	166	173	376
Long gun only	9	44	35	88
Long gun and handgun	7	25	36	68
Total	94	369	365	828
% Armed	78	85	92	87
% Armed with gun	56	64	67	64
% Armed with long gun	17	19	19	19

	Self-Reported Lifetime Assaults			
Weapons Used[b]	*Never or Once*	*A few*	*10 or More*	*Total*
No weapon	21	41	17	79
Nongun weapon	31	94	54	179
Handgun only	47	141	117	305
Long gun only	13	46	22	81
Long gun and handgun	3	35	32	70
Total	115	357	242	714
% Armed	82	89	93	89
% Armed with gun	55	62	71	64
% Armed with long gun	14	23	22	21

[a] Table covers all felons in 10 state survey who reported being incarcerated for an assaultive crime—murder, manslaughter, attempted murder, aggravated assault, or simple assault—and who indicated how they were armed when they committed the crime.
[b] Weapons with which felons were armed when they committed the offense for which they had been imprisoned.
Source: Secondary analysis of ICPSR (1986).

Table 5.5. Weapons and Crime Completion in Rape and Robbery

	Rape		Robbery	
Offender Weapon(s)	*% with Weapon*	*% Completed*	*% with Weapon*	*% Completed*
Gun	9.5	48.7	20.0	78.8
Knife	10.7	41.9	16.7	60.6
Other weapons	4.1	19.8	10.0	55.5
Weapons, type unknown	1.1	42.3	2.4	67.7
Unarmed	63.9	28.1	39.7	56.6
Unknown if armed	3.8	22.0	11.2	60.8

Source: U.S. Bureau of Justice Statistics (1986b, pp. 3–4; adapted from Tables 5 and 10). Covers violent crime victimizations reported in National Crime Surveys, 1973–1982.

Table 5.6. Rates of Attack, Injury, and Medical Treatment in Violent Crimes, by Weapon Type

	Offender Weapon(s)					
	Gun	*Knife*	*Other Weapon*	*Combination*	*Weapon, Type Unknown*	*No Weapon*
% Attacked	36.6	42.7	62.8	58.2	56.1	52.1
% Injured	14.0	24.9	45.0	37.9	42.5	29.9
% Injured, among those attacked	38.3	58.3	71.7	65.1	75.8	57.4
% Received medical care	7.5	13.6	22.0	21.1	18.9	10.4
% Got medical care, among injured	53.6	54.6	48.9	55.7	44.5	34.8
% Received hospital care	6.2	10.1	15.5	14.5	13.3	5.6
% Hospital care, among injured	44.3	40.6	34.4	38.3	31.3	18.7
Median days of hospital care	7.3	5.0	4.1	—	—	3.5

Source: U.S. Bureau of Justice Statistics (1986b, pp. 4, 6; computed from data in Table 12). Table covers violent crime victimizations reported in the 1973–1982 National Crime Surveys.

Table 5.7. Variables in the Individual-Level Analysis

Name	Interpretation	Dataset: NCS Assaults, 1979–85 Mean	SD	NCS Attacks, 1979–85 Mean	SD	NCS/SHR Injuries 1982 Mean	SD
ATTACK	Victim attacked	.495	.500	1.000	0.000	1.000	0.000
INJURY	Victim injured	.258	.438	.522	.500	1.000	0.000
DEATH	Victim killed	0.000	0.000	0.000	0.000	.014	.119
HGUNPRES	O[a] had handgun	.114	.318	.061	.239		
OGUNPRES	O had other gun	.022	.147	.014	.120		
KNIFPRES	O had knife	.122	.328	.107	.309		
OWEPPRES	O had other weapon	.136	.343	.170	.376		
HANDGUN	Handgun used in attack (shot or shot at)	.011	.103	.022	.146	.021	.144
OTHERGUN	Other gun used in attack (shot or shot at)	.004	.065	.009	.093	.004	.060
KNIFE	Knife used in attack	.021	.144	.043	.202	.056	.230
OTHRWEAP	Other weapon used	.061	.239	.123	.329	.168	.374
UNDTWEAP	Undetermined weapon used in attack	.010	.099	.018	.133	.000	.016
HGSHOT	V shot with handgun					.021	.144
OGSHOT	V shot with other gun					.004	.060
KNIFED	V wounded with knife					.056	.230
CLUBBED	V injured with blunt object					.223	.416
OWEPINJ	V injured with other weapon					.017	.131
SERIES	Series incident	.057	.232	.037	.189		
INCOME	V household income	8.120	3.947	8.005	3.962		
EDUCATN	Victim's years of formal schooling	15.790	6.475	15.260	6.420		
MARRIED	Victim married	.329	.470	.286	.452		
GUNOCC	V in gun-carrying occupation	.038	.192	.040	.195		
BLAKVICT	Black victim	.136	.343	.136	.343	.119	.324
MALEVICT	Male victim	.703	.457	.698	.459	.730	.444
AOLE11	O age 11 or under	.010	.099	.014	.116	.004	.062
AOGE30	O age 30 or over	.236	.425	.197	.398	.202	.402
MALEOFF	Male offender	.942	.233	.936	.244	.941	.236
UNDRACEO	O race undetermined	.021	.143	.022	.146	.025	.156
AGEDIF	Age advantage to O	.210	.407	.209	.407	.269	.444
SEXDIF	Sex advantage to O	.257	.437	.257	.437	.228	.420
NUMDIF	Number offenders minus number of victims	.767	2.787	.910	3.219	.814	1.928
ROBBERY	Robbery involved	.286	.452	.317	.465	.335	.472
BURGLARY	Burglary involved	.038	.192	.030	.170	.032	.176
RAPE	Rape involved	.029	.166	.037	.189	.042	.202
POPGE250	Occurred in city of 250K+ population	.324	.468	.331	.471	.307	.461
SUMMER	Occurred June–August	.279	.448	.283	.450	.270	.444
DARK	Dark at the time	.542	.498	.578	.494		
INSIDE	Occurred indoors	.267	.442	.241	.428		

[a] V, victim; O, offender. Blank spaces indicate variable did not exist in that dataset.

Table 5.8. ATTACK Equations

	Coefficients (Ratio, Coefficient/Standard Error)				
	1[a] *OLS*[b]	*2*[a] *Probit*[b]	*3*[a] *Probit*[b]	*4*[a] *Probit*[b]	*5*[a] *Probit*[b] *Reported*
Variable	*All*[c]	*All*[c]	*Nonfelony*[c]	*Nonseries*[c]	*to Police*[c]
HGUNPRES	−.2836	−.7704	−.6084	−.7769	−.9310
	(−22.40)	(−21.64)	(−12.74)	(−21.57)	(−17.00)
OGUNPRES	−.1579	−.4223	−.3040	−.4451	−.6650
	(−5.90)	(−5.76)	(−3.60)	(−5.93)	(−6.02)
KNIFPRES	−.1246	−.3259	−.2264	−.3392	−.3860
	(−10.13)	(−9.94)	(−5.07)	(−10.16)	(−7.05)
OWEPPRES	.0961	.2545	.2702	.2422	.1614
	(8.27)	(8.14)	(7.59)	(7.54)	(2.89)
AOLE11	.1681	.4654	.5135	.4385	.1804
	(4.22)	(4.17)	(3.95)	(3.78)	(0.87)
AOGE30	−.0632	−.1668	−.2092	−.1746	−.0709
	(−6.68)	(−6.56)	(−7.21)	(−6.67)	(−1.59)
EDUCATN	−.0053	−.0741	−.0179	−.0141	−.0074
	(−8.53)	(−8.44)	(−8.92)	(−8.23)	(−2.52)
MARRIED	−.0640	−.1699	−.1799	−.1658	−.1617
	(−7.49)	(−7.41)	(−6.64)	(−7.01)	(−4.12)
GUNOCC	.0769	.2081	.2162	.2528	.2647
	(3.69)	(3.71)	(3.69)	(4.05)	(2.93)
ROBBERY	.0895	.2391	—	.2391	.3112
	(9.70)	(9.60)		(9.47)	(7.30)
BURGLARY	−.0785	−.2056	—	−.1963	−.1917
	(−3.60)	(−3.49)		(−3.27)	(−2.32)
INSIDE	−.0293	−.0820	−.0966	−.0751	−.1759
	(−3.05)	(−3.18)	(−3.42)	(−2.81)	(−3.51)
SERIES	−.1885	−.5075	−.5032	—	−.3922
	(−10.98)	(−10.72)	(−10.10)		(−4.45)
DARK	.8418	.2256	.2609	.2222	.1786
	(10.46)	(10.44)	(10.09)	(9.98)	(4.65)
Constant	.5987	.2592	.2900	.2627	.3031
Log-likelihood	(0.08)[d]	−9704.3	−6830.5	−9167.6	−3030.6
Sample (n)	14,922	14,922	10,420	14,040	4,772

[a] Equation.

[b] Estimation method.

[c] Sample.

[d] Adjusted R^2.

Table 5.9. INJURY Equations

	Coefficients (Ratio, Coefficient/Standard Error)					
	6[a] *OLS*[b]	*7*[a] *Probit*[b]	*8*[a] *Bivariate*[b]	*9*[a] *Bivariate*[b]	*10*[a] *Bivariate*[b]	*11*[a] *Bivariate*[b]
Variable	*All*[c]	*All*[c]	*All*[c]	*Nonfelony*[c]	*Nonseries*[c]	*Reported to Police*[c]
HANDGUN	−.3136	−.9267	−.9257	−1.1858	−.9391	−1.3116
	(−8.03)	(−7.75)	(−7.85)	(−8.22)	(−7.77)	(−5.88)
OTHERGUN	−.3506	−1.1619	−1.1619	−1.1912	−1.1386	−1.2612
	(−5.72)	(−5.40)	(−7.10)	(−6.67)	(−6.82)	(−4.37)
KNIFE	.1357	.3625	.3625	.1674	.3704	.3418
	(4.81)	(4.72)	(4.56)	(1.70)	(4.53)	(2.33)
OTHRWEAP	.2058	.5597	.5597	.4623	.5770	.5747
	(11.81)	(11.64)	(11.18)	(7.95)	(11.15)	(6.56)
EDUCATN	−.0043	−.1142	−.0113	−.0187	−.0116	−.0070
	(−4.76)	(−4.78)	(−4.42)	(−5.50)	(−4.39)	(−1.62)
INCOME	−.0035	−.0094	−.0095	−.0152	−.0104	−.0090
	(−2.40)	(−2.43)	(−2.43)	(−3.17)	(−2.62)	(−1.27)
GUNOCC	−.0799	−.2133	−.2133	−.0851	−.1943	−.1524
	(−2.73)	(−2.73)	(−2.87)	(−1.07)	(−2.41)	(−1.24)
SEXDIF	−.0537	−.1403	−.1403	−.2623	−.1618	−.1494
	(−3.82)	(−3.79)	(−3.79)	(−5.41)	(−4.32)	(−2.43)
AGEDIF	.5592	.1482	.1482	.1113	.1503	.0377
	(3.95)	(3.95)	(3.96)	(2.26)	(3.93)	(0.63)
RAPE	.1324	.3428	.3428		.3544	.2227
	(4.19)	(4.09)	(3.87)		(3.95)	(1.61)
ROBBERY	.0615	.1647	.1647		.1602	.2454
	(4.85)	(4.90)	(4.57)		(4.39)	(4.05)
DARK	.1121	.2943	.2942	.2503	.2940	.1953
	(9.60)	(9.54)	(8.95)	(5.67)	(8.67)	(3.54)
Constant	.5104	.0298	.0298	.3079	.0576	.0775
Log-likelihood	(0.06)[d]	−4800	−14542	−10062	−13796	−4623
Sample (n)	7300	7300	7300	4937	7007	2400

[a] Equation.
[b] Estimation method.
[c] Subsample.
[d] Adjusted R^2

Table 5.10. DEATH Equations

	Coefficients (Ratio, Coefficient/Standard Error)				
	12[a] *OLS[b]*	*13[a]* *Probit[b]*	*14[a]* *Bivariate[b]*	*15[a]* *Bivariate[b]*	*16[a]* *Probit[b,d]* *Reported*
Variable	*All[c]*	*All[c]*	*All[c]*	*Nonfelony[c]*	*to Police[c]*
HGSHOT	.3782	2.964	2.602	3.093	3.282
	(35.28)	(12.49)	(13.53)	(2.97)	(17.59)
OGSHOT	.3948	2.773	2.531	2.654	7.261
	(15.41)	(7.29)	(4.63)	(2.58)	(0.28)
KNIFED	.0438	1.397	1.679	1.728	1.264
	(6.53)	(6.41)	(14.37)	(11.01)	(8.07)
CLUBBED	−.0051	0.013	0.160	0.106	0.054
	(−1.36)	(0.05)	(2.13)	(1.11)	(0.28)
OWEPINJ	.0048	.336	.531	.381	.555
	(0.41)	(0.62)	(2.72)	(1.69)	(1.42)
AGEDIF	.0054	.419	.507	.372	.234
	(1.53)	(2.29)	(6.57)	(3.85)	(1.70)
NUMDIF	−.0027	−.158	−.066	−.052	−.017
	(−3.33)	(−2.63)	(−3.16)	(−1.94)	(−0.33)
ROBBERY	−.0137	−.560	−.199		−.537
	(−4.10)	(−2.80)	(−2.74)		(−3.62)
BLAKVICT	.0165	.716	.264	.318	.626
	(3.37)	(3.65)	(2.45)	(2.15)	(4.18)
UNDRACEO	.0880	1.139	1.425	1.316	.961
	(8.80)	(4.13)	(8.73)	(6.26)	(4.50)
MALEOFF	−.0353	−.723	.018	.193	−1.056
	(−5.38)	(−2.89)	(0.11)	(0.96)	(−5.24)
Constant	.0379	−2.485	0.064	−0.112	−1.702
Log-likelihood	(0.29)[e]	−144.81	−3893.5	−2480.6	−252.1
Sample (n)	4322	4322	4322	2868	3914

[a] Equation.

[b] Estimation method.

[c] Sample.

[d] Bivariate probit estimates could not be estimated because the correction for sample selection created a near-singular estimated variance matrix.

[e] Adjusted R^2.

Table 5.11. Summary of Weapon Effects in Violent Incidents (OLS Coefficients)[a]

Weapon	Attack		Injury, Given Attack		Death, Given Injury		Net Effects, All Incidents, Death	
	b	*B*	*b*	*B*	*b*	*B*	*b*	*B*
HGUNPRES[b]	−.284	−.181	−.314	−.092	.378	.459	.014	.079
OGUNPRES[c]	−.158	−.046	−.351	−.065	.395	.199	.016	.038
KNIFPRES[d]	−.125	−.082	.136	.055	.044	.085	.003[e]	.018
OWEPPRES[f]	.096	.066	.206	.135	−.005[g]	−.018[g]	−.000[e]	−.002
					.005[h]	.005[h]		

[a] Omitted weapons category—incidents in which no weapons were present or used. b, unstandardized OLS regression coefficient; B, standardized OLS regression coefficient.
[b] HANDGUN in Injury equations, HGSHOT in Death (given injury) equation.
[c] OTHERGUN in Injury equations, OGSHOT in Death (given injury) equation.
[d] KNIFE in Injury equations, KNIFED in Death (given injury) equation.
[e] Not significant at .05 level.
[f] OTHRWEAP in Injury equation, CLUBBED and OWEPINJ in Death (given injury) equation.
[g] Coefficient for CLUBBED.
[h] Coefficient for OWEPINJ.

Table 5.12. Prior Studies of the Impact of Aggregate Gun Levels on Violent Crime Rates[a]

Study	Sample	Two-Way Relationship ?	Measure of Gun Level[b]	Crime Rates[c]	Results[d]
Brearley (1932)	42 states	No	PGH	THR	Yes
Krug (1967)	50 states	No	HLR	ICR	No
Newton and Zimring (1969)	4 years, Detroit	No	NPP	THR, TRR, AAR, GHR	Yes
Seitz (1972)	50 states	No	GHR, FGA, AAR	THR	Yes
Murray (1975)	50 states	No	SGR, SHR	GHR, AAR, TRR	No
Fisher (1976)	9 years, Detroit	No	NPP, GRR, PGH	THR	Yes
Phillips et al. (1976)	18 years, U.S.	No	PROD	THR	Yes
Brill (1977)	11 cities	No	PGC	ICR	No
				THR	Yes
				TRR	No

(continued)

Table 5.12. (Continued)

Study	*Sample*	*Two-Way Relationship ?*	*Measure of Gun Level*[b]	*Crime Rates*[c]	*Results*[d]
Kleck (1979)	27 years, U.S.	Yes	PROD	THR	Yes
Cook (1979)	50 cities	No	PGH, PGS	TRR RMR	No Yes
Kleck (1984a)	32 years, U.S.	Yes No	PROD	THR TRR	No Yes
Maggadino and Medoff (1984)	31 years, U.S.	No[e]	PROD	THR	Yes
Lester (1985)	37 cities	No	PCS	VCR	No
Bordua (1986)	102 counties	No[f]	GLR, SIR	HAR, THR	No
	9 regions			GHR	No
McDowall (1986)	48 cities, 2 years[g]	Yes	PGH, PGS	TRR	No
Lester (1988b)	9 regions	No	SGR	THR	Yes
McDowall and Loftin (1988)	36 years, Detroit	No[h]	PGR, FGA	THR	Yes
Linsky et al. (1988)	50 states	No	GMR	GHR	Yes[i]

[a] Table covers only studies and findings in which the dependent variable was a crime rate, as opposed to the fraction of crimes committed with guns.

[b] Measures of Gun Level: FGA, fatal gun accident rate; GLR, gun owners license rate; GMR, gun magazine subscription rates; GRR, gun registration rate; HLR, hunting license rate; NPP, number of handgun purchase permits; PGA, % aggravated assaults committed with guns; PGC, % homicides, aggravated assaults, and robberies (combined together) committed with guns; PCS, same as PGC, but with suicides lumped in as well; PGH, % homicides committed with guns; PGR, % robberies committed with guns; PGS, % suicides committed with guns; PROD, guns produced minus exports plus imports, U.S.; SGR, survey measure, % households with gun(s); SHR, survey measure, % households with handgun(s); SIR, survey measure, % individuals with gun(s).

[c] Crime Rates: AAR, aggravated assault rate; GHR, gun homicide rate; HAR, homicide, assault, and robbery index (factor score); ICR, index crime rate; RMR, robbery murder rate; THR, total homicide rate; TRR, total robbery rate; VCR, violent crime rate.

[d] Yes, study found significant positive association between gun levels and violence; No, study did not find such a link.

[e] Authors modeled two-way relationship, but only report gun impact results for model where this was not done.

[f] A few gun-violence associations were positive and significant, but almost all involved female gun ownership or male long gun ownership. Author interpreted pattern to indicate effect of violence on gun ownership. See text.

[g] Panel design, two waves.

[h] Attempt to model two-way relationship probably failed due to an implausible identification restriction. See text.

[i] Only established an association with *gun* homicide rate. No result for total homicide rate reported.

Table 5.13. Variables Used in City-Level Analysis[a] (n = 170 cities)

		Mean	*SD*	*Sources*[b]
Violence rates (1979–1981 average, rates per 100,000 resident population, natural logs)				
LNMR	Homicides	2.47	.78	a
LNASLT	Aggravated assaults	5.90	.58	b
LNROB	Robberies	5.79	.75	b
LNRAPE	Forcible rapes	4.04	.54	b
LNBURG	Burglaries	7.77	.35	b
LNSUICID	Suicides	2.63	.35	a
LNGUNMR	Homicides with gun	1.98	.88	a
LNNGMR	Homicides without gun	1.42	.72	a
LNGNASLT	Assaults with gun	4.55	.75	b, c
LNNGASLT	Assaults without gun	5.55	.60	b, c
LNGNROB	Robberies with gun	4.87	.76	b, c
LNNGROBR	Robberies without gun	5.22	.84	b, c
LNGNSUIC	Suicides with gun	1.94	.56	a
LNNGSUIC	Suicides without gun	1.81	.47	a
LNFGA	Fatal gun accidents	0.50	1.35	a
Gun ownership indicators				
PGH7982	% gun, homicide, 1979–1982	61.48	11.89	d
PCTGNAST	% gun, aggravated assault, 1979–1980	28.31	11.39	c
PCTGNROB	% gun, robbery, 1979–1980	42.00	13.11	c
PGS7982	% gun, suicide, 1979–1982	53.37	14.91	a
GUNSTOL	Dollar value, stolen guns/ $ value, all stolen property	1.20	.75	e
Instrumental variables				
RGUNMAG	Subscriptions/100K respop, *Guns & Ammo, Sports Afield, Field & Stream, Outdoor Life*, county	6564.74	8656.41	f
HUNTERS	Hunting license holders/100K respop, state	6985.58	4252.36	g
Control variables				
PCTBLACK	% respop, black	19.27	16.69	h
PCTHISP	% respop, Spanish origin	8.82	12.23	h
PCTM1524	% respop, male, age 15–24	10.05	2.30	i
PCTOLD	% respop, age 65+	11.20	3.53	h
RUNM1624	Unemployment rate males, age 16–24	13.18	6.12	i

(continued)

Table 5.13. (Continued)

		Mean	SD	Sources[b]
RPOV	% respop < poverty line 1979	13.97	5.16	h
MFI	Median family income, $s, 1979	19435.52	3592.01	h
INEQUALT	% hshlds w. income <$10k or >$50k	35.51	6.91	h
OWNEROCC	% housing units owner-occupied	54.14	11.19	h
COLLEGE	College enrollment/100K respop	7619.66	4267.42	i
PCTMOVE	% respop age 5+ not in same house as 5 years before	51.01	8.44	h
TRNSIENT	% respop, born out of state	42.74	15.79	h
PCTFOREN	% respop, foreign born	7.68	8.25	i
POPCHANG	% pop change 1970 to 1980	7.32	20.37	h
CNTDIVRT	Divorces per 100K respop, county	639.20	245.25	h
FEMHEAD	% families headed by females	21.21	10.93	h
CHRCHMEM	Church membership per 100 respop, county	20.38	12.02	j
ALCHLSM	Alcoholic liver disease deaths per 100K respop	7.77	4.45	a
ADDICTION	Deaths due to nonmedical accidental poisoning by opiates per 100K respop	.22	.52	a
PCTSMSA	City respop as a % of SMSA respop	34.58	22.73	i
VISITORS	Lodging receipts in dollars/100K respop, SMSA	111.00	269.38	k
INVPOP	Inverse population 1/(respop in 100,000s)	.56	.29	h
HSACTRAT	Household activity ratio—fraction of households not of husband–wife, wife not working type	.71	.05	i
PCRM80	Property crime except burglary per 100K respop, 1980	6072.55	1805.93	b
HOSPITAL	Hospital beds per 100K respop	1013.90	661.20	h

(continued)

Table 5.13. (Continued)

		Mean	*SD*	*Sources*[b]
LIVLONE	% households with 1 person	10.18	2.91	h
STORES	Retail establishments/100K respop	851.72	167.09	h
MAXTEMP	Average daily maximum temperature, July	87.16	6.64	h
CROWDING	Percent of occupied housing units with 1.01+ persons/room	4.89	3.23	h
DENSITY	Persons per square mile	4334.26	3375.96	h
STHNBORN	Percent respop born in South	12.93	6.33	i
SOUTH	South region dummy	.32	.47	h
WEST	West region dummy	.28	.45	h
STHNNESS	Gastil "Southernness Index"	20.24	7.43	l
POLEXP	Police expenditures per capita	70.65	24.92	h
COPS	Sworn police officers/100K respop	207.57	82.40	b
STPRISRT	State prisoners/100K respop	157.90	164.58	m

[a] Unless otherwise noted, each variable refers to a city, as of 1980. In variable descriptions, "county" indicates variable refers to county in which city was located, and "state" indicates variable refers to state in which city is located. Methods of estimating missing values may be obtained from author. respop, resident population.

[b] Sources: a. U.S. NCHS (1983); b. U.S. FBI (1980–1982); c. ICPSR (1983); d. ICPSR (1984a); e. ICPSR (1984b); f. Audit Bureau of Circulation (1979–1981); g. U.S. Fish and Wildlife Service (1982b); h. U.S. Bureau of the Census (1983a); i. U.S. Bureau of the Census (1983b); j. Quinn et al. (1982); k. U.S. Bureau of the Census (1981); l. Gastil (1971); m. U.S. Bureau of Justice Statistics (1982).

Table 5.14. Total Violence Rates and Gun Ownership Levels: Effects of Control Variables

	LNMR	Gun Ownership[b]	LNASLT	Gun Ownership[c]	LNROB	Gun Ownership[d]	LNRAPE	Gun Ownership[e]	LNBURG	Gun Ownership[e]
PCTHISP	−.083[a]									
PCTBLACK					.260*	.420*	.231			
MFI							−.252*	.163		
PCTM1524					−.096*				−.091	
RPOV	.420*		.453*							
INEQUALT			.190		.424*		−.016		.331*	
OWNEROCC					−.249*	.348*	−.428*	.508*		
COLLEGE	.333*	−.161*	−.183*		−.181*				−.176*	
TRNSIENT					.107*					
PCTMOVE									.262*	
POPCHANG					−.110*		.016		−.240*	
PCTFOREN	−.352*									
CNTDIVRT	.207*		.228*	.217*	.063	.440*	.120		.021	.371*
PCRM80									.574*	
CHRCHMEM			.145	.192*	−.142*					
ADDICTRT					.089*					
ALCHLSM			.225*							
PCTSMSA	−.096	.134*	−.141*		−.173*	.205*				

(continued)

Table 5.14. (Continued)

	LNMR	Gun Ownership[b]	LNASLT	Gun Ownership[c]	LNROB	Gun Ownership[d]	LNRAPE	Gun Ownership[e]	LNBURG	Gun Ownership[e]
VISITORS					.180*	−.221*				
INVPOP	−.333*		.065		−.157*		−.093		.036	
WEST					.047		.268*	−.220*		
MAXTEMP			.113	.250*			−.206	.266*		
CROWDING	.611*									
DENSITY	−.099	−.394*					−.164			
STHNNESS	.357*	.478*								
HOSPITAL										
LIVLONE										
PCTOLD										
RGUNMAG		.125*		.017		.118*		.037		−.033
HUNTERS		.203*		.113		.039		.063		.128

[a] Standardized coefficients.
[b] Latent construct with indicators: PCTGNAST, PCTGNROB, PGS7982, GUNSTOL.
[c] Latent construct with indicators: PGH7982, PCTGNROB, PGS7982, GUNSTOL.
[d] Latent construct with indicators: PGH7982, PCTGNAST, PGS7982, GUNSTOL.
[e] Latent construct with indicators: PGH7982, PCTGNAST, PCTGNROB, PGS7982, GUNSTOL.
*$p < .05$.

Table 5.15. Effects of Gun Ownership on Violence Rates[a]

	LNMR	*Gun Ownership*[b]	*LNGUNMR*	*Gun Ownership*	*LNNGMR*	*Gun Ownership*
LNMR		.226*				
LNGUNMR				.164*		
LNNGMR						.232*
Gun ownership	−.604*		−.121		−.673*	
PSI	.256	.076	.239	.088	.310	.117
PSI (2, 1)	.054		−.004		−.046	
df	104		104		104	
χ^2	244.30		227.07		224.43	
GOF	.939		.940		.941	

	LNASLT	*Gun Ownership*[c]	*LNGNASLT*	*Gun Ownership*	*LNNGASLT*	*Gun Ownership*
LNASLT		.073				
LNGNASLT				.048		
LNNGASLT						.088
Gun ownership	−.085		.604*		−.401	
PSI	.492	.272	.423	.239	.524	.281
df	102		102		102	
χ^2	227.65		249.50		226.70	
GOF	.939		.934		.938	

	LNROB	*Gun Ownership*[d]	*LNGNROB*	*Gun Ownership*	*LNNGROBR*	*Gun Ownership*
LNROB		−.051				
LNGNROB				−.099		
LNNGROBR						−.013
Gun ownership	.006		.535*		−.308*	
PSI	.147	.172	.193	.174	.157	.147
df	120		120		120	
χ^2	273.31		286.89		273.10	
GOF	.937		.934		.937	

(*continued*)

Table 5.15. (*Continued*)

	LNRAPE	*Gun Ownership*[e]	*LNBURG*	*Gun Ownership*[e]
LNRAPE		.809*		
LNBURG				−.114
Gun ownership	.586		.267*	
PSI	.527	.494	.319	.375
PSI (2, 1)				
df	139		133	
χ^2	356.83		287.01	
GOF	.909		.919	

Summary of Effects of Gun Ownership on Total Violence Rates

	Model				
	Murder	*Assault*	*Robbery*	*Rape*	*Burglary*
Significant positive effect of gun ownership on crime rates?	No	No	No	No	(Yes)—see text

[a] Coefficients for control variables were reported in Table 5.14. Gun law dummies were also included in these models but their estimated coefficients are not reported until Chapter 10.

[b] Latent construct with indicators: PCTGNAST, PCTGNROB, PGS7982, GUNSTOL.

[c] Latent construct with indicators: PGH7982, PCTGNROB, PGS7982, GUNSTOL.

[d] Latent construct with indicators: PGH7982, PCTGNAST, PGS7982, GUNSTOL.

[e] Latent construct with indicators: PGH7982, PCTGNAST, PCTGNROB, PGS7982, GUNSTOL.

*$p < .05$.

CHAPTER

6

Guns and Suicide

Suicide reduction has not traditionally been regarded as a major object of legal control, although many psychiatrists and public health specialists have argued that it should be (e.g., Browning 1974; Seiden 1977). Although some suicide scholars have proposed gun control measures as an indirect method of controlling suicide through law (e.g., Boyd 1983; Markush and Bartolucci 1984), general studies of gun control usually give only the most cursory attention to suicide (e.g., Cook 1982).[1] Arguments in favor of strict gun control typically place far more stress on anticipated reductions in homicide than on suicide, despite the fact that, in recent years, guns have been involved in more suicides than homicides. For example, in 1985 there was 17,369 gun suicides (representing 55% of all gun deaths) and only 11,621 gun homicides (Table 2.8).

In the United States, guns are by far the most common method for committing suicide, accounting for 57% of U.S. suicides in 1985, compared to only 14% for the next most popular method, hanging (U.S. Bureau of the Census 1989, p. 84). To assess the potential for controlling suicide through gun control it is necessary to first gain some understanding of this extraordinary predominance of gun use among suicide methods. As will become clear, none of the obvious explanations suffices.

Why Do Suicides Use Guns?

When people contemplate suicide, what characteristics of the possible methods influence their choice?[2] Simple availability of the necessary tools of a given method is an obvious logical prerequisite. One must have access to drugs to commit a drug suicide, access to a high place to commit suicide by jumping, and access to a gun to commit a gun suicide. However, the prevalence of gun use in suicide relative to other common methods cannot be explained by relative availability of the required tools, since firearms are less available to would-be suicides than the means for almost any other common method of self-destruction. National surveys indicate that about 47% of U.S. households report ownership of a gun (Table 2.2). In contrast, 84% of U.S. households owned at least one motor vehicle in 1980 (U.S. Bureau of Census 1981, p. 628) and thus could produce the gas necessary for carbon monoxide poisoning. Virtually the entire population is within an hour's drive of a tall building (76% of the 1980 U.S. population lived in a metropolitan area), high bridge, mountain cliff, or other high place suitable for a suicide jump. A large majority live near a body of water suitable for drowning—53% of the population in 1980 lived within 50 miles of a coastal shoreline (U.S. Bureau of the Census 1983a) and most of the rest lived within a short drive of a lake or a river. Virtually every home surely has belts or rope sufficient to commit suicide by hanging, and knives or razor blades adequate for suicide by cutting. Further, in a 1982 national survey of high school seniors, 55% reported that it would be "fairly easy" or "very easy" for them to get barbiturates, and 59% said the same about tranquilizers (U.S. Bureau of Justice Statistics 1984a, p. 294). Prescription drugs, which are easy for most high school seniors to get, are probably at least as easy for would-be suicides to get, especially since suicides are most heavily concentrated among older people, who are more likely to have a legal prescription for treatment of a medical problem, or to know someone with such a prescription.

The foregoing leads to the inference that when people commit suicide with a gun, it is the result of a choice over other more available alternatives that the suicide passed by to use the preferred firearm. Thus, gun use in suicide would almost never be due solely to the gun's availability, nor would it result from shooting being the only reasonable method available. (see also Marks and Abernathy 1974, p. 7).

Besides mere availability, then, firearms must have other characteristics that suicides find desirable. Lester (1988c) surveyed (presumably nonsuicidal) college students as to what considerations might guide the choice of methods. The issue was necessarily an abstract one for this sample, so the information provided is of doubtful relevance. On the other hand, successful suicide attempters (i.e., those who killed themselves), cannot tell anyone after the fact why they chose a given method, and no one has asked survivors of suicide attempts why they chose their method. Therefore one must speculate about what features of suicide methods would-be suicides look for. Although one could extend the list of relevant attributes indefinitely, the following traits would seem to be among the most important ones.

First, persons genuinely intent on self-destruction, as opposed to those who want only to make a suicidal gesture or "cry for help," would want a lethal method, i.e. one technically effective in producing fatal results. Second, most would probably prefer a relatively painless method. Third, many would prefer a method that is relatively easy to carry out, requiring relatively little effort. Fourth, some suicides probably prefer methods with which they are familiar or that do not require considerable expertise. Fifth, serious suicides may prefer a method that is quick, producing fatal results before anyone can intervene. Finally, it has been speculated that some suicides may be concerned about the physical condition of their bodies after death and therefore prefer a method that is not disfiguring (Marks 1977; Lester 1969).

For lack of any better information, one must make informed judgments as to how the various potential methods of suicide are rated on these traits by prospective suicides. Table 6.1 lists each of the seven methods most commonly used in U.S. suicides in 1980, along with their frequency and ratings of each method with regard to each trait. The lethality ratings are based on the data presented in Table 6.2 whereas the ratings of availability are based on the survey research and other evidence discussed above. The other ratings are more subjective and hence debatable. However, Table 6.1 has the merit of making explicit the basis for later judgments of the relative merits of the major suicide methods.

Table 6.2 reports fatality rates of suicide attempts using various methods, i.e., the percentage of attempts that results in death. These rates are only approximate measures of method lethality, since they reflect the seriousness of the intentions of the users as well as method lethality itself, just as was true of assault fatality rates. Somewhat surprisingly, the data show that suicide attempts with guns are only slightly more likely to end in death than those involving hanging, carbon monoxide poisoning, or drowning. Fatality rates for the first four major methods are barely distinguishable, all of them being in the 75–85% range. None of the methods is certain to produce a death, yet all are likely to do so, and to roughly equal degrees. Fatality rates would undoubtedly vary within each broad method category if one made finer distinctions as to exactly how the method was used. For example it can be seen in Table 6.2 that about 89% of gunshot wounds to the head result in death, compared to only 46% for wounds to other parts of the body. Likewise, two or three barbiturate tablets will not have the same effect as an entire bottle, and a 20 foot jump is not as likely to be fatal as a 200 foot jump. Nevertheless, the results make it clear that firearms are not unique in producing high fatality rates, nor substantially different from other common methods.

If guns were not available for some potential suicides, and attempters substituted one of the common methods such as hanging, carbon monoxide poisoning, or drowning, the attempts might be fatal only slightly less often than shooting attempts would have been. Even positing this much difference assumes that the observed small fatality rate differences are at least partly attributable to differences in technical lethality of the methods and not entirely to differences in the seriousness of suicidal intentions of their users.

"Perceived painlessness" is probably closely related to how quick a method is perceived to be. On the basis of the assumption that self-inflicted gunshot wounds, especially those to the head, produce death more quickly than other suicide methods, shooting has been given the highest rating of five on both painlessness and quickness. However, although some other methods such as poisoning by drugs and by carbon monoxide are slower, they nonetheless are evidently relatively painless, according to those who have survived attempts with such methods. They were rated accordingly.

"Ease of carrying out" a method is a function of the effort required to use it, including getting to an appropriate location (if any) and obtaining any necessary implements, and of the courage and resolve required to successfully carry out the suicidal intention. Suicides may shy away from drowning because they fear that an instinct for survival will cause them to swim to safety. Likewise, a fear of heights could preclude a jumping suicide for some. Shooting was rated at 4, just below exhaust gas or drug poisonings, but higher than most of the rest of the methods.

Most people have little idea of how much of a given drug or poison is enough to produce fatal results and this may discourage some serious suicide attempters from using such substances. Likewise, operating the safety and loading mechanisms on long guns and semiautomatic pistols requires some knowledge, which may deter use by those unfamiliar with these weapons. On the other hand, revolvers require very little expertise. Shooting was therefore rated at 4 on "required expertise," drug poisoning at 2, and most of the rest were rated at 5, requiring little or no special expertise or knowledge.

Finally, the methods were rated as to their perceived lack of disfigurement, since cosmetic concerns may persist even on the brink of death. Marks (1977) suggested that such concerns may explain why gun use is so much less common among women. However, an alternative explanation is that women responsible for the domestic chores of cleaning up after others all their lives show a greater concern for those who would have to do the same for them. Among the widely used suicide methods, the ones that seem likely to be perceived as both least disfiguring and least messy are drugs and carbon monoxide poisoning, rated at 5. Shooting was rated low on this factor, at 2, whereas the rest were rated intermediately, at 3.

It is doubtful if these traits all are given equal weight by the average prospective suicide. If they were, a measure of the "technical" suitability of the methods would be the unweighted sum of the separate ratings, found in the penultimate column of Table 6.1. Results for this measure indicate that both carbon monoxide poisoning and hanging are more satisfactory methods of suicide than shooting, and that drowning and drug poisoning are nearly as suitable.

One can assign some admittedly subjective weights to each of the factors, reflecting the hypothesized general importance that the average suicide attaches to each one, and these are listed in the last row of Table 6.1. Each separate rating for each method was multiplied by the corresponding weight and the products were summed to produce the weighted overall ratings found in the last column of the table. Giving greater weight to lethality, anticipated painlessness, and ease of carrying out produces weighted scores that again suggest that carbon monoxide poisoning and hanging are superior suicide methods to shooting.

Although these weights and the more subjective ratings are subject to debate, Table 6.1 indicates that firearms do not have, merely by virtue of their more obvious technical characteristics, any clear superiority over other common suicide methods, and certainly not enough to account for the overwhelming popularity of guns among completed suicides. Thus the question remains: why are guns used in suicides so much more often than methods that are almost equally lethal and even more widely and conspicuously available? The answer requires consideration of some emotional and symbolic aspects of the methods, as well as the possibility of prospective suicides simply misperceiving the attributes of the methods.

The Control Hypothesis

Suicide is not necessarily "the easy way out," a defeatist substitute for solving one's problems. The problems many suicides face are seen as unsolvable, sometimes with good reason—they suffer from an incurable and fatal disease, a loved one has died, or their spouse or lover has irrevocably left them. If solving their problems is not regarded as an alternative, their only remaining choices may be to passively continue their misery or to act to end it by suicide. From their standpoint, to commit suicide is "to take arms against a sea of troubles," an active alternative to passively suffering "the slings and arrows of outrageous fortune." Suicide can be viewed as an affirmative act, in that it affirms that the suicide can control at least one aspect of his or her life—when and how it will end. Indeed, one of the most significant distinctions between suicides and the rest of humanity is this control over their final destiny. The act of suicide reflects not only misery and desperation, but also a final attempt to be in control of events. The terminal cancer patient who kills himself causes his pain to end, rather than waiting for the disease to take its course. Suicide thus can be motivated by a desire to control events, as well as by suffering and unhappiness.

Perhaps what separates some suicides from other equally unhappy people who do not kill themselves is a greater need to have control over their lives. These suicides may prefer shooting over other suicide methods because it is a method that allows maximum control of the final act. All other common suicide methods are surrounded by doubts as to whether they will get the job done, how quickly they will accomplish it, whether it will be painful, and whether others will be able to interfere with the act. If a suicide uses drugs to poison himself, he is not in control of the act, to the extent that he is ignorant of the exact dosage necessary to kill himself. If he hangs himself, he runs the risk of slowly suffocating, unable at the end to either hasten death or avert it. If he tries to drown himself it is likely to be in an outdoor, public location where others can interfere with his attempt. Carbon monoxide poisoning also permits intervention of others, both because it is slow and because it requires creating exhaust fumes that can attract attention.

In contrast, shooting can produce death almost instantly, without risk of interference from others. There are few doubts about necessary "dosage"—one well-placed bullet can suffice. The suicidal shooter can control events right to the very end. Of course all this applies only to suicide attempters who have a relatively unambivalent intent to end their lives. Those who want only to make a suicidal gesture, communicating their unhappiness to others, would want a method with a different sort of control, one that would allow them to avoid death. For them, a method that maximized the likelihood of intervention, such as poisoning with small amounts of drugs, would be preferable. This may partly explain why shooting is less common among nonfatal attempts—not only do guns kill most of the attempters who use them, but also those not truly intent on dying may avoid guns because of their lethal reputation.

Emile Durkheim asserted that the most important cause in the selection of a method of suicide is "the relative dignity attributed by each people, and by each social group within each people to the different sorts of death. They are far from being regarded as all on the same plane. Some are considered nobler, others repel as being vulgar and degrading; the way opinion classifies them varies within the community" [Durkheim (1897) 1951, pp. 292–3]. Guns may be regarded as appropriate for suicide, as customary, or even as relatively socially acceptable tools. For example it has frequently been noted that shooting is particularly prevalent among male suicides (see Table 6.3). The association of guns with masculine sports such as hunting and with aggression could lead to a perception of shooting as the appropriate way to produce death for men, who in turn predominate among suicides. Further, shooting is a more active, affirmative method of self-destruction than the common alternatives. The gun is both a symbol and an instrument of power—to use a gun is to exert power. Consequently, these cultural connotations give shooting a special attractiveness to those who feel they should have been able to effectively direct their own lives but felt powerless to do so.

Suicide motives that are especially characteristic of men may also contribute to gender differences in suicidal gun use. Under traditional sex roles, threats to performance and achievement are more serious for males, whereas threats to personal relationships are more critical for females. Male suicides are often motivated by some loss of effectiveness, such as loss of a job, of sexual virility, or a general loss of physical vigor associated with illness or advancing years. The last thing a man so motivated wants is yet another performance failure. To fail at a suicide attempt would be the ultimate indignity. Consequently one would expect that confidence in the lethality of the chosen suicide method would be especially crucial for men.

Likewise, social groups likely to place great emphasis on the value of control are likely to both favor guns as modes of suicide and to keep guns for self-defense. Having a gun for protection makes one less dependent on the police and others. Thus the same social groups that might be expected to most heavily stress control, and to prefer guns as suicide methods for that reason, are also likely to have higher-than-average access to guns. This makes it difficult at the group level to distinguish effects of cultural preference from those of gun availability. Data that describe gun use in suicide but that control for gun availability will be discussed in a later section.

The cultural emphasis on the ideal of the self-reliant, autonomous individual who is captain of his own fate is especially strong in the United States, and some scholars have asserted further that within the

United States the ideal is given especially strong support in the South (e.g., Cash 1940). Therefore, the control hypothesis would lead one to expect that gun use in suicide should be greater in the United States than elsewhere in the world and greater in the South than in other regions of the nation. This is indeed what is found—gun use predominates more among suicides in the United States than in other nations (Farmer and Rohde 1980) and more in the South than elsewhere (see Table 6.4). However, gun availability is also higher in the United States than in other nations and higher in the South than in other regions (Newton and Zimring 1969), so these patterns also can provide only ambiguous support for the control hypothesis.

Nevertheless, a sociocultural perspective emphasizing the value of control is certainly plausible and reasonably consistent with available evidence. More importantly, it can help draw together and make meaningful a number of otherwise unconnected facts. It is most helpful when comparing use of a given method in one group with use of that method in other groups. However, it is least useful in comparing the overall prevalence of one method with that of another. Males are more socialized into gun use than females, and males use guns in suicides at least four times as often as any other method. Does it follow, then, that for males, gun use (in suicide or in ordinary daily life) is at least four times as "acceptable" as the use of rope, automobiles, barbiturates, bodies of water, or high places? Clearly the control hypothesis must be supplemented to adequately explain the extreme *degree* to which shooting predominates over other methods among suicides in general as distinct from explaining why its use is more common in some social groups than in others.

The Modeling Hypothesis

In choosing a method, prospective suicides may take their cue from killers. Death is the goal of both murderers and suicides, and whatever is effective in achieving that goal for killers will presumably do the same for suicides. At least that may be the general line of reasoning followed by would-be suicides. As firearms increased in popularity as murder weapons, they may have thereby acquired an increasingly lethal reputation.

This hypothesis is at least partially consistent with data on trends in gun use in homicides and in suicides. The fraction of homicides that involved firearms increased from the mid-1950s to the early 1970s, whereas the fraction of suicides involving guns increased from 46.0 to 58.5% over the years 1965 to 1981 (Table 6.5). If the tendency of suicides to model their choice of method after the weaponry of killers persisted over time, so that gun prevalence in suicides continued to increase, in lagged fashion, after the rise in homicide gun prevalence had stopped, then the observed trends would be roughly compatible with the modeling hypothesis. On the other hand, the gun share of suicides continued increasing up until 1981, even though gun use in homicide had sharply declined from 1973 to 1983. It should, however, be noted that most prospective suicides would not know these statistics, and might have been exposed to increasing numbers of mass media news stories about gun violence, even during periods when gun violence was actually declining. The volume of gun homicide news stories may be the more relevant cause of gun use in suicides, rather than actual gun homicide levels, and the former could well have been increasing in the 1973–1983 period.

In any case, quite apart from explaining trends in suicidal gun use, the modeling hypothesis may help explain the extremely high degree to which shooting predominates as a method among completed suicides. Guns do heavily predominate among homicide weapons. This in turn gives them a reputation for lethality and hence for suitability as suicide tools as well.

It is also possible that prospective suicides are simply misinformed about some of the relative differences among suicide methods. Even though there is little factual basis for a belief that guns are substantially more lethal than some alternative suicide methods, their predominance among the weapons used in homicides, both the real ones reported in the news and the fictional ones in television programs, could easily lead to an elevated reputation for lethality, but without any corresponding process operating for other suicide methods. Perceived technical characteristics of firearms would thereby matter more than actual ones, leading persons truly intent on self-destruction to choose a method erroneously perceived to be uniquely lethal.

Who Is Most Likely to Use Guns in Suicide?

Table 6.6 displays three numbers pertaining to each major age–sex–race segment of the U. S. population. The upper number in each cell indicates the fraction of suicides committed with guns. These patterns may be summarized as follows. In the high suicide older ages, males are substantially more likely than women to prefer guns, but this is less true at the younger ages. There are no substantial black–white differences in gun use, although older black women are somewhat more likely to use guns than white women of the same age. There is no consistent age pattern in gun use among men, but gun use declines with age for women.

Table 6.6 also displays, in the lower two entries of each cell, gun suicide percentages compared with the percentages of persons in each group who personally own a gun, and with the percent who live in *households* with a gun. Thus the rates indicate how likely gun suicides were, relative to gun availability. The rates show that in the older ages, where most suicides occur, men are much more likely to kill themselves with guns than are women, even controlling for gun availability. Thus the idea that cultural preferences influence method choice beyond mere availability is supported. At the younger ages the picture is more complicated. Taking into account how few young women personally own guns, a surprisingly large fraction use guns to kill themselves, at a rate even higher than men in the 15–24 and 25–39 age groups. On the other hand, many women who do not personally own a gun nevertheless live in households in which guns owned by men are available. Basing rates on measures of household availability, women are somewhat more likely than men to prefer guns in suicide in the 0–14 and 15–24 age groups, but less likely to do so in older age groups.

Controlling for gun availability, based on either personal ownership or household gun availability, blacks (male and female) are more likely to kill themselves with guns than whites (male and female) at all ages. This is especially pronounced among black men age 15 to 24, who use guns in suicides at a rate more than seven times as high as one would expect on the basis of either personal or household gun availability. Part of this may be an artifact of these men underreporting their gun ownership, but it is doubtful if so strong a pattern is entirely due to such an artifact.

Finally, controlling for gun availability, based on either personal ownership or household gun availability, persons age 15–24 are more likely to prefer guns to use in suicide than persons in any of the other age groups, among both men and women and regardless of race.

These age–sex–race patterns in suicide gun preference may be compactly summarized in a sentence. Controlling for gun availability, the same population groups that show the highest rates of other-directed violence and criminal behavior also show the strongest preference for using guns when they commit suicide. The only exception to this generalization would be the rather minor one of young women, who have low rates of crime, violence, and suicide, but show a preference for guns when they do commit suicide. Thus the results generally support the view that suicidal people may be modeling their method choice after the weapon choices of assaultive persons.

Region and Suicide Method Preference

The aforementioned regional differences in gun use are especially striking and worthy of further attention. It is evident in Tables 6.3 and 6.4 that the predominance of shooting among U.S. suicides is disproportionately accounted for by Southerners and by men. The preference for a more violent, sudden, and dramatic method of self-destruction is of a piece with the portrayal of the "mind of the South" by historian Wilbur Cash, who believed that radical individualism and a special "romanticism" were at the heart of Southern culture. About Southern men, he wrote: "In every rank they exhibited a striking tendency to build up legends about themselves and to translate these legends into explosive action—to perform with high, histrionic flourish" (1940, p. 52). Even the politics of the region was described as "an arena wherein one great champion confronted another or a dozen, and sought to outdo them in rhetoric and splendid gesturing" (p. 54).

Likewise, the Southern exaltation of military virtues has been noted. Throughout the antebellum period, Southerners joined local and state militias, as well as the U.S. military forces, at a rate far exceeding that of Northerners. In these settings and in innumerable military academies, the military spirit and soldierly virtues were inculcated into Southern men (Franklin 1956, esp. pp.146–192). If a man subject to such socialization experiences were driven to suicide, it would seem preferable to leave life as a soldier so often does—by gunshot wound. Faced with a choice between shooting one's self, or quietly swallowing pills or breathing car fumes, it should not be surprising that Southern males overwhelmingly turn to the gun. Southerners apparently would rather end it all "with a bang, not a whimper."

It could be argued, then, that the greater availability of guns in the South and the Southerner's greater familiarity with them do not alone account for the prevalence of shooting among Southern suicides. Rather, both gun availability and the preference for shooting as a suicide method are the common products of a regional culture that stressed individualism, self-reliance, personal autonomy, the soldierly virtues of combativeness and physical activity, and the love of self-dramatization and the grand gesture.

None of this necessarily implies that Southern suicides are inflexibly wedded to shooting, and incapable of substituting another method if guns were not available. They might well simply substitute the next best method, one nearly as lethal but perhaps not quite so dramatic. Rather, the foregoing serves simply as a plausible explanation for the especially strong predominance of shootings among Southern suicides.

To a lesser degree, this cultural argument also applies to suicides in the West, many areas of which were settled largely by migrants from the South and that remain culturally Southern to an intermediate degree. Scholars such as Raymond Gastil (1971, 1976) regard nominally non-Southern states such as Arizona, New Mexico, and Oklahoma as almost as culturally Southern as former states of the Confederacy. And California, Nevada, and Colorado are said to have populations about half or more of southern background and/or had a southern majority at the time of first settlement. The same is noted of large areas of Illinois, Indiana, and Ohio in the Midwest. Thus, geographical patterns of gun use in suicide, seen in Table 6.4, correspond well with geographical patterns of Southern culture. The South itself shows the highest prevalence of shooting among suicides, the West and North Central states are intermediate, and the Northeast shows the lowest level.

Southerners may be more likely to own guns for a variety of reasons previously discussed, including various aspects of regional culture; greater gun availability, in turn, should certainly lead to a higher fraction of suicides being committed with guns. Is there any tendency for Southerners to prefer guns in suicide above and beyond greater gun availability? The penultimate row of Table 6.4 shows the percentage of suicides committed with guns for each region, compared with the percentage of households that report owning a gun in national surveys. Southerners are somewhat more likely to prefer guns, even controlling for gun availability, than persons in the West or Northeast, and substantially more likely to use guns than suicides in the North Central states. When gun availability is controlled, Southerners are only slightly more likely to prefer guns than persons in the Northeast. The latter are much less likely to own guns, but relative to their low level of gun ownership, they are very likely to turn to shooting as a way of taking their own lives. Consequently, the Southern subculture explanation of suicide method preferences is only partially supported.

Ownership and Acquisition of Suicide Guns

Access to a gun is obviously a logical prerequisite to use of a gun in suicide, so it is important to understand why and how suicides acquire guns. Three studies offer unusually detailed information on who owned the guns used in suicides and why they were acquired. All were done in highly urban counties, and thus may yield results unrepresentative as to the prevalence of handguns, the prevalence of protection as a reason for owning a gun, and other urban-associated traits. Indeed, it is less urban places where shooting most heavily dominates as the preferred method of suicide (Table 6.7). Nevertheless, these studies provide important information not found elsewhere, Danto (1972) reported that in two-thirds of suicides the gun was owned, and had been brought into the house, by the suicide. However, in only 1 of 20 cases in which reasons for the gun acquisition could be determined did the suicide get the gun specifically to kill himself. Circumstantial evidence suggested to Danto that the guns were mostly acquired originally for protection. Confirming these conclusions, Browning (1974) found that only 3 of 35 suicide guns in his sample were acquired specifically for suicide; 15 were owned for protection, 5 for hunting, 3 for occupational reasons, and 9 for unknown reasons. Of the 35 guns, 27 were owned by the suicide. Thus, suicide guns were usually originally acquired for defensive reasons, and were not usually obtained for the suicide. Similarly, Frierson (1989) found that only 6 of 62 women gun suicide attempters had obtained the weapon specifically for the attempt. These findings closely parallel those of research on homicide guns, which usually were owned for defensive reasons and were not originally acquired to commit a homicide or any other crime (Chapter 2).

These findings are relevant to estimates of the potential efficacy of waiting period or "cooling off" laws for preventing suicides. These laws require that a minimum period of time pass before a gun sale can be completed, and could prevent impulsive gun acquisitions by prospective suicides who sought to get a gun shortly before a suicide attempt. Given the finding that few suicides get guns specifically to kill themselves, it is not surprising to learn that in Danto's study only 1 of 11 cases (where relevant information was obtained) involved a gun that had been in the home only a short time before the suicide. In the one case in which a gun had been obtained specifically for the suicide, it was in the suicide's home for only 6 hours before his death. Even in this case, the suicide may have decided to obtain a gun long before actually doing so. In all other cases, the gun suicides lived in households that had contained guns for a considerable period of time before the suicide event, making a last-minute gun purchase unnecessary. If these findings are representative of all gun suicides, they indicate that waiting period laws would rarely have any potential for preventing suicides.

Types of Guns Used in Suicides

Because handguns are especially likely to be owned for defensive purposes (Chapter 2), a predominance of defensive guns among suicides could lead one to expect a predominance of handguns over long guns (rifles or shotguns). And in the samples studied by Browning and Danto this was indeed the case—83% of the suicide guns in Browning (1974, p. 550) and 62% of those in Danto (1972, p. 116) were handguns. However, these samples were highly urban, where handguns make up a disproportionately large share of the guns (Table 2.4). For the nation as a whole, long guns are twice as common as handguns and these are predominantly owned for sporting purposes (Chapter 2). If suicides do not obtain guns specifically for the suicide act, their reasons for ownership and types of guns owned should reflect the general population's ownership patterns. This leads us to expect a predominance of long guns in gun suicides, unless handguns have some special attraction or utility for suicides. Further, in nonurban areas, long guns are the preeminent firearm in general ownership even more than in urban areas, suggesting that there should be less of a predominance of handguns in a national sample of suicides than in purely urban samples.

For all the deaths officially registered in the vital statistics system as gun suicides in 1980, information on the type of gun was known for 5101. Of these, 2109 or 41% involved handguns and 59% involved long guns. However, the majority of gun suicide death certificates (10,292 such cases) did not contain sufficient information to code the deaths as to type of gun involved (U.S. NCHS 1983, p. 35). It is possible that when those certifying death failed to record information on gun type, it was disproportionately because the stereotypically expected type, a handgun, was involved. Long guns might seem to stand out as more noteworthy or exceptional weapons, leading to a higher recording rate when they are involved. If true, long guns would actually be involved less often than 59% of the time. This is, however, pure speculation. Taking the national data at face value leads to the tentative conclusion that most gun suicides involve long guns.

Unlike with crime, where concealability is at least sometimes a useful attribute, handguns have no special advantages over long guns in connection with suicide. There is no significant physical difficulty in pointing the end of the barrel of any but the very longest shoulder guns at one's own head, and even in the few cases in which gun length is very long relative to arm length, suicides can simply use a ruler or other stick, or a toe, to push the trigger while holding the barrel to their head.

Handguns are both less common and less lethal than long guns. Therefore, there is little reason to expect availability of handguns to be any more closely related to suicide rates than availability of long guns. Nevertheless, basing their reasoning on data covering unrepresentative local samples of exclusively urban suicides, some scholars have asserted that handgun availability should be more closely related to suicide rates (e.g., Clarke and Lester 1989). One reason they adhere to what seems to be an implausible hypothesis is the difficulty that trends in gun availability pose for the idea that gun availability causes increases in total suicide rates. If one is committed to using survey data as valid indicators of national trends in gun ownership and takes them at face value, one has to deal with the fact that the total and gun suicide rates were increasing over the 1961–1984 period, a time when survey data indicated constant or slightly declining gun ownership (Clarke and Lester 1989, pp. 50, 59). Clarke and Lester attempted to sidestep this empirical embarrassment by asserting that, for reasons they failed to enunciate, handguns do have some special utility over long guns for suicide, and ownership did increase in this subcategory of guns. They cited survey figures indicating handgun increases (p. 59), but half of these "data" were imaginary, produced by interpolations between genuine survey results covering only a few of the relevant years. (The reader is urged to examine their figure on p. 58 to see just how misleading their use of these data was.)

More important, the *real* survey handgun data show no change in handgun ownership from 1959 to 1972. Over the period studied, 1959–1984, 74% of the increase in the total suicide rate, and 68% of the increase in the gun suicide rate, had already occurred by 1972. Thus, even if one both accepted the validity of these survey data (contrary to the evidence reviewed in Chapter 2) and accepted on faith the dubious claim that handguns are more useful for suicidal purposes than the more widely available and more lethal long guns, the 1959–1972 increases in total and gun suicides still could not be attributed to increases in handgun availability. If one believes the survey data, there *were* no such increases—16% of households reported a handgun in both 1959 and 1972. As to the 1972–1984 increase in reported handgun prevalence, the survey data indicate that almost all of this shift took place in the first year, moving from 16% in 1972 to 20% in 1973. The percentage of households reporting a handgun was 21% in 1984, indicating no significant change after 1973. Consequently, the Clarke–Lester attempt to link trends in handgun prevalence and suicide rates turns out to rest on that single 1972–1973 shift in handgun prevalence figures, as an explanation of shifts in suicide rates that took place over the entire period from 1959 to 1984, most of them occurring *before* 1972.

These authors performed a regression analysis on their time series data, even though the gun prevalence data were imaginary for 13 of their 26 time points. Needless to say, this analysis cannot yield any meaningful findings on the guns–suicide connection. For what it is worth, the authors reported a significant positive association between handgun prevalence and the *gun* suicide rate, and a significant *negative* relationship between handgun prevalence and the *total* suicide rate.

What Suicides Might Be Prevented by Reduced Gun Availability?

Some supporters of gun control seem surprisingly willing to accept the arguments of gun control opponents as they apply to suicide prevention, in contrast to the opponents' arguments concerning homicide. The anticontrol argument can be summarized as follows. The majority of suicide attempters who use guns are determined, at least at that moment, to kill themselves. Because essentially all suicide attempters have many other highly lethal means available to them, the absence of guns would make very little difference as to how many of them would succeed in killing themselves. Virtually all would substitute essentially equally lethal methods, hanging or drowning themselves, breathing exhaust fumes, or using some other method if a gun were not available.

Note that the substitution-of-other-means issue is different with suicide than with homicide. Unlike murderers, suicide attempters are largely in control of the violent event, usually able to determine whether the "victim" dies, without interference from others. Further, being both offender and victim, so to speak, they rarely face anyone effectively able to prevent the acquisition and use of available tools for producing death. In contrast, homicides ordinarily involve a victim who does not want to die and who will use any means available to avoid death. This sharply restricts the killer's choice of methods for killing, especially in those homicides that are the impulsive, unpremeditated act of an enraged attacker. Such an assaulter would have a hard time shoving poisons down an adult victim's throat, putting a rope around his neck and hanging him, or even throwing him from a high place or drowning him. Consequently, guns would seem to be essential or very helpful in a much larger share of homicides than of suicides, and substitution of other means should be correspondingly higher with suicides than with homicides.

Nevertheless, there still may be potential suicidal situations in which the availability of guns could make a difference as to whether the attempter lived or died. Therefore, hypothetical gun suicide scenarios where a death could potentially be prevented by eliminating the immediate availability of guns will be described. They will be covered in increasing order of plausibility, based on the existing suicide literature. It should be kept in mind that in real life, suicide situations are often combinations of the scenarios; they are described separately to clarify the elements that might make a suicide preventable through the elimination of gun availability.

1. *A suicide attempter is intent on using only firearms and will not make an attempt of any kind if a gun is not available.* Seiden (1977, p. 274) has argued that at least some suicide attempters are set on using only one particular method and are unable to quickly switch to any other method. If this were true for any prospective gun suicide attempters, eliminating the availability of guns could prevent suicides. Seiden presented no evidence that this is true for any gun users, relying for support on another study's evidence concerning persons who jumped off the Golden Gate Bridge. Rose (1975) interviewed six persons who survived such a jump, and four of them said that they would not have used any other method had that bridge not been available. However these survivors stated that the Golden Gate Bridge had special romance and notorious fame as a suicide locale, suggesting that their views on substitution of other methods may be peculiar to this unique "suicide shrine," as Rosen phrased it. Consequently, it is questionable whether these results can be generalized to any other suicide method.

2. *An impulsive suicide is precipitated by the knowledge that a uniquely quick, easy method of suicide is immediately available; no attempt would have been made without a gun being available.* Newton and Zimring (1969, p. 36) suggested that for a depressed person, "the knowledge of having a quick and effective way of ending his life might precipitate a suicide attempt on impulse." Although an interesting speculation, this ignores the almost universal availability of other quick and effective means for killing one's self. If a suicide attempt by a depressed person could be precipitated by the mere knowledge of the availability of such means,

eliminating gun availability would make little or no difference (assuming scenario 1 does not apply) and such attempts would ordinarily be impossible to prevent.

3. *A nonserious attempter uses a gun because he does not fully understand its lethality. He would not have died had he used a method better suited to his nonlethal intentions.* It might be impossible to prevent people seriously and persistently intent on killing themselves from doing so. However, it is possible that some persons who are not truly determined to die nevertheless use guns in their attempts and ending up killing themselves due to unexpected or misunderstood lethality of firearms. In such suicides there is a mismatch of intention and method, with the lethality of the latter exceeding that of the former. It is unlikely that any sober, mentally healthy person would not be aware of the great lethality of firearms. If anything, their reputation for lethality is probably exaggerated by movies and television. However, at least at the time of the act, some suicide attempters are cognitively disordered or impaired in some way. Estimates of the fraction of suicides who are mentally ill have been as high as 60%, depending on how mental illness is defined, though figures around a third are more common (Lester 1984b, pp. 106–21). This is not necessarily true specifically of those who use guns and it is impossible to tell how often illness distorts thought to the point where the lethality of guns is not adequately understood.

Similarly, use of alcohol and other drugs could impair thought processes in such a way as to encourage nonserious suicide attempters to use guns in a lethal fashion. Shneidman and Farberow (1961, pp. 35–6, 39) found that 24% of the males and 11% of females who committed suicide had at least some alcohol in their bodies at the time of autopsy. It is, however, impossible to estimate from these data how often thought processes were distorted to the point at which gun lethality could not have been sufficiently appreciated. Questioning of survivors of gun suicide attempts could shed light on this matter, but no such evidence has not yet been produced. If a nonserious attempter of this sort could be denied access to firearms, one would not necessarily expect substitution of other equally lethal methods, unless there were similar misperceptions of the lethality of these other methods. Thus reduction of gun availability might prevent some suicides that followed this scenario.

4. *A gun user's intentions are ambivalent and he leaves his death up to chance; gun use tips the odds in favor of death.* Seiden (1977, p. 275) and others have noted that many suicide attempters are ambivalent about whether they really want to die. Such persons may leave it up to chance

whether they live or die. That is, they leave it up to the vagaries and uncertainties of the methods they use or to the unknown chances of someone effectively intervening in their attempt. This scenario is certainly plausible with less lethal methods such as drug self-poisonings, where the lethal dosage is so often unknown, or with self-inflicted cuttings, where it is uncertain how many cuts are needed, how deep they must be, or where they have to be located in order to produce death. However, it seems less plausible with shooting than with almost any other method. Because guns are ordinarily perceived to be so lethal, few prospective suicides are likely to view them as chancy or uncertain tools of self-destruction. And shooting attempts can easily produce death so quickly that intervention is categorically ruled out. However, if scenario 3 is also true, i.e., the attempter's thinking is distorted, then scenario 4 might occur.

5. *A suicide attempter is only temporarily intent on dying. Denied a gun, he substitutes a slow-acting method. This allows others to intervene to prevent death, without the attempt being followed by later attempts.* This scenario's plausibility rests on several premises, which are supported by research evidence to varying degrees. First, most suicide attempts that do not result in death are never followed by subsequent suicide (Dorpat and Ripley 1967). Therefore, preventing suicide on the first attempt is usually tantamount to permanently preventing it. More relevant to the issue at hand, Card (1974, p. 43) found that only 6.25% of suicide survivors who used *guns* subsequently killed themselves. The follow-up period in this study was short, ranging from 0 to 2 years, but it still remains very likely that most survivors of gun suicide attempts do not subsequently kill themselves. Interpretation of these facts, however, is complicated by an obvious problem with sample censoring—only survivors of the initial attempts were "eligible" for a subsequent suicide. If those who successfully killed themselves on the initial attempt were more lethal in their intentions than those who survived, the survivors would not be representative of all attempters and certainly not of serious attempters. It is at least hypothetically possible that if one could somehow separately identify those attempters who had a serious and persistent intent to die, one would find that 100% of the survivors among this group did subsequently kill themselves. Perhaps the 93.75% of survivors of initial gun attempts who did *not* subsequently suicide were never serious in the first place, and had only shot themselves in nonvital areas of their bodies. Eliminating gun availability among this group would not reduce suicide since none of its members would ever have killed themselves anyway. And reducing gun availability among the "serious" attempters

(those who died in the initial attempt and the 6.25% of survivors who later committed suicide) would not reduce suicide since all of these would have made subsequent successful suicide attempts had the initial attempt failed. Card's data do no preclude this possibility. Nevertheless it is possible that some attempters who use guns are seriously intent on self-destruction, but only temporarily so, and thus preventing suicide on the initial attempt could prevent it permanently.

If one accepts that premise for the moment, then it is worth considering how many initial suicide attempts with guns could be prevented by eliminating gun availability. Temporarily serious attempters who otherwise would have used guns would, if unable to get a gun, substitute other methods, some of which are nearly as lethal as guns. (Those who substitute less lethal methods will be considered in discussion of a later scenario). How then could lives be saved? Newton and Zimring (1969, p. 36) argued that some of the methods substituted would be, even if of roughly equal technical lethality, somewhat slower acting, increasing the chances of others intervening to save the attempter's life. Among persons who currently use guns to make serious suicide attempts, would elimination of guns cause them to substitute slower methods? And would such substitution increase successful intervention? In answer to the second question, some of the likely alternative methods are clearly slower than shooting, whereas a difference is not so apparent for other methods. Falls from sufficiently high places are probably fatal almost instantly whereas shorter falls will produce a slower death. Some hangings will produce death instantly if the victim's neck is broken immediately from a drop of some distance, whereas others result in slow strangulation over a span of minutes. Drownings certainly take somewhat longer than the average shooting, as do carbon monoxide poisonings. Therefore, among those prospective suicides who are not careful to substitute methods producing death as quickly as shooting, intervention would be at least hypothetically possible.

Intervention, however, is possible only when the suicide does not isolate himself from others so as to preclude such an eventuality. Is this true for those who currently use guns to kill themselves? Danto's evidence on Detroit gun suicides indicates that persons who used guns made intervention very difficult regardless of the method they had ended up using. He found that in 28 of 29 cases (97%), the gun suicide victim was home alone at the time of the event (1972, p. 117). It is of course possible that in some of these cases, where the suicide did not live alone, someone came home shortly after the suicide, soon enough to effectively intervene had a slower method been substituted. There is no evidence on this point, but to the extent that the speculation is true, at least a few seriously intended suicide attempts could result in life saving intervention. In a general sample of completed suicides using a variety of methods, Maris found that death occurred within an hour of the suicidal act in 66% of the cases in which the time interval was known, leaving a third of the cases in which there was over an hour of potential intervention time (1981, p. 284). Unfortunately, it was not possible to know how many lingering deaths involved seriously motivated attempters. However, the Danto evidence on this matter indicates that causing substitution of slower methods would rarely result in successful intervention. Further, the other methods available as substitutes are all quieter than shooting; thus their use would reduce the chances of others becoming aware of the attempt or being drawn to the scene due to noise.

6. *Substituting a method requiring longer preparation increases the chances of a temporarily serious attempter changing his mind.* This scenario involves a different time issue than the previous one—the time span between when a person decides to commit suicide and when they actually take the first suicidal action (swallow pills, breath car exhaust fumes, pull a trigger, etc.), rather than the time between this action and death. Many suicide attempts are impulsive, with the attempt being made shortly after the idea was first seriously considered, or at least this is the case among some survivors of nonfatal attempts. Kessel (1967) reported that 66% of the nonfatal self-poisoning cases he studied were impulsive, although he did not precisely define impulsivity. However, there is evidence that few of Kessel's attempters were serious about dying, suggesting that they may have been different from the average gun user. For example, very few of the studied survivors said, after recovery, that they still wished to take their lives. Likewise, Fox and Weissman (1975) found that self-poisoners were more impulsive and less intent on dying than those using other methods, including guns.

Nevertheless, there are probably at least some gun users who attempt suicide impulsively. If guns had not been available, they would have had to substitute methods of suicide that required at least somewhat longer preparation time. The Danto and Browning studies concluded that most gun suicide victims had owned their guns for protection, and guns owned for protection, in turn, are especially likely to be kept loaded and in a location where they can be used quickly. Therefore, if a gun owner were home when he experienced a suicidal impulse, he usually could bring a loaded firearm to bear on a vital area of his body very quickly. In contrast, the methods likely to be substituted for guns all require at least a few more minutes of preparation time, at least for some fraction of their users. Hanging one's self entails locating an exposed pipe, a roof rafter, a tree limb, or other strong support from which a noose can be suspended. For those without a sufficient existing supply of drugs, self-poisoning might entail acquiring them from friends or using prescriptions to accumulate a lethal stockpile from pharmacists. For those without a garage or similar enclosed space, carbon monoxide poisoning would necessitate locating a hose of suitable diameter with which to direct exhaust fumes into the interior of a vehicle. For those who do not work or live in tall buildings with openable doors or windows on the upper floors, a fatal jump would require at least a short trip to a suitable jumping place. And drowning would often entail a similar trip to a large enough body of water. In short, for at least some prospective suicides, lethal alternatives to guns would not be *instantly* available, increasing the time in which suicides could reconsider their actions and decide not to attempt suicide at all, perhaps by as much as half an hour or more.

The Fox and Weissman findings suggested that gun users are less impulsive than drug users but left open the possibility that even among seriously intended gun users there may be some whose suicidal intentions are serious for only a short time. This leaves open the possibility of preventing some suicides by reducing gun availability, delaying the execution of suicidal actions, and allowing temporarily suicidal persons to reconsider.

Ordinarily, when suicide scholars speak of "transitory" suicide impulses, they seem to mean those lasting a few weeks or days. However, an impulse lasting even as long as an hour would provide sufficient preparation time for using any of the major alternatives to shooting. Existing evidence does not give any indication as to how many gun suicides experience a suicidal impulse that lasts for less than an hour.

7. *A seriously motivated suicide attempter who otherwise would have used guns is forced by their unavailability to substitute another method that is somewhat less lethal. He survives and makes no subsequent suicide attempts.* This scenario illustrates the most straightforward reason to hope for some savings of lives if gun availability among serious prospective suicides can be reduced. Even if such persons substituted other common, frequently fatal means of suicide, deaths might not occur as often simply

because the methods are not quite as lethal as shooting. As noted earlier, the differences are modest, but there are differences nonetheless.

The critical question here is the same as the one raised in Chapter 5 in connection with assault fatality rates. To what degree are the differences in suicide fatality rates across method categories attributable to differences in the technical lethality of the methods/weapons themselves, as opposed to differences in the seriousness of their users' intentions or motivations to inflict serious harm? It can be argued that suicide attempters who use guns are more serious and less ambivalent about dying than users of other common methods, and the argument has considerable empirical support. For example, both Tuckman and Youngman (1963, 1968) and Eisenthal et al. (1966) found that survivors of nonfatal suicide attempts who had used the "most serious" methods, including shooting, were more likely to subsequently commit suicide (but see Card 1974). Fox and Weissman (1975) found suicide attempts with more serious methods were less likely to be impulsive. Finally, Fox and Weissman also found that among survivors of nonfatal suicide attempts, those who used the more violent or active methods (including shooting) were more likely to say in interviews that their intentions were serious and that they truly wanted to die. And common sense suggests that mentally unimpaired persons who did not want to die but rather wanted only to make a "cry for help" are unlikely to shoot themselves in the head, given the nearly universal perception of guns as highly lethal devices. Consequently there is strong a priori reason to believe that at least some of the difference in fatality rates between gun suicide attempts and those using the less frequently fatal methods (or methods with less of a reputation for lethality) is attributable to differences in the "seriousness" of their users. However, it is not clear whether this would hold very well for a comparison of gun attempts with those involving other frequently fatal methods, such as hanging or carbon monoxide poisoning. Given the limits on relevant evidence, the most prudent working assumption would seem to be that some of the fatality rate differences between gun attempts and hanging, exhaust gas, jumping, or drowning attempts are due to differences in technical lethality and some to user differences in intentions and strength of motivation. This means that the already small intermethod differences in lethality suggested by the fatality rates in Table 6.2 may well be even smaller than they appear, if gun users are more "serious" than users of the methods with similarly high fatality rates. Therefore, savings in lives attributable to the substitution of these competing methods would probably be small, though not necessarily zero.

To summarize, some of the foregoing "preventable gun suicide" scenarios are logically plausible and not contradicted by available evidence. Although there is no evidence that any of them are very common in real life, there is also little solid evidence to the contrary. At best, one can say there is some a priori reason to hypothesize that gun control measures that reduced gun availability among suicide-prone persons might save at least a few lives. It remains an empirical question whether gun scarcity, whether natural or produced through gun laws, could cause anything more than a substitution of nongun methods.

Prior Studies of Method Availability and Suicide Rates

There is considerable evidence that limiting the availability of one means of suicide can reduce the frequency of deaths in *that* category of suicide and cause some prospective suicides to switch from the restricted method to an alternative one. For example, detoxification of domestic gas in England and in Vienna was followed by lower rates of gas suicide and lower percentages of total suicides committed with gas (Kreitman 1976; Farberow and Simon 1969). Likewise, legal restrictions on the size of prescriptions for barbiturates in Australia were followed by reductions in the rate of drug suicides and in the fraction of all suicides that involved drugs (Stoller 1969; Oliver and Hetzel 1973).

Few people would argue, however, that it is a worthwhile goal of public policy merely to shift suicides from one method to another, without producing any net reduction in the total number of suicides. Therefore, establishing the suicide reduction effectiveness of gun control or other policies aimed at reducing availability of one means of suicide must entail demonstrating that such efforts caused a reduction in the *total* suicide rate as well as the rate of suicides using the restricted method. So far, no studies of restrictions on the more lethal suicide methods have accomplished this.

Consider Farberow and Simon's study of gas detoxification in Vienna. Detoxification of the municipal domestic gas supply began in 1965. It undoubtedly reduced gas suicides, since one cannot commit suicide with nontoxic gas. There also was a slight drop in total suicides at this time. However, during the preceding 3 years, from 1961 to 1964, total suicides had already declined 17%, from 347 to 288. Applying simple linear regression to the 1961 to 1964 total suicide figures, extrapolated or expected total suicides for 1965 to 1967 can be computed. Contrary to the claims of the authors that the decline in total suicides after detoxification was "a reduction that far exceeds expectations from the long term trend" (p. 401), their data actually indicated that there were *more* total suicides after detoxification than would have been expected on the basis of the 1961–1964 trends.[3] Obviously, something other than gas detoxification caused total suicides to decline, both before and after detoxification occurred. As far as can be determined from the Farberow–Simon data, prospective gas suicides simply switched over to other lethal methods of suicide, with no evidence of anything less than complete substitution of alternative means, which produced equally frequent fatal outcomes.

Similarly, data for England indicated a decrease in both gas suicides and total suicides that coincided in time with gas detoxification, leading one analyst to conclude that there was "a direct causal relationship between the two phenomena" (Kreitman 1976, p. 92). Unfortunately for this optimistic hypothesis, uncritically endorsed by later suicide scholars (e.g. Markush and Bartolucci 1984), more detailed subsequent analyses using control areas indicated that the total suicide drop was merely coincidental. Using more geographically disaggregated data, Barraclough (1977a,b) found that decreases in total suicides were no greater during this period in towns that had detoxified their gas than in towns in which this had not yet been carried out. Again, something other than "means reduction" was causing total suicides to decline in England at this time and the evidence cannot legitimately be interpreted as indicating that detoxification accomplished anything more than simply causing prospective gas suicides to use other methods. A similar analysis using control areas found that detoxification in the Netherlands also had no effect on the total suicide rate (Sainsbury et al. 1981). Finally, in less elaborate analyses, Stengel (1964), Fox (1975), and Clarke and Mayhew (1989) all reported similar evidence of complete substitution of other methods following gas detoxification in Basel, Switzerland, the Netherlands, and Scotland, respectively. Although gas detoxification certainly reduced gas suicides, the drop in total suicides in England was apparently little more than an interesting coincidence.

It is worth discussing the relevance of the foregoing studies to an assessment of gun control as a technique of suicide control. "Means reduction" strategies can succeed only to the extent that substitution of other fatal methods is minimized. The likelihood of such substitution is in turn a function of how strong and persistent a prospective suicide attempter's desire to die is. Evidence has already been cited indicating that gun users are more strongly motivated to die than users of more passive, less violent methods such as gas or barbiturate poisoning. As lethality of the restricted method increases, the extent of substitution of other methods that one can expect should also increase. Consequently one would expect even more substitution among would-be gun users than has been observed in studies of reduction in availability of lethal gas. The fact that these studies' data indicate complete or near-complete substitution even among presumably less strongly motivated suicide attempters is strong reason to expect the same where gun availability is reduced. In contrast, Stoller (1969) and Oliver and Hetzel (1973) found reductions in total suicides following restrictions on barbiturate prescriptions in Australia, reductions not attributable to any simple continuation of preexisting downward trends. Because self-poisonings apparently are especially likely to be impulsive and weakly motivated, they may be easier to reduce through "means reduction" than domestic gas or gun suicides. In any case, the results of studies of less lethal methods cannot be legitimately used to infer the extent of method substitution one could expect after reducing availability of more lethal methods such as firearms.

The Impact of Gun Ownership Levels on Suicide Rates

Few studies have attempted to measure directly the relationship between gun availability and suicide rates, and these few are methodologically primitive. Some studies purporting to address this subject did not actually measure gun availability, but instead inferred it from the percentage of suicides committed with guns (e.g., Boyd 1983) or simply asserted differing gun ownership levels to exist (e.g., Farmer and Rohde 1980). The studies that measured gun ownership levels are summarized in Table 6.8.

Markush and Bartolucci (1984) computed simple bivariate correlation coefficients between total and gun suicide rates of nine U.S. regions and regional rates of household gun ownership as reported in national surveys. The extremely high level of aggregation and very small sample of just nine regions were necessitated by the fact that survey gun ownership data were not available for any smaller units. The authors found both pistol and total gun prevalence to be significantly associated with gun and total suicide rates. Because bivariate associations of this sort are weak evidence of causal connections, the authors attempted to buttress their claim of an "etiologic" connection by reference to nine previous studies. None of the studies in fact had the alleged causal implications for a suicides–gun connection, but they are worth reviewing for their own sake.

Two of the cited studies, by Boyd (1983) and Boor (1981), were nothing more than components analyses that showed that most of the recent increase in the U.S. suicides had occurred in the gun suicide category. This fact is as consistent with a hypothesis of an increasing cultural acceptability of, or preference for, shooting among suicides as it is with the idea that increased gun availability caused increases in total suicides.

Markush and Bartolucci miscited Cook (1979) to the effect that he found regional gun suicide rates to be correlated with survey gun prevalence data. Actually, however true that may or may not be, Cook merely found that the *fraction* of suicides committed with guns correlated with survey gun prevelance, a fact devoid of causal implications for the impact of guns on the total suicide rate. They also cited two studies that related suicide rates not to gun prevalence but to levels of strictness of gun control laws (Farmer and Rohde 1980; Lester and Murrell 1980). The relevance of these studies' findings to the guns–suicide connection is unclear, in view of the authors' earlier remarks noting that prior studies had failed to establish any connection between gun control strictness and gun prevalence (Markush and Bartolucci 1984, p. 123). Finally, the authors uncritically cited a series of studies of the sort just discussed, which purported to show that decreases in total suicide were caused by restrictions in the availability of a means of suicide (Farmer and Rohde, Kreitman, etc.). None of these studies concerned firearms; rather they concerned methods commonly used by those less strongly motivated to seek substitutes. Some of the studies did not even address the issue of substitution of other methods, and all of them failed to show any causal effect of means reduction on the total suicide rate.

In two short sentences Markush and Bartolucci (1984) noted the possibility that some unspecified "factor common to the southern U.S. culture causes both a tendency toward suicidal behavior and a tendency to have guns" (pp. 125–6). The matter was then dropped and they proceeded quickly to their conclusion that "the firearms suicide correlation is etiologic" (p. 126). It is not hard to imagine exactly what cultural traits could account for both the high suicide rates of Southern and Rocky Mountain regions and their high gun ownership levels. As previously noted, it is possible that depressed persons who place great emphasis on being self-determining masters of their own fate are especially likely to blame themselves for their problems and to consequently take their own lives (Lester 1972, 1984b). Logically, such persons would also be more likely to have guns for protection rather than having to depend entirely on the police. Rural persons have to be more self-reliant than those with close neighbors, and they are also more likely to own guns (Chapter 2). Numerous authors have noted that Southerners and Westerners place especially strong emphasis on the values of self-reliance and self-determination (Cash 1940; Hackney 1969; Gastil 1971; 1976, pp. 184–8). Consequently one would expect a correlation between regional gun ownership and regional total suicide rates even if the former had no causal effect whatsoever on the latter.

In addition, it could be noted that regions that are the most rural have the poorest medical care and the highest fractions of their populations living in places remote from the nearest doctor, presumable causing a larger share of suicide attempts to result in death. Rural areas also have higher gun ownership levels, both of handguns and long guns (Table 2.5) and the South and West are more rural than other regions. Again, regional differences in rurality could completely account for observed differences in both gun ownership and suicide rates.

Other studies have used indirect measures of gun ownership. Lester (1987) used the fatal gun accident rate and the fraction of homicides committed with guns as gun ownership indicators, and, in a later study, rates of gun magazine subscriptions (Lester 1989). The first two had significant positive correlations with state gun suicide rates, but insignificant positive correlations with the total suicide rate, indicating that gun availability might affect method choice but not frequency of total suicides. The third measure was significantly and positively correlated with the rates of both gun and total suicide. Without controls for any variables correlated with both gun magazine subscription rates and suicide rates, it is difficult to interpret these results. It should also be noted that in the Chapter 5 city-level study, among nine different indicators of gun ownership assessed, the only two that had *no* significant association with gun ownership, as measured by regional survey data, were gun magazine subscriptions and the fraction of homicides committed with guns. Consequently, the only result supportive of a link between gun ownership and the total suicide rate was the one that used an unreliable indicator of gun ownership. The various studies reported in Table 6.8 can be summarized as follows. They all had extremely small samples, used primitive measures of gun availability, and usually failed to control for any other likely determinants of suicide rates that might be correlated with gun ownership levels. On the whole, they found that gun ownership levels were significantly and positively related to the *gun* suicide rate, but not to the total suicide rate. Therefore, the results accord with the conclusion that gun availability influences the choice of method for suicide, but not the frequency with which people kill themselves. However, this conclusion is based on very primitive research; more reliable conclusions will have to await the results of the 170 city study reported later in the chapter.

The Impact of Gun Control Laws on Suicide

What impact do gun control laws have on suicide rates? Table 6.9 summarizes the results of 12 previous studies. The best study is also the earliest. Geisel and his colleagues (1969) estimated models of state suicide rates with as many as eight other suicide predictors in addition to their gun control variables. They also measured gun control strictness at both local and state levels, considered eight different major categories of gun regulation, and checked for effects of gun control on total suicide rates as well as gun suicide rates. They found that their index of overall gun control severity had a significant negative relationship with the *gun* suicide rate, but failed to find a relationship with the *total* suicide rate significant at the conventional .05 probability level. This suggests that gun control laws only cause substitution of nongun methods of suicide for shooting, without significantly affecting total suicide. This is precisely what one would expect based on the findings of prior research on the relationship between gun ownership levels and suicide rates.

Scholars who have commented on this seminal study have overlooked its most important findings, probably because the authors themselves underemphasized them so much. Tucked away in an appendix, on the last page of the article, a single sentence of text and an accompanying footnote revealed that when dummy variables separately representing the various types of gun laws were inserted into the regression equations, the authors "could obtain no significant or even meaningful results" (p. 676). Since there were at least eight dummy variables and only one index, this means that the authors relegated the bulk of their findings to a single sentence in the appendix, findings that apparently indicated that gun control was generally ineffective. Contrary to the authors' generally positive conclusions, their findings constitute some of the strongest evidence available to date that gun control laws do not affect suicide rates.

Murray's (1975) analysis of state suicide rates in 1969 improved on the Geisel et al. study by introducing dummy gun control law variables into his regression equations, singly and as a group of dummies, rather than lumping them together into a single index (and by reporting the results of this procedure). Consistent with the dummy variable results in the Geisel study, none of the laws, either singly or collectively, showed a significant relationship to state suicide rates. Murray noted that, like Geisel, he had no measure of states' efforts to enforce the laws. His study also measured gun control only at the state level, an important flaw since the strictest gun laws are often found at the city level (Wright et al. 1983, pp. 247–69). The Geisel et al. city-level regression analyses had produced larger coefficients for the gun control index than the state-level analyses did, hinting that city regulation may be more effective.

DeZee (1983) replicated Murray's study using 1978 data and a regression technique that can estimate models with every possible combination of independent variables. He found that no single gun law or combination of gun laws, considered singly or added together, provided any additional ability to predict rates of gun suicide, nor did the "best" combination of predictors include any gun law variables. These findings are all the more significant given that DeZee used the gun suicide rate as his dependent variable. His results do not even support the idea that gun laws cause some suicides to substitute other lethal methods for shooting. However, all of the criticisms mentioned in regard to Murray's study also apply to this one.

Other studies in this area are weaker, offering little basis for judging the effect of gun laws on suicide. Lester and Murrell (1980) reported research that consisted entirely of computing simple bivariate correlation coefficients between an index of gun control severity and either suicide rates or changes in suicide rates between 1959–1961 and 1969–1971. States with more gun control had lower male suicide rates. However, despite the fact that 30% of female suicides in 1970 were committed with guns and that shooting was the leading suicide method among women, gun control severity was unrelated to the female suicide rate. The authors never provided a rationale for why the amount of gun control measured at a single point in time (1968) should relate to *changes* over time in suicide (and during an earlier period of time at that).

The complete absence of controls for other determinants of suicide rates makes these results uninterpretable. Not surprisingly, the methods used in this study yield absurd or nonsensical findings. For example, the authors did not mention in the 1980 article a finding from the same dataset that Lester reported in his 1984 book: using either 1960 or 1970 data, the gun control severity index had an even stronger negative correlation with the accidental *drowning* rate than it did with the total suicide rate! As Lester admitted, "there is no direct way in which strict gun control statutes could influence rates of death due to those kinds of accidents" (1984, pp. 100–1). Lester and Murrell also lumped together very different laws into a single index, using Guttman scaling. This scaling technique is ordinarily used to combine items that all reflect a singly underlying unidimensional trait, yet Lester's own subsequent principal components analysis later indicated that gun law types reflect at least three different dimensions of control, each of which relates to rates of violence in different ways (1984a, pp. 103, 106). And because the index was to be used in a correlational analysis, which requires measurement at the interval level, Guttman scaling was inappropriate, since it yields only ordinal measures (see Nunnally 1967, pp. 64–66 for a critique of Guttman scaling). This study was also characterized by all of the other problems noted in connection with the earlier studies.

Medoff and Magaddino's (1983) study was a state-level analysis similar to those of Murray and DeZee but they concluded that gun control laws reduce suicide rates. Their most interesting innovation was the inclusion in their model of an "enforcement" variable. They claimed to measure strictness of enforcement of gun control laws, inserting a dummy variable to designate six states that the National Rifle Association (NRA) labeled as being "stringent" in enforcement. No NRA publication was cited as a source and no evidence or rationale for these classifications was offered. The authors' comments on the variable indicate that it measured two things, neither of them enforcement effort. First, it appeared to measure strictness of the statutes themselves, especially how narrowly the laws formally defined who qualified for a handgun purchase permit, rather than strictness of enforcement. Second, the variable seemed to reflect administrative rigor as indicated by supposedly high permit application rejection rates. However, no data on rejection rates were presented or cited (pp. 366–7). A genuine measure of enforcement effort would reflect arrests, convictions, or sentences imposed for violations of the laws, and the authors' measure reflected no such thing. Nevertheless, the variable was significantly and negatively related to total suicide rates.

This study represented a step backward from earlier ones, in that it tested for the effects of just two types of laws—permit-to-purchase laws and waiting period laws. Even these two were lumped together in a single dummy variable representing whether a state had either law, making it impossible to distinguish the separate effects of the two. The authors argued that other forms of regulation are unlikely to affect suicide rates (p. 371), even though one would think that if any law were to have any effect it would be prohibitions of possession by mentally ill persons, a provision on the books in 22 states (Ronhovde and Sugars 1982, pp. 204–5). In contrast, waiting period laws are especially unlikely to affect suicide rates because gun suicides almost never have to purchase a gun at the last minute; nearly all of them use guns they had already acquired in the past for other purposes.

Medoff and Magaddino's model of suicide rates included age, unemployment, income, occupation, the percentage of a state's population that is Catholic, and a West region dummy, but was still seriously incomplete, failing to measure other known correlates of suicide rates that might relate to the existence of gun laws, including population density, population transience, the divorce rate, the rate of alcoholism, fraction of the population living alone, and other indicators of social disorganization, isolation, and instability [see Lester (1972, pp. 131–9) for a partial review of research on these suicide correlates, and the later results in Table 6.10). The omission of so many relevant suicide predictors makes it likely the regression coefficient estimates in this study were biased. These problems also characterized all of the previous studies.

A brief regression analysis by Sommers (1984) represented an even further step backward, in that the author ignored the substitution-of-other-methods issue and tested only for the impact of gun laws on states' gun suicide rates. Even so, his results were surprisingly negative. Only one of the nine types of gun laws evaluated showed a significant negative relationship to gun suicide rates: prohibitions of possession by mentally ill persons (significantly, one of the laws Medoff and Magaddino excluded from their analysis). The waiting period law dummy was negatively related to gun suicide rates, but was only marginally significant at the .10 level.

Sommers' gun suicide regression model included only two predictor variables beside the gun control dummies. The divorce rate, omitted from Medoff and Magaddino's model, was positively and significantly related to gun suicide rates. The unemployment rate, included and significant in the earlier study, was not significantly related in Sommers'. Given the omission of nearly all predictors of state suicide rates, it is almost certain Sommers' estimates were biased, making it impossible to draw any firm conclusions about the impact of gun laws even on gun suicide rates. This study also failed to measure city-level gun regulation, which could well affect state suicide rates, or to measure gun law enforcement activity.

There is one study that yielded evidence suggesting that at least one gun law may have reduced total suicides. Nicholson and Garner (1980) studied the Washington, D.C. Firearms Control Act of 1975 (which went into effect in February 1977). This law is arguably the most stringent gun law applying to any large jurisdiction in the United States, effectively eliminating handguns sales in Washington, D.C. and, more importantly, prohibiting private handgun possession except among those few who had already legally registered their handguns prior to passage of the law (Jones 1981, pp. 141–3). From 1976 to 1977, the gun suicide rate decreased by 38% and the total suicide rate declined by 22%, even though the U.S. suicide rate was increasing at this time. Although the authors did not control for any other determinants of suicide rates, it would be hard to think of any extraneous factors that changed just at this time, were unique to Washington, D.C., and that changed sharply enough to produce so large a 1-year drop. At the very least the results lend plausibility to the idea that this unusually strict law reduced suicides.

It is noteworthy that, despite the authors' assertions to the contrary, the law did not produce drops in total crimes that significantly exceeded those in control jurisdictions (see esp. their Table 10). Favorable effects, then, were limited to suicides. Since few crimes, but most suicides, are committed by persons not seriously criminal, this finding is consistent with the idea that broadly directed gun controls primarily reduce gun possession among the law-abiding, if at all.

Rich et al. (1990) compared the average suicide rates in Toronto in the 5-year periods before and after implementation of more restrictive Canadian gun law provisions. They found a drop in the gun suicide rate, but no significant change in the total suicide rate, concluding that other immediately lethal methods were completely substituted for guns.

On the whole, previous studies failed to make a solid case for the ability of gun controls to reduce the total suicide rate. Table 6.9 indicates that there have been only two studies to establish significant negative associations between gun controls and both gun suicide and total suicide rates, and neither of these had controls for any other determinants of suicide rates that might be correlated with gun controls. Overall, the studies have been about equally divided between those finding an apparent negative impact on total suicide rates and those failing to do so. However, the studies supportive of gun control efficacy have almost all been among the most technically primitive. More reliable assessments of gun law efficacy in reducing suicide will be presented in Chapter 10.

City-Level Analysis of the Impact of Guns on Suicide Rates

The city-level dataset described in Chapter 5 can be used to assess the impact of gun ownership levels on the rate of suicides. The general methods, data, and assumptions remain the same, and the variable names are the same as in Table 5.7. A model was specified in which gun levels could affect suicide rates, and suicide rates could also affect gun ownership levels.

Table 6.10 presents standardized LISREL solutions for estimated effects of gun ownership levels and the control variables on rates of suicide. The control variable results are not discussed here and are left to the interested reader.

The findings indicate that gun ownership appears to have no effect on rates of total, gun, or nongun suicide. Though the associations were not significant, gun ownership was positively associated with the gun suicide rate and negatively related to the nongun suicide rate. Consistent with most prior research, this pattern of findings suggests that availability of guns may (at best) influence the choice of method, but apparently does not affect the overall frequency of suicide.

The effort was also modeled in the opposite causal direction. High rates of suicide (total, with gun, and without gun) had the apparent effect of reducing gun ownership. Perhaps suicides remind some prospective gun buyers, especially those with depressed or other emotionally troubled people in their families, of one of the presumed risks of keeping guns.

Although gun ownership levels do not appear to influence total suicide rates, it is possible that the measures used here do not focus sufficiently narrowly on ownership among high-risk individuals, which might have an impact. Consequently, gun controls might still reduce suicide by reducing gun ownership levels among depressed and other suicide-prone segments of the population, and gun laws might still reduce suicide rates. This issue is taken up in Chapter 10.

Table 6.1. Suitability of Major Suicide Methods

Method	1980 Deaths	*Relevant Characteristics* Availability	Lethality	Painlessness	Quickness	Ease	Required Expertise	Lack of disfigurement	*Overall Ratings* Unweighted	Weighted[a]
Shooting	15420	3	4	4	5	4	4	2	26	115
Hanging	3405	5	4	3	4	4	5	3	28	115
Drug poisoning	3402	4	1	5	3	5	2	5	25	104
CO exhaust	2000	5	4	5	3	5	3	5	32	129
Jumping	880	5	2	2	4	2	5	3	24	90
Drowning	548	5	4	3	4	1	5	3	22	100
Cutting	399	5	1	2	3	3	5	3	22	86
Weights		4	5	5	4	5	3	3		
							Maximum possible score		35	145
							Minimum possible score		7	29

[a] Weighted rating for method m = $\sum_{j=1}^{7} \chi_j \cdot w_j$, where χ_j = method m's score on Relevant Characteristic j, and w_j = weight assigned to that characteristic. Unweighted overall ratings are simply the sums of the separate scores for each characteristic.

Table 6.2. Fatality Rates of Suicide Attempts by Method (Combination of Results of Two Studies)

	Completed Suicides			*Completed plus Attempted*				
	S/F	*Card*	*Total*	*S/F*	*Card*	*Total*	*Fatality Rate (% Completed)*	*Fatality Rank*
Shooting[a]	269	349	618	349	381	730	84.7	1
Head wound	223			250			(89.2)	
Other	46			99			(46.5)	
Hanging, etc.	100	176	276	127	227	354	80.0	2
CO[b] exhaust	84	117	201	111	150	261	77.0	3
Drowning	15	30	45	15	45	60	75.0	4
Jumping/ impact	23	107	130	50	257	307	42.3	5
Poisoning, except drugs	31	22	53	270	95	365	14.5	6
Other gas (besides CO)	15	4	19	95	47	142	13.4	7
Drugs	177	168	345	1450	1476	2926	11.8	8
Cutting/ stabbing	31	23	54	536	561	1097	4.9	9
Total[c]	768	1039	1807	3420	3481	6901	26.2	

[a] Only Shneidman and Farberow separately tabulated gunshot wounds by body location.
[b] CO = carbon monoxide, usually from motor vehicles.
[c] Includes unknown methods, combinations of methods, and other miscellaneous methods, not included elsewhere in table.
Sources: S/F, Shneidman and Farberow (1961, p. 35), approximate frequencies computed from rounded percentages; Card, Card (1974, p. 39).

Table 6.3. Suicide Method by Sex, U.S., 1980

	Sex								
	Male			Female			Total		
Method	Deaths	%	Rate	Deaths	%	Rate	Deaths	%	Rate
Shooting	12958	63	11.77	2462	39	2.11	15420	57	6.81
Hanging, etc.	3004	15	2.73	697	11	0.60	3701	14	1.63
Poisoning	1329	6	1.21	1713	27	1.47	3042	11	1.34
CO, other gases	1639	8	1.49	741	12	0.64	2380	9	1.05
Jumping	581	3	0.53	299	5	0.26	880	3	0.39
Drowning	326	2	0.30	222	3	0.19	548	2	0.24
Cutting	309	2	0.28	90	1	0.08	399	1	0.18
Domestic gas	33	0	0.03	5	0	0.00	38	0	0.02
Other	356	2	0.32	142	2	0.12	498	1	0.22
Total	20541	100	18.66	6377	100	5.47	26918	100	11.88
Resident population (1000s)	110,053			116,493			226,546		

Source: Analysis of 1980 Mortality Detail computer tape from the National Center for Health Statistics.

Table 6.4. Suicide Method by Region of Occurrence, U.S., 1980[a]

	Region											
	Northeast			*North Central*			*West*			*South*		
Method	*Deaths*	*%*	*Rate*	*Deaths*	*%*	*Rate*	*Deaths*	*%*	*Rate*	*Deaths*	*%*	*Rate*
Shooting	1786	38	3.63	3480	54	5.91	3450	55	8.20	6614	71	8.78
Hanging, etc.	1045	22	2.13	960	15	1.63	805	12	1.86	891	10	1.18
Poisoning	545	12	1.11	566	9	0.96	1068	17	2.47	863	9	1.14
CO, other gases	513	11	1.04	937	15	1.59	48	7	1.11	450	5	0.60
Jumping	395	8	0.80	131	2	0.22	227	4	0.53	127	1	0.17
Drowning	144	3	0.29	118	2	0.20	103	2	0.24	183	2	0.24
Cutting	100	2	0.20	89	1	0.15	116	2	0.27	94	1	0.12
Domestic gas	3	0	0.01	6	0	0.01	15	0	0.03	14	0	0.02
Other	158	3	0.32	111	2	0.19	105	2	0.24	124	1	0.16
Total	4691	100	9.55	6400	100	10.87	6466	100	14.98	9361	100	12.42
(% suicide, shooting)/ (% households with guns)		1.21			1.07			1.21			1.26	
Resident population (1000s)		49,135			58,866			75,372			43,172	

[a] The regions combine various census regions (see population source below, inside front cover). The total row includes 12 deaths due to late effects of suicide attempts, not included elsewhere in table.

Sources: Suicides—Analysis of 1980 Mortality Detail computer tape from the National Center for Health Statistics. Population—U.S. Bureau of Census (1984, p. 12). Percent of households with guns—1980, 1982 combined General Social Surveys (Davis and Smith 1984).

Table 6.5. Gun Involvement in Suicides and Homicides, U.S., 1933–1988[a]

Year	*Total Suicide Rate*	*Gun Suicide Rate*	*% Suicides with Guns*	*% Homicides with Guns*	*Firearms per 1000 Resident Population*
1933	15.9	6.2	39.0	64.9	—
1934	14.9	5.8	38.8	63.9	—
1935	14.3	5.4	37.5	61.5	—
1936	14.3	5.3	37.0	58.8	—
1937	15.0	5.5	36.7	58.1	—
1938	15.3	5.7	37.2	57.4	—
1939	14.1	5.3	37.5	57.2	—
1940	14.3	5.3	37.4	56.7	—
1941	12.8	4.8	37.3	57.1	—
1942	12.0	4.5	38.0	54.3	—
1943	10.2	3.8	37.0	51.5	—
1944	9.9	3.6	36.3	52.6	—
1945	11.1	4.0	36.0	54.4	352
1946	11.5	—	—	56.5	344
1947	11.5	—	—	57.5	351
1948	11.1	—	—	57.3	363
1949	11.4	4.8	42.5	55.5	371
1950	11.3	4.9	43.0	55.1	381
1951	10.3	4.5	43.2	54.4	390
1952	10.0	4.5	45.1	54.9	396
1953	10.0	4.6	45.7	54.8	402
1954	10.1	4.7	46.1	55.5	405
1955	10.2	4.7	46.3	53.5	408
1956	10.0	4.7	46.7	55.0	413
1957	9.7	4.6	47.1	54.6	417
1958	10.6	5.1	47.9	56.1	420
1959	10.5	5.0	47.2	56.5	425
1960	10.6	5.0	47.4	56.7	431
1961	10.4	4.9	47.6	57.3	435
1962	10.9	5.1	46.9	56.4	439
1963	11.0	5.1	46.1	57.2	445
1964	10.8	5.1	47.6	57.5	452
1965	11.1	5.1	46.0	59.0	463
1966	10.9	5.3	48.9	60.6	476
1967	10.8	5.3	49.5	63.9	492
1968	10.7	5.5	51.1	65.7	513
1969	11.1	5.6	50.5	67.3	532
1970	11.5	5.8	50.1	67.9	549
1971	11.6	5.9	51.0	67.6	567
1972	11.9	6.4	53.4	69.2	588

(continued)

Table 6.5. (Continued)

Year	Total Suicide Rate	Gun Suicide Rate	% Suicides with Guns	% Homicides with Guns	Firearms per 1000 Resident Population
1973	11.9	6.3	53.0	68.5	610
1974	12.0	6.7	55.4	69.9	637
1975	12.6	6.9	55.0	68.2	657
1976	12.3	6.8	54.9	65.3	678
1977	13.0	7.3	56.1	64.5	697
1978	12.3	6.9	56.4	65.5	716
1979	12.2	7.0	57.2	65.3	721
1980	11.8	6.8	57.3	64.8	738
1981	12.0	7.0	58.5	64.7	754
1982	12.2	7.2	58.7	62.7	768
1983	12.1	7.1	58.7	59.6	778
1984	12.4	7.2	58.4	59.7	788
1985	12.3	7.3	59.0	59.5	798
1986	12.8	7.5	58.7	60.7	805
1987	12.7	7.5	58.9	60.8	816
1988	12.3	n.a.	n.a.	62.8	n.a.

[a] Gun suicide figures were not gathered for 1946–1948.
Sources: Suicides, homicides—U.S. NCHS (1989) and earlier years; firearms—Table 2.1; population—U.S. Bureau of the Census *Statistical Abstract of the United States—1989.*

Table 6.6. The Preference for Suicide by Shooting, by Sex–Race–Age Group, U.S., 1980

% of suicides committed with gun
(% suicides, gun)/(% of persons owning gun)
(% suicides, gun)/(% persons in gun-owning households)

	Male				*Female*				
Age	*White*	*Black*	*Other*	*Total*	*White*	*Black*	*Other*	*Total*	*Both Sexes, All Races*
0–14	54.6	37.5	0.0	53.4	66.7	100.0	0.0	69.2	56.2
	—	—	—	—	—	—	—	—	—
	1.11	1.24	0.0	1.14	1.36	3.31	0.0	1.48	1.22
15–24	65.0	58.0	44.8	64.2	53.8	42.0	41.7	52.6	62.2
	1.62	7.53	[a]	1.78	11.70	6.88	[a]	11.19	3.46
	1.11	7.53	[a]	1.22	1.35	1.68	[a]	1.44	1.43
25–39	59.1	62.3	44.7	59.1	42.6	41.3	30.9	42.2	55.1
	1.17	2.12	1.56	1.22	3.64	4.01	0.93	3.58	1.93
	1.08	1.76	1.56	1.21	0.91	1.76	0.93	0.97	1.16
40 and over	65.7	68.1	25.8	65.4	33.1	44.2	8.2	33.1	56.9
	1.19	1.31	0.39	1.19	1.99	4.65	0.66	2.08	1.76
	1.12	1.27	0.39	1.12	0.79	1.79	0.22	0.82	1.19
All ages	63.5	62.8	42.8	63.2	38.8	42.9	24.2	38.7	57.4
	1.23	1.64	1.28	1.26	2.85	4.66	1.53	2.98	1.98
	1.11	1.51	1.28	1.14	0.90	1.76	0.92	0.96	1.22
Both sexes, all ages	57.7	59.0	37.4	57.4					
	1.91	3.10	1.54	1.98					
	1.18	1.95	1.26	1.22					

[a] Impossible to calculate because there were no sample cases of gun owners these categories.

Sources: Analysis of 1980 Mortality Detail File, National Center for Health Statistics for suicides; combined 1980, 1982 General Social Survey for gun ownership rates (Davis and Smith 1984).

Table 6.7. Suicide Method by Size of Place of Residence, U.S., 1980

	Size of Place of Residence														
	1 million or more			*100,000–1 million*			*25,000–100,000*			*10,000–25,000*			*Under 10,000*		
Method	*Deaths*	*%*	*Rate*	*Deaths*	*%*	*Rate*	*Deaths*	*%*	*Rate*	*Deaths*	*%*	*Rate*	*Deaths*	*%*	*Rate*
Shooting	756	38	4.31	2912	53	7.28	2330	50	5.39	1436	56	5.19	7970	65	8.12
Hanging, etc.	362	10	2.07	769	14	1.92	729	16	1.68	365	10	1.32	1466	12	1.49
Poisoning	319	16	1.82	773	14	1.93	610	13	1.41	313	12	1.13	1020	8	1.04
CO, other gases	73	4	0.42	773	7	0.98	544	12	1.26	254	10	0.92	1115	9	1.14
Jumping	258	15	1.70	252	5	0.63	133	3	0.31	45	2	0.16	144	1	0.15
Drowning	56	3	0.32	143	3	0.36	103	2	0.24	60	2	0.22	185	2	0.19
Cutting	64	3	0.37	102	2	0.25	67	1	0.16	40	2	0.14	122	1	0.12
Domestic gas	6	0	0.03	12	0	0.03	8	0	0.02	0	0	0.00	12	0	0.01
Other	70	4	0.40	88	2	0.22	103	2	0.24	59	2	0.21	175	1	0.18
Total[a]	2006	100	11.45	5448	100	13.62	4631	100	10.71	2573	100	9.31	12211	100	12.44
Resident population (1000s)		17,530			40,007			43,222			27,645			98,142	

[a] Includes 12 deaths due to late effects of suicide attempt, not included elsewhere in table.

Sources: Suicides—Analysis of 1980 Mortality Detail computer tape from the National Center for Health Statistics. Population—U.S. Bureau of Census (1984, p. 27).

Table 6.8. Previous Studies of the Effects of Gun Ownership Levels on Suicide Rates

	Markush and Bartolucci (1984) 9 U.S. regions	*Lester (1987) 48 states*	*Lester (1988a) 6 Australian states*	*Lester (1988b) 9 U.S. regions*	*Clarke and Jones (1989) 26 (13) years*[a]	*Lester (1989) 50 states*
Number of control variables	0	0	0	3	0	0
Measure of gun ownership[b]	S	O	S	S	S	O
Impact on *gun* suicide rate?	Yes	Yes[c]	No	Yes[c]	Yes/No[d]	Yes
Impact on *total* suicide rate?	No[e]	No	No	No	Yes/No[d]	Yes

[a] Time series dataset included 26 years total, but only 13 had real data on gun ownership levels; the rest were interpolations.

[b] S, survey measure—% of households with guns; O, other measures.

[c] Only bivariate association reported.

[d] Handgun prevalence related to suicide rates, total gun prevalence unrelated.

[e] Significant positive correlation was obtained only if eccentric weighting scheme was applied. Conventional unweighted results indicated no significant association.

Table 6.9. Previous Studies of the Effect of Gun Laws on Suicide Rates

Study	*Sample*	*Number of Control Variables*	*Gun Ownership Measured?*	*Number of Gun Controls Assessed*	*Gun Controls Significantly[a] Reduce Rate of*	
					Gun Suicide	*Total Suicide*
Geisel et al. (1969)	50 states, 1960	7	No	1(8)[b]	Yes/no[c]	No
	50 states, 1965	8	No	1(8)[b]	Yes/no[c]	No
	129 cities, 1960	8	No	1(8)[b]		No
Murray (1975)	50 states, 1970	9	No	7	No	
Lester and Murrell (1980; 1986)	48 states, 1960, 1970	0	No	1[b]	Yes	Yes
Nicholson and Garner (1980)	Time series Washington, D.C.	0	No	1	Yes	Yes
Lester and Murrell (1982)	48 states, 1960, 1970	0	No	3(8)[d]	Yes	

Medoff and Maggadino (1983)	50 states, 1970	5	No	1(2)[e]		Yes
DeZee (1983)	50 states, 1978	7	No	7	No	
Sommers (1984)	50 states, 1978	2	No	9	No[f]	
Lester (1987a)	48 states, 1970	0	No	1[b]		Yes
Lester (1987b)	48 states, 1980	1	No	1[b]		Yes
Lester (1988b)	9 regions, 1970	2	Yes	1[b]	Yes[g]	No
Boor and Bair (1990)	50 states, D.C., 1985	9	No	2(8)[h]		Yes
Rich et al. (1990)	Time series 2 cities	0	No	1	Yes	No

[a] Significant at .05 level.
[b] Measured "strictness" of gun control—all control types lumped together.
[c] Overall "strictness" index was significantly and negatively related, but separate gun law dummies yielded no significant results.
[d] Used three factor scores grouping eight gun control types together; individual controls not separately assessed.
[e] Lumped two gun law types together into a single dummy variable.
[f] Only one of nine gun law coefficients significant at .05 level.
[g] Only bivariate association reported.
[h] Grouped eight types of gun control into two summary indexes.

Table 6.10. Effects of Gun Ownership Levels and Control Variables on City Suicide Rates[a]

	LNSUICID	*Gun Ownership*[b]	*LNGNSUIC*	*Gun Ownership*	*LNNGSUIC*	*Gun Ownership*
PCTBLACK	−.091	.499*	[Gun and nongun suicide models contained the same control variables as the total suicide model. Their coefficient estimates have been omitted.]			
TRNSIENT	.211*					
PCTMOVE	−.011					
CNTDIVRT	.226*	.196*				
ALCHLSM	.356*					
INVPOP	−.083	−.203*				
DENSITY	−.321*	−.357*				
HOSPITAL	.171*					
LIVLONE	.098	−.216*				
PCTOLD	.100					
RGUNMAG		.257*				
HUNTERS		.174*				
Gun ownership	−.225		.119		−.379	
PSI	.510	.353	.273	.344	.518	.356
PSI (2,1)	.266*		.172*		.177*	
df	86		86		86	
χ^2	226.44		234.20		226.63	
GOF	.932		.929		.932	

[a] Gun law variables were also included in these models but are not shown; estimates of their coefficients are presented in Chapter 10. Also, the following control variables were tested but found to be unrelated to suicide or gun ownership levels: MFI, PCTHISP, INEQUALT, PCTM1524, RPOV, OWNEROCC, COLLEGE, POPCHANG, PCTFOREN, PCRM80, CHRCHMEM, ADDICTRT, PCTSMSA, VISITORS, WEST, MAXTEMP, CROWDING, STHNNESS, ACCIDENT.

[b] Latent construct with indicators: PGH7982, PCTGNAST, PCTGNROB, GUNSTOL.

*$p < .05$.

CHAPTER

7

Firearms Accidents

Fewer than 5% of gun deaths in 1987 were due to firearms accidents, which numbered about 1400 that year. The significance of accidents therefore is not due to their dominance in the firearms death statistics. Rather, this category of gun misuse is important because of the pivotal role it plays in the debate over whether keeping a gun in the home for protection entails more risk than benefit for the average household. Many people who misuse guns, whether in accidents, suicides, homicides, or other crimes, originally owned the guns for defensive reasons (Heins, et al. 1974; Browning 1974; Burr 1977; Wright and Rossi 1986). Consequently, disarming a significant share of these persons is likely to entail persuading them either that guns are not very useful for self-defense (an issue addressed in Chapter 4) or that there is some serious compensating risk that outweighs any possible defensive benefits.

Most defensive gun owners do not perceive themselves as prone to crime or suicide, so it is difficult to persuade them that such risks apply to them. On the other hand, most people regard accidents as events that can happen to anyone. It is plausible that even the most responsible and law-abiding family can experience a gun accident if they keep a firearm in the home, particularly if it is kept loaded for self-defense. Therefore, the argument goes, because the chances of successfully using a gun for defense against criminals are extremely small, the risk of a gun accident to the average gun owner should outweigh any reasonable estimate of the defensive value of guns.

As noted in Chapter 4, this argument was made in explicit form by Rushforth and his colleagues (1975, p. 504). Noting that fatal gun accidents outnumbered justifiable homicides of home burglars and robbers, the authors concluded from these facts that "the possession of firearms by civilians appears to be a dangerous and ineffective means of self-protection" (p. 505). Although this conclusion was a non sequitur, it has since been repeatedly cited in procontrol propaganda tracts (e.g., Yeager et al. 1976, p. 4) and many others have made similar arguments (e.g., Shields 1981, pp. 49–53; Kellerman and Reay 1986).

This argument is rhetorically important. Without any counterbalancing risk, even the slightest defensive benefit of guns could tip the scales in favor of ownership. Even if *nearly* all crimes occurred in ways that precluded victims from defending themselves with a gun, there would still remain that small minority of cases in which a gun would be usable. Because crime victims cannot know in advance whether they would be among that small minority, they might well decide they should have a gun just in case they did find themselves in such a rare circumstance. The reasoning would be: "If there's no risk to me or my family, why not give myself the option of using a gun, should appropriate circumstances arise?" Consequently, the risk of gun accidents to ordinary people plays a critical role in the gun control debate, serving as the counterbalancing risk to which all gun owners and their families are theoretically subject.

Despite its importance, the topic of gun accidents has been given little attention in books on gun control. Wright and his co-authors (1983) devoted about four pages to it, Lester (1984a) gave it two pages, and Brill (1977) and the authors in Kates (1984) (excepting a single footnote, p. 46), ignored the subject altogether. Newton and Zimring (1969) devoted only seven widely spaced pages of material to the topic, but even that much attention may serve as an indication of the importance attached to the subject by the authors of a report aimed at justifying more restrictive federal gun control laws.

The Frequency of Gun Accidents

In 1987, about 1400 U.S. deaths were officially classified as being due to the accidental discharge of a firearm (Table 7.1). However, this may be an overcount, due to the misclassification of some gun suicides and, to a lesser extent, some homicides as fatal gun accidents (FGAs). The potential for misclassification of suicides is suggested by the high fraction of alleged FGAs that resulted from self-inflicted wounds. Over the period 1969–1978, at least 22% of U.S. deaths officially classified as due to FGAs were self-inflicted (Table 7.1). However, the other 78% included cases "unspecified" as to whether they were self-inflicted, therefore presumably including some that were self-inflicted. Eight more detailed studies covering smaller general samples of FGAs have been done by the Metropolitan Life Insurance Company (MLIC) and others. In three MLIC studies (1953, 1956, 1968) the percentages of FGAs that were self-inflicted were 42, 44, and 65, respectively, and in three studies reviewed by Iskrant and Joliet (1968, pp. 95–6) "most" or "approximately half" of the FGAs were self-inflicted. In Rushforth et al. (1975, p. 502) the percentages self-inflicted were 41% for victims 15 and under, and 70% for adults. Most recently, Morrow and Hudson reported that 45% of North Carolina FGAs in 1976–1980 were self-inflicted (1986, p. 1122). Considering all of the findings, probably about half of all (FGAs) are self-inflicted.

That a death is self-inflicted does not prove it was suicidal; people do accidentally wound themselves. However, the circumstances of many allegedly accidental self-inflicted woundings are highly suspicious. For example, one of the most detailed MLIC studies found that of 66 fatal self-inflicted home gun "accidents," 24 involved the victim allegedly cleaning, oiling, or repairing a gun (MLIC 1968). However, Vincent DiMaio, an expert on gunshot wounds, has written that in his experience as a medical examiner he "has never seen a case of an individual fatally shooting himself while 'cleaning, repairing or oiling a weapon. . . Careful investigation of these deaths (where such an activity was alleged) . . . revealed all to be suicides" (1973, p. 2). He has further stated that most deaths alleged to be single person hunting accidents and many cases of "Russian Roulette" are in fact suicides. Combining data from the three most detailed MLIC studies (MLIC49–51, MLIC53–55, and MLIC64–66 in Tables 7.7 and 7.8), of 327 home FGAs in which circumstance was specified, 38 deaths were self-inflicted and allegedly involved cleaning or repairing a gun; another 20 were self-inflicted and involved Russian Roulette. If it is assumed that half of the Russian Roulette cases and all of the "cleaning, repairing" cases were actually suicides, in line with DiMaio's judgments, then at least 48 deaths, or 14.7% of the home FGAs were actually suicides. Since about 63.5% of all FGAs occur in the home (Table 7.8), about 9.3% (0.147 × 0.635 × 100%) or more of all FGAs may actually be suicides, under the assumptions stated. This estimate is confirmed by more direct evidence provided by Dr. Paul Morrow (1987), whose North Carolina data indicated that 11–28% of self-inflicted fatal gun "accidents" were possible or probable suicides. If half of the U.S. FGAs are self-inflicted, Morrow's figures would imply that 5.5–14.0% of all deaths classified as FGAs were actually suicides. (Note that although these misclassified cases are a substantial share of the relatively rare FGAs, they constitute at most 1–2% of the far more numerous gun suicides and are therefore of little significance for suicide analyses.)

DiMaio (1973) also reported that "incidents in which a gun 'accidentally' discharges during a 'friendly scuffle' or while 'horsing around,' on close examination are usually found to be homicides." If it is assumed that just half of the cases in the three detailed MLIC studied that were other-inflicted and involved "scuffling for possession of weapon" or "playing with weapon," were actually homicides, then another 13.7% of home FGAs, or 8.4% (0.133 × 0.635 × 100%) of all FGAs are homicides. Excluding alleged FGAs that may have actually been suicides or homicides leaves 78–86% of the original total, or about 1090–1204 genuine FGAs in 1987. This is less than 4% of all gun deaths and about 1.3% of all accidental deaths due to all causes. Nevertheless, as this estimate relies on limited information, the official published FGA figures will be conservatively used in subsequent discussions. The estimate of 1090 may serve as the lower limit, and the official figure of 1400 as the upper limit, of a range in which the true number of FGAs in 1987 fell.

The risk of being a victim of a FGA can be better appreciated if it is compared to a more familiar risk. Table 7.2 shows death rates associated with motor vehicle accidents and gun accidents for the United States in 1980. The rates are based on two measures of exposure to risk: (1) the number of households that own at least one of the devices in question, and (2) the total number of such devices in private hands.

The accidental death rate for motor vehicles is 15 times as high as for guns when based on the number of owning households, and 29 times as high when based on numbers of devices in existence. The point is not that guns are safe because they cause accidental death less often than motor vehicles. Cars are very dangerous when handled recklessly, and for an object to be less involved in fatal accidents than cars is not to pass a rigorous standard of safety. The comparison is made only to provide a meaningful point of reference with which readers are familiar. In this connection, it might also be noted that more Americans die each year in swimming pool drownings than die in FGAs, even though guns are far more common than swimming pools—2934 accidental drownings occurred in swimming pools in 1980, compared to 1955 FGAs in the same year. Similarly, the number of accidental deaths relative to the number of objects in existence is also far higher for boats and ships (2121 deaths) and aircraft (1543 deaths) (tabulations from 1980 Mortality Detail File, U.S. NCHS 1983).

The risk of accidental motor vehicle death is routinely taken on each day by millions of Americans. Traffic deaths may occur so often because people so casually expose themselves to the risk, sometimes failing to fully appreciate the lethal potential of cars. Guns, on the other hand, are widely recognized as lethal instruments and evidently treated by most of their users with sufficient caution to prevent accident fatalities. The paradox, then, is that the object that is most obviously dangerous is, perhaps partly for that reason, less likely to actually be involved in an accident.

Frequency of use accounts for some of the difference in accident frequency. Inaccurate perceptions of risk may be the reason people routinely drive their cars two or more times a day, nearly every day, even when not necessary for occupational or other reasons, thereby greatly increasing their exposure to risk. On the other hand, few gun owners casually fire their gun several times or even once a day. Findings from a 1975 national survey indicated that even among active recreational shooters the average number of days of participation per participant per year was only 14 for target shooting, 15 for "plinking" (shooting at tin cans, etc.), and 23 for hunting. Depending on how much these days of participation overlapped and how many of the three activities they engaged in, the average active shooter devoted only 14 to 52 days each year to shooting. Further, the survey figures on number of participants indicated that most gun owners did not participate in any of these activities at all in 1975, i.e., were inactive shooters (U.S. Fish and Wildlife Service, 1977, pp. 54–5, 64, 85). Therefore, exposure to the risk of recreational shooting is rather infrequent among gun owners. And the number of times guns are fired for defensive or criminal purposes is negligible compared to recreational shooting (Chapters 2 and 4).

Table 7.3 provides additional comparative information on the risk of gun accidents. It covers nonfatal injuries rather than deaths and is based on data gathered by the Consumer Product Safety Commission (CPSC) from a national sample of hospital emergency rooms. These figures mostly cover accidental injuries, but also cover intentionally inflicted injuries among persons under 15 years of age and injuries suspected but not confirmed to be intentionally inflicted on persons 15 and over. Based on estimates of the number of nonfatal injuries requiring emergency room treatment, guns accounted for about 60,000 such injuries, ranking behind 35 other products or groups of products, but ahead of 147 others. Various sorts of sporting equipment were the products most often involved in these nonfatal injuries. However, stairs were the number one "product" on the injury list, accounting for more than 12 times as many injuries as guns, even when BB and pellet gun injuries were lumped in with firearms injuries. Bicycles accounted for over eight times as many injuries, while baseball, football, and basketball equipment each accounted for over seven times as many injuries as guns.

Earlier data from the CPSC weighted injuries by their seriousness, producing an injury index that reflected seriousness as well as frequency of injuries involving various products. These data, also presented in Table 7.3, reflect a similar picture, with guns ranked behind 45 other common products or groups of products and ahead of at least 113 others. The rating for the top-ranked product, bicycles, was 15 times as high as that of firearms, which were ranked just behind nonprescription drugs and only three positions ahead of "pens and pencils." The low frequency with which gun owners shoot their guns, and thereby expose themselves and others to risk, probably is largely responsible for these relatively low injury frequencies.

Trends in Gun Accidents

Table 7.1 shows the number and rate of FGAs for the United States from 1933 to 1987, along with the per capita rate of gun ownership for comparative purposes. The data seem to present an anomaly—as the rate of private gun ownership increased sharply from 1967 to 1987, the number and rate of FGAs sharply declined. To some degree this trend is attributable to the same causes driving down accident rates in general; the overall accidental death rate has been declining since the 1930s. However, whereas the general rate declined by only 18% from 1977 to 1987, the FGA rate dropped by 33% (National Safety Council 1988, pp. 18, 21). Thus, factors specific to gun accidents have also been at work.

It should be stressed that these data count only deaths, rather than total accidents. Waller and Whorton (1973) found there were 14.5 nonfatal accidents to every fatal one in Vermont, and Rushforth et al. reported a 13 to 1 ratio in Cleveland (1975, pp. 504–5). Although there are no trend data on nonfatal gun accidents, it is at least possible that total accidents remained the same or even increased over the period in question, but that so much smaller a fraction of them resulted in death, the death total declined.

The peak in the FGA rate, within the last 30 years, occurred in 1967 and the sharpest increases occurred in the 1965–1967 period. One interpretation of these facts is that increases in defensive gun ownership occurred during this period in response to the unusually large increases in crime of the period. Because the increases in defensive gun ownership were likely to have been among persons not raised around guns and not socialized into their safe use (Lizotte and Bordua 1980; Lizotte et al. 1981), they were especially likely to contribute to FGA increases (McDowall and Loftin 1986). The first year or two of such inexperienced ownership might be especially accident-prone. Crime increased sharply during the same years that had large increases in FGAs. The 1963–1964 period showed a 14% increase in the reported rate of violent crime and a 10% increase in burglary, 1965–1966 saw 9 and 10% increases, respectively, and 1966–1967 saw 15% increases in both categories. On the other hand, the largest 1-year crime increase in recorded U.S. history occurred in 1967–1968, during which time the FGA rate declined sharply. This same pattern was in evidence again in 1973–1974. Thus it is difficult to attribute FGA increases solely to general crime increases and resulting defensive gun purchases. However, what distinguished 1965–1967 from the rest of the past 30 years was the outbreak of riots in many of the nation's large cities. Thus riots in particular may have increased new gun ownership among especially accident-prone people as well as increasing the keeping of loaded guns in the home.

The decreases in FGAs from 1967 to 1987 may be partly attributable to improvements in medical treatment of gunshot wounds. Certainly, over a long period of the past, there have been dramatic improvements in survival rates of gunshot victims. The mortality rate for abdominal gunshot wounds treated at a midwestern urban hospital was 60% in the 1930–1938 period, 36% in 1938–1946, 16% in 1955–1962, and 12.7% in 1962–1970 (Taylor 1973, p. 175). It should be stressed that these mortality rates apply only to victims reaching the hospital alive and are therefore not useful for determining the absolute level of mortality. They are cited only to indicate long-term trends in the effectiveness of medical treatment of gunshot wounds. Note, however, that the medical explanation seems insufficient to explain the dramatic declines in the FGA rate after 1967, since the medical improvements apparently had slowed or perhaps even ceased by the mid-1960s, and were probably not large enough to account for a halving of the FGA rate.

The explanation of recent trends may instead involve shifts in the types of guns owned and, more importantly, the types routinely kept loaded. FGAs occur only with loaded guns, and most of the guns routinely kept loaded are handguns owned for self-defense (Chapter 4). The fraction of the civilian gun stock attributable to handguns increased in the past several decades (Table 2.1) and it is possible that an increasing fraction of these handguns were the cheap, small-caliber, low-power handguns known as Saturday Night Specials (SNSs). Since these are less lethal than other guns and are probably mainly owned for self-defense (Chapter 3), an increasing fraction of loaded guns being SNSs could lower the mortality rate among accidental woundings (Kates 1983a, p. 263).

Children and Gun Accidents

The image of a small child finding his parents' gun and killing himself or a playmate is an emotionally powerful one. Advocates of stricter gun control often lay special stress on the risks of gun accidents to children (e.g., Yeager et al. 1976, p. 4). Accidents of this sort can more easily be blamed on the mere availability of guns per se, rather than to correctable problems with how they are handled, since all small children are assumed to be irresponsible by adult standards and therefore cannot be taught safety precautions with the same assurance of effectiveness as would be the case with teenagers or adults. It can be argued, then, that this sort of risk applies to all households with guns and small children, not just those with unusually irresponsible older persons.

Table 7.4 shows the distribution of FGAs by age of victim and gun type involved. The data are from the Mortality Detail File, a computerized dataset containing coded information from essentially all U.S. death certificates. Regardless of how "small child" is defined, it is clear that FGAs rarely involve small children. The victims of FGAs, like victims of intentional homicides, are concentrated most heavily among adolescents and young adults. In 1980, only 122 children under the age of 10 and 45 under the age of 5 were killed in accidents officially classified as FGAs. Assuming that the distribution of FGAs across gun type categories is the same among cases in which gun type was unknown as among cases where it was known, handguns were involved in 61 deaths of children under the age of 10, 24 of these younger than 5.

However, even these figures probably overstate the frequency of FGAs involving small children. It has long been known that abusive parents who seek medical care for their battered children often attribute the injuries to "accidents" (e.g., Kempe et al., 1962). When the children in such incidents die, it is all the easier for parents to sustain the deception, since their victims cannot contradict them. It is therefore likely that some of the FGAs involving small children were actually extreme cases of child abuse. A 1976 national survey found that 3% of children had, in the previous year, had guns or knives (the two are combined in the source) actually used on them by their parents, according to the parents' own admissions (Strauss et al. 1980, pp. 61–2). Since this translates into about 46,000 such incidents per year, it would not be implausible for a hundred or so to result in a gun death falsely reported as accidental.

The frequency of FGAs involving children is sometimes inflated by the inclusion of adolescent FGAs in the "child" total. In some extreme cases, authors have even included 18–24 year old adults in the total. For example, Teret and Wintemute (1983) claimed that "almost 1,000 children die each year from unintentional gunshot wounds," citing the National Safety Council annual compilation *Accident Facts* for 1980 as their source. Examination of this source reveals that the claim of "almost 1,000 children" actually pertained to persons age 0–24, an age span not stated by the authors (National Safety Council 1981, p. 7). Interestingly, Wintemute elsewhere set age 14 as the upper age limit for a study of FGAs among "children" (Wintemute et al. 1987, p. 3107). Even if one defines "children" to include adolescents as old as 14, the national "child" FGA total in 1980 was only 316 (Table 7.4), less than a third the figure cited. The practice of lumping FGAs involving adolescents and even young adults with children FGAs creates an erroneous impression that FGAs are common among small children. This practice is especially common among procontrol propagandists and among physicians and public health specialists (e.g., Rivara and Stapleton 1982; Runyan et al. 1985; Patterson and Smith 1987). Even the federal Centers for Disease Control (CDC) is not immune to the practice, defining "children" and "childhood" as encompassing the ages 0 to 19 (U.S. CDC 1989).

The practice is misleading because it mixes a very low rate population, preadolescent children, in with a very high rate population, adolescents and young adults. It is more informative to keep adolescent FGAs separate from those involving other age groups. Even if adolescents had to be grouped with others it would seem to make far more sense to group them with young adults than with children, since there are only small differences in FGA rates between adolescents and young adults, but very large differences between adolescents and younger children. Grouping small children with adolescents seems to serve no purpose other than the propagandistic one of duping people into believing that accidental gun deaths are common among small children.

This practice of inflating statistics on the frequency of a social problem is not unique to gun control advocates. For example, leaders of the missing-children movement repeatedly cited enormous estimates of the number of children abducted by strangers, sometimes claiming there were as many as 50,000 such incidents a year. The estimates were unreliable and almost certainly far too high. Once their numbers came to be challenged, however, movement crusaders then argued that numbers were irrelevant, frequently asserting that even "one missing child is one too many" (Best 1988, pp. 87–8). Virtually identical defenses are presented when gun control advocates' estimates of child gun accidents are challenged. As Best noted, "activists use statistics to persuade; but these numbers must be understood for what they are—part of the rhetoric of social-problems promotion" (p. 92).

Accidental gun deaths involving a small child as the victim do not necessarily involve a small child as the shooter. In 137 California FGAs with victims under age 15, 88 or 64% were identified as involving a shooter who was also under 15, including self-inflicted cases (Wintemute et al. 1987, p. 3108). If this figure applies to FGAs with victims under age 10 and it were applied to the national data in Table 7.4, it would imply that about 78 ($122 \times 0.64 = 78$) FGAs in 1980 involved children under the age of 10 shooting themselves or other children under age 10, with about half, or 39, of these involving handguns. These figures are upper limit figures, since they assume that all such cases are genuine accidents and not the result of sibling combat or other intentional violence; Strauss et al. estimated there were about 109,000 annual uses of guns or knives by siblings on each other (1980, p. 82).

In 1980 there were about 33 million children in the United States under the age of 10 (U.S. Bureau of the Census 1983b). About half of U.S. households have a gun (Chapter 2). Assuming that gun ownership levels were as high for households with small children as in those without them, around 16.5 million were exposed to the risk of an in-home FGA. Thus the chance of a child-against-child FGA (including self-inflicted cases) occurring to a small (age 0–9) child in a gun-owning household in 1980 was at most about one in 212,000 (78/16.5 million). The probability of *any* kind of FGA occurring to a small child in a gun-owning household was about one in 135,000.

This figure is, of course, an average pertaining to all gun-owning households. The risk would higher among just those households with children. In 1987, there were 280 FGAs with victims under age 15 (Table 7.5), about 103 of these involving handguns (assuming 36.9% of FGAs under age 15 involved handguns—Table 7.4). According to a 1989 national survey (Quinley 1990), 62% of gun-owning households have no children at all, of any age, and therefore are subject to zero risk of a resident child being accidentally hurt by a gun kept in the household. However, of 42.8 million households with guns, and 24.4 million with handguns (Table 2.4), about 16.3 million households with guns and 6.2 million with handguns did have "children," with no age limits specified in the survey source. If the survey's Rs were mainly reporting children in the under-15 age span, the risk of experiencing a child (0–14 years old) FGA in any one year was about 1 in 58,000 for all gun-owning households with children, and 1 in 60,000 for handgun-owning households with children.

The fact that so few child FGAs involve handguns is partially attributable to certain mechanical characteristics of revolvers. For children under the age of 4 or so it may be physically impossible to fire unmodified revolvers of even minimally adequate manufacturing quality, because small childrens' hand spans are too small to gain sufficient leverage and their hand strength is too slight to pull the trigger double-action (i.e., from an uncocked position) or to cock the hammer back for single-action firing (Kates 1982, p. 37). In contrast, long guns, very cheap handguns, guns modified to have very light trigger pulls, and the rarer derringer-type handguns can be discharged more easily, possibly by some children as young as 3 years old. In one extreme case, it was even alleged that a 2-year-old boy had shot himself with a revolver with an abnormally light trigger pull (Wintemute et al. 1987, p. 3108).

A study of newspaper accounts of handgun accidents among children age 16 or younger found that the accidents disproportionately occurred during summer months and afternoon hours, with 66% occurring when no adult was present (Center to Prevent Handgun Violence 1989). Analysis of a subset of these cases indicated that 50% occurred in the victim's home and 30% in a friend's home. In 45% of the 200 cases where the location was known, the child found the gun in the bedroom, presumably their parents' bedroom. This almost exactly corresponds to the 42% of all guns that are kept in the owner's bedroom (Quinley 1990, p. 5). In 47% of the cases, the gun owned by the victim's parents and in 28% of the cases by parents of a friend of the victim (Center to Prevent Handgun Violence 1988). A study of 88 California FGAs with victims under age 15 found that in at least 48% of the residential deaths, the gun was kept loaded and unlocked (Wintemute et al. 1987, p. 3109). Thus a typical handgun accident with a child shooter or victim involved the child finding his parents' loaded and unlocked gun in their bedroom during the early afternoon in the summer school vacation period, while without adult supervision (see also Wintemute et al. 1987).

Although a few such incidents may have occurred, none of the sources reviewed in this chapter cite even a single case of a child victim or shooter who found a locked gun, unlocked it, and shot himself or another person. In practice, keeping a gun locked, whether loaded or not, whether stored away or not, appears to be a near-absolute protection against a child gun accident.

Table 7.5 shows trends in FGAs with young victims during 1974–1987). These sharply declined during this period, especially among children under age 10. FGAs decreased in this group from 227 in 1974 to 92 in 1987, a drop of 59% in just 13 years. The reasons for this dramatic decline probably parallel those discussed in connection with FGA trends in general. If preadolescent victims are defined as those under age 13, then about 190 FGAs with preadolescent victims occurred in 1987 (assuming about half of 10–14 year old deaths involved 10–12 year olds). Based on the gun type distribution among 1980 FGAs with victims under age 15 (Table 7.4), about 37% of these involved handguns. Thus about 70 preadolescent children were killed in fatal handgun accidents in 1987.

Gun Types Involved

Table 7.4 shows the distribution of FGAs by the type of firearm involved. Among cases in which the gun type was specified on the death certificate, 289 or 41% involved handguns and 59% involved long guns; by 1985 the handgun share had dropped to 37% (National Safety Council 1988, p. 13). Since about 33% of the guns in the U.S. civilian stock are handguns (Chapter 2), this means they are slightly overrepresented among FGAs.

However, only loaded guns kill people in firearms accidents. If one considers loaded guns to be the ones primarily "at risk" of a FGA, it is more appropriate to compare handguns' share of FGAs with their share of guns routinely kept loaded. It is reasonable to expect that guns kept loaded in the home all the time should be more likely to become involved in a home FGA. *Most* of the guns kept loaded for self-defense are handguns (Chapter 4), yet handguns accounted for only 37% of FGAs in 1985. Thus handguns were far less likely to be involved in FGAs than would be expected based on their share of guns kept loaded in the home. Some analysts have compared the handgun share of FGAs only with their share of *all* guns owned or produced, rather than the handgun share of guns kept loaded, leading them to the dubious conclusion that efforts to control gun accidents through reduction of gun availability should focus on handguns (e.g., Wintemute et al. 1987, p. 3109).

The lower rate of accident involvement of handguns per loaded gun, compared with long guns, is partly due to technical differences. On a purely mechanical basis, most modern handguns are harder to accidentally discharge than long guns, given a loaded and unlocked status.

Firing a revolver or semiautomatic pistol double-action requires a stronger pull on the trigger than firing most rifles or shotguns. Further, most modern handguns are made in such a way that they cannot discharge without the trigger being pulled, something that is untrue for many long guns (Kates 1983a, pp. 262–3). Cases of guns discharging when they are dropped are more common among hunting accidents, nearly all of which involve long guns (Table 7.11), than they are among home gun accidents, most of which apparently involve handguns (Table 7.9).

Handguns are more likely than long guns to be owned and used for either defensive or criminal purposes (Chapter 2), and criminals own and use guns mainly for defensive and criminal purposes (Wright and Rossi 1985). Further, a larger share of handgun owners are criminals. Tabulations from seven national surveys done between 1973 and 1984 show that 13% of respondents living in a household with only handguns admitted having a nontraffic arrest record, whereas only 10% of respondents in households with only rifles and shotguns reported a nontraffic arrest (analysis of data from Davis and Smith 1984). Criminals, in turn, are more likely to be involved in gun accidents (Waller and Whorton 1973). In sum, handguns are disproportionately owned by the kinds of people who are unusually likely to get involved in accidents. Therefore, were this not the case, the share of FGAs that involve handguns would probably be still lower than it is.

The implications for gun control policy of these comparisons by gun type are straightforward. Measures restricting access to handguns that did not place equally stringent restrictions on long guns would tend to encourage the substitution of long guns for handguns as loaded home defense weapons. Long guns need not be more expensive than handguns, yet are more deadly than handguns (Chapter 3). If the sorts of people who currently own handguns were to substitute long guns as loaded home defense weapons, the rate of accident discharge would probably increase, and the fraction of accidental woundings that resulted in death would almost certainly increase. Further, rifles have greater capacity to penetrate walls and injure persons outside a room where an accidental discharge occurred (Kates 1983a, pp. 261–3). Therefore handgun-only legislation is likely to increase the frequency of home FGAs, to the extent that it is effective in reducing handgun ownership among those likely to get involved in gun accidents. This conclusion parallels the Chapter 3 conclusions regarding homicide and handgun-only controls.

The Victims and Shooters in Gun Accidents

Age, Sex, and Race

The demographic distribution of the risk of an FGA is shown in Table 7.6. The rates of death are expressed in three ways for each age–sex–race group. The upper number in each cell of the table is the rate of accidental death per 100,000 resident population of the indicated group, the middle number is the rate per 100,000 persons of that group who personally own a gun, and the bottom number is the rate per 100,000 persons of that group who live in a gun-owning household. The latter two rates are based on combined data from the 1980 and 1982 General social surveys (GSS) (Davis and Smith 1984). Because these surveys covered only persons at least 18 years old, no rates based on personal ownership were calculated for persons under age 15; those for persons aged 15 to 24 were assumed to be the same as for persons age 18 to 24. The combined both-sex rates of household gun ownership for each racial group were assumed to prevail for persons under 15, whereas the 18–24 year old rates of household ownership were assumed to prevail for those age 15–24.

The Table 7.6 data indicate that males, persons age 15 to 24, and blacks all have FGA rates higher than average. Among victims of FGAs in 1980, 86% were male, 57% aged 15 to 34, and 17% were black, compared to 49, 35, and 12%, respectively, of the 1980 resident U.S. population in those groups (U.S. Bureau of the Census, 1983b, p. 33). The most significant information in Table 7.6, however, is the FGA rates based on numbers of persons in each sex–race–age group who personally own guns or live in households that have guns. The rates indicate that even when one controls for gun availability, males, blacks, and persons aged 15–24 all are far more likely to be involved in FGAs than other groups. For example, based on household gun ownership levels, black males aged 15 to 24 have FGA rates 23 times the national average, and white males of that age group have rates 2.7 times the national average. Thus something about some persons in these sex, race, and age groups inclines them toward involvement in gun accidents beyond mere gun availability. Indeed, the high involvement of blacks is all the more striking once one takes into account their lower levels of gun ownership.[1] The same is true to a lesser extent for persons aged 15 to 24, who personally own guns at a rate lower than the general adult population. These are the same groups that show the highest rates of intentional violence such as homicide, both as offenders and as victims, suggesting that there are some common predisposing factors shared by participants in accidents and participants in acts of intentional violence.

Social Class and Gun Accidents

Given the lower average income of blacks, the disproportionate involvement of blacks in FGAs hints at a disproportionate involvement of lower income persons generally. This issue is in turn wrapped up with that of gun ownership for protection.

Findings from the National Health Survey for 1971–1972 indicate that persons with a family income under $5000 had a rate of injury from the accidental discharge of a firearm nearly four times as high as that for persons with a family income of $15,000 or more. However, the rates had very large standard errors and the original source advised against using these individual income group injury rates (U.S. DHEW 1976, p. 17). Nevertheless, the general pattern has been confirmed in other research. Klein and his colleagues (1977) studied all FGAs of persons under age 16 for Michigan for the period 1970–1975. They found that between 71 and 90% of child FGA victims in Michigan were of lower socioeconomic status. The gun accident patterns parallel patterns for accidents in general. National data indicate that lower income people are more likely than middle income people to suffer home accidental injuries in general, regardless of the activities or objects involved (U.S. NCHS 1985a, p. 44).

Heins and her colleagues (1974) studied a largely lower class sample of urban child gun accident victims treated in a Detroit hospital over the period 1962–1971. The authors remarked that "the lack of safety precautions in households we visited was truly amazing" and noted that both the children and parents involved as victims or as shooters were usually unfamiliar with guns and basic gun safety rules (p. 329). The majority of the guns had been acquired for protection and 60% of the guns involved were kept loaded at all times; yet despite the presence of children in all of the households, only 13% of the families usually kept the gun under lock and key. The parents involved were unusually careless gun owners, in view of a 1989 national survey that indicated that only 24% of all gun owners always kept a gun loaded, and 45% of owners usually kept their guns locked up (Quinley 1990).

Klein and his co-workers stated that it was their "very strong impression" that the guns involved in child gunshot deaths were nearly all kept for self-protection and most of them were kept loaded for use against prowlers. They speculated that "guns used for self-protection are more likely to be involved in accidental shootings because hunting or target guns are much less likely to be stored loaded or to be kept where they are readily accessible" (1977, p. 181). As has been shown, this is true, but is only part of the explanation. Protection guns also seem to be owned by different sorts of people than guns kept for sport, by persons not socialized into safe gun handling as part of a sporting gun subculture (Lizotte and Bordua 1980, Lizotte et al. 1981), and loaded handguns are also, for mechanical reasons, more easily discharged accidentally. Klein et al. concluded that gun control laws are unlikely to be effective because compliance would be low among people who regard a gun as their only protection against crime. They further asserted that gun safety programs, as currently run, are not likely to be effective because they are misdirected at a largely middle class audience of hunters and target shooters.

Klein (1980) elaborated on these points in a later article on childhood accidents, based on his interviews with parents ("most of them with low incomes and little education") who exposed their children to recreational hazards. These parents frequently expressed "a fatalistic attitude towards their child's exposure to hazard," communicating the hope that "Somebody up there is looking out for Johnny." Klein also noted that the predominantly low income urban families of child gunshot victims "kept loaded guns within ready because they had no confidence that the police offered them protection against neighborhood crime." Consequently the guns viewed as a hazard by "the middle class professional" were regarded by their lower-income owners as an essential protection against crime (p. 277). Klein cited previous studies that showed that there is "substantially less supervision of children in lower-class families and spending of time with them in shared activities." He asserted that in general lower class household life is irregular, disorderly and unplanned when viewed from a middle-class point of view. He speculated this may be due to a simple lack of resources, feelings of powerlessness to control one's life, greater stress, an overload of too many children in inadequate housing, and/or a cognitive style that is focused on the immediate present. He concluded that most safety programs seem to be devised by, directed at, and likely to be effective only with middle-class persons, and that effective accident reduction must involve changes in the physical and social environments of lower-class families.

Victim Marital Status, Size of Place, and Region

The Mortality Detail File (MDF) for 1980 included data on marital status of the victim, size of place of residence of the victim, and region of occurrence of FGAs. Analysis of this dataset revealed that 46% of male victims age 15 and over were never married, compared to only 24% of the general U.S. adult male population age 18 and over (U.S. Bureau of the Census 1983b, p. 43). Thus, single males are far more likely to be involved in FGAs than males of other marital statuses, the same as is true with intentional violence.

Table 7.7 indicates that most of the victims of FGAs live in rural areas or small towns, consistent with the fact that gun ownership increases as size of place decreases (Chapter 2). Sixty percent of FGA victims lived in places with populations under 10,000, compared to only 43% of the general population (U.S. Bureau of the Census 1983a, p.27), indicating that rural residents are more likely to be involved in FGAs than urban residents. The data in this table also serve to caution readers that studies of gun accidents based exclusively on urban samples (e.g., Rushforth et al. 1975; Copeland 1984) are likely to overstate the involvement of handguns and therefore of guns owned for defensive reasons, since handguns account for a much larger share of FGAs in large cities than they do in the smaller places where most gun accidents occur.

Finally, the mortality data indicate that half of FGAs in 1980 occurred in the South Atlantic, East South Central, and West South Central census regions, although these regions claimed only one-third of the U.S. population (U.S. Bureau of the Census 1983a, p. 10). Thus, Southerners are more likely to be involved in FGAs, consistent with higher Southern gun ownership.

Shooter Traits

In intentional homicides, killers and victims tend to resemble each other demographically, being nearly always the same in race and usually similar in age and social class. The only major exception is with respect to gender—34% of 1989 U.S. homicides were cross-sex killings (U.S. FBI 1990, p. 10). The same generalizations appear to be true for gun accidents, based on analysis of an admittedly select sample of gun accidents—negligent manslaughters, as described in the Supplementary Homicide Reports (SHR) for 1980. In 228 cases, race of victim and shooter were the same in 96.5% of the shootings. The average absolute difference in ages was 6.6 years. And since shooters and victims in these cases were both overwhelmingly male, gender similarity was inevitable—sex was the same in 74.6% of the cases. Further, in another, nonoverlapping segment of FGAs, the 50% or so that were self-inflicted, shooter and victim were identical in all respects, being the same person.

Therefore, it is fair to say that shooters and victims generally resemble each other in FGAs, allowing us to use characteristics of victims to roughly infer at least some traits of the shooters.

Based on this reasoning, the data on victims indicate that shooters in gun accidents are disproportionately drawn from the same demographic groups that are overrepresented in intentionally violent behavior—males, persons age 15–34, blacks, and lower income persons. Again, these facts hint at the possibility that accidental and intentional killers may share some underlying personality traits, such as poor aggression control, impulsiveness, alcoholism, willingness to take risks, and sensation seeking.

This hypothesis is supported by the findings of one of the most important studies of gun accidents. Waller and Whorton (1973) studied a virtually complete population of accidental gun woundings, both fatal and nonfatal, treated by physicians in Vermont, a state in which doctors are required by law to report all persons treated for gunshot wounds, no matter how minor. They searched for the arrest, traffic citation, and highway accident records of the shooters and victims in accidental gun woundings, as well as the records of a comparison sample of licensed drivers. Whereas victims shot by another person were not significantly different from the licensed drivers, accidental shooters were significantly more likely to have been arrested, arrested for a violent act, arrested in connection with alcohol, involved in highway crashes, given traffic citations, and to have had their driver's license suspended or revoked. Fifty percent of the shooters had been involved in a highway crash in the previous 3 years, compared to 29% for the comparison sample of licensed drivers. After showing that the shooters with nontraffic arrests were also generally the same individuals involved in highway crashes, the authors concluded that a common behavioral model may be applicable to both intentional and unintentional acts of violence, both on the highway and elsewhere, a model that stresses "poor control of aggressive tendencies" (p. 355). This hypothesis was consistent with findings from a Minnesota study of negligent shooters in hunting accidents, which found that although hunters in general were mildly introverted, the accident-involved shooters had low inhibitions (Kuluvar 1953, cited in Diener and Kerber 1979).

Alcohol Involvement

These findings lead one to suspect that alcohol might play a role in gun accidents, since it is commonly believed that alcohol reduces the drinker's control of aggressive impulses. Although no studies have measured alcohol in the bloodstream of accidental shooters, Rushforth et al. (1975, p. 502) report that ethanol was found in the blood of 48% of FGA victims. Of course, in those cases involving self-inflicted wounds, alcohol in the victim's blood means alcohol in the shooter's blood as well. The various drinking-related incidents that Waller and Whorton found in the backgrounds of accidental shooters strongly hinted that many of the shooters were alcoholics. It seems plausible to estimate that perhaps half of the victims and probably at least half of the shooters in FGAs had been drinking prior to the accident. Alcohol may contribute to gun accidents in either of two general ways. It may impair physical coordination, reaction time, judgment, and alertness, and thereby increase the chances of a genuinely unintentional gun accident. However, by reducing control of aggressive tendencies, it may also facilitate less unintentional "accidents" that might be more accurately viewed as acts of sublimated aggression.

Circumstances and Activities Associated with Gun Accidents

Gun accidents may be conveniently divided into two categories—those occurring in the home, which constituted about half of FGAs in 1987, and those occurring outside the home, many of which are hunting accidents (National Safety Council 1988, pp. 7, 84, 93). There are no published police data on the circumstances of gun accidents and only limited unpublished information on negligent manslaughters in the FBI's Supplementary Homicide Reports (SHR). The national vital statistics data say nothing directly about circumstances of FGAs. The best data available come from the life insurance claims files of the Metropolitan Life Insurance Company (MLIC), covering fatal firearms accidents occurring in a variety of periods from 1946 to 1966. The representativeness of these samples is suspect, since they may be biased somewhat in the direction of including more "suspicious" cases worthy of examination by claims investigators. On the other hand, they also cover only insured people, suggesting an underrepresentation of lower income people. Still, some rough hints about the circumstances of FGAs can be derived from these studies.[2]

The relevant data from various studies done by MLIC and from a few other local studies are summarized in Tables 7.8 and 7.9. These studies each classified circumstances differently, although the categories in the various studies overlapped or resembled each other sufficiently so that some can be grouped together to establish new categories that are consistent from study to study. Nevertheless, some of the listed categories were used in only one or two of the studies. There were undoubtedly accidents in the other studies that would have fitted into these categories but researchers grouped the cases with other classes of accidents or lumped them into "other" or "unspecified" categories. Because researchers have not followed a standard classification scheme, categories are not strictly comparable across studies. Consequently, when results from different studies are combined, the results are approximate and should be interpreted with caution.

In these sets of deaths at least, cases involving clearly reckless activities were common. Table 7.8 summarizes results from studies that examined general samples of accidents, both in and out of the home. By far the most common specific circumstance or activity associated with FGAs was one involving reckless or negligent behavior—"playing with a weapon." This is most clearly true for home accidents, but less true for hunting accidents. A large fraction of the cases involved "unspecified" activities. Shooters and other witnesses may be more likely to withhold information in connection with the most suspicious deaths, leading to incomplete information in claims records. Therefore, examination of only those cases in which circumstance could be specified may tend to understate the prevalence of reckless behavior or suspicious circumstances.

Looking just at the three most detailed studies summarized in Tables 7.8 and 7.9, MLIC49–51, MLIC53–55, and MLIC64–66, there were a total of 455 FGAs in which the specific circumstance was listed. Of these, the most frequent circumstances were playing with a weapon (122 cases), cleaning, repairing a gun, (68 total, 38 self-inflicted), handling, examining, or demonstrating a weapon (54), walking into line of fire in hunting (27), tripping while carrying in hunting (26), and Russian Roulette (21). Cases involving playing with a loaded weapon and Russian Roulette clearly were reckless, and self-inflicted deaths while the shooter was allegedly cleaning or repairing a gun were probably mostly suicides. It is impossible to make judgments on cases in the other common categories based only on the sketchy information communicated by the category labels. For example, the "handling or demonstrating" of a loaded firearm that resulted in a FGA might have involved perfectly responsible behavior. On the other hand, some accidental shooters have been known to check to see if a gun was unloaded by pulling the trigger while the gun was pointed at themselves or others (see the example in Heins et al. 1974, p. 329). Likewise, hunting while intoxicated would be reckless and could result in one hunter being caught in the line of fire of another or in a hunter tripping with a loaded gun. It is apparent that, at minimum, a third of the deaths in these samples of FGAs involved obviously reckless conduct, but it is impossible to say how large a share of the remaining cases were also reckless.

The MLIC64–66 study (Table 7.9) contains interesting material specifically relevant to the risks of keeping and using guns for defensive purposes. It is the only study of a general sample of FGAs that counted separately those occurring in connection with attempts to use guns defensively (the Heins et al. study concerned only child cases). In other studies, this type of incident was evidently too rare to merit a separate category, even though separate categories were commonly provided for as few as 2% of the total cases. Of 107 FGAs where the associated activity or circumstance was known, only two involved "searching for prowlers, protection against threats." Thus fewer than 2% of FGAs involved such uses of guns. If this figure applied to the 1987 total of 1400 FGAs, it would imply a rough annual estimate of fewer that 28 FGAs involving attempts to use guns defensively. In Chapter 4 it was estimated that guns are used by civilians to legally kill in self-defense about 1500–2800 times a year in the United States and that the annual number of defensive uses may be as high as one million. Since defensive killings usually require a serious threat to human life to be legally justifiable or excusable, this implies that 1500–2800 lives of crime victims may have been saved by using guns to kill felons. Further, some of the far more numerous nonlethal defensive uses of guns also saved lives. In any case, accidental deaths connected with defensive uses of guns almost certainly amount to less than 1% of the number of legal, potentially lifesaving uses. On the other hand, in the Heins et al. study of Detroit FGAs with child victims, of 43 cases where the circumstance was known, nine cases, or 21% involved "protection against threats." As this result is out of line with the other studies, it probably is due to the peculiarities of the sample, derived entirely from a single inner city public hospital in a high-crime city.

Hunting Accidents

Hunting accidents seem to be a different sort of event from home gun accidents, involving much less clear evidence of reckless behavior. They also are much less common than previously thought. In 1975, the National Safety Council estimated that hunting accidents accounted for 600 to 800 deaths a year, which would have amounted to 24–32% of the 2500 annual FGAs per year, 1971–1973 (1976, p.1). This estimate is implausible, as can be seen by examining Table 7.10. It is known that over 96% of fatal hunting accidents with guns involve long guns (NAAHSC 1982). Hunting by definition is done in outdoor locations. Therefore, almost the only FGAs that can plausibly be hunting accidents are those that involved shotguns or rifles and that occurred in an outdoor locale suitable for hunting. In Table 7.10 there are 601 FGAs in which gun type and place of occurrence were both known. Even if one generously considered all "Other Specified Place" locales to be places appropriate for hunting, along with all farm and miscellaneous places, only 105, or 17.5% of these FGAs could have been hunting accidents. The true figure is almost certainly less, since some long gun accidents in outdoor locations are not connected with hunting.

Another estimate supports this conclusion. The North American Association of Hunter Safety Coordinators (NAAHSC), compiled data annually on hunting accidents, covering 34 of the 50 states in 1980. These 34 states accounted for about 62.7% of the paid hunting license holders in the United States (author's tabulation of data in U.S. Fish and Wildlife Service 1982b). The NAAHSC report counted 167 fatal hunting accidents for the 34 states (NAAHSC, 1982). Extrapolating this to all 50 states, one can divide 167 by 0.627 to get an estimate of 266 fatal hunting accidents for the United States as a whole, or 13.6% of all FGAs that year. A middle estimate would therefore be that about 16% or one-sixth of FGAs are hunting accidents.

Table 7.11 summarizes information from the NAAHSC surveys on the circumstances of gun accidents in hunting, covering over 5000 fatal and nonfatal accidents occurring in the period 1977–1980. The information is unusually detailed and permits several conclusions. First, rough classifications of circumstances indicate that 28% of fatal accidents and 20% of nonfatal accidents involved a safety or law violation or "careless handling." Again, hunting accidents appear to involve reckless conduct less often than home accidents. Second, those accidents that do involve reckless conduct are more likely to be fatal than nonreckless accidents—16.9% of reckless incidents were fatal, compared to 12.5% for nonreckless ones. Third, few hunting gun accidents involve a gun going off by itself—only 11% of the cases clearly involved no one pulling the trigger, as when a gun fell from an insecure rest and discharged or when the trigger caught on an object. Finally, when a person pulled the trigger, it was usually pulled intentionally. The incidents were accidents only in the sense that the hunters involved did not intend to shoot another person, rather than in the sense that the gun was accidentally discharged.

Hunting accidents, then, most commonly involve a hunter intentionally firing a gun but accidentally shooting another person. The events are more genuinely accidental, as opposed to the unsurprising result of reckless conduct, than home gun accidents. At worst, the bulk of hunting accidents may involve poor judgment or momentary lapses in concentration rather than gross negligence. The most common circumstance was a hunter shooting at game, missing, but then hitting, beyond the game, a hunter who was obscured by brush and possibly his own camouflage clothing. In hunting areas with dense growth, this sort of accident would seem difficult to avoid altogether. In the long run, a few such tragedies will occur as long as hunting continues, no matter how responsible hunters are. Other types of accidents may involve debatable errors in judgment, such as those in which the victim was covered by a shooter swinging on moving game or those in which the victim was mistaken for game. Some of these might have been avoided if hunters had been more careful to ensure that the entire area in front of them was clear and by being absolutely sure of the nature of their target. These incidents seem especially avoidable in view of the fact that 60–80% of hunting accidents involve members of the same hunting party, who should be able to keep track of each other (MLIC 1953, 1956).

Defective Firearms

Do defects in the design or manufacture of firearms cause gun accidents? It is clear that the majority of accidents involve persons intentionally pulling a trigger and a gun doing precisely what it was designed to do—propelling a projectile at high velocity. Nevertheless, a few accidents do occur without anyone pulling a trigger, intentionally or otherwise. For example, many single action revolvers and derringers have exposed hammers but no safety device such as a hammer block or rotating firing pin to prevent the hammer from striking a cartridge's primer should the weapon be dropped on its hammer (DiMaio 1972). Although such weapons account for a fairly small fraction of handguns, they can accidentally discharge simply by being dropped on a hard surface, without the trigger being pulled. There is no good reason for a gun to be capable of firing without its trigger being pulled, and inexpensive technologies exist that can prevent such discharges. Therefore, when a dropped gun accident occurs, it is reasonable to conclude that a correctable defect in the gun's design was instrumental in causing the accident. That is, future models could be designed so as to be free of this sort of defect. In particular, many long guns lack these safety devices and thus are subject to a needlessly high risk of accidental discharge.

In the MLIC49–51 study, 5 of 122 home FGAs (4.1%) involved guns being dropped (Table 7.8), and 28 of 626 FGAs (4.7%) described in the NAAHSC hunting accident data involved firearms discharging after a fall from an insecure rest (Table 7.11). Likewise, two of 60 home gun accidents (3.3%) studied by Heins and her co-workers (1974) involved dropped guns (Table 7.8). On the other hand, cases of this type were evidently too rare in the other studies summarized in Tables 7.8 and 7.9 to merit a separate category of accident circumstance. If there were a few such cases, they were probably lumped into the "other" or "unspecified" residual categories. Generally, dropped gun accidents are rare, but are somewhat more common among hunting accidents than among home accidents. In addition to deaths resulting from a gun falling from an insecure rest, the NAAHSC hunting accidents include another 16 FGAs attributed to "defective firearms," without any further explanation. Combining these with the falling gun cases gives 44 cases, or 7% of hunting FGAs that involved some sort of defect in the gun, along with 363 such cases (8%) among nonfatal gun hunting accidents.

For nonhunting accidents, results of the only two studies that included categories for accidents involving dropped or defective guns, MLIC49–51 and the Heins et al. study (Tables 7.8 and 7.9) can be combined. Of 126 cases in which the circumstance was specified, seven, or 5.6% involved dropped guns. The fraction of such cases in the other samples of nonhunting accidents was probably smaller than this, given the absence of an appropriate category. For all studies in Tables 7.8 and 7.9 combined, deaths explicitly counted in dropped or defective gun categories accounted for about 1% of the total of cases with a circumstance specified. On the other hand, Wintemute and his colleagues (1987) found that among a sample of child FGAs (93% of which were residential, and therefore nonhunting, accidents), 8% involved defective guns. This unusually high figure may be due to the fact that many younger children are not physically capable of discharging some kinds of firearms *unless* they are defective. The available data taken as a whole indicate that about 1–8% of nonhunting gun accidents involved dropped or otherwise defective guns. Since about 16% of FGAs are hunting accidents, this amounts to about 224 deaths in 1987 (0.16 × 1400); 7% of the 224 hunting deaths, or about 16 hunting FGAs involved defective guns. Among the remaining 1176 nonhunting FGAs, 1–8%, or 12–94 deaths involved defective guns. Thus, in 1987 a total of about 28–110 FGAs involved defective guns, or 2–8% of all FGAs.[3]

The Nature of Accidents and Those Who Cause Them

An accident is defined in *Webster's Seventh New Collegiate Dictionary* as "an event occurring by chance or from unknown causes", "an unforeseen or unplanned event", "an unfortunate event resulting from carelessness, unawareness, ignorance, or avoidable causes," or "an unexpected happening causing loss or injury which is not due to any fault or misconduct on the part of the person injured" (p.5). None of these definitions exactly fits all of the events officially classified as gun accidents. Many gun accidents are not accurately described by any of them. Most gun accidents do not occur by chance, most involve known causes, many could in some sense be foreseen, and many were not entirely unexpected given the reckless behavior involved. Many were due to misconduct on the part of the person injured. The most applicable of the dictionary definitions is the one that describes accidents as unfortunate events resulting from carelessness, unawareness, ignorance, or unavoidable causes; some gun accidents fit at least part of this definition.

Accidents are not usually chance events that occur at random, without known causes. Rather, they commonly involve antecedent behavior that is predictably hazardous. Although the ultimate consequences of these antecedent behaviors were not necessarily consciously foreseen by the actors involved, an outside observer could have predicted that the behaviors would produce injury or death in the long run, if repeated often enough. Driving while intoxicated does not always or even usually lead to crashes, but in the long run is likely to result in accidents for a significant fraction of those who do it. Likewise, playing with loaded guns, hunting while intoxicated, scuffling for possession of a loaded gun, playing Russian Roulette to impress one's friends, and similarly reckless behaviors with guns carry predictably high risks with them. In the long run, the odds are bound to catch up with those who persistently handle deadly instruments recklessly.

Gun accidents, then, are not totally accidental in the everyday sense of that word. The same observation has been made regarding other types of accidents. For example, Willett (1964) studied 653 persons convicted of motoring offenses, 383 of them involving motor vehicle collisions. Even using very generous criteria, he could classify only 91 cases, or 14% of the total motoring offense cases and at most 24% of the collisions, as genuine accidents due to bad luck or errors of judgment. "In the majority of the other cases the offense was undeniably brought about by the offender's own behavior in consciously taking a risk" (p. 236). Likewise, in 1987, 71% of U.S. motor vehicle accidents with injury involved some kind of improper driving such as driving too fast or failing to yield the right of way (National Safety Council 1988, p. 61).

Personality Traits of the Accident-Involved

Findings discussed earlier indicated that the same individuals who cause gun accidents also were commonly involved in other types of accidental and violent events, including motor vehicle accidents (Waller and Whorton 1973). This appears to be true about those who cause a variety of types of accidents. Persons who cause one type of accident are more likely than others to be involved in other types of accidents and to commit intentional criminal acts, especially assaults and alcohol-related offenses (Haviland and Wiseman 1974; Willett 1964; Whitlock 1971). These facts have been interpreted by some scholars as indicating that all of these behaviors share some causes in common, such as a disregard for the welfare of others or a low estimation of the value of human life (e.g., Porterfield 1960). They also suggest that although information on the sorts of people who cause gun accidents is limited, one might learn something about them from the very extensive literature on motor vehicle and other accidents.

A long series of personality traits has been found to be associated with drivers with higher-than-average rates of traffic citations and accidents, including aggressiveness and a lower capacity for control of hostility and aggression (Conger et al. 1959; Tillman and Hobbs 1949; Shaw 1965), impulsiveness or the tendency to express impulses (Conger et al. 1959; Schuman et al. 1967), immaturity, foolhardiness, and greater dependency needs (Tillman and Hobbs, 1949; Conger et al. 1959), and a lesser ability to tolerate tension without discharging it (Conger et al. 1959). Researchers have also found poor driving records to be associated with a complex of personality traits linked to psychopathy, including overconfidence, self-assertiveness, and an indifference to danger, risk, the consequences of one's actions, or the welfare and rights of others (Conger et al. 1959; Shaw 1965). Finally, alcoholism, frequently linked to criminal and intentional violent behavior, has also been found associated with poor driving records (Waller 1967; Brenner 1967; many others). That is, alcoholism as a persisting trait of the driver at fault has been linked to accidents, as distinct from the fact that the driver had been drinking before the accident.

Other scholars have looked at the social characteristics of bad drivers, finding that they are generally less well-adjusted and integrated into society. Accident-involved drivers are commonly characterized by family disruption and conflict, both in their adult lives and in their childhood (McGuire 1976), poor employment records, fewer friends, sexual promiscuity, and irresponsibility toward their families (Tillman and Hobbs 1949). Of even greater interest is the finding that such drivers are more likely to have police and court records of delinquency and criminal behavior, especially violent criminal behavior (Tillman and Hobbs 1949; McFarland and Mosely 1954; Willett 1964; Waller 1967; Whitlock 1971; Haviland and Wiseman 1974).

If personality traits are viewed as relatively unchangeable, these findings might be interpreted to indicate how difficult it would be to prevent accidents. However, such an interpretation would be an oversimplification. Many accident-linked traits constitute a constellation of characteristics associated with emotional immaturity, which may characterize some individuals only for certain stages of development such as childhood and adolescence. Although it may be difficult to alter such traits deliberately, they may disappear on their own as a result of natural maturation. On the other hand, given that all humans must pass through immature stages of development, this means that a certain fraction of the population is always going to be substantially more prone to accident involvement than others.

Further, personality traits of this sort do not usually produce accidental behavior by themselves. There appears to be an interaction between these traits and the occurrence of stressful life events in producing accidents. Without stressful events such as job and financial difficulties, marital conflicts, and health problems, these personality traits alone do not inevitably result in accidents. Likewise, stressful events alone do not usually cause well-adjusted people to crash their cars or have gun accidents. However, the combination of the two can lead to accidents. Therefore, accident frequency could be reduced by reducing unemployment, preventing illness, improving marital relations, and otherwise limiting the occurrence of stressful events, i.e., by general improvement in the quality of life, without altering anyone's personality. It is not inevitable that a society must always suffer from its current level of stressful life events, a fact evidenced by the sharp variations over time in the frequency of such events that every society experiences.

Similarly, alcoholism treatment programs are sometimes aimed at reducing drinking behavior without necessarily altering underlying personality traits that may cause problem drinking. To the extent that drinking behavior can be reduced, the frequency of alcohol-linked accidents can also be reduced, without necessarily reducing the prevalence of alcoholism itself.

Reducing Gun Accidents

One cannot have a gun accident without a gun. The presence of a gun in the vicinity of risk-taking or reckless persons is a significant additional hazard in the environment of persons who need as few hazards around them as possible. At the same time, gun accidents are not an inevitable by-product of routine gun ownership by ordinary people. They appear to most commonly be the result of reckless or aggressive behavior by the same kind of individuals responsible both for intentional violence and other types of accidents. They are rarely the result of a gun "going off" by itself or someone accidentally pulling a trigger, and rarely involve guns that were defective in design or manufacture or due to wear. Rather, they usually involve someone intentionally pulling the trigger on a gun that performs mechanically exactly as it was designed to do.

The limited information available suggests that many shooters in gun accidents (as well as those responsible for other types of accidents) are "accidents waiting to happen." They are frequently people with histories of prior involvement with other types of accidents, intentional violence, and problem drinking. Gun accidents are but one part of a larger picture of their reckless disregard for their own safety and the safety of others. They frequently place themselves in positions of hazard, exposing themselves to risks of all sorts and defying the odds of being injured. And by doing so, they often place those around them at risk as well. With this background, what measure for reducing gun accidents could be effective?

Gun Safety Training

Gun safety programs aim at informing gun users about general safety principles and rules, such as "Never point a gun at something you do not intend to shoot" or "Always treat every gun as if it were loaded," and about technical matters, such as when a pistol's safety is on and how to safely check to see if a gun is loaded. They do not attempt to alter gun owners' personalities, cure alcoholism, or reduce stressful events in gun owners' lives, nor is it likely they could do so if they tried. Rather, they aim to correct knowledge deficiencies of one sort or another.

The claim that such programs can reduce the frequency of gun accidents is based on two premises. First, it assumes that the programs reach those segments of the population in which accidents are likely to occur. Second, it assumes that some nonnegligible number of gun accidents can be attributed to correctable knowledge deficiencies, to ignorance of safety procedures, rules, or customs. This in turn implies that significant numbers of persons who would otherwise cause gun accidents would, on exposure to the training program, be able and willing to alter their gun-handling habits in the direction of more cautious, responsible, and prudent conduct.

Concerning the first premise, as noted earlier, Klein (1980) observed that gun safety training programs primarily reach middle-class hunters, whereas most gun accidents involve lower-class persons handling guns in their homes. Perhaps this indicates that the programs have successfully reduced the problem within their traditional target population. In any case, it indicates a need to go beyond that population. Concerning the second premise, many gun accidents, perhaps the majority of them, involve chronically reckless people whose impulsiveness, emotional immaturity, or alcoholism cannot be eliminated by a few hours of safety training. Consider the following illustrative case.

Two men and their wives were at a dinner party in rural Northern Florida. One of the men, the host, decided to demonstrate his marksmanship to the other guests by shooting beer cans off the other man's head with a .22-caliber pistol. His guest willingly participated, placing a can on top of his head and even backing off further to increase the challenge. Both host and guest had been drinking. The guest was confident because the shooter had already demonstrated the William Tell stunt *twice* earlier in the evening. This time the shooter fired and the bullet struck the victim in the head, killing him. The shooter was later described in a local newspaper as having a history of "psychological incidents" (*Tallahassee Democrat* 1982a,b).

For this tragedy to occur required an extraordinary lack of prudence on the part of both shooter and victim. It is unlikely that either the shooter or the victim was intellectually unaware of the fact that firing a pistol at a target inches above the head of another human being was dangerous; no detailed knowledge of gun safety is necessary for this to be understood. The event was not in any way due to defects in the gun or to its user's ignorance of how it worked. The shooter knew all too well how it worked, aimed the gun at his intended target, and intentionally pulled the trigger. The event was accidental only in the sense that the shooter did not hit what he aimed at. In all these respects, the event was typical of gun accidents.

Although this case involved unusually reckless conduct, it illustrates the limits of gun safety training in preventing gun accidents. It is unlikely that a few hours of safety training could have prevented this sort of accident. Likewise, safety training is largely irrelevant to gun violence that is inflicted with hostile intent, whether conscious or unconscious. People who want to hurt others (or themselves) with guns cannot be prevented from doing so by safety training.

On the other hand, some gun accidents do involve correctable knowledge deficiencies, especially accidents involving otherwise careful but young or inexperienced shooters. Although safety training cannot change reckless personalities into prudent ones, it can provide knowledge and inculcate habits that encourage safe gun handling among persons motivated to make use of that knowledge and to acquire those habits.

What sorts of gun accidents might be preventable through safety training? Events officially labeled as "gun accidents" are distributed across a continuum of shooter intentionality, from those involving shooters with the least intent to harm to those with the most intent. Figure 7.1 illustrates the continuum and gives examples of events at various points along the continuum. Some acts officially classified as gun accidents are actually intentional homicides or suicides. Others, although not exactly intentional, are "subintentional" or unconsciously intended, as when someone exposes a person they dislike to a high risk of "accidental" injury or when a depressed person does the same to himself. Still other accidents involve individuals such as those in the William Tell incident, who do not intend the outcome, but do intentionally take actions that put themselves or others at high risk. Still lower on the scale of intent, some people handle guns in a way that violates safety rules, but without any willful intent to do so—they just forget or are unaware of the rules. Others momentarily fail to concentrate on their actions or are otherwise not sufficiently careful around their guns, without engaging in any obvious violations of safety rules. Finally, there are accidents that are genuinely beyond the control of the shooters, as when a hunter's bullet ricochets off a rock and hits an unseen hunter.

Safety training is most likely to succeed with the events in the intermediate range of this continuum. The most intentional acts are hard to prevent because the shooters involved are motivated to intentionally ignore safety precautions. On the other hand, the least intentional events are also difficult to control because they are a byproduct of prudent, legal, socially acceptable uses of guns and involve little or no correctable misconduct or errors by the shooters. Therefore, one would expect the greatest payoff for safety programs to be in preventing accidents attributable to ordinary carelessness or the inadvertent violation of safety procedures, as distinct from more extreme misconduct by chronically reckless persons. Safety training might prevent hunting accidents that involved a sober hunter transporting a loaded long gun in a motor vehicle or improperly crossing a fence with a loaded gun, but is unlikely to prevent either the William Tell stunt or, at the other extreme, a ricochet hitting an unseen hunter.

Evidence on the circumstances of gun accidents was often too sketchy to permit a judgment as to the degree of recklessness of intent involved. Therefore, it is difficult to tell what share of gun accidents fall in the intermediate range of intent and are thus more easily prevented by gun safety training. However, information from the NAAHSC hunting accident data suggests that hunter safety programs may produce moderate reductions in accident frequency. Information was recorded for each accident on whether the shooter was a graduate of a gun safety course. It is not known how many graduates and nongraduates never became involved in accidents, but it is possible to determine whether graduates who did get into accidents were less likely to be involved in mishaps attributable to violations of law or safety rules or to careless handling. The data in Table 7.12 indicate that among shooters involved in acci-

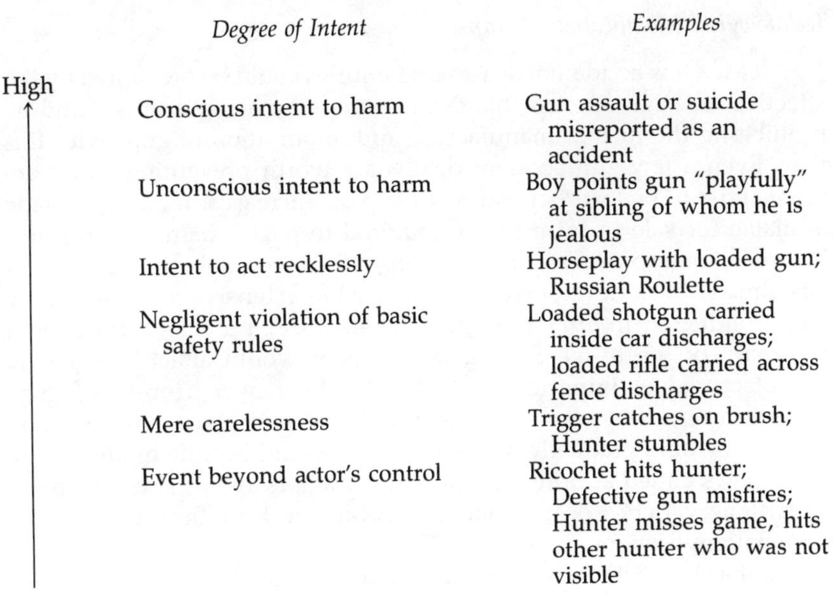

Figure 7.1. Continuum of intent in gun "accidents."

dents, hunters who had graduated from a gun safety course were significantly less likely than nongraduates to have contributed to the accidents with their own reckless behavior. Thus, at least among hunters, safety training programs may have some modest value for reducing the frequency of at least some kinds of gun accidents. On the other hand, it is possible that hunters who start out more responsible and cautious are more likely to participate in safety training and that the training itself had no effect.

For the majority of gun accidents that occur in the home, there is no solid basis for the assumption that correctable knowledge deficiencies of the sort that gun safety training could reduce are important causes. Many of these accidents occur as a result of reckless behavior that may be traceable to personality traits conducive to risk-taking, impulsive behavior, and aggressive action. Because gun safety training programs are not intended to alter personality or cure alcoholism, their ability to prevent many of these gun accidents is limited. Nevertheless, some of the less reckless home accidents may be preventable through safety training, if programs could be successfully extended to reach the relevant gun owners.

Technological Modification of Guns

At least a few accidental deaths and injuries could be prevented by the effective redesign of guns that can discharge by being dropped and by prohibiting the further manufacture and importation of guns with this flaw. Even a few gun accident deaths are worth preventing and there seems little to be lost, beyond modest price increases, if all guns made available for sale in future were required to pass a hammer drop test before being approved for sale. An objective, workable test of this sort has already been developed and was used in extensive handgun safety tests conducted in 1971 (see U.S. Senate 1971, pp. 155–8 for a brief summary of the tests). Such a requirement would affect only newly manufactured or imported guns, but as the newer drop-proof guns came to claim a larger share of the national gun stock, dropped-gun accidents would gradually decrease. There would be little motivation to evade laws aimed at bringing this state of affairs about, since the more hazardous varieties of gun offer no advantage for either defensive or criminal applications.

Another basically technological measure could effectively prevent accidents among children, especially young children. A trigger lock is a simple, cheap device that is placed behind the trigger of a gun, making discharge of most modern guns impossible until the device is unlocked with a key or otherwise disabled. Placing a trigger lock on each gun kept in homes with children old enough to pull the trigger could substantially reduce child gun accidents. Some defensive gun owners would reject this measure since it reduces the gun's readiness for defensive uses. However, it does make it safe to keep a gun loaded, and therefore ready for defensive use, in a household with children. It therefore is a safety measure that many defensive owners could be persuaded to adopt, unlike the suggestion that all guns be kept both unloaded and locked away in a box or cabinet (Center to Prevent Handgun Violence 1989), a practice that would render guns useless in many, perhaps most, defensive situations.

Screening for Proficiency

Testing for gun handling ability, knowledge of gun safety, and of how guns operate before granting a permit or license to purchase or own a gun has some merit, its principal drawback being the considerable expense involved. It could conceivably prevent a few deaths and injuries due to a lack of such knowledge and ability. However, available evidence does not support the idea that a large fraction of gun accidents are attributable to such deficiencies. If this kind of testing would not be capable of reliably identifying individuals with a predilection for engaging in high-risk activities, it is unlikely it could have much impact on the rate of gun accidents.

No states require gun training of all persons possessing guns. New York requires it of persons buying guns and Rhode Island requires it for handgun acquisition (*Federal Register* 6-26-89, p. 26925). For persons applying for a permit to carry a gun, at least five states require evidence of completion of a gun safety or training program or other proof of ability to use a gun safely—Florida, Iowa, Maryland, Minnesota, and Rhode Island. South Carolina requires that applicants for carry permits pass a proficiency test (Nispel 1981, pp. 8–9). These requirements, however, apply only to the very small fraction of the gun-owning population that seeks carry permits, making the administration of the laws far less expensive than if they applied to gun possession or purchase, but also making the requirements far less extensive in their potential effects.

General Gun Control Measures

As an alternative, there are legal means of removing guns altogether from the households of some high-risk individuals. Where successful, such measures could at least eliminate one source of risk from the environment and produce a marginal reduction in exposure to hazard. Rather than testing for knowledge of gun safety rules, license or permit laws prohibit gun purchase or possession by convicted felons or alcoholics and can thereby incidentally prohibit gun possession by many of those at highest risk of gun accidents. The main practical obstacle to the laws' effectiveness is the fact that many accidental shooters own guns for defensive reasons rather than just recreational ones. It is hard to dissuade people from owning guns if they believe their lives or those of family members may one day depend on having a gun for protection. Consequently, voluntary compliance with a permit law might be low among those segments of the population in which the accident risk is highest. Nevertheless, at least some marginal, involuntary reduction in gun ownership might be achieved through such gun laws.

At least five published studies have examined the impact of gun control laws on the rate of fatal gun accidents. The earlier review of these studies' suicide findings indicated that they suffer from serious methodological flaws (Chapter 6); therefore, little confidence can be placed in their accident findings. Geisel and his colleagues (1969) concluded that gun control reduces the FGA rate, but the dummy variable findings mentioned in an appendix to their article indicated that gun laws have no effect. Murray (1975) concluded that none of the types of gun laws he studied had any impact on the FGA rate, and DeZee's (1983) replication of Murray using later data confirmed that conclusion.

Lester and Murrell (1981a; 1986) calculated simple correlation coefficients between state FGA rates and a Guttman scale of gun control laws (critiqued in Chapter 6). They found a significant negative correlation between the two variables, but also found, for their 1970 data, an even larger negative correlation between their gun control index and the rate of fatal drowning accidents. Since the authors conceded it was doubtful that gun laws could have any direct effect on drowning accidents, their finding regarding gun accidents cannot reasonably be interpreted as demonstrating an impact of gun laws on gun accidents.

Gun control laws are aimed primarily at reducing violent crime and therefore do not usually include features specifically designed to prevent gun accidents. However, one major exception was the Washington, D.C. Firearms Control Regulations Act of 1975 (FCRA). This law not only banned local handgun sales and prohibited most civilian handgun possession, but also required persons who legally owned guns to maintain them in their residence in an unloaded and disassembled state, or bound by a trigger-locking device (Jones 1981, p. 40). Unfortunately, it is impossible to tell if this measure was effective in reducing FGAs. Secondary analysis of Mortality Detail File data for 1969–1982 indicates that FGAs had already disappeared in Washington, D.C. before the law went into effect. The law went into effect on February 21, 1977. There were no FGAs in 1977, and only one in 1976, the victim dying in September. From September 1976 until the effective date 5 months later there were no FGAs. From 1968 to 1976 the handful of FGAs had trickled down to nothing (33 in 1968, 14 in 1970, 6 in 1972, 2 in 1975), so it was impossible for the FCRA to produce further reductions, however, effective its provisions might be. The gun accident-related features of the FCRA were a largely unnecessary solution to a largely nonexistent problem.

To summarize, there is, as yet, no credible evidence indicating that gun control laws reduce the frequency of gun accidents. This does not mean that gun laws cannot reduce accidents. Many gun accidents involve alcoholics and/or convicted criminals, and many gun laws prohibit purchase or possession of guns by such persons (Chapter 8). If these laws were somehow effective in accomplishing their intended goal and denied guns to a significant number of high risk individuals, they might reduce the rate of gun accidents. However, prior studies have not yet discerned such an effect, suggesting either that the research is inadequate or that gun laws do not deny guns to high risk persons, or both.

City-Level Analysis of Fatal Gun Accident Rates

The city-level dataset used in Chapter 5 is now used to assess the impact of gun ownership levels on city rates of FGAs. The variable names and data sources are the same as described in Table 5.6. Table 7.13 presents standardized LISREL coefficients representing the effects of gun ownership levels and control variables on city FGA rates. The control variable results are not discussed here and are left for the interested reader.

No impact of gun ownership levels was detected. This result may seem somewhat surprising, since common sense would seem to suggest that where there are more guns, there should surely be more gun accidents. Recall, however, that the simple trend data in Table 7.1 also failed to support this expectation—FGAs declined as gun ownership increased. The null finding may be partly explainable by the extreme rarity of FGAs. The average city has only one or two FGAs a year, and cumulating 3 years' worth of data does not increase the numbers much. Consequently, only gun availability among a very tiny fraction of the population is likely to have any impact on the FGA rate. Further, given the random component in accident causation, it is not that surprising that hardly any variable shows a strong relationship with the FGA rate. The model's PSI indicates that 90% of the variation in rates was left unexplained.

It may also be that many of the cities with higher gun ownership, especially smaller cities and those in the South and West, have many gun owners who were, from childhood, thoroughly socialized into safe handling of guns, in contrast to owners who acquired guns only as adults, and who received little or no safety training. Thus, the same cities that have cultures supportive of gun ownership may also have safer-than-average gun owner populations. If so, high aggregate rates of gun ownership would not necessarily be positively related to city FGA rates, even if gun ownership by high-risk segments of the population did increase the rates. Consequently, it is not certain that gun ownership levels do not affect FGA rates, and it remains possible that gun laws might reduce FGAs. This issue is addressed in Chapter 10.

Summary and Conclusions

Fatal gun accidents commonly involve unusually reckless behavior. The typical accident involves a shooter intentionally pulling the trigger, but hitting someone she/he did not intend to hit. About half of accidental gun deaths are self-inflicted. Most gun accidents occur in the home, many (perhaps most) of them involving guns kept for defense. However, very few accidents occur in connection with attempts to use guns defensively.

Gun accidents are generally committed by unusually reckless people with records of heavy drinking, repeated involvement in automobile crashes, many traffic citations, and prior arrests for assault. Gun accidents, then, involve a rare and atypical subset of the population, as both shooters and victims. They rarely involve children. Instead, the accidents most commonly involve adolescents and young adults. Accident rates are also higher among males, blacks, lower income persons, single people, rural people, and Southerners, i.e., the same segments of the population that show higher rates of intentional violence.

The risk of a gun accident is extremely low, even among defensive gun owners, except among a very small, identifiably high-risk subset of the population. Consequently, it is doubtful whether, for the average gun owner, the risk of a gun accident could counterbalance the benefits of keeping a gun in the home for protection—the risk of an accident is quite low overall, and is virtually nonexistent for most gun owners.

Loaded long guns appear to be considerably more likely to become involved in accidents than loaded handguns. Therefore, with regard to accident reduction, it would be bad policy to restrict only handguns, without similarly restrictive controls on long guns, since this would encourage substitution of more lethal and "accident-prone" long guns as home defense weapons, possibly resulting in an increase in fatal home gun accidents. Gun accidents rarely involve defective guns. City rates of fatal gun accidents are not significantly related to gun ownership levels. Finally, there is, as yet, no credible evidence indicating that existing gun laws reduce gun accidents.

Table 7.1. Trends in Fatal Gun Accidents, U.S., 1933–1987

Year	*Total*	*Self-Inflicted*[a] *(%)*	*Other-Inflicted and Unspecified*	*Rate per 100,000 Resident Population*	*Guns per 1000 Population*
1933	3014			2.40	n.a.
1935	2799			2.20	n.a.
1940	2390			1.80	n.a.
1945	2454			1.84	n.a.
1950	2174			1.43	381
1955	2120			1.28	308
1960	2334			1.30	431
1965	2344			1.21	462
1966	2558			1.30	476
1967	2896	(postwar peak)		1.47	492
1968	2394			1.20	513
1969	2309	568 (25)	1741	1.15	532
1970	2406	523 (22)	1883	1.18	549
1971	2360	524 (22)	1836	1.14	567
1972	2442	538 (22)	1904	1.17	588
1973	2618	516 (20)	2102	1.24	610
1974	2513	512 (20)	2001	1.18	637
1975	2380	520 (22)	1860	1.10	657
1976	2059	448 (22)	1611	0.95	678
1977	1982	450 (23)	1532	0.90	697
1978	1806	384 (21)	1422	0.81	716
1979	2004			0.89	721
1980	1955[b]			0.86	738
1981	1871			0.82	754
1982	1757			0.76	768
1983	1695			0.72	778
1984	1668			0.71	788
1985	1649			0.69	798
1986	1452			0.59	805
1987	1440			0.57	816

[a] Gun accident deaths were separately classified as self-inflicted only while the eighth revision of the International Classification of Diseases was in use, 1969–1978.
[b] This table indicates 1955 fatal gun accidents for 1980, a count of resident deaths only, to maintain comparability with other years. All other tables pertaining to 1980 cover all deaths, including four nonresident deaths, for a total of 1959 fatal gun accidents.
Sources: Deaths—U.S. National Center for Health Statistics (and predecessor agencies), 1988 and earlier; National Safety Council (1988, p. 20). Population estimates—U.S. Bureau of Census, 1983b, p. 6. Guns owned—Table 2.1.

Table 7.2. Risks of Accidental Death from Guns and Motor Vehicles U.S., 1980

	Accidental Deaths per 100,000			
	Gun-Owning Households	*Firearms*	*Vehicle-Owning Households*	*Motor Vehicles*
All guns	5.261	1.188	76.005	34.323
Handguns	4.137	1.592	—	—

Sources: Deaths—Mortality Detail File for 1980 (computer dataset); number of civilian guns, handguns—cumulations of annual totals of guns manufactured, minus exports, plus imports, in Chapter 2; gun-owning households—averages of percentage owning in NORC (1980) and Gallup (1980) surveys in Table 2.2, applied to total households (U.S. Bureau of the Census 1983b, p. 48); vehicle-owning households (occupied housing units)—U.S. Bureau of the Census (1983b, p. 752); registered motor vehicles—U.S. Bureau of the Census (1983b, p. 614).

Table 7.3. Comparison of Injury Hazards of Firearms and Other Products[a-e]

Estimated Number of Injuries Requiring Emergency Room Treatment, 7–1–80 to 6–30–81		
Ranking	*Product Group*	*Injuries*
1	Stairs	763
2	Bicycles	518
3	Baseball equipment	478
4	Football equipment	470
5	Basketball equipment	434
.	.	.
.	.	.
35	Gymnastics equipment	62
36	Guns (including BB, pellet guns)	60
37	Doors and panels	60
38	Hammers	58
.	.	.
.	.	.
.	.	.
	(183 product groups listed)	

Age Adjusted Frequency and Severity Index (AFSI), 7–1–76 to 6–30–77		
Ranking	*Product Group*	*AFSI*
1	Bicycles	40.608
2	Stairs	23.566
3	Foods	20.708
4	Motor vehicles	20.328
5	Football equipment	13.682
.		.
.		.
45	Nonprescription drugs	2.714
46	Firearms (not including BB, pellet guns)	2.435
47	Fireworks	2.435
48	Gas, air, spring operated guns (including BB guns)	2.402
49	Pens, pencils	2.371
.	.	.
.	.	.
	(At least 159 products rated)	

[a] The AFSI is computed by weighting each injury by a rating of its seriousness, on a scale from 10 to 2516. Also each injury to a child 14 or under is given additional weight by multiplying it further by 2.5.

[b] Estimates of injuries include all types, whether accidental, suicidal, or assaultive for persons under age 15, but for older persons exclude injuries known to be intentionally inflicted.

[c] The data on numbers of injuries include those involving BB, pellet, and other spring, gas, or air-operated guns, as well as true firearms; the data on AFSI ratings include a separate category for these types.

[d] All data reflect injuries associated with a given product, not just those in some way caused by the product. Thus the number of injuries caused by the product would probably be lower than the number associated with it.

[e] The gun injury figures count injuries in addition to those involving gunshot wounds. For example, if a clerk in a sporting goods store dropped a rifle on his foot, broke a toe, and went to a hospital emergency room to have it treated, it would count as a gun injury for CPSC purposes.

Sources: Number of injuries—U.S. Consumer Product Safety Commission, (1982). AFSI—U.S. Consumer Product Safety Commission (1978).

Table 7.4. Deaths due to Accident Caused by Firearm Missile (E922) by Age and Gun Type, U.S. 1980[a]

Age	Handgun	Shotgun	Gun Type Hunting Rifle	Military Firearms	Other (Flare)	Unspecified	Total
Under 1 month	0	0	0			1	1
1–11 months	1	0	0			1	2
1 year	1	2	0			1	4
2 years	3	2	1			1	7
3	4	1	2			11	18
4	4	2	1			6	13
5–9	17	13	7			40	77
10–14	25	46	17			106	194
15–19	58	50	28		1	237	690
20–24	47	39	17		1	227	331
25–29	34	26	15			166	241
30–34	38	21	9			106	174
35–39	17	12	6			72	107
40–44	4	11	3			64	82
45–49	4	13	8			57	82
50–54	11	7	1			33	52
55–59	7	9	5			34	55
60–64	5	7	4			29	45
65–69	6	6	3			25	40
70–74	0	4	1			16	21
75–79	1	6	1			13	21
80–84	1	4	0			7	12
85–89	1	2	0			1	4
90–94	0	0	1			0	1
95 and over	0	0	0			0	0
Not stated	0	0	0			1	1
Total	289	283	130	0	2	1255	1959

Gun Accidents by Gun Type by Age Groups, Children Only

Age Group	Total	Gun Type: Type Unknown	Type Known	Known to Be Handgun	Estimated Total Handgun
Under 5	45	21	24	13	24
5–9	77	40	37	17	37
10–14	194	106	88	25	55
Under 10	122	61	61	30	61
Under 15	316	167	149	55	116

[a] Military firearms includes army rifle and machine gun. Hunting rifle includes any nonmilitary rifle, but not air rifles or BB guns. Handgun includes pistols and revolvers. Age refers to age at last birthday (except for infants) of victim.

Source: Analysis of the Mortality Detail computer tape for 1980, National Center for Health Statistics (1983).

Table 7.5. Recent Trends in Fatal Gun Accidents Involving Young Victims

	Victim Age				*Total*		
Year	*0–4*	*5–9*	*10–14*	*15–19*	*0–14*	*0–19*	*Total, All Ages*
1974	85	142	305	476	532	1008	2513
1975	71	120	304	428	495	923	2380
1976	61	104	263	362	428	790	2059
1977	48	104	240	390	392	782	1982
1978	52	87	210	320	349	669	1806
1979	57	87	220	354	372	726	2004
1980	45	77	194	373	316	689	1955
1981	51	64	183	306	298	604	1871
1982	44	81	154	271	279	550	1756
1983	40	45	158	261	243	504	1695
1984	34	66	187	265	287	552	1668
1985	43	58	177	241	278	519	1459
1986	34	57	143	238	234	472	1452
1987	37	66	144	220	247	467	1440

Sources: U.S. NCHS (1990 and earlier).

Table 7.6. Social Distribution of Fatal Gun Accident Victimization, U.S., 1980

Accidental gun deaths per 100,000 resident population
Accidental gun deaths per 100,000 gun owners[a]
Accidental gun deaths per 100,000 persons in gun-owning households[b]

	Male				*Female*				
Age	*White*	*Black*	*Other*	*Total*	*White*	*Black*	*Other*	*Total*	*Both Sexes, All Races*
0–14	0.97	1.01	0.57	0.97	0.04	0.26	0.44	0.25	0.62
	—	—	—	—	—	—	—	—	—
	1.99	3.36	1.90	2.07	0.49	0.87	1.48	0.53	1.31
15–24	2.86	3.24	2.45	2.90	0.36	0.68	0.21	0.40	1.66
	7.13	42.13	*c*	8.03	7.76	11.17	*c*	8.48	9.22
	4.88	42.13	*c*	5.52	0.90	2.72	*c*	1.09	3.82
25–39	1.55	3.80	1.99	1.79	0.24	0.46	0.27	0.27	1.02
	3.06	12.92	6.95	3.69	2.06	4.43	0.82	2.27	3.58
	2.84	10.76	6.95	3.40	0.52	1.94	0.82	0.61	2.14
40+	0.93	1.55	0.31	0.97	0.11	0.24	0.14	0.12	0.51
	1.68	2.98	0.47	1.77	0.65	2.48	1.11	0.76	1.58
	1.59	2.88	0.47	1.67	0.26	0.95	0.37	0.30	1.07
Total, all ages	1.45	2.23	1.24	1.54	0.21	0.38	0.27	0.23	0.86
	2.81	5.81	3.73	3.05	1.53	4.18	1.69	1.78	2.98
	2.54	5.37	3.73	2.77	0.48	1.58	1.02	0.57	1.84
Both sexes, all ages	0.81	1.26	0.76	0.86					
	2.70	6.62	3.14	2.98					
	1.66	4.17	2.57	1.84					

[a] No figures calculated for persons under age 15 who personally own guns.
[b] Figures assume the race-specific household gun ownership rates for all ages and sexes combined apply to persons under age 15.
[c] Rates cannot be calculated because no gun ownership was reported by these groups.
Sources: Gun accident deaths—analysis of 1980 Mortality Detail File computer tape (U.S. NCHS 1983); respondent and household gun ownership—combined 1980 and 1982 NORC GSS (Davis and Smith 1984).

Table 7.7. Gun Type by Population Size of Place of Victim Residence, Fatal Gun Accidents, U.S., 1980

	Size of Place						
Gun Type	*Under 10,000*	*10,000–50,000*	*50,000–250,000*	*250,000 or larger*	*Unknown*	*Total*	*% of Known Gun Type*
Handgun	150	43	41	54	1	289	41
Rifle, shotgun	272	56	45	39	1	413	59
Other	2	0	0	0	0	2	0
Subtotal	424	99	86	93	2	704	100
% handgun	35	43	48	58	—	41	—
Unknown	747	205	155	146	2	1255	—
Total	1171	304	241	239	4	1959	—
% of total	60	16	12	12	0	100	

Source: Analysis of the Mortality Detail File computer tape for 1980, National Center for Health Statistics (1983).

Table 7.8. Activities/Circumstances Associated with Fatal Firearms Accidents—General Samples of Accidents[a]

Study:	*MLIC46–47*	*MLIC49–51*			*MLIC53–55*			*WW67*	*C7282*	*MH76–80*		
Activity/Circumstance	*T*	*O*	*S*	*T*	*O*	*S*	*T*	*T*	*T*	*O*	*S*	*T*
Home (total)	126	63	47	122	77	81	173	—	—	—	—	—
Russian Roulette	—	1	5	6	0	11	11	—	3	—	—	—
Playing with weapon	26+	23	11	35	31	18	49	—	12	30	23	53
Scuffling for possession	"Some"	0	0	5	4	1	5	—	—	—	—	—
Handling, examining, demonstrating weapon	32	12	3	15	16	9	25	15	10	9	2	11
Shooter tripping, falling	—	—	—	—	1	6	7	—	—	—	—	—
Picking up, setting down weapon	—	—	—	—	0	9	0	—	—	—	—	—
Brushing against, moving guns	"Several"	—	—	—	—	—	—	—	—	—	—	—
Dropping weapon	—	1	4	5	—	—	—	—	—	11	18	29[b]
Cleaning, repairing gun	19	5	12	17	8	14	22	5	6	7	12	19
Loading, unloading gun	—	—	—	—	2	7	9	—	—	—	—	—
Unspecified home activity	49	—	—	39	15	6	36	—	—	—	—	—

(*continued*)

Table 7.8. (Continued)

Study:	*MLIC46–47*	*MLIC49–51*			*MLIC53–55*			*WW67*	*C7282*	*MH76–80*		
Activity/Circumstance	*T*	*O*	*S*	*T*	*O*	*S*	*T*	*T*	*T*	*O*	*S*	*T*
Hunting (total)	64	51	30	87	45	24	72	23	4	31	8	39
Carrying loaded in vehicle	—	2	4	7	—	—	—	—	—	—	—	—
Carrying weapon over or through fence	—	2	6	8	0	4	4	—	—	—	—	—
Tripped while carrying	—	3	7	16	3	7	10	—	—	—	—	—
Mistaken for game	—	6	0	6	9	0	9	—	—	—	—	—
Picking up, setting down	—	16	0	16	11	6	11	—	—	—	—	—
Loading, unloading gun	—	6	0	6	—	—	—	—	—	—	—	—
Unspecified hunting	64	16	13	34	21	7	31	—	—	—	—	—
Outdoors public place, not hunting (total)	60	21	15	42	26	14	57	—	—	—	—	—
Playing with weapon	—	—	—	—	7	5	12	—	—	—	—	—
Carrying loaded weapon in vehicle	—	—	—	—	—	—	—	—	—	—	—	—
Walking into line of fire	—	5	0	5	5	0	6	—	—	—	—	—
Examining, demonstrating weapon	—	4	1	5	—	—	—	—	—	—	—	—
Target shooting	18	—	—	—	—	—	—	19	—	11	2	13
Unspecified outdoor	42	11	10	26	14	9	39	—	—	—	—	—
Other and unspecified	—	1	7	16	—	—	—	—	19	17	29	46
Total	250	136	99	267	148	119	302	62	54	116	94	210

[a] For those studies that make the distinction: O, other-inflicted wounds; S, self-inflicted wounds; T, total. Total can exceed sum of O and S because it includes unspecified cases. Dash (—) indicates this category was not used in the study.

[b] Not comparable with other studies—covers "dropped or mishandled gun," including eight cases of tripping and falling while carrying gun.

Sources: MLIC, Metropolitan Life Insurance Company. Numbers following this indicate years in which the studied deaths occurred. The respective publication dates of these studies are 1948, 1953, and 1956. WW67, Waller and Whorton (1973); C7282, Copeland (1984); MH76–80, Morrow and Hudson (1986).

Table 7.9. Activities/Circumstances Associated with Firearms Accidents—Home Accidents Only[a]

Study:	*MLIC56–57*	*MLIC64–66*			*Heins et al. 62–71*	*Wintemute et al.*
Activity/Circumstances	*T*	*O*	*S*	*T*	*T*	*T*
Russian Roulette	5	0	4	4	—	5
Playing with weapon, pointing it in fun	12	18	8	26	14	66
Scuffling for possession	—	5	0	5	—	
Argument	—	—	—	—	8	
Searching for prowlers, protection against threats	—	0	2	2	9	
Demonstrating or examining weapon	5	8	6	14	—	
Dropped	—	—	—	—	2	
Accidental discharge	—	—	—	—	9	6
Target practice, shooting at birds, etc. in yard	—	2	10	12	—	
Cleaning, oiling, repairing, loading gun	13	5	24	29	1	
Other specified	20	3	12	15	0	3
Unspecific, unknown	24	21	15	36	17	8
Total	79	62	81	143	60	88

[a] MLIC, Metropolitan Life Insurance Company. Following numbers indicate years in which studied deaths occurred. O, other-inflicted deaths; S, self-inflicted deaths; T, total deaths. Dash (—) indicates category was not used in that study. The Heins et al. study concerns an exclusively urban sample and is probably not representative of home accidents. The Wintemute et al. study is included in this table because 82 of its 88 cases occurred in a residence.

Sources: MLIC (1959, 1968), Heins et al. (1974), and Wintemute et al. (1987).

Table 7.10. Location of Fatal Gun Accidents by Gun Type, U.S., 1980

	Place of Accident								
Gun Type	*Home*	*"Other Specified Place"*	*Farm*	*Street or Highway*	*Public Building*	*Miscellaneous*	*Total Specified*	*Not Specified*	*Total*
Handgun	179	32	4	21	18	5	259	30	289
Shotgun or rifle	216	73	23	17	3	9	341	72	413
Other	1	0	0	0	0	0	1	1	2
Specified	396	105	27	38	21	14	601	103	704
Unspecified	565	186	50	54	38	19	912	343	1255
Total	961	291	77	92	59	33	1513	446	1959
% of specified	63.5	19.2	5.1	6.1	3.9	2.2	100.0	—	—

Source: Analysis of Mortality Detail File Computer tape (1980), National Center for Health Statistics (1983).

Table 7.11. Circumstances of Gun Accidents in Hunting, 1977–1980

Circumstance	*Fatal*	*Nonfatal*	*Total*	*% of Total*
Shooter intentionally fired gun (I)	282	2226	2508	50.0
Victim out of sight of shooter	69	813	882	17.6
Victim covered by shooter swinging on game	38	616	654	13.0
Victim mistaken for game	121	469	590	11.8
Victim moved into line of fire	49	171	220	4.4
Defective ammunition	0	13	13	0.0
Richochet	5	144	149	3.0
Shooter accidentally fired gun (A)	124	832	956	19.1
Shooter stumbled and fell	99	510	609	12.2
Loading firearm	12	163	175	3.5
Unloading firearm	12	149	161	3.2
Cleaning firearm	1	10	11	0.2
No one fired gun (N)	54	510	564	11.3
Insecure rest, firearm fell[a]	28	210	238	4.7
Trigger caught an object	26	300	326	6.5
A or N	84	228	312	6.2
Using firearm as a club[a]	14	31	45	0.9
Removing or placing firearm in vehicle[a]	50	130	180	3.6
Improper crossing of obstacle[a]	20	67	87	1.7
Unknown whether I or A or N	82	590	672	13.4
Discharge of gun in vehicle[a]	25	84	109	2.2
Defective firearm	16	153	169	3.4
Careless handling[a]	22	228	250	5.0
Horseplay with loaded firearm[a] (may not have known gun was loaded)	19	125	144	2.9
Total	626	4386	5012	100.0
Classified as reckless	178	875	1053	
% reckless	28.4	19.9	21.0	

[a] Indicates circumstance was classified as reckless, involving a safety or law violation or careless handling.

Source: Tabulated from NAAHSC (1982).

Table 7.12. Hunting Accidents and Gun Safety Training Courses[a]

	Was Shooter a Graduate of Gun Safety Course?					
	Yes		*No*		*Total*	
Recklessness in Accident	*Number*	*%*	*Number*	*%*	*Number*	*%*
Safety or law violation	95	7.4	708	15.7	803	13.9
Careless handling	69	5.4	181	4.0	250	4.3
either of above	164	12.9	889	19.7	1053	18.2
Other	1112	87.1	3623	80.3	4735	81.8
Total accidents	1276	100.0	4512	100.0	5788	100.0

[a] $\chi^2 = 33.36$, $p < .005$ ("either of above" vs. "other").
Source: Tabulated from NAAHSC (1982).

Table 7.13. Effects of Gun Ownership Levels and Control Variables on City Fatal Gun Accident Rates[a]

	LNFGA	*Gun Ownership*[b]
PCTBLACK	.591*	.533*
PCTM1524	−.114	
ALCHLSM	.083	
INVPOP	−.190	−.166*
DENSITY	−.264	−.461*
HOSPITAL		−.157*
ACCIDENT	.145	
RGUNMAG		.221*
HUNTERS		.193*
Gun ownership	−.577	
PSI	.905	.392
PSI (2,1)	.289	
df	76	
χ^2	194.35	
GOF	.933	

[a] Gun law dummies were also included in these models; estimates of their coefficient are reported in Chapter 10. Also, the following control variables were tested but found to be unrelated to gun accident or gun ownership rates: PCTHISP, MFI, RPOV, INEQUALT, OWNEROCC, COLLEGE, TRNSIENT, PCTMOVE, POPCHANG, PCTFOREN, CNTDIVRT, PCRM80, CHRCHMEM, ADDICTRT, PCTSMSA, VISITORS, WEST, MAXTEMP, CROWDING, STHNNESS, LIVLONE, PCTOLD.

[b] Latent construct with indicators: PGH7982, PGS7982, PCTGNAST, PCTGNROB, GUNSTOL.

*$p < .05$.

PART III

REGULATING GUNS

CHAPTER

8

Types of Gun Regulation

There is an almost endless variety of ways to regulate guns, with no two legal jurisdictions having the same set of controls. To understand the material in the remaining chapters it will be necessary to understand some of the major legal strategies for controlling weapons. This chapter is devoted to outlining the major forms of gun regulation currently in existence, and describing their enforcement and administration.

Gun controls can be categorized along many dimensions, but the following are certainly among the most important: (1) the gun-related activity that is regulated, (2) the type of gun that is regulated, (3) the categories of persons to whom regulations apply, (4) the level of government that imposes and enforces the controls, and (5) the level of restrictiveness of the controls.

Gun-Related Activity Regulated

Controls have been imposed on each of the following gun-linked activities.

1. *Manufacture.* Federal law prohibits manufacture of some types of guns (e.g., all-plastic guns), tightly restricts manufacture of others (e.g., fully automatic guns), and requires a license for manufacturing almost any type of firearm. In addition, states such as Maryland, Hawaii, Illinois, and Minnesota have banned the manufacture of so-called "Saturday Night Specials," usually defining these as handguns made of cheap metal that melts at a relatively low temperature (U.S. Bureau of Alcohol, Tobacco and Firearms 1980, 1988). Manufacturers are also required to stamp serial numbers on guns so they may be identified for law enforcement purposes.

2. *Importation.* The federal government has exclusive jurisdiction over importation of guns into the country and a federal license is re-

quired for importation. Import controls have never been directed at producing overall gun scarcity, but have, on occasion, been directed at reducing the inflow of specific subtypes of guns. The Gun Control Act of 1968 banned importation of foreign-made handguns that failed to meet a test of suitability for "sporting uses." As it had no impact on the total number of handguns flowing into private hands (Zimring 1975), its main effect appears to have been to shield U.S. handgun makers from foreign competition at the low end of the price range (Sherrill 1973). Similarly, a 1990 federal ban on the importation of certain "assault weapons" was aimed at a small number of foreign-made models (Chapter 3).

3. *Sale/Purchase/Transfer.* When most people think of gun controls, they probably first think of regulations intended to restrict or otherwise regulate the acquisition of guns by private individuals. Some controls over gun purchases focus on sellers, others on buyers. Both the federal government and some state and local governments require retail gun dealers to obtain a license to do business. Dealers have legally imposed responsibilities and limits regarding their sale of guns. They are obliged by federal law to ensure that purchasers of handguns reside in the state in which the business is located and that they are adults, to record the sale of all guns on federal forms, and to maintain these records and make them available for inspection by the authorities. Some licensing requirements, such as licensing fees, have the effect of limiting the number of retail dealers (Blose and Cook 1980, p. 20), whereas others are directed at keeping criminals and similar high-risk individuals out of the gun business.

The federal Firearms Owners' Protection Act, passed in 1986, was widely regarded as a loosening of restraints on gun sales, but for the first time it made it unlawful for *any* person, whether a licensed dealer or not, to knowingly transfer a firearm to a member of various high-risk groups not permitted to possess firearms (the provision previously applied only to dealers). Federal law, however, does not provide any effective way for gun sellers to know whether prospective buyers are disqualified.

Some cities such as Washington, D.C. and Chicago ban the sale of handguns within city limits altogether. Such controls are rare and do not exist anywhere at the state level, although some states forbid dealer sales of some, generally cheap, handguns. Other controls regulate who may purchase or otherwise receive guns. The most common control of this type is a minimum age requirement, most commonly 18 for purchase of long guns and 21 for handguns. Other purchase controls allow for checks of various records to see if a prospective gun buyer falls into a prohibited class, such as convicted felon, alcoholic, drug addict, mentally ill person, alien, or fugitive from justice.

This can be done in several ways. Some laws require prospective gun buyers to obtain a purchase permit, which is not issued until the applicant has cleared all required records checks. Laws requiring handgun purchase permits date back at least as far as 1911, when New York passed such a statute (Kennett and Anderson 1975, p. 182). The requirement that buyers have a permit usually applies to sales by both dealers and nondealers (Blose and Cook 1980).

An "application to purchase" system is different. The prospective buyer fills out an application that is sent to a regulatory agency such as a state law enforcement department. If the seller does not hear from the authorities after a specified time period, the sale goes through. The burden is on the authorities to stop the sale—their silence implies consent (Blose and Cook 1980, p. 13). The records check is optional for them, and is probably often skipped or postponed until after the transfer has been completed, to reduce the number of checks required. Further, most application-to-purchase systems regulate only retail sales by licensed dealers. Since at least one-quarter of gun acquisitions by noncriminals, and a majority of acquisitions by criminals, are by means other than purchases from dealers (Chapter 2), this means that a large share of gun transactions under some application systems are not even theoretically subject to a criminal records check of the applicant. Most waiting period requirements are linked with application systems (although Wisconsin has a stand-alone waiting period). The stated periods range from 1 to 15 days, with 3 and 7 days being the most common.

A license-to-possess or gun owner's identification (ID) system resembles a purchase permit system in that it uses record checks to restrict gun acquisition by prohibited classes of persons, and legal acquisition of a gun requires that the license by obtained first. However, ID requirements commonly also regulate the possession of guns as well as their initial acquisition. A person must have a license to possess a gun, regardless of how it was acquired, and the requirement applies to possession in the owner's home or business as well as in public places. Concerning gun purchases, licenses can be either "open-ended"—good for a certain time period during which any number of guns may be acquired—or one-time-only, requiring that a separate purchase permit be obtained for each gun purchase (Blose and Cook 1980, p. 13).

Some controls over gun purchases do not directly restrict gun acquisition, but merely record it. Many gun registration schemes require that records of purchases be made so that specific buyers, identified by name, address, and other attributes, are linked with the specific guns purchased, identified by make, model, serial number, and so forth. Federal law requires that gun dealers retain such records of their sales on their premises; state and local registration requirements may additionally entail sending records of gun transactions to local or state licensing or enforcement authorities, thereby generating centralized files of gun buyers.

In addition to requiring registration of gun purchases, some local jurisdictions also require that *possession* of guns be registered. This is a much more extensive form of control, since it applies to persons guns that were acquired before the enactment of registration requirements, regardless of when or how the guns were acquired. Theoretically, such a system would allow authorities to link any gun in their jurisdiction to its owner.

4. *Possession.* A few states require that all persons possessing guns must have a license to do so, even in their homes. Possession is also regulated in two other ways. First, possession of guns is prohibited altogether for members of "high-risk" classes such as those listed above in connection with purchase restrictions. The most commonly prohibited classes are convicted criminals (usually just felons, but sometimes violent misdemeanants or even all misdemeanants as well), mentally ill persons, drug addicts/users/abusers, and alcoholics. These restrictions are less prevalent than one might think. Most states do not prohibit possession by mentally ill people, most do not ban possession by addicts, and most do not ban possession by alcoholics (or at least did not as of 1980). Although 37 of the 50 states banned (as of 1980) possession by criminals, these bans were somewhat redundant in that federal law prohibits, everywhere in the United States, possession by convicted felons, as well as by adjudicated mental incompetents and illegal aliens (Ronhovde and Sugars 1982, pp. 204–5; U.S. BATF 1988).

The other main control over possession is the regulation of the carrying of guns. This refers to physical possession of the gun, either on the carrier's person or in a motor vehicle or otherwise under the carrier's control, while moving through a public place, i.e., somewhere other than the carrier's home or business. "Carrying" in the legal sense usually excludes physical carrying of a gun by a licensed hunter during hunting season in a location suitable for hunting, as well as carrying by police, military personnel, and security guards in the performance of their duties. Except in Vermont, concealed carrying of firearms is either prohibited or requires a license. Regulation is typically stricter concerning carrying on the person than carrying in a motor vehicle, stricter concerning concealed carrying than open carrying, and stricter concerning handguns than long guns (Jones and Ray 1980; Blackman 1985).

5. *Use.* Some gun controls regulate the manner in which guns are used. It is commonly unlawful to fire a gun within city limits or in other congested urban areas, with exceptions usually made for self-defense uses. Some forms of open display of guns in public places may be prohibited under measures forbidding "reckless display" of guns. However, the most important controls over gun use concern the use of guns in felonies and other crimes that would be regarded as serious even without gun involvement. Most states, as well as the federal government, have "sentence enhancement" and/or mandatory sentencing statutes that provide for additional penalties or mandatory minimum sentences if one of a class of serious crimes is committed with a firearm. Sometimes the sentencing provisions are discretionary, allowing, but not requiring, judges to impose heavier-than-usual penalties, whereas others are theoretically mandatory. Although none of the sentencing provisions are truly mandatory in operation, sentencing discretion may be limited by requiring minimum sentence lengths, or by prohibiting suspended sentences, probation, parole, concurrent service of multiple punishments, or time off for good behavior.

Gun Types Controlled

All of these forms of gun control vary with regard to what types of guns are regulated. Most gun controls in the United States apply only to handguns or to "concealable" guns. For example, of 19 states that had waiting period laws in 1989, 15 applied the requirement only to handguns or other concealable weapons. Of 22 states requiring a criminal records check before a gun sale in 1989, 18 required it only for handguns (U.S. Department of Justice 1989, p. 26940). Nine of 13 states requiring a permit to purchase a gun in 1980 did so only for handguns. Even prohibitions of gun possession by convicted criminals applied only to handguns in nearly half of the states with such restrictions (Ronhovde and Sugars 1982, pp. 204–5). (The federal ban on possession by felons applies to all gun types, but there is little enforcement of this sort of federal law because only a very limited federal law enforcement apparatus exists.) And among the 26 states requiring a permit to carry guns as of

1990, 24 applied the requirement exclusively to handguns (National Rifle Association 1990). Some controls apply to all gun types, and a few apply just to long guns. Other controls apply to rarer, special gun types, such as machine guns, plastic guns, or SNS-type handguns, as well as sawed-off long guns and more exotic firearms. These were addressed at length in Chapter 3, so no further discussion is necessary here.

Who Is Controlled?

Gun controls can also be distinguished by what sorts of people are targeted by the controls. Although most gun laws use language that prohibits certain acts without regard to who does them, many regulations are in practice aimed at restricting gun acquisition, possession, and use among high-risk subsets of the population. Most controls over purchase of guns, most possession bans, and all sentence enhancement statutes fall into this category. Other regulations are intended to restrict gun acquisition, use, and possession within the general population. For example, controls over gun carrying probably restrict carrying among the noncriminal majority of the population at least as much as among the criminally active subset. Likewise, bans on possession of weapons such as unregistered fully automatic weapons, sawed-off long guns, and silencers typically apply to virtually the entire civilian population, except for specially authorized persons. And possession of guns may be prohibited to the general public with regard to certain places, such as court buildings, prisons, schools, airports, bars, and public meeting places.

There is a fundamental logical dilemma in deciding whether to focus controls only on high-risk groups such as criminals. If controls are directed at everyone, the burden of regulation falls mainly on the law-abiding majority, and reductions in gun use, possession, or carrying are achieved mostly among people who would never use guns to commit crimes. Thus, most of the regulation effort is wasted on people who do not need to be controlled. On the other hand, if controls are directed solely at criminals, they are directed at persons who are as unlikely to obey gun laws as they are to obey laws prohibiting violent crimes. Further, such controls miss people who lack some official record of violence-proneness, yet may nevertheless commit violence in the future. In short, the controls either are directed at people who need to be controlled, but will not obey the gun laws, or they are directed at people who will obey the laws but do not need to be controlled.

The same could obviously be said about most criminal laws. They control crime only to the extent that they affect people who would commit criminal acts in the absence of legal prohibitions, yet who also can somehow be influenced by criminal prohibitions and their associated penalties. In connection with gun control, this means that controls work only to the extent that violent acts are committed by people willing to break laws forbidding crimes such as murder, rape, robbery, and aggravated assault, yet who will obey gun control laws. Although it might seem that criminals of this sort are not very common, they are not nonexistent either. The impulse to commit acts of violence may affect a person's conduct only very intermittently and for very short periods of time. At other times, the person may be disinclined to break the law, unwilling to risk penalties, and likely to give considerable thought to the risks of illegal acquisition, possession, or use of guns. The strong motivation to break the law that prevails for some brief periods of time does not necessarily imply anything about the motivation to do so at other times. Very likely, robbers and even murderers obey traffic laws and feed parking meters much of the time, albeit less than noncriminals.

The more astute advocates of gun control know that their proposals will reduce violence largely to the extent that they can affect this subset of the population. They do not expect to observe the impact of gun control primarily among the sort of "hard-core" career felons who make up a large share of our nation's prison population. Rather, effects are expected among the sorts of presumably more weakly and intermittently motivated violent offenders who are frequently screened out of the criminal justice system at an early stage, e.g., arrestees whom prosecutors decline to prosecute.

It is unlikely that much can be done to prevent highly motivated prospective aggressors from acquiring a gun in a nation with 200 million guns in private hands. However, it may be possible to either prevent acquisition or make possession sufficiently risky that more marginally motivated people would be unable to get, possess, or use guns or would be unwilling to even attempt to do so. If one required a license or permit to buy a gun from a licensed retail dealer, most career felons and strongly motivated intermittent offenders would probably be willing and able to get a gun through other channels. However, there very likely would also be some remaining prospective aggressors who would be either unwilling to seek out other sources, or would lack the personal contacts, time, money, or other resources needed to do so. Although these individuals may well account for a minority of violent crimes, they are not necessarily insignificant in number.

Two centuries ago, Cesare Beccaria [1963 (1764), p. 88] asked "Can it be supposed that those who have the courage to violate the most sacred laws of humanity . . . will respect the less important and arbitrary ones, which can be violated with ease and impunity?" The short answer is "Yes, such a thing can be supposed—for at least a few criminals." Whether this can be supposed for enough criminals to justify the costs of gun control measures is not so clear. Legal control of criminal behavior is a game of small reductions in crime produced through partial compliance with the laws; this is at least as true of other laws as it is of gun laws. As noted in Chapter 1, even among the supposedly hard-core felons interviewed in the Wright–Rossi prison survey, substantial minorities reported registering guns and applying for permits, as required by law. Further, a quarter of the men claimed to have never possessed even a single gun, half claimed to have never committed a crime with a gun, and half said they had never fired a gun at another person (1986, p. 80–1). And 15% of the felons thought they would have to go to "a lot of trouble" to get a handgun after release from prison (p. 212). Presumably these percentages would be considerably higher among less hard-core criminals with fewer well-connected criminal associates. Thus, some criminals appear to obey gun laws, some do not own guns in a nation awash in guns, and many do not use them in crimes. Although there is no way to tell if these criminals would have done any of these things in the absence of gun laws, the point is that it is not self-evident that people willing to violate society's "most sacred laws" would also invariably violate all gun laws.

There are obvious costs to imposing controls that are aimed at an unduly wide segment of the population. People who consider themselves law-abiding citizens are angered when treated like criminals. Some would withdraw respect for the law and those who make and enforce it. Many would resist the controls. An Illinois survey asked respondents if they would comply with a law that required them to turn in their firearms to the federal government; 73% of the gun owners said they would not (Bordua et al. 1979). Further, to the extent that law enforcers feel that controls are imposing unwarranted costs on the law-abiding, they will be less committed to enforcing the law. "Throwing the net widely" may ensure that the law theoretically covers everyone who might commit a gun crime, but it may also make it harder to catch anyone at all, even those you most needed to catch.

On the other hand, restrictions more narrowly focused, as with permissive licensing and purchase permit systems or carry permit, have their own problems. By allowing some to acquire, possess, or carry guns, but not others, the possibility of discriminatory administration arises. Kates (1986) claimed there is considerable discrimination based on race, class, and gender in the granting of permits in some places. He has also argued that when privileged people obtain permits that ordinary people are denied, it undercuts the legitimacy of the laws and reduces voluntary compliance (1984a).

Level of Restrictiveness

Controls also vary with regard to their level of restrictiveness. This is closely related to the preceding issue of who is regulated. Permits and licenses to purchase, possess, or carry firearms can come in four broad varieties, of increasing restrictiveness. First, controls may be completely absent—that is, an activity may be unregulated. Second, there may be limited regulation in the form of a "permissive" licensing system whereby anyone is issued the required license or permit as long as they do not fall within a prohibited category. The burden of proof is on the authorities to show that the applicant should not receive the license, and the applicant need not provide evidence of special need. Third, there may be a much more restrictive control, "restrictive" licensing, which is the reverse of permissive licensing. Not falling into a prohibited high-risk group is not a sufficient basis for getting a license. No one may receive the required license unless they provide special justification and evidence of an unusual need for a gun. The burden of proof is on the applicant. Fourth, there may be the most restrictive level of control, prohibition. A restrictive licensing system is only slightly less extensive than prohibition. Few gun prohibitions are absolute—there are almost always exceptions for military and law enforcement personnel, and sometimes for security guards, body guards, private detectives, federal licensees, and the like. Therefore, the distinction between restrictive licensing and prohibition may be a slight one of semantics.

Neither the nation nor any state or local jurisdiction in the United States prohibits private possession of all types of firearms. From 1910 to 1963, South Carolina, theoretically at least, banned the sale or manufacture of handguns by prohibiting any pistol that was not at least 20 inches long, a category encompassing virtually all handguns (Kennett and Anderson 1975, p. 193). A few cities such as New York City and Washington, D.C. have licensing and registration systems in place that are tantamount to bans on the sale and private possession of handguns. Also, unregistered private possession of so-called "dangerous weapons" such as machine guns and sawed-off shotguns is prohibited everywhere by federal law. Prohibitions on concealed gun carrying are fairly common. Arkansas, Illinois, Oklahoma, Tennessee, and Texas ban the carrying of concealed guns by private citizens almost entirely; many other states require licenses that are very rarely issued (Blackman 1985).

Level of Government

Finally, gun controls can vary with regard to what level of government enacted and enforces them. There is generally an inverse relationship between jurisdictional scope and restrictiveness—the more extensive the jurisdiction, the less restrictive the controls. Thus, the most stringent controls have been enacted by, and apply only to, local jurisdictions such as counties and municipalities, especially big cities. Moderately stringent controls are common at the state level, and controls enacted by the federal government are generally the least stringent.

The patchwork of thousands of gun laws varying across jurisdictions and governmental levels creates confusion and inconvenience to citizens unfamiliar with their legal responsibilities and liabilities. However, the most commonly discussed problem with multilevel lawmaking is the "leakage" problem with local and state controls. Local or state controls over possession or carrying work just as well regardless of whether the implementing jurisdiction borders on areas with weaker controls. However, when strict controls on the acquisition of guns exist in one local or state jurisdiction, their effectiveness is undercut if nearby jurisdictions have weaker controls. The strict local controls can be evaded by motivated gun buyers traveling to nearby areas with weaker controls. Thus, a local jurisdiction might ban possession of guns within its borders, yet have no effective way of preventing its citizens from getting the guns in the first place.

In many local jurisdictions, the issue of what controls to enact has been rendered moot by the passage of state preemption laws. These laws, supported by gun owner groups such as the NRA, are passed by state governments that thereby declare that they preempt the field of gun control, or some subcategory of gun control, claim sole authority to regulate guns, and prohibit local areas from doing so. Preemption laws may wipe out entire categories of existing controls in hundreds of localities, and preclude future enactment of any other local controls. At least 34 of the 50 states had passed one or another kind of state preemption law by 1988 (*U.S. News and World Report* 4-25-88). The political significance of these laws derives from the fact that it is far easier to build the coalitions and popular consensus needed to pass gun controls in smaller local areas than at the state level. State preemption nullifies this political advantage for procontrol forces.

Some Detailed Comments on Specific Control Measures

Waiting Periods

Public opinion polls indicate that the most popular form of gun control is a law requiring a waiting period before a person may buy a gun (Chapter 9). Waiting period provisions were proposed as early as 1926, as part of the Uniform Revolver Act, a measure written and supported by gun owner groups (Kennett and Anderson 1975, pp. 192–3). This control is commonly combined with an application system and thus is usually linked with an opportunity for authorities to check criminal records and other files. Some waiting period requirements apply only to retail sales by licensed gun dealers, but most cover, at least in theory, all sales. Compliance with the requirements as they apply to private transfers is probably limited. Informal inquiries among experienced gun owners in Illinois indicated that "the waiting period requirements as they applied to private transactions were not only not obeyed but were not even known" (Bordua et al. 1985, p. 152).

The rationale for waiting periods per se, as distinct from the commonly accompanying records checks, is conveyed by another name under which they are known—"cooling-off periods." The premise is that some violent people get angry, rush out and buy a gun from a retail source, and use the gun to impulsively commit an act of violence that they otherwise would not have committed, or at least not with an equally serious outcome. It is assumed that more "cooling off" will occur during a 1, 3, or 7 day waiting period than would occur just during the time it would take an angry person to get to and from a gun seller and to complete a purchase.

Cooling-off periods are thought to be especially helpful in preventing impulsive homicides. For a killing to have been prevented by a waiting period, a number of conditions must have existed. (1) The killer used a gun that was the only gun he owned, or at least the only one that could have been used in the crime. (2) The killer purchased the gun from a source that could realistically be expected to comply with waiting period regulations, i.e., a licensed retail gun dealer. (3) The gun was purchased within a span of time before the crime equal to or less than the waiting period minimum, e.g., within 3 days. (4) The killer would not have repeated the act or waited until after the waiting period elapsed, i.e., the act was a one-time-only incident rather than the product of some ongoing relationship accompanied by repeated, serious assaults.

Every once in a while a killing may occur that at least approximately fits this description, but it is apparently an extremely rare event. A 1982 survey of Florida prison system inmates found that of 342 felons who had committed handgun homicides, only 3 (0.9%) had owned only the one handgun, had purchased it from a retail dealer (including pawnbrokers), and had done so within 3 days of the killing (Mannelli 1982, pp. 7–8). Thus, fewer than 1 in 100 handgun killings were even hypothetically preventable through an effectively implemented 3-day waiting period requirement. However, for a number of reasons, even this extremely small number overstates the fraction of gun killings that were potentially preventable. First, these inmates were unusually likely to have gotten their handguns from retail sources, probably because of Florida's weak controls over retail gun purchases. In other states, where purchase controls are generally somewhat stricter, more criminals use nonretail sources. In their 10-state prison survey, Wright and Rossi (1986, p. 185) found that only 16% of handgun-owning felons had purchased their most recent handgun from a retail outlet, compared to 33% among the Florida handgun killers (Mannelli 1982, p. 2). There were 126 retail handgun buyers among the Florida killers; among these, three (2.3%) also owned only one handgun and had bought the gun within 3 days of the killing. Applying this figure to the more nationally representative 16% from the 10-state survey, about 0.37% (0.1565 × 0.0238 = 0.0037) of handgun killers bought their only handgun from a retail source within 3 days of the killing. This figure can be enlarged a bit by assuming a 7-day waiting period instead of 3 days. In the Florida sample 84 killers had gotten their guns within 3 days, and 110 had done so within 7 days. The 0.37% figure can be adjusted by multiplying it by 110/84 to yield an estimate that 0.5% or about 1 in 200 handgun killings were potentially preventable by a 7-day waiting period.

However, even this figure still exaggerates the violence-preventive potential of waiting periods, because it fails to take into account at least four possibilities. First, it is likely that some of the few killers who otherwise seemed "preventable" either also owned a long gun or could have acquired one, and could have used one in their crimes if a waiting period had prevented immediate acquisition of a handgun. Second, some of those who were successfully denied a gun might still have killed with a different kind of weapon. Third, many of the killers had ongoing relationships with their victims, prior confrontations with them, and continuing reasons to attack them long after any waiting period was over (Manelli 1982, p. 9). Fourth, some of the few otherwise "preventable" killers could have obtained guns through other channels, besides retail purchase, that most criminals use—purchase from friends, theft, trade, borrowing, and so forth. In sum, it is not clear that in the Florida sample there was even *one* handgun killer who could have been prevented from killing his victim due to a waiting period. This suggests that it is highly unlikely that waiting periods, by themselves, could prevent even as many as 1 in 200 gun killings. Although criminal records checks may have beneficial effects, the waiting periods that often accompany them are probably superfluous.

Registration

Registration of firearms is a measure that generates records that link particular persons with particular guns. Strong forms of registration require that all guns possessed be registered with a central governmental agency, whereas the more common weak forms usually require only that retail sales be recorded with an agency. The latter measure is only one step removed from federal requirements that prevail everywhere in the nation. The 1968 Gun Control Act required that all gun sales by licensed dealers after October 1968 be recorded. However, the records are kept by the dealers, not the government. Although BATF may inspect these records, they have never been centralized in government hands for quick and efficient access.

Registration does not, by itself, prevent anyone from acquiring or possessing a gun. Its utility for violence reduction is therefore not obvious. Suspicious critics claim that its main result would be to generate lists of gun owners that would facilitate government mass confiscation of firearms, should that become politically possible in the future. Although it is hard to say how likely this eventuality is in the United States, there have been mass government confiscations of guns elsewhere, as when the Soviet Union ordered Lithuanians to turn in their arms in 1990 (*New York Times* 3-22-90, pp. Al. A16). Gun registration was mandatory in the Soviet Union (U.S. Library of Congress 1981, p. 177), so all Lithuanians who legally owned guns knew the authorities had records listing them as a person who should have turned in a gun. This presumably was a strong inducement to cooperate with the turn-in decree. There is no evidence that registration lists were "used" in any other sense, such as leading police to gun-owners' homes in door-to-door confiscations. It has also been claimed that registration lists were "used," in some sense, in mass confiscations in Greece, Bermuda, and the Irish Republic (Bruce-Briggs 1976, p. 59).

Registration supporters assert that their concern is with violence control, not gun confiscation. Blose and Cook (1980, pp. 16–17) provided the most coherent rationale. Registration might provide an incentive for gun owners to be careful to avoid transferring a gun to an ineligible recipient—if the gun were misused, it could be traced back to its previous owner. Registration for this purpose might be useful if it were combined with legal provisions for punishment of illegal transfers once they were discovered. There is no evidence on whether existing registration systems are actually used for such a purpose, or whether any significant numbers of illegal transferors are punished.

Registration records might be used to solve a gun crime in which a gun was left behind at the scene of the crime. For registration to lead to the solution of a crime, all of the following five elements would have to prevail: (1) a gun was used in the crime, (2) the gun was left behind at the scene of the crime, or was lost by the offender somewhere else, (3) the police recovered the gun, (4) the criminal was not arrested at the scene of the crime or on the basis of information unrelated to the gun (if he had been so arrested, the gun would be redundant in identifying the suspect), and (5) either the criminal had registered the gun, using his true name or other uniquely identifying attributes, or the registered owner could somehow lead police to the criminal. Although criminal incidents involving all five of these elements probably have occurred, they surely must be extraordinarily rare; certainly no empirical case has been made to the contrary. Even when such a crime occurs, the accused could simply claim his gun had been stolen and used by others. At best, registration would only help identify a possible suspect, not provide evidence sufficient for conviction.

Gun registration might deter misuse of a gun, if the owner thought that registration could somehow facilitate his punishment. However, for this to be plausible in connection with a given potential instance of misuse, all of the above conditions would have to be met. And for the deterrent effect to occur, the gun owner would also have to somehow consider this issue, and *believe* that the gun's registration would help police catch him. It is difficult to imagine a scenario that would fit these conditions and occur with some nonnegligible frequency.

If combined with gun owner licensing, registration of all guns owned might facilitate confiscations of guns from owners who acquired a legal disability that precluded them from lawfully owning a gun. For example, a person might legally acquire a gun when they had no prior convictions, and then later get convicted of a crime that would make them ineligible to possess firearms. If the authorities knew both who owned guns, and how many guns of what type they owned, registration would make it easier to be sure that they had confiscated all the guns the newly ineligible owner had owned. Of course, it would also make it easier to implement mass confiscations of guns from noncriminals. The facilitation of confiscation from criminals would, however, be mostly redundant if the states simply passed laws requiring gun confiscation as part of the sentence imposed on persons convicted of violent crimes. The authorities could not be certain they had seized all the guns over which the convicted person had control. As a practical matter, however, the same would be true under a registration system, since many guns owned by criminals would not be registered, and the criminal could still acquire other guns after the conviction.

Finally, even some gun control advocates have conceded that registration "would be a cumbersome system to administer" (National Coalition to Ban Handguns, undated), which "would require a massive paperwork and clerical effort" (Brill 1977, p. 146). The benefits that might outweigh its risks and costs have not yet been demonstrated.

Sentence Enhancement for Crimes Committed with Guns

The next most popular gun control measure after waiting periods is a law requiring a mandatory prison sentence for using a gun in a crime (Chapter 9). This popularity probably is due to the fact that this kind of law focuses solely on "bad guys" rather than regulating the general citizenry. These laws are one variant of "sentence enhancement" laws, which provide for add-on penalties for certain crimes (usually violent felonies) when they are committed with a gun. Some laws allow judicial discretion in imposing the penalties. Most, however, require either that convicted gun criminals always be sentenced to prison or that prison sentences be of a given minimum length. These so-called "mandatory" penalty provisions all restrict prosecutorial and judicial sentencing discretion in some way, often prohibiting the use of various lenient sentences such as probation, or tactics such as charge reduction that prosecutors and judges might use to avoid imposing the tough penalties. This kind of law is supported by both the National Rifle Association *and* Handgun Control Inc. (Blackman 1981; Shields 1981, p. 156). Statutes providing for either mandatory or discretionary "sentence enhancement" for committing a crime with a gun existed in at least 39 states in 1980 (Ronhovde and Sugars 1982, pp. 204–5).

Support for the mandatory sentence enhancement is based on the following premises. In the absence of mandatory sentencing provisions, the criminal justice system is lenient on violent criminals, or at least does not impose higher penalties on gun offenders than criminals who do not use guns. Mandatory sentencing provisions can force lenient judges in the "revolving door justice system" to impose stiffer sentences on gun criminals they currently treat "with kid gloves." To this end, laws can be written that eliminate all the loopholes that might be used by judges and prosecutors to evade the intent of the laws. Finally, sentence enhancement laws, whether mandatory or discretionary, reduce violent crime rates, by either deterring use of guns in crime or possibly by deterring offenders from committing the crimes. All of these premises are dubious and lack consistent empirical support.

The crimes that the public fears most are serious violent crimes committed by strangers, and these are probably also among the ones they think are inadequately punished. If it is believed that these crimes are generally treated leniently by the criminal justice system, the perception is inaccurate. The system is rarely lenient with serious violent offenders, especially those who victimize strangers and those with extensive prior records (Walker 1989, p. 30). With respect to stranger violence, sentence enhancements for crimes with a gun are an unnecessary solution to a largely nonexistent problem. Further, judges already treat offenders armed with guns more seriously than those without guns (Loftin et al. 1983; Cook and Nagin 1979; Wright et al. 1983, pp. 300–7; Castellano 1985; but see Lizotte and Zatz 1986), and it is doubtful whether sentencing enhancement laws can be given most of the credit for bringing this about. In some places, the pattern is at least partly due to prosecutorial policy rather than statutory mandate (Cook and Nagin 1979, pp. 24–6; Wright et al. 1983, p. 306). Further, a comparison of sentencing practices before and after enactment of one enhancement law indicated that the gun pattern existed before the law, which had no effect on overall sentencing severity toward gun offenders (Loftin et al. 1983).

Court officials such as judges and prosecutors often have strong motivation to evade legislative intent regarding mandatory sentencing. Mandatory penalties reduce (but do not eliminate) the defendant's incentive to plead guilty, a practice court officials regard as essential to maintaining their ability to handle their caseloads. Some laws even specifically forbid use of plea bargaining or charge reduction. Further, with the prison system operating at full capacity, it could not handle the inflow of prisoners if mandatory penalty laws were fully implemented. It is no overstatement to say that the very survival of the criminal justice system depends on court officials evading the intent of legislatively mandated sentencing enhancements. If legislative intent were actually implemented and long prison sentences were imposed on every person arrested for a violent crime with a gun, (or 1 year sentences imposed on every unlawful carrying arrestee), the system would collapse. Nationally, there were only about 600,000 state and federal prison spaces available in 1988 (U.S. Bureau of the Census 1988, p. 185), but about 155,000 persons were arrested for violent crimes with a gun (computed from U.S. FBI 1989, pp. 12, 21, 24, 168, assuming 10% of rape arrestees used a gun), with another 222,000 arrested on weapons charges (p. 168), most of which are probably unlawful carrying or something similar (Chapter 10). We could empty the prisons of every killer, rapist, drug dealer, and other offender who did not use a gun in the crime for which they were imprisoned, make each weapons violator serve just 1 year, and still would not have enough prison space to make each violent gun crime arrestee serve even 3 years in prison. Legislative intent is obviously impossible to implement, so criminal justice agencies are forced to subvert that intent.

No "mandatory" sentencing law has been written that eliminates all of the loopholes that court personnel can exploit to evade the intent of the laws. Judges already impose harsh penalties on gun offenders where they feel this is appropriate, and are able to avoid imposing "mandatory" penalties where they feel the penalties would be inappropriate (Walker 1989, pp. 84–95). No matter how tightly a law is written to eliminate loopholes, court personnel (and police) always have alternatives permitting them to maintain their preferred sentencing (and arrest) practices. There are numerous ways this can be accomplished. When police officers believe an arrest on a charge subject to mandatory penalties would result in excessive punishment of a person who was, leaving aside the weapons charge, not a criminal, they can either refrain from arresting the person, or arrest them on a related charge not subject to the mandatory prison term. Similarly, if prosecutors think the mandated penalty is too harsh, they can refrain from prosecuting those charges, or reduce them (with or without plea bargaining) to some lesser variant of the charge not subject to the mandatory provisions. Under the more loosely written laws, judges can suspend the "mandatory" penalty, assign probation instead of prison, allow parole or time off for good behavior to shorten the term of incarceration, allow "mandatory" sentences to be served concurrently with other sentences, and so on. Even under tighter laws, judges can find defendants guilty of the original felony but not the gun charge, or find the defendant guilty only of a misdemeanor version of the original charge, so that the add-on gun penalty does not apply. And under any circumstances, judges can dismiss cases, ruling that evidence is inadmissable or insufficient for conviction.

Which of these numerous evasion tactics will be used, and the degree to which they are used, will depend on the specifics of a given law and local court practices, as well as the degree of overload in the system. In any case, it seems reasonable to say that these laws can increase punishment severity only when and where court personnel want them to. In some courts, enactment of such a law might catalyze preexisting opinion that "we need to get tougher on gun criminals," in which case sentencing practice might be altered (e.g., see McPheters et al. 1984, p. 566). It would seem, however, that most courts holding such sentiments would already have acted on them, without legislative prodding.

Michigan passed a sentence enhancement law that mandated an additional 2 years of incarceration for using a gun in a felony, in addition to whatever sentence was imposed for the felony itself. The law closed off many of the loopholes, and in Detroit courts the prosecutor even voluntarily implemented a policy of no plea-bargaining on gun charges. Nevertheless, the "going rate" sentence that prevailed before the law was passed was maintained with little change through a simple "sentence adjustment" strategy. If a judge thought a total term of 5 years was appropriate, he simply sentenced the defendant to 3 years for the felony, then added in the 2 year "mandatory" add-on penalty, yielding the same sentence that would have been imposed before the law. This adjustment was impossible in cases in which the judge would have sentenced the defendant on a felony conviction to less than 3 years, but in those instances judges often simply dismissed the cases altogether (Loftin et al. 1983, 297–300).

Even under the tightest laws imaginable, some loopholes could never be eliminated because the courts could not function without prosecutors and judges having the authority to decline to prosecute or try cases that clearly lacked sufficient admissable evidence to obtain a conviction. Thus, prosecutors will always be able to drop charges or decline to prosecute altogether, and judges will always be able to dismiss cases or charges altogether or to acquit defendants on the "mandatory" charge (e.g., after ruling the search for the weapon was illegal and the resulting evidence inadmissable) (Carlson 1982; Loftin et al. 1983).

The best that can be said regarding implementation of these laws is that they may increase punishment severity for defendants with extensive prior records (Loftin et al. 1983; Lizotte and Zatz 1986). Defendants who already were treated harshly on the basis of their prior record may get punished even more severely due to their use of a gun. However, this applies only to an extremely small subset of criminals. For example, an analysis of a statewide California sample by Lizotte and Zatz (1986) found a sentence enhancement effect due to gun use in a felony only for arrestees on their fourth or later arrest; these constituted only 0.6% of all arrestees. And even this modest pattern may not have been due to the law, since Lizotte and Zatz did not show whether the pattern already prevailed before the law's enactment.

Given that sentence enhancement laws are often not even implemented, and in practice are impossible to fully implement, it would not be surprising if they failed to reduce violent crime. Nevertheless, even partial implementation might produce an impact. Or, a law that was not implemented might nevertheless cause prospective offenders to get the erroneous impression that punishment had gotten more severe for gun crimes. This might cause some offenders to refrain from carrying guns and/or using them in violent crimes, or to refrain from committing violent crimes altogether. Some prior studies of sentence enhancement or mandatory penalty laws in Michigan and Florida found little support for the idea that they decreased violent crime rates. One explanation for the general absence of effects is that, even when the laws are at least partially implemented, an additional 2 or 3 years tacked onto the already severe sentences ordinarily imposed for serious violent crimes may not produce much of a marginal increase in perceived risk among prospective offenders. Also, the deterrent effects of any increase in the severity of punishment may be offset by decreases in its certainty (Loftin et al. 1983; Loftin and McDowall 1984). This is a poor trade-off from a crime control standpoint, since prior research generally does not indicate that longer prison terms exert a deterrent effect (Orsagh and Chen 1988, pp. 159–60). Nevertheless, McPheters et al. (1984) concluded that such laws could reduce robbery. No study, however, has established whether the *mandatory* nature of the penalty structure is responsible for either (1) increased penalties for gun crimes, or (2) crime reductions. Instead, sentence enhancement may do better when it is discretionary than when it is mandatory, since this might increase, or at least maintain, the certainty of punishment by giving prosecutors greater bargaining power to induce guilty pleas.

The National Rifle Association (NRA) and other gun owner organizations have advocated mandatory sentences for crimes with a gun as an alternative to other forms of gun control. This advocacy serves a rhetorical purpose for progun groups that it does not serve for gun control advocates who also support such laws. When the NRA repeatedly opposes even moderate gun control measures, critics can say something like "You have plenty of negative things to say about gun laws—what alternatives do you propose for reducing violence?" Without an alternative, gun owner groups look like unhelpful nay-sayers. Advocacy of harsher punishment of gun crimes provides a ready, and highly popular, response to this criticism. More specifically, this is an alternative that is popular not only with the general public but is also eminently acceptable to the largely conservative membership of gun owner organizations. Each time a highly publicized gun massacre or celebrity killing occurs, a progun spokesman is likely to assert that the problem is not the gun but rather the lenient, "revolving door" system of justice that allowed the killer to roam free, saying something to the following effect: "If this killer had only been sentenced to a long prison term after one of his earlier offenses, he would not have been free to commit this heinous act." There are certainly many implementable alternatives to gun regulation that may prove effective in substantially reducing violence. However, the preceding analysis indicates that it is questionable whether the gun lobby's alternative is one of them.

Mandatory Penalties for Unlawful Carrying

Gun owner groups oppose a superficially similar type of mandatory sentencing law that requires a mandatory penalty for unlicensed or otherwise unlawful carrying of a firearm. This differs from sentence enhancement laws in that there often is no other crime involved besides the gun violation, which is a "victimless crime." Gun owner groups oppose such measures because they are directed not just at career criminals, but also at otherwise law-abiding gun owners who need a gun for protection but are unable to get a carry permit (Blackman 1981). Advocates of the laws support them because they feel they deter the casual carrying of firearms in public places and thereby reduce gun use in unpremeditated crimes (Beha 1977). Evidence is mixed as to whether these laws are successfully implemented, in the sense that the punishment of unlawful carrying or possession is actually increased. Implementation is hindered by the same factors that affect mandatory sentence enhancement for gun crimes.

After Massachusetts instituted a mandatory penalty for unlicensed carrying in 1975, interviews with Boston police officers indicated that 89% of them had become more selective about who to frisk for weapons, because they did not want to risk having to arrest "otherwise innocent" persons. The number of arrests in gun incidents decreased from 1974 to 1976 by 23%, even though weapons seizures without arrest had increased by 120% (Carlson 1982, p. 6). These facts strongly hint that although gun carrying may not have been reduced by the law, police made fewer carrying arrests in order to evade the intent of the law to incarcerate every unlicensed gun carrier.

These laws tend to impede the flow of weapons cases through the courts, to a great extent because they reduce the defendant's incentive to plead guilty. The rate at which gun carrying cases went to trial tripled after Massachusetts passed its mandatory sentence for unlicensed gun carrying, the overall conviction rate was cut in half, and median time to disposition doubled, all largely due to the fact that the rate of guilty pleas was cut in half. More defendants fled rather than face trial, and more appealed their dispositions. Further, dismissals and verdicts of not guilty doubled, consistent with the hypothesis that judges were attempting to avoid imposing the 1 year sentence on defendants they felt did not deserve it or for whom it was not worth expending scarce prison space (Rossman et al. 1980; Carlson 1982). In some cases the ironic result was that defendants who might otherwise have received a short jail term received no jail time at all because judges felt the mandated 1 year sentence was excessive.

The overall effect on sentencing severity was mixed. A reduced fraction of carrying defendants were convicted of felony gun carrying charges in Boston, but within this group the fraction who received prison sentences did increase. However, this increased severity affected only a handful of offenders. Rossman et al. (1980) estimated that the sentences of no more than 40 defendants in Boston courts each year had been changed by the new law. Before New York State's 1980 law calling for a mandatory 1 year term for illegal gun possession, about 4 in 10 people convicted of this charge in New York City were sentenced to 1 year or more in prison. After the law, this fraction was unchanged (*New York Times* 1-29-90). Another study of the New York law found that although sentencing severity did not increase in Manhattan, it did increase in two other areas (Castellano 1985). However, in one of these areas, Rochester, the increase may have been due to a BATF-supported campaign against illegal guns. Similar to the experience with sentence enhancement laws, these measures displaced sentencing discretion rather than eliminating it, with little impact on the overall frequency or severity of punishment inflicted on violators. Whatever marginal gains in punishment severity the laws sometimes produce are counterbalanced by reductions in the certainty of punishment. Consequently, it is unclear whether deterrence theory would lead one to expect the laws to produce any reductions in gun carrying. The effects of these laws on crime rates will be addressed in Chapter 10.

Prohibition and Other Broadly Targeted Measures

Whereas sentence enhancement is targeted solely at people who are criminals even apart from anything they do with guns, many other gun control measures are aimed at somehow regulating the behavior of broad segments of the population, including the large majority who will never commit a serious violent act of any kind, with or without a gun. Prohibitions of the purchase, possession, or use of guns, or some subtype of guns, are such measures. These controls have the merit of at least theoretically regulating everyone, and therefore cover everyone who might do violence with a gun. Further, it has even been argued that since the majority of the people they cover are generally law-abiding, they are therefore more likely to enjoy a high rate of compliance with whatever restrictions are imposed (Newton and Zimring 1969, p. 81). This latter, however, is a somewhat dubious virtue, since there is little direct crime-control advantage in regulating the law-abiding, no matter how easy it is to do it. As noted in Chapter 5, serious violent acts are rarely committed by previously law-abiding people.

On the other hand, broadly directed gun restrictions might make sense if they could indirectly produce a reduction in criminal gun possession by substantially reducing ownership among noncriminals. Certainly, a large proportion of guns that end up in criminals' hands had been stolen at some time in the past, often from noncriminals, even if few criminals become armed with a gun through theft (Chapter 2). Further, there are strong hints in Chapter 10 that criminal gun possession is high in the same places where noncriminal ownership is high. There is, however, little reason to believe that any but the most radical reductions in noncriminal ownership would produce measurable reductions in criminal gun possession. Given their very strong motives, both defensive and criminal, for getting and keeping guns, criminals very likely would be among the last people to be disarmed under general gun restrictions.

As a practical and political matter, a general prohibition on all gun types is impossible, at least at present. Further, voluntary compliance with an all-guns ban would probably be low. One statewide Illinois survey found that 73% of gun owners said they would disobey a federal law requiring them to turn in their guns (Bordua et al. 1979). On the other hand, political and popular support is already high enough to suggest that it might one day reach the point where a national prohibition aimed only at handguns could be enacted (Chapter 9). As demonstrated in Chapter 3, such a narrowly focused measure would probably do more harm than good. Thus, the dilemma is this: this prohibition that, arguably, might do some good is probably impossible to enact and implement, whereas the one that might be enacted in the foreseeable future would almost certainly do no good at all.

There is little benefit and considerable cost in denying guns to people who will never misuse them. Consequently, it seems desirable to attempt to craft gun policies that distinguish those likely to misuse guns from those not so likely. To be sure, it is not always possible to distinguish, in advance of their violent behavior, violent individuals from nonviolent individuals, or to predict future violence without error. Nevertheless, it is possible to distinguish high-risk from low-risk groups. For example, persons who currently have a record of a criminal conviction are more likely to commit acts of serious violence in the future than those without such a record. Thus, it is possible to prohibit legal acquisition and possession among a significant share of those who will eventually abuse guns without restricting gun possession by everyone (Kleck and Bordua 1983). At best, restricting guns among the nonviolent majority might produce the benefit of indirectly reducing gun possession among the high-risk minority by reducing gun transfers between the two groups, through theft or other illegal transactions.

Prohibitionist proposals share other serious difficulties. First there is the needle-in-the-haystack problem noted in Chapter 3. If only a few percent of gun owners will ever use their guns to commit an unlawful violent act, broad-based controls are highly inefficient. A hundred people must be disarmed in the hopes of preventing two or three from doing violence with a gun. Even this is an optimistic assessment that relies on the assumption that gun restrictions would reduce possession at the same rate among violence-prone people as among the nonviolent majority. More plausibly, those most likely to abuse guns would constitute a disproportionately large share of the very last people disarmed, since they are the ones motivated to get and retain guns for the strongest of reasons—self-defense and use in a criminal career.

Nevertheless, even if only a few dangerous people were disarmed while many more law-abiding citizens were disarmed, this still might be a rational trade-off if there were no serious costs to disarming the law-abiding. The evidence in Chapter 4 indicates that there are serious costs to disarming prospective victims. Even if one rejects the more debatable claim that widespread civilian gun ownership deters criminals from attempting certain crimes, the fact remains that each year thousands of crime victims use guns in self-defense to avoid injury and property loss. Under the assumption that prohibitionist controls would reduce gun ownership more among the law-abiding than among criminals, this would mean that the beneficial effects of noncriminal gun use would be reduced proportionally more than the harmful effects of criminal gun use.

The fact that prohibitionist measures are directed so broadly seems to ensure more widespread beneficial effects, yet this same attribute is also responsible for their greater costs and undesirable side-effects. Laws imposing burdens on noncriminals are more likely to be perceived as unjust and to reduce respect and support for the institutions making and enforcing the laws (Kaplan 1979). When the laws result in the arrest of otherwise law-abiding people, these individuals are stigmatized as criminals, may be so regarded by others, and may increasingly come to perceive themselves the same way. Acquiring a criminal record may make legitimate employment more difficult. These effects in turn can increase the chances the stigmatized person will later commit other crimes. It is by no means rare that an otherwise noncriminal person is arrested for violations of gun control laws. For example, 33% of the people arrested for violating Massachusetts' gun carrying law had no prior record of any kind, and 8% had only a minor prior court record (Beha 1977, p. 132; see also Vera Institute of Justice 1981, pp. 127–8). A Chicago judge even stated that *most* gun violators in his court had no previous arrests (Shields 1976, p. 184).

Closely related to these difficulties is the problem of sheer scale in restricting guns in the entire population. With over 200 million guns and over 70 million handguns, banning possession of either all guns or just handguns would be an enormous undertaking. The practical difficulties are compounded by the nature of the objects being controlled. Unlike previously banned commodities such as alcoholic beverages and illegal drugs, which are consumed and must be frequently replaced, guns last indefinitely and do not need to be replaced as long as they are given minimal maintenance. Further, they are sufficiently compact that any losses could easily be replaced through the same forms of smuggling currently responsible for the importation of thousands of tons of illegal drugs (Kates 1984a).

Finally, prohibitionist measures entail all the costs associated with other "victimless crime" laws, and the enforcement of laws concerning possessory offenses. Bans on possession of all guns or of handguns would stimulate the creation of black markets to meet the demand for guns not met by legal sources, and would thereby increase criminal profits. Enforcing the prohibition would be extremely expensive and would overload existing resources or any that could be realistically anticipated in the foreseeable future. It could also divert resources from enforcement efforts aimed at more serious crimes and crimes in which these efforts are more effective. Given the limits on resources and probable high rate of violation, enforcement would inevitably be highly selective, and, very likely, frequently discriminatory. The combination of black market profits and selective enforcement would encourage police corruption, with enforcement steered away from those wealthy enough to buy an unofficial police "license" to sell guns. Finally, as with drug laws, gun bans would require the most intrusive, morally objectionable, and constitutionally dubious enforcement tactics, including a heavy reliance on paid informants, testimony coerced by threat of prosecution, warrantless searches, wiretaps and other "bugging," a covert surveillance, and the intrusion of undercover agents into the lives of people unaware of their status as police officers (Kates 1976; Kaplan 1979; Kessler 1980). In view of these considerations, advocacy of any form of gun prohibition must meet a burden of proof that the measures would produce violence-reducing benefits sufficient to outweigh the serious costs.

On the other hand, it should be stressed that none of the foregoing says anything decisive about whether some benefit might be obtained from more narrowly targeted gun control measures with correspondingly lower costs. The general policy principle to be derived is that gun control measures are more likely to succeed if they are targeted at high-risk groups rather than the entire population.

Enforcement of Current Gun Laws

It is commonly asserted that laws cannot effectively reduce crime if they are not enforced, in the sense of violators being arrested, convicted, and punished. Critics of gun laws also often assert that there is no point to having new laws if we are unwilling to seriously enforce the ones we already have (e.g., Bendis and Balkin 1979). Both assertions have some truth to them, but oversimplify the matter. First, there is nothing theoretically impossible about unenforced laws affecting criminal behavior, and certainly nothing implausible about minimally enforced laws having some impact on crime. Conservative critics quick to doubt the efficacy of gun laws will nevertheless argue the deterrent effectiveness of the death penalty, even though the penalty has never been imposed even as many as 200 times in the entire nation in any given year (U.S. Bureau of Justice Statistics 1987b, p. 541). Further, some analysts have claimed that they detected effects of gun laws before their effective dates, and thus before they could have been enforced at all (Pierce and Bowers 1981). Deterrence of criminal conduct depends on prospective offenders' *perception* of legal risk, regardless of whether there is any factual foundation for that perception. It may seem self-evident that there should a fairly close correlation between actual enforcement levels (rates of arrest, conviction, and incarceration) and perception of legal risk, but there is in fact virtually no empirical basis for this belief. Therefore, actual enforcement of laws may not be an absolutely necessary condition for crime control efficacy, and even unenforced laws could have an impact on crime rates.

Second, even if some existing laws have not been enforced, that does not mean that new ones will not be. Some laws are inherently harder to enforce than others, and the commitment of the authorities to enforcing laws can change over time just as it varies from place to place (Brill 1977, pp. 26–35; Chapter 10). If more sensible laws are passed, enforcers may see more reason to expend their resources on enforcing them. With these caveats in mind, evidence on enforcement of gun laws is now reviewed.

Are gun laws currently on the books seriously enforced? That is, do police arrest people for violating the laws, do prosecutors charge and convict gun violators, and do judges sentence them to significant punishments? Prosecutors and judges commonly evade the intent of sentence enhancement and mandatory penalty laws, and in that sense do not enforce these laws. More precisely, they continue to enforce older laws governing common law crimes such as robbery and assault, imposing the customary "going rate" penalties on criminals, and continuing to impose the customary additional punishment due to gun use, without being influenced by the enhancement laws. These are unusual sorts of gun laws in that they pertain to offenses that would be serious crimes even if they did not involve guns. Most gun control laws more narrowly focus on inherently gun-related conduct such as the sale, purchase, carrying, or possession of guns. These can be called "gun violations" to distinguish them from acts that would still be crimes apart from the use of weapons.

In 1988, police in the United States made about 222,000 arrests for "weapons" offenses, only some of which involved guns (U.S. FBI 1989, p. 168). Weapons arrests accounted for 1.6% of all nontraffic arrests. With about 480,000 sworn police officers in the nation (p. 232; U.S. Bureau of the Census 1988, p. 177), the figures imply that most police officers do not make a single weapons arrest in a given year.

Apart from making arrests on weapons charges, police may enforce laws against unlawful carrying or possession in another sense, by confiscating guns. In Appendix 1, it is estimated that police seize roughly 220,000 handguns and 70,000 shoulder guns per year. However, only about 75–80% of confiscated guns were linked with any crime—the rest were abandoned guns found by officers, guns voluntarily turned in by citizens, and so on. Among the crime guns, perhaps 50–60% were seized in connection with illegal gun possession (which appears to include illegal carrying—Brill 1977, p. 24). Thus, the figures imply fewer than 220,000 crime guns confiscated per year, indicating that the average sworn officer confiscates a crime gun about once every 2 or 3 years. Evidently, police currently devote very little time to making weapons arrests or confiscating weapons.

When police arrest someone for a weapons violation, it can be the result of either of two kinds of police enforcement efforts, reactive or proactive. A reactive effort involves a police officer reacting to either a citizen request that he do something, or the officer himself, in the course of routine activity such as patrol, directly observing a person committing a crime. A citizen could report a robbery in progress or a patrol officer could observe one himself, arrest a suspect, and in the course of searching the suspect, discover an unlawfully possessed firearm. The weapons arrest would thereby be a reactive by-product of activity initially aimed at other crimes. Or a citizen might complain to police about someone recklessly waving a gun around, or brandishing one in a bar, or firing one into the air within the city limits, or an officer might observe such activity in the course of routine patrol ("on view" observations). In contrast, a proactive effort would involve an officer initiating an action, such as a street search of a suspect's outer garments, intended to uncover a weapons violation. Police detectives could even proactively launch investigations aimed at uncovering unlawful trafficking in guns or related offenses. Moore (1980) found, in a five-city survey of police departments, that most weapons arrests were the product of responses to citizens complaints, a large minority were due to "on view" observations by police, and only a few were due to investigations. Although the first category clearly is entirely reactive, it is less clear whether the "on-view" arrests were the reactive result of routine patrol or the proactive result of aggressive patrol activities aimed specifically at discovering weapons violations. Moore also found that 80% of weapons arrests involved handguns, and more than 80% were made by patrol units.

Bordua and his associates (1985) obtained unique information on the combination of charges linked with weapons arrests. They studied arrests made for violations of Illinois' law requiring a gun owner's license or ID to possess any kind of firearm, and found that 91% of "no-ID" arrest charges were accompanied by other charges. This might suggest that there is little police effort aimed specifically at enforcing the licensing law. However, 41% of the accompanying charges were other weapons charges, indicating that many arrests did involve just weapons charges, consistent with the possibility that some arrest activity is motivated by a special effort to control weapons.

Only 18% of the accompanying charges were for violent crimes. (Not surprisingly, the most common violent charge was aggravated assault with a firearm.) This has two important implications. First, it indicates that no-ID arrests were not usually the by-product of police arrest efforts aimed at more serious violent crimes. Indeed, only about 14–29% of accompanying charges ranked higher in the FBI offense hierarchy (see Chapter 10); thus, a gun violation was usually the most serious charge in a no-ID arrest. Second, it indicates that Illinois prosecutors were usually not in a position to use the no-ID charge as either a "bargaining chip" to induce arrestees to plead guilty to violent offenses or as a means of incarcerating violent offenders they could not convict on violent crime charges. Compared to 13,631 arrests for violent Index crimes in Illinois in 1982 (U.S. FBI 1983, p. 238), there were only about 195 no-ID arrest charges accompanying these violent crime charges (Bordua et al. 1985, pp. A.49–A.55). On the other hand, a survey of Illinois prosecutors indicated that most of them claimed they *would* use no-ID charges in this way if they got the chance (pp. 122–4).

These particular weapons arrests may or may not have been the result of enforcement activity directed specifically at weapons offenses, but they clearly were not usually the by-product of enforcement directed at violent crimes. On the other hand, they may nonetheless have been the reactive by-product of a variety of other police enforcement activities. Most no-ID charges were accompanied by a miscellany of minor charges, including substantial minorities linked with traffic violations (10% of accompanying charges) and drug charges (9%). As these are the sorts of charges that often result from stops of motor vehicles, they suggest that a substantial minority of weapons arrests may be a reactive by-product of traffic enforcement.

Once police make weapons arrests, do prosecutors make serious efforts to gain convictions and significant punishment? Answering this question in a meaningful way requires answering the counterquestion, "Compared to what?" Critics have often noted how frequently gun charges are dropped, or otherwise fail to result in a conviction, without showing this to be especially characteristic of weapons charges. For example, Bendis and Balkin (1979) noted that only one-third of gun law violation charges resulted in a conviction in Chicago courts in 1966–1973. This appears to be something of an anomaly peculiar to Chicago, however. A study of New York City courts found that 22 of 28 felony gun possession charges resulted in some kind of conviction, though only two were for the original felony charge or a higher one (Vera Institute of Justice 1981, p. 119). More recent data covering five cities in 1986 indicate that 51–72% of weapons arrests (i.e., a weapons charge was the most serious charge) presented for prosecution resulted in either a guilty plea or trial conviction (Boland et al. 1989, pp. 20–22). However, what these figures fail to provide is a comparative perspective that would allow one to say whether the conviction rates are good or bad. Compared to an unrealistic 100% conviction rate they may look bad. However, compared to felony prosecutions in general, they are about average. In the same five cities, 53–64% of all felony arrests resulted in conviction. Thus, the loss of convictions in a quarter to a half of weapons cases is not a peculiarity of weapons arrests, but rather appears to be merely the norm for felony arrests handled in urban courts. The New York City study in fact found a *higher* conviction rate for gun cases than for other felonies (Vera Institute 1981, p. 118).

One thing that does set prosecution of weapons arrests apart from prosecution of other felony arrests is the reasons why prosecutors sometimes decline to pursue them. Generally, due process restraints on police procedures such as searches, seizures, and arrests have almost no impact on prosecution success in obtaining convictions. In eight cities in 1986, only 8% of all felony arrests that prosecutors declined to prosecute were turned down because of due process problems. However, 19% of the declinations to prosecute weapons arrests were due to such problems (pp. 32–5). Along with drug offenses, weapon violations are among the few crimes that are frequently hard to prosecute because of due process limits on the police. Bendis and Balkin (1979) noted that making legal searches is often difficult in concealed carrying cases. An officer must have probable cause to make a search in the first place. If he does not, the search would usually be illegal and the resulting evidence inadmissable in court. If the gun is not visible, the officer would usually not have probable cause to make a legal search. On the other hand, if the gun is visible, it is not concealed and hence a charge of concealed carrying could not be justified (though open carrying is also unlawful in some jurisdictions). Likewise, a study of Detroit carrying charges found that "illegal search and seizure" was the most common reason for cases to be dismissed (Anonymous 1976, pp. 619, 624; see also Vera Institute of

Justice 1981, p. 120–7). Thus, although complaints about the police being "handcuffed" by liberal Supreme Court due process rulings are generally without much foundation (Walker 1989, pp. 116–27), the exclusion of evidence due to illegal searches and seizures and other due process violations does apparently play a modest role in the failure to get convictions on weapons charges.

Do judges sentence weapons violators as severely as they should? This question is of course something of a matter of opinion, but comparative information is helpful. The general public does not regard gun violations by themselves as very serious crimes, compared with the kinds of crimes that commonly result in prison sentences. The National Survey of Crime Severity, conducted in 1977, found that a robbery murder was assigned an average severity rating of 43.2, rape resulting in the victim's hospitalization was rated at 30.0, and a gun robbery of $10 with no injury was rated at 9.4. However, illegal gun carrying was rated at 4.6, just below the 4.7 assigned to a man exposing himself in public and just above the 4.5 assigned to someone committing federal income tax fraud. Firing a rifle for which the user had no permit rated at 2.1, just below the 2.2 assigned to a $10 shoplifting and the same as the 2.1 rating assigned to a woman engaging in prostitution (U.S. Bureau of Justice Statistics 1984c). In short, the public seems to rate these two gun violations as being about as serious as offenses that normally result in probation or a fine, when they result in punishment at all. Consequently, there is little reason to expect prison terms to be routinely imposed for weapons violations.

Bendis and Balkin's (1979) data on registration law violations and unlawful carrying charges in Chicago indicated that 12.3% of the cases resulted in sentences with some incarceration, with an average sentence of about 36 days (computed from p. 445–6). A Detroit study of concealed carry cases found that 18% of convicted defendants received some incarceration, with the median sentence being about 6 months (Anonymous 1976, p. 625–6). The authors of both these studies described these sentences as "lenient," but it is not clear what standards they used to arrive at this assessment, since they made no comparisons with other offenses. If they were only comparing sentences imposed with the maximum allowed by statute, then their conclusions were foreordained by the severe statutory provisions common in American law. By this standard, *all* offenses, including murder, are treated leniently and always have been, since no major felony always results in the maximum allowable sentence. However, the conclusion of leniency is not evident when direct comparisons with other offenses are made. In U.S. District Courts in 1985–1986, 64.5% of persons convicted of "weapons and firearms" charges were sentenced to imprisonment, for an average of 54.0 months. For federal income tax fraud, a charge rated by the public as being almost identical in severity to illegal gun carrying, only 44.9% of defendants were sentenced to imprisonment, for an average of 32.5 months (U.S. Bureau of Justice Statistics 1988, p. 444). Similarly, in lower courts in 11 states in 1984, 47% of defendants convicted of weapons offenses were sentenced to incarceration, compared to 54% of those convicted of larceny and 37% of those convicted of other public-order offenses, crimes rated by the public as similarly serious (p. 413). In sum, there is no evidence of unusual leniency in the sentencing of weapons violators. Judges impose sentences about as severe as one would expect based on the way they sentence other, similarly serious offenses. Indeed, in view of the fact that prisons are packed to capacity and the public is clamoring for longer prison sentences for serious offenders, it is hard to imagine how the courts could treat weapons violations much more seriously than they already do.

Thus, there is little reason to believe there is an unusual lack of effort in the prosecution of weapons violations or undue leniency in their sentencing. On the other hand, it can be argued reasonably that gun law enforcement is slight at the police stage. There is considerable room for increases in police enforcement effort in the form of weapons arrests and confiscations. Therefore, if police would be willing and able to shift their resources from elsewhere toward more enforcement of gun laws, it is possible that the crime control potential of gun control might be increased. This proposition will be empirically tested in Chapter 10. Note, however, that without some considerable increase in court and prison funding, increased police enforcement activity would have to produce crime control effects largely without corresponding increases in prosecution and incarceration of weapons violators. Deterrent effects of police activity may still be possible, although they are less likely, under these conditions.

Administration of Licensing Laws—Two Contrasting Cases

Whereas enforcement of gun laws involves punishing violators, administering license and permit laws involves screening applicants, collecting fees, and processing applications for licenses and permits to purchase, sell, possess, or carry guns. Administration can be highly discretionary, with administrators exercising very subjective judgments about who gets the license, or largely nondiscretionary, with administrators fairly mechanically processing applications in accordance with clear qualifying criteria requiring little exercise of judgment. Laws requiring that an applicant be "of good moral character" tend to allow considerable exercise of administrative discretion, whereas those forbidding licenses to persons with a conviction for any of a set of specific crimes require very little discretionary decision-making. Generally speaking, restrictive licensing systems tend to be administered in a discretionary fashion because the authorities must make judgments about which applicants have proved they have a special need for the license, and "need" is rarely defined by statute. Permissive licensing systems, on the other hand, tend to be administered in a fairly nondiscretionary way because attributes that would disqualify an applicant from receiving the license are commonly specified in statute, often in great detail.

Two state gun laws nicely illustrate this distinction. Both New York and Illinois require their citizens to have a license to buy or possess a handgun, and the requirement applies to possession in the home or place of business as well as public places. The New York law, however, is a restrictive license law, whereas the Illinois law is a permissive license law. The New York law, often known as the Sullivan Law, after the Tammany Hall political boss who sponsored it, is commonly cited by the gun lobby as a example of what can happen if they let their guard down momentarily and let a moderate, apparently innocuous gun control measure through—let them license guns and eventually the "gun grabbers" will turn it into a ban. There is more than a kernel of truth in this claim regarding the Sullivan Law.

The law initially did three things: (1) it made carrying handguns without a carry permit a felony (it had been a misdemeanor), (2) it required a permit to buy a handgun, and (3) it required a permit to possess a handgun. As originally passed in 1911, the law clearly set up a permissive licensing system for handgun possession in the home. The authorities publicly announced that, although carry permits would be hard to get, permits to possess handguns "would be as easy to obtain as dog licenses" (Kennett and Anderson 1975, p. 182). Although the law apparently reduced gun carrying (p. 184), it had no apparent effect on crime; the number of gun homicides actually increased 5% from 1910 to 1912 (p. 185). When mild measures fail, it often seems reasonable to try stronger measures. This line of reasoning apparently appealed to the New York legislature, for the Sullivan Law was amended "scores of times" in subsequent decades (p. 186), making it increasingly strict. In addition, the law was administered by the New York Police Department

(NYPD) in an increasingly restrictive fashion, so that by the 1950s it had gradually evolved into a de facto ban on the possession of handguns in New York City (Kates 1986). In these respects, New York's experience paralleled the history of gun regulation in Great Britain, which began with very mild measures in 1906 and earlier, and then evolved into de facto bans on possession of handguns first, then eventually rifles as well (Greenwood 1972).

Police "guesstimates" of the number of handguns in New York City have gone as high as one or two million; nearly all of these guns are possessed illegally. As of 1989, only 49,000 civilian residents had one of the four types of permits that authorized handgun possession, in addition to 30,000 permits held by retired police officers (D'Andrilli 1989). Thus, although at least 15% of Americans personally own a handgun (Table 2.4), less than 1% of New York residents legally own a handgun.

The permitting process is administered in New York City by the city's police department. Most of the permits it grants are carry permits that authorize concealed carrying of handguns in public places as well as possession in the permit holder's home or place of business. Few people apply for handgun permits of any kind, and only a small minority of these get them. The application approval rate is low, and has gotten lower, from 34% in 1981 to 21% in 1987 (*USA Today* 10-19-87). Not only are the chances of a successful application slim, but the process is complicated, expensive, and very prolonged. The applicant must fill out a lengthy form on which he is required to provide, among other things, over 28 different pieces of information, including all places of employment for the preceding 5 years and all places of residence for the preceding 10 years. The applicant must get the application notarized and is required to supply two photographs of a specified size, proof of current residence, and in some cases a birth certificate, proof of citizenship, military discharge papers, proof of business ownership, and a notarized letter explaining why the permit is needed. Those who want a permit to keep a gun on their business premises also must supply two copies of their business sales tax reports, daily bank deposit slips, monthly bank statements, payroll information, and sometimes a copy of their personal income tax return as well. Applicants must be fingerprinted.

The permits are also very expensive. As of 1987, the initial application cost $100, plus $19 for the fingerprinting, and renewal every 2 years costs another $100 (New York City Police Department 1987). Thus, to legally keep a handgun for 10 years would cost $519. The application fee is nonrefundable, even if the applicant is turned down, making the application process a very expensive gamble, against long odds. The application process is also very prolonged. In the past it often took over a year before a final decision was made. Even after a state court ordered the NYPD to make its decisions within 6 months of the application date, the average time was still 6–9 months for a carry permit and 2–6 months for the other three types of possession permits (D'Andrilli 1989). In sum, the NYPD makes it procedurally extremely difficult and expensive to get a permit to possess a handgun in New York City.

The key point at which administrative discretion is exercised is in interpreting certain vague phrases in the law. For example, the law forbids issuing a license to anyone who is not "of good moral character." Likewise, there must be "no good cause" for the license to be denied (New York State Penal Law, Section 400.0). Neither phrase is defined by statute, so police are free to decide whether an applicant fits these descriptions, Further, persons who apply for the "carry" type of possession permit must establish that "proper cause" exists for issuance of the license. This is interpreted by the NYPD to mean that the applicant must show unusual need for the gun. NYPD regulations explicitly state that previous victimization or living or working in a dangerous neighborhood is not sufficient to establish special need (NYPD 1988).

Thus, a law that was originally written as (and indeed still appears to be) a permissive licensing law, designed only to prevent a high-risk minority from possessing handguns, has evolved, through gradual legislative amendments and increasingly strict administrative interpretation, increasingly expensive fees, and long delays in processing permit applications, into a virtual ban on the possession of handguns by anyone in New York City. In view of the New York experience, the gun lobby's warnings about gun control being a "slippery slope" do not look all that implausible. However, can the New York (or Great Britain) experience, and in particular, New York City's administration of the permit law, be regarded as typical of what happens when moderate license/permit laws are enacted?

The answer would seem to be "no," largely because gun owner groups have not convincingly documented any other U.S. cases of originally moderate laws eventually evolving into gun bans. If there were other examples, these groups would surely have been motivated to document them. More typical of moderate license or permit laws is the Firearms Owners' Identification Card (FOIC) system in Illinois, enacted in 1968. This system has been thoroughly examined and described in a research monograph written by David Bordua and his colleagues (1985). Carrying a gun is completely forbidden to civilians in Illinois, while buying or possessing a gun of any kind requires an FOIC identification (ID) card. The ID law is clearly a permissive licensing law regarding possession, as the authorities are allowed to deny applications only if the applicant falls into one of six specific high-risk categories: minors with a misdemeanor or delinquency record, minors without parental permission, convicted felons, narcotics addicts, persons who had been a mental patient in the preceding 5 years, and mentally retarded persons. Although any law or rule is subject to interpretation, there is very little subjective interpretation of these disqualifying attributes as the system is administered in Illinois. Less than 1% of applications were denied, and 80% of the denials were due to a felony conviction (Bordua et al. 1985, pp. 34, 38). The authors concluded that the system is fairly administered and that "there is close attention to the due process rights of legitimate firearms owners" (p. 51). Further, "complaints about the system from the ranks of owner organizations have been rare" (p. 45). For their part, gun control advocates mainly complained that the controls did not go nearly far enough.

Other states such as Massachusetts and New Jersey have similar owner ID systems, and many other states have purchase permit or application-to-purchase systems that are similarly administered as permissive systems, i.e., the burden is on the authorities to show that the applicant is not qualified to get a gun. The administration of these other systems appears to resemble that of Illinois more than that of New York. Outside of New York, the systems have not evolved into bans or near-bans on handgun possession, either through legislative amendments or through increasingly strict administration. It cannot be denied that some gun control advocates would like this to happen and that some will work to bring it about. Nor can it be stated with certainty that they will never succeed. However, the best guide to the future is the experience of the immediate past, and the historical record does not support the gun lobby's "slippery slope" criticism of moderate gun controls aimed at making it more difficult for high-risk people to acquire guns. So far at least, the New York experience has been the exception, not the rule.

On the other hand, many gun owners will continue to believe that gun control is a slippery slope, as long as gun control advocates make fundamental attacks on gun ownership in general, rather than just misuse of guns or possession of guns by high-risk groups. For example, efforts to demonstrate that the Second Amendment confers no protection of an individual right to keep and bear arms, or to demonstrate that guns have no defensive value, seem to make sense only in the context of a long-term project to prohibit or restrict gun ownership in the general, largely law-abiding public. They are largely unnecessary to justifying the more moderate regulations. If gun control advocates truly do seek to do no more than regulate guns with moderate measures such as license or purchase-permit laws, they would have more success in allaying gun owners' fears if they foreswore these more fundamental attacks on gun ownership.

CHAPTER

9

Public Opinion and the Bases of Support for Gun Control

In a democracy, public opinion matters. For proposed gun controls to have any impact, they must survive the political process and be implemented first, and this is difficult without significant public support for the measure. Public opinion polls are an important part of the political process and combatants on both sides of the gun control debate use poll results to buttress their positions and persuade policy makers of the popularity of the measures they propose. Polls are commissioned by activists, and by news outlets such as television networks, news magazines, and newspapers, and other surveys are conducted for their own reasons by pollsters such as Gallup and Harris and by research organizations such as the National Opinion Research Center (NORC). Advocates and opponents regularly cite public opinion polls as indicating that "the public" wants stricter controls, or is happy with existing controls, believes the Second Amendment guarantees an individual the right to keep and bear arms, or believes gun controls will or will not be effective in reducing crime. Each side selectively asks questions likely to yield answers favorable to their arguments and imposes interpretations on the answers that stress the "friendly" implications, and ignore the "hostile" implications.

Some Caveats About Interpreting Public Opinion Polls

Survey results do not interpret themselves, and do not always mean what they seem to mean. Caution must be exercised in interpreting public opinion poll results, especially with regard to the exact form and wording of the questions asked. In the February 1989 Time/CNN national survey, 29% favored "making it illegal for civilians to own handguns." However, in a Gallup survey conducted just 7 months earlier,

37% endorsed what appeared to be the same measure the Time/CNN poll asked about. However, there was a critical difference in the wording of the Gallup question, which read: "Here is a question about pistols and revolvers. Do you think there should or should not be a law which would forbid the possession of this type of gun except by police *and other authorized persons?*" (emphasis added). The key difference is that Gallup added a phrase that would allow some respondents (Rs) to believe that they would be among those persons authorized to keep handguns. Whether intentionally or not, Gallup had in effect transmuted a question apparently referring to a handgun ban into one that could be interpreted by some Rs as referring to a handgun licensing law, perhaps even a permissive one allowing most people to have handguns. Yet, it is clear from the interpretation accompanying release of the poll results that Gallup interpreted the findings as if they concerned "a ban on handgun possession" (Gallup 1982, p. 152). Support for the "ban" is as much as 28% higher (37/29 = 1.28) if the Gallup wording is used, rather than the more straightforward Time/CNN wording.

Consider the contrasting wordings used in questions about requiring a police permit to buy a gun. A 1978 national poll commissioned by an anticontrol sponsor asked about "a law *giving police the power to decide* who may or may not own a firearm" (emphasis added)—only 31% favored such a law. However, a national survey the previous year had asked whether Rs would "favor or oppose a law which would require a person to obtain a police permit before he or she could buy a gun"—72% favored such a law (Crocker 1982, p. 240). The differences in results were enormous because the details of the questions implied important substantive differences. In both questions, the measure being asked about was basically a police purchase permit covering all guns. However, the anticontrol wording raised the specter of arbitrary administration of the law by police. Wright (1981, p. 33) argues that results such as these were perfectly compatible, and that they indicated that the public favored a police purchase permit system, but not one in which police can set the criteria for who qualifies to buy guns. Thus, a system such as New York City's, in which police exercise considerable discretion, sometimes in an allegedly arbitrary fashion, would be opposed by a majority of Americans, whereas a system such as that in Illinois (Bordua et al. 1985) would be supported (see Chapter 8 for a comparison).

Survey findings can require a very close reading, as there is sometimes less than meets the eye in the results. Some are based on questions that violate fundamental rules of survey question construction. For example, one rudimentary rule that every beginning student of survey research learns is "Do not ask questions which assume knowledge that Rs are not likely to possess" (e.g., Dillman 1978, p. 112). This rule is routinely violated in gun control polls. For example, consider the results of a CBS "48 Hours Poll"—73% of 663 respondents (Rs) supported a "total ban on military-style assault weapons," with 22% opposed, and 5% missing. Although the findings appear to indicate strong support for a specific gun control measure, their significance is impossible to gauge in the absence of any evidence indicating that Rs knew what interviewers meant by the term "military-style assault weapons." The term is a propagandistic one, disseminated by procontrol activists to stigmatize a class of weapons as "good for only one thing—killing people." It is not a term with any precise technical meaning in standard firearms reference works, and it certainly does not have a universally agreed-on meaning in popular usage. It is likely that many, perhaps most, of the Rs providing affirmative answers believed that the guns referred to were capable of fully automatic fire. This would not be surprising since true assault rifles *are* capable of fully automatic fire. Even if this information about true assault rifles were irrelevant to what Rs believed about so-called "assault weapons," many would still believe the weapons in question were fully automatic, since this view was encouraged by numerous news stories in 1989 that repeatedly blurred the distinction between automatic and semiautomatic fire and that inaccurately insisted that semiautomatic weapons on the market could easily be converted to fire like a machine gun (Chapter 3). It would hardly be major news that a large majority of Americans favor a ban on private possession of machine guns, especially since this is already the de facto law of the land. It is unclear whether Rs opposed weapons with a military appearance, opposed semiautomatic weapons, understood what "semiautomatic" means, or even knew that the guns referred to in the question *were* semiautomatic.

Survey researchers know that most respondents are reluctant to admit they do not know what an interviewer is asking about, and will generally provide responses to questions, however meaningless. They sometimes will even "express an opinion about an issue they could not possibly know anything about, simply because they do not wish to appear empty-headed or uninformed," even giving responses to questions asking about prejudice against imaginary ethnic groups or about nonexistent government officials invented by the surveyors (Lewis and Schneider 1982, p. 42).

Perhaps the most meaningless public opinion results in the entire gun control area are responses to a question asked repeatedly by the Gallup poll (and similar questions asked by others): "In general, do you feel that the laws covering the sale of handguns should be made more strict, less strict, or kept as they are now?" (Crocker 1982, p. 248). If Rs incorrectly believe that there are fewer current controls over handgun sales than there really are, they may give answers implying that they favor controls that are stricter than those they actually favor. Thus if controls are seen as falling on a 1–3 scale of strictness, Rs might think controls are at level 1, and favor controls at level 2, even though the reality is that controls are already at level 3. Three Rs would presumably choose the "more strict" answer even though they actually favored controls *less* strict than the present ones.

Responses to this sort of question cannot be taken at face value unless one assumes that Rs knew how strict such laws were at the time of the interview. This in an implausible assumption. Most Americans know little about how much or how little law of any kind exists, including gun law. For example, in a 1975 national survey Rs were asked five simple, nontechnical questions about federal gun law. The questions were Yes/No items, and therefore even completely ignorant Rs could answer such questions correctly half of the time just by guessing. Nevertheless, 50% of the Rs could not provide correct answers to more than two of the five items; only 29% got better than three right (U.S. Congress 1975a). According to binomial probabilities, one would expect 50% of the Rs to get three or more correct answers even if they were guessing on all five questions. Therefore the distribution of scores on this knowledge test was almost exactly what one would expect if all Rs were in fact totally ignorant and were just guessing. If Rs do not know how strict laws are now, it is impossible to take at face value survey results that indicate that Americans want laws stricter than the present ones. Such results may indicate little more than that many people want "something" to be done about gun violence.

Further, given that gun laws are mostly state or local, there is considerable variation in "strictness" of laws regulating handgun sales. Consequently, for a resident of a strict jurisdiction to want even stricter laws is much more impressive than for a resident of a lenient jurisdiction to want this. In jurisdictions with no state or local controls on handgun sales, an affirmative response might indicate only that the R supported weak controls. Therefore, even if Rs did know the strictness of gun control in their areas, cumulating responses to this question over the nation as a whole would yield uninterpretable results. It is possible that "stricter" responses were provided largely by Rs in no-control jurisdictions, whereas most Rs in strict-control areas answered "less strict" or "kept as they are now." Such results would indicate that the average American wants no more control than the average area already has, although she or he also wants some controls rather than none at all.

A variety of similarly uninterpretable survey results have been generated by questions asking whether Rs favor a "crackdown on illegal sales," making the rules for becoming a handgun dealer stricter, or making the rules for getting a permit to carry a handgun "strict." As Wright (1981, p. 32) wryly noted, "Making existing regulations and laws tougher is what one might call a 'Why Not?' item: the surprising finding from such items is not that so many people say they favor them, but rather that anybody says they do not."

Public opinion on gun control issues seems to be very volatile, supporting the view that gun control is not a highly salient issue for most people. Consider the 1976 Massachusetts referendum to ban private possession of handguns. A June 1976 poll for the *Boston Globe* indicated 55% supported the measure statewide. Three months later, after considerable public debate, news coverage, and dissemination of propaganda, another statewide survey conducted on September 29–30, 1976 indicated that support had dropped to 40%; a survey the next month indicated 51% support. Finally, in the referendum vote itself, on November 2, 1976, only 29% supported the ban. These facts suggest at minimum that gun control opinion can be highly volatile. They also indicated that support generally declined as the public debate progressed. The same pattern was also observed with another state referendum campaign. Although the Maryland referendum to ban cheap handguns eventually passed on November 8, 1988, its support in statewide polls dropped from a 3–1 margin in the Spring of 1987 to a 49–44% margin by October 1988 (*Washington Post* 10-27-88, p. A8).

It might be argued that paid advertising by gun owner groups caused these declines in support, through the use of inaccurate, disproportionately anticontrol propaganda. However, regardless of the accuracy of the anticontrol advertising, its influence was balanced by equally slanted proreferendum paid advertising and, more importantly, unpaid support for the referendum by the state's key mass media outlets. In the words of referendum supporters, the state's leading newspaper, the *Boston Globe,* "crusaded tirelessly against the dangers" of handguns, and most other major media outlets took similarly proreferendum positions (Holmberg and Clancy 1977, p. 1).

Noting this pattern of declining support as discussion and information dissemination increased, Bordua (1983) accounted for it partly by arguing that gun control simply is not a salient issue for most people.

Most do not think about it much, care about it very deeply, or have firm, stable opinions on it. Consequently, it was easy for gun control opinions to be changed. Likewise, Crocker (1982, pp. 263–4) concluded, after the most extensive review ever done on gun control opinion polls, that "very few people appear to see the gun control issue as an important problem facing this country." If asked, people will endorse many gun controls. However, it is not one of the first things that springs to mind if people are asked to list ways they think crime could be reduced, nor is gun ownership considered a major social problem. For example, in a 1975 national survey, Rs were asked the open-ended question, "What steps do you think should be taken to reduce crime?" and only 11% mentioned gun control (U.S. Congress 1975a). A 1986 survey asked "What would you say is most responsible for this country's high crime rate?" and only 1% mentioned availability of guns or weapons. A 1990 national survey asked Rs to identify the two or three most important national problems that they wanted the federal government to do something about. Only 2% mentioned gun control, compared to 25% mentioning drugs and 24% mentioning homelessness; 27 other national problems were mentioned more often than gun control (DIALOG 1990).

This still leaves open the question of why there should be more shifting of opinion from pro- to anticontrol, rather than the reverse, as more information is acquired. Some evidence suggests that procontrol opinion may be more weakly held than anticontrol opinion. Gun control supporters, when asked in surveys about the intensity of their views, provide responses indicating that they hold their views about as strongly as do opponents. However, when researchers tested these claims by inquiring about whether Rs actually did anything tangible to act on their opinions, such as writing a letter to a public official or giving money to an advocacy group, opponents were three times as likely to report doing something like this as were supporters (Schuman and Presser 1981). This suggests that procontrol opinions are not strongly enough held to motivate action likely to have a direct impact on public policy-making as often as anticontrol opinions. Procontrol views, in short, appear to be opinions on which people rarely act, and which are presumably more weakly held than anticontrol opinions.

Schuman and Presser proposed a different interpretation. They tried to save the idea that gun control supporters have beliefs as strong as opponents by hinting that opponents of gun control were more likely to act on their beliefs only because of "the efficiency of the National Rifle Association in mobilizing supporters" (1981, p. 46). This thesis falls afoul of two facts. First, it is inexact to assert that the NRA influences "supporters" in general to act. More precisely, the NRA directly mobilizes only those supporters who are also NRA *members*. Second, in 1978, when these data were gathered, less than 1% of the population were NRA members. At most perhaps 10 of the 1070 persons in Schuman and Presser's sample were NRA members. Even if all of these 10 were among the 85 opponents who reported taking actions (writing letters, etc.), that would still have left at least 75 non-NRA opponents reporting actions, i.e., 18.0% of all opponents, vs. only 7.1% among supporters. Even among people not subject to the NRA's mobilization efforts, opponents were far more likely to have acted on their beliefs than were supporters.

A more credible interpretation than Schuman and Presser's would be that gun owners make up the majority of gun control opponents, and gun owners believe themselves to have far more at stake personally in the gun control debate than nonowners. Those who own, enjoy, and/or rely on guns believe they could personally lose something very valuable if restrictive gun control is implemented, either immediately, or as a result of escalation in controls following initially moderate controls. On the other hand, most supporters could, at best, enjoy only the uncertain and collectively shared benefits of the less dangerous environment that might result from gun control. Concrete and immediate personal costs motivate behavior more strongly than abstract shared benefits that may or may not materialize sometime in the future, and this principle will operate regardless of whether there is an organization that is efficient at mobilizing gun owners.

All of this may help explain the apparent contrast between the large majorities of public opinion poll respondents favoring moderate gun control measures and the failure of supporters to get corresponding laws on the books. Supporters commonly attribute this failure to the considerable (and, it is hinted, unfair) power of the National Rifle Association to "thwart the will of the people" through lobbying and campaign funding. However, an alternative explanation would simply be that most members of the public have few strong, well-formulated views on the subject, and thus in a sense there is very little "will of the people" to be thwarted. The survey-based support for gun control may be less substantial than it appears, and may not be strong enough to translate into the sorts of politically relevant actions that influence legislators: votes, telephone calls, telegrams and letters to representatives, letters to the editor, large numbers of small campaign contributions from individuals, and so on. Sometimes, a survey "opinion" is little more than a response given on the spur-of-the-moment to a stranger who calls unannounced at the respondent's door or on the telephone, and asks a question about a topic to which the R has given little thought. Whether opinions mean any more than that becomes evident to legislators only when people in some way act on their views.

Consequently, with low-salience issues, a large fraction of the public can provide responses supporting a given position without it indicating that there is popular support extensive enough to result in relevant legislation. An interesting comparison can be made with another prohibitionist proposal. Whereas 41% of Americans favored a ban on private possession of handguns in 1975, 10 years earlier an almost identical 42% favored banning professional boxing by law (Gallup 1966, p. 1949). Yet at no time was there any indication of widespread agitation or active mass effort, or a credible legislative push, to actually get such a law on the books. Perhaps the powerful boxing lobby "thwarted the will of the people." More likely, the appearance of support for these sorts of measures can be created by the simple fact that most people will provide an opinion if asked, regardless of whether or not they had a well-formed, stable, or strongly held opinion on the issue before they were interviewed.

An affirmative response to a survey gun control opinion item may indicate little more than that the respondent wants *something* done to reduce violence and crime, but has no strong views on precisely what would be a good way to accomplish this. Gun control opinion poll results should be viewed in a comparative context to more meaningfully judge their significance. National surveys routinely find large majorities of the public supporting almost *any* plausible measure aimed at crime, regardless of its character, crime control potential, or hopes for implementation. Although recent surveys indicate that about 70% of Americans say they support a gun purchase permit law, similar or larger percentages also endorse the death penalty, longer prison terms, building more prisons, mandatory drug testing, raising the drinking age to 21, and so on (U.S. Bureau of Justice Statistics 1988). The public clearly wants something to be done about crime, but whether it has strong opinions on exactly what should be done is not so clear.

Trends in Public Opinion on Gun Control, 1959–1990

Table 9.1 presents findings from various nation public opinion polls in a way that permits valid comparisons of results over time. The findings are limited to those produced by questions concerning specific gun control measures that have figured in a large number of surveys over the years. Comparisons over time can be made legitimately because the question wordings for the relevant items have been identical or very similar from one survey to the next. For gun purchase permits, the exact same wording has been used in all surveys: "Would you favor or oppose a law which would require a person to obtain a police permit before he or she could buy a gun?" Eight of the 12 items concerning handgun bans (specifically, those used in the post-1959 Gallup surveys) were identically worded; the other three post-1959 questions were somewhat differently worded but concerned similar proposals. The 1959 Gallup question was sharply different from later handgun ban questions. The handgun registration items differed in minor ways but all concerned the substantially identical measure—federal registration of all handguns owned.

Overall, there was little long-term trend in support for gun control over the period 1959–1990. Although there were many sharp short-term shifts in apparent levels of support, there was little that could be described as a strong long-term trend. To the extent that there has been any trend, there was a modest erosion in support for purchase permits, from 75% in 1974 to 68% in 1990, and a modest decline in support for handgun registration, from 77–78% in 1975, to 73% in 1990.

On the other hand, consistent with the idea that opinion on gun control has low salience for most Americans, opinion on some specific measures seems highly volatile, with substantial short-term shifts in levels of support. The Massachusetts referendum experience showed that opinion on even as strong a measure as a ban on handgun possession could shift substantially in a matter of months. The figures in Table 9.1 likewise indicate considerable instability in support for controls, with large changes (far in excess of those that could be attributed to random sampling error) occurring in short periods of time. Identically worded questions in two Harris surveys in 1978 and 1979 indicated that support for a federal law requiring registration of currently owned handguns declined from 78% in August 1979 to 67% in December 1980—a drop of 11 percentage points in just 16 months.

Public opinion seems particularly prone to large changes in response to highly publicized acts of gun violence, with support increasing sharply immediately after the event and then dropping as memory of the event fades. Between 1963 and 1966, using identically worded questions, Gallup found that support for gun purchase permits dropped by 12 percentage points, then increased 5 points by the following year. The 1963 survey had been fielded just after the assassination of President John F. Kennedy. Likewise, identical questions yielded results indicating support for a handgun ban which increased from 31% in November of

1979 to 38% in December of 1980, immediately after the murder of John Lennon. Gallup asked identically worded questions concerning mandatory prison sentences for persons unlawfully carrying handguns in January 1980 and again in April 1981. In 15 months, the percentage favoring this measure jumped by 12 percentage points (Crocker 1982). The second survey was fielded just after the attempted assassination of President Reagan on March 30, 1981. Pollsters' predilection for asking gun control questions shortly after well-publicized acts of criminal gun violence all but guarantees that results will have an unrepresentative character, generally tending to show temporarily elevated support. However, the main point is that views on these control measures were weakly enough held for a single event to alter the opinions of millions of people. On the other hand, this pattern is not universal; views on some gun control measures have been reasonably stable over some periods of time. For example, despite earlier instability, support for police purchase permits for handguns was consistently in the 68–75% range after 1967.

What Kinds of Gun Control Do Americans Favor?

Some of the survey results previously discussed were generated by questions whose wording was too biased or vague for results to be interpreted accurately. Other surveys, however, have asked reasonably worded questions about specific gun control measures, and have obtained meaningful results. Table 9.2 summarizes the findings of some of these surveys concerning 38 specific gun control measures. The results are grouped by the general type of control mentioned, and within these categories are ordered from least popular to most popular. For each gun control type, findings from the latest national survey using a reasonably unslanted question wording are reported. A number of control measures cannot be covered in the table because some modes of gun control have never been asked about in national surveys. These generally are uncontroversial measures that have been on the books in most of the country for many years and are therefore not the subject of much public debate—e.g., bans on possession of guns by convicted felons. Nevertheless, those controls that pollsters do ask about also are mostly very mild-to-moderate measures, likely to elicit little opposition. For example, whereas over a dozen surveys have asked about handgun registration, few national surveys have asked about the ultimate gun control measure, a ban on private possession of all guns.

Several clear patterns are evident in Table 9.2. (1) There are a large number and wide range of weak-to-moderate controls that solid majorities of Americans will endorse if asked. (2) This support does not, however, extend to stronger controls. Generally, the stronger the measures, the less support there is. Bans on possession of common gun types do not have majority support, but moderate regulatory measures such as waiting periods, registration, purchase permits, owner licenses, and carry permits all have solid majority support. Similar general patterns very likely are evident with proposed solutions to most social problems—the strongest measure have the weakest support, and vice versa. A clear majority of Americans favor regulation of guns, but they do not favor their prohibition. (3) There is more support for measures limited to handguns than for those regulating all guns or those regulating just rifles or shotguns. This would help account for the predominantly handgun-only character of gun laws in the United States, despite the pronounced crime control problems posed by such laws (Chapter 3). Similarly, there is more support for restricting special weapon types such as semiautomatic "assault weapons" or plastic guns than for applying otherwise similar regulations to more common gun types. (4) There is more support for "getting tough on criminals" than for imposing restrictions that would also affect ordinary gun owners. In particular, there is strong support for imposing more severe or mandatory prison sentences on criminals, either for unlawful carrying or using guns to commit crimes. (5) There is more support for regulating sale and purchase of guns than there is for regulating possession or ownership. Thus, support is greater for measures that would affect first-time gun buyers than for measures affecting those who already have the guns they want. Similarly, there is more support among (adult) respondents for limits on gun use by minors than by adults.

In general, the patterns are consistent with the broad principle that Rs look after their own interests, favoring restrictions that appear to impose little real cost on themselves, and opposing those that might interfere with their own possession or use of guns. Consistent with this generalization, there is more support for restricting carrying of guns, which few Americans do (Chapter 4), than there is for banning the keeping of loaded guns in the home or significantly restricting the acquisition of guns, which many Americans do. Likewise, there is more support for registration of guns and for purchase permits, which would not interfere with ownership or acquisition of guns for most Americans, than there is for any kind of ban on sale or possession of common gun types.

There also are indications in the table that Americans are more supportive of measures that seem to have few significant short-term dollar costs than of measures likely to cost them money. For example, an overwhelming majority favor requiring safety training to buy a gun, though no one has asked about applying this requirement to those who already own guns. Also, most people support registration and purchase permit systems, which are relatively cheap (Blose and Cook 1989). On the other hand, an overwhelmingly majority opposes proposals to buy back and destroy handguns, which could cost taxpayers a great deal of money.

The Nonutilitarian Nature of Much Gun Control Support

Why do people support gun control? The obvious answer is that they want to reduce violence and believe that gun control will help accomplish this goal. Unfortunately, this appealingly simple explanation is inadequate for explaining the positions of many, and possibly most, gun control supporters.

Both Wright (1981; Wright et al. 1983) and Crocker (1982) have noted that even though a majority of Americans favor a variety of moderate gun control measures, large majorities also believe that handgun control will not keep criminals from getting guns, that gun controls cannot prevent assassinations, and (on most questions) that gun laws will not reduce crime or violence. This sort of finding is not peculiar to gun control—the American public holds many such apparently "nonutilitarian" opinions on measures alleged to control crime. For example, although half of the population believes that prison sentences do not discourage crime, 69% nevertheless approve of building more prisons so longer sentences can be given to criminals (U.S. Bureau of Justice Statistics 1984a, pp. 260, 270). Similarly, when a 1981 survey asked death penalty supporters why they favored capital punishment, only 35% gave answers indicating they thought it was a deterrent to killers (p. 278). Most commonly the death penalty was favored for reasons of retribution. Thus, many crime control measures are favored for moralistic or symbolic reasons with no necessary connection with crime control.

Interpreting gun control opinion polls, Wright concluded that "many people support such measures for reasons other than their assumed effects on the crime rate" (1981, p. 35). He summarized public opinion as follows: "Just as licensing and registration of automobiles seem to have very little effect on reducing automobile accidents, so too do most people anticipate that stricter weapons controls would have little or no effect on crime. This, however, does not stop them from favoring at least some stricter gun control measures. The underlying concept here seems to be that weapons, as automobiles, are intrinsically dangerous objects that governments ought to keep track of for that reason along" (1981, p. 39).

Another interpretation of these poll results is that some gun control supporters do favor controls for utilitarian reasons, supporting moderate measures because they expect some *modest* reduction in violence to result, even though they do not expect large decreases. For example, even though they believe that controls may not keep guns from "criminals," some Rs might believe that restrictions will keep guns from basically noncriminal people who may occasionally lose their tempers or who may commit a gun suicide or get involved in a gun accident. Further, clear majorities of Americans believe that at least some specific moderate controls will be effective in fighting crime at least to some degree, even if others are viewed as ineffective (see the 1978 DMI survey results summarized in Crocker 1982, p. 258).

Nevertheless, many gun control supporters do favor controls for reasons other than a belief that they will reduce crime. A 1990 national survey indicated that 46% of people who thought that more gun control laws were needed also believed that if there were more laws, crime would either stay the same or even increase (Mauser 1990). Thus, nearly half supported more gun laws even though they believed the laws would not reduce crime, even slightly. This result was anticipated by scholars who had noted the seeming lack of interest so many gun control advocates showed for assessing the likely magnitude of the crime control effects of measures they supported. Judging from the negligible space they devote to the topic in their propaganda writings, many advocates seem remarkably uninterested in the issue of whether their proposals would reduce violence much (see, e.g., Zimring and Hawkins 1987; Shields 1981). Mark Moore has stated that "gun owners believe (rightly in my view) that the gun controllers would be willing to sacrifice their interests even if the crime control benefits were tiny" (1983, pp. 187–8).

Much support for gun control, then, rests on grounds other than a utilitarian belief that it will reduce crime. What those grounds might be is not clear from the results of individual survey questions. Perhaps some hints can be derived from detailed analysis of the patterns of support for gun control. Knowing who supports gun control may indirectly shed light on why they support it.

Who Supports Gun Control?

As shown in Chapter 8, there is a tremendous variety of types of gun control, most of which have not been assessed in public opinion polling. Many others have been addressed, but analyzing opinion patterns on all of these would be impractical. Instead the results pertaining to one specific, moderate gun control measure are examined—gun purchase permits. Since more polls have asked identically worded questions about police purchase permits than any other measure (Table 9.1), this would seem to be an appropriate measure to examine in more detail.

Table 9.3 displays results from the combined 1980 and 1982 General Social Surveys (Davis 1984). As neither the level (Table 9.1) nor the patterns of support (Smith 1980) for gun control have changed much in recent decades, the choice of years is probably of little importance, and early 1980s results can probably be applied to years as much as a decade earlier or later. Footnote *a* marking some of the numbers in the last column indicates that the bivariate association between support for a police permit and the pertinent characteristic was statistically significant at the .05 level, using Kendall's tau-b. The exact question wording used was: "Would you favor or oppose a law which would require a person to obtain a police permit before he or she could buy a gun?" The measure is seemingly moderate, neither extremely restrictive nor trivial, and it covers all guns, not just handguns.

Close examination of exactly which segments of the population are most likely to favor purchase permits can be used to get a rough idea as to who is most likely to favor gun controls in general. Although levels of support vary sharply across different control measures, patterns of support by respondent tend to be very similar. Thus, the same groups that are most likely to support one measure are generally the ones most likely to support others (e.g., compare results in a 1985 survey on purchase permits with results from polls concerning handgun registration, strictness of controls on handgun sales, a federal ban on interstate handgun sales, and local bans on possession of handguns, in U.S. Bureau of Justice Statistics 1989a, pp. 172–5).

The strongest bivariate associations in Table 9.3 are as follows. Females are significantly more supportive of a permit than are males, urban dwellers are more supportive than are rural inhabitants and small town residents, those not from the South are more supportive than are Southerners, nonhunters are more supportive than hunters, and nongun owners are more supportive than those who own guns. There are other weaker relationships that are statistically significant only because the sample was so large. These bivariate associations could be misleading, of course, since they may reflect the confounding effects of other variables. Further discussion, therefore, will be deferred until after the multivariate analysis.

Because gun ownership is so strongly related to gun control opinion, the former tends to dominate the bivariate associations: whatever relates to gun ownership generally tends to relate the opposite way to support for purchase permits. Groups more likely to own guns are less likely to support permits. Since the correlates of gun ownership noted in Chapter 2 have already been examined, it would be redundant to examine gun control opinion without controlling for gun ownership. That is, it is desirable to know why, in addition to gun ownership, some people oppose permits and others support them. Table 9.4 reports the estimated standardized coefficients of an ordinary least squares (OLS) regression analysis of support for permits. (Independent variables listed in Table 9.3 that do not appear in Table 9.4 were found to have no significant multivariate association with permit opinion.) Although the dependent variable is binary, OLS is an acceptable estimation procedure because the split on the item (72% in favor, 28% opposed) is not an extreme one. Table 9.4 also reports the results for predictors of whether the R hunts or personally owns a gun. These are included to show the possible indirect effects of some variables on permit opinion through hunting and gun ownership.

It is worth noting first some variables that were tested but excluded from the model because they were found to be not significantly related to permit opinion. There was no association between conservatism and permit opinion, once gun ownership and hunting were controlled. Apart from the very small indirect effect it has through gun ownership and hunting, being a conservative does not appear to decrease the likelihood of support for permits; conversely, liberalism does not directly increase support. In fact, persons who think the courts are not harsh enough on criminals (surely a conservative attitude) are actually slightly more likely to favor a permit law, other things being equal. Thus, as suggested in Chapter 1, it may be misleading to discuss gun control opinion as if it clearly divided along ideological lines. The (generally small) bivariate associations noted by many pollsters are misleading because they reflect little more than the slight effect of conservatism on willingness to own guns and hunt, rather than an ideology-based support for gun control. That liberals are not substantially more supportive of gun control is even clearer where a more restrictive measure is involved. A follow-up survey conducted after the Massachusetts referendum to ban handgun possession found that although 66% of conservatives said they voted against the measure, so did a nearly identical 64% of the liberals (Holmberg and Clancy 1977, p. 83).

Being afraid to walk in one's neighborhood and prior victimization in a burglary also were unrelated to permit opinion once multivariate controls were introduced. The positive bivariate association between fear and permit support may have been a spurious one due to the correlation of fear with income—low income Americans are more likely to be fearful and more likely to support gun control. It had been the hope of gun control activists that increasing victimization and rising fear of crime and violence would eventually motivate more Americans to support gun control (Shields 1981). However, support did not increase significantly during the 1960s and early 1970s, when crime rates were rapidly increasing (Table 9.1). The results explain why—apparently fear and prior victimization do not motivate support for gun control. Indeed, indirectly they may tend to have the opposite effect. Chapter 2 results indicated that prior burglary victimization may motivate acquisition of handguns, and the present results indicate that gun ownership in turn discourages support for permits (see Table 9.4). Also, if one accepts as real the ambiguous indications in Chapter 2 that fear motivates gun ownership, then fear would also indirectly reduce support for gun control.

There was no bivariate association between prior victimization and support for a purchase permit. However, where more stringent controls are at stake, victimization and gun control support may be associated. A statewide survey was conducted during the fight over Maryland's referendum to ban "Saturday Night Specials." Rs were asked whether they or a family member had ever been a victim of handgun crime. Although half of the nonvictims supported the ban, only a third of the victims did (*Washington Post* 10-27-88, p. A9). One reasonable generalization from these results would be this—if there seems to be a possibility that a measure would take guns away from people who feel they might need them for self-defense, crime victims are less likely to support the measure than nonvictims. Purchase permits, in contrast, would not disarm most crime victims.

Turning to those variables that relate to support for permits, the standardized coefficients in Table 9.4 indicate that the only strong direct predictors of permit opinion were gun ownership, hunting, and region. That gun owners are less likely to support restrictions on gun purchases is to be expected; self-interest is always relevant in opinion formation. Whereas a modest measure such as a purchase permit by itself would not deprive many Americans of guns, some gun owners may fear that it might be restrictively administered so as to interfere with their future purchases, or they may fear that passing a moderate measure now would make it easier to pass more objectionable and restrictive measures later. Thus a gun owner could feel his own guns were threatened even by measures very moderate in themselves. Conversely, nonowners and nonhunters may support controls because they believe it does not cost them anything of any significance.

Hunters are less likely than nonhunters to support permits, even controlling for gun ownership. Perhaps hunters value their guns even more than do other gun owners, or adhere more strongly to the anticontrol ideology of sporting gun owners than do owners who are less integrated into the sporting subculture. Hunters may read gun magazines, be exposed to more anticontrol information, and discuss gun control more often with other gun owners than owners who are not a part of the sporting gun subcultures. Further, hunters mostly own long guns, which are not covered under most existing purchase permit laws. An all-guns permit would imply new restrictions for many hunters, whereas more defense-oriented handgun owners may have already accommodated themselves to existing permit laws applying to handguns.

Residents of the South and the Rocky Mountain states are less likely to support permits than other Americans, even controlling for gun ownership, conservatism, rural upbringing, and many other variables that might otherwise account for the regional disparity.

Other variables have notable apparent effects on permit opinion, but only indirectly, through their impact on gun ownership and hunting. Men, people raised in the South, wealthier people, and those who were raised in rural areas are all more likely to hunt and to own guns, and hunters and gun owners are in turn more likely to oppose permits. However, these groups are not more likely to oppose permits once their gun ownership and hunting is taken account of. Thus, for example, men who do not own guns are just as likely to support permits as women who do not own guns, other things being equal.

These data were generated by a survey not primarily directed at explaining gun control opinion or gun ownership. Consequently, it is not surprising that little of the variation in these variables is accounted for by the models. The surveys apparently did not measure most of whatever it is that influences gun control opinion formation.

Returning to the culture conflict themes of Chapter 2, it is possible that some people support gun control as a way of stigmatizing another, disliked, group and its culture, using the criminal law to declare that some kinds of activities, such as owning guns, are shameful and morally objectionable, and should be limited for this reason alone. Some gun control support, therefore, would be unrelated to either the specifics of the particular measure asked about, or to concerns about reducing crime. Recall that about half of gun control supporters support more gun laws even though they believe they will not reduce crime. Don Kates has noted the indifference that gun ban advocates show for practical issues such as enforceability, and interpreted this as indicating that "the anti-gun crusader's concern is of symbolic rather than pragmatic value," and concluding that "anti-gun crusaders view a ban on guns as an official or symbolic endorsement of their moral superiority and as a simultaneous condemnation of guns and gun owners" (Kates 1990, p. 10). More generally, procontrol propaganda is notable for what it almost entirely omits—any discussion of examples of successful gun control laws. Surely anyone whose support for gun control was based on a belief that it could reduce violence would place great emphasis on such success stories, even if they were spurious, yet propagandists often devote virtually no space to even making an argument for such a results-based rationale (see, e.g., Handgun Control 1989; Shields 1981).

Some people who do not own guns stereotype gun owners as "gun nuts" and "rednecks," who are thought to be violent, anti-intellectual, racist, reactionary, and dangerous (Kaplan 1979, p. 6). Gun control, then, may be viewed by some supporters not merely as a form of violence control; it is redneck and reactionary control as well. The debate over gun control is merely one reflection of larger status conflicts involving the tactics of the "stigma contest." Guns are merely symbolic of associated people and cultures that are disliked, largely for reasons not directly related to gun ownership (Hawley 1977).

Some observers see in the gun control struggle a conflict between the older, more traditional culture of "bedrock America," and the newer, more urban one of "cosmopolitan America" (*Wall Street Journal* 6-7-72, p. 14). Others have emphasized the regional dimensions of the conflict, seeing the antigun movement as reflecting hostility to Southern culture (Hawley 1977). Still others have stressed a class dimension, interpreting the conflict as one in which predominantly upper-middle class and upper class supporters such as Pete Shields (former executive in the Du Pont corporation) attempt to impose their views on working class people exposed to the daily realities of street crime (Kates 1979).

Finally, still others have stressed a racial dimension. For example, liberal investigative reporter Robert Sherrill (1973) concluded that the object of the federal Gun Control Act of 1968 was black control rather than gun control. Sherrill argued that the ghetto riots of 1967 and 1968 impelled Congress to ban imports of cheap handguns, which they associated with ghetto blacks, while leaving more expensive handguns, along with rifles and shotguns, relatively untouched. Tonso (1985) quoted the founder of the National Black Sportsman's Association as asserting that "Gun control is really race control. . . . All gun laws have been enacted to control certain classes of people, mainly black people, but the same laws used to control blacks are being used to disarm white people as well."

Kates' (1979; also 1986) review of the early history of gun control (discussed in Chapter 1) supports these view in regard to the origins of gun laws. Nevertheless, it should be stressed that however much the impact of gun laws may disproportionately fall on minorities and poor people, this does not necessarily imply anything about the motives of those who support gun laws. It is difficult to distinguish a person who uses a concern about violence control as a mere rationalization for supporting gun controls from one whose support is genuinely based on concerns about the role of guns in violence. Nevertheless, given the nonutilitarian nature of much gun control support, it is likely that some of the drive for gun laws relies as much on concern about controlling despised or feared "dangerous classes" as on controlling crime.

Table 9.1. Trends in Support for Selected Gun Control Measures[a]

Gun Purchase Permits		*Ban on Handgun Possession*		*Federal Handgun Registration*	
Year	*% in Favor*	*Survey*	*% in Favor*	*Survey*	*% in Favor*
1959	75	Gallup	59[b]		
1963	79				
1965	73				
1965	70				
1966	67				
1967	72				
1971	72				
1972	72				
1973	73				
1974	75				
1975	74	Gallup	41	CBS	78
1975		Harris	37	Harris	77
1975				Harris	77
1976	72				
1977	72				
1978		Caddell	31	Caddell	74
1978				Harris	80
1979		Gallup	31	Harris	78
1980	69	Gallup	38	Harris	67
1981		Gallup	39		
1981		Gallup	41		
1982	72	Gallup	45	Gallup	66
1984	70				
1985	72			Gallup	70
1987	70	Gallup	42		
1988	74	Gallup	37		
1989	78			Harris	78
1990	68	CSUR	36	Harris	73
Range	67–79		31–59		66–80

[a] The 1959–1972 (first 1972 survey) purchase permit surveys were all Gallup polls. All subsequent purchase permit results are from NORC's General Social Surveys, except the 1990 result, which is drawn from the CSUR (Center for Social and Urban Research) survey (Mauser and Margolis 1990).

[b] Worded significantly different from later surveys.

Sources: 1959–1980—Crocker (1982); 1982–1987—U.S. Bureau of Justice Statistics (1987, p. 175); CSUR 1990—Mauser and Margolis (1990); other 1988–1990 surveys—computer search of DIALOG database POLL file.

Table 9.2. What Kinds of Gun Control Do Americans Favor? (Generally in Increasing Order of Popularity)

Control Measure	*Date*	*Survey*	*% in Favor*
All-guns bans			
Private citizens surrender all guns to government	1976	NORC[c]	<17[a]
Ban sales of all guns	1985	Roper	22
Making it illegal for civilians to own guns	1989a	Time/CNN	29
Handgun bans			
Buy back, destroy handguns, mandatory basis	1978	Caddell	26
Buy back, destroy handguns, voluntary basis	1978	Caddell	33
Ban further manufacture, sale of handguns	1978	Caddell	32
Ban private possession of handguns	1990	CSUR	36
Ban sales of handguns	1989	CBS	40
Ban handgun possession in high crime areas	1975	Harris	<47
Local ban on sale, possession of handguns in R's own community	1986	Gallup	47
Ban further manufacture, sale of nonsporting handguns	1978	Caddell	48
Federal ban on interstate sales of handguns	1986	Gallup	67
Ban further manufacture, sale of small, cheap handguns	1978	Caddell	70
Federal ban on manufacture, sale, possession of "Saturday Night Specials"	1989	Gallup	71
Other gun bans			
Federal ban (as above) on semiautomatic assault guns, such as the AK-47	1990	CSUR	69
Federal ban (as above) on plastic guns	1989	Gallup	75
Ban on keeping loaded guns			
Illegal to have loaded weapons in home	1965	Gallup	<47[a]
Ammunition purchase permit			
Police permit required to buy ammunition	1965	Gallup	<56[a]
Mandatory penalty, carrying			
Mandatory minimum 1 year jail term, carrying gun without a license	1981	Gallup	62
Ban on use by minors			
Completely forbid use of guns by those <18	1967	Gallup	<68[a]
Purchase Permit			
Required permit to purchase a rifle	1975	Harris	<69[a]
Require police permit to purchase a gun	1990	CSUR	68
Owner's license			
Require license to own a handgun	1978	Caddell	74

(continued)

Table 9.2. (Continued)

Control Measure	*Date*	*Survey*	*% in Favor*
Registration			
Register all guns owned	1989	Time/CNN	73
Register all rifles owned	1989b	Time/CNN	68[b]
Register all shotguns owned	1989b	Time/CNN	65[b]
Register all handguns owned	1990	Harris	73
Register all gun owners	1940	Gallup	74
Register all semiautomatic weapons owned	1989b	Time/CNN	77[b]
Register all gun purchases	1990	Harris	79
Register all handgun owners	1938	Gallup	79
Register all handgun purchases	1978	Caddell	84
Safety training			
Require mandatory safety training to buy gun	1985b	Time/CNN	82[b]
Mandatory prison sentence, crime with gun			
Require mandatory prison sentence for persons using a gun in a crime	1978	Caddell	83
Carry permit			
Require a permit to carry a gun outside home	1988	Gallup	84
Waiting periods			
21-day waiting period to allow criminal records check, handgun purchases	1981	Gallup	91
14-day waiting period, any gun purchase	1989a	Time/CNN	89
7-day waiting period, handgun purchases	1988	Gallup	91

[a] Source only reported percentage opposing measure; 100 minus percentage opposing is maximum possible percentage in favor.
[b] Computed as simple average of separate percentages for gun owners and nonowners.
[c] NORC, National Opinion Research Center, producer of General Social Surveys.
Sources: 1989b Time/CNN—Quinley (1990); 1981, 1986, 1987 Gallup—Gallup (1987); 1988 Gallup—Gallup (1989); 1965, 1967 Gallup, 1975 Harris, 1976 NORC—Smith (1980); 1990 CSUR (Center for Social and Urban Research)—Mauser and Margolis (1990); 1985 Roper, 1989a Time/CNN, 1989 CBS, 1990 Harris—computer search of DIALOG database, POLL file; all others—Crocker (1982). See original sources for exact question wordings.

Table 9.3. Who Supports Gun Control?

Respondent Characteristic	*% in Favor of Purchase Permit Law*	*Kendall's tau-b*
Total	72.0	
Sex		
Male	66.0	−.117[a]
Female	76.5	
Race		
White	70.7	.080[a]
Black	82.1	
Age		
Under 25	75.3	−.042[a]
25–29	74.7	
40–64	67.9	
65 or over	72.3	
Marital status		
Never married	76.9	−.071[b]
Divorced	73.5	
Separated	83.0	
Widowed	74.0	
Married	69.2	
Family income		
Under $10,000	74.8	−.025[a]
$10,000–19,999	72.0	
$20,000–24,999	70.4	
$25,000 or more	71.8	
Occupation		
Service workers	73.5	.046[a]
Farmers, farm laborers	47.3	
Laborers	67.6	
Craftsmen, operatives	66.8	
Clerical	77.5	
Managers, sales worker	69.7	
Professional, technical	78.4	
Education (years of formal schooling completed)		
0–7	68.4	.041[a]
8	71.6	
9–11	69.7	
12	72.4	
1–3 years of college	74.7	
4 years of college	74.7	
> 4 years of college	78.0	

(*continued*)

Table 9.3. *(Continued)*

Respondent Characteristic	*% in Favor of Purchase Permit Law*	*Kendall's tau-b*
Population of place of residence		
Under 5,000	61.1	.132[a]
5,000–49,999	74.7	
50,000–249,999	72.8	
250,000–999,999	78.6	
1 million or larger	84.5	
Region		
New England	93.0	.228[b]
Middle Atlantic	85.9	
East North Central	73.8	
West North Central	74.3	
South Atlantic	64.4	
East South Central	68.1	
West South Central	59.6	
Mountain	42.4	
Pacific	73.0	
Political views		
Liberal	76.6	−.088[a]
Moderate	73.8	
Conservative	66.0	
Hunter?		
Yes	47.5	.254[a]
No	77.3	
Nontraffic arrest		
Yes	64.1	−.067[a]
No	73.1	
Approval of violence (0–5 scale)		
0	73.4	−.038[a]
1	76.5	
2	72.5	
3	68.2	
4 or 5	67.8	
Afraid to walk in area		
Yes	76.3	.089[a]
No	68.3	
Burglarized in past year		
Yes	71.1	−.006
No	72.0	

(continued)

Table 9.3. (Continued)

Respondent Characteristic	*% in Favor of Purchase Permit Law*	*Kendall's tau-b*
Gun-owning household		
Yes	59.6	−.268[a]
No	83.6	
Handgun-owning household		
Yes	52.9	−.236[a]
No	78.2	
R owns gun		
Yes	52.4	.291[a]
No	81.0	
R owns handgun		
Yes	47.3	.247[a]
No	77.5	

[a] Indicates bivariate association (Kendall's tau-b) significant at .05 level. Sample sizes vary across items from 2671 to 2932.
[b] Respondent characteristic was measured at nominal level, as bivariate association was measured using the contingency coefficient; chi-square significant at .05 level.
Source: NORC, Combined 1980 and 1982 General Social Surveys (Davis and Smith 1984).

Table 9.4. Results of Regression Analysis of Support for Police Purchase Permits (standardized regression coefficients)

	Dependent Variable		
Predictor	*Hunts*	*Owns Gun*	*Supports Permits*
R owns gun			−0.19
R hunts		0.34	−0.14
Courts not harsh enough		0.03	0.03
R has arrest record			−0.04
Lives near blacks			0.03
Single			0.03
Conservatism	0.04	0.04	
Income	0.05	0.11	
Education	−0.07	−0.04	
Lives in South			−0.08
Lives Rocky Mountain	0.06	0.03	−0.11
In South, age 16		0.08	
Rural area, age 16	0.11	0.05	
Size of place	−0.07	−0.07	
Protestant	0.09	0.06	−0.08
Jewish		−0.03	0.02[a]
Age	−0.20	0.13	
Sex (female)	−0.33	−0.29	
Black			0.05
Single female		0.03	
Adjusted R^2	0.18	0.33	0.13
valid cases	4202	3848	3969

[a] $.05 < p < .10$, one-tailed; all other coefficients, $p < .05$, one-tailed.

Source: Combined 1980, 1982, and 1984 General Social Surveys.

CHAPTER

10

The Impact of Gun Control on Violence Rates

The appeal of gun control may lie in its apparent simplicity. It appears at first glance to involve only the regulation of a technology of violence, rather than the reform or manipulation of people. By reducing availability of one major, highly lethal tool for inflicting violence, it is argued, the frequency, or at least the seriousness, of violent acts will be reduced (Newton and Zimring 1969). As noted in Chapter 2, however, one difficulty with this reasoning is that persuading people to give up their guns, or to forego acquiring them in the first place, may also require changing human values and attitudes, such as those regarding self-defense and the protection of other people and property. Consequently, it is unclear how many people, among those likely to commit violent acts, can be deprived of guns.

The rationale for gun control, of course, includes the assumption that the availability of guns has a significant net positive effect on violence rates. It was concluded in Chapter 5, concerning homicide and other violent crimes, Chapter 6, concerning suicide, and Chapter 7 concerning gun accidents, that this assumption is not supported by the weight of the best available evidence. Therefore, even if some violence-prone people can be disarmed, it is not obvious that this would result in a net reduction in violence. Nevertheless, these conclusions were all subject to qualifications, caveats, and possible future modification. It is possible that gun ownership in high violence groups may increase some kinds of violence under some conditions and that gun laws can reduce violence by reducing gun ownership in these specific subsets of the population. It is also possible that some gun laws may reduce violence without reducing gun ownership, e.g., by reducing the availability of guns in specific situations, such as carrying in public places, or by deterring criminals from using guns in the commission of crimes. Therefore, the efficacy of gun control laws still is an open question at this point. This chapter assesses the effects of every major type of gun law on each of the major categories of violence that frequently involve guns.

Methods of Prior Research

Two general strategies have previously been used to assess the impact of gun control laws on violence rates: time series analyses and cross-sectional analyses. In the time series design, monthly or annual violence rates for a single jurisdiction are analyzed to see if there is a significant downward shift in crime after a new gun law went into effect. Cross-sectional designs typically compare jurisdictions such as states or cities with each other to see if those having a given type of gun law have lower levels of violence than those lacking the law.

Previous studies of gun control's impact on violence have been characterized by a variety of methodological flaws. The first is the failure to adequately establish *ceteris paribus* conditions, i.e., to control for other variables that can affect violence rates, so as to maximize one's confidence that observed differences in violence rates truly are attributable to differences in gun laws. This is probably, contrary to the claims of some scholars in the field (e.g., Wright et al. 1983, p. 285) at least as much of a problem for time series analyses as for cross-sectional studies. Although it is true that cross-temporal variation in extraneous variables will usually be smaller than cross-jurisdictional variation, it is equally true that cross-temporal variation in the dependent variable (the crime rate) is also usually smaller than between-jurisdictional variation in crime rates. *Relative to variation in the dependent variable,* there can be just as much variation in extraneous variables in longitudinal designs as in cross-sectional ones. When this is true, the need for controls is every bit as great in the former as in the latter.

Data availability is one area in which the two designs differ considerably. Cross-sectional designs can take advantage of considerable data in census years for cities, metropolitan areas, or states on extraneous determinants of crime rates, whereas time series data on most such variables, except at the national level, are virtually nonexistent. Consequently, subnational time series designs usually do not explicitly control for any other important determinants of crime that might show changes coincident with changes in gun laws. Instead they, at best, make do with crude comparisons to "control" jurisdictions that, it is assumed, would show crime trends similar to those in the intervention jurisdiction were it not for the impact of the gun law changes. This was the strategy followed by Pierce and Bowers (1981); Loftin and McDowall (1981, 1984), Deutsch and Alt (1977), and Hay and McCleary (1979) did not use control jurisdictions at all. The Pierce and Bowers "control" jurisdictions, however, may not have served the control purpose very well since they were not chosen in a way that would ensure that their crime trends would have been the same as those of their intervention city, Boston. Rather than being chosen on the basis of similar preintervention crime trends, they were selected simply because they were of the same general population size and/or region as Boston. As there was no reason to believe that either region or population size was consistently related to time trends in crime, there was no reason to believe that the chosen cities were adequate as controls. Other time series studies have instead used trends in *non*gun violence rates within the impact jurisdiction as internal controls, relying on the assumption that gun and nongun rates would follow similar trends were it not for changes in gun regulation (e.g., Loftin and McDowall 1981). Thus if gun violence decreases more than nongun violence, this supports the view that gun laws were responsible.

Time series designs also have another serious problem that does not afflict cross-sectional designs: it is very difficult to tell exactly *when* the effect of a new law is supposed to become evident. The difficulty is highlighted in the study by Pierce and Bowers (1981), whose ARIMA results indicated no significant downward shift in crime in the month when the Massachusetts Bartley–Fox carrying law went into effect, but did indicate a downward shift in the *previous* month. Rather than concluding that the law did not work, these authors hypothesized that the law caused an "announcement effect" attributable to "a dramatic, and not completely accurate, two-month publicity campaign" (p. 124). Of course this could conceivably be true, but use of such ex post facto interpretations makes decisive tests of gun control impact difficult, since equally plausible interpretations could be applied to downward crime shifts that fall almost anywhere else in the time series. [Faced with very similar findings in their Detroit study, Loftin and McDowall (1981, pp. 159–62) concluded that the law did *not* affect crime.] Consider just a few of the possible candidates for the time when a new law's impact could become evident. Effects could begin at the time when the law is:

1. first publicly proposed,
2. formally introduced into the legislature,
3. passed by each branch of legislature,
4. signed into law,

5. first heavily publicized,
6. achieves its peak level of publicity (most air time, print space, etc.),
7. at its effective date, i.e., when it officially goes into effect,
8. first enforced (first arrest, conviction, imprisonment), and
9. first enforced in a publicized way.

And of course, a researcher could plausibly hypothesize that public perception lags, so that the law's impact would first be felt at almost any point within a year or two *after* its effective date. As long as there was at least one significant downward shift in the time series anywhere near in time to the development/passage/initial enforcement period, a researcher could argue it was evidence that the law worked. This renders a gun law effectiveness hypothesis difficult to falsify, even in the absence of any actual causal effects.

Experts in ARIMA modeling also commonly point out difficulties that even experienced practitioners have in specifying time series models. Specification is very much an art rather than a science, so that different researchers, using the same body of data, can make substantially different, even arbitrary, specification decisions, and, as a result, obtain sharply different results [e.g., compare the findings of Deutsch and Alt (1977) with those of Hay and McCleary (1979) re. the effects of the Bartley–Fox gun law on robbery rates; they were sharply different, based on a single change in model specification].

Finally, time series approaches to gun control impact share what might be called a flaw of research efficiency. Such studies usually examine a single law's operation in a single jurisdiction, and thus may have limited generalizability to other circumstances. Unless a jurisdiction adopts, in its entirety and unmodified, the total legislative package previously evaluated in another jurisdiction, the prior evaluation can give only weak hints as to whether the law would work for another jurisdiction. For example, if we accept that the Bartley–Fox law as a whole worked, it would be risky to infer even that other carrying laws with mandatory sentences for violations would work, since it may have been some unique constellation of detailed features of that law, or peculiarities of the Boston setting, that was responsible for its effects. Only when a number of different carrying laws have been assessed, in many different jurisdictions, can one be confident that the type of regulation is generally effective and likely to work in other jurisdictions. In contrast, cross-sectional designs examine many different jurisdictions with a given type of law, offering a stronger basis for generalizing their results.

One might hope that longitudinal evaluations of single jurisdictions will eventually cumulate into the needed body of studies, but this seems a forlorn hope at this point. The experience of the past 20 years of research has been that a total of four types of laws have been evaluated with time series designs, and for three of the four types, only a single example has been assessed.[1] At that rate it could take centuries before a large enough number of studies on each law type cumulated to the point where they would be useful for policy-making.

It is clear, then, that cross-sectional studies of many jurisdictions offer clear advantages over longitudinal designs if one wants to identify what types of gun regulation are generally likely to produce crime reductions. At the very least, they serve to complement single-jurisdiction time series designs, since each of the two designs has different strengths and weaknesses. The one major weakness of cross-sectional studies is one shared by time series studies—the difficulty of correctly specifying a model of how crime rates are generated. It should be noted, however, that the cross-sectional design does *not* require, as Wright et al. asserted, that "the investigator have a fairly complete understanding of how the particular crime rates are generated" (1983, p. 285). This is an impossible standard to meet, and fortunately an unnecessary one. Instead, unbiased estimates of the impact of a gun control measure can be obtained if one includes in the model those extraneous variables that affect crime rates and that *also* have nontrivial correlations with the gun control measures. Omitting crime determinants that are not substantially correlated with gun laws does not substantially bias estimates of gun laws' effects. Although one can never be sure that all necessary variables have been controlled in a model, the same is also true of time-series studies.

With only two exceptions (Geisel et al. 1969; Cook 1979), prior cross-sectional studies have used states exclusively as their unit of analysis. This aggravates the problem of aggregation bias. States are larger aggregations than cities, and are much more heterogeneous with regard to violence rates and variables affecting violence rates. Consequently, a state could have one area with high violence rates but little local gun regulation, while the rest of its component areas have moderately low violence rates and severe local gun regulation, consistent with the idea that gun regulation reduces crime. Yet when the areas are lumped together in the entire state unit, the high violence area could dominate the violence measure so much that the state showed a higher-than-average violence rate despite generally severe local gun restrictions. The aggregation would thus conceal a causal effect of gun laws evident at lower levels of aggregation. Consequently, the best level of aggregation to use would be the lowest one at which gun law is made—the city level.

Only one prior study has measured gun regulation at both the state level and the city level (Geisel et al. 1969), yet the most severe gun regulation in the nation is at the city or county level. Many, even most, of the residents of a given state might be subject to very strong gun laws in the cities in which they reside, yet be subject to little or no state regulation. Consequently, studies that fail to measure local ordinances mismeasure the degree of gun regulation to which the population is subject.

For many gun laws, the presumed reason for any effects they have on crime is that they reduce levels of gun ownership or availability, which in turn affects crime rates. Yet, only 3 of 24 studies published to date explicitly measured gun ownership or availability. Thus it was usually impossible to tell whether apparent gun law effects were produced through reductions in gun ownership or through some other causal mechanism. Further, none of these three studies treated the gun–violence relationship as a simultaneous reciprocal one. This is problematic because there is reason to believe that violence rates can motivate gun acquisition, in addition to gun levels possibly affecting violence levels (Chapter 2).

Finally, close examination of the various surveys and compilations of gun laws reveals significant differences between sources, indicating in each instance that at least one source was in error. Consequently, studies using a single source of information are vulnerable to error in measurement of the key independent variables. This was the case with all prior studies.

Results of Prior Research

Table 10.1 summarizes the results and weaknesses of 29 studies of the impact of gun control laws on crime rates; it will be necessary to discuss only the more noteworthy ones. Studies focusing on suicide or gun accidents have been reviewed in Chapters 6 and 7, so Table 10.1 covers only studies addressing, at least in part, violent crime.

One of the best studies in the field is also one of the earliest. Geisel and his colleagues (1969) estimated models of state and city violence rates with controls for as many as eight other violence predictors in addition to their gun control variables. They also measured gun control strictness at both local and state levels, considered eight different major categories of gun regulation, and checked for effects of gun control on total violence rates as well as gun violence rates. No significant negative effects of an index of overall gun control severity, which combined eight types of gun laws together, were observed for total homicide, aggravated assault, or robbery rates. Likewise, results were negative when regression equations included separate dummy variables representing each type of gun control, though these results were not reported in detail (see Chapter 6 for further comments on this study).

Murray (1975) and DeZee (1983) analyzed state violence rates, improving on the Geisel et al. study by introducing dummy gun control law variables into the regression equations, rather than lumping them together into a single index, and reporting the results of this procedure. Consistent with the dummy variable results in the Geisel study, none of the laws, either singly or collectively, showed a significant relationship to violence rates. These studies both measured gun control only at the state level.

Cook (1979) conducted an excellent study of robbery rates in 50 cities, but studied only one type of law. He found that cities in states with gun purchase permit laws had no less robbery or gun robbery than cities not subject to such a law.

Perhaps the most persuasive evidence concerning a given type of gun regulation concerns laws establishing mandatory add-on penalties for commission of violent felonies with a gun. In separate time series studies of laws in Florida and Michigan, Loftin and his colleagues found no consistent effects of such laws on rates of violent crime (Loftin et al. 1983; Loftin and McDowall 1984).

Nicholson and Garner (1980) studied the Washington, D.C. Firearms Control Act of 1975, which went into effect in February 1977. This law is arguably the most stringent gun law applying to any large jurisdiction in the United States, effectively eliminating handgun sales in Washington, D.C. and, more importantly, prohibiting private handgun possession except among those few residents who had already legally registered their handguns prior to passage of the law (Jones 1981, pp. 141–3). Despite the authors' assertions to the contrary, the Washington law did not produce drops in total crimes that significantly exceeded those in control jurisdictions (see esp. their Table 10).[2]

The summary of prior research contained in Table 10.1 indicates that most studies have found no impact of gun laws on violence rates. Of the eight studies providing at least mixed support of gun law impact, three were time series evaluations of the same law, the Bartley–Fox carrying law. These three found drops in violence which *preceded* the law's effective date, casting doubt on favorable assessments of the law. Further, a fourth study of this same law concluded that evidence regarding the law's impact was inconsistent and that the optimistic conclusions of previous researchers were premature (Hay and McCleary 1979).

The impact of the Bartley–Fox law has been widely misunderstood, partly because commentators have leaned too heavily on evaluators' verbal summaries rather than their statistical results. The three studies that performed sophisticated ARIMA time series analyses of this law are summarized in Table 10.2. Both of the studies that assessed homicide effects agreed: there was no statistically significant effect on homicide rates. Regarding armed robbery, the same two studies reached opposite conclusions, disagreeing over technical issues of model specification. Finally, all three studies agreed that gun assaults declined, although they also agreed that the apparent effect occurred a month *before* the law's effective date. However, only Pierce and Bowers provided data on total armed assaults. Although they did not report any ARIMA results for total or nongun assaults, their simple percentage change data indicated that both the nongun armed assault rate and the total armed assault rate increased far more than the gun assault rate declined. Since nongun assaults are substantially more likely to involve injury than gun assaults (Chapter 5), this means that assault injuries almost certainly increased after the law went into effect. In sum, the best available evidence indicates that Bartley–Fox had no detectable effect on homicide, may or may not have reduced robbery, and *increased* both total assaults and assault injuries. This is why the results of these studies are described as "Mixed" in Table 10.1.

Summarized this way, the law hardly seems like a rousing success, but one would not know this from the summary remarks of many commentators. After a discussion apparently based solely on Pierce and Bowers' percentage change data, Zahn (1990, p. 386) flatly concluded that "gun control can reduce homicide rates." This is a particularly odd conclusion, given the findings of Deutsch and Alt (1977) and Hay and McCleary (1979) that there were no effects on homicide. Even a normally skeptical Samuel Walker blandly noted that the law "apparently had some effect on armed assaults," citing the decline in gun assaults. Although noting the possible substitution of nongun assaults, he nonetheless accepted the positive, though misleading, summary judgement that the law "did have some impact on gun-related crime" (1989, p. 91).

Taking prior research as a whole, it would be fair to say at this point that a credible case for efficacy in reducing violence has not yet been made for any major type of gun control.

Cross-National Comparisons

Many of the same problems afflict the use of cross-national violence rates to assess gun law impact that afflicted the effort to use such data to assess the impact of gun ownership levels (discussed in Chapter 5). Pairs of nations are compared, but are arbitrarily selected so as to prove whatever point the analyst wishes, or many nations are compared and any observed differences in violence are arbitrarily attributed to differences in gun control strictness.

The most common paired comparison is between the United States and Great Britain (GB). The latter does indeed have both stricter gun laws and less homicide than the United States. Certainly the residents of GB rarely kill one another with guns (Killias 1990, p. 171). However, there is little reason to believe that gun controls were responsible for the lower total homicide rates. Conclusions to the contrary typically rely on static comparisons of the two nations in fairly recent years. These comparisons overlook one major fact: GB had far less violence than the United States long before it had strict gun laws. Before 1920, gun control was at least as lenient in GB as in the United States—there were few significant controls on any common gun type. The Library of Congress referred to the pre-1903 period as "the era of unrestricted [gun] ownership" (p. 75) and noted that in the 1903–1920 period, although a license was required to obtain a gun, "licenses were available on demand" (U.S. Library of Congress 1981, pp. 75–6). Since 1920, controls have been made progressively stricter, first in response to political unrest, especially in Ireland, and later as a crime-control measure (p. 76). According to Archer and Gartner (1984), in 1919 the homicide rate for England and Wales was 0.8 per 100,000. The United States had no national homicide counts before 1933, but a usable estimate for 1919 can be calculated. The U.S. Death Registration Area (DRA) consisted of those states that had essentially complete recording of deaths on death certificates. As each state achieved complete recording, it entered the DRA. Among states that were in the DRA in 1910, the homicide rate was 5.3 in 1919 and 5.4 in 1933. The DRA achieved complete coverage of the United States in 1933. At this time the national homicide rate was 9.7, 1.8 times the rate in 1933 just among those states that had been in the 1910 DRA (U.S. Bureau of the Census 1943, pp. 313, 315). Multiplying 1.8 times the 5.3 rate for the 1910 DRA in 1919 yields an estimate that the homicide rate for the entire United States was 9.5 in 1919. This is 11.9 times as large as the rate in England and Wales. By 1983–1986, after more than 60 years of increasingly stringent gun regulation, the homicide rate for England and Wales was still a remarkably low 0.67, whereas the rate in the United States was 7.59 (Killias 1990, p. 171). The U.S. rate was thus 11.3 times as high as the English rate. Therefore, England's homicide rate relative to that of the United States was the same or even slightly worse after fifty years of strict gun control.

Closer to home, the same sort of comparison can be made between the United States and an even more culturally similar nation. Canada has had a national handgun registration system since the early 1920s and further tightened restrictions considerably in 1977 (Bruce–Briggs 1976; U.S. Library of Congress 1981, p. 15). In 1919, the estimated U.S. homicide rate of 9.5 was 13.8 times as large as Canada's 0.69. By 1971, the U.S. rate of 8.50 was only 4.29 times as large as Canada's 1.98 (Archer and Gartner 1984). After the 1977 restrictions went into effect, the ratio was still lower. The average 1983–1986 homicide rate was 2.60 in Canada and 7.59 in the United States, yielding a ratio of 2.92 (Killias 1990, p. 171). As in Great Britain, after Canada implemented its more stringent gun controls, its homicide rate advantage over the United States actually decreased.

These comparisons could be multiplied, but to little purpose. They are not made to buttress a claim that gun controls cause homicide to increase. Pairwise comparisons of arbitrarily selected jurisdictions are useless for judging the impact of gun controls on violence. Rather, the examples demonstrate that these commonly compared foreign nations with strict gun controls had lower violence rates *before* controls were implemented, and that one therefore cannot conclude from such simple cross-national comparisons that stricter gun controls reduced violence.

A City-Level Study of Gun Control Impact

The following analysis of gun law effects builds on the models of city violence rates described in Chapter 5, where the focus was on the effects of gun ownership on violence rates. Now the focus shifts to the effects of gun laws on gun ownership levels and on violence rates. (This section is adapted from Kleck and Patterson 1991.) Only a few additional methodological points need to be made about this analysis.

The dependent variables are the rates of homicide, suicide, fatal gun accidents, robbery, aggravated assault, rape, and burglary. All but the burglary rate are rates of violence. Burglary is a generally nonviolent crime rarely committed with guns. Because it is a crime of stealth in which guns are rarely necessary to complete the crime, it should not be affected much by gun laws. It therefore can serve as a useful test in detecting spurious or coincidental associations between violence rates and gun laws. For example, if a gun law were as strongly associated negatively with burglary as with murder, it would suggest that rather than the law having a causal effect on murder, it might merely be associated with some extraneous, omitted variable(s) which affects crime in general, regardless of gun involvement.

Table 10.3 lists the gun law variables, provides descriptive statistics, and gives their sources. Corresponding information on the rest of the variables was presented in Table 5.5. The following four sources were used for gun law coding, in order of importance, most important first: U.S. BATF 1980, Jones and Ray 1980, Blose and Cook 1980, and Ronhovde and Sugars 1982. Multiple sources were used wherever possible because each source provided some information the others did not, and each served as a reliability check on the others. When sources conflicted, statute books were consulted.

Both state laws and city ordinances were coded. Every major category of existing gun law (19 of them) that could have affected violence rates in 1980 was included in the analysis. The philosophy guiding coding of the gun law variables was to code them in such a way that each variable would measure the presence or absence of a given form of regulation, regardless of what other elements might have accompanied it in a given statute or ordinance, and regardless of the governmental level that imposed the restriction. Thus a variable was coded 1 if the form of regulation applied in 1980 to a given city, either due to a city ordinance or because the city was located in a state with such law, whether the law applied to all types of guns or, as was usually the case, only to handguns; the city was coded 0 otherwise. A single ordinance or statute therefore might result in a city being coded 1 on two or three different gun law variables.

Although Chapter 8 described the major forms of gun control, the coding of the gun law variables requires some explanation. The variables were constructed in such a way that any city subject to a gun license law was also, by definition, subject to purchase permit requirements, since existing license laws all include as a component a requirement that a license be presented in order to buy guns from licensed dealers, in addition to requiring a license for home possession of guns. On the other hand, a city could be subject to a purchase permit requirement without requiring a license for home possession of firearms.

Cities were coded as being subject to waiting periods on gun purchases only if the law specified a particular minimum time period before a buyer could receive a gun. They did not receive such a coding merely because a wait of some length was necessitated by the time associated with the processing of an application or permit to purchase.

Gun registration was liberally defined to include any record-keeping system by which some governmental unit maintained records that linked specific guns to specific owners, beyond the decentralized records mandated by federal law. This could include either the fairly rare systems in which all gun owners were required to register their ownership of all existing guns, or the more common systems in which retail sales of guns were recorded and the records forwarded to some centralized governmental archive.

Penalties were considered to be "mandatory" for illegal carrying or for felonies committed a gun if the statutory language somehow limited sentencing discretion (e.g., "*shall* impose a penalty of not less than . . ."). Laws coded under this standard as providing "mandatory" penalties did not necessarily eliminate use of probation, suspended sentences, assigning sentencing for gun violations to be served concurrently with sentences for other offenses, and so on. Methods for evading legislative intent are universally available, so no law ensures that penalties are imposed in a truly mandatory fashion (Chapter 8).

Cities were coded as subject to a state constitutional right to bear arms provision only if some language in the constitution specified an *individual* right to keep and bear arms. Provisions lacking such language were treated as if they conferred only a right to keep arms for the maintenance of a state militia, and states providing only for this limited right were treated the same as states lacking an arms-right provision of any kind.

It could be argued that levels of violence could influence how much gun control a city has, in addition to the reverse. If violence levels and the presence of gun laws had a simultaneous reciprocal relationship, a nonrecursive model would be called for. However, gun laws were not passed frequently enough for violence in 1979–1981 to have influenced the passage of any significant number of gun laws during the same period (see Jones and Ray 1980, Appendix III, re. the pace of gun law changes). Rather, the level of gun control strictness in 1979–1981 was almost entirely a cumulative product of legislative activity before 1979. Therefore, the relationship was not treated as a simultaneous one in this analysis.

The conditions under which one could tentatively conclude that gun laws reduce violence are as follows. If gun laws are effective, they should meet the following conditions: (1) have a significant negative association with the *gun* violence rate (e.g., the gun homicide rate), (2) have a significant negative association with the *total* violence rate (e.g., the total homicide rate), and, preferably, (3) have a weaker association with the *nongun* violence rate than with the gun rate.

If (1) is true, but not (2), it indicates that gun laws merely shift people from guns to nongun weapons, with no net reduction in deaths or crimes. If (2) is true, but not (1), one might infer that gun laws are merely associated with some omitted variable(s) that have an effect on total violence rates, but that gun laws themselves have no effect, since they should have their effects by, at minimum, reducing rates of violence committed with guns. If (1) and (2) are true, but (3) is not (i.e., if gun laws are as strongly negatively associated with nongun rates as with gun rates), interpretation is ambiguous. This pattern would suggest that either the law variable is nothing more than a correlate of some omitted variable that affects the violence rate, since there is no strong a priori reason why gun laws should reduce the rate of violent acts without guns, or the law does reduce acts of violence with guns, but is also a correlate of some omitted factor that reduces violent acts without guns as well. Interpretation is also ambiguous if (1) is true, (2) is not true, and the gun law was not significantly associated with the nongun violence rate. As noted, the first two circumstances would ordinarily suggest substitution of nongun means for guns, with no net effect on total violence; however, the fact that the gun law did not show any evidence of increasing the nongun violence rate would seem to contradict this interpretation. (Note that this logic is irrelevant to analyses of burglary and rape, since there were no data available to separately measure rates of gun and nongun rapes and burglaries.)

Findings

Effects of Gun Controls on Gun Ownership Levels. Some gun laws are supposed to indirectly affect violence rates by limiting gun ownership. The effects of 19 types of gun regulations on gun ownership levels are presented in the form of standardized LISREL coefficients in Table 10.4 and briefly summarized in the last panel of Table 10.5. It should be stressed that the effect of each gun restriction on gun ownership is estimated multiple times, once in each of seven violence rate models. Because the exact set of gun ownership indicators used varies from one model to the next (to avoid the previously mentioned problem of artifactual associations—see Chapter 5), it is possible for estimated effects of restrictions on gun ownership to vary from model to model.

Of the 19 gun laws, none showed consistent evidence of reducing gun ownership as measured in this study. Each law's effect on gun ownership was estimated seven times, but none of the laws showed a significant effect in a majority of the tests. Only two of the regulations, requiring a license to possess guns (LICENSE), and prohibiting possession by mentally ill persons (MENTAL), showed an apparent effect in even as many as three tests. Nevertheless, there is partial support for the view that these two measures may reduce gun ownership, presumably among "high-risk" segments of the population. Also, if our gun indicators primarily reflect criminal gun ownership, it is possible that some of the other gun laws may have an unmeasured effect on ownership in the general public but not among criminals.

Effects of Gun Controls on Violence Rates

Table 10.4 contains detailed results on this issue, which are then summarized in Table 10.5. Generally, the findings indicate that gun restrictions appear to exert no significant negative effect on total violence rates. Of 121 possible effects tested, only ten are solidly or partially consistent with a hypothesis of gun control effectiveness. Requiring a license to possess guns (LICENSE) appears to reduce fatal gun accidents. Requiring a permit to purchase guns (BYPERMIT) appears to reduce both gun and nongun homicide rates, yet paradoxically has no significant effect on the total homicide rate. The apparent effect was greater for nongun homicides than for gun homicides, undercutting a conclusion that the law itself reduces homicide.

Requiring gun dealers to have a state or local license (DEALER) appears to reduce both gun and total aggravated assaults. This control *may* also reduce total suicides, though the relevant results are more questionable. Although the gun law variable is negatively related to both total and gun suicides, it is even more strongly related to *non*gun suicides than gun suicides. Laws that provide mandatory penalties for illegal gun carrying (MANDPEN) appear to reduce robbery rates (total, gun and nongun). Laws providing additional penalties, either mandatory (ADDONMND) or discretionary (ADDONDIS), for committing crimes with a gun generally seem to have no effect on violence rates. However, discretionary add-on penalties *may* decrease robbery rates, although results in this case are ambiguous because the regulation relates more strongly to nongun robberies than gun robberies. This finding, however, is strengthened in an analysis to be discussed later.

Not only did results rarely indicate that gun laws reduce total rates of violence, they also indicated that most laws do not even seem to reduce the use of guns or induce people to substitute other weapons in acts of violence. For the four types of violence for which data permit a distinction to be made between gun and nongun violence (70 tests), only 10 results indicate that gun restrictions reduced rates of gun violence. These are summarized in the second panel of Table 10.5, indicated by footnote *a*. Prohibitions on gun possession by mentally ill persons apparently reduce gun use in homicide without, however, affecting total homicide rates. Likewise, prohibitions on possession by criminals seem to reduce gun robberies and gun assaults, but without reducing total robberies or total aggravated assaults, and a mandatory penalty for illegal carrying seems to reduce gun homicides without reducing total homicides. On the other hand, these controls did not appear to increase nongun robberies, assaults, or murders, making it unclear whether there was complete substitution, and leaving open the interpretation that the measures work. Similarly ambiguous results were obtained for the impact on suicide rates of prohibitions of gun possession by mentally ill persons.

Interactions with Enforcement Level

It could be argued that gun laws are not always given a fair chance to work because in many places they are not adequately enforced. Kates, for example, has argued that "we could substantially reduce gun crime by simply enforcing our present laws" (1990, p. 63). Perhaps greater resources devoted specifically to gun law enforcement could make some gun laws effective.

This idea was tested by forming multiplicative interaction terms between each gun law variable and a measure of police enforcement effort, the number of weapons arrests per 100 sworn police officers (WEAPARST), and including these terms in the models of violence rates. The resulting estimates confirmed the previous results. The coefficients for the interaction terms were almost never negative and significant, indicating that the effects of gun laws apparently did not depend on the level of police enforcement effort, at least not based on the measure of effort used and not within the range of enforcement effort currently exerted in large U.S. cities. Generally, existing laws showed no violence-reducing effects, regardless of police enforcement effort. Of 121 possible interaction effects tested, only two suggested possible gun law effectiveness when accompanied by sufficient police enforcement effort. Laws providing discretionary add-on penalties for committing crimes with a gun appear to reduce the total robbery rate in cities where police made many weapons arrests. Also, purchase permits *may* have such a contingent effect on the total murder rate—the law appears to reduce gun murder, as well as total murder, but had an even larger apparent effect on nongun murder (results not reported here but available from the author). Given the large number of hypothesis tests performed, these results could easily be due to chance. However, the result regarding add-on penalties does roughly comport with sophisticated research indicating that a law providing higher mandatory penalties for robbery with a gun did reduce both gun and total robbery (McPheters et al. 1984).

It should be noted that these findings are based solely on a measure of police enforcement effort, and do not necessarily reflect effort or emphasis by prosecutors and other relevant CJS personnel. They cannot test a thesis that says gun laws would work if they resulted in prison sentences for violators often enough. Further, FBI data on arrests for so-called "Part II" offenses are flawed as total arrest counts, because of the "hierarchy rule" for counting arrests. When someone is arrested on multiple charges, the arrest is classified only according to the most serious charge—no arrest is counted for any lesser charge. For less serious crimes, this can cause a substantial undercount if arrests frequently occur in connection with other offenses. This is often the case with weapons violations. For example, violations of the Illinois law requiring a license to possess a gun were accompanied by other charges 91% of the time. On the other hand, the accompanying charge was most often another weapons charge, usually unlawful use. In such a case, the arrest would still get counted as a weapons arrest. An arrest with a weapons charge accompanied by a Part I charge would get counted only as a Part I arrest. If it were accompanied only by a Part II charge, an arrest would get counted in the weapons category only if the law enforcement agency making the arrest considered the weapons offense to be the most serious one. FBI rules leave this judgment up to the arresting agency (Florida, no date, p. 115).

Only 14% of the charges accompanying no-license charges were for Part I crimes that would definitely have caused the weapons charge to go uncounted, whereas another 12% were higher ranking Part II offenses, and 3% were for other Part II offenses that at least some agencies are likely to consider more serious (tabulated from Bordua et al. 1985, pp. 99, 103, A.49–A.51, A.54). Thus, 13–26% ($0.907 \times 0.140 = 0.13$; $0.907 \times 0.288 = 0.26$) of the no-ID charges would have gone uncounted due to the hierarchy rule.

The enforcement variable is primarily a measure of unlawful carrying arrests, if Illinois is typical of the United States. In that state, 87% of weapons violations arrests are for "unlawful use" (Bordua et al. 1985, p. 68), which essentially encompasses carrying (Bendis and Balkin 1979). The variable would still serve as a useful indicator of police enforcement of gun laws in general if enforcement of other gun laws were highly correlated with carry law enforcement. However, if enforcement has to reach some minimum threshold level to begin to have an impact, it is possible that this level has not yet been reached for any of the other gun control measures. Therefore, the conclusions regarding enforcement may not be generalizable beyond carry laws.

Nevertheless, it is questionable how much the average city can do to achieve whatever minimum enforcement level is necessary to realize gun control effects. Few municipal governments have surplus revenues or untapped sources of further revenue sufficient to radically expand police services; indeed, many are being forced to cut their police forces back (Walker 1989, p. 133). And it is by no means obvious that police are inclined to shift their existing resources away from other activities and toward increased gun law enforcement, or at least to the degree needed to achieve enforcement levels even higher than the highest levels currently being attained. Nevertheless, Chapter 11 suggests some ways in which existing resources might be used to increase the impact of police enforcement of gun laws.

Collinearity among the Gun Law Variables

As previously mentioned, some of the gun laws overlap somewhat. Also cities that have one regulation should be more likely to have others, to the extent that passage of any of the measures depends partially on general public support for gun control. Consequently there is collinearity among the gun law variables. This could cause inflation of standard errors and thereby bias hypothesis tests in favor of the null hypothesis. To address this problem the violence rate models were reestimated with just four gun law variables thought to be especially likely to show effects, since they were fairly strong measures—licenses, purchase permits, handgun possession bans, and bans on sale of "Saturday Night Specials." This did reduce collinearity, but only one of the previous results was altered so as to support the hypothesis of gun control efficacy. With reduced collinearity, estimates indicated that purchase permits *may* reduce total murders. Gun ownership still showed no positive effect on any of the violence rates. Models with this reduced number of gun law variables were also estimated using the enforcement interaction terms described above, but with uniformly negative results. (Results not shown, but available from the author.)

Discussion

These results generally do not support the idea that existing gun controls reduce city gun ownership or violence rates. No law showed consistent evidence of an effect of gun laws on gun ownership levels (see first panel of Table 10.5). For many gun regulations, such as carry controls or add-on penalties, this is not surprising, since they were not intended to reduce gun ownership. And other controls may operate to restrict ownership only among "high-risk" groups such as criminals or alcoholics. However, results discussed later indicate that gun controls generally fail to reduce gun use in acts of violence, undercutting the idea that gun ownership was reduced even in these limited subsets of the population. One reasonable explanation for this failure would be the huge size of the U.S. gun stock. With over 200 million guns in private hands (Chapter 2), it is difficult to keep guns away from anyone who truly wants one.

Of 121 tests of the direct effects of 19 different major types of gun law on seven different categories of crime and violence, only four tests unambiguously supported the gun law efficacy hypothesis, with six others providing ambiguous support (see second panel of Table 10.5). Thus, 92% of the results indicate no impact of gun control. Note that one would expect a similar number of "significant" hypothesis test results just on the basis of chance, given the very large number of tests. However, it is significant that one of the four clearly supportive results indicated that mandatory penalties for illegal carrying of firearms reduces robbery rates. This result thereby confirms the robbery findings of three prior studies supporting the efficacy of gun control. Beha (1977), Deutsch and Alt (1977), and Pierce and Bowers (1981) all concluded that the Bartley–Fox law in Massachusetts reduced robbery rates (but see Hay and McCleary 1979). Likewise, add-on penalties for committing felonies with a gun appear to reduce robbery, as indicated by the findings of McPheters et al. (1984). Thus the present findings confirm some of the occasional positive findings as well as the more usual negative findings of prior studies.

Carry laws with mandatory penalties appear to reduce robbery, presumably by deterring the carrying of concealed weapons in public places. Why should carry laws work while others apparently do not? One possible reason is that carry laws are not so seriously weakened by the substitution of long guns for handguns (discussed in Chapter 3). Robberies are most frequently committed in public places like a street or highway (U.S. FBI 1989, p. 19). In such places, rifles and shotguns are not easily substituted for handguns by would-be gun carriers. Even when long guns are reduced in size by sawing off most of their barrels and stocks, they are still too cumbersome for most people to routinely carry on a daily basis. Thus, although persons planning a robbery could substitute a sawed-off long gun, the more common opportunistic robber takes advantage of easier robbery targets that present themselves in the course of his daily activities (Conklin 1972, p. 68). A sawed-off long gun could not be used in this sort of unplanned robbery unless the robber had been routinely carrying such a weapon. Thus, in connection with robbery, the benefits of deterring some handgun carrying are not entirely counterbalanced by the costs of substitution of more lethal weaponry. Further, as previously noted, carry laws seem to receive the greatest enforcement effort by police, accounting for the majority of weapons-related arrests (Bordua et al. 1985).

It is doubtful that the mandatory penalty feature of these carry laws is the key to their success, since the penalties are not really mandatory in practice, as there are always loopholes that prosecutors and judges can and do exploit when they think the mandated penalty is excessive (Chapter 8). Nevertheless, carry laws with mandatory penalties seem to reduce robbery, possibly because the mandatory penalty feature may serve as an indicator of a strong level of support, among both lawmakers and law enforcers like police administrators and prosecutors, for fairly rigorous enforcement of carry laws.

Discretionary add-on penalties for committing crimes with guns appear to reduce robbery, while mandatory ones do not. This sort of sentence enhancement may work better when it is discretionary because it increases penalty severity without inadvertently causing reductions in the certainty of punishment. When the add-on penalties are not mandatory, prosecutors retain their ability to induce defendants to plead guilty in exchange for lesser sentences, thereby maintaining conviction rates at higher levels. Further, even though defendants who do not plead guilty receive penalties more severe than those who do plead guilty, the average penalties imposed on defendants as a whole can still be higher than they would be without the law.

Another type of gun law that appeared to have some beneficial effect was a somewhat surprising one. Laws requiring a state or local license to be a firearms dealer were negatively related to both the total and gun suicide rates, and to both the total and gun aggravated assault rates. Because dealers everywhere in the United States are required to have a federal gun dealer license, additional state or local licensing requirements would seem redundant. However, where these requirements are more stringent than federal requirements, they may reduce the number of convenient retail gun outlets. For example, Cincinnati's high dealer licensing fee apparently was sufficient to displace all handgun dealers to the city's suburbs (Blose and Cook 1980, p. 20). Thus, the measure might reduce casual acquisition of guns among persons not sufficiently motivated to seek out less convenient stores or who lack the interpersonal connections needed to get a gun through nonretail sources. Although results summarized in the first panel of Table 10.5 do not support the idea that this law reduces gun ownership levels in general, it may affect a small subset of weakly motivated prospective buyers. Thus, this type of measure may have an effect solely on suicide and assault rates because these violent acts may disproportionately involve such weakly motivated people. On the other hand, given the large number of gun law efficacy hypotheses tested, these may be nothing more than chance findings.

Perhaps what is most encouraging about the pattern of findings concerning which gun laws are effective (Table 10.5) is their congruence with the findings of the best prior research. Previous research generally has failed to find evidence that gun laws reduce total (gun and nongun) violence rates, although some of the laws may reduce rates of gun violence while increasing nongun violence by at least an equal amount (see the studies in Tables 10.1 and 10.2). The present research generally points to the exact same conclusion. Previous research on suicide rates has found that laws prohibiting gun possession by mentally ill persons could reduce the rate of *gun* suicides (Sommers 1984); the present research found the same thing. However, the present research went beyond this previous work and also found that this law had no apparent effect on *total* suicide rates, suggesting that prospective suicide attempters merely substituted other lethal means of suicide when guns are not available. This replicates the findings of Geisel and his colleagues (1969), which indicated that an index of overall gun control strictness was significantly and negatively related to the gun suicide rate but not to the total suicide rate. It likewise confirmed the findings of Lester (1988b) and Rich et al. (1990), who also found gun laws negatively related to gun suicide rates, but not to total suicide rates. One of the few gun laws showing some (albeit very mixed) evidence of effectiveness in prior research was a mandatory penalty carry law, the Bartley–Fox law; the present research indicates that such laws can reduce robbery.

Finally, the present study found partial support for the claim that laws establishing discretionary add-on penalties for committing felonies with a gun may reduce total robbery rates; time series research by McPheters and his colleagues (1984) has also found support for this claim. The more debatable present findings concerning the impact of dealer licensing on assault and suicide rates have no parallel in prior research. Nevertheless, the many specific points of correspondence between the present findings and those of previous studies using very different methods and samples increase confidence in the present findings.

There were no distinct patterns concerning what forms of violence can most easily be reduced through gun control, since most gun regulations apparently do not have any effect on total rates of any form of violence. The nearest thing to an exception would be robbery, since it was the only type of violence possibly affected by more than one type of control—two firms of regulation may affect robbery rates (second panel, Table 10.5).

Where a gun law was negatively associated with a violence rate, it might be hypothesized that this was a spurious association due to the effect of a population's antiviolence sentiments—nonviolent values might reduce violence rates while also encouraging passage of gun controls. However, the individual-level models of support for gun control tested in Chapter 9 indicated that nonviolent attitudes are not significantly related to support for gun control, so this hypothesis can be tentatively rejected.

Limitations

This analysis is subject to the following limitations. First, the models did not include any measure of how strictly license and permit laws are administered, e.g., how narrowly authorities interpret rules defining which applicants are qualified, as distinct from how much effort is put into apprehending and punishing violators. Second, analysts always need to be skeptical about restrictions used to achieve identifiability in structural equation models. The key identification restrictions needed to model the assumed reciprocal relationship between gun ownership and violence rates were the exclusion of gun magazine subscription rates and hunting license rates from the violence equations. Interest in hunting and other gun-related sports was assumed to affect gun ownership rates but not to directly affect violence rates. Some have argued that such interests may reflect, or even generate, proviolent attitudes, but Krug (1968), Bordua (1986), and Eskridge (1986) all found county hunting license rates to have small-to-moderate *negative* associations with violence rates. Third, prior discussion notwithstanding, one might still argue that there is a simultaneous reciprocal relationship between violence rates and gun regulation, with violence rates affecting whether gun laws are passed, as well as the reverse. Fourth, this study covered only cities. Although most of the violent crime in the United States occurs in cities, perhaps gun laws work differently in other areas. However, given the higher rate of gun ownership in rural areas, it would seem that resistance to gun laws in the general public, and indifference or hostility toward them among law enforcement personnel, would be even higher there than in cities, and gun control effectiveness correspondingly lower.

Conclusions

Why do 19 different major varieties of gun control laws appear, with few possible exceptions, to have no impact on any of the types of violence that frequently involve guns? Many explanations are suggested by both the present results and those of prior research. First, some gun laws are intended to have their effects by reducing gun ownership levels, either in the general population or, more usually, within various high-risk subsets. If the gun ownership measure used here is interpreted as a measure of gun ownership in the general public, results indicate that gun laws do not affect general gun ownership. This should not be all that surprising, since most gun laws are not intended to have such an effect. On the other hand, if the gun ownership measure primarily reflects ownership among high-risk persons, as seems likely, the results indicate that gun ownership within high-risk segments of the population also is not affected by gun laws. Thus, some gun laws may fail simply because they fail to achieve their proximate goal of reducing gun ownership. If supporters of these gun laws intended that they produce a reduction in gun ownership, then the laws were failures in this regard. On the other hand, if opponents of these generally mild measures feared that they would impair the ability of the general citizenry to acquire guns, their fears are not confirmed by these results.

The Chapter 5 results indicated that gun ownership levels do not have a net positive effect on crime and violence. Consequently, the underlying premise of many gun laws is not supported. They may fail simply because, even if they did achieve the proximate goal of reducing gun ownership, this reduction would have no net negative impact on total violence rates. At best, the laws may only influence choice of weaponry in violent events, without affecting their overall frequency.

On the other hand, some gun regulations do not necessarily rely on an assumption that gun ownership levels affect crime. For example, carry laws are intended to make guns less immediately available in public places rather than to reduce overall gun ownership levels, and assume only that immediate availability of guns is relevant to violence rates. This may explain why some carry laws appear to reduce robbery.

It may be that gun laws have a strictly short-term effect on violence rates when they are passed, and that the effect then fades. Most of the laws that were evaluated were implemented well in the past, so this possibility cannot be rejected.

It is also possible that some special combination of gun laws would work even where any one by itself does not. Law A may not work unless it exists in combination with laws B and C. As a practical matter, this hypothesis is impossible to falsify because there are many thousands of possible combinations of gun controls. One could test for the impact of each combination and a large number of coefficients would inevitably be "statistically significant" even in the absence of any actual causal effects, due to the enormous number of hypothesis tests conducted. With 18 different measures (excluding right-to bear-arms provisions), there are 262,143 different combinations possible, for each of six violence models. This would not only make the effort impractical, but the results of over 1.6 million hypothesis tests would be uninterpretable. Nevertheless, it is possible that a particularly well-integrated package of gun controls would work better than the combinations that characterize most U.S. jurisdictions, which are commonly rather haphazard amalgams of controls cobbled together piecemeal over a period of decades, often in response to very transitory political concerns.

Most gun laws regulate only handguns, or regulate handguns more stringently than the more numerous long guns such as rifles or shotguns. This permits the substitution of relatively unregulated guns for the more heavily regulated ones. As has been seen, this common feature of U.S. gun laws can have the undesirable effect of encouraging some prospective gun abusers to substitute the more lethal long guns. The implication for the homicide rate is that the beneficial and harmful effects could either cancel out or, worse, the harmful substitution effect could outweigh the beneficial effects and produce a net increase in mortality (Chapter 3).

Finally, one can always argue that no matter how severe current measures are, stronger measures are needed. The level of strictness of firearms regulation varies wildly from place to place in the United States. In a few cities such as New York City and Washington, D.C. local regulations are about as stringent as in Great Britain, whereas in many other cities regulations are very lenient. The preceding analysis indicated that even fairly strong measures such as banning sales of "Saturday Night Specials" and de facto bans on handgun possession did not appear to reduce any violence rates. Perhaps even these measures were not strong enough. Maybe a still stronger "dose" of gun control would work where weaker doses have not. To assess this, one can evaluate what is arguably the strictest gun law in the nation.

The Toughest Gun Law in America: A Case Study

No U.S. jurisdiction has ever completely banned the private possession of all firearms. The closest approximation has been a ban on private possession of handguns. No large U.S. city has done this—Washington, D.C. basically banned any new handgun acquisitions, although allowing legal handgun owners to continue owning. Morton Grove, Illinois (1980 population 23,675) and a number of other small towns have banned handgun possession. Small towns, however, have so few gun crimes that it would be difficult to achieve any reductions no matter how effective the measure might be. For example, the year before its new law, Morton Grove had no homicides, five gun robberies, and three aggravated assaults with guns; for all practical purposes, it had no gun violence problem to reduce. Therefore, as large a city as possible should be evaluated, to give the maximum opportunity for a crime-reducing effect to be observed.

The largest town to totally (or almost totally) ban handgun possession as of 1990 was Evanston, Illinois. Evanston is a suburb of Chicago with a 1980 population of 73,431. The Evanston City Council passed a handgun ban ordinance on September 13, 1982, and it took effect on the 28th. Thus, the full impact of the law should have been evident in 1983, the first full year of the ordinance's operation. The ordinance prohibited possession of handguns within the city limits of Evanston by anyone except law enforcement and private security guards, some gun collectors, federally licensed gun dealers, members of the city's one licensed gun club, and actors requiring guns for theatrical performances. A survey the previous year had indicated that 10% of Evanston adults owned a handgun (*Chicago Tribune* 9-14-82, p. 1–3), compared to 15% of U.S. adults (Table 2.4). Thus, there were some handguns to be banned in Evanston, though not as many as elsewhere in the nation.

Table 10.6 shows the crime rate trends before and after passage of the ordinance, in Evanston and in comparison areas. For the three crime categories that involve gun use with any frequency, the data indicate that Evanston experienced increases in all three categories from 1982 to 1983. However, the percentage change was trivial for assault and the 100% increase in homicide merely reflected an increase from one killing in 1982 to two in 1983. Although armed robbery declined slightly, total robbery increased. Further, the slight decline in armed robbery was smaller than that experienced by the United States as a whole and by other cities of similar size, which had not banned handguns.

The 1982–1983 shift may be distorted by the fact that the last 3 months of 1982 were after the ordinance went into effect. Also, 1984 seemed to show some crime decreases not evident in 1983, suggesting a possible lagged effect. Therefore, 1981, all of which preceded the new ordinance, is compared with 1984. The 1981–1984 change figures also indicate that Evanston experienced statistically trivial increases in homicide and aggravated assault, and a slight decrease in armed robbery. The only change from the previous comparisons is that now a decrease in total robbery is evident. Although similarly sized cities were experiencing a 19% decrease and the United States was experiencing a 21% drop, Evanston experienced a slightly larger 24% decrease. A 3–5 percentage point difference in robbery rate changes could be produced by as little as 6 fewer robberies in Evanston (there were 193 total robberies in 1982), so this can be regarded as a trivial difference—Evanston experienced about the same decrease in robbery as places that did not ban handguns. In sum, both the 1982–1983 and 1981–1984 comparisons indicate that Evanston experienced no discernible crime reductions that could be attributed to the ban on handgun possession.

The Evanston experience thus suggests that even the toughest gun law on the books failed to reduce violent crime. Unlike Morton Grove, this failure to detect an effect cannot be attributed to the absence of any violent crime to reduce—although Evanston had little murder, it had nearly 200 robberies (60–100 of them armed) and a similar number of aggravated assaults in the years before the ordinance. It is possible the law will take more time to show an effect, as more handguns are turned in, but only 116 handguns were handed in or confiscated in all of 1983 and 1984 (Evanston 1986), in a city with over 5000 admitted handgun owners and an unknown additional number of other owners. It is highly unlikely confiscations and turn-ins will increase over time. The ordinance is only lightly enforced: only 74 charges of violating the ordinance were placed in all of 1983–1985 (Evanston 1986). Perhaps more aggressive enforcement might make a difference, but the Evanston police announced that they intended to rely on voluntary compliance to enforce the law—the deputy police chief publicly stated that "police would not actively search out handguns". Finally, evidence of an effect may have been blurred because the ordinance was preceded by "several years of increasingly stringent gun ordinances" (*Chicago Tribune* 9-14-82, p. 1–3), which might have produced gradual crime reductions before 1982. However, Table 10.6 indicates that crime decreases beginning in the late 1970s in Evanston were mirrored by similar decreases in comparison areas, making it harder to attribute the changes to even multiple increases in Evanston's gun control stringency.

It has also been argued that this sort of measure fails because it is local, and that guns from more lenient jurisdictions "leak" into the stricter jurisdictions. This argument is misleading with regard to any kind of possession ban, since the illegality and risks of possessing firearms in a restrictive jurisdiction are unaffected by the presence or absence of controls in surrounding areas—only controls over acquisition of guns are affected by interjurisdictional leakage. Thus, although Evanston's ban on handgun sales would be affected by the local nature of its controls, the efficacy of the possession ban itself would not be affected.

Leaving the Evanston ordinance, gun control advocates have argued that local controls over the acquisition of guns are undercut by the leakage problem, and federal measures are therefore called for (e.g., Newton and Zimring 1969). The present research could not assess federal controls since they apply equally to all cities and thus do not vary across the units. Nevertheless, prior research on existing federal regulations has generally found them to be ineffective (Zimring 1975; Magaddino and Medoff 1984). On the other hand, these controls are very weak, loophole-ridden measures. Consequently, it is possible that stronger federal measures could accomplish what weaker measures have failed to do. Some of the few measures found in this study to be effective were ones that should not be affected by the leakage problem and therefore should be just as effective at a state or local level as at the federal level. Like possession bans, laws providing for mandatory penalties for illegal carrying of guns or for add-on penalties for committing crimes with guns are not affected by the leakage problem because the legal risks of unlawfully carrying or possessing a gun or using it criminally in a given area are the same regardless of whether other areas have similar measures. "Leakage" is an issue relevant to controls on the acquisition of guns, rather than their use (Blose and Cook 1980, p. 19).

Making global summary assessments of a very large body of findings is necessarily somewhat subjective, since it can sometimes depend on whether one views a glass as half empty or half full. An optimist who believed that all or most gun laws reduce violence would be disappointed by these results—ten supportive results out of 121 is less than impressive. On the other hand, to cynics who started with the assumption that criminal laws are passed for political reasons having little to do with crime control effectiveness, ten instances of gun control effectiveness could look surprisingly positive. Although the results are certainly generally negative for the violence control effectiveness of gun control, the significance of the few positive results should not be overlooked. There do appear to be a few gun controls that work, so there is some hope for a rational gun control policy, organized around gun owner licensing or purchase permits (or some functional equivalent), stronger controls over illegal carrying, and perhaps stricter local dealer licensing. Since these measures are both popular (Chapter 9) and low in financial costs (e.g. Blose and Cook 1980), they may well represent sensible public policy.

Nevertheless, favorites of the general public and the gun control advocacy groups, such as waiting periods and gun registration, clearly do not work. On the other hand, the favored gun control strategy of the National Rifle Association, mandatory add-on penalties for committing crimes with a gun, also is clearly ineffective.

Gun Decontrol: A Case Study

Most case studies of changes in gun law are studies of increases in gun control restrictiveness. However, there is as much to be learned about the efficacy of gun controls from decreases in strictness as there is from increases. The following is a brief case study of Florida's experience with easing access to gun carry permits.

Prior to 1987, Florida had a county-administered, highly discretionary, "may issue" state carry permit system. Each county commission *could* issue a carry license to any adult "of good moral character," but was not required by law to do so (Florida 1976). Commissioners (or their designees) were free to interpret "good moral character" as liberally or restrictively as they wished, so there was considerable room for variation across counties in permit issuance. In most urban counties, where the bulk of the crime was committed, permits were almost never issued. For example, in Hillsborough (Tampa) County, only 25 permits were in effect before the law was changed, only 31 in Pinellas (St. Petersburg) County (*St. Petersburg Times* 1-17-88, p. 1A), and just 23 were in effect in Broward (Ft. Lauderdale) County (*Miami Herald* 5-15-88, p. 14A). On the other hand, if Florida's experience followed that of California, which had a similar county-administered discretionary permit system (*San Francisco Examiner* 9-25-86), rural counties probably issued permits at a much higher per capita rate.

As of October 1, 1987, the state law was changed to a uniform, state-administered, largely nondiscretionary, "shall issue" permit system. Unless applicants had disqualifying attributes, the state was required to issue a license if the applicants submitted the $125 licensing fee (for a 3-year license), got themselves fingerprinted, and properly filled out the required forms. A license would be denied if the applicant was a nonresident, minor, convicted felon, drug addict, alcoholic, mental incompetent, or had been committed to a mental institution. The permits did not authorize carrying in bars or other similar "places of nuisance," courtrooms, jails, government meeting places, schools, or colleges (Florida 1987).

Critics of the law had feared that the expected increase in the number of legally authorized gun carriers would result in increased acts of violence involving permit holders, with angry motorists shooting it out over fender-benders on the freeway and the like. Certainly a large number of permits were issued, though far fewer than Florida authorities had anticipated. The Florida Department of State had forecast that 100,000–130,000 applications would be submitted, but as of late July, 1988, less than 40,000 applications had been submitted, and only 34,122 permits had been granted. This was less than 0.3% of Florida's population. Thus, although millions of Floridians were eligible for permits, apparently relatively few wanted one badly enough to go through the required trouble and expense of applying.

Florida changed its methods of compiling crime statistics in 1988, making it impossible to analyze statewide crime trends after the gun law's effective date. However, local data are available for Dade (Miami) County that are superior to any that would have been available statewide. Dade is an especially strong test case. It had the highest violence rate of any Florida county in 1987 (Florida 1988, pp. 58–82), so if increasing the legal carrying of guns was going to have an adverse impact anywhere, it should have done so in Dade County. The Metro-Dade Police Department gathered unusually pertinent and comprehensive data because its Director was especially worried about the impact of the new law. The number of carry permits in Dade County jumped from about 1300 before the new law to 8150 by May 5, 1988. Police officers were required to fill out a form every time they were involved in an incident involving a gun in *any* way, even if it involved neither an arrest nor a violent act. Over a period from February through May 6, 1988, 743 gun-related incidents were recorded. Of these, only six involved verified carry permit holders. Of these six, two involved use by security guards on duty, and one involved a store worker who thwarted a robbery with his gun. The three remaining charges involved some type of crime. One case involved a crime unrelated to the gun—a permit holder was arrested for drunk driving and his gun was impounded. The second case involved an inadvertent technical violation of the carry law—a woman forgot she had her gun in her purse and brought it into an airport, where even permit-holder carrying is forbidden. The only intentional crime of any kind involving a permitted gun was another technical violation of the carry law—a man was arrested for trying to bring his gun into a court building (*Miami Herald* 5-15-88, pp. 1A, 14A). Thus, over a 3-month period, in the most violent county in the state, after a six-fold increase in the number of carry permit holders, there was not a single known case of a permit holder committing an act of violence with a gun.

It is not hard to imagine why liberalizing Florida's carry law had no apparent impact on violence. First, few people wanted to get carry permits. Second, people who were carrying illegally before the change presumably continued to carry, legally or not, after the change. The only people who should have changed their rate of carrying were those who were unwilling to carry illegally before the change, but who were willing and able to get carry permits after the change. This would be some subset of the 130,000 who got permits. Third, among this "affected" group, the Dade County evidence indicates that there were apparently very few who were willing to commit acts of criminal violence. This is presumably because most violent people were either disqualified from getting permits under the new law, by virtue of having a felony conviction or falling into one of the other forbidden categories, or because they voluntarily refrained from applying for a permit. Although one newspaper proclaimed in a headline that "Gun Permits Soar Through Loopholes," the text of the article indicated that only 68 of 1981 permit applicants in a five-county area had ever been even arrested for a crime, and only 50 had been found guilty of any crime (including 25 who had "final judgment withheld"). The article documented only six cases (⅓ of 1% of the applicants) in which the applicant had been found guilty of a crime involving use or even threat of force, and only three of these (⅙ of 1%) involved a gun. And of these three applicants, only one had actually been granted a permit (the other two applications were still being processed) (*St. Petersburg Times* 1-17-88, pp. 1-A, 17-A). In sum, very few people officially known to be violent got permits. Therefore, the law did not change the legal status of gun carrying for more than a handful of people likely to use their guns for an unlawful violent purpose.

Untried Gun Control Strategies

Most of the measures that appear to be effective in reducing violence are already in place in much of the nation. Those places that do not currently have them might benefit from adopting them. However, for the rest of the nation, if violence is to be reduced through gun controls, this will have to entail new control measures, perhaps including measures never implemented anywhere. The impact of measures not yet tried cannot be estimated, but discussion of relevant issues and some pertinent evidence is worthwhile.

National Prohibition of Private Possession of Guns

This strategy was addressed in Chapter 8.

Banning Further Production and Importation

This proposal falls into the category of closing the corral door after the horses have escaped. There are already over 200 million guns in private hands, most of which can easily be kept in working condition indefinitely. Further, the number needed to serve all criminal purposes is only a tiny fraction of this number. In an imaginative effort to get around this difficulty, Zimring (1976) proposed the "new guns hypothesis." He noted that the guns seized from criminals were disproportionately fairly new guns, hinting that criminal use of guns could somehow be reduced merely by slowing the flow of new guns into the stock. Somehow, some criminals either would not be able to get older guns in the absence of newer ones, or would not find older guns suitable for their purposes. The logical flaw in this implied argument is that there is nothing about new guns that makes them inherently more useful for criminal purposes. Indeed, in one respect newer guns are *less* suitable for criminal purposes. Guns first sold after October 1968, when the Gun Control Act of 1968 went into effect, are easier for authorities to trace than older guns (Zimring 1976), and criminals say they prefer guns that are untraceable (Wright and Rossi 1986, p. 163). Criminals do not use new guns because only new guns can be used in crime or because these are the only guns they can get, but rather because criminals are mostly young people who have been of a gun-owning age for only a short period of time. Indeed, all young people, both criminal and noncriminal, disproportionately own newer versions of almost any consumer durable—very likely a high percentage of their refrigerators and televisions are also comparatively new. Nor is there any evidence that criminals are able to get only new guns; the fact that new guns are easy to get does not imply that older guns are hard to get. Consistent with these arguments, the flow of new guns into the stock of guns has no apparent impact on U.S. violence rates (Kleck 1984a).

Banning Manufacture of Ammunition

Unlike guns, ammunition does not last indefinitely. The powder in gun ammunition eventually becomes unusable after 20 or more years, and can become unreliable much earlier. Therefore, some have suggested a ban on the manufacture of further ammunition as a substitute for gun bans. If no further ammunition were made, the existing supply would be used up or become unusable, so eventually it would not matter how many guns there were. Since many handguns and long guns have identical calibers and use identical or similar ammunition, however, this scheme could work only if it applied to ammunition used in any gun type, not just handguns.

The main technical problem with this scheme is that ammunition is even easier to manufacture at home than guns. This is not even a matter of a hypothetical future—already millions of gun owners handload their own ammunition at home, and these owners alone could easily meet the very limited national need for workable cartridges. Given how rarely criminals (or gun-wielding victims) actually fire their guns (Chapters 2, 4 and 5), a dozen rounds replaced every few years would be ample for most criminal or defensive gun owners. Most of the materials in ammunition, such as lead bullets and brass cartridge casings, can be indefinitely recycled. The key item that cannot be reused is the powder. An ammunition ban with any hope of success would have to include a ban on powder, but adequate forms of gunpowder are also easy to home manufacture, and they are certainly easier to make than many widely manufactured illegal drugs or "moonshine" alcohol (Bruce-Briggs 1976; Kaplan 1979; Kates 1984a). The best one could hope for from this measure would be that some criminal gun users would be unable to either make or steal their own ammunition or locate anyone else willing to provide them with some.

Civil Liability for Unlawful Transfer of Guns

The following measure is both politically achievable and at least minimally enforceable. Serious federal gun control proposals have included provisions making persons who knowingly transfer guns to ineligible persons liable under civil law for harm done with the guns (Blose and Cook 1980). Even scholars otherwise skeptical of gun control have endorsed such measures (e.g., Kates 1990, p. 60). This type of measure is aimed at keeping guns away from ineligible persons, rather than attempting the hopeless task of reducing the total supply of guns or ammunition. It regulates all transfers of guns, not just those involving licensed dealers. It creates little cost or inconvenience to responsible gun owners and imposes little new cost on the criminal justice system. The costs of bringing civil suits against persons who knowingly transfer guns to ineligible persons is initially born largely by victims, but this cost in practice can be transferred to losing defendants, their insurance companies (when defendants have relevant insurance), and attorneys who work on a contingency fee basis, as is commonly the case with liability suits brought against gun manufacturers. The measure seeks to influence gun sellers who do not have an overwhelmingly strong motivation to evade its provisions, rather than trying to influence gun buyers such as enraged aggressors or frightened crime victims. Although some illegal transferors will have few assets to seize, others will have considerable assets. In any case, even people with few assets do not want to lose them. This measure would necessitate providing transferors with some means of establishing whether prospective recipients are legally eligible, an issue that is addressed in Chapter 11.

Other Forms of Control over Gun Purchases

Gun control supporters ask how anyone could object to gun owner license or purchase permit systems, which aim only at preventing criminals from getting guns legally. Opponents reply that these systems, along with gun registration, generate governmental lists of known gun owners that could be used to seize guns at some future date. There are ways in which the purposes of permit systems can be achieved without generating the lists to which organized gun owners object, including the federal "instant records check" explored by the Bush administration in 1989. This proposal is discussed in detail in Chapter 11.

Table 10.1. Summary of Previous Studies of the Impact of Gun Control Laws on Violent Crime Rates

Study	Weakness[a]							Gun Control Effective?[b]
	1	2	3	4	5	6	7	
Wisconsin (1960)	X	X	X	X	X			No
Krug (1967)	X	X	X	X	X	X		No
Olin Mathieson (1969)	X	X	X	X	?	X		No
Geisel et al. (1969)			(X)	X	X	X		No
Snyder (1969)	X	X	X	X	?	X		No
Seitz (1972)	X	X	X	(X)	X	X		Yes
Murray (1975)	(X)	X	X	(X)	X			No
Zimring (1975)	X	—	—		—	—	X	Mixed
Beha (1977)	X	—	X	(X)	—	—	X	Mixed[c]
Deutsch and Alt (1977)	—	—	—	X	—	—	X	Mixed[c]
Cook (1979)			X		?			No
Hay and McCleary (1979)	—	—	—	X	—	—	X	No[c]
Nicholson and Garner (1980)	X		—	X	—	—	X	Mixed
Sommers (1980)	(X)	X	X	X	X		X	Mixed
Jones (1981)	X	—	—	X	—	—	X	Mixed
Lester and Murrell (1981b)	X		X	X	X	X		No
Pierce and Bowers (1981)	—	—	—	X	—	—	X	Mixed[c]
Lester and Murrell (1982)	X	X	X	X	X	X		Mixed
Magaddino and Medoff (1982)	(X)	X	X	X	X			No
DeZee (1983)		X	X	X	X			No
Loftin et al. (1983)	—	—	—	X	—	—	X	No
Loftin and McDowall (1984)	—	—	—	X	—		X	No
Magaddino and Medoff I (1984)		X	X	X	X			No
Magaddino and Medoff II (1984)		—	—		—	—	X	No
McPheters et al. (1984)	—	—	—	X	—	—	X	Yes
Lester and Murrell (1986)	X	X	X	X	X	X		No
Lester (1987b)	X	X	X	X	X	X		No
Lester (1988b)	(X)	X	X		X	X		Yes
Jung and Jason (1988)	—		—	X	—		X	No

Summary: 3 Yes, 8 Mixed, 18 No

[a] Weakness codes: X indicates problem existed, blank indicates no problem, dash (—) indicates problem is irrelevant to this type of study, and (X) indicates partial presence of problem, or problem inadequately dealt with. Weaknesses: 1. Omitted needed control variables. 2. State level of analysis used, rather than city. 3. Only state gun control laws were measured. 4. No measure of gun ownership included. 5. Only one source of information on gun control laws. 6. Lumped heterogeneous mixture of gun laws together, without separate measures of gun laws. 7. Studied a single specific law; little generalizability.

[b] "Gun Control Effective?" means "did gun laws appear to significantly reduce total rates of crime?"

[c] These four studies are not independent since they are all evaluations of the same law (Mass. Bartley–Fox law) in the same time period, using the same general methods. They contribute three of the eight studies classified as "Mixed."

Table 10.2. Impact of the Bartley–Fox Carry Law in Boston: A Summary of Three Evaluations

	ARIMA Results—Did Law Reduce Crime Rates?				
			Armed Assault		
Study	*Homicide Total*	*Armed Robbery Total*	*Gun*	*Nongun*	*Total*
Deutsch and Alt	No	Yes[a]	Yes[a]	—	—
Hay and McCleary	No	No	Yes[b]	—	—
Pierce and Bowers	—	—	Yes[a]	No[c]	No[c]
Conclusions	No	Maybe	Yes	No	No

[a] Crime decreases began *prior* to effective date of law.
[b] Analysts concluded effect was only temporary.
[c] No ARIMA results reported, but percentage point changes indicated much larger increase in nongun armed assaults than the decrease in gun assaults, and a 27% increase in total armed assaults from 1974 to 1976.

Table 10.3. Descriptive Statistics for Gun Law Variables in City-Level Analysis[a] (n = 170)

		Mean	*SD*	*Sources*
LICENSE	License to possess gun in home	.11	.32	a,b,c
BYPERMIT	Permit to purchase or acquire	.34	.47	a,b,c
BUYAPLIC	Application to purchase or acquire	.37	.48	a,b
WAITPER	Waiting period to buy, receive, etc.	.44	.50	a,c
CRIMINAL	Prohibit possession—criminals	.82	.38	b,c,d
MENTAL	Prohibit possession, mentally ill, incompetent	.25	.43	b,c,d
ADDICT	Prohibit possession, drug addicts, users	.41	.49	b,c,d
ALCHOLIC	Prohibit possession, alcoholics, etc.	.19	.40	b,c,d
MINORS	Prohibit purchase by minors	.98	.15	b,c
REGISTER	Registration of guns	.47	.50	a,b
DEALER	State or city license, gun dealers	.61	.49	a,b,c
CARYHIDN	Concealed handgun carrying forbidden or permit hard to get	.88	.33	c,d
CARYOPEN	Open handgun carrying forbidden or permit hard to get	.56	.50	c
MANDPEN	Mandatory penalty, illegal carrying	.12	.33	c
ADDONDIS	Additional penalty for committing crimes with gun, discretionary	.58	.50	c
ADDONMND	Additional penalty for committing crimes with gun, mandatory	.61	.49	c
RTBRARMS	State constitutional provision—individual right to bear arms	.43	.50	c
HGBAN	De facto ban on handgun possession	.01	.11	b
SNSBAN	Saturday Night Special sales ban	.04	.20	b

[a] Descriptive statistics and sources for the other variables in the city-level analysis can be found in Table 5.13.

Sources: a. Blose and Cook (1980); b. U.S. Bureau of Alcohol, Tobacco and Firearms (1980); c. Ronhovde and Sugars (1982); d. Jones and Ray (1980).

Table 10.4. Violence Rates, Gun Ownership, and Gun Laws: Effects of Gun Ownership and Gun Laws on Violence

	Total Murder	*Gun Ownership*[a]	*Gun Murder*	*Gun Ownership*	*Nongun Murder*	*Gun Ownership*
LICENSE	−.039[b]	−.051	−.060	−.052	−.035	−.067
BYPERMIT	−.134	−.092	−.167*	−.103	−.325*	−.054
BUYAPLIC	−.225*	.048	−.148	.024	−.198	.051
WAITPER	.125	.011	.042	.037	.035	.018
CRIMINAL	.012	−.017	−.018	−.005	.039	−.021
MENTAL	−.134	−.024	−.180*	−.032	−.251*	−.015
ADDICT	−.022	−.037	.069	−.037	.016	−.025
ALCHOLIC	.116	.059	.073	.063	.086	.056
MINORS	.023	.040	.006	.041	−.012	.051
REGISTER	−.001	.093	.118*	.086	.132	.074
DEALER	−.029	−.120*	−.033	−.125*	−.002	−.131*
CARYHIDN	−.084	.062	.046	.047	.097	.040
CARYOPEN	−.087	−.060	−.050	−.046	−.012	−.073
MANDPEN	−.048	−.006	−.108*	.006	−.042	−.007
ADDONDIS	.001	−.005	−.100	−.010	.021	−.028
ADDONMND	−.083	−.106	−.049	−.105	−.018	−.177
RTBRARMS	−.064	.001	−.019	.005	−.020	.001
HGBAN	−.048	−.011	.059	−.019	.020	−.010
SNSBAN	−.085	−.093*	.062	−.103*	.046	−.105*
LNMR		.226*				
LNGUNMR				.164*		
LNNGMR						.232*
Gun ownership	−.604*		−.121		−.673*	
PSI	.256	.076	.239	.088	.310	.117
PSI (2,1)	.054		−.004		−.046	
df	104		104		104	
χ^2	244.30		227.07		224.43	
GOF	.939		.940		.941	

	Total Agg. Assault	*Gun Ownership*[c]	*Gun Agg. Assault*	*Gun Ownership*	*Nongun Agg. Assault*	*Gun Ownership*
LICENSE	−.044	−.071	−.028	−.075	−.068	−.072
BYPERMIT	.074	−.126	.150	−.126	.017	−.126
BUYAPLIC	.004	.092	−.031	.088	.050	.090
WAITPER	−.075	−.308*	.001	−.304*	−.152	−.312*
CRIMINAL	−.022	.021	−.164*	.027	.068	.012
MENTAL	.079	−.311*	.153	−.302*	.034	−.316*
ADDICT	.162	.161	.198	.174	.129	.170
ALCHOLIC	.029	.037	−.049	.035	.059	.035
MINORS	−.057	.020	−.050	.018	−.059	.020
REGISTER	.153	−.100	.153	−.084	.139	−.106
DEALER	−.188*	.004	−.224*	.001	−.163	.005
CARYHIDN	.018	−.008	.032	−.009	−.016	−.002

(continued)

Table 10.4 *(Continued)*

CARYOPEN	.082	−.134*	.028	−.121	.103	−.142*
MANDPEN	−.050	−.055	−.052	−.057	−.055	−.057
ADDONDIS	−.059	−.015	−.096	−.023	.007	−.023
ADDONMND	.041	−.114	.111	−.115	.013	−.113
RTBRARMS	.064	−.053	.041	−.051	.077	−.055
HGBAN	−.023	−.069	.076	−.066	−.052	−.066
SNSBAN	.031	−.054	.157*	−.061	−.004	−.051
LNASLT		.073				
LNGNASLT				.048		
LNNGASLT						.088
Gun ownership	−.085		.604*		−.401	
PSI	.492	.272	.423	.239	.524	.281
df	102		102		102	
χ^2	227.65		249.50		226.70	
GOF	.939		.934		.938	

	Total Robbery	*Gun Ownership*[d]	*Gun Robbery*	*Gun Ownership*	*Nongun Robbery*	*Gun Ownership*
LICENSE	.011	−.122*	.036	−.126*	−.007	−.125*
BYPERMIT	−.059	−.087	−.023	−.101	−.058	−.082
BUYAPLIC	.010	.027	.005	.034	.005	.018
WAITPER	.082	−.130	.051	−.135	.077	−.136
CRIMINAL	−.071	.120*	−.180*	.119*	.012	.117*
MENTAL	−.041	−.195*	−.013	−.201*	−.078	−.195*
ADDICT	.067	.060	.150*	.096	.030	.060
ALCHOLIC	.084	.010	.105	.007	.043	.006
MINORS	−.010	.028	.007	.026	−.020	.026
REGISTER	.023	−.058	−.048	−.047	.034	−.063
DEALER	−.067	.022	−.094	.009	−.055	.031
CARYHIDN	.068	.111	.108	.124	.039	.113
CARYOPEN	.031	−.091	.042	−.087	−.009	−.099
MANDPEN	−.108*	.022	−.133*	.014	−.102*	.022
ADDONDIS	−.127*	−.040	−.116*	−.060	−.115*	−.046
ADDONMND	−.008	−.124	.082	−.119	−.012	−.124
RTBRARMS	.022	−.003	.071	.007	.008	−.009
HGBAN	.054	−.096*	.140*	−.083	.020	−.097*
SNSBAN	.050	−.042	.097*	−.041	.045	−.038
LNROB		−.051				
LNGNROB				−.099		
LNNGROBR						−.013
Gun ownership	.006		.535*		−.308*	
PSI	.147	.172	.193	.174	.157	.147
df	120		120		120	
χ^2	273.31		286.89		273.10	
GOF	.937		.934		.937	

(continued)

Table 10.4 (Continued)

	Total Suicide	*Gun Ownership*[e]	*Gun Suicide*	*Gun Ownership*	*Nongun Suicide*	*Gun Ownership*
LICENSE	−.105	−.166*	−.078	−.165*	−.059	−.164*
BYPERMIT	−.047	−.025	−.096	−.037	.093	−.024
BUYAPLIC	.132	.055	.139	.051	.088	.065
WAITPER	−.128	−.181	−.105	−.185	−.098	−.179
CRIMINAL	.033	−.039	.078	−.035	−.090	−.032
MENTAL	−.080	−.015	−.119*	−.016	−.005	−.013
ADDICT	.137	.244*	.025	.244*	.208	.253*
ALCHOLIC	−.056	−.038	−.029	−.039	−.092	−.041
MINORS	−.017	−.011	−.008	−.012	−.023	−.008
REGISTER	−.133	−.069	−.106	−.069	−.061	−.054
DEALER	−.240*	−.103	−.165*	−.103	−.178*	−.113
HGBAN	−.024	.124	−.039	.125	−.017	.124
SNSBAN	.047	.002	−.019	.000	.089	.001
Gun ownership	−.225		.119		−.379	
PSI	.510	.353	.273	.344	.518	.356
PSI (2,1)	.266*		.172*		.177*	
df	86		86		86	
χ^2	226.44		234.20		226.63	
GOF	.932		.929		.932	

(continued)

Table 10.4 (Continued)

	Rape	*Gun Ownership[f]*	*Burglary*	*Gun Ownership[f]*	*Fatal Gun Accidents*	*Gun Ownership[e]*
LICENSE	.107	−.128	−.039	−.138	−.245*	−.169*
BYPERMIT	−.044	−.033	.025	−.102	−.035	−.067
BUYAPLIC	−.088	.086	.032	.011	.029	−.044
WAITPER	.074	−.134	.152	−.278*	−.086	−.136
CRIMINAL	.018	.019	.019	.026	.082	−.041
MENTAL	.105	−.194	.160*	−.350*	−.203	−.056
ADDICT	.137	−.042	−.021	.164	.166	.244*
ALCHOLIC	.081	−.077	.067	.089	−.004	−.024
MINORS	.090	−.074	−.030	.055	−.059	−.019
REGISTER	−.011	.013	.118	−.131	−.092	−.060
DEALER	−.077	.059	−.058	.037	−.034	−.132
CARYHIDN	.007	.020	.018	.021		
CARYOPEN	.039	−.080	.145*	−.069		
MANDPEN	−.079	.046	−.048	−.018		
ADDONDIS	−.006	−.019	−.087	−.078		
ADDONMND	.202	−.208*	.022	−.214*		
RTBRARMS	.190*	−.168	−.003	−.012		
HGBAN	−.067	.052	.023	−.056	.051	.136
SNSBAN	.120	.124	−.026	−.041	.042	.031
LNRAPE		.809*				
LNBURG				−.114		
Gun ownership	.586		.267*		−.577	
PSI	.527	.494	.319	.375	.905	.392
PSI (2,1)					.289	
df	139		133		76	
χ^2	356.83		287.01		194.35	
GOF	.909		.919		.933	

[a] Latent construct with indicators: PCTGNAST, PCTGNROB, PGS7982, GUNSTOL.
[b] Standardized coefficients.
[c] Latent construct with indicators: PGH7982, PCTGNROB, PGS7982, GUNSTOL.
[d] Latent construct with indicators: PGH7982, PCTGNAST, PGS7982, GUNSTOL.
[e] Latent construct with indicators: PGH7982, PCTGNAST, PCTGNROB, GUNSTOL.
[f] Latent construct with indicators: PGH7982, PCTGNAST, PCTGNROB, PGS7982, GUNSTOL.
* $p < .05$.

Table 10.5. Summary of Effects of Gun Ownership and Gun Laws on Violence Rates and Gun Ownership

	Model						
Gun Law	*Murder*	*Aggravated Assault*	*Robbery*	*Rape*	*Burglary*	*Suicide*	*Fatal Gun Accidents*
Do gun control laws reduce gun ownership levels?							
LICENSE	No	No	Yes	No	No	Yes	Yes
BYPERMIT	No	No	No	No	No	No	No
BUYAPLIC	No	No	No	No	No	No	No
WAITPER	No	Yes	No	No	Yes	No	No
CRIMINAL	No	No	No	No	No	No	No
MENTAL	No	Yes	Yes	No	Yes	No	No
ADDICT	No	No	No	No	No	No	No
ALCHOLIC	No	No	No	No	No	No	No
MINORS	No	No	No	No	No	No	No
REGISTER	No	No	No	No	No	No	No
DEALER	Yes	No	No	No	No	No	No
CARYHIDN	No	No	No	No	No		
CARYOPEN	No	Yes	No	No	No		
MANDPEN	No	No	No	No	No		
ADDONDIS	No	No	No	No	No		
ADDONMND	No	No	No	Yes	Yes		
RTBRARMS	No	No	No	No	No		
HGBAN	No	No	Yes	No	No	No	No
SNSBAN	Yes	No	No	No	No	No	No
Does gun ownership increase violence? (from Chapters 5–7)	No	No	No	No	Yes	No	No
Do gun laws reduce violence?							
LICENSE	No	No	No	No	No	No	Yes
BYPERMIT	Maybe[a]	No	No	No	No	No	No
BUYAPLIC	No	No	No	No	No	No	No
WAITPER	No	No	No	No	No	No	No
CRIMINAL	No	Maybe[a]	Maybe[a]	No	No	No	No
MENTAL	No[a]	No	No	No	No	Maybe[a]	No
ADDICT	No	No	No	No	No	No	No
ALCHOLIC	No	No	No	No	No	No	No
MINORS	No	No	No	No	No	No	No
REGISTER	No	No	No	No	No	No	No
DEALER	No	Yes[a]	No	No	No	Maybe[a]	No
CARYHIDN	No	No	No	No	No		
CARYOPEN	No	No	No	No	No		
MANDPEN	Maybe[a]	No	Yes[a]	No	No		
ADDONDIS	No	No	Yes[a]	No	No		
ADDONMND	No	No	No	No	No		

(*continued*)

Table 10.5. *(Continued)*

Gun Law	Model: Murder	Aggravated Assault	Robbery	Rape	Burglary	Suicide	Fatal Gun Accidents
RTBRARMS	No	No	No	No	No		
HGBAN	No	No	No	No	No	No	No
SNSBAN	No	No	No	No	No	No	No

The assessments pertaining to gun laws in the panel above were based on the pattern of answers to the following question: Was there a significant negative coefficient for the gun law variable in each violence rate equation?[b]

Violence Rate: Total	Gun	Nongun	Gun Law Efficacy Interpretation
Yes	Yes	No	Yes
Yes	No	No	No—omitted var.
Yes	Yes	Yes, at least as strong as effect on gun violence rate	Maybe
Yes	Yes	Yes, weaker than effect on gun violence rate	Yes
Yes	No	Yes	No—omitted var.
No	Yes	No	Maybe
No	Yes	Yes	Maybe
No	All other combinations in gun and nongun columns		No

[a] Gun law appeared to reduce gun use in this category of violence.
[b] For rape, burglary, and fatal gun accidents, where separate gun and nongun rates were not available, an entry in this table could be Yes based solely on a significant negative gun law coefficient in the total violence rate equation.

Table 10.6. Crime Rates in Evanston, Illinois and Comparison Areas, 1976–1984

Area	1976	1977	1978	1979	1980	1981	1982	1983	1984	% Change for Year 1982–83	1981–84
Evanston											
MNNM[a]	5.2	0.0	2.7	10.8	5.4	5.4	2.7	5.4	8.2	+100	+52
Robbery	230.0	168.3	245.7	235.5	260.5	265.1	249.1	287.4	200.2	+15	−24
Arm. Rob.[b]				99.6	135.7	92.0	112.3	102.5	84.4	−9	−8
Agg. Aslt.[c]	182.7	117.9	188.3	328.4	308.0	307.1	249.1	252.3	339.1	+1	+10
Cities, 50–99K population											
MNNM	6.1	6.4	6.9	7.2	7.6	7.4	6.8	6.3	5.9	−7	−20
Robbery	160.6	159.1	176.0	193.9	228.5	228.0	211.7	184.0	185.2	−13	−19
Arm. Rob.				115.3	136.3	133.6	120.0	97.9	96.4	−18	−28
Agg. Aslt.	223.2	249.5	272.8	287.7	327.7	310.4	305.5	285.4	319.6	−7	+3
U.S.											
MNNM	8.8	8.8	9.0	9.7	10.2	9.8	9.1	8.3	7.9	−9	−19
Robbery	199.3	190.7	195.8	218.4	251.1	258.7	238.9	216.5	205.4	−9	−21
Arm. Rob.				134.9	158.6	162.6	156.3	136.9	126.7	−12	−22
Agg. Aslt.	233.2	247.0	262.1	286.0	298.5	289.7	289.2	279.2	290.2	−3	0

[a] Murder and nonnegligent manslaughter.
[b] Armed robbery.
[c] Aggravated assault.
Sources: Crime data: U.S. FBI 1977–1985; Evanston 1986; population data: U.S. Bureau of the Census (1978, 1983a,b). Linear interpolation was used with 1975 and 1985 Census estimates and 1980 Census enumeration, to get intercensal population figures for use in calculating rates per 100,000 population.

PART IV

POLICY LESSONS

CHAPTER

11

Conclusions

The central rationale for gun control as a means of violence control seems eminently commonsensical—guns are dangerous and their use elevates the risk that a victim of violence will die. Therefore, disarming violent people (including those prone to suicide or accidents) could reduce death rates even if people were not otherwise altered and continued to be violent. The more pragmatic supporters of gun control concede that a given policy might have difficulty in disarming people, particularly seriously motivated violence-prone people. Nevertheless, they show little doubt that the effects of the disarming, however limited in scope, would be beneficial when and where it could be achieved. Based on the preceding chapters, across-the-board faith in this rationale is unwarranted. The most fundamental flaw in advocacy of gun control as violence reduction is not that gun laws could not disarm anyone, but rather that doing so would not necessarily produce any net violence-reducing impact.

The rationale for gun control on which supporters have relied for over 20 years is based on an unduly simplified conception of the role of weaponry in human violence. The ownership and use of guns, even just among violence-prone people, have a complex mixture both of positive and negative effects on the rate of violent incidents and the seriousness of their outcomes, effects that often largely cancel each other out. The picture is complicated even further by the fact that the use of guns by crime victims to defend themselves is effective both in preventing completion of the crime and in preventing injury to the victim. Mass ownership and the frequent defensive use of guns by crime victims make criminal behavior more risky and may have a deterrent effect on criminals, especially on those who would assault intimates, rob retail stores, or commit residential burglaries. It may also displace burglars away from occupied homes, reducing deaths and injuries resulting from confrontations between burglars and victims (Chapter 4).

Levels of general gun ownership appear to have no significant net effect on rates on homicide, rape, robbery, or aggravated assault, even though they do apparently affect the fraction of robberies and assaults committed with guns (Chapter 5). This may be due partly to the counterbalancing effects of gun ownership among mostly noncriminal potential victims and ownership among criminals. Nevertheless, even when aggressor gun possession and use in individual incidents alone are examined, this also appears to have a mixture of counterbalancing effects. In both robberies and other assaultive crimes, the possession of a gun by the aggressor appears to reduce the likelihood of attack and injury to the victim, while at the same time increasing the probability that any injury that is inflicted will be fatal (Chapter 5).

General gun ownership levels also seem to have no net effect on suicide rates, due at least partly to the wide range of alternative methods available to would-be suicides. These methods involve resources that are even more widely available than guns, many are nearly as lethal as shooting, and some are superior in many ways to guns for suicidal purposes (Chapter 6).

More surprisingly, general gun ownership levels also appear to be unrelated to rates of fatal gun accidents. Such acts are very rare, and largely confined to a small, unusually reckless segment of the population. This makes it difficult to detect whatever statistical relationship may exist between gun levels and accident rates (Chapter 7).

Neither the present work nor past research, considered as a whole, offers much support for the view that general levels of gun ownership have any net effect on the rate of any major category of violence. Areas of the country that have higher gun ownership rates do not, as a result, have higher violence rates. Therefore, there appears to be no violence reduction benefit to be derived from restricting gun ownership in the general population.

Nevertheless, there is a valid rationale for some kinds of gun control. A gun is not just another weapon. Firearms probably are more lethal than knives and other weapons that could be substituted for guns, though not nearly to the degree that gun control advocates have claimed. Equally important, firearms have a reputation, however inflated, for lethality. The reality and the reputation both help induce compliance with the commands of those who use guns, for either offensive or defensive purposes. Further, guns allow weaker individuals to successfully attack, or defend against, stronger individuals, thereby facilitating both aggressive and defensive attacks. Finally, guns enable people to attack at a distance greater than arms length, a property that can also facilitate some aggressive or defensive attacks.

For these reasons, even though gun ownership levels in the general public have no apparent net effect on violence rates, gun ownership among high-risk subsets of the population may increase the frequency or seriousness of violent incidents. This conclusion is indirectly supported by evidence indicating that gun laws aimed at screening out high-risk groups (such as prospective killers and reckless, accident-prone people) from gun acquisition seem to reduce some kinds of violence (such as homicides and gun accidents). Thus, gun owner license laws appear to reduce gun accidents, and purchase permit laws seem to reduce murder. Likewise, prohibitions of gun possession by convicted criminals may reduce aggravated assaults and robberies, while bans on possession by mentally ill persons may reduce suicides. Further, the carrying of guns in public places may increase robbery rates. This conclusion is supported by evidence that indicates that robbers are more likely to complete their crimes if they are armed with a gun, suggesting that gun carrying can thereby encourage criminals to commit more robberies, especially impulsive or opportunistic ones (Chapter 5). It is also indirectly supported by evidence indicating that well-enforced laws controlling unlicensed gun carrying reduce robbery and that discretionary add-on penalties for committing crimes with guns may also reduce robbery. Both types of laws presumably reduce robbery at least partly by reducing the carrying of guns in public places. Strict carry laws may also reduce homicide, possibly because they may reduce robbery murders. Finally, state and local licensing of gun dealers may reduce robbery and possibly even suicide. Beyond these exceptions, the gun controls currently in operation seem to have no net impact on total (gun plus nongun) rates of violence (Chapter 10).

The Shape of Effective Gun Controls

Thus, although most controls are without demonstrable impact, there are nevertheless a few that appear to have some modest effects. However, if one wishes to go beyond the few measures that are known to have worked in the past, future development of effective gun control policies could be facilitated if the effort were guided by some broad principles of weapons regulation. The following is a first attempt at a list of such principles.

Based on the research assessed in this book, gun controls are more likely to produce net reductions in total violence rates if they do the following:

1. Regulate long guns at least as strictly as handguns. Their political advantages notwithstanding, controls that restrict only handguns probably do more harm than good. Further, those aimed at rarely used weapon types such as "assault rifles" and machine guns are largely beside the point (Chapter 3).
2. Are popular enough to be politically achievable and to not provoke massive disobedience and evasion (Chapter 9), and sufficiently acceptable to criminal justice personnel that they have a chance of being enforced (Chapter 8).
3. Will be obeyed by a nonnegligible fraction of the violence-prone population, not just by relatively nonviolent, noncriminal people (Chapter 8).
4. Do not depend on the hopeless task of producing overall gun scarcity in a nation that already has over 200 million guns (Chapter 2).
5. Avoid the interjurisdictional "leakage" problem, whereby strict local controls on gun acquisition can be evaded by going to less strict areas (Chapter 8).
6. Address the private transfers of firearms that account for the overwhelming majority of gun acquisitions by violence-prone people (Chapter 2).
7. Are not extremely expensive relative to their benefits.

A Workable Gun Control Strategy

Meaningful reductions in violence using the criminal justice system are difficult to achieve unless people scale down their expectations to realistic levels. Insupportable claims that this or that policy or program produced 30 or 40 or 50% reductions in crime poison the climate for considering policies that may well produce genuine crime reductions, but of far more modest scale. If crime control strategies are rejected because they can produce no more than, say, a 5–10% reduction in crime rates, there is little point in considering most of them.

The following is a tentative policy for regulating the acquisition and possession of firearms, one that is subject to modification as new research indicates the need for revisions. The proposal meets all of the conditions outlined above. One of its chief merits is that it is both politically achievable and practical to implement. Many proposals might theoretically have substantial impacts on violence, yet could never be implemented, and others are easily implemented yet hardly worth the effort because they would be so ineffective. The proposal's main focus is on making gun acquisition at least marginally more difficult, and gun possession more risky, for the most identifiably violence-prone segments of the population.

It is already illegal under federal law for a felon to possess a gun anywhere in the United States. However, there is little federal enforcement apparatus for enforcing this provision, and no street-level federal patrol force comparable to those of city police departments. It is also illegal under federal law for anyone knowingly to sell a gun to a convicted felon, but there is no federally imposed effective way for sellers to know whether a prospective buyer is a felon. Findings in Chapter 10 suggested that gun buyer screening systems, such as owner licensing and purchase permit systems, could reduce homicides and gun accidents. Therefore, a screening procedure of some sort would an important part of any effective gun control strategy.

A National Instant Records Check

The central element of the proposed regulatory strategy is a federal "instant records check" at the point of retail sale. The outlines of such a system have already been laid out in considerable detail in a U.S. Department of Justice report (1989). (The following system is essentially the one designated Option A in that report.) Under the system, a prospective gun buyer would go to a licensed gun dealer, fill out an application (as is already done under existing federal law), and show two pieces of identification, with at least one having a current photo. The gun dealer would be required to make a toll-free telephone call to a designated state or federal law enforcement agency for a criminal records check of the applicant. The agency would scan existing state and federal computerized master name indexes covering persons arrested for felonies and serious misdemeanors. As of 1990, 20 states participated in the FBI-operated Interstate Identification Index, and about 70% of 1988 U.S. arrests were made in these participating states. Using current computer and record-keeping capabilities, it is possible to complete the initial check within a few minutes. If no one with the applicant's description was found (i.e., no "hit" was made), the dealer would be told the sale could go through immediately. If there was a "hit," the dealer would be told that the sale could not proceed.

About half of these "hits" would be false, referring to someone other than the applicant (p. 26912). Rejected applicants could go through a more extensive secondary verification procedure (free of charge), taking perhaps several weeks, if they wished to demonstrate that they did not in fact fall within a disqualified category. They would present themselves in person to a law enforcement agency, present identification, and a more extensive search of criminal records would be carried out. If eligibility could still not be determined, or records indicated the applicant had a disqualifying conviction and the applicant still denied that he or she was the person whom the records indicated had been convicted, then he or she could submit to fingerprinting. (This represents a change from the original Department of Justice proposal, which entailed fingerprinting in all secondary verifications. This is unnecessarily intrusive and expensive.) The prints would be checked against state and FBI fingerprint files to see if the applicant was indeed a convicted felon. If final disposition information (e.g., was there a conviction?) was inadequate, telephone inquiries would be made. The state law enforcement agency would make a final determination as to whether the applicant could be issued a Certificate to Purchase, good for buying guns until revoked. The Justice Department study estimated that 84–88% of applicants would pass the initial records check and be cleared to buy a gun within "several minutes" of the time the telephone call was made (p. 26912). Among the remaining 12–16% who were initially rejected, about half, or 6–8% of the total, would turn out to be false "hits" and could gain a Certificate to Purchase if they proceeded with the secondary verification process.

Note that there intentionally is no delay built into the gun acquisition process, hence the name "instant" records check. This represents no crime control loss, since there seems to be no measurable value to waiting period provisions (Chapters 8, 10). Note also that, being national in scope, this regulatory strategy would avoid the "leakage" problem of gun seekers traveling to less strict areas to acquire guns. By 1990, both Virginia and Florida had state instant records check systems in place, covering retail sales only.

For auditing purposes, the telephone inquiry, along with an inquiry identification number, would be logged by the law enforcement agency, to compare with gun dealer records of inquiries that they had made. This would facilitate checking to ensure that dealers were not selling guns without making the required criminal record checks, and were not using the inquiries for unauthorized purposes. However, names of gun purchase applicants would *not* be retained on the system. This is a crucial element of the regulatory strategy that distinguishes it from gun owner licensing, purchase permit and application systems, and registration systems. It means that the system would not generate a list of known gun owners that could conceivably be used in mass confiscations at some future date. This provision is essential to meeting the objections of gun owners that such lists appear to have little current law enforcement utility but could be used to enforce a government edict to turn in all guns (Chapter 8).

Regulating Private Transfers of Guns

As noted in Chapter 2, most serious felons get their guns by means other than retail purchases from licensed dealers, and thus would not be affected directly by an instant records check provision by itself. On the other hand, about 64% of gun acquisitions by noncriminals are acquisitions of new or used guns from retail dealers. Therefore, a disproportionate share, though by no means a majority, of private gun transfers are to unqualified recipients. It was estimated in Chapter 2 that there were about 3.1 million private transfers a year in the late 1980s. A critical element of the proposed system for regulating gun acquisitions, and probably its most politically controversial provision, would be a requirement that these numerous private transfers of guns be routed through a licensed gun dealer. (The Justice Department proposal did not address private gun transfers.)

Private individuals who wanted to transfer their gun to a qualified recipient would still be able to do so, but would have to do so through a licensed dealer acting as a broker. Prospective transferors would go to a licensed dealer with the prospective recipient, where the latter would fill out the usual application form and submit to the standard records check. As a condition of holding their federal licenses, dealers would be required to act as broker in these transactions. For this service they would be entitled to charge a modest service fee sufficient to cover their costs plus a reasonable profit. Because it provides an additional source of income, few dealers would object to such a requirement. And since less than 6% of gun owners transfer a gun to a private party each year [3.1 million private transfers divided by 52 million gun owners (Table 2.4)], this provision would impose modest costs only very infrequently on a small segment of the gun-owning population. For these few, the cost would be slight—the travel time needed to reach the nearest gun dealer and perhaps a $10–20 broker's fee added on to the price of the gun. The benefit would be that all legal gun acquisitions, everywhere in the United States, would entail a criminal records check, and no gun sellers could complain that they had no way of knowing that a buyer was not eligible to receive a gun. An exception to these requirements could be made for gifts to minors from their parents or guardians.

Violations of the ban on private transfers could be punished by an escalating schedule of penalties, perhaps beginning with a fine and/or a short jail term for a first conviction, with longer jail terms for subsequent convictions. For gun dealers who sold guns without the required records check, penalties could include the suspension or loss of their dealer's license. The potential loss of their livelihood would be a powerful incentive for dealers to comply with the law. Private transferors, as discussed in Chapter 10, could be discouraged from evading the system by making transferors financially liable for any harm done by the person to whom they transferred the gun, if they transferred a gun to an ineligible recipient without using the dealer records check (see Blose and Cook 1980; Kates 1990, p. 60; Kleck 1986a).

This is an important element of the regulatory strategy, since the records check element would obviously be more effective if it was harder to evade through private transactions. It is, however, also the element that gun owner groups are likely to most strongly oppose, and that therefore would be hardest to make into law. Consequently, it is important to note that it is not an absolutely essential element, in the sense that the records check would still have some value without it. There undoubtedly are people who do not know, or cannot easily contact, nondealers willing to provide them with guns, and who therefore could be denied guns through controls on retail sales alone. It is, however, unknown how large a fraction of likely gun misusers fall into this category.

No one should believe that all or even most criminals would abide by the provisions of this or any other set of legal controls over access to guns. Many criminals would still get guns through illegal channels, including theft and purchases from black market sources. Some would make purchases from dealers through a "straw man" with no criminal record, and a few might even bother to use false identification papers. This proposal does not rely on an assumption that career felons and other strongly motivated individuals would be blocked from getting guns, but only that a nonnegligible fraction of the less strongly motivated would-be gun buyers, particularly those lacking criminal connections, would be blocked. To expect total evasion would be as pessimistically unrealistic as it would be optimistically unrealistic to expect no evasion.

It would not take a large violence-reduction benefit to outweigh the financial costs of the instant records check, since these costs would be modest. The Justice Department study (p. 26939) estimated that a point-of-purchase telephone records check would cost about $36–44 million to start up, and about $53–70 million per year to operate. The annual operating costs would amount to about $10 per gun transfer, which could be assessed as a fee on each gun transfer and therefore not cost taxpayers anything.

Who Should Be Disqualified?

In addition to convicted felons, persons convicted of a violent misdemeanor would also be ineligible to possess or receive a gun. Nearly all criminal convictions are obtained as a result of a negotiated guilty plea of some sort, and a common part of plea bargaining is the reduction of charges from felonies to misdemeanor versions of the original felony charges. In these cases, there is no difference in the actual seriousness of the offense, just a difference in how the case was processed by the court. Offenders with violent misdemeanor convictions may differ from those with felony convictions only in that the former was convicted in a court that makes more use of charge reduction to induce guilty pleas. As of 1980, at least 12 states already banned gun sales to violent misdemeanants (Blose and Cook 1980, p. 14). Five years after the last relevant conviction, a person could apply for "relief of disability," to once again become eligible for gun acquisition and possession, if they had no other disqualifying traits.

In 1988, based on court data from a representative sample of 39 of the nation's 75 most populous counties, 49% of murder defendants had a prior conviction and 29% had prior felony convictions; for robbery defendants the corresponding figures were 55 and 39%, respectively (U.S. Bureau of Justice Statistics 1990b, p. 7). Thus, a gun control strategy that effectively prohibited firearms to persons with a prior criminal conviction would probably deny legal access to guns to at least a third to a half of prospective murderers and robbers.

Gun sales would also be forbidden to persons under the age of 18. As of 1980, 33 states already had such a provision covering all guns, and another 13 applied the restriction only to handguns purchases (Ronhovde and Sugars 1982, pp. 204–5). This federal requirement would extend the requirement to the rest of the states, and apply it to long guns as well as to handguns.

Gun acquisition and possession would also be forbidden to persons who had been committed to a mental institution as a result of a violent act that would have been considered one of a specified list of crimes had the person not been found not guilty by reason of insanity. The disability could be removed if a licensed psychiatrist or psychologist certified that the person had not suffered from disability for a period of 5 years.

Even broader prohibitions directed at *all* mental patients are a part of gun laws in over 20 states (Ronhovde and Sugars 1982, pp. 204–5), such as the Illinois law that denies the required gun owner license to "a person who has been a patient of a mental institution within the past five years" (*Illinois Revised Statutes,* Chapter 38, Article 83-8). Likewise, federal law forbids dealers from knowingly transferring guns to persons they know to have been committed to a mental institution (U.S. Internal Revenue Service 1969a). These prohibitions, like others that deny privileges to persons treated for mental illness, create disincentives to seek needed treatment. Further, because wealthier people who seek treatment are less likely to go to institutions, there is a class bias to such prohibitions. The prohibitions also have little violence-control utility. Most psychiatric hospitalizations have nothing to do with violence. Further, although some forms of mental illness such as psychopathy may be related to violent behavior, most are not. It is true that among ex-patients who are rehospitalized, violent behavior is responsible for a significant minority of the cases, and postrelease violent behavior is higher for general samples of released mental patients than for the general public. However, apart from the minority who already had a criminal record prior to hospitalization, and who thus were usually already disqualified for gun possession for that reason, patients released from psychiatric hospitals are no more likely to commit subsequent acts of violence than other members of the general public (see studies reviewed in Brown 1983). One careful study found that among patients without a preadmission arrest, only 3.8% were arrested for *any* crime, including nonviolent crimes, following release, compared to 3.3% among members of the general public (Steadman et al. 1978, p. 1219). Thus, there is little additional violence prevention to be gained, beyond that produced by prohibitions aimed at criminals, from including all ex-mental patients among the prohibited classes; doing so would deny these people the use of guns for self-defense.

At present, only a few states (e.g., Illinois) have computerized records of mental patients, and even these states do not necessarily identify patients hospitalized for violent acts. Thus, federal law at present could not require a standardized check for psychiatric hospitalization. Instead, the law could simply continue the ban on dealers knowingly selling guns to such buyers, while states were encouraged to improve their records.

One other group might be denied the right to acquire or possess firearms—those with more than one conviction for one of a specified list of alcohol-related crimes, including drunk driving and public drunkenness (Kates 1990, p. 60). After a period of 5 years without such a conviction, a person previously forbidden from acquiring guns could seek permission from the relevant state law enforcement agency to once again qualify for acquisition and possession of guns. Although the relationship between alcoholism and violence is extremely complex, an extensive body of research linking alcoholism and drinking with antisocial personality traits and violent behavior (see the review of over 180 studies in Miczek et al. 1990) provides substantial justification for a presumption that a person repeatedly involved in alcohol-related crimes is at a much higher-than-average risk of committing a violent act in the future.

Adequacy of Criminal Records

When a dealer called his state law enforcement agency for a records check, that agency could make use of several resources, including the FBI-operated National Criminal Information Center (NCIC) and the Interstate Identification Index (III). The III is a computerized index of names of persons with criminal records in 20 participating states with automated computerized criminal history (CCH) systems of their own. The NCIC provides criminal history information for the other 30 states, as well as pointing to detailed information available in CCH files of the 20 III states (U.S. Department of Justice 1989, p. 26905). Existing CCH records are far from complete. Some agencies fail to report arrests and dispositions to the appropriate state repositories, and many of the repositories have not yet automated some or all of their records. In a 1984 survey, of 47 states responding, only five had fully automated criminal history files; 30 had partially automated files. On the other hand, 25 reported a fully automated name index, with another 14 reporting a partially automated index (U.S. Bureau of Justice Statistics 1985d, p. 3). These systems would be equipped to inform a law enforcement agency immediately as to whether a person with a given name and description (age, sex, race, address) appeared in their files, even though they might not be able to provide details of a criminal record. Even in those states with CCH systems, coverage of arrests is less than complete, and coverage of dispositions such as convictions is worse (Blose and Cook 1980, pp. 112–26). Perhaps half of all felony convictions in the nation are available in automated form, and thus quickly and easily available (U.S. Department of Justice 1989, p. 26905). For purposes of an instant record check, it is mainly coverage of arrests in a name index that is critical, since an arrest is sufficient to yield a "hit" that would stop an immediate gun sale.

It is the secondary verification process, applying only to about one in eight applicants, that would require information about final dispositions. For this process, full automation would be helpful, and obviously faster and more efficient, but not absolutely essential for implementation now. The CCH systems are continuing to improve their coverage and level of automation (U.S. Bureau of Justice Statistics 1985d). This process could be accelerated by making federal criminal justice assistance funds available only if state CCH repositories submitted to audits of their records and reached minimum standards for completeness, and by providing grants to pay for upgrading the systems.

Currently, computerized criminal records files are still seriously incomplete, thus limiting the effectiveness of this sort of screening somewhat. Of course, the same is true of purchase permit, application-to-purchase, and gun owner licensing systems, all of which rely on the adequacy of criminal records. Certainly these systems would all work better if the records were more complete. Nevertheless, it is a non sequitur to conclude from this fact that the records checks are useless. If the system can detect 50% of prospective gun buyers with prior criminal convictions, this is obviously far better than having no screening at all and detecting 0% of them. On the other hand, the problem of false "hits" would be greatly reduced if the accuracy and completeness of CCH records could be achieved before the records check system was implemented.

Regulating Gun Carrying

Well-enforced carry laws show promise for controlling violent crime, especially robbery (Chapter 10). Since there is no leakage problem with controls on gun carrying, it is not essential that these controls be national in scope. In any case, the strictness of control over carrying that is called for varies greatly from state to state. One reasonable compromise between supporters and opponents of strict gun control would the Florida model. All carrying of guns on the person, concealed or open, is forbidden unless the carrier has a state-issued permit. Issuance of the permit is essentially nondiscretionary in Florida; it is always issued if the applicant does not fall into any of various prohibited classes. The same would be true under the strategy proposed here, except that the groups denied access to carry permits would be the same classes forbidden from acquiring guns under the instant records check system described above. In addition, applicants would be required to pass tests showing their knowledge of gun safety, how guns work, and the law in their state concerning both gun carrying and self-defense.

If the Florida experience is generalizable, few people would apply for permits under this system, and enactment of such a law would not result in any measurable violence involving permit holders (Chapter 10). For some states, this sort of control would represent an increase in strictness of the regulation of open carrying and carrying of long guns, while, for most states, it would be a reduction in unneeded restrictiveness in issuing permits for concealed carrying (Chapters 8, 10). The system would reduce complaints about arbitrary denial of applications, yet encourage improvements in gun safety and reductions in use of excessive force in self-defense among gun carriers. It might also result in increased deterrence of robbery and other crimes that commonly occur in public places.

Improved Enforcement of Carry Laws

Laws punishing illegal gun carrying with mandatory penalties appear to reduce robbery (Chapter 10), even though the penalty provisions appear to have little impact on the actual levels of punishment (Chapter 8). One possible explanation of this apparent paradox is that the mandatory penalty provisions may merely serve as an indicator of serious commitment to enforcement among criminal justice personnel, and that greater enforcement of carry laws produces a net reduction in robbery. It has been argued that more proactive or aggressive police patrolling may reduce robbery (Wilson and Boland 1978). This may be largely due to the impact of frequent street searches on casual weapon carrying.

Therefore, police departments might experiment with increasing street searches and arrests for unlawful carrying, and/or improving the targeting of searches. Even in the absence of increased use of prison sentences for violators, increased carrying arrests might deter the casual, routine carrying of firearms, and thereby indirectly reduce opportunistic robberies. Currently, most police departments show little evidence of a serious enforcement effort. Most police rarely make arrests for any gun violations and confiscate few criminal guns (Chapter 8). Nevertheless, some departments make far more arrests and confiscations, even relative to local levels of gun ownership and abuse, than other departments (Brill 1977, p. 32). This indicates that the generally low level of enforcement is not an inevitable or unavoidable part of police work, and might be altered. Further, enforcing laws controlling the carrying of deadly weapons is a traditional, well-accepted part of police work (as long as it is not punished by excessive mandatory penalties), so there is little reason to expect strong police resistance to doing more of it, or to doing it more effectively (Moore 1980).

One major problem with increased searches is that, to the majority of searched persons who were not in possession of weapons or other contraband, street searches look like police harassment, aimed largely at young men and minorities. Further, because many otherwise law-abiding people carry guns for protection (Chapter 4), poorly targeted searches could result in arrests and criminal records being imposed on people who represent no threat to society. This problem could be minimized by making carry permits available to this segment of the population through the "shall issue" carry permit system previously discussed. Finally, like other warrantless searches, frisking people for weapons in public places raises serious Constitutional questions.

One way to minimize these problems would be to maintain the current rate of searches, but improve the rate at which patrol officers successfully identified weapons carriers. Close observation of large numbers of street searches, combined with the accumulated professional "folklore" of experienced patrol officers, might yield information on the observable suspect traits that are most strongly correlated with gun carrying and strengthen officers' basis for having "probable cause" or a "reasonable suspicion" that someone was unlawfully carrying a weapon. The resulting gun carrier profiles could facilitate more selective targeting and efficient use of street searches and the deterrence of gun carrying, hopefully without damaging police–community relations.

Other Elements

When a person previously without a criminal conviction is convicted of a felony or violent misdemeanor, they would no longer be able to acquire a gun legally, assuming that the conviction is promptly entered into the CCH files available for use in the records check system. However, although their continued possession of firearms would be a violation of existing federal law, there would be no practical way of ensuring that criminals did not continue to possess the guns they already owned before the conviction. Therefore, it should be a standard part of these defendants' sentences (where it is not already) that they be required to lawfully dispose of all firearms in their possession. It should also be a standard part of probation and parole conditions (where it is not already), that persons under correctional supervision for a relevant conviction not be allowed to possess firearms of any kind, including long guns. Police, probation, and parole officers should be authorized to search the homes and vehicles of persons with a relevant conviction and to confiscate any firearms found. While limits on police resources would restrict the frequency of these searches, even a small number of randomly targeted searches might exert a deterrent effect.

Findings in Chapter 10 indicated that robbery rates are reduced by laws providing discretionary add-on penalties for crimes committed with a gun. Sentence enhancement might therefore help reduce robbery, and this sort of law may be a helpful part of a gun control package. It is, however, a minor change from the status quo in that it is probably already in place, in some form, in all but a few states (Chapter 8). It is, however, more likely to avoid counterbalancing negative side-effects if it is discretionary. Therefore, states with mandatory sentence enhancement for gun crimes should seriously consider the merits of changing them to discretionary systems.

Chapter 10 results also indicated, rather surprisingly perhaps, that state and local dealer licensing seems to reduce assaults, and may also reduce suicides. It is unclear why this measure produces these results, and other mild measures do not. It also is unclear *how* the results are produced. It is possible that fairly restrictive dealer licensing reduces the number of dealers and thereby makes casual retail gun purchases marginally more difficult. Stricter dealer licensing might prove to be an effective element of gun control policy, whether imposed at the local, state, or federal level.

Don Kates (1990, pp. 60–1) suggested a number of other useful ways to fine-tune current gun laws. To deter gun theft, he proposed a law that (1) would impose a mandatory 3-year prison sentence on anyone who knowingly possesses a stolen gun, and (2) would rebuttably presume knowing possession if the defendant was found to have possessed two or more stolen guns. Although the mandatory sentencing feature may be inadvisable, for reasons suggested in Chapter 8, this sort of measure in a discretionary form might deter fences from buying stolen guns, and thereby reduce the incentive for thieves to steal them.

Kates also suggested strengthening state laws concerning gun possession by minors, through a uniform ban on "possession of any kind of gun by a person under 18 years of age, except under the supervision of a parent or other responsible adult" (p. 60). As subsistence hunting is not unknown in America, however, and some teenage hunters do not have a parent or guardian capable of supervising their hunting, an exception to Kates' proposal might be made for licensed hunters aged 14–17 possessing firearms during hunting season in a place suitable for hunting.

As a reasonable political compromise between gun control believers and agnostics, all of these control measures could be adopted with a "sunset" provision. The authorizing legislation would expire after, say, 10 years. It would mandate careful evaluation of the legislation's impact at the end of the 10 years, after which the legislature could vote to permanently renew it if it appeared to be effective. Those who truly believed the measures were ineffective would have to face useless controls for only a decade, whereas those who believed the opposite, and supported controls for their violence-reducing value, should be confident that the controls would eventually show their effectiveness and become permanent.

These proposals do not by any means exhaust all possibly useful forms of gun regulation. They do, however, address the core problem of gun control: developing politically acceptable and practically implementable strategies that can reduce gun availability among high-risk individuals at acceptable costs. All of the proposals, or similar ones, have received solid majority support in national surveys. Requiring a permit to purchase a gun or a license to possess one is supported by more than two-thirds of the population, whereas requiring a permit to carry is supported even more strongly (Table 9.2). More specifically relevant to an instant records check proposal, 78% U.S. adults in a 1989 Gallup poll indicated that they thought that prospective gun buyers should have to provide more information to police before being able to buy any firearm (DIALOG 1990). The proposals also meet all of the other requisites previously laid out.

The federal instant records check in some form would seem to be politically achievable. The official newsletter of the National Rifle Association's Institute for Legislative Action (its lobbying wing) in 1990 stated the NRA's qualified support of a version of this type of system: "NRA will also encourage adoption of an instantaneous check system (similar to the Virginia system) to identify those few felons who attempt to purchase firearms from dealers when the criminal history record accuracy and accessibility problem is corrected" (*NRA Action*, February, 1990, p. 3). Although the last clause is an important qualifier of support, the cited problems are correctable. Thus, the organization widely regarded as the principal political obstacle to meaningful gun control is publicly committed to supporting a version of the central element of the proposed regulatory strategy.

It should be stressed that neither this strategy nor any other gun control policy is likely to have a dramatic impact on violence in America. Because gun availability, even among high-risk individuals, seems to have at best a modest impact on violence rates, gun controls only nibble at the edges of the problem rather than striking at its core.

Significant, lasting reductions in violence are not likely to be produced by revisions of the criminal laws, reallocation of law enforcement resources, or tinkering with crime control strategies, whether they involve the conservative panaceas of "getting tough" on criminals and making war on drugs, or the liberal panaceas of offender rehabilitation and gun control (Walker 1989). In the long run, solving the violence problem will have to involve reducing economic inequality, injustice, and the social disorder these generate. It will have to involve improving the life chances of the underclass that contributes the bulk of both the victims and the perpetrators of violent crime (Wilson 1987, p. 120). How that might be done is beyond the scope of this book, but there surely has not been enough done to accomplish it yet, and the nation cannot afford to continue to ignore it as a means of reducing violence. Even if poverty reduction programs failed to prevent a single violent act, many could still be justified on their own merits, something that cannot be said for most gun control, drug enforcement, or crime control programs (Walker 1989). Continuing to delude ourselves that dramatic crime reductions can be achieved through the criminal justice system will doom us to ineffectuality, and to suffering the costs of undiminished violence, crime, and poverty.

Notes

Chapter 2

1. It has often been claimed that Switzerland, due to its militia system, has as high or higher a household prevalence of gun ownership as the United States. Recent evidence contradicts the claim. In a 14 nation telephone survey conducted in 1989, Killias (1990) found that only 32.6% of Swiss households reported a gun, compared to 48.9% of U.S. households. Only 12% of the Swiss households owned a private gun; the rest kept a gun in connection with military service.

2. The second of these studies corrected erroneous results in the first one. It is the findings of the second one that are relied on here.

3. Marginals for question 60 list specific sources of the most recently acquired gun for 90% of gun-owning Rs, and 32% of all gun owners cited a private source (DMI 1979, p. 71). The rest are cited sources that would generally be holders of dealer licenses—a gun shop, sporting goods, or department store, pawnshop, or a seller at a gun show. Therefore, among Rs identifying a specific sources, 35.6% (32/90 = 0.356) indicated a private, nondealer source.

Chapter 3

1. Unpublished BATF data on domestically manufactured and imported handguns were used (U.S. BATF 1989b). It was assumed that 75% of imported handguns were semiautomatic pistols, since 67 of 87 imported double-action revolver or semiautomatic handgun models listed in the 1989 *Gun Digest* were semiautomatic pistols (Warner 1988).

Chapter 4

1. The Cambridge Reports survey stands out as the deviant case among the surveys listed in Table 4.1. It shows far smaller estimates of the proportion of the population that has used a gun defensively. This is due apparently to several technical peculiarities of the study. First, the relevant question was asked only of persons who personally owned a handgun at the time of the survey, thereby excluding former owners and nonowners who had used guns defensively. Sec-

ond, the question was only asked of that subset of handgun owners who owned specifically for defensive reasons, excluding those who owned exclusively for nondefensive reasons but nevertheless may have used the gun defensively. Third, the relevant question was oddly worded, asking whether the respondent had "ever *had* to use" their handgun defensively (my emphasis). This further restricted affirmative answers since some may have used guns defensively without being certain that they "had to" in the sense of having no other alternative.

2. The NCS surveys may uncover gun crimes more completely than gun use surveys discover defensive uses because the former ask many questions probing separately for different types of victimization, whereas the gun-use surveys ask only once about defensive gun uses.

3. The gun accident death figure was obtained from secondary analysis of the 1969–1978 Mortality Detail File (ICPSR 1985) and the 1979 and 1980 Mortality Detail Files (U.S. NCHS 1982; 1983).

Chapter 6

1. Four of the 147 pages of text in the Newton and Zimring (1969) and 2–3 of 324 pages in Wright et al. (1983) were devoted to suicide. A notable exception is the 9 pages in Lester (1984a).

2. None of the following discussion is to be interpreted as an assertion that this choice of method is always completely rational. It is assumed only that enough suicides are at least partially influenced by rational considerations to affect the aggregate patterns of suicide methods used.

3. The expected number of total suicides for each year, 1965–1967, was computed using the following regression equation, estimated from the 1961–1964 suicide counts: $Y = 363.5 - 19X$, where Y = total suicides and X = year minus 1960.

Chapter 7

1. It should be stressed that Table 7.7 figures refer to victims, not shooters. Although the two are nearly always of the same race, they are often not of the same gender. Thus, the high rates for black females are at least partly a reflection of high rates of FGA shooting by black males, some of whom accidentally shoot black females.

2. Because no national data existed on this issue, and no one city would be likely to have enough relevant cases for meaningful analysis of police or coroner files, an attempt was made to gather information from large national insurance companies. Of the 50 largest companies in both the life and health insurance fields contacted, only one indicated any willingness to provide information. Most companies did not even reply to the letter. The single cooperative company could locate only 19 life insurance policy claims based on alleged gun accidents, over a 10-year period. No meaningful analysis of this small sample was possible. Nevertheless, the author thanks this company (which desires anonymity) and its employees for their help.

3. A single small-sample study produced findings substantially at variance

with previous work. Copeland (1984) found that 11 of 54, or 20% of Dade (Miami) County, Florida FGAs involved a defective firearm. Morrow and Hudson (1986) found that 14% of FGAs were linked with a "dropped or mishandled gun," but this included cases in which the trigger was pulled by the shooter, as in some or all of the eight cases in which the shooter tripped and fell while carrying a gun. Therefore, this result is not comparable with those in studies that separately tabulated cases explicitly due to a dropped gun, "gun falling from an insecure rest," or a "defective gun."

Chapter 10

1. Two different examples of laws providing added penalties for crimes committed with guns have been evaluated with a time series design (Loftin and McDowall 1984; Loftin et al. 1983). Only a single law, in one jurisdiction, has been evaluated, for each of the following types of laws: a law providing mandatory penalties for illegal carrying [in Massachusetts, evaluated by Pierce and Bowers (1981) and others], one banning handgun sales and possession (Nicholson and Garner 1980), and a law banning importation of cheap handguns (Zimring 1975; Magaddino and Medoff 1984).

2. These conclusions are based on the simple percentage changes reported by Nicholson and Garner, not their regression results. A reanalysis of their data by the U.S. Congressional Research Service (1980) showed that randomly generated numbers inserted into their regression model yielded results as strong as those reported by Nicholson and Garner, indicating that their methods were invalid.

APPENDIX

1

Production-Based Estimates of the Gun Stock (Chapter 2)

The figures through 1968 were obtained by the Task Force on Firearms of the National Commission on the Causes and Prevention of Violence, using the Commission's subpoena power to obtain gun manufacturers' records going back as far as 1899, supplemented by manufacturing data from the Census of Manufactures and import data from the Bureau of Customs (Newton and Zimring 1969, pp. 171–4). Production by companies no longer in business by 1968 was not counted, nor were imports before 1918, and the import and production figures after those years were not necessarily complete either. Therefore, figures in Table 2.1 understate net additions to the gun stock before 1945, and the true cumulated figures would necessarily be higher than indicated for later years. The figures are probably most useful for understanding trends in the gun stock since 1945, and for getting a very rough idea of the size of the existing civilian gun stock.

This method of estimating the gun stock, even for the post-1945 period, fails to count a number of flows into and out of the civilian stock. Although guns are extremely durable consumer goods, they can eventually wear out or, more likely, corrode into inoperable condition due to neglect. Gun manufacturers claim that the useful life of a gun in terms of shots fired is from 10,000 to 100,000 rounds, depending on the type and quality of the gun (Newton and Zimring 1969, p. 5). In 1982, about 4.4 billion units of small arms ammunition (cartridges and shotshells) were shipped by U.S. manufacturers (U.S. Bureau of the Census 1984, p.34E-13). If this is an adequate, rough estimate of the number of rounds fired, it implies that there were only about 24 rounds fired per gun per year. Even with the shorter life span of only 10,000 rounds, this would imply the average gun would last over 400 years before wearing out from use. Of course a few especially frequently used guns may in fact wear out, but it is doubtful if sheer wear-and-tear on otherwise well-maintained guns is a significant source of gun loss. Newton and Zimring (1969, p. 4) reported that 7 of 328 handguns in a sample of weapons confiscated by police had been manufactured before 1899, suggesting that there was even some criminal use of guns that were over 70 years old. Many guns held by noncriminals are also carefully preserved for decades. For example, Hawley (1988, p. 1481) noted that many Southerners preserve and maintain "ancestral weaponry from 'the war' and subsequent conflicts," as well as family hunting guns passed down for generations, because they "serve as a vital link to ancestors" and as evidence of "who they were." This "totemic significance" is still another reason to maintain even very old guns in working order.

However, guns flow out of the active civilian gun stock in other ways besides wearing out. Given that guns are both valuable and dangerous, it seems likely that their owners are even more careful not to lose them than most other types of personal property, but certainly some are lost. Guns can be lost in the woods while hunting or dropped overboard from a boat, for example. A few guns may be stored away in an attic, basement, garage, or barn, and forgotten. In one sense these guns are still in the civilian gun stock, yet they are no longer available for use. A more important source of loss, however, would be rust or corrosion in poorly maintained guns. If not cleaned and kept dry, some guns can rust or corrode to the point of being inoperable. And although made of extremely strong materials, guns can be broken or damaged to a point where they become not worth repairing. Whether a large number of guns are in fact lost in these ways each year is unknown. There has been an attempt to produce loss estimates that amounted to little more than speculation, as even the estimators themselves conceded (Wright et al. 1983, pp. 31–4). It is difficult to make estimates based on experience with other consumer goods since few products are both comparable with guns and have well-documented life spans. For example, although the lifetimes of automobiles can be documented, they are radically different from guns. Firearms are relatively simple devices, have few moving parts to malfunction, have few or no parts made out of materials that are easily broken or worn out (such as glass or plastic), are used only very infrequently, and thus are subject to relatively little wear and tear, and are relatively cheap to maintain and repair. Motor vehicles are the opposite in all these respects and consequently almost certainly have far shorter usable life spans than firearms.

Guns can also be, at least temporarily, taken out of the civilian stock through police confiscation. A survey of police departments (U.S. National Bureau of Standards 1977) indicated that in the several hundred departments reporting, with about 250,000 full time equivalent (FTE) police officers (estimated from Tables 1.5-2, 11 A-1, and 12 A-1), there were 113,377 handguns and 34,227 shoulder weapons confiscated in 1970 and 1971 combined. This implies that about 0.441 handguns, 0.135 shoulder guns, or 0.579 total guns are confiscated per FTE officer per year. With about 500,000 FTE police officers in the nation in 1987 (U.S. Federal Bureau of Investigation 1988), one can project roughly 220,500 handguns, 67,500 shoulder guns, and 290,000 total guns confiscated per year in the nation as a whole, generously assuming that small town and rural police seize as many guns as the predominantly big city police covered in this survey.

This would represent a significant loss to the civilian stock if all the guns were destroyed or otherwise taken permanently out of circulation. However, many are sold at auction or returned to their owners. In the aforementioned survey, police agencies reported that 19.7% of handguns seized were returned to the owner or resold, and another 8.2% were turned over to another agency, which may have put the guns back into general circulation (Tables 11 C-3 and 12 C-3 combined). However, even these figures may understate recirculation. The profit incentive of selling guns may be too much for fiscally strained police agencies and local governments to resist. For a police agency to admit that it simply puts confiscated guns back into circulation could make the agency appear irresponsible, so many agencies may understate the rate at which they do this. Assuming a minimum 19.7% recirculation rate, at most only about 177,000 handguns, 56,000 shoulder guns, or 233,000 guns total are taken out of the civilian stock each year through police confiscations, representing losses that would have been about 5% of the five million additions to the total stock of guns in 1971, and about 10% of the 1.8 million handgun additions (Table 2.1).

On the other hand, there are also additions to the gun stock that these figures do not take into account. Whereas guns produced by licensed firearms manufacturers are counted, those that are handmade by nonlicensed persons, such as teenage gang members' "zip guns," are not. Likewise, whereas those legally imported under import licenses are counted, those illegally smuggled, or brought into the country by returning servicemen, foreign visitors, and returning tourists are not (Newton and Zimring 1969, pp. 4–5). It has been estimated that 8.8 million guns were brought back to the United States as war trophies over an unspecified period of time (U.S. Government Accounting Office 1978, p. 18). There are no firm estimates of the size of most of these flows, and due to the illegal or quasilegal nature of some of them, there probably never will be. Another major source of additions to the gun stock after the end of each major war is the sale of military surplus firearms. Between 1940 and 1969, there may have been as many as 12 million surplus guns added to the civilian stock (Newton and Zimring 1969, p. 4), or over 400,000 per year, a number that more than counterbalances the guns removed from the stock through police confiscations. Further, guns stolen from military armories presumably find their way into the civilian stock (e.g., *Gun Week* 9-19-75, p. 17). The estimates in Table 2.1, like those produced by Newton and Zimring, are based on the assumption that the uncounted additions to the stock equal uncounted losses. We know of no evidence to either support or undercut this assumption. The assumption's principal attraction is its simplicity, rather than the firmness of its empirical support.

APPENDIX

2

Survey-Based Estimates of the Gun Stock (Chapter 2)

One major flaw in survey-based estimates of the gun stock is that some respondents (Rs) intentionally conceal their gun ownership. The reasons some may do this are not hard to guess. Some Rs may be leery of the strangers who call them on the phone or show up on their doorsteps claiming to be survey workers, suspecting they may be agents of a government laying the groundwork for confiscation of their guns. Others possess guns illegally, or think they do, or have doubts about the legal status of the guns they possess. More mundanely, some Rs may simply feel it is none of any stranger's business whether they own guns. Once they have agreed to be interviewed, such Rs can conceal gun ownership by refusing to answer the question, by saying they do not know whether there are any guns in their household, or by simply lying and giving a false "no" answer. It is doubtful if many Rs take the first two alternatives since these would make them stand out as uncooperative Rs and make it appear they had something to conceal. Some Rs must anticipate that such behavior would make interviewers regard them as gun owners anyway, so it would be an ineffective way of concealing gun ownership. Indeed, some survey researchers have applied precisely this interpretation to refusals and "don't know" responses, noting that Rs who give these responses closely resemble Rs who admit gun ownership (U.S. Congress 1975a). In contrast, a simple "no" response should elicit no interviewer skepticism, since an inaccurate "no" would look the same as an accurate one.

Only one set of researchers has gathered evidence directly bearing on whether significant numbers of survey Rs conceal gun ownership. In a 1977 survey of Illinois adults, Bordua et al. (1979) asked Rs in an early part of the interview whether they personally owned any guns, had owned guns in the past 5 years, and whether there were any guns in their household. Then in a later part of the interview, after a long series of intervening questions about other topics, Rs were asked whether they had a Firearms Owner' Identification Card (FOIC), the license every Illinois gun owner was required to have in order to legally possess any kind of firearm. One possible indication that Rs had concealed gun ownership was if they replied "no" to the gun ownership question, but "yes" to the FOIC question. Of 141 Rs who reported a license, 13 had earlier claimed that they did not personally own a gun, had not owned one in the previous 5 years, lived in a household where no else owned one, and thus apparently had no reason for possessing the license (Bordua 1982; survey described in Bordua et al. 1979).

There are a number of possible reasons for this apparent discrepancy besides an inaccurate response to the gun ownership question. First, it is possible an R had obtained the license in anticipation of getting a gun, but had not yet acquired one at the time of the interview, around May 1977. In Illinois, as of May 1, 1977, there were about 1,133,549 valid licenses, 16,094 of which had been issued in the previous 3 months (Bordua et al. 1979, p. 243). Therefore, we would expect about 1.4% of our sample license holders to have gotten the licenses in the previous 3 months. Even if as many as half of these had still not obtained a gun by the time of interview, this would amount to only about 0.7% of the 141 licensees, or perhaps one person of the 13 "discrepant" Rs. This still left 12 Rs with no apparent reason for having a license. Second, it is also conceivable that some of these Rs obtained a license for occupational reasons, e.g., to work as a security guard (police officers do not need a license to have a gun), even though they did not own guns themselves, or to demonstrate to a prospective employer that they could pass the criminal records check associated with the licensing process. However, given that only about 0.7% of employed persons in the United States work as "guards" of some sort (U.S. Bureau of the Census 1987, pp. 376–7), and most of these probably own guns of their own, it is doubtful if many of the 12 "discrepant" Rs had an occupational need for a license for a gun they did not own. Therefore, in addition to 122 license holders presumably honest in admitting gun ownership, there were another 12 license holders who denied gun ownership with no other apparent reason for having a license. These figures imply that the true rate of gun ownership was at least 10% (12/122) higher than the admitted ownership figures suggested. However, this may be an underestimate of underreporting of gun ownership, since the detection method can uncover only underreporting Rs who failed to give consistent answers on the license and ownership questions. Many other Rs may have falsely denied gun ownership but also denied (accurately or not) possession of a license.

In addition to Rs providing false "no" responses, the few Rs who refuse to answer the ownership question are probably also mostly gun owners. Researchers analyzed the 5% of the Rs who refused to answer the gun ownership question in a 1975 national survey and concluded that "their attributes are so much like gun owners (and in many cases are even more intense than those of gun owners) that the bulk of these people could not be classified as non-gun owners" (U.S. Congress 1975a, p. 8). Thus, in addition to the 41% of their sample who admitted household gun ownership, the majority of another 5% who refused to answer the ownership question were also probably gun owners, implying that another upward adjustment in measured gun ownership would be called for. At this point, it seems reasonable to conclude that true household rates of gun ownership could easily be 10 to 20% higher. That is, the rates might be 5–10 percentage points above the reported rates averaging around 46%.

Another reason to suspect that survey figures understate gun ownership would be if there were a major discrepancy between the production-based estimates of the gun stock and the survey-based estimate. Table 2.3 presented figures drawn from those national surveys that asked how many guns were owned in gun-owning households. The 1968 Harris survey was used by Newton and Zimring to estimate the total number of guns in the United States. They simply calculated the average number of guns per gun-owning household, multiplied it by the number of U.S. households, and by the fraction of survey households reporting a gun.

A critical step in this process is choosing a category mean for the highest category. For example, among households that fall into the "five-or-more" handguns category, what is the average number of handguns owned? None of the survey sources used in Table 2.3 reported this sort of figure. Newton and Zimring simply arbitrarily assigned a number, and a rather low one at that, but Wright et al. showed that the estimated gun stock could be made far higher than the Newton and Zimring estimate simply by choosing a higher mean for the upper category (1983, pp. 37–8). In Table 2.3 more generous, empirically based means were assigned to the highest categories, yielding higher survey-based estimates of the gun stock, reducing the discrepancy between survey and production estimates.

It is conceivable that the means to the highest categories are still too low. However, unlike those of Newton and Zimring, these means are empirically based. They were computed directly from the results of the 1977 Illinois survey (Bordua et al. 1979, p. 99). The mean number of guns of all types per gun-owning household was 6.935 for four-or-more households, 8.520 for five-or-more households, and 15.286 for ten-or-more households. These figures have been rounded and used in the Table 2.3 calculations. The Illinois results for all guns have also been used for handguns only, although the mean number of handguns in the higher categories would not be as high as the mean number of all guns. This results in a generous survey-based estimate of the number of handguns. Note, however, that the upper category mean could be increased considerably without bringing most of the survey estimates anywhere near the production-based estimates.

The Table 2.3 figures still indicate that most survey-based estimates are far lower than the production-based estimates in Table 2.1. For example, production cumulations indicate about 102 million guns and 28 million handguns by the end of 1968, but the Harris survey results implied only about 82 million guns and 16 million handguns. From 1968 to 1983, this discrepancy worsened. The cumulated production figure by the end of 1975 for all gun types was about 140 million, whereas the 1975 Gallup survey results implied only about 76 million guns. More recently, the handgun cumulations had reached nearly 59 million by the end of 1983, but the 1983 Gallup survey results implied only about 28 million, less than half as many. Although the discrepancy for the 1968 Harris survey results is not as great as Newton and Zimring found when they assigned excessively low means to the highest categories (1969, p. 6), there is still an enormous discrepancy remaining between these four surveys and corresponding production estimates. Given the empirical evidence of underreporting of gun ownership in surveys, and the lack of any firm evidence of a net undercount in the production-based estimates, the latter seem more credible for judging the size of the U.S. gun stock.

More recently, very different survey results were obtained. The December 1989 Time/CNN national telephone survey of gun owners found that the mean number of guns owned per gun-owning household was 4.41 (Quinley 1990). If the 1989 figure of 48% (Table 2.3) is used for the fraction of households with guns, and is applied to an estimated 92,830,000 U.S. households *Statistical Abstract of the United States 1990*, p. 45, this implies about 196 million total guns by the end of 1989 ($4.41 \times 0.48 \times 92.8$ million $=$ 196 million). If one extrapolates the Table 2.1 production-based estimate for 1987 to the end of 1989, by assuming the same annual net additions to the gun stock as in 1987, an estimate of

207.1 million guns results. Thus the latest survey data implied an estimate that was only 5% lower than the production-based estimate. Using this 1989 survey, the two data sources do not diverge very much, and both figures imply over 200 million guns by the end of 1990. On the other hand, data from the 1989 Gallup poll imply only 3.501 guns per gun-owning household. Using the same estimation procedures as above, these figures imply 149.4 million guns, only 72% of the production-based estimate. Thus, although the surveys do generally appear to understate the size of the gun stock, the Time/CNN poll was a notable exception. Both 1989 surveys, however, strongly support the idea that the number of guns owned by each gun-owning household increased substantially from 1975 to 1989.

Besides the generally enormous discrepancies in estimates of the gun stock, the most noticeable inconsistency between survey data and the production cumulations is that the survey estimates do not indicate any increase in the prevalence of household gun ownership from 1965 to 1990, despite huge net inflows of guns, especially handguns, into the civilian stock. Survey-measured household handgun prevalence showed substantial increases, but even these largely ceased after 1978. According to the surveys, the prevalence of household gun ownership has been quite stable from 1959 to 1990, fluctuating around a mean of 46%, and rarely more than three or four percentage points higher or lower.

Of course it is hypothetically possible for the fraction of households owning to remain the same and for these already-owning households to absorb *any* number of new guns. However, given the magnitude of the inflow, it is hard to believe that demand for guns could increase enormously among those already owning guns, without the fraction of the population wanting to own a gun also increasing to some degree, since at least some of the factors causing the former should also influence the latter. In any case, the data in Table 2.3 indicated that shifts in the average number of guns owned per household were not sufficient to account for much of the inflow of guns before 1983. Whereas the average number of handguns did increase rapidly from about 1.3 in 1968 to about 1.9 in 1983, the average number of guns of all types would appear to have actually dropped a bit from 1968 to 1975, from about 2.7 to about 2.3.

It can be concluded tentatively that survey data are generally inadequate for judging either the size of the current gun stock or trends in gun ownership over time. One way to account for the discrepancy in these assessments of recent trends in gun ownership is to assume that over the past three decades an increasing fraction of survey Rs have incorrectly denied gun ownership. This has also been the conclusion of Newton and Zimring (1969, p. 6), Erskine (1972, p. 456), Kennett and Anderson (1975, p. 253), Stinchcombe and his colleagues (1980, p. 115), and many others (though not Wright et al. 1983).

APPENDIX

3

Substitution of Long Guns for Handguns

For purposes of analyzing the effects of regulating a specific type of weapon, there are three categories of weapons: (1) the restricted weapon, (2) possible substitute weapons more lethal than the restricted one, and (3) possible substitute weapons less lethal than the restricted one. Let us assume the most optimistic possible scenario—a handgun-only control policy successfully deprives all violence-prone persons of handguns. These individuals can adapt in one of three ways: (1) refrain from committing violent acts altogether, (2) do violence with putatively more lethal substitute weapons such as rifles or shotguns, or (3) do violence with putatively less lethal weapons such as knives, blunt objects, or personal weapons such as hands or feet. Although the analysis is directed at handgun-only policies, the general logic of the following analysis would apply to policies focusing on any weapon type. The following notation will be used:

AFR_1 = attack fatality rate, restricted weapon (handgun)
AFR_2 = attack fatality rate, more lethal substitute weapons (long guns)
AFR_3 = attack fatality rate, less lethal substitute weapons (e.g., knives, blunt instruments, hands, feet)
D_2 = AFR_2/AFR_1—deadliness ratio of more lethal substitute weapons (long guns) compared to restricted weapons (handguns)
D_3 = AFR_3/AFR_1—deadliness ratio of less lethal substitute weapons compared to restricted weapons (handguns)
S = fraction substituting more lethal weapons (long guns) in attacks, among attackers who otherwise would have used the restricted weapons (handguns) but were denied that weapon (the fraction substituting less lethal weapons would therefore be $1 - S$)
N = total number of persons wounded with restricted weapons (handguns), in the absence of the restrictions

An equation can be derived that expresses how these parameters are related to one another at the point at which the number of handgun homicide deaths under existing conditions, with handguns relatively available (left side of equal sign), exactly equals the number of homicides that would occur if handguns were completely eliminated (right side of equal sign). This is the "tipping point" where the handgun-only control policy neither helps nor harms, because it results in the same number of deaths as previously occurred without the policy:

$$N \times AFR_1 = (N \times S \times AFR_2) + [N \times (1 - S) \times AFR_3] \qquad (1)$$

Substituting $AFR_1 \times D_2$ for AFR_2 and $AFR_1 \times D_3$ for AFR_3,

$$N \times AFR_1 = (N \times S \times AFR_1 \times D_2) + [N(1 - S)AFR_1 \times D_3] \qquad (2)$$

$$N \times AFR_1 = (N \times S \times AFR_1 \times D_1) + (N \times AFR_1 \times D_3) - (N \times S \times AFR_1 \times D_3) \qquad (3)$$

Dividing both sides by $N \times AFR_1$,

$$1 = (S \times D_2) + D_3 - (S \times D_3) \qquad (4)$$

$$1 - D_3 = S(D_2 - D_3) \qquad (5)$$

$$S = (1 - D_3)/(D_2 - D_3) \qquad (6)$$

Equation (6) expresses how the substitution fraction S is related to the two deadliness ratios, at the "tipping point" where a policy restricting only handguns neither reduces nor increases the number of homicide deaths. The larger S, D_2, and D_3 are, the more likely it is that deaths with the handgun-only restrictions will exceed deaths without them.

Deadliness Ratios

In Chapter 5, the data in Table 5.3 indicated that the gun wounding fatality rate was four times as large as the rate for knife woundings. At least some of this 4–1 difference in death rates reflects differences in motivation of gun attackers compared to knife attackers. Therefore the corresponding *deadliness ratio*, D_3 (based on an assumption of equal motivation), would necessarily be less than 4–1 (see Chapter 5). The deadliness ratio would be only 1 if all of the death rate difference was due to attacker motivation differences, but this is implausible. The deadliness ratio is therefore probably somewhere between 1 and 4; a reasonable working assumption would be to set D_3 at 3. This would be consistent with medical studies that show that gunshot wounds are three to four times as likely to result in death as knife wounds, noting, however, that the difference is smaller if one examines only wounds inflicted in the same area of the body (Wilson and Sherman 1961, p. 640; Ryzoff et al. 1966, p. 652).

What is the deadliness of long guns relative to handguns? Rifles fire bullets at much higher velocity than do handguns, whereas shotguns fire a larger number and mass of projectiles with each round. Long guns are also more accurate than handguns, and thus are more likely to hit a victim at which they are aimed. Although medical experts on gunshot wounds and firearms experts agree that long guns are more deadly, on average, than handguns, they have not produced any agreed-on quantitative measure of this difference, so the issue must be addressed here.

In comparing different guns with one another, experts actually compare ammunition types with each other, since the lethality of a gun is largely a function of the power of its ammunition. Although factors linked to the gun itself, like its barrel length, can affect the velocity and accuracy of the bullet fired, lethality is largely a function of ammunition characteristics, such as the weight, width, and length of the bullet (the projectile part of the cartridge), the shape of the bullet (hollowed-out bullets are more damaging than flat-nosed ones, which are in turn more damaging than rounded or pointed ones), and the velocity at which it can be propelled (a function of the power of its powder charge, among other things—Kleck 1984b and sources reviewed there). The evidence indicates that D_2 could easily exceed 5, but that ratios as low as 1.5 to 3 are plausible as well.

Substitution Fraction

Substitution of one weapon for another can occur in several ways. After handgun restrictions were imposed, a long gun might be acquired to substitute for a handgun seized by police or voluntarily surrendered. Or a person without a handgun, who would have acquired one had there been no legal restrictions, might acquire a long gun instead. Then, once in possession of the substitute weapon, a violence-prone person may or may not actually substitute it in violent acts that otherwise would have involved handguns. That is, such a person might substitute a long gun in possession, but not in violent use. Here, the parameter S refers to the level of substitution of long guns for handguns in violent acts.

Long guns cannot be substituted in some homicides that involve handguns because long guns are too big and thus not sufficiently concealable. Some handgun homicides occur in a way that requires the attacker to either carry the gun concealed or in some other way required a small gun. However, this does not generally seem to be the case. Most homicides occur in one of two circumstances: (1) as a result of a premeditated crime, either the attack itself or another crime like a robbery, or (2) in connection with an unpremeditated crime that occurs in or near the aggressor's home. In the first situation, a long gun can be made available by prearrangement, for use in the planned crime; in the second situation a long gun would be available by virtue of daily routine. In either situation, there is little to block substitution of a long gun for a handgun.

The most common location for a homicide is in the home of the killer, where concealability would be unnecessary for violent use of a gun. This would be especially true of the domestic homicides that handgun controls are supposedly best able to prevent. Other common locations are near the offender's home, in or near the offender's car, and other places near to locations where long guns could easily be kept (Kleck 1986b).

Even when the killings occur in other settings, it is often unnecessary for a gun to be as small as a handgun in order to be used. Both rifles and shotguns can be shortened by sawing off most of their barrel and/or stock, a process requiring only a few minutes' effort and a hacksaw. A double-barreled shotgun can be cut down to a total length of as little as 9 inches; minimum lengths for other long guns would be 20 inches for a pump or semiautomatic shotgun, and as little as 7 inches for some rifles (Fields 1979). These weapons would still not be quite as small as most handguns, but they would certainly be small enough to be completely concealed inside a sport jacket or raincoat without attracting the attention of a police officer passing in a patrol car. They would therefore have *sufficient* concealability for most violent purposes (Kleck 1986b).

There is only one class of situations in which substitution of long guns would be difficult. If a homicide was committed without premeditation, in a setting distant from the attacker's home or car, the only way a gun is likely to be involved is if the attacker routinely carried one on his person. And although there would be little difficulty carrying sawed-off long guns on a short-term basis for committing a particular premeditated crime such as a robbery or burglary, most people would probably find it uncomfortable and inconvenient to carry such a gun on a routine basis. Nevertheless, homicides committed in this type of situation are in the minority. Perhaps 54–80% of homicides occur in circumstances in which it would be easy to substitute long guns for handguns, either because the killing occurred in or near the killer's home or car, or because it was planned or was the by-product of some planned crime like a robbery (Kleck 1986b).

It might be thought that some people would not substitute long guns for handguns because the former are more expensive and would be beyond the means of at least a few violence-prone persons. For those who acquire guns by stealing, this consideration would be obviously irrelevant. However, even among those who purchase their guns, price would be little obstacle to substitution. Based on data contained in the 1987 Census of Manufactures, the average net selling value at the factory was $176.22 for handguns, compared to $182.81 for rifles and $210.55 for shotguns ($193.66 for rifles and shotguns combined; U.S. Bureau of the Census 1989, p. 4). Thus long guns cost only 10% more than handguns. However, even this much difference reflects only aggregate averages—there are many specific models of long guns available that are cheaper than the average handgun.

Although it is clear that long guns *could* be substituted for handguns in most homicides, with neither cost nor circumstances preventing it, the question remains as to how often prospective killers would actually do so. Relevant information was obtained from the Wright–Rossi survey of prisoners, who were asked: "If you wanted to carry a handgun but you just couldn't get your hands on one, which of the following do you think you would do?—Carry knife or club, Carry sawed-off (shoulder weapon), or Not carry?" Among men who had used handguns many times in past crimes, 72% said they would carry sawed-off shoulder guns, and even among those who had used handguns only a few times in crimes, 51% said they would carry long guns (Wright and Rossi 1986, p. 217). Since it is less convenient to carry these guns on the person than it is to keep them in one's home or vehicle, substitution in home possession would presumably be even higher than in carrying on the person. Although not inconceivable, it would seem, at the very least, to be optimistic to expect that the substitution fraction would be less than half. A more reasonable educated guess of its size, consistent with available evidence, would be about two-thirds, the midpoint of the 54–80% range mentioned before.

APPENDIX

4

Alternate Estimates of the Number of Defensive Uses of Guns (Chapter 4)

There are many technical differences between the surveys asking about defensive gun use (Table 4.1), but their results can be made more comparable with each other with some adjustments. For example, the Field poll did not separate uses against animals from uses against people. The December 1978 DMI survey found that 12% of gun owners reported a defensive gun use, but only 7% had used a gun against a person. Therefore, one can adjust the Field result that 1.4% of Rs reported use of a handgun for protection in the preceding year by multiplying it by $7/12$: $1.4\% \times 7/12 = 0.817\%$. Multiplying this by the 1976 U.S. population, age 18 and over, of 149,459,000 (U.S. Bureau of the Census 1979, p. 27) yields an estimated 1.2 million defensive handgun uses per year. This is 89% *higher* than the estimate based on the Hart survey, and higher by any even larger margin than the estimate derived from the Mauser survey.

Note that California had a rate of household handgun ownership, 20.5%, that was almost identical to that of the United States as a whole in 1976, 21% (Table 2.2). Nevertheless, it could be objected that the Field poll was only a single-state survey, and was not necessarily representative of the nation. California did have a higher reported crime rate than the United States in 1976, resulting in more occasions for defensive actions.

Therefore, it is useful to compare the estimates based on the Hart and Mauser surveys to estimates derived from two other national surveys. First, the May–June 1978 DMI survey found that 15% of U.S. households reported ever using a gun for protection. One can adjust for the difference in recall periods between "ever" vs. the past year by using Field survey information based on the two recall periods. That survey found that 1.4% of Rs reported defensive gun use in the past year, whereas 8.6% reported "ever" using. Multiplying 15% by 1.4/8.6 yields an estimate that 2.442% of DMI households had used guns in the past year. One can then adjust for the failure to exclude uses against animals by multiplying 2.442% by 7/12, yielding 1.424%. Finally, one can adjust for the fact that the inquiry was as to all gun types, rather than just handguns, dividing by the 1.214 ratio of defensive uses of all guns over defensive uses of handguns (discussed in Chapter 4): 1.424 × 1.214 = 1.173%. Multiplying by the 76,473,000 U.S. households in 1978 gives an estimated 897,014 households with at least one defensive use of a handgun in 1978. This too is higher than the estimates based on the Hart and Mauser surveys.

Finally, the December 1989 Time/CNN survey found that 9% of gun owners had ever fired a gun for self-protection. Using data from the May–June DMI survey, which found that 15% had ever used a gun for defense but only 9% had ever *fired* one for defensive purposes, 9% is multiplied by 15/6 to get 22.5%. Adjusting for "ever used" vs. past year use, 22.5% is multiplied by 1.4/8.6 to get 3.66%. Next, to adjust for the failure to exclude uses against animals, 3.66% is multiplied by 7/12 to get 2.14%. Finally, to adjust for the question covering all guns rather than just handguns, 2.14% is divided by 1.214, yielding 1.76%. About 28% of the U.S. population age 18 and over personally owned a gun in 1987 (Table 2.2), and there were about 182,628,000 persons of this age in 1988, projected to grow by 1% to 184,266.633 in 1989 (U.S. Bureau of the Census 1989, p. 23; 1990, p. 24). Multiplying by 28% yields an estimated 51,594,654 persons who personally owned a gun in 1989. Multiplying this by 1.76% yields an estimated 908,061 defensive uses of handguns per year in 1989. Again, the figure is higher than those yielded by the Hart and Mauser surveys, perhaps differing by this much because of the differences in recall periods covered. Needless to say, because these numerous adjustments are all subject to question, these alternative estimates should not be given as much weight as the Hart and Mauser poll results. The purpose of the foregoing was merely to show that the Hart and Mauser surveys were not unique in yielding high estimates of defensive gun uses.

APPENDIX

5

Legal Classification and Counting of Defensive Homicides (Chapter 4)

Classification of homicides can be very complex, so this Appendix outlines some of the major distinctions. Table A-1 indicates that some accidental killings are considered criminal homicides, and vice versa, whereas some intentional killings are noncriminal. Negligent manslaughters are accidental, but criminal, as when a drunken Fourth of July celebrant shoots into the air and unintentionally kills a bystander. Justifiable homicides are intentional but noncriminal, as when a robbery victim kills a robber. Some excusable homicides are accidents without negligence (and therefore noncriminal), whereas others are noncriminal intentional defensive homicides, as when a victim of an assault defends himself and kills the aggressor. Nearly all killings by on-duty police officers are treated (correctly or not) as justifiable homicides, so these noncriminal killings are the only subcategory of killings by police.

For the most part, the national vital statistics system and the FBI Uniform Crime Reporting system classify homicides in fairly comparable ways. The vital statistics system counts intentional homicides separately from accidental killings, and the FBI similarly classifies "murders and nonnegligent manslaughters" (all intentional) separately from criminal, but accidental "negligent manslaughters." Both data systems separately classify killings by police, the vital statistics system classifying them as homicides "due to legal intervention," and the FBI counting them as police justifiable homicides. The only noteworthy difference between the two systems is in the way they treat civilian legal defensive homicides (CLDHs). The FBI provides a separate classification of "civilian justifiable homicides" that covers a portion of these killings, though in practice the majority of them may get misclassified as "murders and nonnegligent manslaughters." The vital statistics system has no separate category for these homicides—these are simply lumped into the various

Table A–1. Classification of Homicides

Civilian				Police
Intentional		*Accidental*		*Intentional*
Criminal	*Noncriminal*	*Criminal*	*Noncriminal*	*Noncriminal*
Murder; nonnegligent manslaughter	Justifiable homicide; excusable-defensive homicide	Negligent manslaughter	Excusable-accidental homicide	Justifiable homicide

"death due to intentional assault" categories—gun homicides, knife homicides, and so on.

Each of the 50 states has its own definitions of the different types of noncriminal civilian homicides. Attempting to use a definition spanning these variations, the FBI Uniform Crime Reporting Handbook defines a civilian justifiable homicide as "the killing (during the commission of a felony) of a felon by a private citizen" (U.S. Department of Justice 1980, p. 6). The associated discussion also contains this admonition to police officers filling out Supplementary Homicide Report (SHR) forms: "Do not count a killing as justifiable or excusable solely on the basis of self-defense or the action of a coroner, prosecutor, grand jury, court." Thus it is clear that homicides are treated as nonjustifiable when initial police investigation labels them so, even if a prosecutor, judge, or jury later declares them to have been justifiable.

It is less clear what the parenthetical phrase "during the commission of a felony" means. One would think the phrase is redundant regarding any genuine self-defense killing, since the person attacking the defender would be committing a criminal assault and thus would, by definition, be a felon. Evidently the FBI intends this phrase to refer to other felonies besides assaults. Thus they would not count a self-defense killing as a civilian justifiable homicide (CJH) unless there was some other felony such as robbery or rape involved. This view is supported by the Handbook's inclusion of two hypothetical scenarios of "pure" self-defense homicides not involving other felonies besides an assault, both of which are scored as criminal, i.e., nonjustifiable, homicides (examples 1.a-2, 1.a-4, pp. 7, 8).

California's annual report on homicide also confirms the impression that most civilian self-defense homicides are not treated as CJHs by the

FBI. The report notes that although the California Penal Code treats self-defense killings as justifiable, "the national UCR (Uniform Crime Reports) Program does not" and that "for the most part, self-defense cases are treated as willful rather than justifiable homicide" (California 1983, p. 32). By "willful" homicides, the report was apparently referring to criminal homicides, since the report's count of 2778 "willful homicides" for California in 1982 was virtually identical to the 2779 "murders and nonnegligent manslaughters" reported from California in 1982 to the FBI (U.S. FBI 1983, p. 50). Therefore, most CLDHs fall outside the FBI's count of CJHs.

The criminal law defines two major types of noncriminal homicides: justifiable and excusable. The legal definition of justifiable homicide only roughly parallels the FBI definition. According to *Black's Law Dictionary* a justifiable homicide is a killing "such as is committed intentionally, but without any evil design and under such circumstances of necessity or duty as render the act proper, and relieve the party from any blame" (Black 1951, p. 867). Although self-defense may be involved, there is also some implication of social obligation or duty as well—the killer was obligated to kill and acted "as a matter of right." *Black's* gives an example of a killing that is part of an "endeavor to prevent the commission of a felony which could not be otherwise avoided," thus paralleling the FBI definition; however, the legal definition is not limited to such cases.

Most CLDHs appear to fit better into the other major legal category of noncriminal homicide, "excusable homicide." This category encompasses two quite different types of killings, only one of which involves self-defense. The other type is "homicide by misadventure" or "homicide *per infortunium*"—accidental killings "as where a man doing a lawful act, without any intention of hurt, unfortunately kills another." Thus the accidental killing of one person by another, in the absence of criminal negligence, is one type of excusable homicide. The second type is a variety of self-defense killing, "homicide *se defendendo*." This is "the killing of a person in self-defense upon a sudden affray." *Black's* notes that the name excusable homicide "imports some fault, error or omission, so trivial, however, that the law excuses it from guilt of felony."

The way local police agencies use the terms justifiable and excusable often differs from both the FBI definition and that of the law dictionary. For example, some departments label as justifiable cases that appear to fit the law dictionary definition of excusable homicide. Examination of homicide narratives in one study indicates this was the case in Dade County, Florida in 1980 (Wilbanks 1984, pp. 193–374). Other departments seem unwilling to label any civilian self-defense homicides as either justifiable or excusable. The only cases labeled by Philadelphia police in 1948 to 1952 as excusable homicides were accidents (i.e., homicide by misadventure) and the only cases labeled justifiable homicides were killings by police, despite the fact that police had recorded "self-defense" as the motive in eight civilian killings, all of which later resulted in verdicts of not guilty (Wolfgang 1958, pp. 24, 228, 301–2).

FBI counts of homicides are based on how the events are classified as a result of initial police investigations (U.S. Department of Justice 1980). However, these classifications are frequently contradicted by decisions at later stages of the legal process, as when a prosecutor drops a case or a court dismisses a case or finds a defendant not guilty of criminal homicide because the killing was in self-defense. Many more homicides are eventually declared noncriminal by prosecutors and courts than are so defined by police in their initial investigations. Wilbanks reported that 72 civilian homicides in Dade County in 1980 were ultimately declared "justifiable," but examination of the 1980 national SHR (ICPSR 1984a) dataset shows that only 24 civilian justifiable homicides were reported to the FBI from Dade County police agencies.

Even if available, counts of CLDHs based on the final decisions of prosecutors and judges might themselves understate the frequency of defensive killings. Various researchers have found as many as 38% of criminal homicides involve victim precipitation, i.e., the ultimate victim was the first party to use physical force in the incident (Curtis 1974, pp. 82–3). Although not all are instances of legally permitted self-defensive action, all of these acts are behaviorally defensive in the sense that the killer was responding to the victim's initial use of violence against him. It is possible, then, that some cases of "criminal homicide" should have been defined as legal defensive killings by the judges and prosecutors involved, but were not, possibly due to the killer's prior criminal background, involvement in morally questionable activities at the time of the killing, etc.

APPENDIX

6

Technical Problems in Using National Crime Survey Incident Files Data (Chapter 5)

Distinguishing Victims and Offenders

It has frequently been argued that the primary distinction between persons identified in NCS violent incidents as victim and offender is that the "victim" in the incident is the one who happened to be interviewed by the NCS interviewer (e.g., Block 1981). Many assaults are mutual combat, with both parties attacking and defending and both bearing some moral and perhaps even legal responsibility for the violence. In such cases, both parties are both victim and offender. This is probably not true in most robberies and rapes, where moral asymmetry is more likely to prevail, but is surely not uncommon in "pure" assaults.

The NCS makes no effort to establish blameworthiness in violent incidents, even though one party might be much more culpable than the other. However, although NCS interviewers do not explicitly tell respondents not to report incidents for which they were to blame, they do make it clear that they want to hear only about "crimes," or at least those events the victim is likely to label crime. The NCS respondent (R) is exposed to the word "crime" or "crimes" as many as seven times, four of them before the first question is even asked: once in the introductory letter mailed to Rs, once in the recommended Introductory Statement read when the interviewer arrives at the R's housing unit, twice in the sentence preceding the first question, twice in the household screen, and once more in the crime incident report (U.S. Bureau of the Census 1987; U.S. Bureau of Justice Statistics 1987a, pp. 94–9). The word "crime" implies culpability, and for victims to conceive of an event as a crime in which they were a victim, they probably at least believe they were relatively blameless in that incident. This should narrow Rs' focus largely to events in which they believe they were not at fault.

For purposes of assessing the impact of weaponry on assault outcomes it is not essential to know whether the R bore some responsibility for the violence and was to some extent an aggressor. Rather, the impact of weaponry in the hands of the so-called "offender" is assessed, regardless of that person's blameworthiness. For convenience, the quotation marks are dropped and hereinafter the conventional terminology is used to denote the participants.

Weighting Cases

For NCS cases, the incident weight, which averages about 1500, was used. For SHR homicides, each case was weighted approximately one. Since the SHRs encompass a virtually complete population, each case is essentially self-representing. However, although SHR homicides are not sampled according to a probability scheme, they are also not quite the entire population of homicides. The vital statistics count of all intentional homicides recorded on death certificates was about 10.2% higher in 1982 than the SHR total (negligent manslaughters excluded and civilian and police justifiable homicides included in both counts). A few homicides get recorded on death certificates but not by the police, while others are recorded by police but not on SHR forms submitted to the FBI. To weight the SHR cases up to the highest known national total therefore called for a weight of about 1.102. However, analysis was also limited to homicides known to the police as stranger homicides. A large number of homicides do not have a known victim–offender relationship, a problem almost entirely due to the absence of any information concerning offenders in those killings not cleared by the arrest of a suspect. These cases are probably disproportionately stranger cases, since the lack of a known relationship between the killer and his victim would itself be a major obstacle to police identification of the killer. Therefore, the known stranger homicide count understates the true total. In the 1982 SHR there were 3721 known stranger homicides and another 5141 homicides in which victim–offender relationship was unknown. Although many, perhaps most, of these "unknown relationship" cases were not stranger cases, nevertheless anywhere from 3721 to 8862 SHR homicides could have been stranger killings. This implies the need for weights anywhere from 1 to 2.3816 (8862/3721) to adjust for this undercoverage. Multiplying by the 1.102 weight gives minimum and maximum weights of 1.102 and 2.625. Both weights were tried in estimation for the DEATH analysis, but because homicides are so small a fraction of all assaults with injury (only about 1%), the different weights produced only negligible differences in estimates. Results reported here are based on the larger weight.

Design Effects

The NCS is based on a stratified multistage cluster sample, so the conventional computer formulas used for calculating standard errors, which are based on the assumption of a simple random design, produce biased estimates. Alexander (1987) proposed a rough adjustment for estimating regression coefficient standard errors in the NCS: multiply the computed standard errors by the square root of the design effect, DEFF, where DEFF = b/SI, b is the "generalized variance parameter" reported in an appendix of each annual NCS report, and *SI* is the sampling interval. For stranger assaults in the combined 1979–1985 incident files, Alexander (1988) estimated the DEFF to be about 1.8. Thus, to adjust for the DEFF, the reader could multiply reported standard errors by 1.342 or, equivalently, divide the ratios of coefficients to standard errors by 1.342. Put another way, to achieve significance at the .10 level (two-tailed; .05 one-tailed) would ordinarily require a ratio of 1.645. The unadjusted ratios reported in Tables 5.7–5.9 would therefore have to exceed 2.21 (1.645×1.342) to achieve significance at the .10 level, 2.63 at the .05 level, and 3.121 at the .01 level (two-tailed).

Missing Data

There were few missing data in the NCS samples, so the ATTACK and INJURY analyses would be little affected by deletion of cases with missing data. However, large numbers of SHR cases had missing data and listwise deletion would have eliminated as much as a third of the sample, potentially producing serious sample bias in the DEATH analysis. Instead, all missing data were recoded to zero for all variables. For each variable in which this was done, another variable (the "undetermined" variable) was created—a dummy indicator variable coded one when data were missing on that variable for a given case and zero otherwise (Cohen and Cohen 1983, pp. 281–9). For example, if the weapon type was missing, each weapon dummy would be coded as zero, and the UNDTWEAP variable would be coded one for that case, indicating that weapon type was missing. Thus, no cases were deleted due to missing data. The "undetermined" variables were included in equations along with the rest of the variables, and retained if their coefficients were significant. Their coefficients reflect whether cases with missing data on a given variable were different regarding the dependent variable, indicating a nonrandom missing data pattern.

Measurement of Variables

Household income was measured in its original NCS 14-category form, and education was measured as years of formal schooling. Three other variables require explanation. AGEDIF, SEXDIF, and NUMDIF are all measures of some type of power advantage to the offender(s). AGEDIF was coded one when there was an offender age 15–29 and no victims of this age and zero otherwise. SEXDIF was coded one if there was a male offender and only female victims and zero otherwise. NUMDIF equals the number of offenders minus the number of victims.

References

Albright, Joseph, and Associates. 1981. *The Snub-Nosed Killers: Handguns in America.* Pamphlet reproducing a series of articles appearing in the Cox Newspapers. Washington, D.C.: Cox Newspapers.

Aldrich, John H., and Forrest D. Nelson. 1984. *Linear Probability, Logit, and Probit Models.* Beverly Hills: Sage.

Alexander, Charles H. 1987. *Workshop on the Design and Use of the National Crime Survey. Session 10: Use of NCS for Estimation.* Unpublished paper. Statistical Methods Division, Bureau of the Census. Suitland, Maryland.

______. 1988. Telephone conversation, July 5, 1988.

Alviani, Joseph D., and William R. Drake. 1975. *Handgun Control . . . Issues and Alternatives.* Washington, D.C.: U.S. Conference of Mayors.

Ambler, John. 1982. Telephone conversation 6-24-82 with John Ambler, analyst with the Industry Division of the Bureau of the Census.

Anonymous. 1976. "Some Observations on the Disposition of CCW Cases in Detroit." *Michigan Law Review* 74:614–43.

Archer, Dane, and Rosemary Gartner. 1984. *Violence and Crime in Cross-National Perspective.* New Haven: Yale University Press.

Astrophysics Research Corporation. 1986. "Linescan Stops the Glock." Advertisement in *The Gun Owners* 5:7 (June).

Audit Bureau of Circulation. 1979–1982. *Supplementary Data Report,* covering county paid circulation figures for gun/hunting/outdoor magazines. Chicago: ABC.

Bakal, Carl. 1966. *The Right to Bear Arms.* New York: McGraw-Hill.

Bandura, Albert. 1973. *Aggression: A Social Learning Analysis.* New York: Prentice Hall.

Bankston, William B., Carol Y. Thompson, and Quentin A. L. Jenkins. 1986. "Carrying Firearms: The Influence of Southern Culture and Fear of Crime." Paper presented at the 1986 annual meetings of the American Society of Criminology, Atlanta, Georgia.

Barraclough, Brian. 1977a. Unpublished study. Results reported in Sainsbury et al. (1981, pp. 57–8) and Sainsbury (1986, p. 35).

______. 1977b. Unpublished study. Results reported in Sainsbury et al. (1981, pp. 58–60 and Table III.8).

Beccaria, Cesare. [1764] 1963. *On Crimes and Punishments.* Indianapolis: Bobbs-Merrill.

Beha, James. 1977. "And *Nobody* Can Get You Out." *Boston University Law Review* 57:96–146, 289–333.

Bendis, Paul, and Steven Balkin. 1979. "A Look at Gun Control Enforcement." *Journal of Police Science and Administration* 7:439–48.

Benenson, Mark K. 1982. Memorandum recording telephone conversation with Kennesaw, Georgia Police Chief Ruble, November 4, 1982.

Bensing, Robert C., and Oliver Schroeder. 1960. *Homicide in an Urban Community.* Springfield, Ill.: Charles Thomas.

Bentler, P. M., and Chou, C. 1988. "Practical Issues in Structural Modeling." In *Common Problems/Proper Solutions,* edited by J. S. Long. Beverly Hills: Sage.

Berk, Richard. 1983. "An Introduction to Sample Selection Bias." *American Sociological Review* 48:386–98.

Berkowitz, Leonard, and Anthony LePage. 1967. "Weapons as Aggression-Eliciting Stimuli." *Journal of Personality and Social Psychology* 7:202–7.

Berman, Lamar T. 1926. *Outlawing the Pistol.* New York: H. W. Wilson. [Reprinted pp. 249–52 of Newton and Zimring (1969).]

Berry, William D., and Stanley Feldman. 1985. *Multiple Regression in Practice.* Beverly Hills: Sage.

Best, Joel. 1988. "Missing Children, Misleading Statistics." *The Public Interest* 92:84–92.

Black, Donald. 1983. "Crime as Social Control." *American Sociological Review* 48:34–45.

Black, Henry Campbell. 1951. *Black's Law Dictionary.* St. Paul, Minn.: West.

Blackman, Paul H. 1981. "Conceptual, Constitutional, Enforcement and Experiential Problems Involved in Mandatory Sentencing for the Unlicensed Carrying/Possession of Handguns." Paper presented at the annual meetings of the American Society of Criminology, Washington, D.C.

———. 1985. "Carrying Handguns for Personal Protection." Paper presented at the annual meeting of the American Society of Criminology, San Diego, California.

———. 1989. *Affadavit of Paul H. Blackman, Ph.D.* Affadavit in Keng's Firearms Specialty, Inc. vs. Nicholas Brady, U.S. District Court for the Northern District of Ga.

Block, Richard. 1977. *Violent Crime.* Lexington, Mass.: Lexington Books.

———. 1981. "Victim-Offender Dynamics in Violent Crime." *Journal of Criminal Law & Criminology* 72:743–61.

———. 1984. "The Impact of Victimization, Rates and Patterns: A Comparison of the Netherlands and the United States." Pp. 23–28 in *Victimization and Fear of Crime: World Perspectives,* edited by Richard Block. Washington, D.C.: U.S. Government Printing Office.

Blose, James, and Philip J. Cook. 1980. *Regulating Handgun Transfers.* Durham, N.C.: Institute of Policy Sciences and Public Affairs, Duke University.

Blumstein, Alfred, Jacqueline Cohen, and Daniel Nagin (eds.). 1978. *Deterrence and Incapacitation: Estimating the Effects of Criminal Sanctions on Crimes.* Washington, D.C.: National Academy of Sciences.

Boland, Barbara, Catherine H. Conley, Lynn Warner, Ronald Sones, and William Martin. 1989. *The Prosecution of Felony Arrests, 1986*. Office of Justice Programs, U.S. Department of Justice. Washington, D.C.: U.S. Government Printing Office.

Bollen, K. A. 1989. "A New Incremental Fit Index for General Structural Equation Models." *Sociological Methods and Research* 17:303–316.

______, and Liang, J. 1988. "Some Properties of Hoelter's CN." *Sociological Methods and Research* 16:492–503.

Boor, Myron. 1981. "Methods of Suicide and Implications for Suicide Prevention." *Journal of Clinical Psychology* 37:70–75.

______, and Jeffrey H. Bair. 1990. "Suicide Rates, Handgun Control Laws, and Sociodemographic Variables." *Psychological Reports* 66:923–30.

Bordua, David J. 1982. Unpublished tabulations done for the author.

______. 1983. "Adversary Polling and the Construction of Social Meaning." *Law & Policy Quarterly* 5:345–66.

______. 1986. "Firearms Ownership and Violent Crime: A Comparison of Illinois Counties." Pp. 156–88 in *The Social Ecology of Crime*, edited by James M. Byrne and Robert J. Sampson. New York: Springer-Verlag.

______. Undated. Unpublished tabulations from Illinois survey. Department of Sociology, University of Illinois.

______, and Alan J. Lizotte. 1979. "Patterns of Legal Firearms Ownership: A Cultural and Situational Analysis of Illinois Counties." *Law and Policy Quarterly* 1:147–75.

______, Alan J. Lizotte, and Gary Kleck, with Van Cagle. 1979. *Patterns of Firearms Ownership, Regulation and Use in Illinois*. Springfield, Ill.: Illinois Law Enforcement Commission.

______, Mark Beeman, and Debra Kelley. 1985. *Operation and Effects of Firearm Owner Identification and Waiting Period Regulation in Illinois*. Urbana: Department of Sociology, University of Illinois.

______. 1988. *Firearms Ownership in Illinois: An Informational Report*. Working Papers in Sociology, Department of Sociology, University of Illinois.

Boyanowsky, Ehor O., and Curt T. Griffiths. 1982. "Weapons and Eye Contact as Instigators or Inhibitors of Aggressive Arousal in Police-Citizen Interaction." *Journal of Applied Social Psychology* 12:398–407.

Boyd, Jeffrey H. 1983. "The Increasing Rate of Suicide by Firearms." *New England Journal of Medicine* 308:872–74.

Braithwaite, John. 1981. "The Myth of Social Class and Criminality Reconsidered." *American Sociological Review* 46:36–57.

Brearley, H. C. 1932. *Homicide in the United States*. Chapel Hill: University of North Carolina Press.

Brenner, Berthold. 1967. "Alcoholism and Fatal Accidents." *Quarterly Journal of Studies on Alcohol* 28:517–28.

Brill, Steven. 1977. *Firearm Abuse: A Research and Policy Report*. Washington, D.C.: Police Foundation.

Brown, Phil. 1983. "Mental Patients as Victimizers and Victims." Pp. 183–218 in

Deviants: Victims or Victimizers?, edited by Donal E. J. MacNamara and Andrew Karmen. Beverly Hills: Sage.

Brown, Richard Maxwell. 1969. "The American Vigilante Tradition." Pp. 144–218 in *Violence in America,* edited by Hugh Davis Graham and Ted Robert Gurr. New York: Signet.

Browning, Charles H. 1974. "Epidemiology of Suicide: Firearms." *Comprehensive Psychiatry* 15:549–53.

Bruce-Briggs, Barry. 1976. "The Great American Gun War." *The Public Interest* 45:37–62.

Burr, D. E. S. 1977. *Handgun Regulation.* Tallahassee: Florida Bureau of Criminal Justice Planning and Assistance.

Buss, Arnold, Ann Booker, and Edith Buss. 1972. "Firing a Weapon and Aggression." *Journal of Personality and Social Psychology* 22:296–302.

Cahoon, Delwin D., and Ed M. Edmonds. 1984. "Guns/No Guns and the Expression of Social Hostility." *Bulletin of the Psychonomic Society* 22:305–8.

______. 1985. "The Weapons Effect: Fact or Artifact." *Bulletin of the Psychonomic Society* 23:57–60.

California. 1983. *Homicide in California, 1982.* Sacramento, Calif.: Bureau of Criminal Statistics and Special Services.

Cambridge Reports. 1978. *An Analysis of Public Attitudes Towards Handgun Control.* Cambridge, Mass.: Cambridge Reports, Inc.

Campbell, Donald T., and Julian C. Stanley. 1963. *Experimental and Quasi-Experimental Designs for Research.* Chicago: Rand McNally.

Caprara, G. V., P. Renzi, P. Amolini, G., D'Imperio, and G. Travaglia. 1984. "The Eliciting Cue Value of Aggressive Slides Reconsidered in A Personological Perspective: The Weapons Effect and Irritability." *European Journal of Social Psychology* 14:313–22.

Caras, Roger. 1970. *Death as a Way of Life.* Boston: Little, Brown.

Card, Josefina Jayme. 1974. "Lethality of Suicidal Methods and Suicide Risk: Two Distinct Concepts." *Omega* 5:37–45.

Cash, Wilbur J. 1940. *The Mind of the South.* New York: Alfred Knopf.

Carlson, Kenneth. 1982. "Mandatory Sentencing: The Experience of Two States." Washington, D.C.: National Institute of Justice.

Castellano, Thomas C. 1985. "If You've Got the Gun, We've Got the Room: New York's Experience with Mandatory Minimum Sentences." Paper presented at the 1985 meeting of the American Society of Criminology, San Diego, November 13–17, 1985.

Center to Prevent Handgun Violence. 1988. "Child's Play." Washington, D.C.: Center to Prevent Handgun Violence.

______. 1989. "The Killing Seasons." Washington, D.C.: Center to Prevent Handgun Violence.

Chaiken, Jan M., and Marcia R. Chaiken. 1982. *Varieties of Criminal Behavior.* Santa Monica, Calif.: Rand Corporation.

Clarke, Ronald V., and David Lester. 1989. *Suicide: Closing the Exits.* New York: Springer Verlag.

ınd James Blose. 1981. "State Programs for Screening Handgun Buyers." *als* 455:80–91.

and Daniel Nagin. 1979. *Does the Weapon Matter?* Washington, D.C.: LAW.

d, Arthur R. 1984. "Accidental Death by Gunshot Wound—Fact or Fic-." *Forensic Science International* 26:25–32.

wspapers. 1989. *Firepower: Assault Weapons in America.* Pamphlet re-lucing series of articles. 32 pp. Washington, D.C.: Cox Enterprises.

Royce. 1982. "Attitudes Toward Gun Control: A Survey." Pp. 229–67 in *al Regulation of Firearms,* edited by Harry L. Hogan. Washington, D.C.: Government Printing Office.

ham, William C., and Todd H. Taylor. 1985. *Crime and Protection in rica—A Study of Private Security and Law Enforcement Resources and Rela-hips—Executive Summary.* National Institute of Justice. Washington, .: U.S. Government Printing Office.

ynn A. 1974. *Criminal Violence: National Patterns and Behavior.* Lexington, s.: Lexington.

li, Stephen L. 1989. Letter to the author, 2-9-89, from D'Andrilli, Presi-of Guardian Group International Corp., New York City.

ruce L. 1972. "Firearm Suicide in the Home Setting." *Omega* 3:111–119.

mes A., and Tom W. Smith. 1984. *General Social Surveys, 1972–1984.* hine-readable data file]. Principle Investigator, James A. Davis; Senior y Director, Tom W. Smith. NORC ed. Chicago: National Opinion Re-h Center, producer, 1983; Storrs, CT: Roper Public Opinion Research er, University of Connecticut, distributor. 1 data file (17,052 logical ds) and 1 codebook (483 p.).

cision-Making-Information). 1979. *Attitudes of the American Electorate to-Gun Control.* Santa Ana, Calif.: DMI.

, James. 1979. "Fear of Crime and Handgun Ownership." *Criminology* 1–39.

W. Edwards. [1944] 1978. "On Errors in Surveys." Pp. 233–47 in *So-ical Methods: A Sourcebook,* edited by Norman K. Denzin. New York: raw-Hill.

Stephen Jay, and Francis B. Alt. 1977. "The Effect of Massachusetts' Control Law on Gun-Related Crimes in the City of Boston." *Evaluation terly* 1:543–68.

latthew R. 1983. "Gun Control Legislation: Impact and Ideology." *Law olicy Quarterly* 5:367–379.

1990. Computer search of DIALOG database, POLL file of public on survey results. Palo Alto, Calif.: DIALOG Information Services, Inc.

dward, and Kenneth W. Kerber. 1979. "Personality Characteristics of rican Gun Owners." *Journal of Applied Psychology* 107:227–38.

ry Lorenz. 1983. *Killing for Profit: The Social Organization of Felony Homi-*Chicago: Nelson-Hall.

Don A. 1978. *Mail and Telephone Surveys.* New York: Wiley.

Clarke, Ronald V., and Peter R. Jones. 1989. "Suicid of Handguns in the United States." *Social Scien*

______, and Pat Mayhew. 1989. "Crime as Opport Gas Suicide in Britain and the Netherlands." *Bri* 35–46.

Clotfelter, Charles T. 1981. "Crime, Disorders and t *Law & Policy Quarterly* 3:425–46.

Cohen, Jacob, and Patricia Cohen. 1983. *Applied M Analysis for the Behavioral Sciences.* Hillsdale, N.

Cohen, Lawrence E., and Marcus Felson. 1979. "So Trends: A Routine Activities Approach." *Americ* 608.

Conger, J. J., H. S. Gaskill, D. D. Glad, L. Hass Sawrey. 1959. "Psychological and Psychoph tor Vehicle Accidents." *Journal of the Americ* 1581–7.

Conklin, John E. 1972. *Robbery and the Criminal Just* pincott.

Cook, Philip J. 1976. "A Strategic Choice Analysi *Sample Surveys of the Victims of Crime,* edited by Ballinger.

______. 1979. "The Effect of Gun Availability on Ro Pp. 743–81 in *Policy Studies Review Annual,* edit Bruce Zellner. Beverly Hills: Sage.

______. 1980. "Reducing Injury and Death Rates 6:21–45.

______. 1981a. "The 'Saturday Night Special': A Definitions from a Policy Perspective." *Journal* 72:1735–1745.

______. 1981b. "Guns and Crime: The Perils of Lo *Analysis and Management* 7:120–25.

______. 1981c. "Making Handguns Harder to Hide May 29, 1981, p. 23.

______. 1982. "The Role of Firearms in Violent C *Violence,* edited by Marvin E. Wolfgang and N Sage.

______. 1983. "The Influence of Gun Availability o 49–90 in *Crime and Justice: An Annual Review,* v and Norval Morris. Chicago: University of C

______. 1985. "The Case of the Missing Victims National Crime Survey." *Journal of Quantitati*

______. 1986. "The Relationship between Victim commercial Robbery." *Journal of Legal Studies*

______. 1987. "Robbery Violence." *Journal of Crimi* 76.

DiMaio, Vincent J. M. 1972. "Accidental Deaths Due to Dropping of Handguns." *The Forensic Science Gazette* 3:1–2.

______. 1973. "The Frequency of Accidental Gunshot Wounds." *The Forensic Science Gazette* 4:2–3.

Dixon, Jo, and Alan J. Lizotte. 1987. "Gun Ownership and the 'Southern Subculture of Violence.'" *American Journal of Sociology* 93:383–405.

Dodge, Richard. 1981. "The Washington, D.C. Recall Study." Pp. 12–15 in *The National Crime Survey: Working Papers, Volume I: Current and Historical Perspectives*, edited by Robert G. Lehnen and Wesley G. Skogan. U.S. Department of Justice, Bureau of Justice Statistics. Washington, D.C.: U.S. Government Printing Office.

Dorpat, Theodore L., and Herbert S. Ripley. 1967. "The Relationship between Attempted Suicide and Committed Suicide." *Comprehensive Psychiatry* 8:74–79.

Drinan, Robert F. 1976. "Gun Control: The Good Outweighs the Evil." *Civil Liberties Review* 3:44–59.

Durkheim, Emile. 1951 [1897]. *Suicide.* New York: The Free Press.

Eisenthal, Sherman, Norman L. Farberow, and Edwin S. Shneidman. 1966. "Followup of Neuropsychiatric Patients in Suicide Observation Status." *Public Health Reports* 81:977–990.

Ellis, Desmond P., Paul Weinir, and Louie Miller III. 1971. "Does the Trigger Pull the Finger? An Experimental Test of Weapons as Aggression-Eliciting Stimuli." *Sociometry* 34:453–65.

Endicott, William. 1981. "The Times Poll: Fear of Crime Triggers Rise in Gun Sales." *Los Angeles Times*, 2-23-81, p. I-1.

Erskine, Hazel. 1972. "The Polls: Gun Control." *Public Opinion Quarterly* 36:455–69.

Eskridge, Chris W. 1986. "Zero-Order Inverse Correlations between Crimes of Violence and Hunting Licenses in the United States." *Sociology and Social Research* 71:55–7.

Evanston. 1986. Letter to the author from the City Attorney of Evanston, Illinois.

Ezell, Edward Clinton. 1983. *Small Arms of the World.* Harrisburg, Pa.: Stackpole Books.

Fackler, Martin L. 1989. Declaration of Martin L. Fackler, Amicus Curiae Brief, Castillo v. City of Los Angeles, California Court of Appeal, 1st Appellate District, Division 5.

Fackler, Martin L., J. A. Malinowski, S. W. Hoxie, and A. Jason. 1990. "Wounding Effects of the AK-47 Rifle Used by Patrick Purdy in the Stockton Schoolyard Shooting of 17 January 1989." *American Journal of Forensic Medicine and Pathology* 11:185–9.

Farberow, Norman, and Maria D. Simon. 1969. "Suicides in Los Angeles and Vienna." *Public Health Reports* 84:389–403.

Farmer, R., and J. Rohde. 1980. "Effect of Availability and Acceptability of Lethal Instruments on Suicide Mortality. *Acta Psychiatrica Scandinavia* 62:436–446.

Feagin, Joe R. 1970. "Home Defense and the Police: Black and White Perspectives." *American Behavioral Scientist* 13:797–814.

Feeney, Floyd. 1986. "Robbers as Decision-Makers." Pp. 53–71 in *The Reasoning Criminal: Rational Choice Perspectives on Offending*, edited by Derek B. Cornish and Ronald V. Clarke. New York: Springer-Verlag.

———, and Adrienne Weir (eds.). 1973. *The Prevention and Control of Robbery.* Davis: University of California, The Center on Administration of Criminal Justice.

Felson, Richard B., and Henry J. Steadman. 1983. "Situational Factors in Disputes Leading to Criminal Violence." *Criminology* 21:59–74.

Field Institute. 1976. *Tabulations of the Findings of a Survey of Handgun Ownership and Access among a Cross Section of the California Adult Public.* San Francisco: Field Institute.

Fields, Sam. 1979. "Handgun Prohibition and Social Necessity." *St. Louis University Law Journal* 23:35–61.

Firebaugh, Glenn, and Jack P. Gibbs. 1985. "User's Guide to Ratio Variables." *American Sociological Review* 50:713–22.

Firman, Gordon R. 1975. "In Prison Gun Survey the Pros are the Cons." *The American Rifleman* 23 (November):13.

Fischer, Donald G., Harold Kelm, and Ann Rose. 1969. "Knives as Aggression-Eliciting Stimuli." *Psychological Reports* 24:755–60.

Fisher, Joseph C. 1976. "Homicide in Detroit: The Role of Firearms." *Criminology* 14:387–400.

Florida. 1976. *Florida Statutes Annotated.* St. Paul: West.

———. 1987. *West's Session Law Service. 1987 Laws.* St. Paul: West.

———. 1988. *Crime in Florida. 1987 Annual Report.* Tallahassee: Florida Department of Law Enforcement.

———. 1990. *Florida Assault Weapons Commission Report.* May 18, 1990. Tallahassee, Fl.: Florida Department of State.

———. No date. *Florida Uniform Crime Reports Guide Manual.* Tallahassee: Florida Department of Law Enforcement.

Fox, K., and M. Weissman. 1975. "Suicide Attempts and Drugs: Contradiction between Method and Intent." *Social Psychiatry* 10:31–38.

Fox, R. 1975. "The Suicide Drop." *Royal Society of Health Journal* 95:9–14.

Fraczek, Adam, and Jacqueline R. Macaulay. 1971. "Some Personality Factors in Reaction to Aggressive Stimuli." *Journal of Personality* 39:163–77.

Franklin, John Hope. 1956. *The Militant South, 1800–1861.* Cambridge, Mass.: Harvard.

Frierson, Robert L. 1989. "Women Who Shoot Themselves." *Hospital and Community Psychiatry* 40:841–7.

Frodi, Ann. 1975. "The Effect of Exposure to Weapons on Aggressive Behavior from a Cross-Cultural Perspective." *International Journal of Psychology* 10:283–92.

Fyfe, James J. 1979. "Administrative Interventions on Police Shooting Discretion." *Journal of Criminal Justice* 7:309–23.

Gallup, George. 1966, 1976, 1982, 1984, 1987. *The Gallup Poll—1965* (and 1975, 1981, 1983, 1986). Wilmington, Del.: Scholarly Resources.

Gallup, George, Jr. 1989; 1990. *The Gallup Poll-Public Opinion 1988 (1989).* Wilmington, Del.: Scholarly Resources.

Garin, Geoffrey. 1986. Telephone conversion with Geoffrey Garin of Peter D. Hart Research Associates, Inc., Washington, D.C., April 30, 1986.

Gastil, Raymond D. 1971. "Homicide and a Regional Culture of Violence." *American Sociological Review* 36:412–27.

______. 1976. *Cultural Regions of the United States.* Seattle: University of Washington Press.

Geisel, Martin S., Richard Roll, and R. Stanton Wettick. 1969. "The Effectiveness of State and Local Regulations of Handguns." *Duke University Law Journal* 4:647–76.

Gibbs, Jack P. 1971. "Suicide." Pp. 271–312 in *Contemporary Social Problems,* edited by Robert K. Merton and Robert Nisbet. New York: Harcourt Brace Jovanovich.

______. 1975. *Crime, Punishment and Deterrence.* New York: Elsevier.

______, and W. Martin. 1964. *Status Integration and Suicide.* Eugene, Oregon: University of Oregon Press.

Gillespie, Cynthia. 1989. *Justifiable Homicide.* Columbus: Ohio State University Press.

Glaser, Daniel. 1978. *Crime in Our Changing Society.* New York: Holt, Rinehart.

Goode, William J. 1971. "Force and Violence in the Family." *Journal of Marriage and the Family* 33:624–36.

______. 1972. "Presidential Address: The Place of Force in Human Society." *American Sociological Review* 37:507–19.

Gove, Walter R., Michael Hughes, and Michael Geerken. 1985. "Are Uniform Crime Reports a Valid Indicator of the Index Crimes? An Affirmative Answer with Minor Qualifications." *Criminology* 23:451–501.

Green, Gary S. 1987. "Citizen Gun Ownership and Criminal Deterrence." *Criminology* 25:63–81.

Greene, William H. 1985. *LIMDEP.* Manual for econometrics software package, Version IV.2. New York: Author.

Greenberg, Stephanie W., and William M. Rohe, and J. R. Williams. 1984. *Informal Citizen Action and Crime Prevention at the Neighborhood Level: Synthesis and Assessment of the Research.* National Institute of Justice. Washington, D.C.: Government Printing Office.

Greenwood, Colin. 1972. *Firearms Control: A Study of Armed Crime and Firearms Control in England and Wales.* London: Routledge.

Greenwood, Peter W., and Joan Petersilia. 1977. *The Criminal Investigation Process.* Lexington, Mass.: D.C. Heath.

Gross, Jan T. 1984. "Social Control under Totalitarianism." Pp. 59–77 in *Toward A General Theory of Social Control.* Volume 2. *Selected Problems,* edited by Donald Black. Orlando: Academic Press.

Gulevich, G. D., and P. G. Bourne. 1970. "Mental Illness and Violence." Pp.

309–26 in *Violence and the Struggle for Existence*, edited by D. N. Daniels, M. F. Gilula, and F. M. Ochberg. Boston: Little, Brown.

Gun Owners of America. 1987. *The Gun Owners*, newsletter of the Gun Owners of America, Inc. March/April and September/October issues. Springfield, Va.: GOA.

Gusfield, Joseph R. 1963. *Symbolic Crusade*. Urbana: University of Illinois Press.

Hackney, Sheldon. 1969. "Southern Violence." *American Historical Review* 74:906–25.

Halderman, Brent L., and Thomas T. Jackson. 1979. "Naturalistic Study of Aggressive Stimuli and Horn-Honking: A Replication." *Psychological Reports* 45:880–2.

Hancock, Michael. 1985. "The Convertible Submachine Gun Boondoggle." Letter to the Editor, *New York Times*, 6-15-85, p. 22.

Handgun Control. 1989. Undated, untitled fund-raising letter (in author's files).

Hardy, David T., and John Stompoly. 1974. "Of Arms and the Law." *Chicago-Kent Law Review* 51:62–114.

Harvard Medical Practice Study. 1990. "Harvard Medical Practice Study." Unpublished report to the State of New York. Cambridge, Mass.: Harvard Medical School.

Hassinger, James. 1985. "Fear of Crime in Public Environments." *Journal of Architectural Planning Research* 2:289–300.

Haviland, C. V., and H. A. B. Wiseman. 1974. "Criminals Who Drive." *Proceedings of the 18th Conference of the American Association of Automotive Medicine* 18:432–49.

Hawley, Fred. 1977. "The Gun Control Debate: Stigma Contest, Social Science, and Cultural Conflict." Unpublished paper. Shreveport: Department of Criminal Justice, Louisiana State University.

———. 1988. "Guns." Pp. 1480–82 in *The Encyclopedia of Southern Culture*. Chapel Hill, N.C.: University of North Carolina Press.

Hay, Richard, and Richard McCleary. 1979. "Box-Tiao Time Series Models for Impact Assessment." *Evaluation Quarterly* 3:277–314.

Heckman, James J. 1979. "Sample Selection Bias as a Specification Error." *Econometrica* 45:153–61.

Heins, Marilyn, Roger Kahn, and Judy Bjordnal. 1974. "Gunshot Wounds in Children." *American Journal of Public Health* 64:326–30.

Henry, Andrew F., and James F. Short, Jr. 1954. *Suicide and Homicide*. New York: Free Press.

Higgins, Stephen E. 1986. Testimony before the Subcommittee on Crime, House Committee on the Judiciary, February 19, 1986. Serial No. 131, Part 2. Washington, D.C.: U.S. Government Printing Office.

Hill, Gary D., Frank M. Howell, and Ernest T. Driver. 1985. "Gender, Fear, and Protective Handgun Ownership." *Criminology* 23:541–52.

Hindelang, Michael J. 1976. *Criminal Victimization in Eight American Cities*. Cambridge: Ballinger.

Hogan, Harry. 1986. "Gun Control Amendments, 1986." Report No. 86-704G. Congressional Research Service, The Library of Congress.

Holmberg, Judith Vandell, and Michael Clancy. 1977. *People vs Handguns.* Washington, D.C.: U.S. Conference of Mayors.

Howe, Walter. 1987. "Firearms Production by U.S. Manufacturers, 1973–1985." Pp. 101–12 in *Shooting Industry—Shot Show Issue 1988.*

Inter-University Consortium for Political and Social Research (ICPSR). 1983. *Uniform Crime Reports: National Time Series Community-Level Database, 1967–1980.* Study 8214 [MRDF]. Principal Investigators—Glenn L. Pierce, William J. Bowers, James Baird, and Joseph Heck. Ann Arbor: Inter-University Consortium [distributor].

———. 1984a. *Uniform Crime Reporting Program Data.* Study 9028, Parts 3, 7, 11, 15 [MRDF]. Supplementary Homicide Reports, 1979–1982. Federal Bureau of Investigation. Ann Arbor: Inter-University Consortium [distributor].

———. 1984b. *Uniform Crime Reporting Program Data.* Study 9028, Parts 2, 6, 14 [MRDF]. Property Stolen and Recovered, 1979–1981. Federal Bureau of Investigation [producer]. Ann Arbor: ICPSR [distributor].

———. 1985. *Mortality Detail Files 1969–1978, External Deaths Subfile.* Study 7633 [MRDF]. National Center for Health Statistics [producer]. Ann Arbor: ICPSR [distributor].

———. 1986. *Armed Criminals in America: A Survey of Incarcerated Felons.* Study 8437 [MRDF]. Principal Investigators—James Wright and Peter Rossi. Ann Arbor: ICPSR [distributor].

———. 1987. *National Crime Surveys: National Sample, 1979–1985 (Revised Questionnaire).* Study 8608 [MRDF]. Washington, D.C.: Bureau of Justice Statistics [producer]. Ann Arbor: ICPSR [distributor].

Iskrant, Albert P., and Paul V. Joliet. 1968. *Accidents and Homicide.* Cambridge, Mass.: Harvard University Press.

Iveson, H. Todd. 1981. "Manufacturer's Liability to Victims of Handgun Crime: A Common-Law Approach." *Fordham Law Review* 51:771–99.

James, Garry (ed.). 1975. *Guns for Home Defense.* Los Angeles: Petersen.

Jarrett, William S. 1986. *Shooter's Bible* No. 78, 1987 Edition. South Hackensak, N.J.: Stoeger.

Johnston, John. 1972. *Econometric Methods.* New York: McGraw-Hill.

Jones, Edward D., III. 1981. "The District of Columbia's 'Firearms Control Regulations Act of 1975': The Toughest Handgun Control Law in the United States—Or Is It?" *Annals* 455:138–149.

———, and Marla Wilson Ray. 1980. *Handgun Control: Strategies, Enforcement and Effectiveness.* Unpublished report. Washington, D.C.: U.S. Department of Justice.

Joreskog, Karl. 1973. "A General Method for Estimating a Linear Structural Equation System." Pp. 85–112 in *Structural Equation Models in the Social Sciences,* edited by Arthur S. Goldberger and Otis Dudley Duncan. New York: Seminar Press.

Joreskog, K., and Sorbom, D. 1981a. *LISREL—Analysis of Linear Structural Relationships by the Method of Maximum Likelihood. User's Guide*. Version V. Chicago: National Educational Resources.

———. 1981b. "The Use of LISREL in Sociological Model Building." In *Factor Analysis and Measurement in Sociological Research*, edited by D. J. Jackson and Edgar F. Borgatta. Beverly Hills: Sage.

Jung, Roy S., and Leonard A. Jason. 1988. "Firearm Violence and the Effects of Gun Control Legislation." *American Journal of Community Psychology* 16:515–24.

Kaplan, John. 1979. "Controlling Firearms." *Cleveland State Law Review* 28:1–28.

Kates, Don B., Jr. 1976. "Why a Civil Libertarian Opposes Gun Control." *Civil Liberties Review* 3:24–32.

———. 1979a. "Toward a History of Handgun Prohibition in the United States." Pp. 7–30 in *Restricting Handguns: The Liberal Skeptics Speak Out*, edited by Don. B. Kates, Jr. Croton-on-Hudson, N.Y.: North River Press.

———. 1979b. "Some Remarks on the Prohibition of Handguns." *St. Louis University Law Journal* 23:11–34.

———. 1982. *Why Handgun Bans Can't Work*. Bellevue, Washington: Second Amendment Foundation.

———. 1982a. "Criminological Perspectives on Gun Control and Gun Prohibition Legislation." Pp. 3–76 in *Why Handgun Bans Can't Work*, edited by Don B. Kates, Jr. Bellevue, Washington: Second Amendment Foundation.

———. 1983a. "Handgun Prohibition and the Original Meaning of the Second Amendment." *Michigan Law Review* 82:204–73.

———. 1983b. Personal Communication.

———. (ed.). 1984. *Firearms and Violence: Issues of Public Policy*. Cambridge, Mass.: Ballinger.

———. 1984a. "Handgun Banning in Light of the Prohibition Experience." Pp. 139–65 in *Firearms and Violence: Issues of Public Policy*, edited by Don B. Kates, Jr. Cambridge, Mass.: Ballinger.

———. 1984b. "Conclusion." Pp. 523–37 in *Firearms and Violence: Issues of Public Policy*, edited by Don B. Kates, Jr. Cambridge, Mass.: Ballinger.

———. 1986. "The Battle Over Gun Control." *The Public Interest* 84:42–52.

———. 1990. *Guns, Murders, and the Constitution*. Policy Briefing, Pacific Research Institute for Public Policy. San Francisco: Pacific Institute.

———. n.d. Unpublished m.s. on defensive use of guns by police and civilians.

———, and Mark K. Benenson. 1979. "Handgun Prohibition and Homicide." Pp. 91–118 in *Restricting Handguns*, edited by Don B. Kates, Jr. Croton-on-Hudson, N.Y.: North River Press.

Kellerman, Arthur L., and Donald T. Reay. 1986. "Protection or Peril? An Analysis of Firearm-Related Deaths in the Home." *New England Journal of Medicine* 314:1557–60.

Kempe, C. Henry, Frederic N. Wilverman, Brandt F. Steele, William Droegemueller, and Henry K. Silver. 1962. "The Battered-child Syndrome." *Journal of the American Medical Association* 181:105–12.

Kennett, Lee, and James LaVerne Anderson. 1975. *The Gun in America: The Origins of a National Dilemma*. Westport, Conn.: Greenwood Press.

Kessel, Neil. 1967. "Self-Poisoning." Pp. 345–72 in *Essays in Self-Destruction*, edited by Edwin S. Shneidman. New York: Science House.

Kessler, Raymond G. 1980. "Enforcement Problems of Gun Control: A Victimless Crimes Perspective." *Criminal Law Bulletin* 16:131–49.

______. 1984. "The Political Functions of Gun Control." Pp. 457–87 in *Firearms and Violence*, edited by Don B. Kates, Jr. Cambridge, Mass.: Ballinger.

______. 1988. "Ideology and Gun control." *Quarterly Journal of Ideology* 12:1–13.

Killias, Martin. 1990. "Gun Ownership and Violent Crime: The Swiss Experience in International Perspective." *Security Journal* 1:169–74.

King, John W. 1987. "Situational Factors and the Escalation of Criminal Violence." Paper presented at the annual meetings of the American Society of Criminology, Montreal, Canada.

Kleck, Gary. 1979. "Capital Punishment, Gun Ownership, and Homicide." *American Journal of Sociology* 84:882–910.

______. 1981. "Racial Discrimination in Criminal Sentencing." *American Sociological Review* 46:783–804.

______. 1983. Unpublished tabulations from National Center for Health Statistics Mortality Detail File computer tape.

______. 1984a. "The Relationship between Gun Ownership Levels and Rates of Violence in the United States." Pp. 99–135 in *Firearms and Violence: Issues of Public Policy*, edited by Don B. Kates, Jr. Cambridge, Mass.: Ballinger.

______. 1984b. "Handgun-Only Gun Control." Pp. 167–99 in *Firearms and Violence: Issues of Public Policy*, edited by Don B. Kates, Jr. Cambridge, Mass.: Ballinger.

______. 1986a. "Policy Lessons from Recent Gun Control Research." *Law and Contemporary Problems* 49:35–62.

______. 1986b. "Evidence That 'Saturday Night Specials' Not Very Important for Crime." *Sociology and Social Research* 70:303–7.

______. 1986c. Unpublished tabulations from the National Crime Panel Survey and the Uniform Crime Reports for 1980.

______. 1988. "Crime Control Through the Private Use of Armed Force." *Social Problems* 35:1–21.

______. 1990. "Gun Ownership in America." Unpublished paper, School of Criminology, Florida State University.

______, and David J. Bordua. 1983. "The Factual Foundations for Certain Key Assumptions of Gun Control." *Law & Policy Quarterly* 5:271–98.

______, and Karen McElrath. 1991. "The Effects of Weaponry on Human Violence." *Social Forces* 69:1–21.

______, and E. Britt Patterson. 1990. "Measuring Gun Ownership Levels." Unpublished paper, School of Criminology, Florida State University.

______. 1991. "The Impact of Gun Control and Gun Ownership Levels on Violence Rates." Unpublished paper, School of Criminology, Florida State University.

———, and Susan Sayles. 1990. "Rape and Resistance." *Social Problems* 37:149–62.

Klein, David. 1980. "Societal Influences on Childhood Accidents." *Accident Analysis and Prevention* 12:275–81.

———, Maurice S. Reizen, George H. Van Amburg, and Scott A. Walker. 1977. "Some Social Characteristics of Young Gunshot Fatalities." *Accident Analysis and Prevention* 9:177–82.

Koumjian, Robert (ed.). 1973. *Shooter's Bible.* No. 65, 1974 Edition. South Hackensack, N.J.: Stoeger Industries.

Krahn, Harvey, and Leslie W. Kennedy. 1985. "Producing Personal Safety: The Effects of Crime Rates, Police Force Size, and Fear of Crime." *Criminology* 23:697–710.

Kreitman, Norman. 1976. "The Coal Gas Story: United Kingdom Suicide Rates, 1960–71." *British Journal of Preventive and Social Medicine* 30:86–93.

Krug, Alan S. 1967. "A Statistical Study of the Relationship between Firearms Licensing Laws and Crime Rates." *The Congressional Record* (July 25, 1967), pp. H9366-H9370.

———. 1968. "The Relationship between Firearms Ownership and Crime Rates: A Statistical Analysis." *The Congressional Record* (January 30, 1968), p. H570-2.

Kuluvar, H. L. 1953. *Minnesota Hunter Casualty Study.* Safety Committee of the Minnesota Conservation Federation.

Law Enforcement Assistance Administration (LEAA). 1972. *The San Jose Methods Test of Known Crime Victims.* Statistics Division Technical Series, Report No. 1. Washington, D.C.: U.S. Government Printing Office.

Lester, David. 1969. "Suicidal Behavior in Men and Women." *Mental Hygiene* 53:340–45.

———. 1972. *Why People Kill Themselves.* Springfield, Ill.: Charles Thomas.

———. 1984a. *Gun Control.* Springfield, Ill.: Charles Thomas.

———. 1984b. *Why People Kill Themselves: A 1980's Summary of Research Findings on Suicidal Behavior.* Springfield, Ill.: Charles Thomas.

———. 1985. "The Use of Firearms in Violent Crime." *Crime & Justice* 8:115–20.

———. 1987a. "Availability of Guns and the Likelihood of Suicide." *Sociology and Social Research* 71:287–8.

———. 1987b. "An Availability-Acceptability Theory of Suicide." *Activitas Nervosa Superior* 29:164–6.

———. 1988a. "Restricting the Availability of Guns as a Strategy for Preventing Suicide." *Biology and Society* 5:127–9.

———. 1988b. "Gun Control, Gun Ownership, and Suicide Prevention." *Suicide and Life-Threatening Behavior* 18:176–80.

———. 1988c. "Why Do People Choose Particular Methods for Suicide?" *Activitas Nervosa Superior* 30:312–4.

———. 1989. "Gun Ownership and Suicide in the United States." *Psychological Medicine* 19:519–21.

———, and Mary E. Murrell. 1980. "The Influences of Gun Control Laws on Suicidal Behavior." *American Journal of Psychiatry* 137:121–2.

———. 1981a. "The Influence of Gun Control Laws on the Incidence of Accidents with Guns: A Preliminary Study." *Accident Analysis and Prevention* 13:357–9.

———. 1981b. "The Relationship between Gun Control Statutes and Homicide Rates: A Research Note." *Crime and Justice* 4:146–8.

———. 1982. "The Preventive Effect of Strict Gun Control Laws on Suicide and Homicide." *Suicide and Life-Threatening Behavior* 12:131–40.

———. 1986. "The Influence of Gun Control Laws on Personal Violence." *Journal of Community Psychology* 14:315–18.

Lewis, I. A., and William Schneider. 1982. "Is the Public Lying to the Pollsters?" *Public Opinion* 5:42–7.

Levine, Howard. 1987. "Berkeley Eyes Checkpoints for Weapons." *San Francisco Examiner,* December, 18, p. A-1.

Leyens, Jacques-Phillippe, and Ross D. Parke. 1975. "Aggressive Slides Can Induce a Weapons Effect." *European Journal of Social Psychology* 5:229–36.

Link, Mitchell. 1982. "No Handguns in Morton Grove—Big Deal!" *Menard Times* (prison newspaper of Menard, Illinois Federal Penitentiary) 33:1.

Linsky, Arnold S., Murray A. Strauss, and Ronet Bachman-Prehn. 1988. "Social Stress, Legitimate Violence, and Gun Availability." Paper presented at the annual meetings of the Society for the Study of Social Problems.

Lizotte, Alan J. 1986. "Determinants of Completing Rape and Assault." *Journal of Quantitative Criminology* 2:203–17.

———, and David J. Bordua. 1980. "Firearms Ownership for Sport and Protection: Two Divergent Models." *American Sociological Review* 45:229–44.

———, David J. Bordua, and Carolyn S. White. 1981. "Firearms Ownership for Sport and Protection: Two Not So Divergent Models." *American Sociological Review* 46:499–503.

———, and Marjorie S. Zatz. 1986. "The Use and Abuse of Sentencing Enhancement for Firearms Offenses in California." *Law and Contemporary Problems* 49:199–221.

Loftin, Colin, Milton Heumann, and David McDowall. 1983. "Mandatory Sentencing and Firearms Violence: Evaluating an Alternative to Gun Control." *Law & Society Review* 17:287–318.

———, and David McDowall. 1984. "The Deterrent Effects of the Florida Felony Firearm Law." *Journal of Criminal Law & Criminology* 75:250–9.

———, and David McDowall. 1981. "'One With a Gun Gets You Two': Mandatory Sentencing and Firearms Violence in Detroit." *Annals* 455:150–67.

———, and Ellen J. MacKenzie. 1990. "Building National Estimates of Violent Victimization." Paper read at the National Research Council Symposium on the Understanding and Control of Violent Behavior, Destin, Florida, April 1–6, 1990.

Los Angeles Police Department. 1989. "Quarterly Report of Firearms Booked into Evidence." Gun Detail, Detective Headquarters Division.

Luckenbill, David F. 1977. "Criminal Homicide as a Situated Transaction." *Social Problems* 25:176–86.

———. 1981. "Generating Compliance: The Case of Robbery." *Urban Life* 10:25–46.

———. 1982. "Compliance under Threat of Severe Punishment." *Social Forces* 60:811–25.

Lundsgaarde, Henry P. 1977. *Murder in Space City: A Cultural Analysis of Houston Homicide Patterns*. New York: Oxford.

Magaddino, Joseph P., and Marshall H. Medoff. 1982. "Homicides, Robberies and State 'Cooling-off' Schemes." Pp. 101–12 in *Why Handgun Bans Can't Work*, edited by Don B. Kates, Jr. Bellevue, Wash.: Second Amendment Foundation.

———. 1984. "An Empirical Analysis of Federal and State Firearm Control Laws." Pp. 225–58 in *Firearms and Violence: Issues of Public Policy*, edited by Don B. Kates, Jr. Cambridge, Mass.: Ballinger.

Mallar, Charles, Stuart Kerachsky, Craig Thornton, Michael Donihue, Carol Jones, David Long, Emmanuel Noggoh, and Jennifer Schore. 1978. *Evaluation of the Economic Impact of the Job Corps Program*. Princeton: Mathematica Policy Research.

Mannelli, Ted. 1982. "Handgun Control." Unpublished report to the Executive Office of the Governor, State of Florida. Tallahassee, Florida.

Maris, Ronald W. 1981. *Pathways to Suicide*. Baltimore: Johns Hopkins.

Marks, Alan. 1977. "Sex Differences and Their Effect upon Cultural Evaluations of Methods of Self-Destruction." *Omega* 8:65–70.

———, and Thomas Abernathy. 1974. "Toward a Sociocultural Perspective on Means of Self-Destruction." *Life-threatening Behavior* 4:3–17.

Markush, Robert E., and Alfred A. Bartolucci. 1984. "Firearms and Suicide in the United States." *American Journal of Public Health* 74:123–7.

Matulia, Kenneth J. 1982. *A Balance of Forces*. Gaithersburg, Md.: International Association of Chiefs of Police.

Mauser, Gary A. 1990. Unpublished tabulations from a 1990 national survey, produced at the author's request.

———, and Michael Margolis. 1990. "The Politics of Gun Control." Paper presented at the annual meetings of the American Political Science Association in San Francisco.

Mayhew, Pat. 1987. *Residential Burglary: A Comparison of the United States, Canada and England and Wales*. National Institute of Justice. Washington, D.C.: U.S. Government Printing Office.

McClain, Paula D. 1983. "Firearms Ownership, Gun Control Attitudes and Neighborhood Environment." *Law & Policy Quarterly* 5:299–323.

McDonald, John. 1975. *Armed Robbery: Offenders and Their Victims*. Springfield, Ill.: Charles Thomas.

McDowall, David. 1986. "Gun Availability and Robbery Rates: A Panel Study of Large U.S. Cities, 1974–1978." *Law & Policy* 8:135–48.

______, and Colin Loftin. 1983. "Collective Security and the Demand for Legal Handguns." *American Journal of Sociology* 88:1146–61.

______. 1986. "Collective Security and Fatal Firearm Accidents." *Criminology* 23:401–16.

______. 1988. "Firearm Availability and Homicide in Detroit, 1951–1986." Paper presented at the annual meeting of the American Society of Criminology, Chicago.

______, Brian Wiersema, and Colin Loftin. 1989. "Did Mandatory Firearm Ownership in Kennesaw Really Prevent Burglaries?" *Sociology and Social Research* 74:48–51.

McFarland, Ross A., and A. L. Mosely. 1954. *Human Factors in Highway Transport.* Boston: Harvard School of Public Health.

McGuire, Frederick L. 1976. "Personality Factors in Highway Accidents." *Human Factors* 18:433–42.

McNamara, Joseph D. 1986. "Statement of Joseph D. McNamara, Chief of Police, San Jose, Ca." Pp. 981–93 *Hearing Before the Committee on the Judiciary,* House of Representatives, 99th Congress, 1st and 2nd Sessions on Legislation to Modify the 1968 Gun Control Act, Part 2. Testimony 2-19-86. Serial No. 131. Washington, D.C.: U.S. Government Printing Office.

McPheters, Lee R., Robert Mann, and Don Schlagenhauf. 1984. "Economic Response to a Crime Deterrence Program: Mandatory Sentencing for Robbery with a Firearm." *Economic Inquiry* 22:550–70.

Medoff, Marshall H., and Joseph P. Magaddino. 1983. "Suicides and Firearm Control Laws." *Evaluation Review* 7:357–72.

Mendoza, Alicia. 1972. "The Effects of Exposure to Toys Conducive to Violence." *Dissertation Abstracts* 33A:2769–70A.

Mericle, J. Gayle. 1989. "Weapons Seized during Drug Warrant Executions and Arrests." Unpublished report derived from files of Metropolitan Area Narcotics Squad, Will and Grundy Counties, Illinois.

Metropolitan Life Insurance Company (MLIC). 1948. "Firearms a Hazard Indoors and Out." *Statistical Bulletin* 29:7–9.

______. 1953. "Firearm Accidents Can Be Prevented." *Statistical Bulletin* 34:7–10.

______. 1956. "How Firearm Accidents Occur." *Statistical Bulletin* 37:6–8.

______. 1959. "How Fatal Accidents Occur in the Home." *Statistical Bulletin* 40:6–8.

______. 1968. "How Fatal Home Firearm Accidents Occur." *Statistical Bulletin* 49:12–13.

Miczek, Klaus A., J. F. DeBold, M. Haney, J. Tidey, J. Vivian, and E. M. Weerts. 1990. "Alcohol, Drugs of Abuse and Violence." Paper presented at the National Research Council Symposium on the Understanding and Control of Violent Behavior, Destin, Florida, April 1–4.

Miller, Terry. 1989. Telephone conversation with Terry Miller, National Safety Council, Statistics Division, June 9, 1989.

Milton, Catherine H., Jeanne Wahl Halleck, James Lardner, and Gary L. Albrecht. 1977. *Police Use of Deadly Force.* Washington, D.C.: Police Foundation.

Mohler, David G. 1989. Testimony before the Committee on Public Safety, New York State Legislature.

Moore, Mark H. 1980. "The Police and Weapons Offenses." *Annals* 452:22–32.

———. 1981. "Keeping Handguns from Criminal Offenders." *Annals* 455:92–109.

———. 1983. "The Bird in the Hand: A Feasible Strategy for Gun Control." *Journal of Policy Analysis and Management* 2:185–8.

Morrow, Paul L., and Page Hudson. 1986. "Accidental Firearm Fatalities in North Carolina, 1976–80." *American Journal of Public Health* 76:1120–3.

Moynihan, Daniel Patrick. 1988. Untitled fund raising letter, 1988 campaign for U.S. Senate.

Murphy, Linda R., and Richard W. Dodge. 1981. "The Baltimore Recall Study." Pp. 16–21 in *The National Crime Survey: Working Papers, Volume I: Current and Historical Perspectives*, edited by Robert G. Lehnen and Wesley G. Skogan. U.S. Department of Justice, Bureau of Justice Statistics. Washington, D.C.: U.S. Government Printing Office.

Murray, Douglas R. 1975. "Handguns, Gun Control Laws and Firearm Violence." *Social Problems* 23:81–92.

National Coalition to Ban Handguns. 1988. Untitled membership solicitation letter, c. May 26, 1988. Washington, D.C.: NCBH.

———. Undated. "Twenty Questions and Answers on Handgun Control." Pamphlet. Washington, D.C.: NCBH.

National Rifle Association. 1990. "Your State Firearms Laws." Batch of pamphlets summarizing gun laws in each of the 50 states. Washington, D.C.: NRA Institute for Legislative Action.

National Safety Council. 1976. *Safety Education Data Sheet No. 3, revised. Firearms.* Chicago: National Safety Council.

———. 1981. *Accident Facts, 1981 Edition.* Chicago: National Safety Council.

———. 1988. *Accident Facts, 1988 Edition.* Chicago: National Safety Council.

———. 1989. *Accident Facts, 1989 Edition.* Chicago: National Safety Council.

New York City Police Department. 1987. "Pistol License Application." Application form and instructions. New York City: NYPD.

———. 1988. "New York City Police Department Guidelines for the Issuance of Firearm Licenses." New York City: NYPD.

———. 1989. "1989 Firearms Discharge Assault Report." New York City NYPD Police Academy Firearms and Tactics Section.

New York Times. 1985a. "22% Drop Reported in Crime on Subways." March 22, p. B4.

———. 1985b. "Subway Felonies Reportedly Down." April 18, p. 87.

Newsweek. 1985. "A Goetz Backlash?" March 11, pp. 50–53.

Newton, George D., and Franklin Zimring. 1969. *Firearms and Violence in American Life.* A Staff Report to the National Commission on the Causes and Prevention of Violence. Washington, D.C.: U.S. Government Printing Office.

Nicholson, Robert, and Anne Garner. 1980. *The Analysis of the Firearms Control Act of 1975.* Washington, D.C.: U.S. Conference of Mayors.

Nispel, David H. 1981. *Gun Control: A Look at the Various State and Federal Laws.* Wisconsin. Legislative Reference Bureau. Informational Bulletin 81-IB-3.

Normandeau, Andre. 1968. *Trends and Patterns in Crimes of Robbery.* Unpublished Ph.D. dissertation, University of Pennsylvania.

North American Association of Hunter Safety Coordinators (NAAHSC). 1982. *1977 Through 1980 Hunting Accident Report,* NAAHSC.

Nunnally, Jum. 1967. *Psychometric Techniques.* New York: McGraw-Hill.

O'Connor, James. 1973. *The Fiscal Crisis of the State.* New York: St. Martin's.

O'Connor, James F., and Alan Lizotte. 1978. "The 'Southern Subculture of Violence' Thesis and Patterns of Gun Ownership." *Social Problems* 25:420–29.

Ohio. 1982. *Ohio Citizen Attitudes Concerning Crime and Criminal Justice.* The Ohio Statistical Analysis Center, Division of Criminal Justice Services. Columbus, Ohio: Ohio Department of Development.

Olin Mathieson Company. 1969. Unpublished study summarized in Newton and Zimring (1969, p. 182).

Oliver, R. Graeme, and Basil S. Hetzel. 1973. "An Analysis of Recent Trends in Suicide Rates in Australia." *International Journal of Epidemiology* 2:91–101.

Olmstead, A. D. 1988. "Morally Controversial Leisure: The Social World of Gun Collectors." *Symbolic Interaction* 11:277–87.

Orsagh, Thomas, and Jong-Rong Chen. 1988. "The Effect of Time Served on Recidivism." *Journal of Quantitative Criminology* 4:155–71.

Page, David, and Edgar O'Neal. 1977. "Weapons Effect without Demand Characteristics." *Psychological Reports* 41:29–30.

Page, Monte M., and Rick J. Scheidt. 1971. "The Elusive Weapons Effect." *Journal of Personality and Social Psychology* 20:304–18.

Patterson, Patti J., and Leigh R. Smith. 1987. "Firearms in the Home and Child Safety." *American Journal of Diseases of Children* 141:221–3.

Pierce, Glenn L., and William J. Bowers. 1981. "The Bartley-Fox Gun Law's Short-Term Impact on Crime in Boston." *Annals* 455:120–37.

Phillips, Llad, Harold L. Votey, and John Howell. 1976. "Handguns and Homicide." *Journal of Legal Studies* 5:463–78.

Porterfield, Austin L. 1960. "Traffic Fatalities, Suicide, and Homicide." *American Sociological Review* 25:897–901.

Quinn, Bernard, Herman Anderson, Martin Bradley, Paul Goetting, and Peggy Shriver. 1982. *Churches and Church Membership in the United States 1980.* Atlanta: Glenmary Research Center.

Quinley, Hal. 1990. Memorandum reporting results from Time/CNN Poll of Gun Owners, dated 2-6-90. N.Y.: Yankelovich Clancy Shulman survey organization.

Reiss, Albert J. 1971. *The Police and the Public.* New Haven, Conn.: Yale University Press.

Rengert, George, and John Wasilchick. 1985. *Suburban Burglary: A Time and Place for Everything.* Springfield, Ill.: Charles Thomas.

Rich, Charles L., James G. Young, Richard C. Fowler, John Wagner, and Nancy A. Black. 1990. "Guns and Suicide: Possible Effects of Some Specific Legislation." *American Journal of Psychiatry* 147:342–6.

Richardson, H. L. 1975. "Myth #2: Criminals Won't Have Guns." *True Magazine* (July):32ff.

Rieder, Jonathan. 1984. "The Social Organization of Vengeance." Pp. 131–62 in *Toward a General Theory of Social Control Volume 1, Fundamentals*, edited by Donald Black. Orlando: Academic Press.

Rivara, Frederick P., and F. Bruder Stapleton. 1982. "Handguns and Children: A Dangerous Mix." *Developmental and Behavioral Pediatrics* 3:35–8.

Ronhovde, Kent M., and Gloria P. Sugars. 1982. "Survey of Select State Firearm Control Laws." Pp. 201–28 in *Federal Regulation of Firearms*, Report prepared by Congressional Research Service for U.S. Senate Judiciary Committee. Washington, D.C.: U.S. Government Printing Office.

Rosen, David H. 1975. "Suicide Survivors." *Western Journal of Medicine* 122:289–94.

Rossman, David, Paul Froyd, Glen L. Pierce, John McDeritt, and William J. Bowers. 1980. "Massachusetts' Mandatory Minimum Sentence Gun Law." *Criminal Law Bulletin* 16:150–63.

Runyon, Carol W., Jonathan B. Kotch, Lewis Margolis, and Paul A. Buescher. 1985. "Childhood Injuries in North Carolina." *American Journal of Public Health* 75:1429–32.

Rushforth, Norman B., Charles S. Hirsch, Amasa B. Ford, and Lester Adelson. 1975. "Accidental Firearm Fatalities in a Metropolitan County (1958–1975)." *American Journal of Epidemiology* 100:499–505.

———, Amasa B. Ford, Charles S. Hirsch, Nancy M. Rushforth, and Lester Adelson. 1977. "Violent Death in a Metropolitan County: Changing Patterns in Homicide (1958–74)." *New England Journal of Medicine* 297:531–8.

Ryzoff, Ronald I., Gerald W. Shaftan, and Horace Herbsman. 1966. "Selective Conservatism in Penetrating Abdominal Trauma." *Surgery* 59:650–3.

Sainsbury, Peter. 1986. "The Epidemiology of Suicide." Pp. 17–40 in *Suicide* edited by Alec Roy. Baltimore: Williams & Wilkins.

———, J. Jenkins, and Andre Baert. 1981. *Suicide Trends in Europe*. Geneva, Switzerland: World Health Organization, Regional Office for Europe.

Schetky, Diane H. 1985. "Children and Handguns." *American Journal of Diseases of Children* 139:229–31.

Schmidt, William E. "Town to Celebrate Mandatory Arms." *New York Times*, April 11, 1987, pp. 6–7.

Schneidman, Dave. 1982. "Gun-totin' Town Gets an Apology." *Chicago Tribune*, April 8, 1982, p. 15.

Schultz, Leroy G. 1962. "Why the Negro Carries Weapons." *Journal of Criminal Law, Criminology and Police Science* 53:476–83.

Schuman, S. H., Donald C. Pelz, Nathaniel J. Ehrlich, and Melvin L. Selzer. 1967. "Young Male Drivers: Impulse Expression, Accidents, and Violations." *Journal of the American Medical Association* 200:1026–30.

Schuman, Howard, and Stanley Presser. 1981. "The Attitude-Action Connection and the Issue of Gun Control." *Annals* 455:40–7.

Schur, Edwin. 1965. *Crimes Without Victims*. Englewood Cliffs, N.J.: Prentice-Hall.

______. 1974. "Crime and the New Conservatives." Pp. 228–42 in *The New Conservatives: A Critique from the Left*, edited by Lewis A. Coser and Irving Howe. New York: Quadrangle.

Seiden, Richard H. 1977. "Suicide Prevention: A Public Health/Public Policy Approach." *Omega* 8:267–276.

Seitz, Steven T. 1972. "Firearms, Homicides, and Gun Control Effectiveness." *Law and Society Review* 6:595–614.

Shaw, L. 1965. "The Practical Use of Projective Personality Tests as Accident Predictors." *Traffic Safety Research Review* 9:34–72.

Sherrill, Robert. 1973. *The Saturday Night Special*. New York: Charterhouse.

Sherman, Lawrence W., and Ellen G. Cohn. 1989. "The Impact of Research on Legal Policy." *Law and Society Review* 23:117–44.

Sherman, Lawrence W., and Robert H. Langworthy. 1979. "Measuring Homicide by Police Officers." *Journal of Criminal Law and Criminology* 70:546–60.

Sherman, Lawrence W., Leslie Steele, Deborah Laufersweiler, Nancy Hoffer, and Sherry A. Julian. 1989. "Stray Bullets and 'Mushrooms': Random Shootings of Bystanders in Four Cities, 1977–1988." *Journal of Quantitative Criminology* 5:297–316.

Shields, David J. 1976. "Two Judges Look at Gun Control." *Chicago Bar Record* 1976:180–85.

Shields, Pete. 1981. *Guns Don't Die—People Do*. New York: Arbor House.

Shneidman, Edwin S., and Norman L. Farberow. 1961. "Statistical Comparisons between Attempted and Committed Suicides." Pp. 19–47 in *The Cry for Help*, edited by Norman L. Farberow and Edwin S. Shneidman. New York: McGraw-Hill.

Silver, Carol Ruth, and Don B. Kates, Jr. 1979. "Self-Defense, Handgun Ownership, and the Independence of Women in a Violent, Sexist Society." Pp. 139–69 in *Restricting Handguns: The Liberal Skeptics Speak Out*, edited by Don B. Kates, Jr. Croton-on-Hudson, N.Y.: North River Press.

Simons, Lynn Stanley, and Charles W. Turner. 1975. "A Further Investigation of the Weapons Effect." *Personality and Social Psychology Bulletin* 1:186–8.

Skogan, Wesley. 1978. "Weapon Use in Robbery." Pp. 61–73 in *Violent Crime*, edited by James A. Inciardi and Anne E. Pottieger. Beverly Hills: Sage.

______. 1981. *Issues in the Measurement of Victimization*. U.S. Department of Justice, Bureau of Justice Statistics. Washington, D.C.: U.S. Government Printing Office.

Sloan, John Henry, Arthur L. Kellermann, Donald T. Reay, James A. Ferris, Thomas Koepsell, Frederick P. Rivara, Charles Rice, Laurel Gray, and James LoGerfo. 1988. "Handgun Regulations, Crime, Assaults and Homicide." *New England Journal of Medicine* 319:1256–62.

Smith, D. A., and E. B. Patterson. 1985. "Latent-Variable Models in Criminological Research: Applications and a Generalization of Joreskog's LISREL Model." *Journal of Quantitative Criminology* 1:127–58.

Smith, Douglas A., and Craig D. Uchida. 1988. "The Social Organization of Self-Help." *American Sociological Review* 53:94–102.

Smith, Tom W. 1980. "The 75% Solution: An Analysis of the Structure of Attitudes on Gun Control, 1959–1977." *Journal of Criminal Law & Criminology* 71:300–16.

Snyder, John M. 1969. "Crime Rises under Rigid Gun Control." *The American Rifleman* 117:54–5.

Sommers, Paul M. 1980. "Deterrence and Gun Control: An Empirical Analysis." *Atlantic Economic Journal* 8:89–94.

———. 1984. "Letter to the Editor." *New England Journal of Medicine* 310:47–8.

Stapleton, D. C. 1977. "Analyzing Political Participation Data with a MIMIC Model." Pp. 52–74 in *Sociological Methodology,* edited by Karl F. Schuessler. San Francisco: Jossey-Bass.

Steadman, Henry J., Donna Vanderwyst, and Stephen Ribner. 1978. "Comparing Arrest Rates of Mental Patients and Criminal Offenders." *American Journal of Psychiatry* 135:1218–20.

Stengel, E. 1964. *Suicide and Attempted Suicide.* Baltimore: Penguin.

Stinchcombe, Arthur, Rebecca Adams, Carol A. Heimer, Kim Lane Scheppele, Tom W. Smith, and D. Garth Taylor 1980. *Crime and Punishment—Changing Attitudes in America.* San Francisco: Jossey-Bass.

Stoller, Alan. 1969. "Suicides and Attempted Suicides in Australia: Implications for Prevention." *Proceedings of the Fifth International Congress for Suicide Prevention.* London.

Strauss, Murray A., Richard J. Gelles, and Suzanne K. Steinmetz. 1980. *Behind Closed Doors: Violence in the American Family.* Garden City, N.Y.: Anchor Press.

Sumner, William Graham. 1904. *Folkways.* New York: Ginn.

Tallahassee Democrat. 1982a. "Beer-can Target-Shooting Ends in Death of St. Marks Man." July 22, 1982, pp. 1A, 11A.

———. 1982b. "Wakulla Man Convicted in William Tell Gun Stunt." December 12, 1982, p. 1A.

———. 1985. "Subway Robberies Drop." 1-25-85, p. 1A.

Tannenbaum, Percy H. 1971. "Emotional Arousal as a Mediator of Erotic Communication Effects." Pp. 326–56 in *Technical Report of the Commission on Obscenity and Pornography,* Vol. 8. Washington, D.C.: U.S. Government Printing Office.

Taylor, Frederic W. 1973. "Gunshot Wounds of the Abdomen." *Annals of Surgery* 177:174–7.

Teret, Stephen P., and Garen J. Wintemute. 1983. "Handgun Injuries." *Hamline Law Review* 6:341–50.

Thompson, James W., Michelle Sviridoff, and Jerome E. McElroy. 1981. *Employment and Crime: A Review of Theories and Research.* National Institute of Justice. Washington, D.C.: U.S. Government Printing Office.

Tillman, W. A., and G. E. Hobbs. 1949. "The Accident-Prone Automobile Driver: A Study of the Social Background." *American Journal of Psychiatry* 106:321–31.

Tonso, William R. 1984. "Social Problems and Sagecraft: Gun Control as a Case in Point." Pp. 71–95 in *Firearms and Violence: Issues of Public Policy,* edited by Don B. Kates, Jr. Cambridge, Mass.: Ballinger.

______. 1985. "Gun Control: White Man's Law." *Reason* (December): 22–5.

Trahin, Jimmy L. 1989. "Congressional Testimony on Assault Weapons." Unpublished copy of testimony given 5-5-89.

Trends. 1984. "Megatrends." *American Firearms Industry.* March 1984.

Tuckman, Jacob, and William F. Youngman, 1963. "Suicide Risk among Persons Attempting Suicide." *Public Health Reports* 78:585–7.

______. 1968. "Identifying Suicide Risk Groups among Attempted Suicides." *Public Health Reports* 78:763–6.

Turley, Windell. 1981. "Manufacturers' and Suppliers' Liability to Handgun Victims." *Northern Kentucky Law Review* 10:41–6.

Turner, Anthony. 1981. "The San Jose Recall Study." Pp. 22–27 in *The National Crime Survey: Working Papers, Volume I: Current and Historical Perspectives,* edited by Robert G. Lehnen and Wesley G. Skogan. U.S. Department of Justice, Bureau of Justice Statistics. Washington, D.C.: U.S. Government Printing Office.

Turner, Charles W., and Diane Goldsmith. 1976. "Effects of Toy Guns and Airplanes on Children's Antisocial Free Play Behavior." *Child Psychology* 21:303–15.

Turner, Charles W., John F. Layton, and Lynn Stanley Simons. 1975. "Naturalistic Studies of Aggressive Behavior: Aggressive Stimuli, Victim Visibility, and Horn Honking." *Journal of Personality and Social Psychology* 31:1098–1107.

Turner, Charles W., and Lynn Stanley Simons. 1974. "Effects of Subject Sophistication and Evaluation Apprehension on Aggressive Responses to Weapons." *Journal of Personality and Social Psychology* 30:341–48.

United Nations. 1982. *Demographic Yearbook 1980.* New York: United Nations.

U.S. Bureau of Alcohol, Tobacco and Firearms. 1975–1984. *Alcohol, Tobacco and Firearms Summary Statistics.* Annual issues covering fiscal years 1973 through 1982. Washington, D.C.: U.S. Government Printing Office.

______. 1976a. *Project Identification: A Study of Handguns Used in Crime.* Washington, D.C.: BATF.

______. 1976b. *Project 300.* Washington, D.C.: BATF.

______. 1977. *Concentrated Urban Enforcement.* Washington, D.C.: U.S. Government Printing Office.

______. 1980. *State Laws and Published Ordinances, Firearms—1980.* Washington, D.C.: BATF.

______. 1988. *Federal Firearms Regulation 1988–89.* Washington, D.C.: U.S. Government Printing Office.

______. 1989a. "Statistics Listing of Registered Weapons." Sheet prepared 4-19-89. Washington, D.C.: BATF.

______. 1989b. Letter to author dated 6-29-89 detailing 1984–1987 gun production figures.

______. 1990. "Bureau of ATF Tape Analysis." Copy of computer printout page on trace requests by crime type, dated 2-9-90.

U.S. Bureau of the Census. 1943. *Vital Statistics Rates in the United States, 1900–1940.* Washington, D.C.: U.S. Government Printing Office.

———. 1975; 1976; 1978; 1981; 1982; 1983; 1984; 1986; 1987; 1988. *Statistical Abstract of the United States 1976* (1977; 1979; 1981; 1982–83; 1984; 1985; 1987; 1988; 1989). Washington, D.C.: U.S. Government Printing Office.

———. 1972. *1967 Census of Manufactures—Industry Series, Small Arms.* Washington, D.C.: U.S. Government Printing Office.

———. 1978. *County and City Data Book 1977.* Washington, D.C.: U.S. Government Printing Office.

———. 1979. *1977 Census of Manufactures—Industry Series, Small Arms.* Washington, D.C.: U.S. Government Printing Office.

———. 1981. *1977 Census of Service Industries—Geographic Area Series—United States.* Washington, D.C.: U.S. Government Printing Office.

———. 1983a. *1980 Census of the Population. Volume I: Characteristics of the Population.* Chapter B—General Population Characteristics, United States Summary, Table 46. Washington, D.C.: U.S. Government Printing Office.

———. 1983b. *1980 Census of the Population, Volume I: Characteristics of the Population.* Chapter C—General Social and Economic Characteristics, Table 118. Washington, D.C.: U.S. Government Printing Office.

———. 1983c. *County and City Data Book 1983.* Washington, D.C.: U.S. Government Printing Office.

———. 1983d. *National Crime Survey: Interviewer's Manual.* NCS-550. Part D—How to Enumerate NCS. Washington, D.C.: U.S. Government Printing Office.

———. 1984. *1982 Census of Manufactures—Industry Series. Small Arms.* Washington, D.C.: U.S. Government Printing Office.

———. 1989. *1987 Census of Manufactures—Preliminary Report, Industry Series, Ordnance and Accessories, N.E.C.* Washington, D.C.: U.S. Government Printing Office.

U.S. Bureau of Justice Statistics. 1978. *Criminal Victimization in the United States, 1976.* Washington, D.C.: U.S. Government Printing Office.

———. 1980. *Intimate Victims: A Study of Violence among Friends and Relatives.* Washington, D.C.: U.S. Government Printing Office.

———. 1981. *The Prevalence of Crime.* BJS Bulletin. Washington, D.C.: U.S. Government Printing Office.

———. 1982a. *Criminal Victimization in the United States 1980.* Washington, D.C.: U.S. Government Printing Office.

———. 1982b. *Prisoners in State and Federal Institutions on December 31, 1980.* Washington, D.C.: U.S. Government Printing Office.

———. 1983. *The Prosecution of Felony Arrests, 1979.* Washington, D.C.: U.S. Government Printing Office.

———. 1984a. *Sourcebook of Criminal Justice Statistics 1983.* Washington, D.C.: U.S. Government Printing Office.

———. 1984b. *Capital Punishment 1983.* BJS Bulletin. Washington, D.C.: U.S. Government Printing Office.

______. 1984c. *The Severity of Crime.* BJS Bulletin. Washington, D.C.: U.S. Government Printing Office.

______. 1985a. *Household Burglary.* BJS Bulletin. Washington, D.C.: U.S. Government Printing Office.

______. 1985b. *The Risk of Violent Crime.* BJS Special Report. Washington, D.C.: U.S. Government Printing Office.

______. 1985c. *Criminal Victimization in the United States 1983.* Washington, D.C.: U.S. Government Printing Office.

______. 1985d. *Reporting Crimes to the Police.* BJS Special Report. Washington, D.C.: U.S. Government Printing Office.

______. 1985e. *State Criminal Records Repositories.* BJS Technical Report. Washington, D.C.: U.S. Government Printing Office.

______. 1986a. *Prison Admissions and Releases, 1983.* BJS Special Report. Washington, D.C.: U.S. Government Printing Office.

______. 1986b. *The Use of Weapons in Committing Crimes.* BJS Special Report. Washington, D.C.: U.S. Government Printing Office.

______. 1987a. *Criminal Victimization in the United States, 1985.* Washington, D.C.: U.S. Government Printing Office.

______. 1987b. *Sourcebook of Criminal Justice Statistics, 1987.* Washington, D.C.: U.S. Government Printing Office.

______. 1987c. *Lifetime Likelihood of Victimization.* BJS Technical Report. Washington, D.C.: U.S. Government Printing Office.

______. 1988. *Sourcebook of Criminal Justice Statistics, 1988.* Washington, D.C.: U.S. Government Printing Office.

______. 1989a. *Criminal Victimization in the United States, 1987.* Washington, D.C.: U.S. Government Printing Office.

______. 1989b. *Criminal Victimization 1988.* BJS Bulletin. Washington, D.C.: U.S. Government Printing Office.

______. 1990a. *Handgun Crime Victims.* BJS Special Report. Washington, D.C.: U.S. Government Printing Office.

______. 1990b. *Felony Defendants in Large Urban Counties, 1988.* Washington, D.C.: U.S. Government Printing Office.

U.S. Bureau of Labor Statistics. 1973; 1980. *Producer Price Index.* Issues for 1973, 1980. Washington, D.C.: U.S. Government Printing Office.

U.S. Centers for Disease Control. 1989. "Firearm Mortality among Children and Youth." *Advance Data from Vital and Health Statistics of the National Center for Health Statistics,* no. 178, 11-3-89. Washington, D.C.: U.S. Government Printing Office.

U.S. Congress. 1975a. "Gun Control." *Congressional Record* 121 (December 19):1–10.

______. 1975b. "The Escalating Rate of Hand Gun Violence." Subcommittee to Investigate Juvenile Delinquency of the Senate Committee on the Judiciary, 92nd Congress, 1st Session.

U.S. Congressional Research Service. 1980. Unpublished memorandum reporting results of a reanalysis of U.S. Conference of Mayor's evaluation of D.C. gun law. Washington, D.C.: The Library of Congress.

———. 1991. "Semiautomatic Military-Style Firearms: Statistics and Issues." Washington, D.C.: The Library of Congress.

U.S. Consumer Product Safety Commission (CPSC). 1978. *Consumer Product Hazard Index*. Washington, D.C.: U.S. Government Printing Office.

———. 1982. *1982 Annual Report—Fiscal Year 1981*. Washington, D.C.: U.S. Government Printing Office.

U.S. Department of Defense. 1980. *Small Arms Identification and Operations Guide*. Washington, D.C.: U.S. Government Printing Office.

U.S. Department of Health, Education and Welfare (DHEW). 1976. *Persons Injured and Disability Days by Detailed Type and Class of Accident: United States—1971–1972*. Vital and Health Statistics, Series 10, No. 105. Washington, D.C.: U.S. Government Printing Office.

U.S. Department of Justice. 1980. *Uniform Crime Reporting Handbook*. Washington, D.C.: U.S. Government Printing Office.

———. 1989. "Draft Report on Systems for Identifying Felons Who Attempt to Purchase Firearms; Notice and Request for Comments." *Federal Register*, June 26, 1989, pp. 26901–41.

U.S. Federal Bureau of Investigation (FBI). 1962–1975; 1981; 1983; 1984; 1985; 1986; 1987; 1988; 1989; 1990. *Crime in the United States (year)—Uniform Crime Reports* (Covering years 1961–1974, 1980, 1982–1989) Washington, D.C.: U.S. Government Printing Office.

———. 1971–1989. *Law Enforcement Officers Killed and Assaulted (Year)*. Annual issues, 1970 to 1988. Washington, D.C.: U.S. Government Printing Office.

U.S. Federal Bureau of Prisons. 1971. *National Prisoner Statistics Bulletin Number 46*. Washington, D.C.: U.S. Government Printing Office.

U.S. Fish and Wildlife Service. 1977. *1975 National Survey of Fishing, Hunting and Wild-life Associate Recreation*. Washington, D.C.: U.S. Government Printing Office.

———. 1982a. *1980 National Survey of Fishing, Hunting and Wildlife-Associated Recreation*. Washington, D.C.: U.S. Government Printing Office.

———. 1982b. *Federal Aid in Fish and Wildlife Restoration, 1980*. Washington, D.C.: U.S. Government Printing Office.

U.S. Government Accounting Office. 1978. *Handgun Control: Effectiveness and Costs*. Washington, D.C.: U.S. Government Printing Office.

U.S. Internal Revenue Service. 1969a. *Gun Control Act of 1968*. Publication 627 (1–69). Washington, D.C.: Department of the Treasury.

———. 1969b. "Factoring Criteria." Form 4590, Department of the Treasury. Washington, D.C.: U.S. Government Printing Office.

U.S. Law Enforcement Assistance Administration (LEAA). 1972. *The San Jose Methods Test of Known Crime Victims*. Statistics Division Technical Series, Report No. 1. Washington, D.C.: U.S. Government Printing Office.

U.S. Library of Congress. 1981. *Gun Control Laws in Foreign Countries*. Law Library. Washington, D.C.: U.S. Government Printing Office.

U.S. National Bureau of Standards. 1977. *LEAA Police Equipment Survey of 1972, Vol. VI: Body Armor and Confiscated Weapons.* Washington, D.C.: NBS.

U.S. National Center for Health Statistics (NCHS). 1976. "Persons Injured and Disability Days by Detailed Type and Class of Accident, 1971–72." *Vital and Health Statistics.* Series 10, No. 105. Washington, D.C.: U.S. Government Printing Office.

______. 1981. *Vital Statistics of the United States, 1978. Volume II, Motality, Part A.* Washington, D.C.: U.S. Government Printing Office.

______. 1982. *Public Use Data Tape Documentation: Mortality Detail 1979 Data.* Hyattsville, Md.: U.S. Public Health Service.

______. 1983. *Public Use Data Tape Documentation: Mortality Detail 1980 Data.* Hyattsville, Md.: U.S. Department of Health and Human Services.

______. 1985a. *Persons Injured and Disability Days Due to Injury: United States, 1980–81.* Vital and Health Statistics, Series 10, No. 149. Washington, D.C.: U.S. Government Printing Office.

______. 1985b. *Vital Statistics of the United States 1980.* Volume II: *Mortality,* Part A. Rockville, Md.: NCHS.

______. 1988. *Vital Statistics of the United States 1985.* Volume II: Mortality, Part A. Washington, D.C.: U.S. Government Printing Office.

______. 1989. *Vital Statistics of the United States 1986.* Volume II: *Mortality,* Part A. Washington, D.C.: U.S. Government Printing Office.

______. 1990. *Vital Statistics of the United States 1987.* Volume II: *Mortality,* Part A. Washington, D.C.: U.S. Government Printing Office.

U.S. National Criminal Justice Information and Statistics Service. 1975–1979. *Criminal Victimization in the United States* (year). Issues covering 1973–1978. Washington, D.C.: U.S. Government Printing Office.

U.S. National Criminal Information Center. 1983. "A Breakdown of Gun Records in NCIC by Type as of 10/6/83." Unpublished information sheet provided to author by NCIC. Washington, D.C.: NCIC.

U.S. Senate. 1971. "Proposed Amendments to the Gun Control Act of 1968 to Prohibit the Sale of 'Saturday Night Special' Handguns." Hearings on S.2507 before the Senate Committee on the Judiciary, 92nd Congress, 1st Session.

U.S. Small Business Administration. 1969. *Crime against Small Business.* Senate Document No. 91-14. Washington, D.C.: U.S. Government Printing Office.

Van de Ven, P. M. M., and Bernard M. S. Van Praag. 1981. "The Demand for Deductibles in Private Health Insurance: A Probit Model with Sample Selection." *Journal of Econometrics* 17:229–52.

Vera Institute of Justice. 1981. *Felony Arrest,* revised edition. New York: Longman.

Walker, Samuel. 1986. *Sense and Nonsense About Crime.* Pacific Grove, Calif.: Brooks/Cole.

______. 1989. *Sense and Nonsense about Crime,* 2nd edition. Pacific Grove, Calif.: Brooks/Cole.

Waller, Irvin, and Norman Okihiro. 1978. *Burglary: The Victim and the Public.* Toronto: University of Toronto Press.

Waller, Julian A. 1967. "Identification of Problem Drinking among Drunken Drivers." *Journal of the American Medical Association* 200:115–20.

———. and Elbert B. Whorton. 1973. "Unintentional Shootings, Highway Crashes and Acts of Violence." *Accident Analysis and Prevention* 5:351–6.

Wallerstein, James S., and Clement J. Wyle. 1947. "Our Law-Abiding Law-Breakers." *Probation* 25:107–12.

Warner, Ken (ed.). 1988. *Gun Digest 1989—43rd Annual Edition.* Northbrook, Ill.: DBI Books.

Weber, Max. 1922. *Economy and Society.* New York: Bedminister Press.

Wheaton, B. 1988. "Assessment of Fit in Overidentified Models with Latent Variables." In *Common Problems/Proper Solutions,* edited by J. S. Long. Beverly Hills: Sage.

Whitehead, John T., and Robert H. Langworthy. 1989. "Gun Ownership and Willingness to Shoot: A Clarification of Current Controversies." *Justice Quarterly* 6:263–82.

Whitlock, F. A. 1971. *Death on the Road.* London: Tavistock.

Wilbanks, William. 1984. *Murder in Miami.* Lanham, Md.: University Press.

Willett, T. C. 1964. *Criminal on the Road.* London: Tavistock.

Williams, J. Sherwood, and John H. McGrath. 1976. "Why People Own Guns." *Journal of Communication* 26:22–30.

Wilson, H., and R. Sherman. 1961. "Civilian Penetrating Wounds of the Abdomen." *Annals of Surgery* 153:639–49.

Wilson, J. Harper. 1990a. Letter dated 6-20-90 from J. Harper Wilson, Chief, FBI Uniform Crime Reporting Program.

———. 1990b. Letter dated 9-5-90.

Wilson, James Q. 1975. *Thinking about Crime.* New York: Vintage.

———. 1976. "Crime and Punishment in England." *The Public Interest* 43:3–25.

———, and Barbara Boland. 1978. "The Effect of the Police on Crime." *Law & Society Review* 12:367–90.

Wilson, William Julius. 1987. *The Truly Disadvantaged.* Chicago: University of Chicago Press.

Wilt, G. Marie, J. Bannon, Ronald K. Breedlove, John W. Kennish, Donald M. Snadker, and Robert K. Sawtell. 1977. *Domestic Violence and the Police: Studies in Detroit and Kansas City.* Washington, D.C.: U.S. Government Printing Office.

Wintemute, Garen J., Stephen P. Teret, Jesse F. Kraus, Mona A. Wright, and Gretchen Bradfield. 1987. "When Children Shoot Children: 88 Unintended Deaths in California." *Journal of the American Medical Association* 257:3107–9.

Wisconsin. 1960. *The Regulation of the Firearms by the States.* Research Bulletin 130. Madison, Wisc.: Wisconsin Legislative Reference Library.

Wolfgang, Marvin E. 1958. *Patterns in Criminal Homicide.* Philadelphia: University of Pennsylvania Press.

Wright, James D. 1981. "Public Opinion and Gun Control." *Annals* 455:24–39.

______. 1984. "The Ownership of Firearms for Reasons of Self-Defense. Pp. 301–27 in *Firearms and Violence,* edited by Don B. Kates, Jr. Cambridge, Mass.: Ballinger.

______. 1990. "In the Heat of the Moment." *Reason* (August/September):44–5.

Wright, James D., and Linda Marston. 1975. "The Ownership of the Means of Destruction: Weapons in the United States." *Social Problems* 23:93–107.

Wright, James D., and Peter H. Rossi. 1985. *The Armed Criminal in America: A Survey of Incarcerated Felons.* National Institute of Justice Research Report. Washington, D.C.: U.S. Government Printing Office.

Wright, James D., and Peter H. Rossi. 1986. *Armed and Considered Dangerous: A Survey of Felons and Their Firearms.* New York: Aldine.

Wright, James D., Peter H. Rossi, and Kathleen Daly. 1983. *Under the Gun: Weapons, Crime and Violence in America.* New York: Aldine.

Wrong, Dennis H. 1988. *Power.* Chicago: University of Chicago Press.

Yeager, Matthew G., and Joseph D. Alviani, and Nancy Loving. 1976. *How Well Does the Handgun Protect You and Your Family?* Handgun Control Staff Technical Report 2. Washington, D.C.: United States Conference of Mayors.

Young, Robert L. 1985. "Perceptions of Crime, Racial Attitudes, and Firearms Ownership." *Social Forces* 64:473–86.

______. 1986. "Gender, Region of Socialization, and Ownership of Protective Firearms." *Rural Sociology* 51:169–82.

Zahn, Margaret A. 1990. "Intervention Strategies to Reduce Homicide." Pp. 377–90 in *Violence,* edited by Neil Alan Weiner, Margaret A. Zahn, and Rita J. Sagi. San Diego: Harcourt Brace.

Ziegenhagen, Eduard A., and Dolores Brosnan. 1985. "Victim Responses to Robbery and Crime Control Policy." *Criminology* 23:675–95.

Zimring, Franklin E. 1968. "Is Gun Control Likely to Reduce Violent Killings?" *University of Chicago Law Review* 35:721–37.

______. 1972. "The Medium Is the Message: Firearm Caliber as a Determinant of Death from Assault." *Journal of Legal Studies* 1:97–123.

______. 1975. "Firearms and Federal Law: The Gun Control Act of 1968." *Journal of Legal Studies* 4:133–98.

______. 1976. "Street Crime and New Guns." *Journal of Legal Studies* 1:95–107.

______. 1977. "Determinants of the Death Rate from Robbery. A Detroit Time Study." *Journal of Legal Studies* 6:317–32.

______. 1988. Review of *Armed and Considered Dangerous,* by James D. Wright and Peter H. Rossi. *American Journal of Sociology* 93:224–5.

______, and Gordon Hawkins. 1987. *The Citizen's Guide to Gun Control.* New York: Macmillan.

______, and James Zuehl. 1986. "Victim Injury Death in Urban Robbery: A Chicago Study." *The Journal of Legal Studies* 15:1–40.

Zimring, Franklin E., and Gordon J. Hawkins. 1973. *Deterrence: The Legal Threat in Crime Control.* Chicago: The University of Chicago Press.

INDEX